The Mediterranean Area

Where the central part of this story takes place

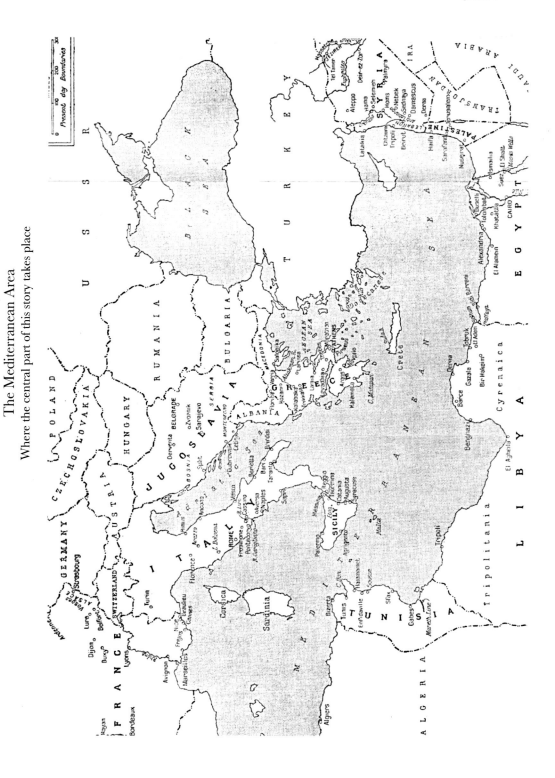

An Exacting Mistress
The Friends Ambulance Unit 1940 -1944

Seen through the eyes of one of the FAU's most Senior Officers, this book recounts the CO's story from the inside. Through the private correspondence of Ralph and Joan Barlow, it tells the story of the war from both the Pacifist's viewpoint and from that of a mother left at home.

"It might be worth keeping these letters, as they could be of interest after the war."
From one of my father's letters to my mother, 1942

My father, Ralph Barlow, was Officer in charge of the Middle East section and later Deputy Director, visiting India and China. He describes the FAU as 'An Exacting Mistress', and in his letters he confides his thoughts and doubts on being a Conscientious Objector; describes the carnage he witnesses, as well as the beauty of the places he visits; he tells of an hilarious meal with a Bedouin chief and an embarrassing incident in a hotel; and all written in memorable prose. My mother replies equally movingly, of the heartache and the struggle of bringing up two children in war-torn England with an absent father.

"With this beautifully illustrated and meticulously researched book, Antony Barlow has added an important chapter to the history of the Friends Ambulance Unit."
From the Foreword by Rupert Cadbury

Quacks Books
Q

This book is written in honour of my parents
Joan and Ralph Barlow
whose courage and love for each other shines
through every page,
and whose dedication to Quaker principles
is an example to all.

Stephen Tanner (1936-2019)

As this book goes to press, I learn of the sad news
of the death of Stephen Tanner from leukaemia.
Stephen was an enormous help to me when I set out
on this project, supplying me with photographs and
family history of his father Tom.

I would like to dedicate this book to him, which
seems especially apposite, as my father considered
Tom the Unit's 'greatest man', and the person,
who more than anyone else, set the path
for the future of The Friends Ambulance Unit.

Published by Quacks Books
7 Grape lane, Petergate, York YO1 7HU

British library cataloguing in Publication data
Antony Barlow
An Exacting Mistress
Great Britain

ISBN 978-1-912728-35-0
Obtainable direct from the publishers, bookshops or Amazon
Published by Quacks Books

Set in Baskerville and printed on an 80gsm book wove,
section sewn and bound with a hard back cover by
Quacks the Printer, 7 Grape Lane, Petergate York YO1 7HU
t 0044 (0) 1904 635967 info@quacks.info www.radiusonline.info

Acknowledgements

I am deeply indebted to the generosity of spirit of the descendants of those Unit members who were colleagues of my father, who have been so helpful in completing this book. Also to all who have kindly allowed me to quote from their books:

Roger and Annabel Barlow, for the photograph of John and Enid Barlow and for their patient checking of family dates.

Daniel Barratt Brown for a photograph of his father Michael and for permission to quote from Michael's autobiography *Seekers*.

Duncan Cadbury, who allowed me to see his father Michael's FAU archive and found a photograph of his parents, Michael and Heather.

The Edward and Dorothy Cadbury Trust for permission to use their photos of these two remarkable people.

Richard Cadbury, who helped me with a photo of his father Paul, and lent me a copy of Paul's visionary book '*Birmingham 50 Years On*'.

Rupert Cadbury, for his help with details of his father, Brandon's postwar life, plus photographs, and for kindly writing such a generous Foreword.

Mark Davies and **Allen and Unwin** to quote from Tegla Davies' *The Friends Ambulance Unit*.

Edinburgh University Press to quote from Geoffrey Carnall's biography of Horace Alexander.

The Friends Service Council for John Turtle's book *Quaker Service in the Middle East*.

Sanvu Gumede, for the photograph of his grandfather, Dr Innes Gumede.

Stephen Hill for information on Keith Linney in *Somerset Cricketers 1919-1939* (Halsgrove).

Ruth Hunnybun for generously searching family archives to find me a photograph of her great aunt, Noel Hunnybun.

The Imperial War Museum for permission to reproduce paintings by Edward Ardizzone.

Emily Kirige, Senior Archivist of the Campbell Collection, KwaZulu-Natal for the photograph of Maurice Webb from the Webb family archive.

Anthony and Christopher Loukes and their late sister **Susan Mary Waters**, the children of Harold and Mary Loukes, who tended my sick father so lovingly in Darjeeling, for providing photographs and biographies of their parents.

Rachel Malloch, for permission to quote from *Birds and Binoculars* about Horace Alexander by her father Duncan Wood, and for patiently answering my questions.

Metro Publishing for quoting from Stanley Aylett's *Surgeon at War 1939-45*.

John Murray for a photo of Joyce and Sydney Loch from JL's autobiography *A Fringe of Blue*.

The Newmarket Local History Society to quote from *One Afternoon in February*.

Graham Peet for permission to use prints from his father Stephen's films of the FAU.

Rooftop Publishing for use of the image of Freddy Temple.

Quaker Tapestry Museum, Kendal for use of the FAU tapestry panel.

Rob Reichelt for friendship in good times and bad and for permission to use his photo of me.

Sir Michael and Marjorie Rutter, for permission to quote from private family interviews.

Carol Saker, for her encouragement and supply of photos of our family from her own archive.

Jessica Sinclair-Loutit, for details of Angela's postwar life, and for the photo of her mother.

Hilary Skelton, daughter of Jack Frazer, for help with JF's post-war life and for photos of him.

Stephen Tanner, the son of Tom Tanner, who died in the North Atlantic, and who lent me a photograph of his father and generously told me details of his father's early life.

Rodney Vincent for *Evacuees in Wood Ditton* from *A Tanner Will Do*.

Teresa Waugh for the use of a photo of Lord and Lady Dillon and for allowing me to publish FRB's stories about her grandmother Lady Dillon.

Anthony Wilson, for his encouragement and permission to use a photo of his parents Roger and Margery as well as putting me in touch with his Uncle Geoffrey Wilson's family, who kindly found photos of him and allowed me to reproduce them.

Most importantly, **Libby Adams, Lisa McQuillan & all at Friends House,** and especially **Melissa Atkinson** for her help in patiently tracing documents and photographs from the FAU archive.

The Genesis of a Book
With thanks and gratitude

I have always suspected that the letters that my parents wrote to each other during the troubled years of the war, would not only illumine a story of which I knew only part, but reveal more about two remarkable people, which I could only guess at. Both these facts were proved true in all respects, but I also discovered my father's remarkable writing talent, which could bring everywhere he visited instantly to life; and shining through every page of my mother's letters is her love of our father and of the family.

I began this project some five or six years ago, never imagining that I would still be working on it many years later. But as I soon discovered, it proved a much more difficult undertaking than I had originally anticipated. Although my father had tentatively embarked on an autobiography and had even edited his letters home into a sort of travel journal, it never materialised into anything approaching a narrative of his time in the FAU.

However, it quickly became obvious to me, even on a preliminary canter through these letters, that here was not only an incomparable historical archive of a relatively untapped insider's view of the Unit, but together with my mother's letters to him, formed a unique picture of how the war tore apart a newly married couple, dispatching my father to distant parts of the world, and my mother to leave the beloved marital home and live in first one and then another house, as she brought up my brother and me and kept our absent father alive for us. Her letters are stoic survival notes of loss, heartache and longing, whilst my father's while recording times of great depression, are also wonderfully crafted accounts of the sights and sounds of hitherto unknown parts of the globe, as he strives to co-ordinate groups of CO's working in clinics, medical units and refugee camps.

The difficult part comes in trying to splice them both together to make a coherent whole. The vagaries of war time postal services, often using the facilities of the military, could well mean that letters took several months, leaving my mother ignorant not only of my father's whereabouts, but whether he was sick - several times – depressed – much of the time – or, just about coping. Additionally, my father's frequent movements, meant that even when a letter did eventually arrive, he might not get it till he returned to base days or even weeks later. Further, although they numbered their letters so that each would know if any were lost, my father would happily head a letter 'Sunday', followed by 'continued next day', making precise dating an additonal struggle. All this meant that for most of the time they were writing into the blue, not knowing when a letter would arrive, and very often replying to the letter before last. So I have had to guess at dating from internal evidence, juggle with the best sequential order, and make a speculative arrangement that hopefully makes a story.

On top of this is my father's often scrawly writing, best described as characterful when he was taking care, spidery when tired, and bordering on the illegible when depressed. Like many of his generation he would also frequently refer to colleagues by their initials from PSC to HGA, familiar to my mother, but only a few to me, leaving one floundering in hours of research. The Unit was also rich in men of identical first names, so that identifying which Peter or John is being referred to can be yet another challenge.

Perhaps the most important task I had in writing the book was to set it in its historical context, so that readers would be able to determine how the Unit's activities dovetailed into the chequerboard of the war's progress. For this I have been indebted to Tegla Davies' 1947 first draft of the Unit's history, in his book *The Friends Ambulance Unit,* and to his son Mark for his permisson to quote from it.

In fact, the help I have received from the descendants of the Unit members who were colleagues of my father, has been truly wonderful. Sometimes this has been very moving, as in the case of the children of Harold and Mary Loukes, who looked after my father when he fell ill in India, and who had no knowledge of this part of their parents' life; or of being able to show Stephen Tanner the eulogy that my father had written of his father Tom, so tragically killed in the North Atlantic.

Such co-operation has come from both near and far: South African Quakers, who had been so welcoming to my father and his FAU colleagues for photos and information; the small band of remaining Lebanese Friends who put me in touch with the Cortas family; the Haverford College of Quaker Collections in Pennsylvania, who furnished me with pictures of Jack and Tessa Cadbury; the many members of English Quaker families from the Cadburys, Taylors and Woods to my own relatives, the Rutters, Braithwaites, Sakers and Barlows. Of these, I must make special mention of Clare Norton (Taylor), Mary Penny (Taylor), Carol Saker (Braithwaite), Roger Barlow and his daughter Annabel, and my brother Nicholas, who has doggedly read draft copies, picking up typos, errors and obfuscations and given great support; to my other siblings David, Stephen and Rosemary for kindly letting me publish the letters, and to my publisher Michael Sessions for bearing with me throughout a long gestation period and for his advice and meticulous proofing. To all a huge thank you.

Of course no Quaker research would be possible without the inestimable help of all at Friends House Library, but especially Melissa Atkinson for chasing up the many photographs that have so helped to illustrate this book, which I just about completed before Coronovirus shut the library down. I am also greatly indebted to the many friends, relatives and members of the public who have helped me trace the postwar lives of those members of the FAU mentioned in the book.

Finally and most importantly, none of this would reach publication were it not for the generosity of the following Trusts, Societies and many individuals, to whom I am indebted not just financially, but above all for their kindness to me and their forbearance while I struggled to complete the book:

The Alfred W Braithwaite Trust
The Juniper Hill Fund
The Pollard and Dickson Trust
The C B and H Taylor Trust
The Southall Trust
The Westcroft Trust
The William A Cadbury Charitable Trust

The Friends Historical Research Grant
The Sessions Book Trust
Sutton Quaker Meeting
The Wainwright family

Nicholas and Caroline Barlow
Helen Brockley
Sir Dominic Cadbury
Duncan Cadbury
Sean Cathie
Alan Cooklin and Gill Gorell Barnes
Mark Davies
Alnoor Dhanji
Roger H Gillett
Harry Headley
Rosemary Howells
Richard Hoyland
Anthony Loukes
Jessica Sinclair-Loutit
Caroline Tanner
Simon W and Elaine J Taylor

If I have inadvertently omitted to mention anyone, I offer my heartfelt apologies.

A Victorian Family
The Cash Family and Aunt Lou

The photograph below shows how relative time can be. We like to pigeon-hole history into neat compartments: Victorian, Edwardian, pre-war, post-war. But in reality there is no clean break. This photograph was taken just before the turn of the 20th century, only 10 years before my father was born in 1910. The Second World War had its roots in the past, and its effects were felt long after it ended. When this photograph was taken, Aunt Louisa (Lou for short), to whom my father refers in Chapter 11 is 39, while FRB's grandfather, Frederick Goodall Cash was 71 and his grandmother, Martha Cash was 64. They were all very much Victorians, born just before the Queen's coronation in 1838. My father's own parents, John Henry and Mabel Barlow, were born in the middle of the century, and were themselves brought up in a Victorian household.

Little wonder that dear Aunt Lou in a letter written in 1941 to my father about her 80th birthday, does not once mention the war! Born in 1861, she had lived through seemingly endless 19th century European wars, the Franco Prussian war, the Crimean war, the Boer war and then in the 20th century the First World War; she'd seen too many already. Her 80th birthday would certainly have seemed more important than more war news!

The Cash family
My father's maternal grandparents with their children and spouses.
Seated left and right at the front are the grandparents FG Cash and Martha (née Bowly)
Back row l to r are: Herbert, Gertrude and John Taylor, John Henry Barlow with Mabel Barlow (née Cash) seated in front, Louisa (Aunt Lou) and Ernest Hutchinson.
Herbert Cash emigrated to America to join his brother Oliver (not present) and they both married Americans.
Photograph courtesy of Carol Saker

List of illustrations

———

Contents

Names of those frequently mentioned in this book

FAMILY MEMBERS RELATED TO F. RALPH BARLOW, THE AUTHOR'S FATHER

John Henry Barlow (1855-1924) – FRB's father
Mabel C Barlow (née Cash) (1868-1956) – FRB's mother

John C Barlow (1901-1972) – FRB's brother
Enid Barlow (née Priestman)(1900-1991) – married to John C Barlow
Roger Barlow (b.1930) – son of John and Enid Barlow
(m. Mary Biddle 1933-1997. Daughter – Annabel b.1963)

M Millior Braithwaite (née Barlow) (1904-1993) – FRB's sister
Alfred Braithwaite (1901-1975) – married to Millior Barlow
Anna M Braithwaite (later OHerlihy) (1942-2011)   ]Children of Alfred and Millior
Carol M Braithwaite (later Saker)   (b.1948)   ]Braithwaite.

Joan Barlow (née Barber) (1914-2007) – married to Ralph Barlow
David J Barlow (b.1937)   ]
Antony R Barlow (b.1941)   ]
Stephen H Barlow (b.1945)   ]   Children of Ralph and Joan
Rosemary J Barlow (later Howells) (b.1947)]   Barlow.
Nicholas P Barlow (b.1958)   ]

Dorothy (aka Bobby) Hazel (née Barber) (1901-1965) – Joan Barlow's eldest sister
Leslie Hazel (aka Les) (1902-1976) – married to Bobby
Barbara Hazel (later Stuart)(b.1931)]   Children of Les and Bobby
Susan Hazel (later Boyce) (b.1942)   ]

Winifred (aka Win) O Rutter (née Barber) (1904-2007) – Joan Barlow's 2nd sister
Dr Llewellyn (aka Llew) Rutter (1907-2003) – married to Winifred (Llew's father Dr
Hubert Rutter taught first aid to FAU members at Manor Farm, Birmingham)
Michael Rutter (b.1933)]
Priscilla Rutter (b.1935)]   Children of Llew & Win. Michael and Priscilla (later
George Rutter (b.1943)]   Sidrak) were sent to the US to escape the bombing.
Richard Rutter (b.1946)]

Reginald (aka Reg) Barber (1906-1965) – Joan Barlow's brother
Vera Barber (née Lunt) (1917-2017) – married to Reg
Graham Barber (1936-1979)]   Children of Reg and Vera Barber
Christopher Barber (b.1942)]

BOURNVILLE VILLAGE TRUST
Leonard P Appleton (aka LPA) – 2nd Director of the BVT

Annotations

In the main text, there are many indices that refer to a further explanatory note at the back of the book, on a particular word or phrase that I feel would so beneift. Each chapter has its own notes, and each new chapter starts its numbering over again, from number one thus - [1].

In addition there are 12 such indices that refer to footnotes which are explained at the bottom of the page in question. To differentiate these from the group aforementioned, I have added an asterisk , thus - *[1], and also highlighted them in a bold typeface.

Friends Ambulance Unit Members and Lifelong Friends of FRB

Paul S Cadbury   -   (aka PSC) Responsible for re-launching the FAU in 1939
(1895-1984)   Son of Barrow Cadbury and great nephew of George Cadbury,
                     Chairman of Cadbury Bros – married Rachel Wilson. 4 children:
                     Catherine, Edward, Philipa and Charles (see Ransome)

Brandon Cadbury –   Grandson of Richard and great nephew of George Cadbury
(1915-2011)   married to Flavia (née Freeman). Son Rupert

Horace Alexander – (aka HGA) - Leading Quaker teacher; Staff at Woodbrooke; Joined
(1889-1989)   FAU to lead India section; friend of Gandhi and influential in
                    India independence. Knowledgeable and important ornithologist.
                    m. 1 – Olive Graham. m. 2 Rebecca Bradbeer

Michael H Cadbury - Descendant of Joel Cadbury. Married Heather Chambers.
(1915-2007)   3 children. Andrew, Duncan and Janine. Duncan was Chairman of
                    BVT until 2018. Michael was Managing Director Cadbury Fry
                    (Export Ltd). Joined FAU 1940 working in hospital Units and at
                    Gordon Square at China desk, and at Failands.

J Duncan Wood   -   Son of theologian Herbert G Wood (aka HG) and Dorothea, who
(1910-2006)   had been wardens of Woodbrooke Quaker College.
                    Duncan (JDW) 2nd of 4 children. Went to Downs Sch and Leighton
                    Park Sch with FRB, and best man at his Wedding. Joined FAU, and
                    became Senior member of China Convoy. Post war, taught at LP
                    then ran Geneva Quaker Summer School and worked for UN.
                    Keen Ornithologist often with FRB.
                    Married Katharine Knight. Daughter - Rachel Wood (now Malloch)

Michael H -   Son of Arnold Rowntree, nephew Joseph Rowntree. Helped Paul
Rowntree   Cadbury and Michael Barratt Brown re-establish FAU. He worked
(1919-2007)   alongside FRB in Middle East, later in Italy and Germany. Post war
                    Journalist and General Manager Oxford Times and Mail. Worked
                    on many charities including Oxfam. m. Anna Crosfield. 3 children.
                    Ornithologist.

FAMILY FRIENDS

Joseph (aka Jeph) - Long time Quaker friends in Birmingham. Jeph was a solicitor,
& Margaret Gillett but for part of the war both he and Margaret were wardens at a
(née Hicks)   childrens' home in Barnt Green, for those bombed out of their
                    homes.

Ernest and   -   Next door neighbours at Linden Road, amateur musicians
Dolly Keen   -   and knowledgeable art collectors

Edwin and   -   Close family friends. Edwin Director of Barrow Stores, died young.
Hilda Ransome   4 Children – Mary, Jill, Robert and Dinah. Jill married Charles
(née Stafford Allen) Cadbury, son of Paul & Rachel Cadbury and is mother of MP Ruth
                    Cadbury.

In the course of this book I have taken the liberty of introducing extracts of reports or letters of my father's and mother's. Rather than insert my name above or below each, all the italic sections are my own exegesis.

Ralph Barlow's Wartime Timeline

September 1938
FRB joins AFS part time

September 1939
JMB and David evacuated to Sibford to join her sister and family
January 1940 – they returned home

May 1940
FRB and JMB and David holiday in Dunster

June 1940
FRB joins AFS full time

End of September 1940
FRB leaves AFS

October 1 – 14 1940
Break at 26 Linden Road

Mid October 1940
Tribunal

End of October 1940
FRB joins FAU at Northfield Camp

Autumn 1940
JMB moves to Beaconwood

December 1940
FRB joins Hospital in Whitechapel

January 19 1941
ARB born at 'Beaconwood'

Jan 29 – March 29 1941
FRB in Cheveley near Newmarket

March 31 - April 6 1941
FRB & JMB week's holiday at 'Spinneyfields' Nr Lydiate Ash/Lickey Hills (Lent by George Cadbury jnr)

April 7 – June 30 1941
FRB in charge of 11th Camp at Northfield

July 1 – 12 1941
FRB & JMB break at Ewyas Harold, Nr Abergavenny - (stayed in 'Ivy Cottage' which belonged to LP Appleton then CEO BVT)

July 1941 – June 1942
FRB in charge of London Relief Section based in Poplar

July 1941 – November 1943
JMB moves to Wolverhampton

July – August 1941
For a period of about 3/4 weeks, Joan staying in Monmouth with ARB and DJB (House belonged to Mr and Mrs Dobinson.)

September 1941 – January 1942
Tom Tanner in America.
FRB becomes Deputy Director

November 1941
Bournemouth Conference

May 1942
Holiday at Stottesdon, Nr Bridgenorth with FRB, JMB and DJB

June 1942/43
FRB sails via Durban to Cairo - where he is based for next 18 months

November 23 1942
Tom Tanner and Peter Hume leave for China – torpedoed in the South Atlantic December 2nd. All bar one lost

Christmas 1942
FRB goes to Teheran to find homes for Polish refugees

March 1943
FRB to Ethiopia - where he probably contracted the encephalitis which later developed en-route to India

May/July 1943
FRB to India. Laid low for 3 months with encephalitis. Recuperated in Darjeeling

July/August 1943
FRB to China completing Tanner's mission

October 1943
FRB Sails home – still low from illness

November 1943 – January 1944
FRB on Sick leave.
Moves to 6 Swarthmore Rd

January 1944 – December 1944
FRB Officer for Overseas work and Deputy Chairman Gordon Square.

December 1944
Leaves Unit on Doctor's orders

Code
FRB – Ralph Barlow
JMB – Joan M Barlow
DJB – David J Barlow
ARB – Antony R Barlow

Commonly used abbreviations in this book

Organizations

AFS	Auxiliary Fire Service
BRCS	British Red Cross Society
BVT	Bournville Village Trust
CAB	Citizen's Advice Bureau
CO	Conscientious Objector
FAU	Friends Ambulance Unit
FH	Friends House
FRS	Fire and Rescue Service
FVRS	Friends Victims Relief Service
FWVRC	Friends War Victims Relief Cte

FRSC	Friends Relief Service Council
NAAFI	Navy, Army and Air Force Inst
NCSS	National Council of Social Services
RAMC	Royal Army Medical Corps
UNRRA	United

People

FRB	F Ralph Barlow
HGA	Horace G Alexander
HGW	Hubert G Wood (or just HG)
JDW	J Duncan Wood
JMB	Joan M Barlow
PSC	Paul S Cadbury
TLT	Tom L Tanner

———

FAU Mobile Operating Theatre
Photograph Friends House Library

The Friends Ambulance Unit
by Antony Barlow

The FAU tapestry panel on the Friends Ambulance Unit
by kind permission of the Quaker Tapestry Museum, Kendal

This book does not tell the story of the fighting that took place throughout the Second World War, not only here but worldwide. To most that is well known and well documented, with its tales of heroism, of 'the few' fighting alone against the might of Germany; of the horrors of the blitz, destroying the homes and livelihoods of the ordinary person in terrifying nightly bombardment; of their suffering as they were badly wounded or killed; of the pluck of those who rescued the hundreds of trapped soldiers at Dunkirk; of the gallantry of the military at Alamein; of the starvation and loss of human life at the siege of Stalingrad. Nor does it tell of Nazi atrocities or, for that matter of the equal loss of life sustained by the axis powers.

Instead this book tries to tell the story in between these spaces, where in the midst of battle, there are people trying their best to save the lives of the wounded, whether they be civilians caught in the crossfire of enemy bombing, or soldiers wounded in what Wilfred Owen calls the 'cess of war'. This is the story of those who joined the Friends Ambulance Unit in 1939 and 1940, not to fight, but to make a difference whilst at the same time, standing against 'the truth untold/The pity of war, the pity war distilled.'

My father started a memoir which begins as follows: "In the course of the war, I was fortunate enough to travel rather widely and I have ventured to think that extracts from my letters to Joan might be of interest." I have tried my best to complete his work as he envisaged it and in addition to add my mother's replies in as well, forming a fuller picture of the way the war unravelled for one family.

Foreword
by Rupert Cadbury

With this beautifully illustrated and meticulously researched book Antony Barlow has added an important chapter to the history of the Friends Ambulance Unit; one which admirably complements the official record 'The Friends Ambulance Unit' written by Tegla Davies and published in 1947.

The letters from Ralph Barlow to his wife, Joan, on which the book is based are full of carefully observed detail which, with warmth and humour, bring to life his experience as he progresses from school to married life and then, having made the difficult decision to register as a conscientious objector, to his service in the FAU, and a temporary but painful separation from his wife and children.

The letters from his time overseas are particularly vivid and reflect his wide ranging fascination with every aspect of life – from the flora, fauna and landscape, to the people he encountered with their culture and social conditions.

Like Ralph Barlow, my father Brandon Cadbury was part of the Quaker community in Birmingham and a conscientious objector, who also joined the FAU. For us, his children, it was his time with the China Convoy that held a particular fascination. He rarely talked about China, although on special occasions he would cook the most wonderful Chinese meals, so completely different from the English food of the day. FRB's letters give a clear, unfiltered and unsentimental view of life in the FAU, which do much to dispel the sense of mystery surrounding my father's war time experience.

The book concludes with a compilation of the very moving tributes he received on being invalided out of the FAU in 1944. To win respect is an achievement, to be so obviously loved is quite remarkable.

Finally, this foreword would not be complete without a tribute to Joan, on whose love and support he so clearly depended.

Rupert Cadbury, Tansor House, July 2020

Father and son: Brandon Cadbury and Rupert
Photograph courtesy of Rupert Cadbury

Introduction
The FAU and Friends

The initials FAU and the words they stood for, The Friends Ambulance Unit, were inextricably woven into the fabric of our family life and in many ways came to be synonymous with the values my father, Ralph Barlow believed in. He served in the Friends Ambulance Unit from 1940 to 1944 when he was invalided out, and later wrote a short memoir of that time for the benefit of his children. But typical of my father, it leaves as much out as it tells. Attempts to find out more about his time in the Unit when we were young, did not elicit a great deal more. Naturally shy, he was not one to volunteer information and my suspicion has always been that his time in the Unit was as taxing and demanding as that of many an army officer, and possibly more harrowing than he ever let on. One of the reasons, therefore, for my writing this history is to discover more about his contribution and also to document a largely unwritten section of Quaker history. When after my father's comparatively early death, in 1980, I came across his memoir that he had written for us children and typed it out, I sent a copy to his lifelong friend, Duncan Wood. His comments were revealing.......

'Typical Ralph; underplaying his role, which of course was much more significant than he makes out. His notes say little about his most important appointment as C-in-C of all the work in the Middle East, based in Cairo. And just to add to his burden of responsibility, he was sent to China to sort out the problems of the China Convoy. In military terms he had the rank of Field-Marshal: he played a very important part indeed in the life of the wartime FAU."

This is a friendship that goes back to their childhood when they were at The Downs School [1] together in the 1920's, and it might be apposite to cite a section of Duncan's Foreword to his own book on their friend and mentor, Horace Alexander [2].......

"Ralph and I met in the early twenties at The Downs School....Horace had been at school there twenty years before us....Every Wednesday afternoon was devoted to a 'hobby' which was compulsory in that you had to choose which branch of Natural History you would study. When I went to The Downs....I had no interest whatever in any branch of natural history...until by chance, I saw a Nuthatch. I had no idea that there existed a bird capable of coming down a tree-trunk head first. I was fascinated...but I needed a true companion who shared my suddenly new-found interest. So at the beginning of the next term Ralph Barlow – bless him - took me on. He was already a budding birdwatcher and recognised that by signing up for birds, we would have the freedom to explore the countryside on our own and unsupervised. We used that freedom productively...thus we began a close partnership in the pursuit of what became a lifelong absorbing interest....and it was our good fortune to be members of the large Quaker community in south Birmingham and thus neighbours of Horace...who invited us two to join him in birdwatching....From then on he became our much cherished companion in all birdwatching expeditions."

Their friendship and birdwatching enthusiasm is well illustrated in a letter from Duncan to my father dated 1927, which is just signed 'Love From Me', and though I had it authenticated by Duncan's daughter Rachel [3], there was little need, as it could only be from Duncan to my father. In five pages, he discusses nothing else but how many birds each has seen and is very miffed that my father has seen a Serin [4] and he hasn't! The friendship was a deep and enduring one and when my father married my mother Joan in 1936, it was naturally to Duncan that he turned to as his best man.

At the outset of war they joined the Unit together, but after initial training, their work was to take them apart, with my father in the Middle East and Duncan in China. It might, therefore, be appropriate here to quote from a note that Rachel had found amongst her father's papers, which my father wrote in 1941 just before Duncan left for China, anticipating perhaps more in hope than expectation, that it would be ended by 1943! .....

"My dear Duncan...In memory of a friendship which has been one of the best things in my life. In gratitude for this and all that it has meant. In remembrance of so many good times – of laughter and birds and walking. With the most sincere good wishes for the success of your venture. Success which I know you will achieve because you so richly deserve it. With the most sincere and heartfelt prayers for your safety and looking forward eagerly to your return. Whatever may have come by 1943, Joan and I will be overjoyed to see you and there will be a home and welcome for you in our house wherever it may be and whenever you may need it. If there is anything I can do for you, however small, do not hesitate to ask. I shall miss you more than I can say. God bless you. Yours ever Ralph."

In the front of the FAU Annual report for 1939 – 1943, the Unit boldly states its credentials: "A venture in faith, in the midst of war" and in many respects it was that idealism that imbued those early recruits. In my father's accounts he talks of his first memory as a member of the Unit, turning up at Manor Farm, Northfield for the first training Camp and being introduced to other members gathered round the mess table....

Anyone who arrived then must think with affection of the people he met there and throughout my time in the Unit I have been glad to think that amongst those potential section leaders were John Burtt, Harold Kempster and Duncan Wood. The camp was full of enthusiasm...in fact we were all imbued with the general enthusiasm of those days and the Unit was still very much our unit. At that time the FAU was in a very formative stage and had not by any means resolved in its own mind, if it was to become an efficient relief organization or whether it wanted to be some sort of religious order.

———

Instead of going to Oxford or Cambridge as Duncan did, my father went to Birmingham University, as I think his mother, having lost a child in infancy as well as a much revered husband, became over protective towards her next child. So in many ways this was his University 'away from home', where he matured and showed his worth. Here he writes about the experience of FAU life in general.......

I am grateful for the friends I made and the life that existed in the London Hostel. It gave me something new, something that I might have got had I gone to a University away from home. A chance to talk about everything from books, films and plays to history and religion, Quakerism and war. And what a fantastic world I had to deal with, ranging from homosexuality and birth control to the problems of the war, such as protection from gas or even the mundanity of beetles in the kitchen. And such a mixture of people, with Anglicans, Methodists and Quakers - from State schools and Public schools; snobs and democrats. And a day might start with my interviewing an Italian refugee, followed by a Quaker Committee meeting at Friends House and ending with supper with two high-ranking BBC officials......I boasted in a letter to Joan, that after the war I felt I could run anything! It has given me experience and self-confidence. I have made my way, stood on my own feet and done a job. I have gained knowledge of all sorts of people and places.

But as he describes, service in the Unit meant separation from family and loved ones.........

Unit members, like everyone else in this war, know what separation means. Often, although away from home, the husband has the more interesting job, seeing people and getting about, whereas the wife has the harder job of looking after the children and a dull daily round. I saw many relationships grow apart. But Joan was wonderful......and thank God, we did not grow apart. For a time, I think she thought I was growing away from her, but she was quite mistaken.

As for many people working in places such as the Middle East, China, India or North Africa, disease was an ever present danger and one of the most taxing episodes of my father's war years, was in 1943 when he contracted Epidemic-Encephalitis in Ethiopia. This was a life-threatening illness and seriously weakened him for the rest of his life. But typical of my father, who tended to try and disregard illness, he refused to succumb, insisted on carrying on after a very short convalescence, and far too prematurely, returned to work, some thought to the detriment of his well-being in later life.

For my mother it was undoubtedly a period of enormous strain, giving up her own home, moving from house to house, first to Honor and Christopher Cadbury's[5] where I was born and then to Wolverhampton, and bringing up two children in someone else's house albeit her sister's and brother-in-law's. In addition, all through the period of nearly four years, letters to and from this country took uncertain and variable lengths of time to reach their destination, with the constant worry of not knowing the danger my father might be in, or, when he was very ill, whether he would recover. That their relationship survived and that they were able to regroup after the war, says a great deal for both of them and their mutual loyalty and devotion, as shown in their many letters written during this extremely testing and difficult time, which clearly show their trust and love in each other, many of which form the bulk of this book.

After the war, for my father, there was the necessary readjustment to civilian life. Starting back at the Bournville Village Trust after five years away, during which time he had seen continuous action during an adrenalin filled time, travelled continuously from place to place, lead his mission and been responsible to HQ, could not have been easy. It was a long period of great camaraderie, with people of shared values and a common desire to serve in trying and often impossible conditions, with whom he had observed scenes of unimaginable carnage and terribly wounded soldiers, many of whom died horrific deaths. It is little wonder that he didn't talk much to us children about his wartime life and even his memoirs, written specifically for us, are mere outlines of these years; the deeper experience is scarcely touched on. How humdrum the running of an inner city housing estate must have seemed initially.

As a child after the war, I can remember dressing up in my father's FAU uniform, so from an early age, I was very much aware that my father had been in the FAU and a Conscientious Objector, even if I didn't fully understand its implications. At the end of his memoirs my father talks about returning home and living with the family again............

I was very doubtful about the rightness of leaving the Unit and as long as they wanted me at Gordon Square, I felt I could have carried on. I did not want my health to be an excuse for getting me back to Bournville. But I was not well and perhaps did not fully realise how far from well I was. So, although I had many regrets about leaving, I did not share other people's forebodings that I should find my life at home dull. To live at home again, without fear of further partings hanging over my head, was marvellous. A reunion and a return after so long wandering and waiting, seemed almost too good to be true.

I might end this introduction by quoting from Tegla Davies' book on the FAU, which I think sums up the feelings of most of those who were in the Unit during the war.

"It was our Unit, and we were proud of it, not with uncritical pride, but with the pride of those who for better or worse, had made it what it was. The Unit started with the war and we who became its members were the Unit....We all had ideas of what we wanted it to be, of what we wanted it to do. We argued and we laughed and we sweated over it: for the war years it became our life: it bounded our horizons: our friends were in it: we talked little of other things: and only when we left it did we realise fully what it had meant to us."

What follows is a history of the Friends Ambulance Unit as told through my father's words, partly from the memoir he wrote for his children, partly through reports he wrote for HQ and perhaps mostly through the letters he and my mother wrote to each other throughout the troubled years of the Second World War from 1939 to 1945, which I hope will shed a new light on the work of the Unit, my father's and other's contribution, and the relationship of my parents.

———

"If you can fill the unforgiving minute with sixty second's worth of distance run....."

During my father's time in the Middle East he travelled in all 30,000 miles in 11 months:

England to Cairo via Durban (12,000 miles)
Three desert trips:
   a) Barq al Arab]
   b) Martuba   ] (2,600 miles)
   c) Tobruk   ]
Four visits to Alexandria (1,500 miles)
Visits to Buseli and Darmanham (1,500 miles)
Three week trip to Syria, Ismailia, Beersheba,]
Haifa, Beirut, Broumana, Damascus, Sednayeh,]
Selimiyeh, Hama, Aleppo, Tel Tamar, Aleppo,   ] (3,000 miles)
Latakia, Beirut, Jerusalem, Cairo   ]
Four day trips to Ismailia, Tel Aviv, Haifa, Beirut, Jerusalem, Cairo (1,100 miles)
Two week-end visits to Jerusalem (1,400 miles)
Journey to Teheran by air (3,000)
Journey by air to Addis plus various trips to Ambo, Bishoftu, Hadama, Debra Birhan and Ficce (4,000 miles)

Family Benefactors

Edward and Dorothy Cadbury
My father's cousins, who were so kind to my parents when they got married.
Dame Elizabeth Cadbury said of them:
"I do not know of any other two people so devoted to each other as Edward Cadbury and his wife Dorothy, so thoroughly in harmony in every intention both in life and work."

Photograph courtesy of the Edward and Dorothy Cadbury Trust

My parents' first home, 26 Linden Road,
A wedding present from the Edward Cadbury family

Lifelong Friends - Ralph Barlow and Duncan Wood

Ralph and Joan's wedding September 1936 with Duncan Wood as best man.
Vera Barber as bridesmaid, and Barbara Hazel and Roger Barlow as pages.

Lifelong birding companions since their schooldays.
First at The Downs School, and later at Leighton Park School.

Dedication
Antony Barlow

Although I have edited these letters and deleted repetitions, I make no apology for keeping in the many endearments with which my parents have filled their correspondence. In some places these are quite intimate, and some may be surprised that I decided to leave them in, but it seems to me that they express an essential part of the story – their feelings for each other. They are after all, a young married couple with a child, torn apart by the exigencies of war, and 'love, and missing and longing' are a large part of that narrative.

It has been an enormous privilege to collaborate on editing these letters with my family and friends, and I believe it to be a very valuable heritage I am bequeathing to history. As I worked with the descendants of the many Unit members who served with my father, it has been borne in on me that within a few short years, not only has my father's generation long since gone from us, but we now in our 80's, will shortly have died too. This, therefore, is the eleventh hour to preserve memories as near to first hand as possible.

I trust everyone who reads these pages will enjoy not only an important part of Quaker history, but the wonderful descriptions, the joyous humour and the loving tenderness, that kept this relationship of two very special people together.

Joan and Ralph together on my father's 70th birthday in 1980

Ralph and Joan Barlow's wedding 1936

Chapter 1
Family Background

This is the story of two people from very different backgrounds, and how they coped with the problems and hardships thrown at them by the Second World War. It is the story of my father from a famous old Quaker family, who while not being, as he describes 'a rabid pacifist', has nonetheless been imbued with the pacifist creed of Quakerism handed down through generations of his Quaker ancestors. He therefore, almost backs into being a Conscientious Objector, and finds himself in the Friends Ambulance Unit, in which he discovers unsuspected qualities of leadership and ends up as Deputy Director, when his predecessor is torpedoed in the North Atlantic.

His trajectory takes him abroad to the Middle East, to Iran and Ethiopia, before going on to India and China, witnessing the excesses of war as he supervises the setting up of mobile hospitals and operating theatres, blood banks and rest homes; of resettling refugees, relieving the casualties of the Sino-Japanese war and helping with the casualties of the Bengal famine. For nearly two years, my father is away from my mother and two young children – my brother and me – and they both have to learn to cope with separation.

It is also the story of my mother, from a totally different Quaker background, from a family with little money and few privileges, who finds an inner strength and resolve to survive, living away from home, bringing us up, and living off the half salary of my father.

So I think it would be instructive to begin this story with a short account of both my parents' early lives, as I believe their backgrounds and upbringing reflect greatly on how they conducted themselves during these difficult years of the war. Both my parents came from Quaker backgrounds, both were the youngest child of four and both lost their fathers when they were still very young, but that is about the end of the immediate similarity. Although they were both members of the Society of Friends, they were from very different families. My father's family was from very old Quaker roots, whereas my mother's family were more recent converts.

The Barlows were an evangelical family, well off and moved in elite Quaker circles, whereas my mother's family, the Barbers were by comparison poor and scraped a living by taking in lodgers. Both my parents had been to Quaker schools, though my father went to an all-boys school, whereas my mother went to a co-ed; my father studied at Birmingham University, while my mother, though she would have loved to, wasn't able to, as she had to earn a living.

Their characters too, were very different. My father was somewhat shy and retiring and would do anything to avoid confrontation. He was remarkably tolerant and understanding, born in many respects, as he later admits, from his years in the Friends Ambulance Unit, when he experienced more than he ever tells. This time away from home, having to take responsibility for a group of men from backgrounds, often very different from his own, separated from their families in far-away places, was the sort of experience he might have enjoyed had he gone away to University and lived away from home, rather than with his mother in Birmingham. But it was probably the making of him.

My mother, on the other hand, was an outgoing person, vivacious and full of fun, who made friends easily. She enjoyed tennis and acting in plays and as a pretty young girl, was obviously the life and soul of the party. Before she got married she went out to Broumana in the Lebanon, to stay with her newly married sister and brother-in-law, and like my father, obviously relished the first time away from home in a very different country.

While she was there, she was much admired by the men folk, and indeed experienced an affair with a young Lebanese man. It all left a lasting impression on her, and in many ways was her surrogate university experience. When later she and my father did get married in 1936, my mother was a great home maker and made their house a welcoming place for all their friends, perhaps prompted by a remark from my father in a 1935 letter from central Europe, where he was on a birding holiday, in which he expresses the hope 'that they will have a spare room when they get married, so that they can have friends to stay.' But generally she was a more sociable person, whilst my father was far more diffident.

My father, came from one of the old Quaker families, which dated back to the very beginning of the Society. Both his parents, John Henry Barlow and Mabel Cash, came from a long line of distinguished Quakers and were related to many of the well-known Quaker names such as Cadbury, Cash, Darby, Nicholson and Taylors, whose children my father had grown up with, in the wide Quaker diaspora. He was born in 1910, the youngest of four children, one of whom, Phyllis, had died aged only two, which had caused much heart ache. Their mother Mabel, wrote in a family memoir "A great sorrow came to us in 1909, when on June 9th our darling daughter, Phyllis Deborah[1] was called to another home. We were indeed sorely stricken as she was so full of brightness, so loving and gay." *But a year later another child, my father, was born and his birth was the occasion of great joy,* "given us by God to help heal the sore hearts", *wrote his mother.*

My father in a typically Eeyorish way, was wont to say that he was 'a replacement child', but I think the evidence is that he was all the more loved for that very reason. He was christened Frederick Ralph; Frederick after his grandfather Frederick G Cash, and Ralph just because his parents liked the name! Indeed Ralph became the name by which he was henceforward to be known and throughout his life; never Frederick!

His father, John Henry was at that time, possibly the most well-known person in the Society of Friends; Clerk of Yearly Meeting throughout the war years, the go-to person to head delegations such as leading the fight to secure the conscience clause in the 1916 Military Service Act; or the enquiry into the Black and Tans[2] in 1920; or as representative for the five year conference in 1922 at Richmond, Indiana, as well of course as being the director of George Cadbury's housing project, the Bournville Village Trust. And although he was undoubtedly a father who doted on his children and loved to read stories and play games with them, John Henry was of quite a severe demeanour, as is apparent from photographs of the period and it was certainly a very religious household. Despite the many calls on my grandfather's time however, my grandmother writes…….

"Home was to him, and to me, the very centre of our lives….what pleasure it was when there was a free evening at home. After the children had been read to or played with, we would settle down to work or to read aloud to each other. It was a peculiar delight to listen to his reading, particularly when he assumed a scots accent*, to which he gave exactly the right lilt. He and I also loved to entertain and at some of the parties, John used to act excellently in charades, making a capital actor. How Selly Oak Friends used to enjoy seeing him in this unfamiliar role." (*He had been born in Edinburgh)

So there were the two sides of this extraordinary man, both devout, serious and committed, as well as the loving family man. As a cousin observed on his death……..

"We shall not look upon his like again. His dignified eloquence and his powerful speaking, always finding 'le mot juste', are my outstanding memories of him and above all, the deep feeling and experience behind all that he said. Then too, his humour and appreciation of it were in such contrast to his dignified and almost apostolic public deliverance, one wondered at the great qualities of this man."

The Grandparents

Mabel Barlow (née Cash)

John Henry Barlow

William Barber

Ellen Barber (née Eyre)

My father went away to Quaker boarding schools, first to The Downs School near Colwall in the Malvern Hills and later to Leighton Park in Reading. It was at these schools that he met his life-long friend Duncan Wood, the son of the eminent Quaker theologian H G Wood. Both Duncan and my father, through the help and advice of the Quaker eminence grise, Horace Alexander[3], became devoted and expert bird lovers, a hobby they pursued throughout their lives and later Duncan was best man at my parents' wedding.

My grandfather, died in 1924, after a long illness, when my father was only 14 and still at school. His mother thought it better he shouldn't be upset and so he wasn't able to say his farewells, as his siblings had. I think there is evidence that his mother often over protected him, possibly since the death of Phyllis and then the death of his father. After school, for instance, he went to Birmingham University to study history, rather than to Oxford as his friend Duncan did. As a result, he didn't have the normal teenage freedom to experiment in the way Duncan had, a fact he draws attention to in his wartime memoirs, stating how he wished he had been more worldly wise when he joined the Friends Ambulance Unit.

Having read History at Birmingham, one of his former masters at Leighton Park, Tom Elliott, thought he might take up teaching, as did Duncan when he took up a post at Leighton Park..........

"I hear from Duncan that you had thoughts of teaching....this gave me a sudden glow of pleasure. The need in Friend's Schools particularly, for the right sort of man is so great and the opportunities, so vast. I think we are on the eve of a great new era in education with scope for new ideas and enthusiasms. And I think you are exactly the right sort of person, as you have enthusiasms, wide interests and ability. Above all, you know already that schoolmastering is not class room teaching only and that the spirit of man needs fostering and feeding as well as the intellect."

However, whatever ideas of teaching my father had himself contemplated, it was not long after he graduated in 1932, that he decided to join the Bournville Village Trust. But here again there is evidence of pressure from his mother that he should follow in his father's footsteps at the BVT, as seen in a letter dated March 16th 1932 from Dame Elizabeth Cadbury[3], who it should be recalled was his mother's first cousin........

Dear Ralph
I reported to the Trustees the conversation which I had yesterday with you and your mother...and they are very pleased that you would like to come to the Estate Office in the summer. Affectionately, Cousin Elsie

So I suspect the proposition may well have emanated from the family, but my father seems happy enough to have acquiesced and by the autumn of 1932, on the Trust's initiative and with some additional financing, he is busy travelling through Europe, including a visit to Russia, looking at various housing projects. The engagement letter offers £25 towards the travelling and a remuneration of £125 for the initial training period under his father's successor, Leonard Appleton. My father always acknowledged the great help LPA gave him in those early days and often paid tribute to him........

I began at the Estate Office for the BVT in 1932, latterly as Assistant Secretary to Leonard P Appleton. My debt to him is great; he taught me to work hard and thoroughly; he taught me too what I know of administration; and taught me above all that the man in charge was responsible. Never say 'well it's not my fault'; everything should be known or foreseen. Bournville, I felt had outlived its usefulness and much of its reputation as a housing experiment. We attended housing conferences and meetings but we had less to give. But under LPA the Estate was well run and the assets grew.

My father worked conscientiously at the Trust in those early years, and probably around 1933 or 34 he met my mother through the Quaker circles centred on Woodbrooke and the Midland Institute. My mother, Joan Barber, had grown up in a quite different family background. She was born in June 1914, the youngest of four children of William and Ellen Barber, then living in Bournville. Both her parents - her mother's family the Eyres and her father's family the Barber's - were from very humble backgrounds and distinctly on the wrong side of poverty. My mother's sister, Winifred talking in later life of their mother said [4] *............*

"Our mother had a very hard life. Her parents had died when she was young (she and her sister and brothers grew up in an orphanage) and soon after she married my father, they found out that he had a weak heart. It was an awful blow to her that he wasn't strong but I never heard her grumble. No Insurance Company would insure father because of this and so we really were quite poor after he died. Mother would never let anyone say that we were, but we were poor. Mother used to take in paying guests to earn extra money."

From her days in Crowley's Orphanage, run by a Quaker, Ellen Eyre as she was then, and her sister, Emily had been greatly helped by the influential Birmingham Quakers through Edward Cadbury, who had been on the board. The children at the orphanage received a good education and it was through them that she first met her husband, William Barber, a printer by trade, who had grown up in the Coleshill area of Birmingham. So the story went, he described my grandmother as having the most beautiful eyes, "that could fetch the ducks off the water". They were eventually married, and set up home in Smethwick, where their first child, Dorothy was born.

With Quaker assistance Ellen's children were enabled to go to the Quaker school of Sibford near Banbury in Oxfordshire. After her time there, my mother went on to train at a secretarial college in Birmingham and in 1934 got a job working for two remarkable Quaker Headmasters, Charles Dobinson and Tom Rogers of the two King Edward's schools at Five Ways, to the West of the city and Camp Hill, close to the city centre respectively, both of whom remained close friends. My grandmother was always very conscious of and grateful for the enormous assistance she received from Quakers, as a result of which she joined Friends herself and her children began mixing in Quaker circles. As already stated, my mother had a very lively personality, and enjoyed playing tennis and acting, and joined the Quaker dramatic society. This is where she first met my father, when he was aged 20 and up at University and she was 17, studying at Gosling's Secretarial College in Birmingham. It is clear from letters dated 1933, that she was already very fond of him, and they continued to act together in a variety of plays, in the years leading up to 1936, when they got married.

In one of his wartime letters my father comments on the death of the playwright, Mary Lucy Pendered who wrote 'The Fair Quaker', which they had both acted in..........

What fun that play was and how blessed, because it was then that I first fell in love with you. For that reason alone I shall always treasure the play and remember it with gratitude. I'm not sure that I was any good, but you were enchanting.

The relationship was not popular with my father's mother, who like her cousin Elizabeth Cadbury, could be rather grand, and undoubtedly thought my mother unsuitable, as not coming from what she would regard as 'Quaker royalty'! But my father always reassured my mother, by telling her "to have patience; you'll see, it will be alright in the end." *So although by this time there had obviously been an understanding, they were not in fact, formerly engaged until the beginning of 1936. In an extract which gives the background to this period as well as the time they were apart during the war, my father writes.......*

Joan and I were married in 1936. It was a step opposed by some, but I knew then and time has confirmed, that it was the right thing to do. We loved each other then, and love each other still more now; in every way she is the perfect wife and the more I know her the more do I love and admire her. Her courage throughout the war years has been beyond praise. Our married life since 1936 has been completely happy.

They were married in Selly Oak Quaker meeting house and with a generous gift of a home from their wealthy cousins, Edward and Dorothy Cadbury, who had no children of their own and treated them as if they had been theirs, they moved into a lovely house in Bournville at 26 Linden Road. Their first child, David, was born in 1937 and with some domestic help, they led a quiet and happy middle class life within a close-knit Quaker circle. During those pre-war years my parents enjoyed several holidays abroad including in 1938, a wonderful fortnight in Switzerland, while my mother's mother kindly looked after David. They visited Grindelwald, Wengen and Kandersteg and my father describes their time there with affection......

"Mountains always fascinate me, with their incredible height and snowy purity. Up in the high Alps we found gentians and soldanellas[5] and I shall never forget Joan's delight at finding them. As always she had an overpowering temptation to pick them and often we had wonderful bowls in our rooms. We walked over from Grindelwald to Wengen and down to Interlaken and then up from there to Kandersteg by train. On our return we had two days in Paris and saw some of the French housing at Suresnes[6] and we visited the Louvre, a great highlight of our trip."

Then the next year 1939, they went to Stockholm for a housing conference.......

"In 1939 we travelled to Sweden in a luxurious boat from Svenska Lloyd[7]. We were both thrilled with Stockholm, a city beautifully situated and containing so many lovely modern buildings. We shall both of us remember the reception given to members attending the conference in the Town Hall. The beautiful rooms, filled with people in evening dress, the lights glittering on the water outside, the light nights and the wonderfully dressed shop windows linger forever in my memory."

My parents were at that time very loyal members of Selly Oak Quaker Meeting, with my father as both Clerk of the Meeting, Chairman of Birmingham Young Friends and Secretary of the Woodbrooke Settlement Committee. They busied themselves with work and friends, only dimly aware that it was being threatened and likely to come to an end. My father writes of the work of conservation he undertook at the Trust, acquiring and managing large agricultural estates just outside the city, working closely with the National Trust; and how at home he and my mother took on many of the social problems presented by the huge municipal estates in Birmingham, starting a mixed social club on the rather run down Weoley Castle estate, remarking that - 'It was tragic that so much of this effort was soon to be interrupted by the war."

They lived at the Linden Road house from 1936 to 1939, which my father describes with great fondness as – "a house of great character both within and without, and the view from the windows out over the then open country of the Estate and the slopes of Frankley Beeches[7], was a fine one, with a glorious Beech in the fore-ground."

He also talks more generally of his beliefs at this time...... "Before Joan and I were married we had done a good deal of pacifist propaganda, but as we settled down, we became more conservative. Generally we gave our time to a number of good causes. We read all the gloomy 1936 prognostications in the New Statesman and News Chronicle but hoped that our little comfortable world would not be shattered.

We could not whole heartedly disapprove of Munich[8], because it gave us a year's respite. How little we then understood of world politics and how much more do we know now."

*As they settled into their home, they both liked to entertain friends and often had people in to supper and my mother, as I remember from later in life, was a very fine cook, always preparing excellent and well-served meals. Thus the early years of their marriage were wonderfully happy and secure; a lovely home and garden, a young son, and a job my father enjoyed doing; a small group of friends, mostly Quaker whom they had known, often since childhood and pastimes they both relished. Then, as my father recalls, it all ended......"*Such was our world, when the war came and shattered it; how bitterly we resented its going. Would we have it back now if we could? In essentials, it is all we wanted back, but how different we are now."

However, from September 1939 after the blitzkrieg on Poland, and after Neville Chamberlain had declared war, till April 1940, seemingly nothing happened and it became known as the 'Phoney War'. But because of the perceived danger of a German invasion at this time, many families were evacuated and it was widely considered possible that they would all be there for some time. Indeed, my mother and her sister, Winifred, along with their mother and my brother David, and cousins Michael and Priscilla, were all evacuated to 'Burdrop Farm' near Sibford. My mother often told how, thinking it would be a long stay, they had all taken vast quantities of belongings with them, including their potted bulbs! My father stayed behind and he describes visiting them at this strange farm which belonged to an eccentric couple, a Mr and Mrs Poulton...

My mother still got petrol for her car* at that time before the days of rationing, and I drove them all over there. They shared a dirty, inconvenient, old fashioned farm house with an outside toilet. I later visited them there some weekends and though I quite enjoyed my weekends in the country, I don't know how they stood it for three months.

However, in Western Europe very little of military importance did take place. In fact, so little occurred that many of those who had been evacuated at the start of the war, had returned to their homes as did my mother and the rest of the family. But to assume that nothing was going on, would be wrong, as Poland was in the process of being occupied, with all that brought for the Polish people, one of the results of which was that my parents generously let their house to a family of Polish refugees, the Tritches[9]*.*

In fact, many things were happening, but the British public or very few of them, were largely unaware of them. However, the sinking of the 'Athenia' by a German U boat, sent a clear message to Britain that Germany was prepared to sink passenger liners and not just ships of military importance, and the sinking of the 'Royal Oak' also soon brought the war home to everybody. Such was the shock to the government of the 'Royal Oak's' sinking, that many people only learned about it from the propaganda broadcasts of William Joyce, better known as Lord Haw Haw.

My father remembers how: "In some ways the first months of the 'phoney war' meant little change. My mother kindly moved into 26 Linden Road with her maid Bessie and looked after my brother John and me, as Enid[10] (sister-in-law) was evacuated too. The breakup of everything that seemed to matter to us, was shattering. I shall never forget the misery of those weeks nor the hopelessness with which one evening down at Sibford, we heard the Prime Minister announce that the Cabinet were calculating on a three years war."

———

*My father's mother owned a car, which was looked after by a driver, a Mr Dutton, and she had first call on his services. If Mrs Barlow or my father didn't need the car, Mr D could use it to drive others about.

AFS Certificates and a dismissal

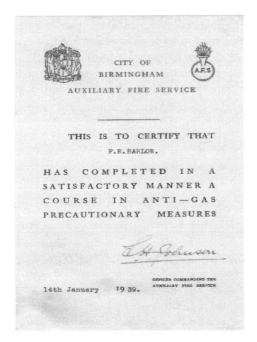
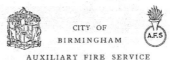

My Father's two certificates gained during his time in the AFS

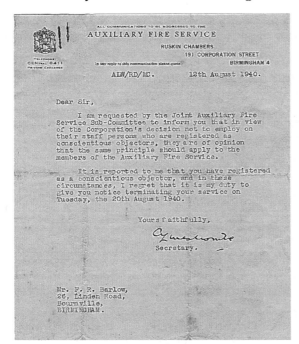
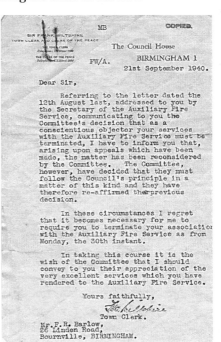

Letters of dismissal from the AFS for being a Conscientious Objector

Chapter 2
The Auxiliary Fire Service
September 1939

The Auxiliary Fire Service (AFS) was formed just prior to the Second World War as part of the government's Civil Defence Service plans, to supplement the work of the local fire brigades. In the beginning their work was often made more difficult by the incompatibility of equipment used by different brigades. The most obvious example was the lack of a standard size of hydrant valve.

Initially, some people wrongly saw firemen as trying to dodge joining the forces, but as soon as the bombing started, their value was soon realised. Throughout the war, especially during the blitz, fire became a huge threat to the British people and emergency water tanks were installed in many towns and, where any large water supply, such as a river was available, pipes were laid to provide water for fire-fighting. Members of the AFS were unpaid, part-time volunteers, who could, if necessary, be called up for whole-time paid service. Both men and women were able to join, the latter mainly in an administrative role. By 1941 The Auxiliary Fire Service and the local brigades were superseded by the National Fire Service and after the war the AFS was again reformed along with the Civil Defence Corps, to form part of the UK's emergency response to nuclear attack. But in 1968 it was disbanded altogether.

Gas attacks were widely predicted and all households were issued with Gas masks and I can remember playing with ours after the war along with trying on my father's FAU uniform!

AFS firemen damping down the remains of the fire in the Bull Ring area, Birmingham.
Photograph Birmingham City archives

My father writes at some length about his time in the Auxiliary Fire Service......

At the time of Munich in September 1938, I had joined the AFS in a voluntary capacity, and by September 1939 I was supposed to be trained. In those last tense days when war was expected and the street lamps started to go out, we were given respirators and tin hats. All that autumn we were at a post under Ward's[1] shop on the Green and in the early days we slept on a bare concrete floor, but later comfort increased when beds were provided. Our night duty was not unpleasant, for though it meant a long cold stand on the job, it gave the next day free.

I remember those early nights when the future seemed utterly and impossibly black and the company hopelessly uncongenial. Later however, I came to enjoy the camaraderie of my fellow firemen. They were a mixed lot, mostly working class or clerks, but on acquaintance they were very likeable and we had our jobs and our gossip. One day we had a flower show and were at home to our wives and friends. It was with considerable satisfaction that I won some prizes.

At first there was little work; polishing and cleaning the cars and engines along with drill and practice in the yard. It was a fairly easy life in which the afternoons were mostly free. Although starting with extreme distaste, I soon quite enjoyed it. We turned out to various practices in cars that might or might not start. Once, early on, the telephone rang in the small hours. We all leapt up expecting a call - but it was a wrong number! There were rumours of raids, rumours of everything, but in fact my time at that post and later at another in Raddlebarn Road[2], were undisturbed by fires.

In January 1940, Joan and David returned from Sibford and life became more normal again. We went to Dunster for a week in May. The country was unbelievably lovely and we walked everywhere. The trees were all in fresh green with bluebells, primroses and cowslips in profusion. While we were there, we heard that Germany had invaded the low-countries and the calling up of my class was foreshadowed. It was a rude shock amidst that rural calm.

We returned home, but it did not seem to me right or possible to remain at the Bournville Office. I felt that on the whole I ought to be a pacifist, but my first choice, The Friends Ambulance Unit, with which I had been and still was associated, were still not doing much and initially were not recruiting married men. I had been trained in the AFS and the service needed men, so after much thought I decided, with considerable reluctance, to join up full time. Through all these difficult months Joan was a tremendous help and strength to me. In accordance with their practice, the Bournville Trustees agreed to make up half of my salary and I left the BVT with a heavy heart, wondering when or if I should ever return.

At that time I think the AFS were inefficiently organised. There were too many people in responsible positions who had got there because they knew the right man. Many were inefficient and few Station Officers knew how to command. Our own S/O was however a happy exception; he was very keen, very efficient, conscientious and hardworking. In many ways it was a narrow, restricted life and chances of promotion or increased responsibility were very vague, but I enjoyed it. And although I was not a leading fireman, I worked hard and was anxious for promotion. I remember with pride my name going up on the board in charge of the big 700 gallon pump and just after the outbreak of war, I recall the S/O and I talking with Joan outside the station and he said – that he was now 'glad that we had declared war.'

One day we had to go to a 'do' in Cotteridge Park and I felt a real thrill driving on the fire engine with the bell ringing! I seem to recall spending a good deal of time on the telephone, but on the whole I enjoyed it. With the family back in Linden Road, I was now living at home too, able to garden and cultivate my allotment. Looking back, I am surprised I was so satisfied, but I was.

Dunkirk[3] in May and June of 1940 was a different story, of course, and then came the air raids, and warnings which got us out of bed at night. Firstly, I had to see Joan and David down into the cellar that we had adapted and then I bicycled down to the station. Often we waited for a while with nothing happening, so then we went back home. In the August, raids became worse and the market hall burnt down. A few nights later High Explosives and Incendiaries were dropped in the Bull Ring area of the city and we were sent off to Great Charles Street[4]. We were towing our pump behind an Austin which would not go properly and I wondered if we should ever get up Suffolk Street. I can remember now the glow of the fire against the night sky.

Eventually we somehow arrived, ran out our hose and fought a fire in a partially gutted factory building. Although we were not in real danger, bits of the glass roof kept falling near us and once the full force of the hose was directed into my face when the man holding the branch[5] fell. Hardest of all was rolling up the wet rubber hose in the cold early morning and then returning home as the light slowly grew. I remember the people going early to work, staring curiously at us and all our paraphernalia. But we had worked hard for many hours. It was our first taste and we were elated and in all I was glad that I had not volunteered to go to fight an oil fire in South Wales as some of the others had!

Then everything started to go wrong. We were asked to join the Home Guard[6] to defend the station. Although I had, with much hesitation registered as a Conscientious Objector, I felt that by refusing, I might let down my fellows, especially as the AFS had agreed to take me on even after I had made it clear that I should register as a CO. It showed the difficulty of trying to be a consistent CO and yet continuing to work with authority. I often looked back, wondering if I was making a mistake. But then the City Council decided to dismiss all COs. At first I got a reprieve as the Trust kindly agreed to pay me my full half salary and the Council allowed me to stay on as a volunteer. We all saw people and I wrote a letter to the Town Clerk saying that I thought the decision was neither wise nor just and I still think so. Christopher Cadbury and Donald Veitch, with whom I had been at university, were also much involved, and despite the fact that we had been fully trained and the AFS still lacked suitable people, the Council, after much lobbying against us, finally adhered to its original decision and dismissed some 12 or 15 trained and reliable workers.

My AFS Station Officer, Mr Stacey, and Section Officer, Mr Burman were both very kind and got up a petition, asking that I should be retained. I was very tempted to do so, but Horace (Alexander) persuaded me not to and, I think on the whole rightly. It was a difficult time and eventually I left at the end of September and touchingly all my colleagues at the station made me a presentation. I had a fortnight's break and did what I could to make it possible for Joan to stay on at No.26 alone and then came my tribunal.

———

Letter to the Town Clerk

> 26 Linden Road
> Birmingham

To the Town Clerk

14ᵗʰ August 1940

Dear Sir

I am grateful for your expression of appreciation of the services which I have given, but I cannot help feeling somewhat surprised that after 12 months of what on your own admission is 'very excellent service', I should now be considered unsuitable for further employment. It is also a matter of regret to me that I should now be debarred from putting my experience and training at the disposal of my native city, especially when we had been informed that 'we are serving where there is most need for our skills and experience'......I also fail to see why a man who has relinquished his own employment to become a member of the AFS should be so dealt with. In view of this, I cannot think that the committee's decision is based either on reason, common sense or justice and feel bound to make this protest against it.

Yours sincerely
F Ralph Barlow

Letter from Paul Cadbury re FRB's Tribunal

FRIENDS AMBULANCE UNIT.

All communications
should be addressed
to the Secretary.

Telephone: PRIory 1863

Training Camp,
Manor Farm,
Bristol Road South,
Birmingham 31.

(Tram No. 69, 70, 71 or 72
from Navigation Street.)

To the Chairman of the Birmingham Tribunal

30th September, 1940.

Dear Sir,

I understand that F. Ralph Barlow is coming before you to-morrow.

At the beginning of the war he gave great assistance in the forming of the Friends' Ambulance Unit and was an original member of the Council. At that time as a married man of 30 he felt it his duty to remain in his job and do spare time A.F.S. work. Later he took on full time A.F.S. work, but has now been asked by the city to relinquish his position.

I have known Ralph Barlow since he was a boy and have the highest regard for his sincerity. I believe under certain circumstances he might have been willing to join the R.A.M.C. This was at a time when there seemed little chance of active medical work with the Friends' Ambulance Unit. Now that a considerable proportion of the work of the Unit is in the East End of London, and such work has become both arduous and dangerous, Ralph Barlow is very anxious to join the Unit which he helped to form.

I hope the Tribunal may place his name on the Register of Conscientious Objectors, and that if there is a condition it may be 'ambulance work under civilian control'.

Yours truly,

Paul S. Cadbury

Chairman.

A letter from PSC backing my father's application to be a Conscientious Objector in 1940

Paul S Cadbury, the father of the FAU

Paul, almost single-handedly was responsible for the reformation of the FAU in 1939
Photograph courtesy of Richard Cadbury

After my father had been dismissed from the Auxiliary Fire Service for being a Conscientious Objector in 1940, he joined the Friends Ambulance Unit. He had been involved with setting up the fledgling FAU from the start and on the Executive, but in those early days, they were reluctant to take on married people. But by 1940, the Unit was more established and that barrier was lifted, and so he finally submitted his application letter to the authorities......

26 Linden Road
Birmingham

28th September 1940
Dear Sirs
In June I gave up my employment and joined the Auxiliary Fire Service. On August 12th I was informed by the AFS Committee that as I had registered as a Conscientious Objector, I could no longer continue in their employment, although I had previously been told that this would not be a problem. I arrived at this decision with considerable doubt, but I hope that the sincerity of my conscientious objection is borne out by the fact that I have come out of the AFS - work which I enjoyed - rather than recant my views.

Since work with the AFS is now not possible, I should therefore like to ask that - if the Tribunal grants me exemption - I might be allowed to work in the Friends Ambulance Unit rather than in the non-combatant services of the army. I might add that I have a close connection with the FAU - I am on its Council and acted as a Secretary for a short while after the outbreak of war and would have asked to join them previously had I not known that at that time they were experiencing difficulty in accepting married men and in finding work, both of which have now largely been overcome.

Yours sincerely
F Ralph Barlow

He was duly summoned before a tribunal and writes in his memoir.......

I have never been a very rabid pacifist. I have seen so clearly the belief of most men that Germany represented a power of evil which if not stopped would have dire effects for the world. I realised that hard as it was, this country was bound by treaties to help Poland. I understood and was grateful for the protection given by the Navy, Army and Air Force. I did not want to shirk or have an easy time. Yet I was a Quaker, born of many generations, strictly brought up, and I could not believe that for me war was right. I believed war to be so utterly wrong that even though short term results seemed to justify it, it would be wrong in the long term. So I registered as a CO and though I have learnt much, I do not regret it.

I put my traditional Quaker pacifism in my first tribunal statement and followed it by another explaining why I had volunteered for the Home Guard. The tribunal was very easy and gave me AFS or FAU. I had looked forward to it with dread but it was simple. I had then decided to apply for and had been accepted by the FAU. It was a cruel wrench leaving home. To part from Joan and David, to give up my home and garden was very hard. Shortly before I left, Joan decided to go to Beaconwood[7] for a short while, at Honor Cadbury's kind invitation as the raids were trying her. She was expecting Antony at the time. So reluctantly we shut up our beloved Linden Road house.

Ralph Barlow
From raw Recruit to Officer in Charge of the Middle East

Ralph aged 29 in 1939
My father looking very much the young, slightly insecure FAU recruit

But by 1942 he was a confident leader in his FAU uniform, about to sail as Officer in Charge of the Middle East Section – here with my mother and brother, David.

Chapter 3
The Friends Ambulance Unit WW2

"We all recognize that there are many people who have perfectly genuine and very deep-seated scruples on the subject of military service, and even if we do not agree with those scruples, we respect them as honestly held. (And) it is the view of the Government, where scruples are conscientiously held, that they should be respected and there should be no persecution of those who hold them."

The PM, Neville Chamberlain in the House of Commons, May 1939

I suspect that when people think of Quakers or the Society of Friends, apart from familiarity with a certain brand of cereal, they will probably think first of pacifists and Conscientious Objectors or 'Conchies' as they were derogatorily named. And indeed pacifism has been one of the abiding principles of the Society, deriving directly from their beliefs, since the Peace Testimony was established under King Charles II. In 1660 a declaration was made to King Charles II by 'The Harmless and Innocent People of God called Quakers'...........

"We utterly deny all wars and strife and fightings with outward weapons, for any end, or under any pretence whatever; this our testimony to the whole world. The Spirit of Christ by which we are guided is not changeable, so as once to command us from a thing as evil and again to move us unto it; and we certainly know and testify to the world, that the Spirit of Christ, which leads unto all Truth, will never move us to fight and war against any man with outward weapons, neither for the kingdom of Christ nor for the kingdom of the world."

And in the Quaker book of Advices and Queries, which are read from time to time in the Society's meetings for worship, it says....

"Be faithful in maintaining our testimony against all war as inconsistent with the spirit and teaching of Christ. Live in the life and power that takes away the occasion of all wars. Seek to take your part in the ministry of reconciliation between individuals, groups and nations."

This teaching was fundamental to Quakerism, as established by their founder George Fox and derives directly from their understanding of Christian teachings. Fox had already broken away from the established church and the Society of Friends as we know it today, was beginning to take shape. It was Fox's belief that ritual was not a necessary part of worship, no more than a formal church building was, which is why Quakerism does not have any written creed or dogma or elaborate church building. From the earliest days, Quakers have worshipped in simple meeting houses, mainly in silence, believing that 'God can be found anywhere'; as it says in Matthew "Where two or three are gathered together in my name, there am I among them."

In the succeeding centuries, despite relatively small numbers, the Society of Friends has been hugely influential in the history of reform and Quakers have played a significant role in such movements as the abolition of slavery, promoting education and equal rights for women, the humane treatment of prisoners and most recently on behalf of gay rights. But throughout its history Quakerism, despite other modifications has always maintained at its core its central belief in pacifism, from which the FAU naturally developed.

The Friends Ambulance Unit - or the FAU - was founded as The First Anglo-Belgian Ambulance Unit at the start of World War 1 in 1914 by Philip Noël Baker and other like-minded people, including my Grandfather John Henry Barlow, but which was later renamed the Friends' Ambulance Unit.

Members were trained at the Quaker centre, Jordans, in Buckinghamshire, sometimes referred to as the 'Canterbury of Friends'. Altogether, it sent over a thousand men to France and Belgium, where they worked on ambulance convoys and ambulance trains with the French and British armies. The FAU was administered under the jurisdiction of the British Red Cross. It was eventually dissolved after the war in 1919. In the late thirties, with the rise of fascism and the Nazi party and as war again appeared to be likely, a number of Friends had felt a concern for some time that there was a need for an organisation with a religious background, which could find active work for young Friends and others who shared Quaker views on war. As in 1914, there were a great number of young men who, on the grounds of conscience refused to enter the fighting forces, but felt a deep concern to give service no less onerous and were anxious to relieve the suffering caused by war.

It was with the object of providing opportunities for work of this type, that action was taken to re-form the Friends' Ambulance Unit and several who had been involved in the original FAU formed a committee, led by Paul Cadbury, who had served in the original Unit in WW1 and was the man, almost single-handedly responsible for re-establishing the FAU in 1939.

Paul Strangman Cadbury was born in 1895, the son of Geraldine Southall and Barrow Cadbury, and the grandson of John Cadbury, who first started the family-run chocolate business in the centre of Birmingham in the late 1840's. When John retired in 1861, his sons George and Richard (Paul's grandfather) took over the business, re-locating it to Bournville in 1879. Paul married Rachel Eveline Wilson in 1919, and was one of several Quakers, including Arnold Rowntree, who for the first time had been given exemption from military service on the grounds of conscience as a result of the so-called 'Conscience Clause' in the 1916 Military Service Act, that my Grandfather had helped to secure with his MP cousin Sir John Barlow, and so was able to join the fledgling Friends Ambulance Unit (FAU) in 1915, or the Friends Emergency and War Victims Relief Committee, as it was first called, which provided help for refugees and victims during the war. In the period after 1918 he worked for the family business and by the time the Second World War was over, he was to become Chairman. He became a Trustee of the Bournville Village Trust in 1922 and remained one for the next 60 years, working both with my Grandfather and later after 1935 with my father.

Paul Cadbury and Arnold Rowntree re-formed the Unit with the intention of again enabling conscientious objectors to undertake civilian service in a military context. One of the aims of the Unit was to assist those conscientious objectors who were not members of the Society, and thus less likely to be granted exemption from military service. Paul had been encouraged by Rowntree to set things in motion once again and for vigour, tireless energy and sheer determination to get things done, Paul was the ideal man. He wrote a letter to The Friend [1] in September 1939 putting forward details of procedure:

"We are concerned that young Friends and others who wish to undertake civilian service shall be able to do so…..There are, however, a number of our members of military age who wish to give proof that, although they register as CO's they have no wish to be exempt from a period of constructive labour as a result of their convictions.

If, however, there is a real demand, we believe that it may be right for a group of individuals acting on their own responsibility to start a scheme of work which would be approved by the Minister of Labour as meeting requirements of this Sub-Section of the Act….If war comes such a scheme could be rapidly developed to train men for relief and ambulance work."

Events were moving with frightening rapidity. The letter had been written in late August and related to military service, but by the time most people read it, it was already out of date, and as Tegla Davies wrote in his book on The Friends Ambulance Unit......

"Since the above letter was written the international situation has become ever more grave. We understand from Paul Cadbury that plans are under consideration by him and others for a camp at which ambulance training could be given, and he would be willing to receive the names of Friends wishing to undergo full-time training, and those concerned for such work should write to him. He points out, however, that the number with whom it might be possible to deal would be strictly limited to begin with.

Two days later, Britain was at war. The following week a further letter appeared in The Friend. The Committee, now a provisional Council of a Unit still unnamed, had met at Manor Farm[2], kindly lent by Dame Elizabeth Cadbury for an initial camp. The response to the letter of 1st September had been immediate: 300 applications came in the first few days."

By mid-September 1939, six pioneers had arrived at Manor Farm to convert farm buildings into a camp, helped by many local Friends and valuable assistance from the Bournville Village Trust, led by my father. The mainspring, however, was undoubtedly Paul Cadbury. He busied himself here, there and everywhere, interviewing prospective members, attending tribunals, seeing officials, turning up at all hours of the day and night with new pieces of equipment for the camp. Indeed, in claiming to have made the Unit what it was, people sometimes forgot how much had been done in those early days by PSC, as he was generally known, as well as other volunteers, in order to make it possible. It is never easy to sell a new idea and it was doubly difficult when a war had already begun.

The name of the new organisation was still uncertain, but two days later the Council, now firmly established, decided that what had so far been called "Ambulance Training Camp for Friends " should adopt the old name of The Friends Ambulance Unit. As was fitting, Paul Cadbury was confirmed as Chairman of the Council, with Arnold Rowntree, the elder statesman who had urged him on, as Vice-Chairman. It had all taken a matter of days.

There were inevitably several dissenting voices, particularly from those who felt that the work of the Unit in WW1 had compromised the Society's peace testimony and that with its khaki uniform it became too close to the military. Much correspondence followed in The Friend, with some feeling that such a set up could prejudice tribunals against the absolutist case. However, when the Unit realised that the tribunals were saying that the FAU was the only acceptable alternative, it made representation saying that 'The Unit could not accept members merely because a tribunal gave an applicant no further alternative.' Those who joined the Unit were particularly anxious that any work they undertook should not be used to prejudice their fellow pacifists who felt called to a different type of witness. The Ministry of Labour eventually agreed, and the Unit retained its independence and the right to reject applicants. The Friends Ambulance Unit was on its way. This question of the Unit's autonomy was to crop up again with the 'Agreement' drawn up by the War Office for those in the Middle East.

My father writes on this subject later in the war...."How far is there a place for voluntary societies in the twentieth century? Still more, what place is there for voluntary societies in a world totally organised for war? I think that the experience of The Friends Ambulance Unit, both at home and overseas, during this war shows that there still is a place for them.

Its basis for existence and perhaps its main justification is that its members are all young pacifists both men and women, who, because of their religious convictions, feel unable to fight but who are nevertheless anxious to give service when they can, and to share to some extent the hardships and sacrifices which their fellow countrymen in the forces are bearing. Many Friends must wonder how far the Unit overseas succeeds in making any pacifist witness. On my way back from overseas, a man on the boat, who was in fact most sympathetic to our point of view, told me he thought the Unit's position untenable, and that a real pacifist witness can only be made by completely standing aside. I know that certain Friends feel that our compromise has been too great.

They may be right; but after visiting all Unit sections overseas, I have come to the conclusion that the Unit does succeed in making a very real witness. This is particularly the case in our co-operation with the Army in the Middle East, where the whole basis of our work depends on the authorities accepting our position as pacifists and appreciating what we can and cannot conscientiously do. To those who do not share our view, it is not the degree of compromise but the fact of our pacifism that matters.

However infinitesimal, comparatively speaking, the Unit's achievements may be, it is impressive that a band of young and largely inexperienced young men, holding unpopular views, has been able to build up the work it has, in centres so widely separated as Whitechapel, Beirut, Addis Ababa, Calcutta and Kutsing. It is also a remarkable tribute to the liberal mindedness of the country in which we live. Irrespective of what has been achieved, and this is by no means negligible, it has value and meaning as an indication of what men of goodwill can do in a world of war.

It has also enabled nearly eight hundred CO's to give service where it is needed, which was the hope of Paul Cadbury when he re-founded the Unit at the beginning of the war. It has enabled them to share the life of those millions of our fellow countrymen and women who are serving overseas."

"Tom Tanner's parents, Herbert and Dora kindly lent part of their home 'Failands' near Bristol, as a mechanics training school. Its aim was to make driving and maintenance of vehicles as much part of routine Unit training as hospital work." (left)
(Right) The FAU badge designed by Frank Gregory.
Images Friends House Library

Chapter 4
Getting started
September 1940

From the very beginning, Dame Elizabeth Cadbury's help and interest in the work of the Unit was invaluable. She provided the site of the first training camp at their home, the Manor farm, Northfield, Birmingham, using converted cow-sheds and stables for bunk-houses, a large barn for lectures and the lake and stream and nearby fields and woods for manouevres. Indeed the Manor Farm came to be so greatly appreciated by the hundreds of members who were subsequently trained there, that along with Whitechapel in the East End, it became one of its two spiritual homes.

A small group of pioneers started work on September 11th 1939 and with much assistance from the Bournville Village Trust led by my father, converted the old farm buildings into a Training Camp, to which the first sixty men were called on September 27th 1939. By the end of the war, more than 1,300 members had been trained there and went on to serve as ambulance drivers and medical orderlies in London during the Blitz, as well as overseas in Norway and Finland and Sweden (1940), the Middle East, (1940–1943), Greece, (1941, 1944 and 1946), China and Syria, (1941-46), India and Ethiopia (1942-1945), Italy (1943-46) France, Belgium, Netherlands and Yugoslavia (1941–1946).

The system of training adopted, consisted of six weeks or more in Camp and was designed to prepare members mentally and physically for their future work in the Unit. Each camp modified and improved the programme of its predecessors, but it was the first camp that set the pattern, and each subsequent camp by and large followed its format. There was a Commandant and Quartermaster, and later camps introduced a Training Officer. There were six sections each with its appointed leader and its own stable or cow-shed, with instruction in First Aid, Stretcher Drill, Home Nursing and Air Raid Precaution [1] (ARP) forming the main items of the programme.

The lectures in first-aid were from Dr Hubert Rutter [2] and Sister Margaret Gibbs, who were untiring in the energies they devoted to training members, so that at the end of their period of training, they were able to take the St John Ambulance Association Exams in First Aid and Home Nursing. There were lectures from members of the old First World War Unit on working in the field; PT classes, and runs and route marches became a regular feature; and there were mechanical classes and devotional services after the manner of Friends, which helped to bring spiritual togetherness. In fact Manor Farm became the nursery of the Unit and was the home to twenty successive camps.

One of the initial problems of the FAU was to find work for those who had joined, which during the so-called 'Phoney War' seemed illusory. But in 1939 after hostilities had broken out between Russia and Finland, a party was dispatched, with the assistance of the Red Cross. They were only there for six weeks as after Russia annexed part of Finland and invaded Norway and Denmark it ended in some confusion. One party under Brandon Cadbury eventually managed to get back to England, but others like Martin Lidbetter, were stranded in Sweden for some months. With help from the Russian Ambassador in London providing passports, and the British Red Cross in Cairo, who urgently needed extra drivers, twenty six Unit members were enabled to escape via Moscow, Odessa, Istanbul and Beirut to Cairo. While Martin was in Sweden, he became friendly with a certain Eva Ternström, hardly expecting ever to meet again. And once in Cairo, he was soon working on rebuilding ambulances for the Red Cross, ultimately bound for Greece, where he was taken prisoner. Released in 1945 however, he was repatriated via Sweden and by chance met up with Eva again, whom he married after the war.

Dame Elizabeth Cadbury

"Dame Elizabeth Cadbury, took a great interest from the very beginning in the early FAU and provided the site of Manor Farm at their home in Northfield, Birmingham, which became the de facto base of the Unit."

Dame Elizabeth was a first cousin of our Grandmother, Mabel Barlow, and the author aged 7 (right) is watching the cake cutting at the great lady's 90th birthday in 1948 watched by her son Laurence and his wife Joyce (née Mathews) and cousins Virginia Cadbury and Bryony Cadbury.

Both photographs - Barlow family archives

This illustrates well the essential mobility of FAU personnel throughout the war, when people had to be prepared to up-sticks and move to wherever the next emergency was at short notice, thus necessitating meetings and separations, groupings and re-groupings. My father for instance was forever working with people like Brandon Cadbury, Richey Mounsey, Ronald Joynes or Mike Rowntree, all of whom as it happened had been in Finland or Sweden with Martin, and who were destined to meet up with each other in several different parts of the globe.

It is amazing that friendships managed to flourish under such circumstances, even when lack of permanence mitigated against them, but they did, which says a great deal for the camaraderie engendered by a common cause.

Though the Finnish project had not been entirely successful, it was as Tegla wrote, hugely influential in the subsequent life of the Unit.....

"Lives were saved and people helped; and that was after all what they had gone for....Much more important was the fact that it evoked, in many for the first time, qualities of initiative and resourcefulness which, when later grounded in longer and more systematic training, were responsible for the Unit's finest work. It also established a tradition and made the Unit better known. It was more likely to be asked to do other work in the future, and not unimportant for a voluntary society, it would make it easier to raise funds for further enterprises."

However, even after Finland, there was still considerable frustration, as anticipated work abroad came to nothing, and so initially members began working in hospitals across the country and in rest centres and relief work. During this time of relative quietness the Unit began to establish itself on a more constitutional basis, when in August of 1940 a series of Staff Meetings were set up, which worked out a system of democratic governance that survived for the rest of the war. (see Chapter 6) Suffice it to say that when my father joined the FAU in September of that year, the Unit was still very much caught up in this process and finding its feet. He writes in his memoirs of the early days........

I first came into contact with the Unit in the very early days when Paul Cadbury was starting it off, and at that time, although only Secretary of the Council, I had something to do with the alterations and preparations at Manor Farm, converting stables into sleeping-quarters, constructing bunks, making shelves and light-traps for the black-out and generally helping to make the farm ready for human habitation. The Unit now was becoming more established. The Finnish party had returned and were now acting as wardens, Relief was under the inspiration of Tom Tanner and the executive committee was becoming established, though as yet Tom had not been elected Chairman.

Tom Tanner had joined the Unit in July 1940. He was rather older than most members, and had been an Oxford Rugby Blue and undoubtedly possessed a strong personality, which at the same time drew out the best in those around him. Tegla writes....

"He was impatient of inefficiency, and possessed the true Friend's impatience of all injustice and insincerity. Tom Tanner combined a shrewd idealism and a passion for action which, once it had got going, no-one could stop. He worked on a large canvas, took the Unit in hand and organized the work. In December 1940 he was appointed Chairman of the Executive. The reign of TLT had begun. It lasted almost exactly two years. What he had brought in weight of body into the pack as an Oxford Rugger Blue, he now brought in weight of mind, in energy and vision to the Unit's work. He had the over-powering personality which, while it dominates, does not dwarf; he drew out the best from those around him. Some were critical of his methods, but ultimately all seemed to agree, that he was undoubtedly the Unit's greatest man."

Thomas L Tanner
The FAU's 'Greatest man'

Tom Tanner, who dominated the Unit from 1940-1942.
"He laid the foundations of its future success."
Here pictured outside the family home 'Failands', Bristol - photo courtesy of Stephen Tanner.

In December 1942, Tom Tanner and Peter Hume were torpedoed in the North Atlantic on their way to China (see Chapter 28). Following this tragic loss, my father wrote an appreciation of him, and it is worth including here in full to indicate the calibre of the man who set the Unit on its path.....

From the first meeting with Tanner it was apparent that here was someone out of the ordinary run of Unit members. He was mature, a man of the world, he was a big man in so many senses and he had a personality which made itself felt wherever he was.

At Trinity College, Oxford he read law and won a rugger blue. He travelled widely, especially in America, where he had many friends. Soon after coming down from Oxford, he went into the business of which his father was Managing Director, and in the years immediately preceding the war he had held an important position in one of the firm's subsidiaries, John Laird in Glasgow.

From his tribunal he got complete exemption and joined the FAU's 5th Camp in Birmingham. It was clear that a man of his ability was bound soon to make a mark in the Unit. His opportunity came with the heavy air raids in London in the autumn of 1940 and he saw immediately that here was work that the Unit could do and it was out of his initiative and drive that the relief work of the Unit grew. Many have considered that this was one of the finest contributions that the Unit has been able to make and certainly the chance to do so was given to it by Tanner.

In the early months of 1941 he became Chairman of the Executive Committee and he had continued in this post ever since. During this time he has been in daily contact with the affairs of the Unit, save for the four and a half months when he was absent in America. He gave the Unit all those qualities which had made him successful in business. He had real drive which could produce results where others had failed. He had energy that would keep him at work from morning to late at night. He had a certain ruthlessness, which was perhaps no bad thing in a Unit such as ours and he was an administrator of no mean ability. But he was more than just a successful business man, he had the vision to see what the Unit might become and what it might do not only in relief work but also abroad. He understood the Unit and the Society of Friends and although he frequently criticised them, I think that he sincerely believed in them. He would have had a great contribution to make to Friends' work in the post war years.

He was a man whom it was impossible to disregard. One remembers him in so many circumstances, strolling out of his car in his masterful way, carelessly lighting a cigarette, taking the chair at a meeting, obviously quite clear what solution to the problem he wanted, or greeting some Friend or visitor to the Gordon Square HQ in his charming way. He was a man who commanded great loyalty from his colleagues, although his strong personality sometimes tended to overshadow them so that they did not always give of their best. Often too it was difficult to know what was in his mind and sometimes one became exasperated, wondering what game he was playing. He was quick to realise this however, and he could be so charming that, when he really tried, it was rare that he failed to get his way.

He had an immensely wide circle of friends to which he was continually adding. He always felt that contacts were worth following and so often, at some future date, one of Tom's contacts would be able to produce the very thing he wanted at that moment. He himself has confessed that to his own loss, he was not keenly interested in certain aspects of life.

He was not a great reader or especially interested in the arts, but he was immensely interested in people and in life and events. He liked to meet people and he liked to talk to them and he talked well. So often, late at night, just when one wanted to go to sleep, one has heard him coming down the passage almost with a sense of despair, but as soon as he was in the room, one realised that he had something to say that would be interesting and worth hearing and that the next two hours would be immensely entertaining.

In his loss the Unit has suffered an irreparable blow and those of us who knew him well have lost a friend whom we shall not forget. Our sympathy goes to his parents in England and to his wife and children in America.[3]

F Ralph Barlow

The FAU Executive Committee 1941,
Chairman Tom Tanner (centre) with colleagues outside Gordon Square HQ.

Back Row: Ralph Barlow, Peter Gibson, Freddy Temple, Dick Symonds
Front Row: Richey Mounsey, Peter Hume, Tom Tanner, Brandon Cadbury, John Bailey
Photograph Friends House Library

———

Chapter 5
FRB joins the FAU and his first Camp at Manor Farm
October 1940

After he joined the FAU in September 1940, my father remembers his early experiences and writes at some length in his memoir of these times......

My first memory as a member of the Unit was of turning up at Northfield for the 9th camp, being welcomed by David Tod and introduced to the potential section leaders of that camp, who were gathered around one of the tables in the mess room.

That camp was also memorable for the blitz, which often made life rather too exciting. In November 1940, Birmingham had what must have been among the city's worst raids. One bomb fell just behind bunkhouse A, and another one burst the water main in the road, and in the morning the crater was occupied by a fire engine which had driven in by mistake in the dark. The Camp turned out in force for the blitz nights and on one night I was sent out as a stretcher party in the Camp's Austin 10, driving through debris-littered streets, practically the whole night.

Another night in Douglas Mackenzie's car we did much the same thing, and we had a puncture with me having to change the wheel. I remember waiting in a shelter under the car park and hearing a really big bomb come down, and on yet another day some of us went over to the Coventry Road area, to help in the Rest Centres. I shall always remember the wrecked houses, the dust everywhere and pathetic groups of people salvaging what they could from the ruins. That whole area of Birmingham was terribly badly damaged, and the Centres themselves were a total shambles. Whether we relieved or increased the prevailing shambles, I am not quite sure!

The Birmingham FAU Relief Section was getting going at that time, and at the request of Keith Linney[1], four of us made a survey of courting couples in the suburbs of Birmingham, to see whether or not people were trekking out to the suburbs at night. On one occasion I walked all over the Lickeys and back again, and found no-one, yet alone young lovers - just one man and his child in a shelter at the Rednal tram terminus!

The 9th Camp was full of the enthusiasm of the early days of the war. We were prepared to work hard. The Unit was still small enough and in a sufficiently formative stage to be our Unit. We all hoped to run it, and the older among us regretted what were perhaps considered as the unwise rule of younger men. We heard how the 8th Camp had conducted itself at Buckhurst and how later it had moved up to London and made itself even more felt, and we all thought we had a Field Marshal's baton in our knapsacks.

At that time the Unit itself was in a very formative stage and had not by any means resolved in its own mind whether or not it was to become an efficient relief organisation or whether it wanted to be some sort of religious order. The camp numbered 60 and was full of personalities such as Peter Tennant, who was the Commandant. In my opinion this was not the position for him, as he was away too much, constitution-making in London. Also, although he was a man of great integrity, conviction and sincerity, his judgement was not always good and he lacked the essential qualities of a sense of humour and sufficient imagination to cope with such a camp.

Then there was David Tod as training officer, who bore the brunt of the work. Some disliked his manner, but I liked him and always did, and I could never understand why a man of his undoubted abilities had not gone further in the Unit.

Others included able people such as Michael Cadbury as Quarter Master and section leaders Duncan Wood and John Burtt, both of whom had made a well-deserved mark in the Unit. Finally, there were Douglas McKenzie, a man of considerable charm and ability, but perhaps not a Unit leader, and Harold Kempster, an excellent, hearty and very good second rank leader.

Taken as a whole I much enjoyed my time in the camp, even though it was a tremendous change from my sedentary family life, and working in a community of men with regular and violent exercise, was like going back to school, with all of one's ideas being upset. And I confess that my self-confidence was not greatly increased, as I still keenly regretted being out of the AFS, which I had come to love both for the company and the work. Indeed I missed it so much, that on learning that some of the men were tired out, I went back to the station on a couple of nights and acted as a telephonist for them.

I also made various visits over to 26 Linden Road, which was now a sad and silent house. As always we had vast stocks of apples and those that had not gone bad, I took up to camp, plus some cabbages from my allotment. Joan was at Beaconwood, unable to get out much, and I visited her whenever I could, especially at weekends. Honor (Cadbury) was always very kind, but I know it was not easy for Joan living in someone else's house, expecting a child and with David needing much of her attention. But she bore it all with great courage.

If anything the enforced separation, only increased their love for each other, as witness this letter from the Northfield Camp. It is perhaps worth emphasizing that this is 1940, and while modern readers may baulk at such phrases as 'so good at running the house and looking after our friends', my father was not in any way a chauvinist, and strongly supported the introduction of women to the Unit. It wasn't that 'a woman's place is in the home', so much as a practical matter of looking after a young son, with another on the way. In fact later my mother writes to my father how much she wishes she could get out and do more (p229)……….

Tuesday, September 17th 1940 – Northfield Camp

 My very dear wife

We have been married 4 years today, and I want to say what a wonderful time it has been. The longer I am married to you, the more I love you. You have been such a perfect wife in every way: so loving and tender, such a good companion, so good at running the house and looking after our friends, such a good mother and always so interested in my interests. Thank you a thousand times.

We have had such a lovely time too; such fun with our garden, reading books together and buying pictures; enjoying the cinema and theatre and having some wonderful holidays. It's all been perfectly grand - even better than we could ever have hoped.

Now you are expecting another baby and you are so brave about it in your own dear way. I do so admire your courage and I know that it will all go well. I enclose a trifling trinket, and I so wish it were more, but it is a remembrance. We will celebrate on Thursday.

All my love
Ralph

Members of the FAU with whom FRB served

Keith Linney
Photo courtesy Somerset Cricket
Museum

Michael Cadbury
Photo courtesy Duncan Cadbury

Peter Tennant
Photo Friends House Library

Douglas Mackenzie, John Gough and Richard Wainwright
Manor Farm Training Camp

Photograph Friends House Library

Early Days

"There were lectures in first-aid from Doctor Rutter, who served the Unit to the end and showed more briskness in retirement than most men in their working lives, while Sister Margaret Gibbs (below) from Bournville, combining charm and unembarrassed firmness, taught many an awkward youth the intricacies of envelope corners on the beds, of Nelson inhalers and roller bandages. The Unit's debt to both of them cannot be measured."

Photograph left Friends House Library

Dr Rutter teaching first aid at Manor Farm

Sister Margaret Gibbs giving a first aid talk
Photograph courtesy of Stephen Peet and IWM

More familiar FAU faces with whom FRB worked

Peter Gibson

John Bailey

Brandon Cadbury
(photo courtesy of the family)

Michael Rowntree

Tegla Davis (rt) and David Tod

Michael Barratt Brown

Apart from Brandon Cadbury, all other photographs Friends House Library

"The normal healthy young pacifist is not a freak. He feels the same passions and emotions as his fellow men. He does not enjoy being classed as odd or different. When war comes he is in a dilemma. If he joins the army, he violates his deepest convictions: if he refuses, he is in danger of cutting himself off from the community, of becoming a too self-conscious rebel, a segregated being.........they would be unnatural if they did not. Men of their own age, men who were their friends, men with whom but recently they had shared a desk or bench or common room, were being despatched into the very fury of the battle. Why should they, simply because the law had granted them exemption, avoid the danger and the unpleasantness? It may be argued that mingled with this feeling was the anxiety to avoid any suspicion of cowardice, to justify themselves in their own eyes and in the eyes of their fellow men."

The Friends Ambulance Unit by A Tegla Davies

The East India Dock Road and Poplar Hospital

The East India Dock Road in the 1940's

Poplar Hospital for Accidents, East India Dock Road
Established near Blackwall tunnel in 1855 on the initiative of Quaker banker Samuel
Gurney, to deal with victims of accidents at the nearby docks. Following damage due to
enemy action the hospital was eventually demolished.
Photographs Historic London

Chapter 6
Poplar Hospital
December 1940

In the beginning it had been assumed that once recruits were trained, work would come in, but it proved extremely elusive. As briefly mentioned in Chapter 4, when hostilities broke out between Russia and Finland in December 1940 instead of disbanding, Finland was grasped with eagerness as a worthwhile project, and brushing aside such small organisational difficulties as finance and transportation, the Finnish convoy by 'indirect and crooked means' eventually reached their destination. The weather was terrible, the conditions worse, and the venture a short-lived one. But something had been achieved and lives and people were saved. As Tegla writes in his history of the FAU......

"It fired the Convoy's imagination and gave it confidence. They had had a shot at a difficult job, and found that, though things had gone wrong, on the whole, they did it reasonably well. For the Unit it did two things: it made the Unit better known, and also made it easier to raise funds."

But on their return to the UK, things had already changed. The Unit no longer had an adventurous foreign enterprise ahead of them and funds were short. There was a feeling of frustration that the work they had trained for had not opened up. Nonetheless a frantic search for overseas openings continued, including such possibilities as working with the Australian forces, with the South African forces, in Belgium, in France or anywhere. But the work was simply not there. Meanwhile, the Unit was growing fast with recruits still knocking at the door. And so slowly, but surely the Unit reconciled itself to undertaking work at home rather than abroad. Hospital work, relief work, committee meetings all became the routine. Eventually the Unit settled down to make the best of it and started to examine itself.

The most important outcome of this introspection was that it was quickly realised that what was urgently needed was to set up a proper administrative structure for a Unit, no longer in its infancy, but that had now grown to over 300 members. To quote Tegla again:

"It was one of the Unit's main achievements that it managed to hammer out for itself a system of democracy that worked, which combined an effective voice for its members, under the supervision of its Council. So started a series of Staff meetings."

At the fourth Staff meeting, a minute read as follows.......

"After long and sincere discussion, we as members and as representatives of the various sections of the Unit feel that the time has come when the members of the Unit themselves should assume control of their own affairs, both spiritual and executive. We feel that the Unit is lacking in spiritual life, both in the Training Camps and in the Hospitals, and that the spiritual drive which in the Unit's inception came from the Chairman must now come from the members themselves."

They set up an Executive Committee to decide policy and put it into effect; a written constitution was settled upon and on October 2nd a final form was ratified – the Unit's Magna Charta, as it became known, which lasted with the odd modification for the next six years. The Executive was to meet every week, and would be responsible for the Unit's administration and for the management of its affairs. Tom Tanner, a newish recruit, but by far and away its leading figure, became the Chairman of this new committee, which comprised John Bailey, Brandon Cadbury, Peter Hume, Richey Mounsey, Freddy Temple, Peter Tennant and Ralph Barlow.

As Tegla wrote "The reign of TLT had been inaugurated."

At the same time an office administration was slowly being built up. To begin with Peter Hume set up a Unit office in one of the hospital wards, which was pretty inadequate, with no telephone and no proper filing cabinets. As Peter delightfully described it - "one of the problems was finding enough pennies for the public telephone box in Stepney Way, and then on some days when we made so many calls and blocked it up, requesting the Post Office to come and empty it again!"

Soon, however, the admin was put on a more professional footing and premises were found in respectable Bloomsbury at No 4 Gordon Square. Brandon Cadbury became Joint Secretary, Richey Mounsey Finance Officer and by the end of the year with Tom as the Unit's Chairman, the Unit had become a very different body and as Tegla Davies writes:

"Much of the old shuffling and despondency had gone. The blitz was on, and in hospital, shelters and Rest Centres it had found a job to do in England, which tightened every nerve."

By September 1940, with the blitz at its height, there were FAU members stationed in hospitals throughout London's East End, and as the air raids continued, more and more FAU staff began to be transferred from hospitals until, by the end of that year, some 200 men were engaged in air-raid relief work. By now too, all the official government Civil Defence services were well prepared to provide fire-fighting, first aid and rescue services. But by far and away the most important need was in the provision of adequate shelter for the thousands of people who were losing their homes. The Friends War Victims Relief Committee, with their great experience of wartime refugees, took on this work. For those who could not be evacuated to the country, Rest Centres became their only home, and the FAU took over the running of ten centres, working in shifts around the clock. After each air raid, more and more people had to be provided with food, beds, blankets, comfort and company. After my father's time at the Northfield camp, he moved down to Poplar Hospital in the East End of London and here he describes the general background in his official record for Gordon Square......

From Camp I went to Poplar Hospital, where our primary work was in the Out-Patients department and although there was only work to do in the mornings, with the rest of the time being spent waiting for emergencies which rarely arose, the training was good, and we soon became familiar with simple dressings. The nurses were very helpful, and kept us pretty busy, giving us good general experience. In the evenings we were on duty from 5.0 to 8.30 with time spent waiting for any emergencies which arose.

We were also responsible for fire-watching and the roof of Poplar Hospital at that time tended to be an exciting, if dangerous place, especially when, as on one occasion, we were straddled by a stick of five bombs. I spent that Christmas of 1940 in London and it was generally a very dismal occasion, except for one evening when David Tod, who was then working on shelters, took me round the shelters on his round, and the London shelters that Christmas hit a high level for merriment with liquor flowing in buckets.

———

[Textual: A number of my father's early letters are undated, so I have had to rely on internal evidence to place them. The next one is a case in point. It is headed 'Students Hostel, Poplar', so I think it is likely to be more or less about the time my father went to work with the FAU in the East End hospitals. Since in his memoirs he describes the blitz being especially bad in Birmingham in November while he was still at Camp, he probably went to the East End in the December, at roughly about the same time JMB went to stay at Beaconwood, pregnant with me, which was a primary reason for her move.]

Sadly, many of my mother's letters from this period have been lost, but mostly they can be intuited from my father's replies. In this rare survival quoted on the next page, my mother gives voice to one of her most frequent requests, which is to know what sort of things my father is doing, so that she can picture him in her mind's eye and feel that bit closer to him. In these next letters he details his daily routine and paints a clear picture of life in the East End.........

c. Saturday, December 7th 1940 - Student's Hostel, Poplar

 My dearest

I hope you got my note sent yesterday. I wonder if the 'Midland town' mentioned in the newspapers was Birmingham. I do hope you are safe.

The play the 9th Camp produced at Fircroft College[1] went very well and was quite a success. I didn't think it was a very good play, but everybody seemed to appreciate it and I think we did it rather well. Cameron (Cathie) directed as well as being in it and was excellent, but Heather (Cadbury) was a little weak, especially as she didn't speak loud enough....you would have been much better!

We had a good, though terribly slow journey down to London. The section leader, Alan Horsfield picked me up from the Hostel and we travelled together down East India Dock Road to the Hospital. Unfortunately, John Burtt and I are now working in separate places, with him in Bethnal Green and me at Poplar, though my new companions – four of them – are pleasant enough. The day starts with breakfast at 8.0am, followed by duty roster in the Out-patients from 10.0 till 12.45. Then there is a break till 5.0pm, after which we are on duty in Casualty till 8.30pm, and roof-watching until 1.0am, when we can finally get to bed! It is all quite good experience. The evening shift is generally quiet, but the morning one is very busy with people coming in with cuts and fractures, boils and abscesses and all variety of complaints.

We all sleep in a Ward and are really very comfortable, sleeping – can you imagine - in REAL beds, with warm surroundings and hot water. Such an amazing change from being in Camp at the Manor! We have dinner and tea at the Hostel and are free between 1.0 and 5.0 and have one day off in every five. It's all very strange and new and I don't feel particularly settled yet, but no doubt we shall all get used to it. The work is interesting enough, though rather limited, but I expect I shall see things more clearly before long. The real trouble is that I am missing you so much. I also miss the companionship of Northfield and the fresh air and exercise, and although everyone is quite nice here there is not the same camaraderie that we had at Northfield. And we are hardly here long enough to get to know people properly. But enough of me. How are you my dear heart? I think of you so much and always with such admiration. You are so brave to cope with all the trials of moving from house to house and with a baby on the way too. God bless you for being so patient and uncomplaining. More tomorrow....

Continued Sunday, 8th December...........

The war news seems a little better than might be expected and our forces in Egypt do seem to have done wonderfully well. Down here too, thankfully, though there has been a lot of gunfire, not much was dropped and the nights have been relatively undisturbed. In my free time I have been passing the time in reading Henry Williamson's *Tarka the Otter*, which I bought the other day in a Penguin edition. I think it is very good and feel sure you would love it too. I think I will end this now and get it to the post. Tomorrow is my day off, and I am hoping to go and have lunch with Millior and Alfred (Sister and brother-in-law). Take care of yourself and remember I love you dearly. Love, Ralph

This lone surviving letter of my mother's from this period sets the pattern for later letters, trying to keep my father in touch with the day-to-day life he has left behind. It is here quoted in full........

Monday December 16th 1940 – Beaconwood, Rednal

My darling

It was lovely to get your letter this evening and to hear a few more details of your work. It sounds interesting and I am sure as time goes on you will meet more people and make more friends. I am so thankful you are comfortable and have a real bed and hot water again, which will be a welcome change from the primitiveness of Camp! It must also be pleasant to have definite hours and some time off, and perhaps you will even have more free time than you did up at the Manor. I wonder whether you might be able to get down into Kew, or any such place for a breath of country air and maybe some birds, though I suppose travel cannot be easy at the moment. It will be nice for you to see Millior and Alfred. I hope they are alright.

The last few nights here have been fairly quiet. On the Wednesday you went to London, a great deal of damage was done when a huge land mine landed in Hole Lane and windows as far apart as Woodbrooke and Weoley Hill were broken. Your mother had a window broken too, and Mr Appleton told her that they had over 100 houses to see to after this raid. Actually I don't think this raid was as bad as the two previous ones, only they were this side of town.

Honor (Cadbury) and the children and I stayed up, as we were only just recovering from our various ailments. We are both on the mend now, though I find it so difficult to get really comfortable. I feel so huge and unsightly!! However, not much longer now, and then I shall see you. I can hardly realise that when I next see you the baby will be born. I think perhaps Diana Mary would be rather nice for a girl? What do you think?

By the way Horace and Olive (Alexander) called in on Saturday morning to see how I was getting on and to hear if I had any news of you. It was nice to see them. Horace said that there was a special meeting of the Woodbrooke Settlement Committee today to decide what to do about Woodbrooke next term. I think that after Wednesday's raid, everyone was a little nervous, and there is some talk of moving away if possible. In which case Horace and Olive would move too. I wonder if you have heard anything?

Margaret (Gillett) called in to see me for a few moments on Saturday as well and we are hoping to join them for Christmas dinner. Hilda (Ransome) came over too and we had a good long chat. They have at last got a cottage at Aston Cantlow between Stratford and Henley-in-Arden. She says it is pretty small with a couple of tiny bedrooms and an even tinier sitting room, but is sure they'll be able to manage. It has only been let to them for just six months, but if it turns out to be suitable, they are hoping that perhaps they can take it for longer. They are trying to let their house in Wellington Road to someone, and Edwin will stay on as a paying guest.

Life seems very dull at the moment, but I am very, very, lucky and I cannot complain, as I am as comfortable as I should be anywhere away from you and friends, though I do terribly miss having a home of my own, but we must count our blessings. I know it is much more difficult for you, and I do wish I could help you darling one. But cheer up: the time will pass and then perhaps you will have a job nearer to me. Oh how I long for you my dear one. I love you so dearly, which makes being separated so hard to bear. I think of you every moment and pray that God may watch over you and guard you safely.
My dearest love, goodnight from David and me. Joan

The hospital work they undertook at the Hospital, was not without its dangers, as the East End was constantly under attack from air raids, with one night's bombing having near fatal results. Here my father describes in his memoirs the life of the Hospital.........

During my time at the hospital, we also did fire-watching, and the roof of Poplar Hospital afforded us, as it were, a grandstand view, and we saw bombs falling continually, especially those which came down across the river. Regularly, every night the warning went and we would hear the thunder of the guns and the falling bombs; and I remember still the glow, smell and smoke from the city. And though there was undoubtedly a sort of excitement, the hospital roof was a dangerous place, especially when on one night we were straddled by a stick of five bombs and the hospital was hit. By some miracle I had left only minutes before, but two of our members were thrown off the roof, though amazingly neither of them was killed. The next day I walked back and saw the damage, with the still smoking ruins, and the tired firemen surrounded by a tangle of hose.

Every day during the air-raids we were on duty, and the casualties would come in and we would help deal with them. Particularly, I remember two soldiers who were brought in already dead from an "ack-ack" battery, and had to be disposed of; a badly wounded policeman and a poor woman who came in, only to find her husband who had been in the AFS had been killed, and I remember escorting her home. I was immensely impressed by the courage of the injured and the devotion of the staff.

From time to time we were called in to help on the wards with difficult cases. Once I remember it was a smithy, injured by bomb splinters, concussed and paralysed all down one side, but still immensely strong and restless. I rather dreaded my turns on duty with him, lying there injured and bloody, unconscious and snoring dreadfully. The screens were placed round his bed down at the far end of the ward with the wireless turned up loud onto jazz. Eventually he died without recovering consciousness, with his wife beside him.

The staff were friendly and one of the sisters particularly kind, but mostly they left no particular impression. We had a ward to ourselves, a good fire, hot water and we were reasonably comfortable. We collected our food from the Hostel and cooked it ourselves each evening and I remember a young RC priest, who was living with us, whose presence kept us intellectually alive.

(Left) Relief workers attending a fire in 1940 in London's East End
Photo courtesy of IWM

(Far left) Dermot Cameron Cathie, known by his stage name of Dermot Cathie, who often organised the Unit entertainments.

Photo by kind permission of Sean Cathie

Then as now, post at Christmas could be erratic, especially with every service person sending letters and parcels to their loved ones……

Tuesday, 17th December 1940

My very dear Joan
Thank you so much for your letter. It is always a joy to get your letters. But I am so sorry you have not had any of mine as I have written three times.

This is only a note that I have sent under separate cover the following Christmas presents.

1. H. A. L. Fisher's[2] autobiography – well reviewed and as you like autobiographies, I hope you will enjoy this one.
2. A life of the naturalist, Richard Jefferies. I could always change this, if it's not to your taste, though I think you will find him an interesting man.
3. A book for David, which is too old for him at present, but I thought you would like it too, and hope he will also later on. So this a present for you as well.

They are not quite what I should really like to have sent you, but I do hope you will enjoy them. Know that they come with my dear love for a happy Christmas and prayers that the New Year will be a better and happier one than the last.
Dearest love, Ralph

My father was always a fan of the cinema, or as he often used to call it 'the flicks'. Chaplin's masterpiece was not recognised as such until much later in the century, so it says a lot for my father's perspicacity to have spotted its genius early on………

Thursday, 19th December 1940

My dearest Joan
I do hope you have now got over your cold and I trust that the last few weeks before the birth will be easy for you.

Yesterday was my day off, so I went to see Chaplin's 'The Great Dictator'. It is certainly a triumph of acting for Chaplin, who is brilliant both as the little Jewish barber and as Hynkel the Dictator. It is extremely funny and it is a plea for justice, kindness and sanity in man's dealings with his fellow man.

He weaves the two stories together very cleverly – the brutal story of the dictator and the life of the common man – and by a set of strange coincidences, at the end they swap places and instead of the usual speech, the 'common man' delivers an eloquent plea for brotherly love, which is rather splendid. The little Jew is Chaplin at his best – a wonderful picture of the ordinary man, and while very funny, the fun is less farcical than usual and more connected to the story. Some of the reviews said that the final speech was out of place, but I did not feel that. I found it a very powerful affirmation of hope over despair. It is well worth seeing and I'd love you to see it too.

I went up to Bethnal Green the other day for supper and on my way to and from the West End saw more of the damage from the bombing of Sunday night. There is still quite a lot of the city standing unharmed, but there are so many premises that are burned to the ground. Of all the property round St Paul's, very little has escaped and some streets are mere shells of houses. It is a miracle that the cathedral itself is undamaged. There were still some fires burning on Thursday and many buildings must be completely unsafe as all the inside has gone with just the walls standing gauntly up with an ominous lean outward and inward. There is much damage at Aldgate too, and we were lucky to be on the outside edge of the target area and thankfully did not suffer much. When I saw all the fires raging I did rather hanker back to my time with the Fire Service.

I saw Millior this afternoon and we had tea together. She says she hopes to come up and see you. Also I have been thinking some more about letting the house; not to anybody of course, but if we can find the right person, it would be a possibility. But for how long and when would we want it back again?

I'm glad you are enjoying the Jefferies' book. I should like to read it myself. Excuse more now.

All my love now and always, Ralph

Chaplin's 'The Great Dictator'
"It is certainly a triumph of acting for Chaplin."
Photo Universal Pictures

Chaplin's final speech from the film; and if we interpret 'fight' in its widest sense as 'struggle for', then it is surely a belief that we can all embrace. A belief of hope not despair......

"Then - in the name of democracy - let us all unite. Let us fight for a new world - a decent world that will give men a chance to work: give youth a future, and old age a security. By just the promise of these things, brutes have risen to power. But they lie, as they do not fulfil that promise, and they never will!

Dictators free themselves, but they enslave the people! Now let us fight to fulfil that promise! Let us fight to free the world - to do away with national barriers - to do away with greed, with hate and intolerance. Let us fight for a world of reason, a world where science and progress will lead to all men's happiness. Soldiers! In the name of democracy, let us all unite."

As my mother's pregnancy drew closer to the birth date, my father expressed his hopes for a safe delivery and his wish to be with her. Always a voracious and wide-ranging reader, while enjoying Roger Fry's [3] autobiography, he compares and contrasts Fry's very similar Quaker upbringing to his own, and in so doing contemplates what he wishes for his eldest son.......

Saturday, December 21st 1940 – Poplar

My dearest

Thinking of you so much at this time and wishing I could be with you. You have not too long to go now and I so hope you will have an easy birth this time, and that all will go well. You mothers who are having children right now, are the real heroes of the day! Far more so than we men, certainly more than I am. Oh my dear I do love you so very much; take especial care of yourself.

We had a very heavy raid on Friday night as you will no doubt have seen from the papers. There was much gunfire and a salvo of bombs that appeared to 'straddle' the hospital. The noise was simply frightful. We had just finished supper, when they sent for us to go the Casualty Department. About fifteen people were brought in altogether, two of whom were dead already and the rest in varying degrees of trauma. Some were just about managing to walk, while others were very badly wounded. Mostly the wounds were caused by bomb splinters; high explosives are such fearsome weapons.

I was so glad to get your letter and I am so sorry that you have not been well. I hope you are now fit again. Perhaps out of a sympathetic reaction I was very sick on Friday night and felt pretty miserable all day yesterday, so I stayed in bed and slept most of the day. Happily, today, Sunday, I seem to be alright again. The Sister from the Ward below, has been most kind and looked after me very well. Don't worry about me – it's happened before, and already I feel almost fit again.

But being in bed gave me a chance to catch up with some reading, and I have found Roger Fry's autobiography most interesting. He has such knowledge and understanding, that he makes me feel so ignorant; and he delves into such realms of experience, quite outside my ken, that I feel a complete nincompoop. What emphasis he lays on appreciation of spiritual values and in comparison, how little on moral values. But what energy and enthusiasm and sympathy and open mindedness. What queer fads and mad ideas. How curious that a man who comes from such a very similar Quaker background to my own, and whose early life has so many echoes of my own childhood, should break away so completely into a life of such contrast to that of his upbringing. His family, so religious and high-minded and upright and ordered, and yet so narrow and limited; his own life so full and eager, open-minded and unlimited.

Contemplating Fry's life I got to thinking about our son. I am so anxious that David should have a full life. I want him to be self-reliant and not hampered as I have been, by shyness and diffidence. I want him to love the open air, walking and camping; and I want him to appreciate art and literature of all sorts. I want him to meet interesting people and do interesting things and to be able to travel. But more than all these I want him to have a serious purpose and moral backbone and to be able to distinguish between good and evil.

The Roger Fry book inspired me and I went and bought a copy of T S Eliot's *East Coker*. At the moment I find it quite difficult, but Desmond McCarthy reviews it most highly in today's Sunday Times, so I must try again. And then on my way to Hoddesdon I also bought a Penguin 'New Writing', which is a fascinating account of the modern movement in poetry and drama.

The Editor, John Lehmann, explains that the aim of such poets as Auden, C Day Lewis and Spender is to get away from what he calls 'the unreality and artificiality' of the Georgian poets, to a style which expresses more explicitly the times in which they and we live, which is one of disillusion: a time of communism and fascism; a machine age, of unemployment and poverty; but also a time where there is still beauty and hope.

I think that maybe they are trying to find in poetry what Roger Fry was looking for in art – a beauty of form and spiritual content, which lies deeper than merely superficial beauty. A meaning which is more than just story telling or sound and prettiness. I don't pretend to fully appreciate them, and I find them very difficult, yet I believe they are after something important.

There is so much in myself that I am dissatisfied with, and I feel I fall short so often of what I should like to be. But in one thing only I know I have really succeeded, and that is in finding the best wife in the world. You mean so much to me, and I so long to be reunited with you and resume the life we had together, when we would talk and discuss, laugh and cry and share our joys. May that time not be too far away once again.

All for now, my dearest and praying that all goes well for you, I send all my love, Ralph

In his memoirs my father writes of how, after a while, he gradually became attached to the area, but here as on many future occasions he worries as to whether he has made the right decision about joining the FAU………

Strangely enough, during the time I was in the East End, I became quite attached to the district. Across the road was East India dock and Blackwall tunnel and a short walk in the morning brought one out to the river. Sometimes we slept at the Hostel but found it a strange inhospitable place, where we knew few people. I was still very homesick, missing Joan and David terribly and not being able to be there during Joan's pregnancy, and my conscience was troubling me. I kept wondering if I was doing the right thing? Was I making a difference? The only consolation is, that the alternative was the prospect of staying on at the Estate Office and just going on in the same old rut, whereas as it is, I have been given the unexpected opportunity to do entirely different work, meet new people and gain fresh experiences.

But slowly life in the East End settled down and here my father contemplates the problems of the daily life of the Unit, including trying to placate everyone with suitable jobs, as well as his wider family concerns such as whether his brother-in-law, Alfred Braithwaite might be called up, and what should happen to his mother now she is on her own in Birmingham, and will he be able to spend some time with his sister at the Braithwaite family home known as 'Sheredes' in Hoddesdon, Hertfordshire, not to mention an incident with Mrs Churchill……….

Sunday, December 22nd 1940 – Poplar

My darling
I think of you so much and so long to be back together with you. I do admire you so much, and know you have by far the more difficult job. You are doing the real war work in bringing up David and another soon on the way, while I have the good time. How I wish I could help you.

Everything here has been very up and down, with peoples' hopes and plans being at sixes and sevens. Many of my group are very uncertain. David Tod has not been given the job he expected and has come to London to do shelter work for a time and though disappointing for him, it is very nice to see him. Michael Kirby has not got his job either and has gone to Gloucester for hospital training.

Yesterday I had lunch with Millior and Alfred which was very pleasant. They are expecting to stay at Hoddesdon for some time yet, but manage to come up for 2 or 3 nights per week and I expect to see them again next week. Mrs Braithwaite (A's Aunt) has asked me to go down for a part of a day over Christmas if I can, but I don't yet know if that will be possible. Millior is rather worried about what our mother ought to do. She would like, I think, to get somewhere in the country, where she could maybe live with them. But it is almost impossible to find anything at the moment. M&A are also keen, she said, to 'start a baby', though I am not sure if she is serious about the latter, so don't tell anyone.

It seems quite possible if further classes are called up, that Alfred[4] might have to join the FAU or something. Their flat in Gower Street has been quite shaken with several windows broken, but it is otherwise undamaged, even though a house opposite them has been demolished. Millior says she is not giving Christmas presents this year, though they threaten to give us another cheque and says she has sent you a parcel. But I think perhaps we need not send them presents this year either.

Peter Tennant was telling me the other day how his mother had arranged for Mrs Churchill to go round some FAU shelters when she came on a tour of inspection. Winston had sent an armoured car as shelter in addition to her own car, in case of an air raid, plus three police cars. Slightly unfortunately, the FAU pilot car took them up the wrong turning by mistake and led the procession up a cul-de-sac. But by chance there happened to be a shelter at the top of the cul-de-sac as well, and so they were able to hide their mistake, inspect that one first and then walk on to the one they were supposed to have visited! When the situation was explained to the chauffeur, he said "Oh, that's alright. Mind you, the old man would have had a few words to say, if he'd been there!"

Mrs C made a very good impression, asking lots of intelligent questions, because, as she said, "It's no good my telling my husband anything, unless I get my facts right"! In fact her visit bore fruit apparently, because soon after, Malcolm MacDonald (Minister of Health) and Herbert Morrison (Home Secretary) were 'on the mat' before Winston, while he berated them – "My wife tells me….etc etc" !

I will close now ready to post this tomorrow. God bless you my dearest. All my love, Ralph

Mrs Churchill visited some FAU Shelters in December 1940. Later the PM berated the Home Secretary "My wife tells me…!"

My father's brother and sister and families

(Above) My father's elder brother, John and his wife Enid (née Priestman), with their son Roger (b. 1930) and (right) his sister Millior and her husband Alfred Braithwaite, with baby Anna (b.1942).

Both siblings had married into old Quaker families: John and Enid in 1926 and Alfred and Millior in 1939.

John worked for Cadbury's and Alfred was a solicitor, and acted as Treasurer for many Quaker institutions. One of Enid's brothers, Basil was an honorary treasurer for the FAU.

The siblings formed a close family unit, but there was an especially close tie with his sister, and whilst my father was in London at the Poplar Hospital or working at Gordon Square, they often visited each other. On occasions my mother would come to London to see my father, and stay at the Braithwaite's flat in Gower Street.

My father also stayed on several occasions at the Braithwaite's family home 'Sheredes' in Hoddesdon, Hertfordshire.

Photographs courtesy of Roger Barlow and Carol Saker (née Braithwaite).

Life in the Shelters

Edward Ardizzone – Life in the shelters
Reproduced by kind permission of the Imperial War Museum

My father's interests ranged far and wide and in his more discursive letters he would often cover a whole range of subjects from books and cinema to exhibitions, philosophy and theatre. Here he talks of religious discussions with a Catholic Priest, a visit to the National Gallery, modern art and war artists, coping with a colleague's girlfriend and a visit to the Braithwaite home for Christmas. It is interesting that in his visit to the National Gallery, he comes across the war artist Edward Ardizzone, whom he greatly admires, and who he is later to encounter again in an exhibition in Cairo. His evening with Peter Hume is also full of redolence, as ere long he is to be lost at sea with Tom Tanner……..

Friday 20th December 1940 – Poplar

My dearest Joan

Thank you so much for your lovely letter of December 16th. It is always a joy to get your letters, but you praise me too highly. You are the one who is making all the sacrifices. I do hope by now you will have received some of the other three letters I sent, as well as the parcel of books which I sent for Christmas for both you and David, which should also have arrived by now. They are not what I should really like to have sent you, but I do hope you will enjoy them. Know that they come with my dear love for a happy Christmas and prayers that the New Year will be a better and happier one than the last.

Two more people from the Northfield Camp have now joined us at the Hospital and both seem quite nice, which will be a great help. One of them is called Roy Tyldesley, who is an artist of considerable ability, mostly a commercial artist I think, but he does landscapes too and has, I understand painted a colossal mural in the mess room at the Manor Farm. He is certainly an interesting man to have on board.

Did I tell you about Father Keen, the Catholic Priest, who has supper with us at the Hostel every night? He has been bombed out of his church and the hospital have taken him in. He is quite young, only just out of college and I imagine still a curate. He is very friendly, and at first encounter somewhat ingenuous, but we have considerable discussions together, which in fact are most thought provoking. He is very well up on Catholic apologetics and is broad-minded up to a point, but you can't really argue with Catholics for very long, as sooner or later you come up against the brick wall of fundamentalism. They will make a statement which depends on some argument which you are supposed to fully accept, but which of course is impossible for a free-thinking Quaker! But it makes for interesting discussions, even if ultimately they get nowhere!

Yesterday I went into London with David Tod to see two exhibitions in the National Gallery, which is otherwise empty at the moment. One was a collection of drawings by Augustus John and the other of British artists over the past 50 years. They were both very interesting and contained much that I liked. My taste is probably more conservative, tending to appreciate more realistic art, whereas David likes a picture as much for its form and design as for its content. I think he considers my 'likes' suitable for guide books and chocolate boxes, whilst I consider his 'likes' too stylised and 'modern'!

Actually, that is an overstatement, as I am more and more coming to appreciate so-called 'modern' painting. Eric Ravilious and the Nash brothers, Paul and John for instance, I find very powerful. And, of course, I realise that a picture should not just be a copy of whatever it is, but an expression of the artist as well. I do think though that if the artist wants the public to take an interest in his work, he should try to make his art intelligible, whether that be in design, colour or form.

Nevertheless, I do often feel much more sympathetic with some exponents of 'modern' art than I do for many more conventional painters. There was one very interesting contrast of two paintings both of ships: one by Muirhead Bone, who has been an official war artist in both world wars, and the other by John Nash. The Bone was a very competent almost photographic picture, whereas the Nash, which was a more formal and simplified, even slightly cubist picture, was infinitely more effective. On the other hand there was another picture called 'The Renown in action', which was neither like a ship nor was it a picture!

The government has had the intelligence to employ modern rather than conventional and traditional painters, with many names I did not know – Edward Ardizzone, who has numerous brilliant drawings of life in shelters, barracks and towns. They are almost 'Punch' like drawings, but full of understanding of life, with people sleeping in shelters, soldiers with their girl friends, or Officers on duty, all done in an unusual but impressive style. Then there were numerous paintings of army life by Anthony Gross with little detail and apparently very rough, but most vivid. Other pictures of the AFS at work on air raid damage are also very telling.

Mercifully there were remarkably few pictures of the typical 'handsome war hero' variety, though there are some perfectly competent, if dull ones by William Rothenstein and some excellent ones by Eric Kennington. Altogether it was a most stimulating exhibition of a nation at war, with civilians and soldiers doing anything but fighting. Not perhaps the greatest art, but so much more interesting than it might have been, with contemporary artists trying to deal with the subject in their own way and often succeeding.

Last night I went up to see the FAU HQ at Gordon Square, and was persuaded to stay the night. I had a pleasant time there and had a long talk with Peter Hume, now the Secretary, about Unit matters in general. I have come to like him very much as a person. I think I told you about Michael Kirby, who was in my section at the Manor, and who was semi engaged to a girl in London. He was most miserable at being sent to train up at Gloucester and not in London, and very anxious for me to meet his semi fiancée, who is working at the Ministry of Information and was, he said, very lonely. It seemed rather odd, as I have never met the lady, but I wrote to her suggesting that we meet up along with my sister, so that is what we are doing – having lunch with Millior tomorrow. I will let you know what she is like!

There were some air raid casualties in the Hospital today, the men told me, who had had a rather gory time, and since I returned from my leave, we have been taking it in turns to sit with one of them who has a lacerated brain and has become violent in his pain, poor man, and is sinking fast. It's a rotten job and in a way I'd rather fight dozens of fires than watch someone die in agony.

It looks as though I will be free on Boxing Day after all, so I will be able to spend the day with Millior and Alfred at their cousin's home 'Sheredes', which will make a change, though I'd much rather be with you. What about our house? Should we try and let it for a few weeks or months, or are you planning to go back in the spring? I do hope you are keeping alright. I think about you all the time, and miss you terribly. Well, I must end now. I send you all my love. God bless you and all love to David. Ralph

PS. Apropos names for the new baby, I don't care much for Diana Mary. What about Gillian or Rosalind? If it's a boy, Antony I think would be good.

PS2 Later....As promised I had lunch with Millior, and Michael's lady friend, Miss Abbie Chisholm. She is a young girl – only 21 I think – Scottish, and though not especially good looking, is nonetheless very charming. She has an Oxford degree and her first job was with Chatham House and now is with the Ministry of Information in the American Department. She was most grateful to us for asking her out and if you don't mind, we may repeat it again before Christmas, both for her own sake and because I promised Michael.

As will become even more of an issue when my father goes abroad, correspondence even at home often took a long time. Here my father wishes my mother and David a Happy Christmas and discusses emergency preparations in case of an invasion when the new baby is born........

Monday 23rd December 1940 – Poplar

Dearest Joan

 I have been thinking of you so much of late. You are very dear and mean the whole world to me. I can never repay you for all you are and do. I don't expect you will receive this till after Christmas, and I do so hope that you manage to have as happy a time as possible under the circumstances. I trust you received my last two letters and parcel in time for Christmas. I had a card from the Keens, wishing me a happy Christmas and I had a lovely pullover from Winifred, which she had knitted. It is very beautiful, and I like it very much. I also had a card from your mother, which was sweet of her. Do say thank you to both of them for me, and of course I will write as soon as I can.

When the baby is born, I think it would be best if Honor would kindly send me a wire, as phones are so uncertain at the moment. There seems an indefinite delay and if I am not at the Hostel, I will ask them to phone me here at the hospital and tell me that they have a telegram. I will then come as soon as I can arrange it, either the same day or the next and return the same day if possible. I will then get special leave to come and stay as long as possible, probably about 2 weeks later.

If by chance an invasion does take place – and the papers seem to have started talking about it again – it is quite probable that communications will be badly upset. So try not to worry if you don't hear anything from me for some days. We remain very busy here at the Hospital, and continue to take it in turns to sit by the critically wounded man as I told you. He is still desperately ill and unconscious, but miraculously he remains alive, and he is now much less violent than he was. I found it quite hard to bear to begin with, as head wounds can be so terrible, but I am a little more used to it now. How terrible these times are.

This is just a brief note as we have been very busy lately, having quite a lot of fresh work owing to a number of our nurses and staff being down with 'flu. So we have assumed much of the routine work, such as taking meals round and washing up and making beds. Some of us have also been in the receiving room, where all the casualties first arrive.

Mr Tritsch, by the way, has agreed to take the Linden Road house, and Alfred is preparing an agreement. I do hope all is well with you, and wonder so much what you will be getting up to this Christmas, wishing as ever that we could have been together.
Dearest love, Ralph
PS I had tea with Millior and Alfred yesterday and hope to go down to Hoddesdon on Sunday, where they are staying for the time being with Alfred's cousins Fred and Marjorie at their home 'Sheredes'.

Here, as my father's first Christmas away from my mother arrives, he describes two contrasting occasions. To begin with he paints a picture of a rather sober Boxing day spent with the Quaker Braithwaite household at their home 'Sheredes' in Hertforshire, before going on to depict the raucous Christmas day party he spent in the air raid shelters and a very convivial meal back at the Hostel. Not an overtly sociable person at the best of times, my father never found such 'family occasions' easy, even when with my mother.

Here, selecting his words carefully, he describes the Christmas gathering with friends and relatives in minimalist language using words such as 'pleasant', 'nice' and 'sweet', none of which would offend, but are also hardly effusive! But while his descriptions of the family capture perfectly the personifications of good, but dull old Quakerdom, his language ups a gear when describing the jollity of the down-to-earth-ness of the festivities in the Hostel and the shelters......

Thursday 26th December 1940 – Poplar

My dearest Joan
I have now received two lovely long letters from you. Thank you very, very much; it is wonderful of you to write so often, especially as it must now be getting quite uncomfortable for you. Please do not worry about my welfare: you have quite enough to cope with as it is. There is a laundry near here, where I am getting all my clothes washed and Milli has very kindly said she can do any mending I may need. I did love the photo of David, which is extremely good, and I'm only sorry my Christmas parcel hasn't yet arrived, though I feel sure it will soon.

Yes, I had a very pleasant day up at Hoddesdon today with the Braithwaites. I arrived about 10.30 at their house 'Sheredes', which is quite nice and of a good size, with large rooms and windows and some lovely furniture. Hoddesdon itself is really quite a fine, small historic town and the countryside round is most pretty. They own about 70 acres, which they farm in a small way. Alfred's cousins, Fred and Marjorie are both very kind people, and have already asked me to go down again sometime soon, which is sweet of them.

He is short and stout and perhaps a little pompous, and she is very strong-minded, forthright and capable. They have two daughters; the elder, Joan is short and neat and quite pleasant to look at and very friendly, while the younger one Mary, rather dumpy and plain. Arthur, the eldest child and his wife are staying there too, but he had to go up to London and I only just saw his wife briefly.

Apparently, they used to have a maid, but she left rather abruptly just before Christmas, and now they are having to manage both the housework and run the farm on their own. The farm seems to provide them with quite a lot of their food and they gave us a very nice dinner of home produce, including cream from their own cows – quite a luxury in these rationed times. Millior and Alfred seem very happy there and F&M obviously enjoy having them around. Millior thanked me very much for the book you sent and for your letter. She said that she and Alfred are going up to Birmingham next weekend and hoped to be able to come out and see you.

Last night, being my night off, I went with David Tod to three of the shelters for which he is responsible. They were packed with people and both were having parties, with everyone appearing in a happy mood, and despite all the privations they are suffering because of the war, Christmas hit a high level of merriment. There seemed to be plenty of food to go round, liquor flowed in buckets and the children were all playing games, while the young couples cuddled in corners, and everyone sang carols. It was an amazing sight to behold and in these difficult days gladdened the heart. The FAU chaps were there giving out medicines where needed, and tending to anyone suffering and are inevitably known by everyone as 'Doctor' as a consequence! I didn't get back to the Hostel till after midnight.

Earlier on at the Hostel we all somehow had a good old traditional Christmas day lunch with roast beef and some, if not all the trimmings, and Christmas pudding to follow and some silly home-made crackers that someone had made. It was all very jolly and as they say 'a good time was had by all'! I did keep wishing though, that I could have shared it with you and the family. I do hope you all managed to have as good a time as possible up at Beaconwood.
Bless you my dear
With all my love,
Ralph

Christmas passed and the work at the Hospital became more hectic as people were off with 'flu and coughs and colds, but the FAU came into their own and were almost single-handedly keeping the Hospital operating effectively. FRB writes:

During the last weeks of the year, with so many people ill, we made tremendous progress. I visited nearly all departments and the Unit has become really useful to the hospital. On some occasions we were nearly the only staff in Out Patients. With one man in the receiving room and another helping on the ward, it was admirable experience for the men and all the time we were improving and gaining in confidence. Everyone seemed very appreciative of our efforts. So for once, I felt more cheerful and that what we were doing was proving worthwhile.

——

Chapter 7
A New Year Dawns and the Arrival of a New Child
January 1941

With Christmas 1940 over, my father's letters from Poplar turn to the birth of his second child, as he worries about not being close to my mother at such a time. This also leads on, as so often, with him considering his own convictions and, with the world as it is, whether he has made the right decision. He distracts himself, as always, with reading, the occasional visit to the cinema and unusually for my father, socialising – indeed sometimes surprising himself..........

Sunday, January 5th 1941 – Poplar

My very dear Joan

Last night was my night off and Michael Kirby and his friend Abbie and I went to a film and afterwards for supper. We couldn't go until she had escaped from the Ministry of Information, where she is working until about 5.30, and the only cinema we could find open had an amazing Wild West film on. It was actually quite enjoyable in a sort of way, with its galloping horses and crazy shootings, but unintentionally very funny. We then had quite a good supper at a funny little snack bar and afterwards coffee back at her flat. It was so nice of them to ask me and I do appreciate being able to escape sometimes to a more civilized atmosphere.

Today, I had again intended to try and go over to Richmond, but was once more diverted, this time by Cameron (the actor, Dermot Cameron Cathie). He kindly asked me to his home for dinner, but before eating we decided to go for a walk up on Hampstead Heath, which was fine apart from being bloody cold and bleak. But one is practically in the country up there, which has a semi-wild splendour all its own, with limpid near frozen pools, bordered by clusters of trees, and scatterings of over-wintering ducks and gulls, searching hopefully for food. I was about to say it reminded me a little of the Lickeys, but here in mid-winter it's harsher and more remote, with none of the Lickey's intimacy.

Cameron is a dear, and really very nice, but I never feel quite at ease around him. It's always a bit as though I am stepping on eggshells, as he has some distinctly odd views on certain subjects, and I am always afraid of saying something which he might consider rather shocking! His wife, Dinah who is an actress too*, is rather a surprise at first, being quite elaborately made up, dressed in flannel bags and a gay, tight-fitting waistcoat, but is actually very likeable and great fun. She is quite small and exotic looking, and though not exactly pretty or even beautiful, is excellent company and a most vivacious talker and deliciously outspoken. (*Professional name Dinah Martin)

At present she is working for the Ministry of Supply, and the two of them are living out at Finchley in a house belonging to Cameron's mother, who is now in a nursing home. I'm always fascinated by other peoples' surroundings and somehow, I don't know why, I expected Cameron would be living somewhere totally different. This is a rather ugly, pokey, down-at-heel, middle class Victorian house. But I mustn't complain as they provided a very good dinner, that's to say it was very well-cooked, if hardly very well served! You would not have approved at all, as it bore no resemblance whatsoever to how you would have done it. I wished you could have been there, as I so often feel out of place on such occasions, and dearly want you with me to help and hold my hand and laugh along with me. However, we had some good conversation about plays, particularly J B Priestley and his time plays, about how difficult it was to find any work at the moment, which I can well believe; about actors and whom we admired, and actually it was an altogether fascinating day, and I enjoyed myself much more than I had expected to.

Now, here I am back at Poplar. I suppose it's not such a bad life, and I shouldn't complain. But it's all so imperfect. What are we working for, and when will it all end? How dull life is without you. Everything is only half as good as it should be. I do wonder how David is and hope that he is well and being good. Please give him my love. You must be so close to the birth now. I do so pray for you and that all will go well.

I have been asked by the Trust to call in on cousin Margaret Graham, when I am next up – Horace's mother-in-law - concerning the damage she has suffered in the air raid and assess it all, but otherwise I shall try and stay within easy reach of the Hostel in case you want me. I saw that Horace's mother, Josephine had just died; I must write him a note.

As you know, I usually think that 'The Friend' is rather a poor affair, but do try and look at this week's edition, as there are a number of very interesting things in it. The letters recently sent to The Times and now reproduced in The Friend, written by the Archbishop of York, William Temple (Freddy's Uncle) and others, are excellent. He is a man that has a real gift for resolving conflict and that is a talent that we need in abundance at this time. I should also like to get hold of H G Wood's inaugural lecture at Woodbrooke, I so respect his knowledge and scholarship and spirituality. I note that the college is remaining open over Christmas. There was another article in 'The Friend' which also rather appealed to me, on *Pilgrim's Progress'.* I really must re-read PP; I do think it is one of the masterpieces of English literature.

I wonder if you saw that the playwright, Mary Lucy Pendered, who wrote *The Fair Quaker,* which we both acted in, had just died. What fun that play was and how blessed, because it was then that I first fell in love with you. For that reason alone I shall always treasure the play and remember it with gratitude. I'm not sure that I was any good, but you were enchanting.

Joan Barlow (centre in a suit) in a play,
This is when, as my father writes: "I first fell in love with you."

A play called 'The Quaker'
The start of a lifelong love affair

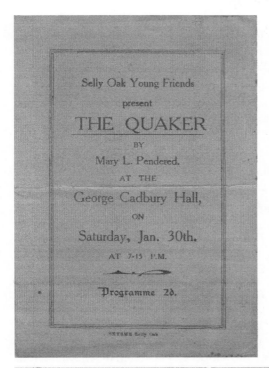

YOUNG FRIENDS' DEBUT AS ACTORS

BIG SELLY OAK AUDIENCE.

ALTHOUGH never before had a public dramatic performance been attempted by the Selly Oak Young Friends, they had the privilege and encouragement of playing before a packed house at the George Cadbury Hall on Saturday evening, when they presented "The Quaker," by Mary L. Pendered.

The play ran remarkably smoothly, and the several minor flaws that might well have been expected, detracted in no way from the general effect of the production. No anachronisms were evident, nor did the beautiful eighteenth century costumes betray any false or jarring detail.

The technique of the play, indeed, was excellent, the settings simple but effective, the exits and entrances timed nearly always accurately, and the costumes attractive. From near the front, however, the make-up on the faces of several of the actors was a good deal too apparent.

To make the duelling scene really convincing, it is certain that expert fencing would be needed. Possibly the play would have gained even if the scene had been omitted altogether. This part was the one obviously weak spot in the play, and burlesque was approached dangerously close. Neither of the swordsmen gave the appearance of being seriously bent upon taking the life of the other, while their slipping shoes on the smooth stage floor provoked misplaced amusement.

Sound rehearsing must have been the basis for the smooth action of the play, but not all the actors were word-perfect. A very polished and accurate rendering of her part was given by Miss Joan Barber in the role of the Hon. Laetitia Coverley. Mr. Frank Westlake, too, interpreted the character of young Nathaniel Harlock with sincerity, enunciating his words with meaning. His treatment made the part very convincing.

Mr. A. Ronald Ford's suave tones eminently fitted him in the role of Mr. Tripp Dapperley, a court gossip; but Mr. Sidney Fountain was not so successful as Baron Milcombe. He spoke too quickly, with a lack of dramatic emphasis in either speech or gesture. As the Hon. Peregrine Coverley, Mr. Alfred W. Davison was effective, but was inclined to over-act, noticeably while expressing surprise when Nat refuses to finish the duel.

Accurate and sympathetic acting marked the performance as Amos Harlock by Mr. Ivor B. Groves. Although his tones were impressive, Mr. Groves must have found the usual difficulty in assuming the character of a person so much older than himself. That the difficulty was not entirely overcome was revealed by his occasional too hasty movements.

Other Performers.

Captain Montague Lushington (Mr. F. Ralph Barlow) could with advantage have put more fire, more of the reckless spirit, into his part. Mr. Barlow did not completely sink his own personality. Other parts were taken by Miss Miriam Carter as Hannah Harlock, Miss May Hobby as Anchoret Harlock, Miss Sadie A. James as Mrs. Tabitha Prewde, the widow; Mr. Edwin O. Ransome as Lord Charles Byng, and Miss Hilda B. Jenks, a maid.

Mrs. Dobbs was the producer of the play, which was stage managed by Miss N. Piele. Miss Barlow was responsible for the costumes. Music was played at intervals by Miss Warrington (violin) and Miss Bristol (piano). The proceeds of a collection which was made were in aid of a boys' camp, which is run regularly by the Selly Oak Young Friends.

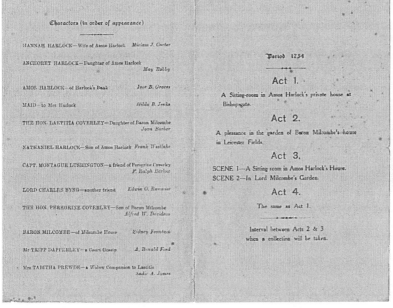

The Quaker, a play my parents were both in at a Quaker gathering in 1935.

"It was in this play that I first fell in love with you," writes my father.

The review in The Birmingham Post commented on a spirited performance by Joan Barber, but thought that 'Ralph Barlow could have shown more fire' !

You mentioned in one of your last letters that some kind person had given us a 7/6 book token. If you have no other ideas, what about 'Drama' by Desmond McCarthy, published by Putnam at 9/6. It is a collection of his dramatic criticism, stretching back over 20 years, dealing with a wide variety of plays which he has seen and reviewed in The New Statesman. I have always appreciated his criticisms and it was very well reviewed both in The Spectator and The Observer. If you have other ideas, I don't mind at all, of course, but I think this is the sort of book that we would both enjoy. Let me know what you think.

Although I haven't been to meeting for two weeks now, I do feel that religion - though I'm not quite sure how I define that – means more to me now than usual. I feel it is a bond between you and me, and I value it because of that. I am convinced that there is a purpose to life, and I am sure God means us to find it, and I believe he will help us to, though it may just be something very humble. I sometimes go to the service in the Hospital wards of an evening, which is very simple and rather moving – just hymns, a short talk and a prayer. I always think of you and say a little prayer for you.

I still see so clearly the difficulties of the pacifist position, but I am glad that I decided to be a CO. For much as I admire the wonderful fight that Britain and the Empire are putting up, yet I can't conceive of a situation in which it could ever be right for me to take a life. And though I don't feel I am doing anything very heroic as a CO, I firmly believe that I have done the right thing.

I'm not sure I should ever enjoy Hospital work as a career, though I must confess that at times it can be really most interesting. I really ought to try and take it more seriously and read the subject up in medical books. My knowledge is really most superficial. Did I tell you that the Sister in the Outpatients department, who is such a nice person, used to be the Matron at Sidcot School[1] and had nursed John and Enid's Roger when he was at school there. Isn't that extraordinary? I must tell John and Enid, they'll be very amused.

There is an air raid on at the moment, and the Germans have lit a fearfully big fire in the City again. We have all been out on the roof, but things seem to be a bit quieter for the time being. I better end this now and get it off to the post. I send you my prayers and love. Ralph
PS Did you ever see Millior, I wonder.

The air raids he refers to were particularly severe that night, so he quickly sends another brief letter the very next day, to reassure Joan that he was alright.....

Monday, January 6th 1941

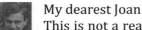

My dearest Joan
This is not a real letter; just a note to say that I am alright after last night's raid, which was very heavy. The whole sky was alight with the fires, and the damage in the city very serious, including a lot near the Hospital. Luckily for us, not too near. I got up about 4.0 yesterday morning to have a cup of tea, and instead of going quietly back to bed, we were all busy with fire-watching, getting meals and taking in casualties, including many fireman, some with serious injuries.

Today, I am supposed to be off, but went to wander round the smouldering fires with Michael Kirby and also pay a visit over to the FAU people in Bethnal Green. The Hospital there seems to be probably the best of all those where the FAU are stationed, and they also get a wide variety of work, which makes it interesting for the chaps. It's now about 7.30pm and seems as though hopefully it might be a quiet night for a change; at least there have been no warnings.

I have just received another letter from you, which is dated Boxing Day, for which so many thanks my darling. I am so sorry about your cold; what bad luck at such a time, as it must make you feel so miserable. I do hope it will clear up soon and that you will start to feel more cheerful. I also had a letter from my mother, who said how nice it was to see you at Innage Road with John and Enid and that you seemed to be coping well. How kind of Jeph and Margaret to have you over too, and I am glad David was so well behaved! Thank you for all the news. I must end this now, as it was just to let you know that I was safe and quite untouched by the raids. Dear love, Ralph

Despite his conviction in an earlier letter that he was glad he had decided to be a CO, here my father is wavering again, contemplating whether his life is too easy compared with those at the front. This is a debate that he has continuously with himself during his time in the Unit, going this way and that, and is a subject that obviously troubled him. He also mentions The Unit Chronicle, to which he contributed throughout his time in the Unit, as well as reminiscing about the many happy times he had shared with my mother.......

Wednesday, January 8th 1941

Dearest Joan
I have just received a letter from you, written last week; letters do seem to be taking a long time these days. Thank you so much for it and for the lovely photo of David. I am so glad my mother came over to visit you; she wrote to me saying how good it was to see you. I went to see cousin Margaret Graham this afternoon, as the Trust asked. The problem seems to have been a misunderstanding between her and the Estate Office over payments, and there wasn't a great deal that I could do. Sadly she is getting rather vague in her old age.

I am sending you some recent copies of the FAU Chronicle, which you may like to see. I think they are really quite good. There is also an FAU report which has been published, which I will let you see in due course. I do think the FAU is doing good work, but I just wish I could be sure that I am in the right place. It seems so wrong that being a CO should enable us to have a much easier time than the others, especially while our fellow countrymen are fighting for a cause. What are we standing for or working for? And is it right for us to stand aside when our country, to whom we owe so much is involved? I wish I could reach a greater degree of certainty in my own mind and satisfaction with myself. Of course, Father Keen, whom I mentioned, is full of certainty as a Catholic, and I must say we do all appreciate his company over supper. He has thought deeply on all sorts of problems and is remarkably well informed, also amazingly broad-minded for a Catholic. We have some very interesting discussions over supper with him, and I only wish they helped to resolve my dilemmas!

Oh I do so hope that everything is going alright for you. You have made me so happy - I have such a clear picture of you in my mind, on so many occasions – in different dresses and coats and hats; and in so many places – when you came over to see me at No 6 Swarthmore, or when you met me in Weoley Park Road when I first kissed you. Then, as you were in *The Fair Quaker,* or you in your orange beret when we first had tea in town. And of course, how could I ever forget you coming into the Meeting House when we were married, or you in your going away dress; or your lovely black evening dress....and a thousand other times. I think of your tenderness and love and understanding; of your cheerfulness and playfulness. I think of you at home and in the garden and your love of flowers. And your intense pleasure in things you enjoy, when you say – "I am so enjoying this". Like Rupert Brooke's 'The Great Lover' I say 'these I have loved'! How dear you are to me....I'll add more in the morning.

Next morning........

We had a man in to supper last night who was in the 9th Camp and is now working at Bethnal Green. He told me that Duncan and one or two others are going to Oxford to learn Chinese. I had already heard from elsewhere that he had put his name down to go to China. I shall miss him. David Tod has been appointed House Steward at the Hostel, which means he is in charge of cleaning, heating the bedrooms etc. I don't think he is very keen, but I'm sure he will do it very efficiently. That is at least the third job he has been suggested for. The Executive Committee don't seem to know their own minds from one day to the next. The job that Michael came down to London to do, has now been filled by someone else! Another of our number has been in bed with a similar bug that I had, but is being well cared for.

I must finish now, dear love. May all go well for you. My love to David and to you my dearest.
Ever yours Ralph

Two letters just expressing thanks for a book received, and saying how much he is looking forward to seeing her very soon....

Sunday, January 12th 1941 – Student Hostel, Philpot Street E1

 My very dear wife
Thank you so much for getting the Desmond McCarthy book I had mentioned. I am delighted to have it and in such a lovely format. I shall greatly enjoy reading it.

And thank you a thousand fold for ringing the other day. It was a real tonic to hear your voice again. As I said, we are busy getting the Annual report out, and I still have a lot of letters to write to various people to go out with it. It is our major fund-raising appeal and with personalised letters, brings in a considerable amount. So what with that and the probability of a meeting on Sunday, it looks like being a busy weekend.

Thank you again so much for the book. Please give my love to David. I do hope he is quite better now. All love, Ralph

Monday, January 13th 1941 – Poplar, London

 My darling
Excuse me for not having written a longer letter since yesterday, but I am expecting to see you any day now, so this too is another short note. But I wanted to say that you are constantly in my thoughts and prayers and I do so pray that all will go well for you. God keep you safe my dear one. We had more heavy raids last night and you will no doubt have seen from the papers the terrible damage done. Happily we are unhurt.

Just to say, that I will stay with mother when I come up, as I can't expect Honor to put me up.

God bless you, much love Ralph
PS1. You will be pleased to hear, after you going on about my old shirts, that I have finally got round to buying some new ones! They refused to wrap them up, so I had to carry them back 'naked' as it were!
PS2. I have just written to Duncan, and I hope the reserve party will be able to take the letter out to him in China.

———

The Unit Chronicle

Stanley Mackintosh, the first Editor of the *Unit Chronicle* with Assistant, possibly Edna Bailey.
The *Chronicle's* purpose was 'the free expression of news and thought in the Unit.'

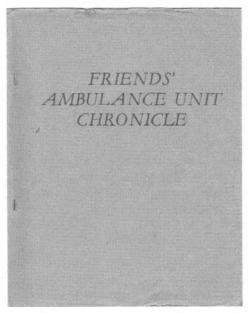

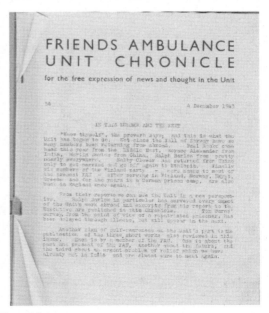

The Unit Chronicle
A monthly publication from 1939 -1945, comprising some 83 issues.
FRB contributed requently to this. My mother received a regular copy, which helped to keep her abreast of the news when FRB was abroad and correspondence was slow getting through.

Beaconwood
The home of Christopher and Honor Cadbury
Near the Lickey Hills, Northfield in Birmingham, where the author was born in 1941.
Photograph courtesy of Peter Cadbury

My father was now nervously awaiting the birth of his second child, feeling helpless back in London, and to add to his worries, the weather was fast deteriorating, with deep snow falling everywhere, making travel increasingly difficult. Most of the country was soon covered with snow and with very strong winds blowing, deeper and deeper drifts were forming. It quickly became apparent that he would somehow have to travel to Birmingham in ever worsening conditions, with Monument Lane, where Beaconwood was situated, on the edge of the Lickey Hills, deep in layers of compacted snow.......

Friday, January 17th 1941 – Poplar

My dearest

I have been thinking of you so much this week and everyday have been expecting news. I have taken some clothes all packed and ready to the Hostel each day, so that I can go straight from there up to Birmingham, and I have tried to phone you several times without success. I feel so sorry for you my darling, having this long and weary wait, which must be miserable and now having to see a specialist on top of everything. You sounded so sad on the phone when I finally got through tonight, and so fed up and I don't wonder. I am very worried and anxious about you and do pray that everything may go alright. God bless you and keep you my dear one.

I feel so useless and helpless and as though I were doing nothing to help and shirking my responsibilities. I pray that when this arrives, all will be over satisfactorily. All I can do is to say how much I love you and that you are absolutely everything to me. Life would be nothing without you. If only I could find more adequate words to express what you mean to me, but words are often such poor things. My God if anything happened to you I don't know how I would cope. But it won't and shan't. May God watch over you.

Dearest love, Ralph

My father wrote in his memoirs...........

On 19th January, Antony was born safely: a happy event in a bleak world. I somehow managed to travel up to Birmingham through the deep snow, and having borrowed a pair of skis, I ploughed my way up Monument Lane through feet of snow, not knowing if I was on the hedge tops or the road till I arrived at Beaconwood on the edge of the Lickey Hills. Thanks to the blizzard, the doctor did not arrive and all the work had been done by the nurse. Honor Cadbury was amazingly kind and I shall always remember seeing Joan sitting up in bed holding our new son.

Back in London my father was obviously delighted and conveys as much to my mother, but counts his luck, knowing that others are not so lucky.........

Wednesday, January 22nd 1941 – Poplar Hospital

 My dearest

It's pretty dull being back here after such a marvellous two days, and it was marvellous two days. To find you so happy and so well and with everything having gone so smoothly was wonderful. Thank you a thousand times for producing such a fine young son. I am sure we did right to go ahead, and we shall be so pleased in years to come. I shall never forget seeing you there, looking so radiant and holding our new child. I am so thankful that all went so well.

I went over to 26 and visited the Keens, who were delighted to hear your news and sent you their love and good wishes. I also rang Edwin Ransome concerning registering Antony with Monthly Meeting – but he had already seen it in The Birmingham Post. He says Hilda is well and comfortable, but rather isolated and lonely, with the baby due in March. 26 looked remarkably tidy, and all things considered, in good condition. Mother does exaggerate so! Oh how I love the house and how I wish we could go back.

Mother made me very comfortable, fed me beautifully and seemed delighted to have me. She was at her very best. I think she must be very fond of me, and even if my being a CO has had no other good results, it has at least pleased her, whereas if I had done anything else, it would have broken her heart. We are in very good odour just now, and she wanted to know all about you and Antony. She will keep a copy of the Birmingham Post for you.

I rang up your mother again and she will find out from Honor before Sunday if the roads are passable. They will be very glad to have David at Wolverhampton while you are at 'Beaconwood' and whenever you want a change, they will be glad to have all three of you. But we can resolve that later. David was an absolute angel and it's completely heart-breaking to have to be away from him. Just think how many children are saying "Daddy, don't go back – I miss you so", and so many of those Daddies are going to hell to be killed, and will never come back. What a wicked tragedy war is.

I met up with Mr Tritsch at King Edward's Five Ways. He is teaching unevacuated boys and Mr Fulford is acting Head while Charles Dobinson[2] is away. He seemed a nice man and in considerable difficulty because of the war. I made him a generous offer, partly because I want the house lived in and because even a little money would help us with the rates, and partly because it does seem a chance to help refugees in difficult circumstances. He is going to let me know if he wants it. I am anticipating letting it for a period of three months or hopefully 6 at 21/- per month. He knows he would not get so good an offer again, but has doubts whether a) they can afford it, b) if his wife can look after it properly and c) if it is safe to bring his children too. Our mothers will prepare it.

My train going back was late starting, but otherwise it was an easy journey. It was very dull at first, with everywhere dirty white fields and overcast sky; no colour at all. I thought for once the English countryside was really dull, but then suddenly there was a gap in the clouds and the sun broke through, and the whole scene took on colour and distance and became its own lovely incomparable self. I must end now as I feel tired, but it was marvellous seeing you.

God bless you and keep you. Thank you so much for everything and dear love and kisses to both the children, Ralph

"I ploughed my way up Monument Lane through the snow."

―

Honor and Christopher Cadbury

Honor and Christopher Cadbury
Top left – Honor. Top right - Honor and Christopher with baby Jamie 1936.
Bottom – Christopher in the Lickey woods.
"They kindly invited Joan to stay at Beaconwood for the birth of our second child as the air
raids were becoming difficult to cope with."
Photographs courtesy of Peter Cadbury

Family Photo album

Baby David with his Granny, father and aunt in 1937.

David and Antony with our mother

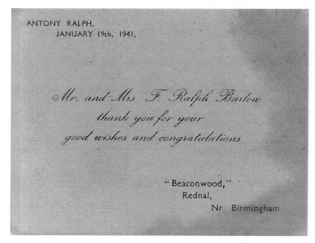

David and Antony at Wolverhampton during the war, and baby Antony 1941

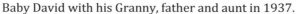

ANTONY RALPH,
JANUARY 19th, 1941.

Mr. and Mrs. F. Ralph Barlow
thank you for your
good wishes and congratulations

"Beaconwood,"
Rednal,
Nr. Birmingham

Fred and Marjorie Braithwaite's house 'Sheredes' in Hoddesdon and Family Braithwaite

Mary, Marjorie, Joan, Arthur, Magnhild and Fred
with young Bevan in the foreground.
Photographs courtesy Carol Saker

In today's world of mobile phones, it is easy to forget how difficult communication could be back then, and having returned to London following my birth, and not having heard from my mother, who is perhaps not yet up to writing letters, and unwilling to use someone else's phone, my father is anxious to know if all is well. My brother David is moving to stay with our Aunt and Uncle in Wolverhampton for a short while, until my mother was up and about and able to cope with two children.

As always my father reads, and not just his favourite novels, but James Joyce, a book of drama criticism, Chekhov and a book on pacifism. Often struggling to convince himself that he is doing the right thing by being a CO, or whether he is having it too easy, he finds 'Christian Pacifism' a help......

Monday, January 27th 1941 – London Hostel

My dearest
I have not heard from you and I hope and pray that everything is going alright. I trust David went off to Wolverhampton quite happily. I thought about you all so much.

Large numbers of people at the Hostel have gone down with 'flu, and at the hospital both porters and nurses are ill. This has meant quite a lot more work for us as we have been helping in the Receiving room, which is actually very interesting, because you see cases coming in and hear something of the diagnosis. We have been sitting up with the old man I mentioned with head injuries, who is now nearly dead, the poor fellow. He was a ship's plumber and might perhaps have pulled round, but he had been unwell for week s before the accident, and had lived largely on alcohol, so he was suffering from a mild form of DT's, as well as the brain injuries. He said some extraordinary things in his semi delirium, condition. The nurses are glad that we are there to help, because I think they are a little frightened of him. This morning I helped with dressings on the ward, which was interesting too in a slightly gruesome way, with broken legs, appendicitis and fomentations (hot poultices).

The night staff nurse - who is quite pretty - has a fiancé who is a doctor on a destroyer on the North Sea patrol, and she is so worried and anxious about him. Another of the nurses knew someone on HMS Illustrious[3], so they are all worried about their dear ones.

Last night we had Stanley Mackintosh in to supper, who is the new Editor of the Unit Chronicle. He is only 21 and very clever I think, with an interesting and unusual mind. He has some arresting views about what the Unit should be. For instance he believes that while the work is important, the life and growth of a Christian Community spirit in the Unit is more important. He and Father Keen had some very fascinating discussions. I am really not very good at close arguing or philosophical discussions, and the rest of us just dropped out and listened! He stayed so late that he had to spend the night here, and I cooked everyone a good supper of macaroni cheese. You would have been proud of me!

I have just finished Dr Cecil Cadoux's book *Christian Pacifism Re-examined.* It is a very fair consideration of the whole position of the pacifist. He holds that there have been righteous wars, and that there is a relative justification for it with the world as it is, and men as they are. But at the same time, he believes that war is contrary to Christian teaching and that pacifism is the right course for those who can accept it. It is a brave book to write at this time and I have found it most helpful.

I am also trying to read James Joyce's *Ulysses*, which Alfred lent me. You may have seen that Joyce died the other day. It is a most obscure book; difficult to follow and difficult to understand. It has very little in the way of description, and principally comprises long accounts of the characters' thoughts. It is also very 'down to earth' and basic. I can't say I cared for it terribly, but it is certainly brilliantly original.

The Desmond MacCarthy book is very interesting. It may perhaps suffer a little from being devoted to certain performances of certain plays, and quite often plays I don't know. But he has many fascinating things to say about acting and drama, about Shakespeare and Ibsen, and about the interpretations of various parts by different actors. He has a great opinion of Ibsen and Chekov, and although I know Chekov quite well, my knowledge of Ibsen is slender.

I am enjoying Dorothy Sayer's *Busman's Honeymoon* very much. It is delightful, daring and funny, plentifully sprinkled with apt quotations, and is a most charming and good detective story. Did you read *Gaudy Night*, because if so, you will remember that at the end of that, Harriet and Peter Wimsey became engaged? This book is about their honeymoon and what happened to them.

There has been yet another Unit change. Theo Willis, who was Warden of the Hostel, is going to China with the advance party and David Tod has taken his place, who will, I think do the job well, and I am very happy about it.

I shall ring Millior after dinner and perhaps go and see her tomorrow. What a curious lull there has been in the raids. We have had nothing for several nights. Isn't the news from North Africa good? I'm afraid it may only be a side show though, and nothing matters as much as beating Germany.

How do you feel now and how is the baby? It was so lovely seeing you, looking so well and happy, and I shall never forget it. You should feel very pleased with yourself. Have you had many letters and flowers or presents? I hope your family were impressed! Has mother been out to see you yet and was she nice? And have you heard from Hilda or Margaret? Do write when you can and tell me how you are. Thinking of friends, I see that they are going to tighten up the ages and classes of reserved occupations, and I wonder if it might affect Jeph (Gillett).

Talking of flowers, someone had put a bowl of daffodils in the Out Patients this morning and they looked so lovely. I can't express how much they affected me, reminding me, as they always do, of you.

One or two young architects and a few others are forming an architectural planning group at the Hostel. I think it might be quite interesting and useful. I think I must end now. I do love you so dearly.
Love Ralph.
PS Could you kindly let me have Horace's letter back, as I forgot to make a note of the address he sent?

———

Norman Booth
The first war casualty from the Unit

Norman was killed by a stray bomb as he was having lunch at the Middlesex Hospital.
"The Unit has lost a man whose simplicity and cheerfulness made him an admirable
companion."
Photograph Friends House Library

A sad end to the year 1941 occurred on January 31st, which brought the war immediately very close to home, when FAU man Norman Booth was killed by a stray bomb as he was having lunch at the Middlesex Hospital. The bomb fell on a corner of the hospital, and a piece of detached drain pipe went straight through the window and killed him outright. He had joined the Unit in July 1940 and returned from working in a provincial hospital to work in London, when the blitz came.

A friend of his wrote: "Those who knew him well, need no reminder of his qualities and will recall what a good friend he was. Those who did not know him, should know that the Unit has lost a man whose simplicity and cheerfulness made him an admirable companion. To any work he brought an equal energy and reliability. Such people form the backbone of any group of men."

Also the death of a close Cadbury Cousin, Geraldine who was Paul Cadbury's mother would have upset him. Finally, he has been able to let the Linden Road house to Josef Tritsch, a Polish refugee, escaped from Austria, which will help with the finances.....

Wednesday, January 29th 1941 – London Hostel

My dearest Joan

[..........] You have probably seen from the newspapers that three hospitals were hit yesterday. One was the Middlesex where three FAU men were living. One FAU man, Norman Booth was tragically killed and another Jack Harris badly injured. It is very sad, as Norman was a fine man and will be much missed. It is amazing in a way that these should be the first serious casualties of the Unit.

I was also sorry to hear that Cousin Geraldine Cadbury died on Thursday. She was a splendid woman. I shall write to Cousin Barrow and Paul expressing our sorrow. How sickening all this separation is, but we mustn't let it get us down. Thank you so much for the two lovely letters I have had from you. I'm so glad you have had lots of nice letters following A's birth, and so happy that he is developing well. I should love to see all the letters sometime. It's great that you have good news from Win about David.

My mother tells me that you are up already. Is this wise? Please don't be in too much of a hurry. Take it easy. I am so sorry that you are finding it dull out at Beaconwood. I do understand how quiet it must seem all by yourself and with so few visitors, and I wish I could be with you more. However, I have told Gordon Square that I really must have some leave very soon.

During the last few weeks with so many people ill, we have made tremendous progress in the hospital filling in, and have been able to work in nearly all the departments and have in fact, been really useful to them, This morning we were about the only staff in Outpatients and we had a man in the Receiving Room and another helping on the Ward. Everyone is really appreciative of our help. It is all admirable experience for us and we are improving and gaining confidence all the time.

It is rather pleasant to get out of the stage when you are frightened to do anything, to one in which you know the ropes. It is splendid that the work here has opened out so much because when we first came, it was practically entirely Outpatients, which is fine, but limited. We are a very happy community here at the London Hostel, and our evening meals round the fire are pleasant occasions, especially as we have the company of Father Keen. I shall miss it all. Life since the war has been one long uprooting from one place to another.

There has been a lot of interesting reading in the press recently. The News Chronicle even had an article on the FAU yesterday. I wonder if you have seen the series of articles by André Maurois in The Telegraph on the collapse of France. They are really most interesting and enlightening. He depicts a country in which the government is dictated to by big business, where months were wasted in shilly-shallying because of petty rivalries, and where Germany succeeded because of France's disastrously ill-equipped forces. The mistakes made are really incredible. There have also been a series of articles in the News Chronicle entitled 'God and the War' introduced by J B Priestley, which are very worth reading. The views include those like Julian Huxley who are sceptical of God, and those who wonder how God can answer both German and British prayers, but the majority seem to think that by resisting violence and tyranny and championing justice and freedom at such a time, we are 'championing the things of God'. It has been suggested that I should try and write an essay on this for the Unit Chronicle.

John Bailey, the chief Personnel Officer of the Unit, came here to supper last night. He is a nice fellow. Apparently, he told someone afterwards that ours was one of the tidiest hospital sections of the Unit that he had visited. I feel that my efforts have been rewarded! Some of the chaps need continual looking after, while some have absolutely no idea how to do simple things like washing up! You won't believe it, but I have become unbelievably domestic! Married life has obviously been of enormous value to me in managing to live a communal life. Truly, I am sure that your training has made me much more useful (cooking, cleaning etc) and much more thoughtful for and careful of looking after other people. It is the virtue of family life in another sphere that helps in a community like this. Virtues such as thoughtfulness and unselfishness etc. No doubt I still leave much to be desired, but thanks to you, I am better than I was before I married you. You would be proud of me! So many young unmarried people are quite unintentionally thoughtless.

Did I tell you that Mr Tritsch has agreed to take the house? That should help us considerably financially. Well, well, I must stop now. I will write again soon. Dear love, Ralph

PS If you do have a moment and have registered A's birth, could you kindly fill in and send off the birth note that I enclosed in my last letter.

Dr Franz Josef Tritsch, was a Jewish refugee, who had fled Poland to live in Austria and then came to this country about 1940/41. My parents rented out Linden Road to him and his family. He had gained a teaching post at King Edward's, Five Ways, where my mother had worked prior to her marriage. In 1943 he left KE and went to Birmingham University.

My father thought him 'a loveable rogue'.

Photo courtesy Birmingham City Library

Chapter 8
A country posting
January – March 1941

Still in the after-glow of the successful birth of their second child, my father's letters reflect a new contentment as he begins to settle in, and to relish the company and discussions with his fellow members. However, this state of affairs is rudely interrupted by instructions from Gordon Square to move to a small village near Newmarket to find more shelters.

With the need for shelters becoming ever more acute, the Unit became involved in finding suitable properties outside London and away from the bombing. The problem, of course, was persuading families bombed out of their homes in Wapping or Stepney, to leave London. So my father, with his experience in housing, was suddenly despatched in late January 1941, to go somewhat hastily, as it turned out, to explore evacuation possibilities in Cheveley near Newmarket. Meanwhile Patrick Armstrong was moved to London to act as Evacuation Officer. Before leaving, my father was told to meet Peter Gibson, then the Relief Officer, to receive his rather abrupt instructions. Here my father writes of his new instructions in his memoirs......

Life in the Unit was never dull! Suddenly, one evening when I got back to Poplar, John Bailey arrived out of the blue at the hospital, and informed me that I was to go to Cheveley, near Newmarket, to negotiate for and prepare the rectory to receive evacuees from London. Patrick Armstrong, who had been working on an ambulance train in Newmarket staffed by the Unit, sent in reports that he had come across many vacant properties in and around Newmarket. In particular there was an old Rectory in the little village of Cheveley, which could be suitable for the huge numbers of people who had been displaced during the London Blitz. I was told to meet Peter Gibson at 2.0pm but he didn't turn up until 5.0pm! Knowing Peter as I do now, I can guess better at his whereabouts than I could then! I hardly had time to do more than collect some clothing and belongings, let alone tell Joan the change of plan. So I scribbled a quick letter for Peter to post to her.......

Saturday, February 1st 1941 – London

My dearest

I am writing this in great haste, as I have suddenly been informed that I am to go to Newmarket. I really hardly know any details myself yet, but apparently there is an old Rectory there to be leased, and prepared for evacuees to live in and to provide a centre where other evacuees in the district can go. They have asked me to go as I know something about property. I gather it is not a permanent job, unless I get keen on it and it grows. But probably only for 6 or 7 weeks. The FAU man doing it at present, is not very successful, they told me. It's probably all soft soap to get me to go! Still, I think it is probably a good move, and it's not that far out of London. Anyhow, it will be a change, and it is in my line, so that although I'm absolutely sick of being continually uprooted, I am nonetheless, quite pleased. We humans are an odd lot. Firstly we dread a change and we hate the first days of a new place; then we settle down and loathe the prospect of moving away again!

I have told them I will need some leave and will let you know when, as soon as I get a feel for the scope of the new job. I'm sorry it is so far away, but it's really no greater separation than my being in London. I suppose we must put up with it. As soon as I know more details and an address, I will write. Try not to be too glum about it. You have been so wonderful about it all. Don't let Newmarket get you down either. I shall see you before very long.

I gave a talk at the Hostel yesterday on 'Housing and Planning', which went fairly well I think. We had quite a good discussion afterwards, so I am actually rather sorry to be going, as a Study Group and a group of architects and planners was being set up, and I was just beginning to know more people and feel more at home, especially with David Tod as Warden. However, change is inevitable, and it is a chance for me. I gather that there is still a chance of my going as supervisor of the 11th Camp in Northfield later in the year, though the China party may have to go there to train. I am so sorry this letter is such a poor one, but I'll write at greater length when I get settled. Lots of love Ralph.

Following my birth, my father took a few days off to spend a little more time with my mother and his new son at Beaconwood, but from his letter afterwards, it is apparent that he had been rather tense, which had somewhat upset my mother. Yet another example of the problems of living in other people's houses and the cost of separation. A shy man, he was not naturally at ease in large company, and there were few things he hated more than constant upheavals. Here my father attempts to apologise, before describing his arrival in Cheveley.......

Thursday, February 6th 1941 – The Rectory, Cheveley

My dearest
This is by way of an apology, for I realise I must have seemed a little cold on my last stay, but believe me it was so grand to see you. If only I could tell you how I love you. I need you so much and I want shelter with you so terribly, that if I gave way I should weep like a child, and that wouldn't help either of us. I felt in the depths all day yesterday, as I am so sick of uprooting and saying goodbyes and meeting fresh people, when all I want is to come home to your protection like a tired child. I'm sorry to say all this, but don't be miserable as I am alright really.

I had a good journey to London and was in excellent time to see Peter Gibson at 2.0pm, but he did not materialise until about five. I was not best pleased, and even less so as he insisted I journeyed up to Cheveley that night. So having collected my bicycle, I didn't get away until 6.0pm, and rushed to Liverpool Street to catch the train to Cambridge, which was freezing cold with a bitter wind blowing outside, and I felt like cutting my throat. But I managed to get a cup of tea and a bun, and felt a little bit better.

I then had to wait about in Cambridge for an hour for another train, and didn't arrive in Newmarket until gone 10.0 o'clock. By this time there was a blizzard blowing and I had no idea where Cheveley was, but a kind person took pity on me and gave me directions. Then feeling anything but friendly towards Gibson, I cycled for 3 miles straight into the blizzard, by which time I was so desperate that it was almost funny.

I arrived in this little village about 10.45 where there were no lights on, nobody around, and I had no idea where the Rectory was. If it hadn't been funny, it might have been tragic. I had visions of sleeping in a haystack, and being found a frozen corpse in a ditch. As it was I found a big house and struggled up the drive and knocked loudly on the door and rang the bell, fully expecting to have the dogs set on me. I felt like the traveller in de la Mare's poem *The Listeners,* "Knocking on the moonlit door" shouting "Is there anybody there?"! But after some while, which seemed like hours, the Vicar appeared rather sleepily at a side door. – "What do you want?" still half expecting him to open fire on me, but he didn't. Instead, he very hospitably invited me in and gave me a bed. They were in fact very pleasant and had been waiting for me and expecting to put me up. I breathed prayers of gratitude as I snuggled very relieved under the sheets and blankets, listening to the gale howling outside. I'll write properly very soon.
Dear love, Ralph

Cheveley Rectory

"I set out to bicycle the three miles to Cheveley in a snowstorm, feeling anything but friendly towards Peter Gibson. I could well have been found a frozen corpse in a ditch."

"Life became daily more and more fantastic. Here am I staying in this grand 18th century Rectory, with some lovely wrought iron gates, enclosing a fine garden."
Photograph courtesy Juddmonte Farms

And so in the winter of 1940/41, my father was moved rather suddenly out of London to the little village of Cheveley, near Newmarket to supervise finding accommodation for the hundreds of people bombed out of London. Never happy at being uprooted, he soon felt depressed and emotionally low.

The blitzkreig by the German Luftwaffe was causing devastation in London's East End, and people were taking refuge in their hundreds of thousands wherever they could: in railway arches, church crypts, warehouses or derelict property. As each day brought new horrors, the official Rest Centres soon became overcrowded, thus aggravating the problems of homelessness. With personnel already stationed in hospitals in the area, the FAU were in the thick of it. As the air raids continued, and conditions worsened, urgent decisions had to be taken. Tom Tanner and Michael Barratt Brown were relieved from hospital duties to make a survey of the situation and on the 18th September 1940, it was agreed that the Unit should thenceforward embark upon relief work. Numbers grew rapidly and by the end of the year some two hundred men were engaged in relief work financed by the American Friends Service Committee organized by Henry J Cadbury who came on a visit to Britain in 1941.

The official government Civil Defence services were well prepared to provide fire-fighting, first aid and rescue services. But the most important need lay in the provision of adequate shelter for those who had lost their homes. London was already over-crowded and so many were evacuated to the countryside. For those who could not be evacuated, Rest Centres became their only home. The FAU ultimately took over the running of ten centres, working in shifts around the clock. After each air raid, more and more people had to be provided with food, beds, blankets, comfort and company. Some centres had to be established from scratch, making use of empty buildings. FAU staff would set up offices, stores, kitchens, dining and sleeping accommodation and recreation facilities. At night, many East Enders sheltered from the bombs in railway warehouses, arches and wharves. With hordes of people regularly sleeping, packed together, night after night, conditions deteriorated rapidly. FAU members began to attend the shelters as medical aid workers, but their responsibilities gradually expanded.

In Wapping, where the FAU was the only voluntary society operating, they took over many of the shelters, turning them into community centres and organizing parties and cultural events, for it became apparent that the shelterers had nothing to do night after night. So CEMA [1], the forerunner of the Arts Council, took a hand and there was co-operation from Adult education groups, children's play centres and amateur entertainers. In the City, 'model' shelters – Lloyd's shelters - were established in places like the basement of banks and one in Derbyshire Street was visited by the King and Queen. But space was a problem and evacuation became more and more the only solution, where families could be kept together and places were found not too far away in order that husbands could pay visits at weekend.

After my father's rather sudden departure and late arrival in Cheveley, he stayed first at the rather splendid Rectory, before moving up to Banstead Manor, where for the rest of his stay, he was the guest of a Mrs Morris - always referred to as Mrs M - and tried to make the best of it. But being now even further away from home, he is often lonely and depressed, though in fact, once he had settled in, it turned out to be one of the more light-hearted episodes of this period of his FAU life.

My father writes in his memoirs......

I'm afraid the whole affair of my departure and eventual arrival, like much of the FAU at the moment, was chaotic and I didn't really know what I would be able to do. In fact life became daily more and more fantastic. Here was I staying in this grand Rectory, more like a luxury hotel than anything, with central heating, servants and God knows what. No air-raids, and long peaceful nights. I wrote to Joan, saying "God it's awful! It will probably demoralise me completely!"

I spent two nights at the Rectory, a lovely 18th century house with splendid wrought iron gates enclosing a fine, if neglected garden. The rooms were large with high ceilings and big windows, and there were wide staircases and roomy kitchens. It was the sort of vicarage that one of Jane Austen's parson's with £10,000 a year, might have lived in. It's really too big for our needs, but we'll see. In a letter to Joan I described the Rector........

Friday, February 7th 1941 – c/o Mrs Morris, Banstead Manor, Cheveley.

My dearest
[....] The Rector is a queer old bird, with an odd, forgetful manner, rather like Dr Grantly in Trollope's *Barchester Towers,* often making strange remarks that seem to relate to nothing at all. But take as you find. To me he is very pleasant and extremely helpful, and has a quite remarkable appreciation of the pacifist point of view. In fact we had a most interesting discussion on Quakerism and pacifism last night, and I think I just about kept my end up. His wife, less well-educated than her husband, is quite a lot younger and really quite nice looking, though Mrs M snootily `insists - 'she's just a farmer's daughter!' But to me she is very friendly and very practical minded. They have a son away at prep school.

Yesterday I went over to see the Ministry of Health officials in Cambridge, and had quite a satisfactory interview. I hope they will agree to rent us the house and then let us use it. This would be much cheaper from our point of view, than if we were to rent it ourselves, and of course mean much less work for me – though I don't think this is quite what FAU HQ envisaged! Shhhh!

Later........February 8th.....Following my visit to Cambridge yesterday, today I spent the morning writing a bunch of follow-up letters, and then went back into Cambridge to deliver them – it's only about 30 mins away from Newmarket – where I had lunch. But for some reason, I returned to Newmarket feeling acutely miserable. Everything I did seemed to be chaotic: I really didn't see what I could do to be of practical use and I was totally fed up with meeting a never-ending round of new people. I was lonely and homesick; and the countryside around suddenly seemed dull and uninteresting. Apart from all that.....I'm fine!

Later I went on into Wood Ditton, where there is another vicarage, housing evacuees, and run by Friends, Alan and Mary Pickard, who act as wardens. He was out, but she was so kind and helpful and greatly cheered me up. It was like talking to one of one's own kind - someone who felt and thought like I did! There are about 20 mothers and children there already and all seem to be happy and contented. She did say, however, that thanks to a deal of FAU bungling, it was total chaos when they arrived, and they both had a great deal to do to get it running smoothly. I must say I was not entirely surprised, but it's vital that I avoid anything like that happening at Cheveley. But they seemed to relish the task, and I have to say, it is now very clean and efficiently run. She greatly cheered me up and as I left, everything suddenly seemed different - the sunset was absolutely ravishing and the countryside started to look beautiful again. Life was starting to look up. All, I needed was to have you here beside me.

When I got back, I moved all my stuff up to the Manor, which is a biggish, modern house with every comfort and at least three maids. Mrs M is married, but her husband is out in China, and only gets back home for three months every year. She is tall and good looking, about fifty with a pleasant way, very capable, kindly and generous, if rather managing. Then there is her mother, who is a queer old stick, but I suspect there may be more to her than at first appears. Mrs M is very keen on the evacuation scheme in the Rectory, and my instructions are to cultivate them! "Get to know the people in the village," she instructed me, "and interest them in your scheme." So that evening I inspected the Rectory properly, and it may well do very well. Mrs M manages a stud farm, breeding and selling bloodstock. I presume, this consists of buying, hiring and leasing mares and putting them with pedigree stallions, but I can't believe it's all that profitable a business in the midst of war.

I find my life here alternates between being sometimes engaging and funny, and sometimes totally miserable. Occasionally - poor little conchie that I am – I feel like Daniel in the lion's den, as though I don't belong in this world and wander about wondering all the time what everyone thinks. At other times, I can laugh at it all and rise above it. I hope I don't have to stay here too long; it would drive me mad.

Well, dearest, it's now midnight and I must stop. I think of you all the time, my dear one. God bless and keep you safe and my love to David.
Dear love as always,
Ralph

PS I haven't forgotten about taking some leave, and as soon as things start to shape up here, I will sort something out.

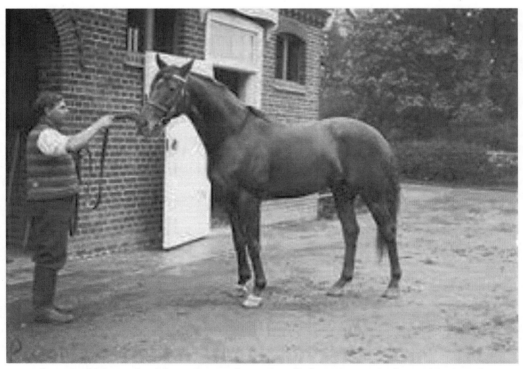

Banstead Manor Stud farm during the war with their prize race horse 'Tai Yang'.
Photograph courtesy Juddmonte Farms

The Cheveley Set

Mrs Vera Morris - outside Banstead Manor
"She is tall and good looking, about fifty with a
marvellous pleasant way, very capable, kindly
and generous."

Eric FitzGerald Dillon, 19th Viscount Dillon
"He came down to dinner in full uniform – a close
fitting blue uniform, loaded with decorations!"

Lord and Lady Dillon with their daughter Pamela and grandchildren, Teresa and Michael
(photograph courtesy Teresa Waugh – see end note)

Banstead Manor turned out to be a very odd establishment, presided over by the splendid Mrs M, who considered herself to be quite the Lady of the manor. My mother, still unhappy up at Beaconwood, suggested that she might come out there to join my father...

Saturday, February 8th 1941 – Cheveley

My dearest

I've just had a lovely lot of letters from you and thank you so much for them. I am glad to know that you are up and well, but I guess now that the nurse has gone, you will be kept busy with two children to look after now. I am sure David will love being back with you from Wolverhampton. I also had a letter from my mother, who says she so much enjoyed coming over to see you and Antony.

In response to your question, I too had thought of the possibility of you coming to stay out here near Newmarket. But on further thought, I really don't think it would be very good for you. It is miles and miles from anywhere or anyone you know. It's surrounded by large aerodromes and if it should happen that the Germans were to land in East Anglia, you would be on the front line in next to no time. There are German planes flying over every night, and we continuously hear the thud of bombs, whilst during the day our own planes are flying over.

I also thought about the possibility of the two of us being wardens of the new hostel. But again, I don't honestly think it would be feasible for you to look after two children, and run a big house with 30 to 40 people; that in itself would be a full time job. At Wood Ditton for instance, Mr Pickard does all the cooking as well as much of the house work. If we didn't have two children, it would, of course, have been grand. But I am really hoping that I shan't be here very long. The Unit have now decided that they will go ahead on their own without waiting for the Ministry to make up their mind, so I have been busy buying things - lino for the house for £12, a stove for £6 and a wringer for 30/-, as well as some seeds for the garden. I'm now negotiating with the Rector about the lease.

On Thursday, I met up with the well-known social worker, Noël Hunnybun who I'd invited to come down from London, to get her advice. I had met her briefly before, and she is highly regarded, about 45-ish I would guess, very efficient and an exceptionally nice person. She comes from an old country family near Huntingdon, and is very much the lady. She works for one of the Lloyds model shelter schemes, and is in charge of all the evacuation, finding the families and then travelling up with them and settling them in.

Mrs M likes her very much too, which is good news, and I was able to have a very useful talk with them both about the evacuation plans for the vicarage, and eventually we managed to sort everything out, so the scheme is now fairly well settled and I hope will not be troubled by any more of Mrs M's red herrings! It is so difficult negotiating with the vicar; not to be too easy on the one hand nor too hard on the other. But I like Mrs M – and I think she quite likes my being here. Her mother is leaving on Tuesday, after which she would have been quite alone were it not for me. So I serve some useful purpose!

Miss H and I went round the stables in the morning. Their most valuable horse at present is 'Tai Yang'[2], which is worth £18,000, and is kept in a completely rubber-lined stall, which in itself cost £2000 to build. I believe this is one of the best stud farms in England. All the mares' boxes have cards up outside – with the name of the mare and the parents – 'covered by such and such a stallion' - with the date when the foal is expected. They have about 400 acres of land, all beautifully kept. Racing may be a luxury and an extravagance, but it does provide good employment round here and it does look after the land. 'Tai Yang' is a lovely chestnut and his foal by some mare or other, is also the same gorgeous colour. They have about 15 delightful fillies in a field all together. They really are beautiful.

Peter Gibson, who is now in charge of relief work came down here on Friday and was a great help in settling various prices suggested by the Vicar. Then he and I along with Miss H and Mrs M went over in her car to Bury St Edmunds to see an evacuation scheme there. A big school has been taken over for about 60 families, with three or four families sharing a living space, but with separate sleeping accommodation. About 8 people have to share a gas stove for cooking. But it was clean and well run, if a little cold and cheerless.

All in all I felt it an admirable idea and an answer to the terribly difficult problem of billeting. It was run by the local billeting officer on quite a lavish scale with every family being provided with full equipment and furniture, which seemed rather excessive largesse. However, we could not but admire the man's vision and energy in bringing the scheme into being, but we did regret his extravagance and wondered if the Ministry would bring him to book about it. He was only a local shopkeeper and we uncharitably wondered if he were making something out of it! Our schemes will be much smaller, but we hope will have a more homely atmosphere and be much more a part of the village.

Peter G tells me that the FAU have already got Wardens in mind by the name of Mr and Mrs Edmunds, so I pressed for them to come as soon as possible. I'm hoping to start alterations this week and expect to go to London for a night on Wednesday or Thursday to arrange for a party of FAU fellows to come up and do some whitewashing and papering the following week. They will enjoy the change and it will save on labour. Thus if all goes to plan the place will be ready quite shortly and people can start moving in.

The countryside has been just lovely these last few days. All soft colours, with spring's promise, and grand sunrises and splendid sunsets. Today, was all blue sky and billowing clouds - the grass bright green and the ploughed earth a deep red brown. Everywhere glossy black Rooks cawing, white Gulls flying, Partridges calling, Yellow Hammers finding their voices, Larks singing, and Thrushes, Robins, and Tits all in full voice. What a glorious month this February has been.

I must say Mrs M's local contacts are very impressive – writing to Lord Astor for this, and Sir Alfred Butt for that and Lady North for something else! She even has the local builders at her command. She is very modest about her racing career, but in fact they have trained and owned Derby winners, won many classic races, and had many first class horses. Actually her son is supposed to manage the place now, but I think she keeps a very close eye on things.

Things are better now that I can go ahead and see an end. It will also keep me pretty busy. Miss H and Peter cheered me up a lot too, and it will be a change to go to London for a night. The Warden should be in by the end of March and I don't think I shall stay much after that, as I can't see much work developing in the district. I met some other local men who have been trying to run a centre for evacuated women. But their leader has rubbed everyone up the wrong way. Everywhere you go, the whole country is thoroughly upset. I dare say one or two of the centres will survive, but I think they should survive on their own. I don't think we should run them. I doubt too if it's worthwhile – while it is generally a good idea, it should not be a separate FAU activity. The hostels are much more useful.

I do so miss you my dear. How grand it will be when I get a week's leave. Mrs M thinks the community revolves round her – and so it does – but she also thinks it would come to a halt without her - which it wouldn't! I must stop now…very dear love. Much love, Ralph.

PS. I have written to FEB (Friends Education Board) applying for the same policy for A as we have for D. We can't afford it, but I think we ought to try and do it. It provides about £20 pa for 4 years from the age of 18. It would certainly help with the boy's education.

Peter Gibson and David Tod and Flaunden

Peter Gibson   David Tod

Two people my father thought highly of in the FAU.

Peter was a key figure in the Unit and he worked closely with my father, both in this country and later in the Middle East. In the early days PG as Relief Officer supervised FRB. Later FRB took over his job as Relief Officer when PG went abroad, and then when FRB took over the Middle East, PG reported to him!

David Tod was initially Training Officer, who bore the brunt of the work. My father wrote - "Some disliked his manner, but I liked him and always did, and I could never understand why a man of his undoubted abilities had not gone further in the Unit. He and his wife Molly later became well regarded Wardens of Flaunden Camp. He and FRB became close friends.

Photographs Friends House Library

Flaunden looking towards the Village Hall – "In the middle of riding country"
Photograph courtesy of Shaun Burgin and the Flaunden Parish Council

Cheveley Village

"Cheveley, is a small village about 3 miles from Newmarket
...and only 30 minutes from Cambridge, right in the heart of racing country....

....and all around is flat, but pleasant, rural and well-farmed country, as in this aerial view."
Illustrations courtesy of Newmarket Local History Society

My father is concerned that no news is getting through, and he's worried that my mother is alright again after my birth.....

Wednesday, February 12th 1941 - The Manor House, Cheveley

My dearest

Wednesday and still no letter from you, and I really feel rather worried about you. I do hope there is nothing the matter. Have you had my three letters? How are you my dear, now that you are downstairs, and do you still feel very shaky? How is Antony and is David happy? What do you feel about the future, and what can I do to help?

I've got a rotten cold and felt very miserable yesterday. I hope I shall feel better today, but I won't worry you with all that. I have little more news since my last letter. I am still waiting for the Ministry of Health to make up their minds, and until this happens, I am held up. I have, however, nearly completed a plan of the house, and expect to go into Cambridge today.

It is good to be here at this time of the year, as the spring is coming on and we have had some beautiful, mild days and the whole world is coming alive again. Larks have been singing, Yellow Hammers too, and the Thrushes' song is perfectly lovely. The Elm flowers are nearly out, as well as Snowdrops, Primula Wanda and Crocuses already in the gardens. I even heard Blackbirds as I bicycled on my tours around the countryside. It certainly is a compensation being in the country. On the other hand, having lived with people for so long, it is rather lonely living with just two women in this big house and seeing none of the people I am used to. But the Pickards came over from Wood Ditton yesterday to see the Rectory, and Mrs M has roped me in to give a talk about the AFS to her local Air Raid Precaution (ARP) workers tonight. I hope my cold will have improved by then.

You ask about my reading, but in truth I'm so busy, I don't seem to get any time at the moment, as I am always running about seeing people, or writing reports, or drawing up plans, and after supper, Mrs M comes in and wants to talk. I suppose it must be a bit of a change in a rather lonely life, for her to have someone to talk to. And we hear the news at 8.0am (I don't because its's in her room), at 1.0 during lunch and at 6.0pm (again I don't because I am not usually in) and then at 9.0pm!

I am sorry this is such a rotten letter, but I feel a bit like that at the moment – and I so want a letter from you.

Later......

Hurrah, at last a letter from you. We only get one post a day and they do seem to be taking a long time just now. But it was lovely, lovely, lovely to hear from you, it has cheered me up no end. It's great news that you will have David back with you. Please give him my love, and I'm glad you managed to register Antony. Thank you so much for doing that my dearest. I am glad you are now up and about and 'looking slim again!

Here I'm still waiting for the infernal Ministry to do something, and it's so sickening hanging around waiting for them. I've half a mind to go off to the cinema at Newmarket this afternoon instead! Did I tell you that my talk to the local AFS and ARP seemed to go very well.

No more news.

God bless, Ralph.

Though the work was often frustrating, it's plain from his memoirs that after a while, my father settled down and became rather attracted to the area. Here he comments on his redoubtable landlady Mrs Morris and the nearby Banstead Stud, and recalls one day when Mrs M was in a good mood because the Duke of Portland was booking an appointment for one of his mares.......

I fear Mrs M is not quite the lady she imagines herself to be; she's only what they call 'county' by virtue of her wealth, and don't her neighbours know it. Her husband, Henry is a bullion dealer based in Shanghai, and they have one son, too delicate for the army and married to a county lady, who helps run the estate. Mrs M herself is full of good works, very capable and very managing, but I must say she was very kind to me and genuinely anxious to get the evacuation scheme going. However, things, especially air raids, often seemed to get on her mind, and so any ideas had to be presented to her gently.

The nearby Banstead stud, was justly famed, having owned several notable horses such as Hanna, bred from Pasch the 1938 winner of the 2000 guineas, and their champion stallion, the aforementioned 'Tai Yang', a beautiful animal worth about £18,000, I'm told. Seeing racing from this perspective – the employment it provides, the lovely foals and strings of horses at exercise, the well run farms - all make for a very fine impression. The whole atmosphere is horses and racing and I got a lot of pleasure just watching them, especially their prize stallion, and I came to have quite a soft spot for it.

One day the Duke of Portland wired for an appointment for one of his mares with 'Tai Yang'. She thought it was a good sign if a man in his position considered it worth bothering about these things. Mrs M told me "'Tai Yang' charges 48 guineas for his services you know." Then, in case I thought this cheap, she added. "And that's not all. To be damned sure she really is in foal, the mare nearly always stays for some time after, so they have to pay for her full keep plus another guinea a week for a groom if he comes too. Good money!" I shall probably be an expert on horses by the time I leave here.

Here in a letter to my mother, my father naughtily compares problems with their mothers, and as always comments on local goings on with Mrs M, not to mention looking ahead to a possible Labour government and nationalisation.......

Sunday, February 16th 1941 – Cheveley

My dearest
[.....] I am starting to settle down a bit now, and am really very comfortable in the Manor. I do like Mrs M. She has exactly the same problem with her old mother, as we do with ours. In fact she seems to be your mother and mine rolled into one! Very exacting, jealous of her daughter's friends, very managing and very easily hurt. We went out to tea and Mrs M asked her mother if she'd like to come too. "No dear. I don't think I will." "But it's a lovely place, and I'm sure you'll enjoy it." "Well dear," says mother, "It's very kind of you, but I think I'll stay by myself." So she stays at home by herself and is miserable, just like your mother. She said to me privately – "I lost my son when he married, you know. He became very independent and exclusive, as you all do. But he's beginning to come back now."

One day we went out to tea, so that I could meet some of the locals. I felt such a small Daniel amongst this particular lot of lions. Although Mrs M is only semi-County, she really imagines she is the full County lady and acts accordingly. But there were others there who were the proper thing. A Mrs Dora Tharpe was one, who is a fully signed up County member, and her sister and brother-in-law, Colonel and Mrs Bridge are too.

He was a military attaché at the British Embassy in Rome before the war, and they own a real old country house nearby, with ancestral portraits, family heirlooms and glorious grounds with sheets of aconites and snow drops out already. I thought of you, as I always do with flowers. I think I behaved passably well. Anyway, they all seemed interested in the scheme, which was the object of the exercise.

If these old families are taxed out of existence, the country will be the poorer. They have a real sense of Trusteeship. Even if the land is nationalised, they ought to be left to manage it. They look after their people and care for their land, and sit on committees. And, of course, service in the armed forces of the Crown is part of their code. Town problems, as I am learning, are very different from country ones. Half of Mrs Tharpe's house is used as a hospital for evacuee children suffering from skin diseases, and as she farms her own land, she must be kept pretty busy. Mrs Bridge's house is a Nursery School. They both made pointed remarks about Mrs M having no evacuees, which rather rankled with her. "Really Dora's insinuation was so uncharitable. Most unlike Dora!" Of course, Mrs M should have evacuees, though I realise that she prefers to have people like Lord and Lady D. Life is constantly amusing.

I went to church this morning, and the old Vicar preached a remarkably good sermon. I'm afraid there were only a handful of people there including a lot of children, to whom the service probably meant very little. It's a fine old church, but very dank.

The rest of the day I have been writing a report. I do hope to get a letter from you tomorrow.

Continued.......Monday, February 17th

Still no more letters from you. I do so long to get your letters. But there's only one post a day here.

I seem to be kept pretty busy and not really accomplishing very much. Everything is held up for one reason or another, such as whether we or the 8 from Bury St Edmunds are going to take the house over.

People said there was a warning last night and that bombs were dropped, but I didn't hear anything. Today is a lovely day and I was up early at the Vicarage, which looked particularly beautiful. It has a delightful, partly walled kitchen garden looking across to the old church. If only one had the money. The Vicar was very appreciative of my going to Church.

Well, my dearest I must stop now. The countryside is beginning to look grand, and I am at least a bit happier now, but how I miss you. I will write again tomorrow.

Dear love Ralph

Though living comparatively peacefully in the country, and pedalling around here and there on various missions, the war is never far away. Here my father recalls the terrible damage that was done to Newmarket on the afternoon of the 18th February, when a single plane dropped a stick of high explosive which badly destroyed a large part of the High Street with serious loss of life. Lord Dillon, a Brigadier from the First World War and his wife, who had been staying at the White Hart Hotel in Newmarket had suddenly to find elsewhere to live after being bombed out, with the loss of all their luggage, and moved into The Manor House, so becoming fellow guests of my father. Here he introduces his redoubtable fellow guests for the first time, not to mention his own lucky escape, and writes to Joan in the same vein.....

Bombing in Newmarket

"At about 3.0pm on the afternoon of February 18th 1941, a stray plane dropped a line of bombs down Newmarket High Street." The photograph clearly shows the damage to the shops.

Damage to The White Hart Hotel in Newmarket, where Lord and Lady Dillon had been staying.
Photographs courtesy of the Newmarket Local History Society

According to my father's account, the bombing in Newmarket was a random attack by a stray plane, but in the booklet 'One Afternoon in February' published by the Newmarket Local History Society in 2000 on the 50th anniversary of the raid, it suggests that it may well have been a deliberate raid targeting the military and so by extension Lord Dillon himself.

First my father's account..........

During my stay at Cheveley there was a serious air raid in Newmarket at about 3.0pm on the afternoon of February 18th, when a stray plane dropped a line of bombs down the main street, which is always full of people on market day during the afternoon, causing a great deal of damage to shops with several people sadly killed. By pure chance I was in Cambridge, or else it's more than likely I would have been in Newmarket myself at that time. But the Brigadier General and his wife were not so lucky, as they were sitting in the White Hart Hotel when a bomb dropped next door and all the plaster on the walls and ceiling collapsed on them. Luckily they emerged unscathed, but all their luggage was buried, and she lost everything, including jewellery, and he a good many of his possessions. I have just lent the Brigadier my razor! Now there's a first!

Miraculous to relate, practically all the Dillon's luggage was recovered from the Hotel after the bombing. Some helpful Czech Pioneers (Scout movement) had been working in the wreckage, and everything, even the things which were not in their suitcase, were found. I'm afraid Newmarket suffered badly though, with some twelve dead and many more casualties of varying degrees of severity. It's was a terrible mess, with ruined buildings and rubble everywhere.

Then from 'One Afternoon in February'.......

"From, the German airforce records in the Bundersarchiv Militararchiv we can see that Newmarket was already on the German pilots map before the fateful raid took place in Feb 1941. Why was the High Street, Newmarket, the target for a deliberate attack? Two very good reasons come to mind. At that date the main trunk roads from the North West and the South East known at that time as the A11 and A45 converged on Newmarket Heath and passed through the town before dividing again at the far end to continue to Norwich and Bury St Edmunds.

Also the main telecommunications route from London and Cambridge ran alongside both of these roads carried on over-head open wire supported by huge telephone poles. Both of these features would have been easily visible from the air and made Newmarket a strategic target to disrupt both road and communication traffic. This in itself was a good enough reason for the raid.

But why Feb 18th 1941 at 3.10 pm? February 18th was of course market day in the town, with the High Street lined with market stalls. But could the real reason for this time and date have been a military conference that was in progress at the Memorial Hall in the High Street? Present at the conference were two Lt Generals and over 500 Officers; if this hall had been hit then the armed forces would have suffered a severe blow to their ranks. The Civil Defence Report noted that the Lt General speaking at the time of the raid was deaf and did not hear the explosion; this was not the case among the officers sitting nearest the door.

For some years this air-raid was considered by officialdom to be a 'perfect raid' for the following reasons. All communications were cut, along with damage to all Utility Companies except transport. An all-important main road was blocked for 3 days, with serious damage to property; nearly 250 people were seriously injured, and 27 people were killed, and many made homeless."

So the reason Lord Dillon had come to Newmarket and was staying in the White Hart was likely to have been in order to attend a high level military conference, but although Lady D may have been in the Hotel, it's possible that he was actually in the Memorial Hall further up the High Street, which due to secrecy, he couldn't disclose.

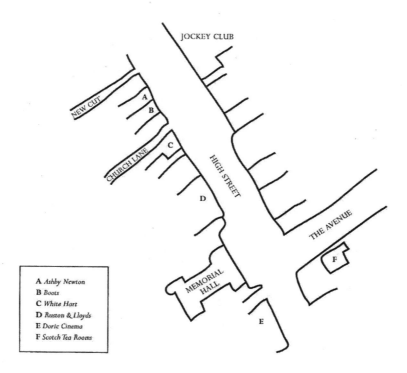

Plan of Newmarket High Street in 1941
showing the positions of the White Hart Hotel (C) and the Memorial Hall.

For whatever reason, the new guests - the splendid Lord and Lady Dillon [3] arrive - who for the rest of my father's stay in the area become the source of many good stories ......

Wednesday, February 18th 1941 – Banstead Manor, Cheveley

My dearest Joan

[.....] Things get stranger by the day here. We've now got a Brigadier General and his wife staying in the Manor House – Lord and Lady Dillon no less! They had both been staying in a very uncomfortable hotel in Newmarket, but were bombed out yesterday. He's recently returned from North Africa to take up a command here and as he couldn't find any suitable married quarters, he has moved in here. Mrs M is very glad to have them, because they bring in money – about £4.4 per person per night. In addition, of course, they have a chauffeur, maid and batman, who all have to be housed and paid for as well. Lord D's a nice old boy, a regular, who's been in the army all his life – "Last here on manoeuvres in 1910" he chortled. Lady D is frightfully aristocratic and very officer's wifeish!

Her conversation is peppered with such remarks as 'Bloody awful Germans' or 'Our splendid soldiers.' God knows what she makes of a CO like me! So Mrs M killed the fatted calf for dinner last night in honour of the Dillons' arrival. Sherry before and Champagne during. Don't tell mother! [.......] Love from Ralph

In this following extract from his memoirs my father expands on the description of his fellow guests and relishes in their eccentricities in a manner worthy of P G Wodehouse:

Mrs M's new guests, Lord and Lady Dillon arrived along with her maid and his batman, who to Lady D's scorn had once been a dancing master. "Would you believe it," she said in her most exasperated voice "a dancing master in Blackpool. Just imagine it! When Eric was in Algeria, he had a proper Jock from a real regiment at his side. Damn fine man too." And on and on she goes. She is so hilarious sometimes - quite unconsciously, of course.

Lord D was a Brigadier, a soldier of the 1914-18 war, recently returned from a mission to General Noguès in N. Africa. He claimed to be in direct descent from Barbara Palmer, the Duchess of Castlemaine, Charles II's most notorious mistress. Lady D - Nora Juanita - known as Nita, was pleasant enough, and must once have been something of a beauty. She's still good looking and attracted to anything in trousers.

Here my father writes to my mother all about his new fellow guests with great delight...

Friday, February 21st 1941 – Cheveley

Dearest Joan

[.....]I seem to be spending quite a lot of time now with Lord and Lady D. Lady D is probably quite nice, and underneath I think she is really quite good-hearted, but she is very Tory, very Army, very Aristocratic and very prejudiced and irrational. "The working classes are all far too spoon-fed," she proclaimed the other day. "We spoil them: they should learn to fend for themselves," and such like pronouncements.

I'm afraid there are very few matters on which we would agree, so I just keep quiet. For all that, one can't help but like her. She is still a fine looking woman, and must once have been quite a beauty. She now has lovely grey hair, which her maid does beautifully for her. They both seem very devoted to each other. Her son-in-law is Lord Cranley, who wrote those articles in The Sunday Times about shelters recently. They have a place in the country – Dorset, I think. She is a magistrate and full of good works.

Lord D is quite different, though very much what you'd expect, but he is a very interesting person. He has travelled a great deal and knows a great many people. Last night he came down to dinner in full uniform – a marvellous, close-fitting blue uniform with red stripes and loaded with decorations! God knows what he makes of me.

I had an interesting talk with him the other evening, while he was in bed, about all sorts of things; birds, Shakespeare, deer stalking, John Buchan, more Shakespeare, the Pyrenees, Algeria & Morocco. He is a friendly sort of man and a jolly good story teller. It's odd that with so much distinguished ancestry, he is far from well off. He told me that he has some very good portraits of his Stuart ancestors and of Charles II by Sir Peter Lely, no less, which he inherited like his title from an Uncle, but has been left poor by death duties, so that he now owns hardly any land and their home - belonging to his wife. [..] Love Ralph

My father had an exceptional talent for descriptions and characterisations, and in his memoirs expands at some length on his time with the Brigadier and his wife.......

On one occasion I had an amusing evening telling both Lord and Lady D about Quakerism, and about the FAU and pacifism. He was quite understanding and could appreciate our refusing to fight abroad, but couldn't understand our refusal to defend our own country. Being a Quaker does have its advantages sometimes, and seems to smooth one's way. Being a CO is definitely looked down on, but being a Quaker is OK – really it's quite astonishing. Even Lady D, when I said I came from ordinary Quaker middle class stock, said "Damn good stock too"! I believe she quite likes me, but mainly I suspect because I'm something in trousers. She was quite concerned when I told her I was going to London.

"But you <u>are</u> coming back, aren't you?!" People seem to accept one's pacifism if one is a Quaker, and having been in the AFS also helped my credibility a lot. Lady D was often full of mischievous chat and that night she was being particularly outrageous about the Germans. She looked at me and laughed saying - "I can't stand all this rot about loving one another. Do you think I would make a good Quaker?" Lord D looked at me and said "Do you take recruits?" I'm afraid I played for time, and replied - "Well, yes, but I am not sure I could really recommend Lady Dillon as a member!" She was very disappointed, so I had to point out that her views on 'not loving one another' did not greatly improve her chances!

She was perfectly priceless about her son Michael's sudden engagement to a French girl from an old colonial family, Irène Merandon du Plessis. She described going to interview Père du Plessis, the girl's father, and how after they'd had tea ("very cheap cake you know!") their son and Mère du Plessis and the two sons were sent out into the hall while she talked business. "One of the sons was an absolute foreigner", she said "but the other had been in England for 5 years so at least he had had a good wash! I made it quite plain to them that there would have to be a substantial dowry!"

Lady D is always full of gossip, recounting how she was "Very amused to see in The Times yesterday that a daughter of Viscountess, Edith Kelmsley (née du Plessis, hence an aunt by marriage) had played host to a Marquis." She continued "Really, Aunt Edith has surpassed herself. She's got the Marquises for herself and a Viscount for her niece!" Then a bit later, apropos nothing in particular, she remarked "You know Ralph, Mrs Simpson and Ribbentrop definitely used to go to bed together. But as for the Duke of Windsor, well! He is a thoroughly bad lot, and never stayed with the best families."

Another time she told me that "The Duke of Marlborough, is a very rude and ill-mannered person; far too fond of women and even kissed somebody's daughter while out hunting, which caused a frightful row and the girl's father wrote demanding an apology. Marlborough wrote back saying that 'kissing the girl wouldn't have any effect on her character. She will be a tart anyway, just like her older sisters.' He had to pay £10,000 in damages. Girl's father was reputed to have said 'I wish I had 10 daughters.'"

I never know how reliable her stories are; probably about 50% I should think. I remember her being quite outrageous, and probably equally unreliable, about their time in N. Africa. She was describing how Lord Gort,[4] a Senior British Army Officer and Duff Cooper[5] turned up to see General Charles Noguès,[6] the C in C North Africa and the French Minister in Algeria after the government's collapse, following the allied invasion.[7] Noguès would not see them, so Lord Dillon arranged for them to see the Civil Governor. As they were leaving, she said - "Little Duff Cooper – minor Cabinet Minister or some such, isn't he, and Gort, C in C British Army, and Eric (Lord Dillon) were held up by a damned Lance Corporal, if you please. Was there ever such an insult?

So Eric went back, picked up a phone, and in the hearing of a roomful of officers, told the Civil Governor exactly what he thought of him and ordered him to make an apology. After a lot of huffing, he did, and they all stood to attention and saluted while he read out the apology, and Gort kept turning round and saying to Eric "Shall I shake hands now?" and Eric said 'No, absolutely not !' Finally Duff Cooper came forward and said on behalf of the Cabinet that 'the incident will be overlooked', and then they all saluted again, shook hands and kissed each other on both cheeks. Don't have any opinion of Gort. 'Fat Boy Gort' they used to call him. Very fat. Very pompous. Terribly brave, but quite stupid. Only got his job because he was bloody rude to Lord Belisha[8], who thought he must be brilliant."

Characters in one of Lady Dillon's stories

Field Marshal, 6th Viscount Gort VC,GCB, CBE

Painting by Regibald Greville Eves

General Charles Noguès
Commander-in-Chief in French North Africa
Photo Bibliothèque Nationale de France

Alfred Duff Cooper
1st Viscount Norwich, GCMG DSO PC

Photograph private collection

General Maxime Weygand
Governor General Algeria

Photo Bibliothèque Nationale de France

Lady D was really rather fun when you got used to her. She was a great talker, very forthright and amusing. She was so funny about the French generals and officers and their wives, when she and her husband were out in Algeria and Morocco. "The French women didn't know whether to call me Madame la Générale or Madame la Vicomtesse," she said. "The old army are perfectly grand and the new army perfectly bloody. Thank God for the Navy." She used to call all the English 'perfect gentlemen', the Italians 'poor macaronis' and the French 'bloody frogs'.

Lady D told me about when she had once run a club for factory girls and their goings on. "One of them said to me 'is your 'usband a corporal milady?' I suppose it was the highest rank the poor lady knew of!" And on another occasion she told me how "one of the members of my girls' club happened to see Lord D when he was walking away from the War Office with the Duke of Athlone. They were both dressed up in morning dress and toppers, and she shouted out 'Watcha Guv' to Lord D or some such vulgar familiarity, and the two men just raised their top hats and continued on their way without saying a word!"

My father continues his descriptions of them in another letter...........

Late February 1941 – Cheveley

Dearest Joan

[......] One day I went for a walk in the afternoon, and when I got back found heaps of women in the house! You couldn't very well escape visitors there, as the front door opened straight into the hall, which acted as a sort of hiring room, where Mrs M did all her business deals. I was overcome with shyness, and stood outside, but it turned out they didn't bite and I survived! Actually, they'd all come in to see Lady D and they left shortly afterwards. Lady D rattled on and on as usual about this and that – such as whom she had been staying with - "Just had a perfectly splendid few days with the Marlboroughs – John and Mary. Do you know them? Lovely couple." One is never quite sure how seriously to take her. But she amuses me and that cheers me up.

Lord D is at present in bed with awful sciatica and I am deputed by Lady D to 'go and cheer Eric up'! The other day an Army doctor arrived to see him, who looked a mere boy. Lady D met him at the door and greeted him with "How old are you?" which did nothing for his confidence. She then told him exactly what he was to do with the General and practically pushed the lad in to examine him. I'm not sure whether the poor chap was more frightened of Lady D or the prospect of meeting the General – "H-h-h-how are you Sir" he stammered in a faint voice!

Lord D became very depressed with the 6.0 o'clock news one night, concerning Maxime Weygand's collaboration with the Vichy regime, and signing an armistice with the Germans. He says "This means the end of French colonial resistance. We should sink their damned fleet immediately." An Air Force friend of Lord D's thinks that by later this year we will have supremacy in the air, and that then "we shall bomb the Germans off the earth, invade them next year and the war will end in 1942". Hmm, I wonder. [.....]
My very dear love, Ralph

Together, Mrs M and the Dillons kept my father amused during his time in Cheveley, keeping his mind off being away from home, and the work, was close enough to his previous work at the BVT to keep him interested. But problems connected with home, such as where my mother was to stay more permanently, began to trouble them, as we shall see in the next chapter.

Cheveley and Wood Ditton

St Mary's Church, Cheveley dates from approximately 1260
"I went to the local church for the funeral of one of the victims of the Newmarket bombing raid. I thought I ought to, as she came from the local village. She was a mother of two, with a husband."

Wood Ditton village and the surrounding countryside.
"A film maker from the Unit came up here last week to take films of Cheveley, and Wood Ditton to show the people in London shelters the sort of place they are coming to."
Photographs Local History Societies

Chapter 9
Finding a home for JMB and the end of Cheveley
February to March 1941

One of the on-going problems for my parents was where my mother should live following my birth. She found 'Beaconwood' quite lonely and away from friends and family, so there were frequent discussions about other possibilities, including my father's Aunt Lou in Carlisle, living with his mother in Swarthmore Road, with his brother John and family, or perhaps with various close Quaker friends such as the Ransomes or the Gilletts. There was also talk of asking the Tritsch family to leave 26 Linden Road and for my mother to move back in with David and myself. Eventually it was decided that they would move to Wolverhampton to stay with my mother's sister and family, the Rutters, which they did in the August of 1941.......

Monday, February 24th 1941 - Cheveley

Dearest Joan

[.........] I am so sad about your letter of today. It must be perfectly bloody for you. It makes me think we were foolish to let our house, but you shouldn't go back there on your own, it will only upset you. How very kind of Cousin Edward to offer to help us out financially; it would certainly help if we could find somewhere. I feel so useless and helpless stuck away here in the country, and it has made me miserable all day. Perhaps you could talk it over with Honor and suggest that you move to Wolverhampton. I believe you might be happy there, and it seems as if where they are, is fairly safe. After all David has been there a month. Even if you only went there for a few weeks, while we tried to find somewhere else. I don't want to press you against your better judgement, but it does seem the best option at the moment.

I should feel much happier if you were there, because you would know you were welcome and you would be with your own people. Best of all from my point of view, I could come and stay with you on leave. It's not very feasible for me to land myself at Beaconwood, and it wouldn't be much fun if I have to go back to Swarthmore Road every night and stay with mother! I do realise that you want to be among people you know and to some extent you would be at Wolverhampton. It might be only for a short time, while we look for somewhere else.

Mother suggested her cousins Maurice and Helen, but they live so far away. It is much better for you to be in the Midlands, where you could have either mother or Hilda Ransome near you. I'm also sure John and Enid would be happy for you to stay with them, but I really think Wolverhampton is a safer bet. Try and cheer up my dear. You are forever in my thoughts and prayers.

It's still bloody cold, though the colours in the sun are lovely. I picked some snowdrops and aconites in the rectory garden on Sunday. How I thought of you and wished they had been for you. They are the only flowers in the house and look so lovely. I always think of flowers and you together. Both so lovely and exquisitely rare, precious and miraculous. A special gift from God to man.

I went to the local church for the funeral of one of the victims of the Newmarket bombing raid. I thought I ought to as she came from the local village. She was a mother of two, with a husband. I fear it was a pretty drab service. It could have been so beautiful, but it was really rather pathetic.

I've no more news. God bless, thee, Ralph

Apart from the daily drudge of sorting out the Rectory, funny things, it seemed were also the order of the day at Cheveley and here he writes to Joan of yet another incident......

Friday, February 28th 1941 – Cheveley

Dearest Joan

[......]The other day at breakfast, a maid ceremoniously brought my washing in on a silver salver! Imagine it! Some bloody fool in London had sent my dirty washing on here, and instead of having the sense to wrap it up properly, had just sent it wrapped up in an old pillow case which I use as a dirty linen bag. Think how embarrassing that could have been in front of Lord and Lady D! Fortunately I was the only person at breakfast!

Of course, I have to say, Mrs M looks after all of us pretty well, especially when we are with Lord and Lady D, when the cooking is excellent. The quantity is not terrific, but then it is wartime. One can't complain at bacon and eggs for breakfast, with tomatoes and mushrooms, followed by toast and marmalade, even if there is no porridge. Lunch is adequate, though tea is very slight. Supper is also slight, but quite enough, and since Lord and Lady D arrived, we have Sherry before and Port after. For God's sake, don't tell my mother! In fact generally we all got on reasonably well, and they were prepared to be friendly, though I am not sure they entirely approve of me. However, Lady D did say to me one day - "Do you know Ralph, you'd have made a damned good officer."

I'm off to London tomorrow for a night or so, so that will give me a slight respite from this place. I hope to get a lot of things settled while I am there tomorrow. I hope they won't think I am letting them in for too much expense. I will finish this letter in London and post it from there.

Saturday February 29th 1941

[......]I got away in quite good time this morning and had a rather long and cold journey down to London. But it is a very pleasant break to be back in London again. I have had a talk with David Tod, which was nice, and I have been able to see a number of other people too. I also had a useful talk with Peter Gibson and Miss Hunnybun[1] and tomorrow I am seeing Roger Wilson. I saw Miss H at the model Lloyds shelter where she works, which really is extremely good.

I also managed to spend about an hour with Milli, which was extremely nice. Have you heard any more from Edwin? How long do you think you can continue to stay at 'Beaconwood'? Don't take this as final, but I should get some leave between now and March 21st, that is sometime within the next month. I absolutely can't wait. I must end now and go to bed. Dear love, Ralph.

PS. I have learnt from Duncan that the China camp at Northfield, starting at the end of February is to have full time studies in Mandarin, along with knowledge of oriental diseases etc.

From his memoirs, my father here returns to his feeling of loneliness away from Joan, as well as his familiar concern about his work being too easy and not really 'war work'.......

A lot of the time I felt quite lonely and depressed, both by the job and the frustrations. I couldn't help feeling that it was all too easy and comfortable. In one way, of course, it was interesting work, and not at all easy. In fact much of it was damned complicated at times, but somehow it didn't seem like war work. Just a succession of meeting people, discussing, arranging things, bicycling miles and miles, talking to Mrs M, and then the next day doing the same all over again. I got depressed and became very homesick and wrote to Joan how much I resented pulling up painfully grown roots. It seemed so isolated and far away and all the time I ached for Joan and home.

Most of the next letters continue to be undated, but are around the beginning of March. Here my father expounds his philosophy of, in Kipling's words, 'of meeting triumph and disaster just the same' as both will pass in time.........

Early, March – Banstead Manor - Cheveley

Dearest Joan

[.....] The more we can make of the present and the less time we spend thinking how endless it is, the quicker it will pass - and it will pass. I remember after a night watch in the AFS, thinking how endless and how bloody, but I knew that it would pass, that I should be relieved and that I should be in a warm bed again soon and the same applies now. I don't say live entirely on hope or you may have a shattering blow, but I do say live courageously in the present and better things will surely come [....] All my love, Ralph

From my father's memoirs......

Nonetheless, I soldiered on continuing my negotiations with the Rector concerning the Rectory, which seemed to be eminently suitable as premises for the evacuees from overcrowded London shelters. It was a fine, quite large old house with 3 good sized sitting rooms, 10 bedrooms and 5 in the attic. There was a large area of garden, enclosed by a brick wall and some lovely wrought iron gates, with a splendid view of the flint church tower. The Rector however, is an eccentric gentleman and a difficult customer to deal with, always trying to get the most out of every bargain.

My father wrote several letters to my mother about some of the bizarre incidents that happened at Cheveley, describing all the amazing characters he had encountered, so that they wouldn't be forgotten, often adding a note to the effect that this may be of interest to later generations......

Early March 1941 – Cheveley

My dearest Joan

[.....]I must say life with Mrs M is never dull, and what with Lord and Lady D and Noël Hunnybun, it's one incident after another. The other day Mrs M was describing in her usual grand manner how she and Noël Hunnybun had been out together looking at various rooms for further evacuees. "I went out with Hunny," - as she calls her –"and we took bicycles from the kitchen maids to go and see two half-dead old fossils, Colonel and Mrs Praed, who live in a big stately house near the Rectory.

We asked them if they had any rooms to spare for the evacuees. 'Where do these people come from?' Mrs Praed enquired haughtily. The old fossils were actually quite nice, but terribly pompous. "Limehouse, Wapping and Poplar" said Hunny with her sweetest smile. "Oh!" and then, as it slowly sank in, they said - "I see. Do you mean these people actually go out to work?" "Really", said Hunny, "some people live completely in another world! You know, I sometimes feel that they are just like children, and need humouring." And then turning to me, she said "I should think your wife will really die of laughter when you write to her about all this".

There was another night when Miss H was up staying with us, and we were all together with Lord and Lady D and another lady. The conversation turned to Quakers and this lady said she had never heard of them. Mrs M then repeated a story I had told her casually one day, about our old family Bible which mother has, dating right back on father's side, and which is stained with sea water from when it was dropped as our ancestor James Lancaster was fleeing persecution along with George Fox. Do you remember mother showing it to us? Mrs M was most impressed. "Old family my dear, and so modest about it." The snobs! [..........]

Mrs M and Lady D seem to have many mutual friends and Lord D knows everyone, calling them by their Christian names - "Spoke to Archie Wavell[2] this morning." I think I shall need a rest after all this carry on. Mrs M's mother has gone home to Seaford, and I don't blame her! Without me she would now be on her own. So I have my uses! Dearest love Ralph

Keeping in touch with the Unit HQ at Gordon Square from distant Cheveley was also important. He was on the Council and so had to attend meetings there from time to time, but also needed to keep them informed of progress on the evacuee situation......

During my time in Cambridgeshire, I managed to keep in touch with the Unit and indeed had visits from both Peter Gibson and Roger Wilson. With the former, Mrs M and I drove over to see a big evacuee centre at Bury St. Edmunds. Mrs M. didn't think much of PLG (Peter Gibson) but she quite liked RCW (Roger Wilson)!

I also kept in contact with the Unit through the members on the Work Squad in the Rectory and by a small section of FAU members working in a hospital in Newmarket, which Brandon Cadbury had come up to settle in. In addition, I managed to get up to London once or twice, where of course Peter Gibson had by now become head of the Relief Section, since Tom had become Chairman, and the section was really very busy. I also attended my first staff meeting at the regular Unit conference and reported on my time in Newmarket. I wasn't sure whether I'd achieved anything worthwhile; but in myself, I was enjoying dealing with houses again and having builders to look after and gardens to think of and tools and seeds to buy and motor mowers to look at. It was quite like old times to wander round watching men work!

Negotiations with the Rector concerning the lease continued, but after much to-ing and fro-ing were eventually concluded. It then became necessary for a number of alterations to be carried out which would be essential to make it suitable for the evacuee families to move in. Whilst my father was in London, he organised for a team of FAU men to come up from London to undertake the necessary decorating and rewiring work. Here in a long letter he keeps my mother up to date......

Friday, March 7th 1941 – Cheveley

My dearest Joan

[.......] When I returned from London, the weather had turned suddenly very cold again and in Newmarket it was snowing hard, which continued throughout the night, and the next morning there was about 2 inches on the ground. Some of it had thawed by yesterday, but it was still jolly cold, though it was a glorious day with a clear blue sky and the bright sun shining on the snow. [........]

These negotiations have not been easy and the Rector has been difficult, but with Mrs M's continual assistance and advice and much wrangling, I have eventually succeeded in renting the house on behalf of FWVRC and hopefully with the help of an FAU Work Squad, who are coming up, it will be made ready, so I have written a positive note to Gordon Square:

"Rectory going on well, and FAU men painting and wiring and laying fires. Two rooms very dirty and are being painted in a very nice cream, rather a daft colour perhaps for these families, but what else will lighten up the dark rooms? I'm sure it will look very nice eventually. The view from the top rooms is quite beautiful and the sun streams in through the windows. Just now two builders' men are putting in a bath and WC and the gardener, who arrived yesterday, seems to be stealing manure from somewhere to improve the soil."

On the Friday after I got back, I had to go to Cambridge to see a couple of people, which didn't take very long, so you'll be pleased to hear that I had a haircut, and I now look quite kempt for a change! When eventually I got back to Newmarket, I had to walk all the way back to the Manor, as Mrs M had driven me out to the train in the morning, so I didn't have my bicycle with me. Actually I quite enjoyed the walk, and it only took me about ¾ of an hour. I must say it is such lovely country round here, and each morning I awake to see the strings of beautiful horses being ridden or walked round Newmarket.

Mrs M's stud here is really a most distinguished one, and they have not only owned and trained one Derby winner, but they have bred another. They now have 20 mares all booked to one stallion at £24 apiece. They come and live here for a few months, to ensure that they are really in foal. It would be so lovely if you could come over and see it all, but travelling is so expensive and awful at the moment. Also I fear there wouldn't be any room here right now, and should there be an invasion, this is a daft place to come to.

During the terrible air-raid the other afternoon, the telephone exchange received a direct hit, which has made life extra difficult, ringing anyone up impossible, and inevitably this meant cycling everywhere. However, matters do seem to be moving in the right direction now and yesterday I opened a bank account for the scheme. I then had one final - I hope - long session with the Rector about the lease, before going over to conclude matters with the builder, who I've fixed to start on Wednesday, by which time the furniture will all be out of the house.

After that, the FAU squad I corralled in London, will arrive up here next Tuesday to undertake the decorating and wiring, with Noël Hunnybun coming on Wednesday, and the new Warden for a short visit on Thursday.....if I'm still alive! I should really like to move down there while the work is going on to keep an eye on it all, but perhaps I ought to stay here with Mrs M. I hope the wardens will be here by mid-March and then the evacuees soon after that. Then my work here will be drawing towards an end.

Although the work has been interesting, I have often found it rather lonely and isolated out here, and as I've often wondered, was it all too easy and comfortable a way of life. I do miss you terribly, and thank you so much for your letter of last Wednesday, which I received on Saturday after I'd got back here. Like you I do often feel very miserable, but we are so close in spirit that we shall get through this, and someday we will be able to look back on it all as a bad dream. We just have to make the best of it right now. We shall be together again and happy with each other and the children, and life will be as it was and we must pray for that. As Sonia says at the end of *Uncle Vanya*, after all the troubles and upheavals - *"Don't cry Uncle, we shall, rest, we shall rest."* The more we can make of the present, the quicker it will pass, and it will pass. I don't say live entirely on hope, or you may have a shattering disappointment. But I do say live courageously in the present, and better things will surely come. And I know just how courageously you do live. I think you are wonderful. You are such an inspiration to me for which I thank you so much. I find it so wonderful that you are always there and always loving me. God bless you for that. I know you must often be lonely, and that it is much worse for you than for me, but I shall be home before very long on leave, and I can't wait for that time.

I'm hoping, though it's not yet confirmed, that I will get my full leave at the end of March or beginning of April, when I shall be due for a fortnight. Of course quite a lot will depend on what they want me to do afterwards, and indeed where you will be at the beginning of April. But wherever you are I can come and stay with you, though I should feel much happier if you were with my mother, or better still at Wolverhampton. All my love as ever, Ralph

Helping Hands with the Evcauation

Noël K Hunnybun
"...known as 'Hunny' - a very nice and
efficient, leading social worker..."

Photo courtesy of Ruth Hunnybun

Roger Wilson
"We had a very good visit from Roger,
who seemed to approve of our work."

Photo courtesy of Bristol University

A cheerful group of evacuees outside their temporary classroom.
Many of them had never seen the country before.
Photograph Rodney Vincent Wood Ditton

A break in routine, with the Rector telling my father that 'he wouldn't like the service' – because it was to be too High Church! – This gives him time to write to my mother.......

Sunday, March 9th 1941 – Cheveley

My darling Joan

I am writing this on Sunday morning, as the Rector said I shouldn't like the service this morning! So I have a good time to write you a long letter instead! I was so pleased to get your letter of Wednesday. Thank you so much for it: and knowing that you are now happier, made me feel so much happier too. I do hope that you feel more settled now. Hang in there dear heart, as I am sure that we shall live to see better times. I did wonder if you'd rather go to my mother's, if you could bear it. At least you would be in Selly Oak. I am so glad that David is now with you again and that he is being good. He is such a dear boy; do give him all my love.

After more than a week of the lousiest cold weather, it has suddenly become warmer and Thursday, Friday and Saturday were beautifully mild days with the whole world coming alive again. Larks, Blackbirds and Yellow Hammers all began to sing and Song Thrushes' 'careless rapture' was perfectly glorious; the Elm flowers are nearly out, as are snowdrops and aconites, with primula wanda and even crocuses making an early appearance too. I have been very busy this week. Tuesday and Wednesday I was making a detailed survey of the house with the Diocesan Surveyor, who was such a nice man. I really enjoyed myself. The survey, which was an exact description of the house when we took it over, and ran to 16 pages! Then on Tuesday, the working party arrived from London; they really have done very well indeed and are now well on with the painting and wiring and should be out in about ten days' time. I think they quite enjoy being here after being stuck in London.

On Wednesday, the builder, who is also doing the plumbing, started work and is making progress, if rather slowly. On Thursday, I had another long sitting with the Rector and a solicitor friend of his about the lease. I really get on very well with both the Rector and Mrs Abbott, and I hope they feel that I have dealt with them fairly. It has not been easy to represent the FAU on the one hand and on the other, to avoid doing them down, because while the Rector is rather grasping and most averse to spending money, he is very impractical and unbusinesslike.

On Thursday afternoon Mrs Edmunds arrived with her husband, who are to be the new wardens. They have been in charge of the University settlement in Glasgow, an organisation in a slum district of the city, where they have run clubs of all sorts, advice bureaus, clinics and nursery schools. There was also a residential wing, where University students took social courses under Mrs Edmund's care. She is extremely well qualified having been in charge for about 4 years and then about 18 months ago, the man now her husband came to do boy's club work and last August they were married. He is only about 30, while she is about ten years older. I found her very nice and efficient, if strong-minded, with very clear ideas of what she wants. It was most helpful to have her around and to get her ideas before it was too late. I think she appreciated coming up too.

I managed to find Mrs E a room in the village, and we spent hours discussing the Rectory, and talking to various people including the billeting officer Mrs Andrews, the local School Master, the District Nurse and Uncle Tom Cobley, as well of course as Mrs M. She went down well with everyone, except Mrs M, who was not over enthusiastic! She thought Mrs Edmunds was too strong-minded – that makes two of them! I can see it is not going to be easy, because Mrs E knows exactly what she wants and Mrs M has very decided ideas of her own, which can't be disregarded as she takes such a keen interest in the scheme.

Only the other day she said "In these dark times, it really cheers one up to see a constructive scheme developing." Though I says it as shouldn't, I do think it has great possibilities. Mrs E hopes to get the hostel up and part running, with 7 or 8 families at first, and gradually developing it with a baby welfare clinic, a playroom for children, a boys' and girls' club and a community centre for all evacuated mothers, providing room for village activities such as Women's Institute and WVS. It is exciting, not only as a partial answer to the problem of the evacuees, but also as a centre for the village and perhaps as a place where the village and the evacuees could meet and get to know each other, instead of disliking each other.

Mrs E liked the Rectory and seemed pleased with all that was being done and thought her visit had been useful. Mrs Andrews is an excellent person, who has an invalid husband who teaches music. She is like a rather superior Mrs Carter (a Birmingham Friend), white haired, with a pleasant face, and one of those quiet efficient people round whom the life of the village revolves. She is always ready to help and always working quietly and efficiently behind the scenes, just getting things done. I also took her over to Wood Ditton, and we were able to get some useful suggestions from Mary Pickard. Her poor husband, Alan was in bed with tonsillitis and appears to be really quite ill with it. I think they ought to go away for a week or so, just in order that Alan can convalesce, but they don't really seem to want to. I must try and persuade them, especially as London could easily send a temporary relief warden.

A film maker from the Unit came up here last week to take films of Cheveley, and Wood Ditton in order to show them to the people in London shelters and let them see what sort of place they are coming to. At Wood Ditton one of the women had her husband, an AFS man, staying with her for a week's holiday. So they dressed him up in his uniform and had him walking down the drive, carrying a suitcase, while they filmed him, as his wife came out to greet him with a kiss. The film man was delighted and the couple loved doing it. Everyone happy!

The Edmunds will move in around March 12, with their furniture arriving shortly before and then the first evacuees about the 20th. I can't believe that it should have taken me so long just to get one house ready, but there has been so much to sort out, from the terms of the lease, the rewiring, plumbing and redecoration, with so many people to placate, it has been quite an intricate jigsaw to solve. It has kept me so busy these last few weeks, often staying up until midnight, writing letters and making lists of people to see and things to do, that I need a rest myself now, but no such luck, as I shall be going down to London next week-end for a round of meetings.

Meanwhile things at the stud farm are not too bad, with about 10 nominations for 'Tai Yang' and 20 for 'Valerian', the other stallion, and the mares are starting to arrive now. I must say one sees the best end of racing here, as these horses are so lovely. But Mrs E points out the reverse of the coin, describing the harm it does in such places as the Glasgow slums, where she has been up till now. "So many go betting, which is quite a shocking waste of the little money they have. It is unbelievable the destitution they get into." Of course she is right. Mrs M is kindly giving the Rectory a lot of brushwood out of her coppices, (Ed: possibly to light fires with) which I went to see with her. The trees were quite lovely in the sun. You might like to show some of this letter to mother. I am afraid I haven't had time to write much to her of late, as I am so busy, and without a typist, there is masses of correspondence of an evening that I have to get through on my own. Someday, people may be interested to read or re-read these letters. It is the only diary that I keep. You are forever in my thoughts. Much love dear one, Ralph

People Remembered

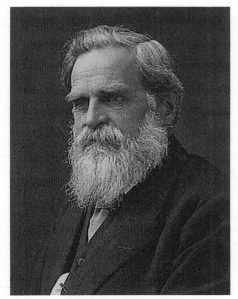

Rendel Harris (1852-1941)
Biblical Scholar and Director of Studies
at Woodbrooke 1903-1916
Photograph Friends House Library

Charles Evans (1866- 1941)
Headmaster at Leighton Park 1910 -1928

Photograph courtesy of Leighton Park School

Friday, March 14th Banstead Manor - Cheveley

My dearest Joan

[........] I see that Rendel Harris has died. There was an interesting note in The Times. I only remember him as an old man, given to rather queer theories and talking too long in meeting, so I never really appreciated him quite as much as others did. But clearly he was a most eminent scholar, and those who knew him well, loved and respected him dearly.

I also see that my old headmaster at Leighton Park, Charles Evans has died. He was a fine man and wonderfully good to Duncan and me in all our bird work. He was always most interested in all we did and saw, and it crowned any day we saw a rare bird, 'to tell the Duke', as we used to call him. He was always intelligently interested and full of encouragement.

In The Friend of February 21, the article 'The Gathered Meeting' is very good and worth reading, saying that the 'gathered meeting' is 'one of the great gifts Friends have to offer the world', referencing back to the first 'gathered meeting' of Christ's 'where two or three are gathered together in my name, there am I in the midst of them'. There is also a rather disquieting article by Oswald Garrison Villard[3], a one-time liberal, who here argues for American disarmament – "always provided that we are not going to be so insane as to go to war in Europe again."

Before we were married, I often used to have on my mind the words of the song 'Dreams I know can never come true'[4] but I used to be so sure that my dream could, would and should come true, that I altered the words to 'will someday come true'! I found myself saying that again the other day – they will too. I am so sure that we shall be making our own home again before so very long. Our love is so strong that I know we shall come through all this and rekindle what we had in our own home again.

Here in Cheveley, we are not quite as happy as we were, as Mrs M and Lady D are getting on each other's nerves! Mrs M says "her Ladyship is altogether too managing and too outspoken, trying to run my house for me. She hasn't enough to do, that's her problem."!

Lady D on the other hand is annoyed with Mrs M for "getting so het up about the air raids and being far too nervous." She has discovered what I said in the first place, that Mrs M is only 'county' by virtue of her money. "She does such peculiar things," says Lady D, "things we would never do," sounding every inch like Lady Bracknell! [5] But as I always say, 'take as you find', and Mrs M is very nice to me. They both confide in me, which I find terribly amusing. Lady D is sometimes a deliberate mischief maker, and I have to be careful. The other day she told me "Doing all this pacifist work is a terrible waste of your talents, as you would make such a splendid officer." It's a very nice compliment, but Lady D likes having men round her and is naturally nice to them, whoever they are! I don't think I trust her an inch!

The Rectory is at last going on well, with 5 FAU men now busy painting, wiring and plumbing and generally transforming the old place. The top rooms were really very dirty and are now being painted in cream, which will lighten up what were previously very dark rooms, and the occupants will get a marvellous view from the windows where the sun streams in. There are also a couple of builders installing a bath and WC, and two elderly gardeners doing what they can: one old chap of 75 wheeling in manure, and another of 65 digging it in. I think eventually it will look very nice.

This afternoon I was leaving to go over to Wood Ditton, when I was stopped by a soldier in the street asking for the Vicar. So I said "I am the Vicar", or something to that effect. How can I help you?" It turned out he was a Major looking for billets for his men for a night. So I said "Come to the Rectory!" So here am I, a good FAU man, giving hospitality to the Army. Well, why not?

I must say I have enjoyed dealing with houses again and having builders to look after and gardens to think of and seeds to buy, and motor mowers to look at. It's like old times wandering around watching men work; and my how the septuagenarians can work. It's all such fun to see the garden taking shape, it reminds me of when we made Linden Road. I wish you could see it all. I have a hundred letters to write and Miss Hunnybun is coming up again tomorrow, so I am being kept very busy. But I'll try and write again at the weekend. I do miss you so much and love you forever. Love to you my dearest and to the children, Ralph.

PS I attach a copy of a letter I wrote to mother about other places to stay.

Dear mother

It is very kind of Aunt Lou to write, and there's much to be said for Joan staying with her for a while, if she feels she could. But, and it's a big but, I shall be in Birmingham for the better part of two months soon, in charge of the 11th Camp at Northfield, and I should really like her to be near me.

I have thought it round and round and I can't think of an ideal solution. I also wondered if either Jeph and Margaret or John and Enid, would have them, while I am at Camp. That is if their offer still holds good. But in either case Joan would then be reasonably close. I also thought that when I get my long leave, we all might perhaps have gone with Joan and the boys for a short holiday. Then afterwards she might either stay on with one of them, or return to Beaconwood, or indeed if the raids are less severe, we might ask Mr Tritsch to leave so that we can move back to Linden Road. I'll discuss it all when I return at the end of next week. Ralph

Here as on several other occasions, particularly at times he wishes to be more personal, my father reverts to the old Quaker form of address – 'thee and thou'.....

Wednesday, March 19th 1941 – Banstead Manor – Cheveley

 My dearest Joan

Thank thee so much for your dear letter, which I was so happy to get. I fear I haven't written as often as I would like, as I had such a heavy lot of correspondence at the end of last week, but my letter of last Sunday, you must admit was a good long one!

I met up with Miss Hunnybun this morning, and have spent most of today going round with her – first over to the Rectory and then after lunch to Wood Ditton. Alan Pickard joined us, but tried to do too much, and is now back in bed again with a temperature. Our solicitor, who is drawing up the lease, has raised yet more points. I wonder if we shall ever get it settled.

The soldiers I mentioned, to whom I gave a temporary home, hospitable man that I am, left the Rectory this morning. I must say, they were a decent lot; very clean and very tidy. Many of the villagers then came in and held a jumble sale in the dining room. We managed to raise £6.10.0. It was really good to see the house being well used, as the Vicar never used to allow anyone in. Hopefully, they will be delighted to rent a room for their various functions in future.

It is good to see the garden coming on as well. The older of the two gardeners, has spread his muck all over, and is hard at work digging it in, while the other old boy is making good progress with the very rough patch. I suppose I am very lucky to be doing work I enjoy, but I so wish I was nearer to you.   No more news tonight. I'll write again tomorrow.

Contd.....Thursday, March 20th

The latest thing from Lady D is that she thinks we are 'spoon-feeding the refugees,' and then asked if I would look after her and Lord D after the war and provide them with an almshouse!

I've had quite a good day today. Hunny is always helpful and very understanding of our difficulties. She thinks the situation here is perfectly priceless. I have spent most of the day at the Rectory, while she has been going round billets with Mrs Andrews, the billeting officer. Hunny says that Mrs M likes me – well that's a relief! There is another awful woman here, who is a thorn in the side of the Pickards. She is 'very well meaning', but as Miss H says 'Quite ignorant of anything but dogs and horses, and behaves just like a child.' As I mentioned before, unlike Mrs M, who is only anybody by virtue of her wealth, Lord and Lady D are certainly the real thing. They were most upset when J B Priestley[6] was broadcasting one of his 'Postscripts' the other night. "That awful man, going on about the ruling classes."! So I said to her "You know, we Barlows do appear in Burke's Peerage." Lord D riposted 'Oh, you mean the Book of Snobs'! Mrs M said 'You are like a lot of children and need humouring as such.' You have to laugh sometimes, though it's quite difficult when you are used to dealing with rational people. As Hunny said to me the other night "I should imagine your wife nearly dies of laughter, when you write and tell her all about the goings on."

After I have so carefully nursed this project, I earnestly hope the Edmunds won't muck it all up. Mrs M wasn't too impressed with them, especially as they have written rather stupid letters, including one to me which she ends "Yours in fellowship". Blah! Blah! Blah! Fellowship! Yours in buggery. There was a chance I might become a good man while I was in London, but I am afraid it is quite hopeless now!

More tomorrow.......Friday March 21ˢᵗ

An awful day today – raining incessantly all day and night. I went with Hunny and Mrs M to see various other houses. One was quite a good vicarage in a very pretty village, with a stream running through it. But it was dank and gloomy and far from the village, and on these grounds I am afraid it would prove to be unsuitable. Also it had been recently occupied by troops and had been left in an absolutely appalling condition.

I spent the rest of the time at the Rectory doing various jobs – seeing the piano tuner, paying the gardener etc etc. The bathroom is now finished and the decorations to the top floor look very nice. The cream paint has made all the difference.

Then I went with Mary Pickard, in her car to Cambridge to see the Ministry of Health about this and that. Not a very satisfactory interview, and the woman we saw, a Miss Bundle, was rather a foolish person.

Then I was off back to London, which was a good journey. There is nobody very thrilling to meet down here, though I have seen David Tod and one or two others, which was pleasant.

All love for now Ralph

[Textual: This has no date, but mention of his brother, John's new post, which he refers to in the next letter too, and buying daffodils point to early spring, and I'm guessing at c. March 23rd.]

c. Sunday, March 23ʳᵈ 1941 – London Hostel

My dearest
I really seem to be very busy at present. I am out a good deal during the day and I am working most evenings, right up to 10. O'clock last night.

John appears now to have got this job of being in charge of relief hostels in the Midland region. The offices are in Viceroy Close, Edgbaston, so he will be able to live at home, which he is pleased about.

I bought a lovely bunch of daffodils the other day and they look so beautiful in my room and remind me so much of you, my dear wife. God bless you dear heart, and love to the children.
Dear love, Ralph

PS I had a note from mother saying that Edwin and Hilda (Ransome) have a son[7]. I am glad, they will be so pleased

[Textual: This letter has no dating at all, not even a day, but several references – viz: jonquils, which are spring flowers; Olive Alexander's illness – she died the following January – (but jonquils are not generally out in January!); up-coming meeting with Robin Whitworth; meetings with the Indian High Commissioner. Although this is at least a year before Dick Symonds and Horace actually went to India (May 1942), firstly, Horace would not have gone abroad whilst Olive was ill, and secondly such remarks as the talks made 'little progress', only show what long planning such projects could involve. So over all March 1941 makes sense.]

FRB comments on the amazing life he leads.....certainly, as he says elsewhere, the University experience he never had, living at home........

Mid to late March 1941

 My dearest Joan

Just a quick line to thank you for the lovely jonquils. They are a joy on my table and I am more than grateful. It is lovely of you to send me flowers, and I appreciate them more than I can say. Thank you a thousand times. It is a lovely token of our love - Joan and flowers go naturally together.

I heard that Olive (Alexander) is very ill and not likely to live very long. I am so sorry. She is a remarkable person and Horace will miss her terribly. [.......]

What a fantastic world I deal with. People from all denominations - Anglicans, Methodists, Friends; from all backgrounds – state schools and public schools; all classes – from snobs and democrats! Then think of it, I start the day by interviewing an Indian in company with leading Quakers, Paul Sturge and Richard Symonds; I dictate letters to the daughter of an Indian Colonel; I attend a Quaker committee at Friends House; and I finish before supper with two high up ex BBC officials Robin Whitworth and Roger Wilson. Quite fantastic – a sort of Arabian Nights or Alice in Wonderland! I think I could run anything after the war! A thousand thanks again for the flowers, and thank David for his delightful drawings, which I am so glad to have. Dearest love Ralph.

PS. Still no letter from you

Olive Graham Alexander and Horace, close friends of my father and Duncan Wood

"I heard that Olive (Alexander) is very ill and not likely to live very long. I am so sorry. She is a remarkable person and Horace will miss her terribly."
Olive's father, John Graham was a leading pacifist in WW1
Photographs HGA archive PA

Sometime in mid to late March 1941 my father takes a long week-end's leave to join my mother and the family in Wolverhampton, where they have now finally decided to move, to be with Win and Llew. From there they make trips out into the countryside, especially to a favourite spot of theirs, Belvide Reservoir, not too far from Wolverhampton, in South Staffordshire.

Renowned for its amazing bird population, Belvide was largely popularised by my father's mentor Horace Alexander who founded the West Midland Bird Club which manages and cares for the Reservoir and its wild life. My parents' youngest son Nicholas follows in Ralph's tradition and is an active member of WMBC to this day.

Belvide Reservoire, North Staffordshire – famed for its birding life.
Photograph by permission of The Canal Trust

Mid to late March 1941

My dearest
I did so enjoy my week-end. Thank you very much for everything. What a joy it was to get out into the country. God bless you for being such a perfect wife. You looked so young and charming and always so nicely dressed, with the children so well looked after and neat as well. You really are perfect.

I have to thank you also for the books too, which I am delighted with. Please say a big 'thank you' to Winifred for looking after me so nicely. I do enjoy staying with them. One other big thank you, of course, to your mother for so kindly doing all my mending. She has repaired my coat beautifully and I am most grateful.

I had a good journey back, and met up with Alfred and Keith Linney and we had breakfast together. All quite fatiguing! I had lunch with Robin Whitworth and then there was an Executive meeting. Since when nothing much has happened, though there always seems to be something to occupy the time. I may have to come up to Birmingham on Thursday, but only for the night, and I don't think I shall be able to get out to Wolverhampton to see you all.

Thank you for your letter. Give my love to David – he really is an angel.
Dear love, Ralph

The ongoing problems between the Dillons and Mrs M came to a head, and Lord and Lady D decided to leave and move in with some friends nearby. Two opinionated groups of people could not long last in close proximity! But there's more gossip before she goes......

Wednesday, March 26th 1941 – Cheveley

My dearest

Well his Lordship and her Ladyship are leaving us! It's been brewing for some time. The ostensible excuse is that the Doctor insists Mrs M must have some quiet and get rid of visitors. So they are moving on to stay with Lady Amherst, who lives about 5 miles away.

We had a nice farewell to Lord D, who moved out first. He hopes we shall meet again etc etc! Probably not! The next day I had dinner with Lady D alone, as Mrs M was in bed. We had a very entertaining evening together, with Lady D being her usual gossipy self. The society magazines would have a field day with her stories and tittle tattle.

First it was Unity Mitford [8] : "She would do anything for publicity. She was tremendously pleased with herself some years ago, when she did something absolutely daft and her name was all over the placards. She said to my daughter 'Pam, isn't it marvellous, I'm famous for the first time.' I fear ever since she tried to shoot herself, she is not at all the same person. The poor girl still has the bullet lodged in her head."

A bit later she was off again about Mrs Simpson and von Ribbentrop. "Mrs Simpson was first introduced to the Duke by Ribbentrop you know, as part of his plot against the Empire, and later by one of the Duke's other ladies, who wanted a fortnight off. When she returned she found Mrs S already well in. The old Queen was quite marvellous. She was frightfully angry about the whole business, terrified in case the Duke abdicated. Before the abdication happened, the Duke of Gloucester was talking to his brother David, who proceeded to be very rude about his mother, Queen Mary, and Gloucester knocked him down." I must say Lady D is very good value, as long as one takes it all with a pinch of salt.

Subjects of Lady D's gossip

Joachim von Ribbentrop	Unity Mitford	Duke and Duchess of Windsor
German Ambassador to the UK.	Socialite, fascist & friend of Hitler, she was sister of Diana, Jessica & Deborah, and in 1939 attempted suicide. Photos Newsweek	In 1936 the Duke abdicated to marry divorcee Wallis Simpson.

Lord D's batman is still here and he has very kindly pressed all my suits for me! Lady D had to go to hospital for a check-up and I went to bring her back this morning, arriving just as she was ready, which was fortuitous, as she really hates being kept waiting. As indeed do I.

Roger Wilson came down the other day, and we had a very good visit. He went down very well with Mrs M and he seemed to approve of what had been done. The works squad have made a wonderfully good job of the house and the parts that have been decorated look awfully nice. I expect the Edmunds to move in on Friday, as their furniture has already arrived. I went and bought some more seeds this morning, and a few more young plants for the garden. The old gardeners have made excellent progress. My how they do work!

We had a welfare committee meeting there this afternoon, and I had arranged such a nice bowl of flowers for the occasion. Primroses, primula, snowdrops, crocuses and scylla. I wished I had been arranging them for you.

I took the train down to London today as I have an orgy of meetings over the week-end. A staff meeting of the FAU tomorrow, and a General Meeting of representatives of FAU sections on Sunday. In addition I've got to see Roger W and various other people too. I read the New Statesman and the News Chronicle on the train and felt very depressed with the world. Mankind seems to be either dirty and feckless and easily led, or grasping hard-faced capitalists, who either grind down the work force, or are charming people like Lord and Lady D, whose minds are set in one groove and who don't see the need for all the things people like us are concerned about. And people like us seem a poor, idealistic, unpractical, and harmless group – or else dangerous lunatics – as the case may be! Will we ever be able to make a more satisfactory world? I don't think I ever shall. I'm too easy and I agree with people too readily.

I will return to Cheveley via Cambridge on Monday, probably by car, as I believe they are at last supplying me with one, which will be such a convenience, as I won't have to cycle everywhere anymore! I do hope there will be a letter from you awaiting me on my return.

It's so grand to think I shall be seeing you before very long now. I do love you so very dearly. I feel as though the great refuge and strength in my life is my dear, dear wife. You are everything that is good and lovely in the world. You are flowers and birds, skies and clouds, books and poetry, gardens and distant views, love and friendship, beauty and charm, home and shelter, food and drink – everything. Oh my dear, if I could only tell you all you are to me. Come what may, your love for me has made my life worthwhile and glorious. And there is a better time coming.

I must try and find out what they intend me to do next while I am in London.

All love for now, Ralph

After my birth, as my mother slowly recovered her figure – often too slowly for her - inevitably her life became more and more hectic, now having to look after two children, one just starting school and the other still a baby. But my mother, a highly intelligent, well read and active lady, no doubt found the constraints of domestic life during the war living in someone else's home, difficult to contend with. Sometimes her frustrations boiled over in letters to my father. Really all she needed was reassurance from my father, which he supplied very well. But visits could be infrequent and telephone calls expensive. Here my father tells her off for belittling herself, and informs her of his new appointment in Birmingham at the 11th Camp, when he will be near her.....and an increase in salary!........

Thursday, March 27th 1941 – Banstead Manor, Cheveley

Dearest Joan

In great haste. [.....] I get really very angry with you, when you start putting yourself down, worrying about how you look after A's birth. When I saw you at Beaconwood just afterwards, you were neither plump, plain nor lacking in charm. I shall never forget how charming and pretty you looked – quite as pretty as you ever were. Lacking in charm? Good God, just look in the mirror and see how young and pretty you still are. Don't talk such rubbish.

Nor are you dull and shy. I remember just how well you held your own when we were at the housing conference in Sweden in 1939. And now you have every cause to be proud, as the mother of two fine sons, and one born in the midst of war. You are truly courageous to have done that. And I marvel every day at how wonderfully you manage, carrying on bravely, living in a strange house, never complaining. You are one of the heroes of the war, far better than I, who by comparison has an easy time. Your husband will love you to your dying day, even as we both get old and lose our youth. But right now he just wants to hold you in his arms and kiss the most beautiful woman he knows. Shut up and don't talk any more rubbish!

You will be pleased to know that I have just been appointed as Officer in charge of the 11th Camp at Northfield, starting on Monday, April 21st. So I will not be far away. I don't yet know about what leave I am due, but it will certainly be before then, and I should probably get away from here about the start of April. So not long at all. Hooray! In haste – and don't be foolish.

I have had a formal note saying that the Trustees have increased my salary to £600*1 and that I shall get half of this – ie 13 monthly cheques of £21. It's good of them to do this, and it will be a help. When did you last have a cheque? All my love to you and David. Ralph.

PS. I have just had a most amusing letter from mother; unusually so for her – warning me against the 'wicked aristocracy'!! That would amuse the Dillons!

[Textual: This next letter is helpfully just headed Saturday! I had initially thought it must be later, but as he talks of the new wardens, the Edmunds having arrived, and in the next letter of showing them around, I am assuming it must be sometime after the last and before the next letter, towards the end of March and as he heads it Saturday I'm plumping for the Friday, 29th March 1941.]

Still worrying about where JMB should live; new Wardens arrive; Lord and Lady D depart.......

Saturday, March 29th 1941 – Banstead Manor - Cheveley

My very dearest

It was so lovely to hear your voice last night and it made me so happy to talk to you. Bless you for being such a dear.

I am so worried about thee my darling, and wish I could be more help. I have thought and thought about it all and can't see a way out. It would make all the difference to me if you could be near while I am at Northfield. It would be so marvellous. I expect John and Enid would have you to stay if they can manage with Roger at home, or Jeph and Margaret. After Camp, could we all go for my next lot of leave to Helen (unknown) and perhaps you stay for a month or so, and then perhaps you could return to Beaconwood. That would be quite a break for both of us as Michael and Heather live within reach of lovely country.

---

*1 About £25,000 in 2020 money.

But also think about J&E or J&M. Then you would be near and I could come up to see you quite easily from Camp, which would be grand. I am actually rather thrilled about being in charge of the Camp, but half the pleasure will be because you will be near me again, and I can ring you, or you can ring me and ask for "The Camp Commandant"! I know you wouldn't mind, but if, of course, you don't feel it's safe for the children, then we must not do it.

I do think and worry about you so much, and if my letters seem full of my own affairs, it is only because I think you may be interested, and not because I am not for ever thinking of you.

The Edmunds are now here and I met them at the station today. It is such a glorious, glorious day, so they could not have seen things under better conditions. I had their room tidy with a nice fire burning and I prepared a special high tea with poached eggs and cake. I had bought some daffodils and arranged them in a vase together with pussy willow and witch hazel, and they looked so lovely. I also put a pretty little bowl of scyllas, primroses, primulas, crocuses and snowdrops on the mantelpiece, which were really rather glorious. I did it partly for them, but in truth, I only ever pick and arrange flowers for one person, and that's you. All flowers are you when I arrange a bowl of them, which is my little act of worship and remembrance and gratitude to the only woman in the world. Joan and daffodils and scyllas and beds of crocuses, and Joan and cherry blossom at Kew, and Joan going mad over blue gentians, and Joan picking apple blossom, and Joan and all the lovely, lovely flowers there are; my dear, dear wife.

The work squad should be out at the weekend, and then we can get the house cleared for the evacuees on Thursday. Lord and Lady D have gone. Lady D made a very affectionate farewell, and thanked me for making their life tolerable at Banstead. She asked for our address and said that if they had a house after the war they would certainly invite us. She was really very likeable, though sometimes the devil seemed to enter into her, and she became quite outrageous. But I think she quite liked me, and I liked her. So now we are just Mrs M and me again, and as Mrs Morris is not very well, I have breakfast and dinner all alone. Mrs M is really a very, very nice person, and I think she is quite relieved that the Dillons have now gone.

Mr Edmunds is a funny little man with a great, booming voice. I think he is probably quite a nice fellow, but probably not much of a manager. I imagine his wife will do all that side of things. I intend to leave here as soon as I can, and get to Birmingham by the end of next week. Won't that be grand? There seems such a lot still to do here even though the Edmunds are here.

I wonder if you have seen mother or Millior and Alfred at all, as I expect that they were up in Birmingham for the Woodbrooke Council meetings.

Excuse such a short note, but I just wished to write and say how much I think of you and to thank you so much for ringing.

May God keep you, my dear one. All my love, Ralph.

PS I have written a long letter to mother. I hadn't written for ages, so I owed her one, especially as I have had 4 from her!

[Textual: Frustratingly, this letter has no date again, only a day – Monday. But my mother mentions in her diary for Friday, April 11th that they all went to cousin George Cadbury's cottage 'Spinneyfields' near Bromsgrove, for FRB's leave, so I am guessing it must be around April 7th 1941]

Final arrangements are made prior to the first evacuees' arrival; and my father is doing everything for the last time.......

Monday, April 7th 1941 – Banstead Manor, Cheveley

My darling

Thank you so much for your dear letter received this morning. I do love to hear from you. How kind of Cousin George to offer us 'Spinneyfield Cottage' for my leave. I will write to him. I have been thinking of you so much and wondering what is best for us to do. I do hope that soon you may feel happier about your future. It is rotten for you and I am so very sorry.

After several glorious days, it has gone dull and heavy and cold today. Perfectly miserable in fact. On Sunday I wrote letters in the morning, and then went into Newmarket to see Brandon Cadbury, who had come out to make arrangements about some FAU men who have started work in the hospital there. He is a nice man, though very slow in saying anything. He told me that the African party, the Egyptian reinforcements and the China convoy are all expected to leave this week, which means, I am afraid I shan't see Duncan before he goes.

In the afternoon I went to Cambridge with Mary Pickard. She had to take a woman into hospital to have her 16th child - can you believe? She is an evacuee living nearby with her husband and five or six of her children. The other five were sent to America, but tragically sunk in one of the liners taking evacuees across the Atlantic. I accompanied Mary, as she wanted to see the house that I visited near Cambridge the other day, to see if it would be suitable in case she and the people she looks after, have to get out of the house at Wood Ditton.

Today I have been clearing up various jobs and taking the Edmunds round and showing them things and people to help familiarise them with the area. They are quite nice and will, I think probably do well enough, though personally I don't take to them frightfully. He seems terribly young, rather a blunderer and not that good at what he does, which probably makes me sound awfully conceited. She is pleasant, but rather cold, hard and efficient. As I say, pleasant, but that's all. Not at all like you. But still there is only one Joan.

Mrs M says that if we like, we can take firewood from her woods. I had hoped to have some spare men to help do it as those who had been helping had piled it all rather badly. Now the men have left, so I had to spend Saturday afternoon and this evening, cutting and piling it myself. Even so, I seem to have done it more efficiently and better in 5 hours than they did in 15. I shouldn't blow my own trumpet, but really your husband isn't such a fool as he looks!

But at the moment your husband is rather worried lest the reception arrangements for the evacuees does not go alright. There is so much to do and get right, and it is so difficult to get any news quickly to and from London. Thank you for the nice things you say about me, and I am very happy that you are so proud of me, but really I am a poor thing, and just at present feeling very nervous about being in charge of the 11th camp. I'm sure I shall make a complete mess of it. However, on another score I am very happy. I am doing everything here for the last time, and am crossing off the last items from my list. I am tearing up letters and thinking of packing AND BEST OF ALL, I SHALL SOON BE WITH YOU. Won't that be grand, grand, grand? I can't tell you how happy I am at the prospect. I shall arrive either Friday evening or early Saturday, but will wire with details. Shall I come straight out? Send me a wire Friday c/o The London Hostel if there is an alternative plan.

All my dearest love Ralph

A leave at Spinneyfield Cottage

'Spinneyfields' cottage on the edge of the Lickey Hills, belonged to cousin George Cadbury jnr, and his wife Edith, which they kindly lent to my parents for a week's leave at the start of April 1941.

My father writes:

"It was like having our own home again, with Joan greeting me at the door and a good meal laid out in the dining room. It was magical, with wonderful views over Worcestershire. We did nothing much but walk in the garden and on the Lickeys all covered in bluebells. The semblance of home life was quite wonderful."

Photos Cadbury family archive

George and Edith Cadbury (née Woodall), parents of Christopher Cadbury.

And so Banstead Manor with its cast of dramatis personae of aristocracy, local odd bods and visiting experts came to an end.

Chapter 10
The 11ᵗʰ Camp and the Mechanics Camp
April – June 1941

The first camp opened in 1939 with fifty eight members, comprising Quakers and those who had been at Quaker schools as well as those with similar pacifist views. As Tegla Davies says "Manor Farm became the nursery of the Unit" *and following the first camp, apart from two at Buckhurst Hill, became the home to the twenty or so successive camps. As a result of Paul Cadbury's letter in The Friend, the many who responded were deployed to Manor Farm and the FAU trainees at the first camp issued a statement expressing their purpose in 1939.....*

"We purpose to train ourselves as an efficient Unit to undertake ambulance and relief work in areas under both civilian and military control, and so, by working as a pacifist and civilian body where the need is greatest, to demonstrate the efficacy of co-operating to build up a new world rather than fighting to destroy the old. While respecting the views of those pacifists who feel they cannot join an organization such as our own, we feel concerned among the bitterness and conflicting ideologies of the present situation to build up a record of goodwill and positive service, hoping that this will help to keep uppermost in men's minds those values which are so often forgotten in war and immediately afterwards."

As already described, my father's first experience of joining the FAU after his time with the AFS, was at the 9ᵗʰ Camp in 1940. Having later spent time in the East End at the Poplar Hospital and later at Cheveley, he then came back, after a period of leave, into the mainstream of Unit life as Commandant of the 11th Camp and later the Mechanics Camp in Northfield. Being in Birmingham, there was not quite the urgency to write letters as he could easily get up to Beaconwood or even phone. But we have his memoirs and here, in describing the scene, his tone is now an almost ironic resignation to the non-stop bombing........

During my time at Northfield, once again our fate was to be troubled by air raids, as sticks of bombs fell in the field across the stream. Mercifully the premises remained undamaged and whilst I was there, the Camp did not get called out. I always tried to maintain quite strict discipline, as I believe the experience of the Unit has shown that members appreciate the rudiments of drill. So each morning we had a morning run and PT sessions, followed by route marches, which proved to be very worthwhile, although I have always had bad memories of a 20 mile route march that we had, which was one of my most vivid memories of this camp.

On this occasion I had instructed the unhappy members of the Camp, to undertake a night route march and I recall with a shudder, two particularly tricky moments. The first, already some way into the march, was when I suddenly realised to my dismay, that our direction of travel was taking us further and further away from Birmingham, on a route that could very well extend the march to at least another thirty miles; and the second only a few hours later, well after the first streaks of dawn had appeared on the horizon, I seriously began to wonder if I should ever manage to get everyone home without having a total revolution on my hands! Indeed one of the company, decided that every time we halted, he would lie down on the road and go to sleep! This turned into a very long night's route march indeed, and has long remained on my conscience. As these events often have their own built in irony, it was our determined road-sleeper who later became our Transport Officer!

In both the 11th Camp and the Mechanics camp which I attended, I recall many outstanding personalities. First amongst these has to be Jack Frazer, to whom I owe an enormous debt. An admirable person in every way, it was my good luck that he should be the Training Officer during my time there, for our association, begun at Camp, was the start of a lifelong friendship for which I shall always be grateful. Other people who stood out were Sandy Parnis, a most meticulous and hard-working man and a wonderful Section Leader, who with his age and experience, became the mainstay of the camp. And then there was Barty Knight, the Quarter Master of the 11th Camp, a very capable and likeable man. Sadly, he suffered badly from fits of depression, which often made working with him quite difficult.

By the end of my time there, thanks to them all, I did feel that I knew at least a little more about running training camps than at the start. And as time went on, I began to have a clearer idea of the objects of camp. Firstly, of course, these must be to familiarise everyone with the Unit itself; then to teach them certain basic skills, be it first aid or mechanics; to ensure that they are all fit; and finally to find out what sort of people they are. In this respect the traditions already established in previous camps, as well as the reports handed down from earlier leaders to us new chaps, were all immensely helpful. I insisted on tidiness and as a result of innumerable odd job periods we kept Northfield pretty tidy. Altogether, though I found it very wearing, nonetheless it proved rather stimulating, and one of the joys of being near home, was that I was able to see Joan and she came several times to camp, including to the last night party bringing a lovely bunch of bluebells. After the party we were on a peak of elation, from which we rapidly fell next day when the Mechanics Camp Section Leaders arrived.

A volume might be written on the Mechanics' Camp, which seemed to me to be very formidable, as its personnel seemed to be all old sweats with everyone being much longer established in the Unit than I. I dreaded it, especially as the Section Leaders proved not to be much help either. But with the help of Sir Louis Matheson, the head of Engineering at Birmingham University, we managed to work out quite a full curriculum. I owe him a great debt of gratitude for all he did to facilitate the training. He started each day with a formal lecture, which was followed by practical work in which each section had to complete a particular task. A number of old cars had been set out in the barn at Northfield which were ideal for the men to practice on. With Sir Louis' assistance, we also laid on driving instruction, which sometimes proved to be a perilous business.

Of the many disastrous things that happened, I especially remember fastening a tow-rope to the steering bar of one of the cars, which I had somehow managed to bend with disastrous results, and poor Alan McBain spending several hours taking the bar out and straightening it and putting it back again. Another time, we attempted to reassemble the engine of an old Ford lorry, which we owned, but because of an unfortunate mistake in our assembly, we managed to fill the cylinders with water, which then proceeded to spurt out in gushing fountains. On yet another occasion, after one section had undertaken much long and patient work on a Vauxhall car that was there, and actually inducing it to work, the hand brake mysteriously slipped to the off, and we watched horrified as the newly fixed Vauxhall trundled all the way down the Manor drive, fast accelerating under its own steam – mercifully ending in the hedge, with no serious damage inflicted on anyone. Nonetheless, despite such follies, the Camp was memorable as one of the Unit's first attempts at serious driving and mechanics training. Everyone worked hard, with a full time-table and though it was ultimately too short a course, the results were not negligible and it also served its purpose of freshening up some by then rather stale Unit members.

The 11ᵗʰ Mechanics Camp

The old barn at the Manor House, Northfield, where the FAU originally trained.

FAU recruits learning to repair vehicles at Manor Farm, Northfield 1941
Photographs Friends House Library

The Mechanics Camp

Sir Louis Matheson

"With the help of Sir Louis Matheson, we managed to work out quite a full curriculum. I owe him a great debt of gratitude for all he did to facilitate the training."

Sir Louis was a British engineer and University administrator. Born in Huddersfield, he graduated from Manchester and Birmingham Universities, and eventually took up a position at the latter, before emigrating to Melbourne where he succeeded in radically modernizing the University system.

During his time at Birmingham he became involved with the FAU Mechanics Camp, working with my father in helping the Unit to devise a curriculum as well as giving formal daily lectures.

Photo University of Birmingham

Mechanics Camp, Northfield 1941 FRB standing 4th from left.
"The mechanics camp seemed very formidable; as its personnel appeared to me to be all sweats….."
Photograph Friends House Library

At the end of the Mechanics Camp in June 1941, I was appointed as Relief Officer in London to take over from Peter Gibson. It was at this time that I heard news of Germany's attack on Russia, and at the end of what had been in all 3 months of Camp, I began to feel very weary.

Many Good Friends

"In both the 11th Camp and the Mechanics camp.......I recall many outstanding personalities.

"First amongst these has to be Jack Frazer (left), to whom I owe an enormous debt. An admirable person in every way, and it was the start of a lifelong friendship.

"Other people who stood out were Sandy Parnis (bottom left) a most meticulous and hard-working man and a wonderful Section Leader, who with his age and experience, became the mainstay of the camp.

"And then there was Barty Knight (bottom right) the Quarter Master of the 11th Camp, a very capable and likeable man."

Photograph courtesy of Hilary Skelton (née Frazer)

Sandy Parnis - Section Leader   Barty Knight - Quarter Master
Photographs Friends House Library

Relief Work in the East End

The Student's Hostel
"Behind the London Hospital showing our odd collection of vehicles."
Photograph Friends House Library

A mobile Citizens Advice Bureau converted by the Work Squad, advising local residents.
Photograph Friends House Library

Chapter 11

A Holiday in Ewyas Harold and Relief Officer
July 1941

Ivy Cottage in Herefordshire
"The whole holiday was a dream of beauty"
Photograph Hereford County archive

After the Mechanics Camp, Leonard Appleton[1] kindly lent us their house, Ivy Cottage in the little village of Ewyas Harold half between Abergavenny and Hereford, quite near the Welsh border. LPA and his wife took us down with David and Antony in the car and both of us will forever remember the first view of that garden. The whole holiday was a dream of beauty, a blazing garden, the common at the door and within bicycling distance of the Black Mountains.

We did very little but we had a wonderful time; housework, getting meals, looking after the children and gardening. It went all too quickly. One day I went up to London for an Executive meeting, bicycling about 10 miles to the station in the early morning. I remember the curlews crying as I rode through the cool lanes, and Joan welcoming me back in the evening. The end was somewhat marred by the tragic death of LPA's wife Peggy.

From there I went to the Relief Office and Joan went back to Wolverhampton. There save for a not very successful visit to Monmouth, she stayed until November 1943. It was a hard time for her, and moving about and living with two children in other people's houses was very difficult, but she bore it with wonderful courage, fortitude and cheerfulness and owing to her loving care, I think that the children suffered very little.

The London Relief Section and the Relief Office were in the Students Hostel behind the London Hospital in the East End. The regular inhabitants there were Relief staff, Relief workers, work squad and garage men, which at the start numbered usually some 130, but by the time I took over in July 1941, the whole Relief Section for which I was responsible was above 200. The FAU first got into relief work soon after September 1940 at the beginning of the blitz and were very quickly right in the midst of it.

Tegla Davies describes the situation well:

"On Saturday, 7th September 1940, the sixty-five members of the Fifth and Sixth Camps, working in East End hospitals, went to their work as usual. That day, as terrible as unexpected, came the blitz. East-Enders took refuge from the terror by the tens and hundreds of thousands in cavernous basements, railway arches, church crypts, large warehouses that looked more adequate, or at least less inadequate, than their own flimsy dwellings. Night after night the terror was repeated; with every new dawn families emerged from their packed and fetid shelters to find their homes no longer there. Constantly there poured into the Rest Centres bewildered men and women and children with nowhere else to go; each day aggravated the problems of destruction and homelessness."

The need spoke for itself, and following a report by Tom Tanner and Michael Barratt Brown, it was decided almost immediately that the FAU should henceforward embark upon urgent relief work, for which Tanner was asked to make the initial arrangements. Soon there were about twelve men from the Unit working in Rest Centres, and gradually more and more members were transferred from hospitals and by the end of the year two hundred men were engaged on air-raid relief work.

———

As so often with my father, he starts a new posting with grave apprehension, unsure if he will ever be capable of doing it, followed by a period of depression and then a gradual awareness that he's quite good at it……….

The months during which I was at Cheveley and Northfield had been formative ones in the history of the Unit. Tom (Tanner) had undertaken his great work as Relief Officer and thanks to his efforts, the Relief Section was now quite large and not a little conscious of its own importance, and he had moved on to become Chairman of the whole Unit. It is difficult to estimate the debt which the Unit owes him for all that he did for it.

My memories of the Unit are punctuated by recollection of periods of extreme and utter depression, when it seemed as though nothing in the world would ever go right again, and I remember that such a period coincided with my arrival at the Student's Hostel in Poplar to take over the Relief Office from Peter Gibson. People who knew the Hostel came to love it, but it became well-known for its lack of friendliness and visitors found it cold and inhospitable. There was a permanent hostility to Gordon Square and it had gained a reputation as a centre of political intrigue.

It was in this state of great depression, following directly on from the Mechanics' camp, that I went down in July 1941 to assume responsibility for the London Relief Section. Peter Gibson was about to go overseas, and how well I remember sitting in his room while he did his best to explain it all to me, feeling terrified as a complete newcomer, full of trepidation. I knew nothing of relief work, and faced with a self-confident, hard and rather truculent Relief Section, found it initially quite daunting to cope with.

This was especially so in the late summer of 1941, when there was a lull in proceedings, with the worst of the raids over, the nights still light and the heat great. In addition to the Relief Office and its staff, there was a house staff consisting of a Warden, House Steward and Quartermaster; but the Relief Officer was the senior person. Everyone was expected to do orderly duties, which was a perennial problem, as the slackness and untidiness of some members was depressing and a constant battle, giving rise to perpetual criticism.

I worked in Room 115 with Michael Barratt (Barry) Brown, which was quite a pleasant corner room and I slept in one of the nicer bedrooms Room 224. This had a telephone, though that proved not to be the boon one might have expected, with calls at all times of the day and night, it was altogether a mixed blessing. Shortly after I took over, women moved in, and overnight the atmosphere completely changed, becoming a quite different and strangely exciting community. But living so much on top of one's work, meant long hours, usually till 9.0 or 10.0 at night, and being available at all times. It was wearing, and though at first I was acutely miserable and had awful periods of depression, in many ways, in the end I found it oddly enjoyable. In a letter to Joan I tried to explain my new responsibilities.......

Sunday, July 13th 1941 – Students Hostel, Philpot Street.

My dearest

I do apologise for the shocking way in which I have treated you letter-wise this week, but things have got rather on top of me. The end of leave, the hot weather, the new job and the East End have all conspired to pull me down. It was so lovely to get your card. I felt badly in need of your loving thoughts.

Being Relief Officer comprises doing the following:

    a.   Generally being head of the section - that means all the FAU work and personnel in London or the provinces engaged in relief.

    b.   Relief constitutes

- Shelter Work – Medical patrols of shelters and social work
- Rest Centre Work – staffing of 8 rest centres, where homeless people can come after an air raid.
- The work which Keith Linney is doing in Birmingham.
- The Queens' Messenger Convoys – our own canteens which do a nightly round.
- The Work Squad and Transport Sections

Each section has a man in charge:

Rest Centres - is Arnold Curtis – youngish, Oxford and very pleasant.

Shelters - is Richard Symonds – 23, married, capable.

Research - is Michael Barratt Brown – 23, very capable, pleasant and rather sure of himself.

Canteens and Queens' Messengers – is John Goss

My job seems generally to be supervising their work, correlating and thinking out policy and attending innumerable committees with War Vics. They have all been very nice to me, though they must rather resent an outsider coming in and telling them what to do. The difficulties are:

    a.   Deciding the exact value of the work.

    b.   Keeping things going during this lull in the air raids.

    c.   Keeping a sufficient grip of everything in such a large section.

I have a very pleasant office with women typists and telephonists, so that in some respects it's just like the Bournville Estate Office all over again! It's nice to have John Burtt here, but I do miss you and your comfort terribly, and often feel rather lonely.

I eat most of my meals at the Middlesex Hospital or in the Mile End Road, where we also have a hospital and relief section. Sometimes I go along to the War Vics Hostel in Cannonbury, though they are rather an odd lot there! The women members of the Unit are a friendly lot, but certainly no beauties!

It looks as though I shall probably be in Birmingham sometime during the next fortnight, and will try and spend a night with you. I don't suppose you could leave the children with your mother in the near future could you, and come up to London for a week end, whilst this lull lasts? I expect Millior would lend us her flat for a night.

The Egypt and Syria convoys will be off as soon as they can get shipping, and an Abyssinian convoy is also in the air.

I will write again soon. Remember me to your family and my love to David. Tell him I loved his drawings of caterpillars.   Dear love Ralph

[Textual: This next letter is undated, but internal evidence suggests June or July 1941. My father was put on the Executive Committee in June 1941, and Jeph and Margaret Gillett became wardens of Upwood House in Barnt Green sometime in mid-1941.]

As my father writes above, the move to London coincided with one of his periods of depressions, as this letter also shows......

Wednesday, early July 1941

My dear Joan

We had a Council meeting this afternoon, with Paul Cadbury (PSC) in the Chair. He really can be most tiring at times, with meetings going on for hours. Jeph (Gillett –Treasurer) came up for the meeting too, and asked after you. He says that he and Margaret are both very busy as Wardens of Upwood, which now has some 30 children.

I do hope you are coping alright these days, and that David is well. I know how difficult it must be now with the two children, and I pray that life is tolerable for you. I do think of you so much and wish I could do more. How long will this damned separation last? Being apart is almost unbearable and I confess it has made me very depressed of late.

On top of which, things just don't seem to be going very well at this end, and I have made more than my share of mistakes, which I can't help feeling pretty bad about. I had supper with Millior and Alfred the other day, but I wasn't in the best of moods and can't have been very good company. I realise my letters of late have been really rotten and I am so sorry. I will try to do better in the future. Think of me and don't be too hard on me.
Love to D&A and of course to you my dearest one, Ralph

My father continues in this downbeat mood in his memoirs, but finds help and loyalty in the team around him.....

Fortunately for me, Tom had collected a very strong staff together, among whom were Sam Marriage, Michael Barratt Brown, Richard Symonds, Arnold Curtis, Lawrence Darton, Jack Goss, Michael Hacking and John Burtt. These able men were now joined by a very unconfident me. I remember discussing my despair with a sympathetic John Burtt - the Warden - which was greatly reassuring and much appreciated. I had always liked John, although perhaps as a Warden, he was a little too vague and indecisive to be really effective.

Of the other staff, I was eternally grateful to my deputy, Michael Barratt Brown. Young, cocksure, arrogant and conceited he may have been, but brilliant and a great worker, who was really keen, with good judgement and great loyalty. He was always such good company too. Then there was Arnold Curtis in charge of the Rest Centres, a very able man and nobody's fool, but often given to fits of laziness; Laurence Darton in charge of shelters, on the other hand was a great worker and meticulous organizer, though not always terribly good with people. And who could forget Richard Symonds, who had been shelter officer in the great days, a young Rugby scholar not long down from Oxford, brilliant with heaps of drive, thoroughly loyal and honest, but on the down side easily depressed, with no great staying power, but so very likeable in every way. The day to day running of the office was under the careful supervision of Leonard Elliott and Clarence Dover.

Frank Gregory, an excellent man, along with the ever reliable Henry Headley, ran what was known as the Work Squad: practical men, good with their hands, a vital component of Unit life. In fact it was Frank who had designed the FAU logo with its intertwining letters, which became so familiar to us all. And how soon they proved their worth, restoring the Student's Hostel to somewhere approaching a habitable state, and then the more lengthy task of renovating the dirty, dingy and dilapidated older Rest Centres. Essential to the whole enterprise was the Garage section, run by Leslie Gardner, who took over from Derryck Hill when he went abroad, and did a really good job putting the whole section onto a much stronger footing, with a seemingly ever increasing staff.

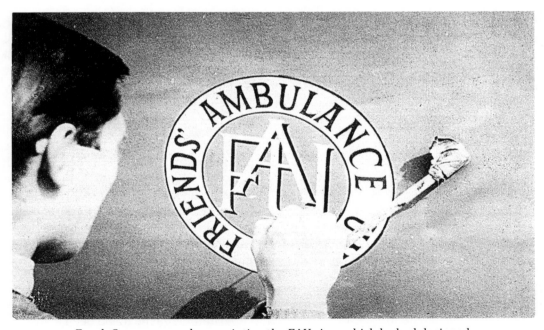

Frank Gregory, seen here painting the FAU sign, which he had designed.
"An excellent man, who ran what was known as the Work Squad: a practical man, good with his hands, a vital component of Unit life."

Photograph Friends House Library

Transport, of course, was crucial to all our emergency work. We needed cars for visits round the shelters, and we needed more cars for use by the canteen. We needed lorries for carrying equipment and supplies around London, and we needed more lorries in the big cities. And both the cars and the lorries had to be serviced, ready for immediate use.

By the end of 1941 we seemed to have accumulated an exceedingly odd collection of twenty seven vehicles of all different makes and sizes, and the section never seemed to stop growing. New vehicles were arriving every other day, including two 3 tonners from the Ministry of Health. Each of the vehicles we acquired seemed to have a distinctly obstinate character unique to itself. The only way we could ever get them going was to call one of the Unit's mechanics to come over, who somehow managed to gently coax and wheedle them back into life.

The increase in numbers meant that very soon the original garage in Raven Row became too small and we moved to a large rented, commercial garage at the end of Philpot Street near the Hospital, which Leslie (Gardner) had found, where there was plenty of parking space as well as a workshop for the constant daily repairs and maintenance.

But it was essential that we kept everyone employed and with our personnel officers, first Glan Davies, then William Barnes and Annette Caulkin, we made successful efforts to do so. Citizen Advice Bureaux, provided some useful training and spare time occupation, but our principal work was now in the Shelters and Rest Centres.

In all, the Unit provided staff for eight Rest Centres, which kept us all very busy. I made a point of visiting them all, often with Arnold Curtis, and inevitably we would encounter all sorts of problems, often of a personal and sexual nature, which we tried our best to deal with. I also arranged to send out regular patrols to visit nearly all the shelters, particularly those in Stepney, Wapping and Poplar, and of course our canteen was forever busy serving them food and gallons of tea.

By now the large London Section was completely filling the overflowing Students' Hostel, but in many ways it proved to be one of the truly remarkable features of the Unit's work. There was so much that was good in it, and those of us who lived there at that time look back on it with great affection. It is, of course, difficult to ultimately estimate the value of the work done there, but in my opinion I think the first six month's work of the Relief Section, was among the finest things the Unit ever accomplished. Our reports really helped to improve the conditions in the East End shelters and together with the work force made an invaluable contribution to the life of those living there. Just when it was most needed the Unit provided the brains and hands that made all the difference.

Indeed at first I felt the work was of a really positive value, but slowly as my twelve months in charge wore on, the medical and raid-relief aspect declined, and it became apparent that much of our work was becoming superfluous. Maybe it had been a mistake for us to barge into the world of social work as we did, because though we accomplished much useful work, it was vastly less successful than the relief work, and I think continuing the Relief Section at such a strength, was almost certainly a mistake. By Christmas 1941 we did start to cut down, and in the end of course, we came out altogether, but we should have done so much sooner. In our defence, it should be said, we had no means of knowing whether the air raids had really come to an end or not.

—

In those last weeks, running such a big section became a thankless job. By this time, I was not only trying to maintain the running of the Unit in an orderly fashion, but I also had to cope simultaneously with drastically reducing staff numbers. On the one hand it was vital to keep people employed and make an increasingly disgruntled staff feel that they were being taken seriously, yet on the other hand, having to justify keeping such a large section to an ever critical Gordon Square.

My father wrote home in a down mood, of trying to cope on a reduced staff and keeping up morale with no definite offer of new work. And, adding to his troubles an in-growing toenail and a boil. But he bolsters himself with some of his favourite verses......

Mid July 1941

Dearest

[........] If only we could find new work or see some definite prospect of some in the future. I do think my job is by way of being one of the lousiest in the Unit at the moment. To begin with it was the biggest section, but now we are cutting back and cutting back and trying hard to justify what remains, as well as working hard to keep people up to the mark, when it all seems so futile. On top of everything, I have a bad in-growing toenail and a boil and am feeling thoroughly sorry for myself! So life is fairly bloody, but I'm still fighting and by God I'll go on fighting!

To lose courage is the crowning sin. So don't pity me, because though I'm fed up, I'm not down and I don't pity myself. I know I am lucky in many ways. I have health and comfort and plenty to do and friends. And most importantly I have you and the children. All of which give me some courage.

So often lines of verse come to me as encouragement. Hugh Walpole's [2] "*Tisn't life that matters, 'Tis the courage you bring to it.*" Or W E Henley's[3] famous lines from Invictus "*I thank whatever gods may be, for my unconquerable soul. In the fell clutch of circumstance ......my head is bloody, but unbowed.*"! Finally there's always Masefield's[4] "*But tomorrow, by the living God, we'll try the game again*"! These are surely worthwhile things to hang on to aren't they?"

[......] as always,

All my love Ralph

One possibility of such new work came with the rapid development of work outside London. Although the blitz had hit London badly, it was far from the only city to suffer the effects of air-raids and soon the Unit turned its attention to provincial cities as well, setting up sections with mobile squads that could be deployed in an emergency. By working in close collaboration with the local authority, they were best able to assist the already existing administrations. In Birmingham for instance, twelve men started shelter work, beginning in early December and following the raid on Coventry, a team was immediately sent there too in order to help organize Rest Centres.

The work in Birmingham started as in London, by providing medical services, but soon extended to welfare and a canteen round. The team surveyed some five hundred shelters which they followed up with reports to the city officials and the Ministry of Health. Similarly in Liverpool, where the Unit had already established local links earlier in the year, a section was sent in October 1941 under Robin Whitworth. Housed first in the Waterloo area of the city and later in Sefton Park, they undertook Rest Centre surveys, provided travelling supervisors for their re-organisation and ran a camp for children near Mold in North Wales.

My father writes in his memoirs..........

We began to establish provincial sections in Birmingham under Keith Linney, in Liverpool under Robin Whitworth and in Newcastle under Arnold Curtis. This was important work and I visited them all several times, in particular the Birmingham section, first in Kingsmead Close, then later when they outgrew that, in Selly Wood, kindly provided by Christopher Taylor. Here through the Unit's strong Quaker connections they did a tremendous job and the initial twelve men soon increased to twenty, thus necessitating the move to new premises.

The team proved so successful setting up shelters and Rest Centres that the work soon expanded to include a Citizens' Advice Bureau, a small Mobile Squad and a group organizing summer camps on the Lickey Hills for children from the shelters. Similarly in Liverpool where the creation of the section was a tour de force by Robin, who fired everyone with his enthusiasm. I think one of the best and most interesting developments by the Unit anywhere was the one Robin set up in the Scotland Road area of the city. This contained some of their very worst slums, beset with poverty, violence, and sectarian divisions. They took over a large and very dilapidated corner shop and together with the Work Squad spent weeks cleaning, repairing and decorating, till the centre was complete, all ready for a variety of club activities. Very soon its influence and success so grew that in the end responsibility for it was taken over by local Friends.

We also helped to staff the Food Flying Squads, which became known as the 'Queens Messengers', after Queen Elizabeth, who had reviewed the convoys at Buckingham Palace. Well managed by Jack Goss, they were a mobile squad under the aegis of the Ministry of Health. They were for use in badly blitzed towns and were particularly effective during the so-called 'Baedeker raids'[5] on Exeter and Norwich; and later in Liverpool, Plymouth and Coventry, where Michael Rowntree was doing sterling work with the Public Assistance Office, helping the overworked Rest Centre managers, following the devastating bombing of that city. All in all, I have to confess, that the work was never less than challenging, and I am grateful for the Friends I made and the life that existed in the Hostel. It gave me something new, something that I might have got had I gone to a University away from home, with discussions and chit chat and gossip.

Meanwhile back in London a whole year had passed since my father had taken over and the longer nights of the winter produced no further activity on the scale of the blitz. And so the Unit was beginning to feel more and more that while provision should be made for those whose primary concern was in social work, for the rest, the only sensible answer was an orderly retreat. Here his letters home talk enthusiastically of the sort of camaraderie he experienced in the Unit Hostel...

Mid July 1941

My dearest

[........] You ask me what we talk about? - Oh, everything - the Unit, of course; its shortcomings, what it can do, what it can't do, what it does. Unit news from abroad, Unit gossip, FWRS [6] affairs and their iniquities. Meetings with outside people. Books occasionally, history, religion occasionally. Are Quakers Christians? Are we Christians? Our friends, our relations. Films, occasionally plays. The war sometimes. Everything and nothing. [........]

All love Ralph

And here he writes further about how he learned to get along and manage, all a prelude to imbuing him with the confidence and leadership skills to go abroad. A drink at the famous Prospect of Whitby didn't hurt either…….

Above all, somehow we all learned to rub along together and I gradually learnt how to manage, starting every morning at 9.0am with an officers' meeting held in Room 115, discussing the day's plans with Michael (Barratt Brown) and the rest, while every Saturday we'd have longer ones to plan further ahead, with once a month meetings of all the provincial Section Leaders. As for the Hostel itself, although we had all sorts of crises from bugs in the women's bedrooms to £15 being stolen from someone's locker, nonetheless we were able to enjoy ourselves too.

We entertained many visitors and, unless they were Quakers, no 'shelter crawl' was complete without a visit to the Prospect of Whitby, the Good Samaritan or the London Tavern. And then there was the East End itself. We were always out and about and got to know it well, often driving in the blackout down the wide, straight roads to Whitechapel with their wonderful Jewish shops, past the rather grimy parks en-route to Wapping and the towering warehouses, and so on to the Prospect of Whitby, overlooking the river and the passing ships making their way to the East India Docks. In an odd way we came not only attached to it but also to love it.

"No 'shelter crawl' was complete without a visit to the Prospect." The Prospect of Whitby is an historic public house on the banks of the Thames at Wapping. It lays claim to being the site of the oldest riverside tavern, dating from around 1520.
Photograph Green King

[Textual: This is another of my father's undated letters but the clues are that he was still visiting some of the camps such as Flaunden in the Chilterns, which puts it late July and the end of the 11ᵗʰ camp and the 12ᵗʰ coming down to London also dates it about then. With help from local historian Shaun Burgin I learned that the camp site was at Stagg Farm Holiday Camp, which from 1929 had been owned by a John and Johannah Major. It had started out as a mix of wooden chalets and tents for holidaymakers and was sold in 1950.]

My father was still watchful over the out of town Rest Centres and obviously enjoyed visiting them, and joy in the love of my mother keeps him buoyant as always……

Saturday 26ᵗʰ July 1941

My dearest

I have been out to our camp at Flaunden to see David and Molly Tod, the wardens there, about various things. It was a perfectly lousy day, pouring without cease all day. But it's a wide straight road and it was a pleasant drive. They have a tough job, keeping a campful of young people amused, especially on such a day as this. The Edmunds, wardens at Cheveley have not proved very successful, and so the Tods will shortly be badly wanted to take over from them at Cheveley. In turn we will urgently need to try and find people to replace David and Molly at Flaunden. Oh the whirligig!

Tomorrow (Sunday) I am on orderly duty and then hope to go to tea with Millior. Things are not easy here, in the present absence of blitzes, everyone tends to get slack and it's all rather too easy going. The 12ᵗʰ Camp has now ended, and they have gone on to further hospital training, and the 11ᵗʰ Camp are coming here by lorry from Birmingham.

Did I tell you that I have been reading *A Memoir* by Neave Brayshaw? [7] He died last year in sad circumstances, when hit by a car in the black-out near his home in Scarborough. My parents knew him at Woodbrooke in the very early days and thought highly of him. He was a fine man I think, and if you can get hold of a copy, I do recommend it.

I am so sorry that my letters to you are so poor of late. It's mostly that life is made up of a round of rather similar and unimportant things, which are of no particular interest to anyone, such as writing letters, endless dull meetings, talking to people about apparently trivial matters, and meal times with people all grumbling about this and that.

There are only a few things in life that really matter I suppose: sleep and food of course; but books and poetry and some special people, and special memories, and a hope that there will be an after the war, and the thought of you. You are such a tower of strength to me, a true rock of ages, and anchor. You are ever in my thoughts as the one real true good thing in life.

Just the fact of you being there and loving me, means that there is still love and truth and beauty and goodness and joy. It gives me faith in God, because I experience his love through knowing you. You are a great inspiration and strength to me. How can I ever thank you enough?

May God keep you safe always.
Your ever loving Ralph.

———

Flaunden Holiday Camp

Above and below - Flaunden Holiday camp 1940's

A ready-made holiday camp was found at Flaunden in the Chilterns where summer camps were organised for children from bombed out areas of London. David and Molly Tod were the first wardens.

Photographs by courtesy of Shaun Burgun and Flaunden Parish Council

Flying Squads and Vans at the Ready

The Queen's Messenger Flying Squads
Preparing food for distribution to those made homeless by the blitz,
with FRB third from left inspecting the set up.
Photograph Friends House Library

Vans at the ready in Gordon Square for ambulance and relief work.
Photograph Friends House Library

Chapter 12
Relief Work – Part 2
July –November 1941

From the end of July until November, when Tom Tanner went to America, my father continued being Relief Officer and visiting centres, and trying to find more overseas work.

My parents must have had a weekend together towards the end of July, probably in London, with just the two of them, for here my father expresses delight at the 'perfect visit', when cares seems to vanish under my mother's love and support......

Wednesday 30th July 1941

My dearest
I thank thee so much for your letter. I too thought that our last time together was a perfect visit. I do love you more every time I see you and feel a wonderful happiness and freedom when we are together. God bless you for being such a perfect wife.

Whilst I was up in Birmingham I had lunch with Keith Linney at Kingsmead College[1] and sorted out some business and then went over to the Northfield camp for a short time to do one or two things and saw Llew's father, Dr Rutter, who kindly ran me into town.

There was no food on the train, so I had to have something at Euston, when I got in. Since then I have been pretty occupied as I am now on the Executive and General Purposes Committee. Don't forget that you were going to have your photo taken. I am so glad to have that picture of David with your mother, which is such a good one. He really is an angel now.

I think it is a great idea for you to go down to Monmouth, and hope you have a lovely time. With a bit of luck I might be able to come down for a week end. All my love to David and thank you again for a glorious stay.
I'll write again soon, dear love, Ralph

———

But even when my father was stationed in London, and getting leave from time to time, arrangements could be difficult, as is obvious in the following exchange of letters. My mother had gone for a short break to Monmouth, and had expected my father to follow her, as he had hoped to do. But the exigencies of war time travel proved the trip impossible, much to the chagrin of both sides and some recriminations. This was part of the reality and heartache of war.

The house in Monmouth belonged to Charles Dobinson, who was Headmaster of King Edward's School, Kings Heath. Before my mother got married, she had worked as secretary to him, and he had become and remained a close friend, attending their wedding and indeed in later years I was at Leighton Park with their son, Humphrey. They kindly lent the house in Monmouth to my mother and Grandmother in the summer of 1941, hoping that it would be a nice get away for all the family.

Unfortunately, it proved a somewhat contentious issue on two counts. Firstly, my mother had expected my father to join her there, so making it a time for a family reunion. But due to the logistics of travel and his FAU commitments, it proved impossible during a short leave period, for him to get there in a reasonable time, before needing to get back again. So, much to Mum's disappointment, it just wasn't feasible. Secondly it proved not to be a very suitable place for children. So all in all it was not the happiest of times. It's just one of many incidents where, due to separation, reliance on letters, not phone calls, small things can be blown up out of proportion.

Saturday, 2nd August 1941

Dearest
[.....] As if life wasn't difficult enough already...I am so sorry for all your troubles in Monmouth dear one, and you are a brick to take it all so philosophically. I have been trying without success to get you on the telephone, and will go on trying.

I'm afraid I won't after all be able to get up next week-end due to work here. But even if I could, the trains are impossible, as there appear to be none from Monmouth on the Sunday. Then I thought I might be able to come to Birmingham on Thursday week and come on to you on the Friday and then come back with you on the Saturday, returning to London on Sunday. And I will certainly do that if you'd like, though as far as I can see, I wouldn't be able to get to Monmouth before 3 or 4 in the afternoon. However I do it, it appears that it would involve 5 or 6 hours of a short week-end travelling there and as long again getting back. But either way, unfortunately next week-end is impossible, as I have just got too much on.

I'll try ringing you again and discuss all this tomorrow.

Thanks again for your letter and card.
God bless you, Ralph

My father explains further the logistical difficulties of joining up in Monmouth and manages to soothe the situation.....

Thursday, 7th August 1941

My darling
[.....] I am afraid you are rather cross with me about this week-end business. But as I mentioned, to get down to Monmouth from here, will take rather more than 6 hours and getting back almost the same. And even if I put off my Saturday engagement, I can't get away before late Friday evening, which makes things almost impossible. Believe me I have tried it every which way and it really seems as though it can't be managed. I'm so very sorry that this disappointment should have come now, as you have had such a tough time coping in Monmouth, and I am truly upset that things should have gone so wrong. As usual, you have coped wonderfully well and been so good about it, that I am full of admiration and gratitude for your courage.

Truly, Unit life is just so busy at the moment that I seem never to be free. I work all day, often right up to 7.0 o'clock in the evening and after supper too, with people coming into ones room till all hours. I do get very tired and very fed up. Some days everything seems to go wrong and I ache to be with you so much, that I feel I can't go on. You mean so much to me and are all the world to me, and what makes life worth living. Honestly, if I could drop everything and be with you, believe me I would.

I get so fed up with myself sometimes, with all my shortcomings, making silly mistakes. I think I am just a failure. I don't know why you are so nice to me? I don't deserve it. But the one bright spark, is that you do still love me, and that is all that matters. So be kind and just go on loving me, and all will be alright.

I must finish and go to bed now, as it's nearly 11.30 and I feel so tired. All my love to you and to David and Antony. Ever yours Ralph.
PS Rumour has it that Churchill is in America, though I can't say if it is true or not.

———

During this time, the question of overseas projects was also developing, but as always with such FAU schemes, the time between conception and execution was lengthy. Ethiopia or Abyssinia as it was still known then, was a case in point. The possibility of sending an ambulance Unit out there, had been first mooted back in April of 1941, while the war in East Africa was raging. It was discussed with the War Office and in September of that year a party of 40 was assembled who would assist the British Army doctors, and training in tropical medicine began at Livingstone College in Leytonstone. Transport was arranged to ship them out there for September, but delays began almost immediately, as negotiations continued between the War Office and the Foreign Office, as to where responsibility lay, now that the Emperor, Haile Selassie had returned, following the defeat of the Italians. Meanwhile the group continued their training at Moorfields Eye Hospital as well as learning about venereal and tropical diseases at Guy's, St Thomas's and Middlesex Hospitals.

After months of waiting, an agreement was at last signed at the end of January 1942, involving the British Army standing down, with a small contingent helping to train the Ethiopian Army. This meant the FAU would be more independent, and with two doctors - Michael Vaizey and Anthony Husband – available, they were formally invited by the Emperor and prepared to set sail in late July 1942. However, no sooner had they left Liverpool than they broke down.

Following extensive repairs, they set off again three weeks later, only to break down a second time! In fact there were a further thirty hold ups, before they all eventually arrived in November of 1942. Even then, with most of the thousand or so Italian doctors having left, the country was desperately short of doctors and with the agreement of the Emperor, many more were recruited. So the Medical Directorate had its hands full with the problems of a country which was trying to stagger to its feet after eight years of war and foreign domination.

Emperor Haile Selassie
Following the Italian invasion of his country in 1935, he lived in exile in the UK.
After the defeat of the Italians in 1941, he returned to Ethiopia.
Photograph Alamy

The next letter is one of my father's long letters and covers a wealth of topics, from questions of leave, to where my mother should live – even a suggestion about Banbury, which although a pleasant place, its only other relevance would be that it was possibly equidistant between London and Wolverhampton! – choosing a party for Ethiopia, the possibility of his own appointment abroad, and making peace with Germany........

Saturday, August 9th 1941

My dearest

Thank you so much for your letters. I am sorry that Monmouth has not proved to be all that it might. I love the photo you sent me of you and I would love to have an enlargement. It is so good of you.

I am so sorry that I couldn't get away, but as I said on the phone, I have so much on at the moment and Monmouth is such a long journey that I would scarcely be with you, before I had to return again. From London to Monmouth takes nearly 7 hours, which seems a waste of valuable time, if I can see you at Wolverhampton. Next week is not going to be very convenient either, so I think the best arrangement would be for me to go to Birmingham on August 21st and spend that night at the Camp, and then come on to you at Wolverhampton on the Friday the 22nd, if Win can kindly put me up. I must go to Northfield, as I can't very well be away twice and it seems most sensible really to combine the two visits, don't you think?

Regarding where you should live.....it's very kind of Winifred to offer to have you, though I can't say that I think you'd be altogether happy there, nor is it what I would call an entirely safe area. But I do see that it has its advantages. On the other hand if you are going to Wolverhampton, you might as well go back home, where we have a better shelter and at least it is in a no more dangerous area than Lea Road. If you stay at Wolverhampton until I get my next leave, then I could help you move back to Linden Road. By then we should know better what the autumn and winter have in store.

The point about Banbury (possibly an intermediate place) is that it would be a house to yourself and it is not that expensive as houses go and is fairly near London. I understand that you are reluctant to make another move, and that it may be lonely, and that we might have to take it for longer than we want. But I don't think we should turn it down out of hand. We had rather a bad week trying to choose the Ethiopian party. There were three long Executive Meetings, and what with all the other work as well, I was just about finished. So I was doubly glad to get your letter on Wednesday, which was a happy end to a bad day. It has now been decided that Richey Mounsey is going to be in charge of the Ethiopian party with Jack Frazer as second in command. I have got to like Jack enormously, and shall miss him very much. I know he would love me to have gone with him, and I should really like to have gone with him too. I think it will be an exciting job. But the committee didn't ask me, partly because I've only just started on this job, and I don't quite see who else could have taken over from me if I'd gone.

If they had asked me, I should have refused, as while there is hard work here, I ought to do it, especially while there are single men who can go abroad. Besides, I should miss you and the children so dreadfully. No, you are not holding me back. I know you'd let me go if the time comes when I must. But it hasn't come yet. I'd go if I had to, but how I'd face leaving you, who mean all the world to me, I do not know. Poor dear, it would be even harder on you. But it hasn't come yet. I am afraid Jack's girl will miss him very much. How hellish it is with all the good chaps going abroad. What's the work going to be and who's going to be left to do it? War Vics want a woman with children to look after a small hostel containing other children at Godalming. There would be assistance. Don't suppose you'd like to take the job, would you?!!

Have you seen the edition of The Friend about Yearly Meeting? I haven't, but it appears to have been quite a good one. Smaller than usual, of course, but more compact or 'gathered' in Quaker language! Roger Wilson gave a very good account of it at a War Vics lunch on Friday. He said that the session on Industrial conscription of all sorts was good, and that the meetings were held in a spirit of deep concern, although no-one could see the future at all clearly. Many at YM were anxious that India should be given a definite date when she should have Dominion status granted and a deputation is being sent to the PM.

Apparently there was quite a division over an immediate peace. Some felt that with our obligations as a country, a peace with Hitler was out of the question. I whole heartedly agree. Peace now would only mean that we would become a martyr nation. There were some, however, who seemed to think that a peace with Hitler could be negotiated. I am quite certain that they are totally wrong.

I see in today's paper that one of the Birmingham firemen who was there with me, has been awarded a decoration. He is the same man who saved John Terry's life. They were together in the cellar when the station was hit.

I can't wait to see you in a fortnight's time. You are such a perfect wife and have made my life very special: it is glorious for me to realise that such a person as you exists and loves me. May God keep you safe.

Give my love to David, and I am so glad that he was brave about the injection.

Dearest love, Ralph

PS love to your mother and thank her for being so helpful. But then she always is.

Dr Llewellyn Rutter and Win with our Grandmother in Lea Road garden.
Barlow family archive

Joan Barlow 1941

The photograph that my father loved of my mother
"I love the photo you sent me. Can you send me an enlargement, please ?"

[Textual: Another letter completely undated and with not too many clues, but seeing the reference to Duncan's departure having being cancelled, places it somewhere between the last letter and the next!]

I'm not quite sure as to why they are cancelling Mr Tritsch's letting, unless they had at this point decided to go back to Linden Road themselves. Indeed, they did later change their mind, which illustrates how difficult it was for them to decide where exactly would be best or indeed safest for my mother to stay with us two children.......

Probably late August 1941 – Students Hostel.

My dearest

I am so sorry to have been such a bad correspondent this week, I do hope that you will have got safely home to Wolverhampton by the time this reaches you.

In reply to the various points in your letter:

- No, I really hope I shan't have to stay in this damned job for ever. I do get so fed up with the Unit at times, and wonder how on earth I'll be able to stick it indefinitely. I am enclosing a copy of the latest Chronicle, though it's not one of our better editions.

- No, the Abyssinian party hasn't gone yet, and the China party has been cancelled again. I was expecting to see Duncan to say good bye, and no-one yet seems to know when they will get off.

- Yes, I wrote to Mr Tritsch to give him notice, and said we shall be wanting the apples – though he is welcome to some as we won't be able to take them all away.

- You didn't comment about Banbury as a possibility. What are your thoughts?

I went up to Northfield on Wednesday night, for a short visit, arriving about 6.45pm, and getting back here at 1.30am the next day. They were having a very good end of camp supper, and it was very pleasant to be there again, if only for a short time, and without any responsibility. I even got to know one of two of the camp members, and Heather Cadbury and the Poulters (Quaker family) were also there. I made a short and completely fatuous speech on the Unit and wished them all well!

On the train back I read an excellent Penguin on *European Sculpture and Painting*[*2] by Eric Newton which is very good, if inevitably rather potted. Do try and get hold of it, as it's well worth reading.

It almost looks as though we are going to let the Russians be beaten without doing anything, just as the Poles were. Oh God, how I wish I were with you. I get so down sometimes, with the state of the war, and the Unit and missing you. When will it all end?

My dearest love, Ralph

Still continued uncertainty about getting the Ethiopian party off, or even a possible Russian group, necessitating more high level talks at the FO and the Russian Embassy, throwing more doubt on any FAU overseas trips. There are worries about Unit members' marital problems, and as my father talks so much about some of his colleagues, he hopes that my mother can come to London to meet them. With the thought that both of them are now much wiser than pre-war, he contemplates what sort of world they will both come back to, and in which his children will grow up. Having been over-protected himself, he wants them to have a good University education and to travel when they grow up and be more independent than he was......

[*2] I still have the book, now somewhat fragile with much reading!

c. Saturday, September 5th 1941 – Students' Hostel

 My dearest

[.......] It seems as though the Ethiopian party may not go after all. We have spent some time recently in the War Office and the Foreign Office, but there are very difficult hitches to deal with. It's very worrying and disappointing for everyone concerned. However, we are going to the Russian Embassy on Monday, but I am very doubtful if anything will come of it.

It's been a fairly full week, though not as bad as some, except for the orderly day I did, which was quite fun, but it made for a long day.

Please thank David very much for his card. [....] I presume that you still have that book for me to give David on his birthday.

I walked down to the river the other night with Richard Symonds. I must say Tower Bridge looks so grand at night. I've come to like Richard more and more. He is a clever person, in fact almost brilliant, and has considerable charm. If anything he is perhaps, a bit unsure of himself, and I am afraid he is not very happy in his marriage, poor lad. He went to Rugby and Oxford and then spent some time in Spain during the civil war. I think he is keen to go abroad, but his wife is against it. God knows how we shall manage to get people abroad if Ethiopia is off. Sometimes I feel very weighed down by so much responsibility, but people are very kind to me.

I do wonder what life will be like after the war. We have both learnt so much, that it should be richer. I think we must try and travel and see more of the world, and meet more people. I'd like you to meet these Unit people that I have got to know. I also want David to have a full life and to get about more and do more than I did. I grew up too late and was too long under mother's influence. I never really grew up till we married. My God what a lot of good that did me, and how grateful I am to you for it all.

Today is such a lovely day, I have decided to take the day off and to go out. I'm so looking forward to next week-end and to seeing you all. I hope nothing crops up here to stop that happening. Dear love, Ralph

It seems that the proposed weekend leave of August 22nd was postponed until September 13th weekend, presumably because my mother was still in Monmouth. And perhaps because of the disappointment of my father being unable to get there, he was on extra good behaviour, as on this occasion his leave in Wolverhampton seems to have been a particularly happy one........

Saturday, September 20th 1941 – Students Hospital

 My dearest

Thank you so much for your letter. It was very sweet of you to write so soon. Thank you too for such a glorious weekend. I enjoyed every minute of it: the long walks we had and the theatre. I love you so much and it is heaven to be with you. David too is quite adorable and Antony is fast growing up. I do miss you all terribly. I will come again as soon as I can. Tell David that I was so proud of him and thank him very much for the postcard, I am glad that you are going to see mother; she always loves to see you and the children.

Since my return I have been desperately busy, often up until midnight as well as Sunday and Monday nights, and will probably be so again tonight. But I don't mind, as it stops me thinking how much miss you.

The journey home was fine, and although the carriage was full, I got a seat and enjoyed a comfortable trip, reading the Russian history, which is excellent and also the John Buchan book, which you so kindly gave me. As always his books are very readable, and there is something about his writing that appeals to me very much. You should try and read it. Happily, I managed to get a bit of supper at Euston on arrival.

I have not so far been able to write to all the people I said I would, but will try and do so this evening. Seeing you so settled with W&L, I've come round to thinking that it would after all be best if you continue to stay at Wolverhampton, so I hope your talk with Honor about this will be an easy one. As soon I know how this went, I will write to her and thank her for all her kindness. Your letter requesting the Ration book didn't arrive in time, but I now enclose it.

Dear love, Ralph

Left and right:
Duncan Wood in 1941. Not long before he went out to China.

My father and he had been close friends since school days and remained so all their lives.

Duncan could be smoking the pipe my father gave him as a farewell gift! (see next page and end note)

Photographs: (left) Friends House Library; (right) courtesy of Rachel Malloch.

My mother was very intuitive, and knowing that my father's oldest friend, Duncan was coming to say his 'good byes' before travelling to China, would have sensed how saddening this would have been for him, and that being able to speak to each other directly, would cheer him up!

Duncan's daughter Rachel, found a quote from her father's own war time diary for September 28th: "We arrived at Euston with heaps of time to spare [...] and managed to get a table compartment, where I wrote my will, which Ralph and Brandon (Cadbury) signed. (Brother) Ross, John Burtt, Edna Bailey, Freddie Royal and others were also there to see us off."

The 'girl from Moffatt' (in Dumfries) mentioned in the next letter, was Katharine Knight, who after the war became Mrs Wood and so Rachel's mother........

Sunday, September 28th 1941 – London Hostel

My dearest

It was very clever and sensible of you to ring me last night, and it cheered me up a lot just to hear your voice, as I am sure you guessed it would. The last few days seem to have been very hectic in one way or another. All quite minor crises, but not always easy to settle. I don't think I'm doing that well, but with so much to cope with, I do feel as if I could run anything after the war!

As I told you Duncan came in to see me late last night and didn't leave until about 12.30. As always it was very good to see him. Just after he left there were planes flying over and gunfire; thankfully no bombs, but by the time I got to sleep it was after 1.0 o'clock, and then I had to be up by 5.30am for orderly duty. I then went over to Euston to see him off.

It will be very hard not having him here, and I shall miss him terribly. He is my oldest and next to you, my dearest friend. So many of my and our good times have been with him and he is in so many of my memories. I do hope he will get back safely. I gave him a pipe[2] as a small token of friendship. Ross was there to see him off as well. Duncan told me that he has a girl who lives in Moffatt, though he didn't tell me anything about her, except that he is obviously pretty happy about her, and I am so glad for him. He sent his love to you.

I had a card from Horace, who seems to have been having a good time. And I have had a letter from mother who has kindly sent me a cheque for £5.0, which all helps. All being well, I will come up and see you on the w/e of October 18th. Give my love to David and Antony. Your ever loving Ralph.

Tuesday, 30th September ....Sorry, this should have been posted yesterday. Thank you so much for the very welcome chocs and cigarettes.

The start and end of this next letter concerns itself with comparative trivia – thanks for the gift of a tie, and sending out the Annual report - but the central body of it deals with serious matters of the day. An instance of authority in the shape of my father, having to cope with the everyday problems of young people living in London during the war, exhibiting how changing morals reflected the times in which they lived – one chap carrying on with a married woman, another soliciting for homosexual [3] men in Piccadilly - then and for years after, a famous pick up area. In retrospect of course, with changes in the law, it now seems sad, but then quite a problem for someone like my father, fairly inexperienced in such matters, but showing considerable compassion on his part, I think..........

Thursday, 2nd October 1941 - Gordon Square

Dearest
Just a quick note to thank you so much for your letter and the tie. It is such a nice one, and I did need it. Yesterday, Horace had a meeting with us, to talk about post-war training. All very interesting, but right at the moment somewhat impracticable! But as always, it was good to see him.

We have had a couple of crises here recently. Firstly, one of the Unit men has been carrying on with a married woman. We decided it would be best to move him, and after some protestations, he has agreed to go to Birmingham. So you had better watch out!

Secondly, another Unit man was arrested in Piccadilly, for making 'improper advances to male persons'! What happens? FRB – who else? - bails him out of Savile Row Police Station at 11.15pm for £25. I then take him round to Alfred's, who is naturally in bed asleep and none too thrilled to be woken! FRB gets home at 1.30am. Poor chap, I felt sorry for him. We arranged for him to be represented in court and he has now been remanded in custody for a week.

It is still pretty busy here, especially at week-ends. We have a meeting tomorrow, Sunday, to discuss who should receive copies of the Annual Report. The list so far includes, Sandy Parnis, Treasurer, myself, the Editor of the Chronicle, Robin Whitworth (formerly of the BBC), but because the Report contains our main annual appeal, well-known people are especially useful. So everyone vied as to who knew the most celebrities!

It has now been decided, following the success of Coventry, to send a new section up to Liverpool to do relief work, under Robin's supervision. I am booking the weekend of the 18th October, and will try and come on the Friday, fairly early. I hope mother's visit is a success. Thinking of you…dear love to you and to D&A. Love from Ralph

My mother has obviously written suggesting that she would like to be doing something useful that utilised her gifts, finding unlike my father's busy life, that hers is dull in comparison. My father rebukes her, saying that she is doing the most important and most difficult job of all in bringing up 'the world of the future'. Living away from my father, on whose support she relies, she is really seeking reassurance that she is loved and valued for what she is doing……

Thursday, October 9th 1941 – London Hostel

My dearest
Thank you for your letter, though forgive me for saying that you are being plain stupid. You may think you'd like to have a more interesting, or as you see it 'more useful' job, such as the one I am doing. But in many ways mine is so much easier. You, my dearest, have the real job and if I may say so, by far the more difficult. I know that sometimes it may seem dull in comparison, but part of the world of the future will be in the hands of David and Antony, and so much depends on their present upbringing, which you can do better than anyone. There can be no question that the job you are doing is one which only you can do, and one which is immensely worthwhile. Have courage and don't let it get you down. The lives of our two children owe everything to you.

My dearest one, thou knows how I love you. As the mother of two fine children you look younger now than ever – more so. You remain as young, charming and intelligent as the Joan I first met. So don't be silly and stupid my darling. You are ever lovely in my eyes.

Please thank David for his card and give him my love. […..] I do hope you are over your cold and feeling better now. I am so glad mother's visit was a success. When I next come up, let's go to the theatre and perhaps a drive out in to the country. We must cheer you up!

We are pretty busy this end, and Roger Wilson and I are aiming to go and see the wife of the Russian Ambassador, the redoubtable Madame Agniya Maisky, to sort out what is needed in her country. Incidentally, I have quite enjoyed being an Orderly, as I am in a pleasant shift, with Eric Green, Leonard Elliott, William Barnes and Angela and myself. I'll have you know that I have peeled more carrots than you would have believed possible!

The chap I mentioned who got arrested in Piccadilly, thankfully got off without being locked up, which is very fortunate and I am pleased about. So life here is full of unusual problems, which though occasionally wearing, are nonetheless challenging. I am already pretty tired and still have several things I have to do before supper. I think I will take part of this Sunday off, as sometimes one just needs to get away from the place. I'm so looking forward to being with you on the 18th.
Dear love, Ralph

Both my parents loved the theatre, and passed the love on to me, and Sir Barry Jackson's famous repertory theatre (widely known as 'The Rep') in Birmingham, was amongst the best in England, where they loved to go and in later life took us too.......

Tuesday, October 14th 1941 – London Hostel

My dear, [....] This will only be a short note, as I shall be seeing you on Friday. Yes, do meet me in Birmingham and then we can go to the Rep, which would be grand. I shall come up on Thursday and go first to the Camp at the Manor and spend that night with Keith Linney. I have various things to do Friday morning, and then I will meet you in town for tea on the Friday, which will be splendid. I am looking forward to seeing you so much. All my love, Ralph

[Textual: Again this next letter is undated, though references to Liverpool places it somewhere around the month of October, and as Duncan left on September 28th, to have reached Singapore and written to Horace would probably place it at least mid-October.]

My father left straight after Wolverhampton to go to inspect the Unit section in Liverpool under Robin Whitworth. The reference to 'the new baby' is to his sister, Millior, being pregnant with their first daughter, who grew up to be cousin Anna......

Tuesday, 22nd October 1941 – on the train back from Liverpool

My dearest

Please excuse my writing, but I am doing this on the train on my way back from Liverpool. I immensely enjoyed our weekend together. It was perfect. Thank you so much for being such a wonderful wife to me.

After I left you I had a good journey up to Liverpool and, arrived at all my destinations punctually. In fact everything went off well, and I had lunch with Robin Whitworth on Monday and attended a FWRS meeting that afternoon. Tuesday morning I spent with Roger Wilson and Russell Brayshaw (Chairman FRSC [4]). They are a good lot and I have full confidence in them. I eventually got back home about 7.0pm, by which time I was pretty exhausted.

Since my return I have not really done anything of interest. I enclose a letter from Millior and I will try and ring her this evening and have a talk about borrowing her flat for when you next come down. Failing that, Richard Symonds would probably lend us his place for a week-end, which I believe could work, though it might present catering and other difficulties if David joins us. I'll write again when I have spoken with Milli.

Thank you for the bird cutting. Horace has also forwarded a long bird letter of Duncan's, written from Singapore. He seems to have seen a fine lot of birds. I'm most envious!

I really did enjoy my visit so much – you are an angel and I love you more and more, if that's possible. I am glad the visit to Swarthmore Road was a success. I'm very pleased about Millior and her new baby. All my love to David and see if he remembers the 4 things he has to do with his tricycle!

Dear love Ralph

––––

My father now Deputy Chairman has many new responsibilities, which involve meeting high ranking people from the FO and the Embassies in an endeavor to place FAU men overseas. My father worries that the power may go to his head. Indeed later on, when Tom returns in the New Year, he momentarily forgets he is no longer number one! However, anyone less power hungry than Ralph Barlow would be hard to find! Already planning Christmas together, but a plea to be exempted from the annual pantomime.......

Saturday, 25th October 1941 – London Hostel

My dearest

It was lovely to hear your voice last night. Thank you so much for ringing, and I am sorry I sounded rather glum, but life is so full of problems at the moment, that everything just seems black and difficult. However, I am alright really.

I have not done anything very noteworthy lately. On Thursday I had quite a useful interview with the RAMC Colonel, who suggests that the Unit might undertake vocational guidance work in the army. Yesterday I had an interview with an extremely efficient and friendly woman, who is high up in the BRCS [5] - a snob organisation! (as Lord Dillon used to say!) – about whether or not our women could be considered as VADs (Voluntary Aid Detachments).

She told me all about Lady Limerick's[6] and Lady Louis Mountbatten's[7] recent visit to the USA, where they went to raise funds for the Red Cross, and "how busy they were and how well they had done", especially the former. Dick (Symonds) says the BRCS, to whom Lady L belongs, really hate Lady Louis like poison and are barely on speaking terms! They accuse her of carrying on with black men, or some such unspeakable crime!! As Mrs M would say – 'Imagine'!

As I mentioned the other day, various crises have arisen recently connected with the kitchens and orderlies and homosexuality and section meetings. But in a way I actually enjoy this job, but being Deputy Director, the power goes to one's head, which is bad. I don't know when Tom will get back, as clippers are being delayed in Lisbon. But the sooner the better, as I seem to do everything very badly. I am continually making all sorts of stupid mistakes, and I'm often not nice enough to people or sufficiently thoughtful. And I don't pay enough attention to my religion. Perhaps if I could get back home again with you, I might be a better person.

I went out with Angela on Thursday for the first time in weeks. We went to Oxford Street, Studio 1 to see *Mayerling,* a French film with Charles Boyer and Danielle Darrieux, which was quite good. We had a meal afterwards, which was quite pleasant. She is good company, but she is not you and never could be. God bless you my dear. I do love you so much and you are such a good influence on me. I just long to see you and to be back home again. It will be so lovely seeing you at Christmas, and I will try and behave nicely! But do I really have to go to the pantomime?! Dear love for now, Ralph

Air raid shelters were being established all over the country – Birmingham, Coventry and in October 1941 in Liverpool, under Robin Whitworth. Though my father had just come back from Liverpool, the bombing there had been so severe, the work had greatly increased with many more Unit people needed. So following a request from Robin my father makes another visit there……

Tuesday, 27th October 1941 – On the train back from Liverpool

Dearest

[…..] At Robin's request, I came back up to Liverpool yesterday, as it is such a busy time with all the bombing going on here. I've just interviewed all 20 of the new section men separately and been to see one of the shelters and talked at length to Robin (Whitworth). I am beginning to like him more than I thought I would. He is friendly, amusing and I think very capable. He had a very good job with the BBC, arranging feature programmes, before he joined the Unit. He and his wife have a house over near Saintbury in the Cotswolds, not far from Chipping Camden.

I must say the section is wonderfully happy and content under his guidance and seems to be doing excellent work. The shelter is in Birkenhead, and can hold about 2,000. It already has a great number of people in it, but it is pretty squalid. There is obviously a great opportunity here, but it's going to be a big job for Robin.

They are quite close to the sea, which is pleasant, but the damage along the docks is absolutely horrific. Houses and warehouses have either been totally demolished or are completely burnt out, though there is still a tremendous quantity of shipping using the port. Liverpool is a cold wind swept place, and the weather has been miserable, raining the whole time I have been here.

I am writing this in the train, which is absolutely packed. I expected I would have to stand, but I walked through the train and luckily managed to find a seat in the dining car and had some tea. It looks as though I shall be able to stay put until dinner, which I shall also have as we don't get in till 10.0pm. It will give me a little time to finish reading E M Forster's *A Passage to India*, which I am greatly enjoying. I think he is a wonderful writer. All my love, Ralph

The Liverpool Docks, showing some of the terrible damage done to the docks on May 3 1941.
"[....] the damage along the docks is absolutely horrific."
Photograph Liverpool Library

———

[Textual: This next letter is dated just as Sunday, and the internal clues are tricky, but it is definitely during his time as Deputy Director while Tom was still away in America, viz. the reference to "I am in charge of the Unit" and the "responsibility of that." Other clues are the reference to Roger Wilson's brother Geoffrey being in Russia with Stafford Cripps, which he was from May 1940 till mid-1942, while he also refers to Lord Beaverbrook (aka 'the Beaver') attending a high level conference in Moscow, which he did with Avril Harriman, Roosevelt's special envoy to Europe from September 29th with a communique being issued on October 1st 1941.]

It would seem that this rather sad letter is referring back to my father's last visit, and my mother's feelings must have been building up for a while. It is a typical example of the tensions of being apart, and the difficulties of adapting to a week-end leave in Wolverhampton after the adrenalin filled tribulations of being Chairman. My mother was obviously eagerly anticipating having him home, and expecting him to suddenly be the bright happy husband from before the war, playing with the children. My father, weighed down with all the responsibilities of suddenly being number one, and coping with all the concomitant problems, and then having to adapt and fit in with his in-laws in a strange house, and be the pipe-smoking contented family man, inevitably found it difficult.......

Sunday, November 2nd 1941 – Students Hostel

My darling

[.....] I must say I was pretty upset by your letter and I think I ought to try and say a few things about it. First of all let me apologise for myself last week-end. I know I was a failure, and I am so sorry. Please don't blame yourself. Why was I such a failure? I will try and explain.

a. Life here is all absorbing and very narrow. We eat, live and sleep in the Unit. I don't have time for much else.
b. As Deputy Director, my job is very responsible and rather wearing. I am in charge of the Unit and that implies a good deal.
c. I do sometimes get very tired and very depressed, and physical tiredness does often produce shocking mental reaction, which makes one feel pretty awful.
d. I work very long hours and I get a fair amount of criticism.

I won't say I don't get something of a kick out of it, because I do. But generally, while as a job it is, undoubtedly, of great interest, as a life it's very narrow. It leaves out most of my former pleasures: no wife, no children and little reading; no flowers, no birds or garden; hardly any real friends, though heaps of good chaps. As a result there tends to be a generally hard-boiled, pseudo-cynical outlook, which perhaps one too readily adopts. Your life is so different.

For all you say, you are still in touch with normal relationships. When I come to you, my own life seems so unimportant; the things I spend my time doing, seem trivial. I feel that you are carrying all our responsibility, of money and children, while I am shirking it. My horizon is so narrowed, that I am dull and uninteresting. In London my job looks important, but in Wolverhampton it seems pretty trivial.

On this occasion I can only plead that I was desperately tired and not very well, and somehow I couldn't adjust myself. I felt a worm, unworthy of your life and useless as a father. It wasn't that I was too bored to talk, just that I was running on empty. My dear one, it's not your fault. How could it be? Our love is not drifting; you were **not** to blame. You are still the same brave, capable, loving and charming Joan. Our love is there and always will be. If anything it's I who have changed.

No, not in essentials, not in my enduring love for you, but my life is so narrow and so full, and I don't have enough time to devote to those things that are really eternal, such as our love. Darling, I am so sorry, but bear with me. Keep our love where it has always been. Go on loving me as I love you. Sometimes I dare not love you too much, as the expectation and aftermath of a leave period, exhausts me so much. Dearest, we can never grow apart; we cannot, not now. Our love is too firmly grounded and you are too good. Dearest one I love you as much and more than ever. Do not blame yourself. You are an angel still. Blame me, but go on loving me as you always have. Don't worry about my 'clever friends' as you call them.

They are all as narrow as I am, and life doesn't consist of Oxford and Cambridge cleverness. A dear wife and children are the only things that matter. You need never ever fear comparison. I may go out with some of the women here occasionally, they cheer me up. But you are the only one I love or could ever love, now and always. You are my wife, married for five years; married in the face of opposition. You are my Joan, the mother of our children. Hell, do not be silly. Do you really think I could ever stop loving you? If anyone's stupid it's me. If anyone's clever, it's you. Above all you are more beautiful and lovelier than anyone in this hostel. If you could only see most of them, you would not worry!

I know your life can be pretty bloody, and I have to say that too much of living in someone else's house, would leave me pretty low too. But you have courage and cheerfulness and all the qualities and virtues a man wants. All I want anyway. So forgive me for being such a bloody fool, but that's no reason why you should be one too. Please don't write me any more such letters. How can I be bored with you – with Joan? Christ, my dearest. Don't be so silly!

Thank you for all the little things you have sent, and please thank mother for the mending and socks she sent too. I am, so sorry you had a fall getting off the bus. How terribly worrying for you. My darling, I'll ring you tonight to see that you are alright. Do take extra care my dearest. What should I or the children ever do without you?

Dick Symonds had rather an amusing time yesterday with a Colonel from the RAMC. I have been wanting for some time to arrange for some of our own chaps to have training with them. The Colonel who has been most obliging, asked Dick in return if the Unit could use its influence with the War Office to get him promotion. What on earth would Friends House say to that?! Roger had a very interesting letter some days ago, from his brother Geoffrey, who is working in the Embassy in Moscow with Stafford Cripps. He says that the Beaver's (Lord Beaverbrook) visit, was a great success and that the volume of our and American aid to Russia is really remarkable, though the Russians are still told very little about what we are doing to help them. The Beaver's visit, apparently, concluded with an enormous banquet in the Kremlin.

I've been working most of today, in an effort to get things cleared off before going away on Tuesday. A second letter from Tom has come in, in which he says he is not too cheerful about the prospects of getting American money. We mentioned you coming up to London for a week-end, so why don't you try. Not next week-end, but perhaps the one after, if raids have not started again. I am sure Millior would let us use her flat. Come down Saturday and return Monday. Please do it. It would be so grand. Surely you could leave the children for two nights with your mother? I think that is all for now. God bless you and please go on loving me. Dearest love, Ralph.

Lord Beaverbrook

Stafford Cripps
Photographs Cripps and Wilson archives

Geoffrey Wilson

[Textual: This next letter is somewhat perplexing. My father mentions a letter from his Aunt Lou, and her talk of a birthday, which would have been her 80th on October 21st, being born in 1861. So this must be 1941. He also mentions looking forward to seeing my mother on November 22, so this must be somewhere in early November, and as it is dated Sunday, I am guessing the 9th. The perplexing bit is that he mentions my mother going for an interview re call up – from which as a mother with children, she would have automatic exemption. But this is mentioned again in a letter in early 1942, so I am assuming the interview must have been postponed from 1941 to 1942.]

In this, one of my father's long letters - a peace offering of some flowers from my mother, a letter from Aunt Lou, a trip to Gloucester, a visit to a depleted BVT, news of Tom in America and a visit to a poor amateur dramatic production! ....

Sunday, November 9th 1941

My dearest

Thank thee so much for the glorious flowers. They are among the loveliest roses that I have had. They have lasted until today, and have been a continuous joy. You are a dear extravagant child! Thank you also for all the various cuttings you sent with your last letter. I do hope your interview went off alright and that you got exemption without any difficulty. I am so sorry that you can't come until November 22nd, but it will be so nice to see you then.

Aunt Lou's letter (see p vii) is marvellous. I love it. In a world where all things seem to be sliding, it's grand to find a household and a person where the old traditions really matter, even if they seem silly to us. You really wouldn't think there was a war on. It might be a description of a birthday any time since 1850. All so seemingly trivial, yet all so important.

Richard and I had quite an amusing trip to Gloucester, and I must say I do like his company. In fact the journey and the company were the best part. We had a very nice little Standard, which went like a bird and was a joy to drive. It went without a hitch all the way. We called in at Barnsley Hall Hotel, just off the Birmingham Road, for lunch and then on to Gloucester. The countryside was looking especially lovely with the Elms and Beeches and Willows all in their autumn splendour of reds, golds and silvers, and the Malverns looking superb as always with round about, farmers busy ploughing the fields.

Although my mother was born there, and my great Grandfather one of the city's most revered citizens, I regret to say that I had never been to the city before. The country round is quite lovely, especially near Chosen Hill where my mother was born. But having visited some of the hospitals in the city, I must say I should not relish doing hospital work there, as it does all seem a little uninspiring, emptying pig-swills, dustbins and cleaning corridors. Though quite how far it is right for members of the Unit to be doing completely stooge hospital work, I don't know. But there were some who thought a willingness to perform humble tasks, was part of the pacifist's witness in time of war. Others thought it a waste of talent. However, they have good living quarters and seem fairly contented with life. Richard Wainwright is in charge there and seems a nice person.

The Gloucester section of the Unit had in the past built up quite a tradition of music and the arts, as an antidote to the humdrum nature of much of the rest of their daily work, with audiences from the nearby slums as well from the Cathedral. But most of the men who made its work famous, have now gone, and today it has more than its share of dimwits. They were all living in accommodation in the slums of Sherborne Street, where I gave a talk which I thought was rather dull and uninspired, but everyone said had gone down well. Richard was much more interesting and started quite a good discussion on the value of hospital work.

I spent the night there and found it quite pleasant, though rather cold. I've come to the conclusion that all camps look much the same until you get to know them. Everyone being ever so keen, and full of inspiring enthusiasm, so unlike the rather jaded atmosphere of the rest of the Unit!

Then coming back from Gloucester on Thursday morning, we set off at 7.30 and all over the Cotswolds we were driving straight into the sunrise, with a golden glory in the sky and all the fields dim, until gradually they took on the morning colour. We went on through Northleach to Burford, and I wonder if you remember coming out with mother, Millior and me to Northleach, long before we were engaged?

When we got back to Birmingham, there was a constitutional crisis at Selly Wood (Quaker College), which took some time to settle and people got a little over-heated, but I think we parted friends. They all seem to be very comfortable in that house. I also went on to the Trust office, which is becoming more and more depleted in personnel, and soon there will only be LPA and a few women left. Aylward has gone and Bailey and Pratt may soon go too. But LPA was in amazing form, quite like his old self. They have given him a year's extension. He is quite wonderful. Being back there made me feel quite sad.

Now back in London we are getting a few things sorted, and on my initiative we have appointed Richard as a sort of Public Relations Officer, and also set up a planning committee for the future work of the Unit, as TLT (Tom) I now learn, is not planning to return until the New Year unfortunately.

Yesterday evening, I went at the special request of Laurence Darton, who is in charge of Shelters, to a number of one act plays being performed in a Jewish Girls Club. It was fair as amateur drama goes, which is, I suspect, much the same the world over. But why is it that working class people always choose to act in plays about snobbish upper class people? I suppose they were quite funny, though more often it was unconsciously. I'm afraid it was largely a wasted evening.

I'm so glad you enjoyed hearing Mrs Cecil Chesterton. I have always heard what a remarkable person she is. Oddly enough, I have just borrowed a history of America by her late husband Cecil Chesterton, GK's brother. Factual, but sterile I think is the verdict. [....]
All my love Ralph

As suggested, my mother came down to London, and stayed the weekend of November 15th/16th. Eventually, it seems she came down on her own, so that they could be together. It also gave her a chance to meet my father's colleagues, and so discover for herself that they were just normal, friendly, down to earth people like my father, and not 'remote and clever' as my mother sometimes imagined......

Tuesday, November 18th 1941 - London Hostel

My dearest
Thank you for your card. It was lovely having you here for the week-end and I enjoyed it all tremendously. I am so glad that you have now seen where I live and work and have been able to meet some of those I work with. It was all perfect. Please thank your mother for looking after the children while you were here, and thank thee for all the gifts you brought: I particularly liked the book of Nature poetry. Bless you. I am glad David was so pleased to see you back. Do give him my love.

We continue to be very busy, but there is very little else of note that has happened since you were here. As you know I am off to a conference in Bournemouth at the end of the month and I will write again from there. Take care and God bless.
All my love Ralph

It seems my father suddenly had to go to Birmingham on Unit business, and so made it an excuse to stay at Wolverhampton again. Recalling his previous visit, he would have made a special effort to be on best behaviour, but even so can't resist a little jibe at the in-laws.....

Tuesday, November 25th 1941 – London Hostel

My dearest

It was so lovely seeing you unexpectedly last weekend and I did enjoy seeing you again. We were both in quite good form and it all went very well. Though how you stand Wolverhampton as well as you do, I don't know.....and the wireless on all the time! But still, I suppose it is less of a strain than being at Beaconwood.

I had quite a good journey back, though I did get rather wet walking to the station. But I managed to get some breakfast and by chance I also bumped into Keith Linney on the train, which was good company, but useful too as I had quite a lot of things to discuss with him.

[....] Please thank Win for putting me up at such short notice. Please also thank your mother for all she did looking after the children.

This week we are pretty busy getting the Annual Report ready to post off this week-end. We write letters to accompany it as well, as the Report is the mainstay of our subscribed income. The generosity of people is really quite humbling, sometimes threepenny pieces from a pensioner's tin, and sometimes large business donations.

Think of me this coming weekend when I am in Bournemouth for a marathon conference about amalgamation - the Civilian Relief Service with the Friends War Victim Relief Committee - chaired by Christopher Taylor. It will no doubt drag on for ages – "in the manner of Quakers"!

All for now, my dearest. Always in my thoughts,
Ever yours Ralph.

Before the days of mobile phones and answer phones, you can be sure that an important phone call would inevitably happen when you were out! On this occasion my mother rang when my father was entertaining an American friend of Tom Tanner's, which seems to have involved a lot of ferrying to and from the East End to the Ritz!

Christmas plans are afoot, though he tries his best to explain why he finds Wolverhampton such a strain, and though he wants nothing more than to be with my mother, he begs at least to be exempted from the Pantomime........

Thursday, November 27th 1941 – London Hostel

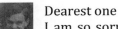

Dearest one

I am so sorry I was out when you phoned last night, but we had an American Congressman here, who is one of a small delegation who have been over. He is a friend of Tom's, and someone from the Embassy asked us to take him to supper and show him some of our shelters. He was a nice chap and Dick and I took him to several shelters and then on to the Prospect of Whitby pub in Wapping, which I'm sure I mentioned to you before. It claims to date from 1520, and he seemed suitably impressed, as Americans often are with our history, being such a relatively young country themselves!

He flew over on a Boeing Clipper, and they are all staying at The Ritz – of course! – and we went up for a drink and were introduced to another Congressman, who came over with him. Tom's friend had seen him recently in New York and said he was fine, which is good news.

The Ritz is a long way West from Wapping, so there was a lot of driving - to the Ritz to meet up with him; then all the way back East to Wapping; and all the way back West to the Ritz, and finally back East again to the Hostel! It's also very exhausting driving in London at night, and we didn't get back finally till pretty late.

On Tuesday Arnold Rowntree was here for the night. He is a nice person, and we held a coffee party for him, but dear oh dear, he kept telling stories about his two parrots and some eccentric friends, which was all crashingly boring! On Wednesday we had a Council Meeting and Paul C was here, and being at his most provoking. I do like him, but sometimes Dick is quite right about how infuriating he can be.

This afternoon we are off to Bournemouth for our week-end conference. I can't say I'm greatly looking forward to it.

Thank you for your dear letter. Indeed it was grand seeing you the other week-end, and thank you for coming: you looked lovely in your new dress. I'm glad you enjoyed it too. The worst of life is that one exists by looking forward to things, and then they either come off or fall through, and afterwards everything is so flat. Or else one uproots oneself and starts a new life and hating it; and then gradually one begins to take root and it becomes tolerable, and then one has to uproot again and begin by hating that, and so it goes on!

My dearest, I will try my very best to get some leave over Christmas, because I do need a rest. I wish when you were here, we could have gone right away somewhere. I don't somehow feel that a few days at Wolverhampton are quite what I want. I know that sounds selfish, because of course you want a change too. But I do tend to get restless whenever there are fresh people to meet, and I have to be polite and cheerful, when I just want to be really lazy. I'm very sorry my dear, but I find it so difficult to adjust myself to Lea Road and hard to be what I ought to be.

Partly it's over-tiredness, partly the sort of life I lead, partly lack of outside interests, partly being separated from normal responsibilities. I'm sorry, but I should love to come to a house of our own, with someone to look after us or even without that, but I'm not sure Wolverhampton will help much. But I do long to be with you and that will make up for everything, and I'll try and behave…but make allowances for me! Do I really have to go to the Pantomime? I think that might be almost more that I can bear! I know it's selfish, because I know you put up with it all the time. So I apologise in advance.

Dear love, Ralph

Arnold Rowntree (left) was here for the night. He is a nice person, and we held a coffee party for him, but dear oh dear, he kept telling stories about his two parrots.....so boring!
And….. Paul C was here too, and being at his most provoking. I do like him, but sometimes Dick is quite right about how infuriating he can be.
Photo Richard Cadbury and Rowntree Trust

Chapter 13
The Bournemouth Conference
The Amalgamation of
Friends War Victim Relief Committee and Civilian Relief Service
November 1941

Ever since the beginnings of the FAU in WW1, there had been serious differences of opinion amongst Friends, as to how close the Unit should get to the military. Now more than ever with ambulance groups going abroad to work alongside the army, and with many of the men wearing a khaki uniform, the better to blend in, the controversy would soon surface again.

But for now concentrating on relief work, none of the work the Unit was involved with, could be said to have any sort of military connection or indeed anything about which Quakers could possibly have any qualms of conscience. The relief work, through the good offices of Henry Cadbury, was financed by the American Friends Service Committee, (see Appendix 4 on Finance) contributed through the FWVRC, and even though the FAU and the FWVRC did not overlap greatly in their work, they were nonetheless tackling many of the same problems from different angles.

It seemed inevitable that sooner or later there should be some form of integration. So in the last weekend of November 1941, a conference was held at Bournemouth with ten representatives of the Unit and 'War Vics' as they were known (War Victims Relief) and as a result, in the following February an amalgamation took place between the FWVRC, (which ceased to exist) with the Civilian Relief Section of the FAU, to be known as the Friends War Relief Service and later just the FWRS.

From then on the Unit concentrated on hospital and training work throughout Britain and its rapidly developing service overseas and for the first time, a piece of work begun by the Unit became the official responsibility of the Society of Friends. Those FAU members mainly interested in relief work were transferred to the new organization, and those who wanted to continue, while waiting for an opportunity to go abroad, worked on a seconded basis. My father continued as Emergency Relief Officer for FWRS until the Unit sent him abroad in the summer of 1942.

Not at all impressed by a down-at-heel wartime Bournemouth, he writes in his memoirs, of the conference and the amalgamation:

As 1941 drew on with no raids it seemed to some of us that the Unit should not be involved in work of a permanent nature, which the Unit's shelter work was rapidly becoming, and that this ought to be handed over, while leaving the pure emergency work to the Emergency Section, which would continue with FAU personnel.

The idea was born at a conference in Bournemouth, hosted by Christopher Taylor, the newly appointed Chairman of FWVRC. Others apart from CT, were - Roger Wilson, Jack Cadbury, and Tessa Rowntree (Michael's sister) for FWVRC, and Brandon Cadbury, Michael Barratt Brown, Richard Symonds, Keith Linney, Laurence Darton, Michael Hacking and myself for the FAU.

We stayed as Christopher's guests in a very comfortable hotel, but Bournemouth in that grey November weather was a deadly place. An ugly town with ugly cliffs and a deserted beach, barricaded with barbed wire.

I wrote to Joan...............

Sunday, November 30th 1941 – Bournemouth

My dearest Joan

[....] We are staying in a very comfortable and respectable hotel with plenty of good food, but it's oh so dull, and Bournemouth seems to me one of the most God awful places anyone ever went to. Frightful, nightmarish hotels, pseudo Gothic churches, formal ugly gardens, endless shops, muddy cliffs with roads and lamp posts and summer houses along the tops and bottoms. Houses and hotels of every imaginable style except good – just plain ugly and vulgar; the scaffolding and barbed wire along the shore were beautiful by contrast. Even the birds were not that exciting, as I only saw three gulls, two cormorants and heard a thrush sing. Most of the time we were in conference, except for Saturday afternoon and evening.

Saturday evening the party split and the soberer elements - Vic and Brandon, failing to get into a cinema - went for a walk. The rest of the Unit gradually disappeared until only I was left. Making the excuse that they all needed looking after, I followed, finding them of course, where you would expect....in a pub! Everyone had a merry evening and nobody really disgraced themselves, though Dick Symonds did find one very happy soul who, being tipsily over talkative kept pointing at me saying - "Don't talk to him, he's reading for the Church"! Well someone did tell me I was looking more miserable than usual!

All love Ralph

Bournemouth Pier seen through barbed wire in 1941
"Bournemouth just now must be the most God awful place anyone ever went to. [.........] Houses and hotels of every imaginable style except good – just plain ugly and vulgar; the scaffolding and barbed wire along the shore were beautiful by contrast."
Photograph courtesy Bournemouth History archive

At the end of the war, one of the things my father criticized was the Quaker committee process, which is fine and admirable in normal circumstances, but in war time, when quick decisions are needed, they are not always fit for purpose. Here he writes about just such interminable meetings that took place in Bournemouth 'in the style of Friends', which took all day………

The upshot was that the amalgamation came about. FWVRC became FWRS. Our work was handed over to a Committee of Meeting for Sufferings. None of us liked it much and there was great opposition from the Society and the Unit. But looking back in cold blood on the conference at Bournemouth and the subsequent amalgamation between the FAU Civilian Relief Section and FWVRC, I realise what a herculean task we had set ourselves. I am not sure whether Michael Hacking or I attended more meetings, but I am equally certain that he spoke more! I also have some vivid memories of Richard Symonds challenging Stephen Verney to explain what prayer was. But one way and another it was accomplished and on the whole, I think it was justified and that we did the right thing.

A word must be said of FWVRC under Roger Wilson. We had worked very closely with them and they financed us. Indeed much of our work was in parallel - their workers were seconded to us for Shelter and Rest Centre work, and our members to them for Hostel work. I have often criticised RCW in the past for not being straight, for personal ambition, for being a poor administrator and a bad judge of men. But of his brilliance there can be no doubt and in those early months he was FWVRC. We were in adjacent rooms at the Hostel, sharing the same bathroom, and through this close contact I came to know him better and subsequently to greatly value his advice. Without him the amalgamation would certainly not have been so smooth.

The Bournemouth Conference 1941

"Bournemouth in that grey November weather was a deadly place."

"Christopher Taylor (left), the head of FWVRC hosted the Bournemouth Conference, and we stayed as his guests in a very comfortable Hotel."

"I have vivid memories of Richard Symonds (below right) challenging Stephen Verney (below left) to explain what prayer was."

Photo Christopher Taylor - courtesy Clare Norton
Other photos Friends House Library

Familiar Faces

Roger Wilson and his wife Margery
Seen here outside their cottage in the Wye Valley after the war. FRB writes - "of Roger's brilliance there can be no doubt and in those early months he was the FWVRC."

Barty Knight, "the Quarter Master of the 11th Camp, a very capable and likeable man."
Photo BK Broumana High School
Photo of Roger Wilson and Margery courtesy RW
Other photos Friends House Library

Henry Headley
"An ever reliable and practical man, and a good friend."

Ronald Joynes
"He reduced the art of getting parties overseas to a fine art."

Chapter 14
Deputy Chairman 1941-42 and Missions hither and yon
September 1941 – February 1942

For two years from December 1940 to November 1942, as Tegla Davies remarks "Tom Tanner ruled", except when he visited the United States in the winter of 1941/42. During that period my father became Deputy Director, in addition to his own work as Officer in charge of Relief. These four months coincided with the amalgamation of the Civilian Relief Section with the Friends War Victim Relief Committee, and with many difficult decisions on the Executive, especially trying to find openings for work overseas. My father was first put on the Executive Committee in June 1941. This consisted primarily of departmental heads, and he says "was one of the best things the Unit produced, as it was fully *au fait* with Unit business and understood exactly what was required." *He remained on it until December 1944, when he was invalided out. In my father's memoirs he writes.....*

Tom (Tanner) was determined to go to America and he departed very suddenly in September of '41, and from September 1941 to January '42, we attempted to carry on without him. I was asked to take over and was initially very reluctant to do so, as the Relief Officer's job was already a very considerable one, and no doubt it was probably a mistake to try to combine this with the Chairman's. However, I did it and consequently greatly overworked, going up to Gordon Square every day.

At that time the Relief section was, as it were, a unit within a Unit. We were, to a considerable extent our own Personnel Officers. Under Tom's regime in charge of the Relief Section, it had been more or less independent of the Unit and Tom had kept a close grip on Peter Gibson as his Assistant, but with Tom in America and Peter in charge of the first Middle East section, I could do more or less as I liked.

Perhaps here I might say a word about Tom. He inspired amazing devotion. In every way he was a really big man; perhaps the only one that the Unit produced and he put the Unit on the map. Though he liked to keep things very much in his own hands, he had immense capacity for work, self-confidence, good judgement and flair; he was a natural leader and administrator, always able to see and seize an opportunity. It also has to be said that Tom loved company and celebrities, was always fond of going places and doing things, and dare I say, was addicted to the sins of the flesh. But none of us could have done for the unit what Tom did. He liked to boast that he was in no sense cultured and in many ways we had little in common. But I think we liked each other.

In fact Tom's American trip produced little but, and it is a big but, it achieved a new and far better UK/US understanding of each other's points of view. He seems to have had a strenuous time over there, but succeeded in making a wonderfully good impression. He met heaps of people and perhaps his chief achievement was to get to know, and be respected by, the American Friends Service Council. Following the heavy losses at Pearl Harbour in December of '41, America was now taking the war seriously and Tom believed, would soon begin to make herself felt. However, with American Friends so fully committed to existing projects such as the Relief work, Tom did not manage to get agreement to much in the way of new finance.

While Tom was in America we attempted as best we could to carry on without him. While he was away, I spent a lot of time visiting sections out of London. I went several times to Birmingham and Liverpool; drove with Richard Symonds on visits to camps in Barnsley Hall and Gloucester; and to a place near Cambridge to see the first course of the Royal Army Medical Corps under John Gough and Jack Frazer.

Richard Symonds was a great help to me both with ideas and sympathy and in making contacts and arrangements to see people. Brandon Cadbury, who was twice the man with Tom away, and might just as easily have been Deputy Chairman in my stead, was very loyal and his influence on the right for caution and conservative ways, balanced Richard on the left. Both were invaluable.

The Unit was then going through a difficult time. Relief was in many ways coming to an end, and we were now desperately in need of overseas work. All sorts of enquiries were made and many ideas were mooted. Some scarcely got off the ground, while others started and then faltered. Each proposed overseas expedition was inevitably a major enterprise, involving months of preparation, fund-raising and just waiting around for shipping to become available. Quite often this ended with everyone's initial, buoyant enthusiasm being dampened by constant disappointment and frustration. The main problem was that when the war was not going well, with whole army divisions having to be shipped half way around the world, the needs of a handful of pacifists did not amount to 'a hill of beans' on the list of priorities.

[Textual: This letter is also undated, but my father mentions the new FWRS which was only formed after the Bournemouth Conference at the end of November. So this must be roughly the beginning of December]

Quite happy to be back in London after the long weekend in Bournemouth, my father enjoys a party along with some good news concerning fund-raising.......

Monday, December 1st 1941 – London Hostel

Dearest Joan

Well we got back from Bournemouth last night, having had quite a useful time, trying to work out a closer collaboration between the two bodies – the FWVRC and the Civilian relief Section of the FAU. The outcome was that the former has now ceased to exist by that name, and the new body is to be called the Friends War Relief Service, with me continuing as Relief Officer, but now for the FWRS...if you follow!

Bournemouth itself, as I mentioned before was exceedingly drab. Saturday evening was our only evening of relaxation, which was a fine, beautiful, night, with a bright moon, and had anyone been in romantic mood, or had you been there, would have been perfect. But it was, we all agreed, wasted on us!

Since getting back, various crises have developed while I was away, but nothing too serious I think. Nonetheless, we all stayed up rather late discussing business, so I really must go to bed.

More later............Wednesday, December 3rd 1941

Sorry yesterday was so hectic, I had no time to finish my letter. Thank thee so much for your two letters, which arrived this morning. I so love hearing from you and news of the children.

I don't think I have much more news since yesterday, except John Gough gave a party last night, as he is going away on a training course with the Royal Army Medical Corps. Before the war he and a lot of friends used to live in three 17th century houses in Chelsea. They face the river, and really are beautiful old houses with big rooms and wide stairs. Some of his friends still live there, and so they laid on some entertainment for us.

It made for a very pleasant time with drinks and light refreshments. There were some of John's friends there, as well as a lot of Unit people and their wives including Barry (Michael Barratt Brown) and his wife, Richard Symonds, Arnold Curtis, Sandy Parnis, Brandon, Angela and myself.

Since then we have been having endless section meetings, and everyone has been criticising the executive, sometimes quite rightly in my opinion, for failing to be decisive, and it all becomes rather wearing. I had a cable from Tom to say that he is expecting to be home on January 3rd, and it will be good to have him back as well as quite a relief.

Our Annual Report, which as I think I mentioned before, is the basis of our annual appeal, has raised about £2,000 so far, which is amazing. We are very pleased after so much work getting it out.

It's been such a busy time of late, and reading has often gone by the board, but I've just started re-reading the plays of Chehkov in the new Penguin edition, and enjoyed them tremendously all over again. They really do give an amazingly arresting picture of the Russian mentality.

All my love for now my dearest and love to David and Antony. Ralph

With plans being laid for several different groups to go overseas, my father is obviously aware that sooner or later he will be required to go abroad too, which is not a prospect he anticipates with any relish. But a disquisition on values to be upheld alongside the tragedy of war, and a belief in God, all contrive to help him through troubled times.......

Thursday, December 6th 1941 – London Hostel

My dearest
I fear I have no further news on whether they want me to go abroad or not, but feel I ought to write to you tonight, else you will not hear from me before Monday. We had a very long executive committee about who should go to China and who to the Middle East, but we could not reach a decision. Brandon wants **me** to go and so I think do others, but there are some who feel I ought to see the newly formed Friends War Relief Service, which we decided on at the Bournemouth Conference, through to the end. I have a feeling that this amalgamation bids fair to keep me pretty busy for some while yet.

All I really want is for us to get together again. I need you so much, especially your love and quietness. What wouldn't I give for a peaceful life with you – as it says in Job: *"Where the wicked cease from troubling, and the weary are at rest."* I could say much more, but we both know how we each feel, and to dwell on it, only makes it worse.

Sometimes the tragedy of war and the tragedy in the lives of those about us, seems unbearable and despite all the explanations of the 'value of suffering', one must I suppose set against it such unalterable values as the beauty of nature, beauties of character such as kindness, trust, love and happiness, the joy of children, all of which are as real and strong as tragedy. Life, of course, has its terrible side but it has its splendours too. If only we weren't continually faced with these insoluble problems. Everything seems so bleak and cold at the moment and I find it difficult to be enthusiastic. But whatever happens, we must keep faith and be true to one's self; keep courage and try and hang on to self-respect and the principles, which experience shows us matter. What are they? Unselfishness, thoughtfulness, courage, reliability, humility. Where does God come in? I am sure there is a God, and we need him and cannot disregard him – but what or how I do not know.

Next Saturday, I have to go to Cambridge, and it will be good to be able to relax on my own for a bit. I will write again soon. God bless you and keep you safe.
Give my love to the children, Ralph

PS I had lunch with Michael and Heather (Cadbury) on Sunday. John (brother) comes up for a fortnight very soon, and I must try and see him.

In contemplating overseas trips, if some Unit group had already established a foothold in another country, it was a great deal easier to send others after. But being the pioneers was often fraught with difficulties, as my father writes in his memoirs........

It was often easier to send additional men to an area where the Unit was already at work, rather than to break new ground. I remember the delight, therefore, with which we greeted Peter's request for reinforcements in the Middle East in January, although predictably the party which was to have gone out under Freddy Temple to swell the hospital staff, did not actually leave until July, again due to shortage of shipping.

Then again, it was much the same story with the party delegated to go out to Ethiopia under Richey Mounsey as Commandant: continual hold ups. The two of us went frequently back and forth, first to the War Office then to the Foreign Office, trying to sort matters out. Some projects seemed doomed from the beginning, and even when Richey, along with Michael Vaizey as Senior Medical Officer, did eventually manage to set sail in August 1942, still more disasters awaited them.

First one boat and then another broke down. Twice they had to return to the UK. Finally, embarked on yet a third boat, they set sail again. But even as they docked in Cape Town harbour, there was an explosion as a vital part of the engine blew up, raining metal pieces down on the deck.

India also was suggested, as with both Burma and Malaya now in enemy hands, Calcutta and the whole eastern seaboard of India was in the front line. By this time the FAU had acquired a considerable body of expertise, and it was widely felt that this should be placed at the disposal of Indian cities in need, as soon as possible.

Dick Symonds was the moving spirit and he and I went to see the Deputy High Commissioner and had long discussions with Horace Alexander, who knew the country well, being a long-time friend of Gandhi. Many high level talks followed, both with Sir Stafford Cripps[1] and the Viceroy, Lord Wavell. Eventually, after long discussions, it was agreed that Horace should lead a deputation out to India with Dick as Executive Officer. Arrangements were made for him to take temporary leave from his position at Woodbrooke, and they left England in May 1942.

My father is in one of his down moods; having anticipated, as he wrote on the 6th, a quiet get away to Cambridge on his own – this was thrown overboard when Brandon insisted on accompanying him! Not best pleased...........

Thursday, December 11th 1941 – London Hostel

My dearest
Thank you so much for your long letter. I am sorry to hear that Edith (home help) is going. I am afraid it will mean a fearful lot more work for you all. How sickening for everybody that the children have colds again. I feel so sorry for you having to cope.

The war news is pretty awful at the moment, and I must say that life here is pretty bloody too, trying to arrange trips that never seem to happen. It's mostly that I'm tired I suppose, and I'm here just on my own with everybody either out or away. You may say that I am never happy, which is probably true, unless I'm with you. On the one hand I complain when I'm on my own, and then I moan when I'm here, having to eat with herds of people, like being back at school! Perhaps I'm sick of being here all the time, which is why I was so looking forward to enjoying a peaceful ride to Cambridge all by myself, but now Brandon says he wants to come with me on Saturday. Oh hell!

I had an interesting lunch at the centre for Political and Economic Planning (PEP) yesterday. Violet Markham[2] (Social reformer) was the guest and spoke very well on the 'Work of the Assistance Board,' and helping the sick and aged. PEP sponsors research groups, which produce some excellent reports – as well as doing excellent lunches! It is partially financed I think by the Sieff family (M&S) and Mrs Sieff was there, as was Kenneth Lindsay MP, the PEP Chairman, who is a friend of Tom's (another!). It was well attended, with quite a distinguished audience there, including G L Pepler, a past President of the Town Planning Institute who has written extensively on the subject.

Tom's girl, Ann Channer is a secretary typist for PEP and seems very pleasant. Tom, of course, is happily married (wife and two children, now in America), and Barry is quite worried about this affair, but I'm quite sure that Tom has far too much sense to make a fool of himself publicly.

I'm sorry about my remarks on pantomimes, but I don't think I shall ever enjoy them, whoever I go with. And it wasn't a Panto I went to with Angela, it was a sort of revue that I saw with her, and going with her had nothing to do with my enjoying it! I was never in love with her as you well know and never thought I was!

It will be so grand seeing you and the children at Christmas. I can't wait. I've told Horace that I will be up over Christmas and that perhaps we could meet on Saturday 27th, or if that's impossible on Boxing day. I'm glad you enjoyed the Bird film.

I am writing to the Tritsch's saying that they can have the house for a bit longer, now you are staying on at Wolverhampton.

Remember I love you very much – Ralph

There seem to be a couple of letters missing here, but Christmas appears to have been a happy time, as an extract from my mother's diary which she kept on my early years, helps to fill in a little………

Ralph came for a week over Christmas, which made our Christmas a real family one, even though we were not in our own home. Antony enjoyed the excitement of his first Christmas and loved the bright paper decorations and lanterns in the Nursery, and of course the Christmas tree, and David was very helpful in giving out the presents to everybody.

And a New Year's letter from my father later confirms this………

January, Saturday 3rd 1942 – London Hostel

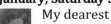

My dearest
I send you all my best wishes for the New Year and may it be as happy as possible under the circumstances, and may it bring us nearer being back in our own home again. I must thank you very much for making me so happy over my Christmas leave and generally being such a darling wife. I really did enjoy it and please thank Win and Llew for having me. I will write to them before the end of the week.

As I mentioned on the phone, the train was hot and overcrowded, and generally rather unpleasant, but it was nice to be able to get a meal, and I got back here at about 9.45. Everything seems to have been fairly quiet in my absence. Barry is in Liverpool and then goes on leave, and Richard is in bed with a cold. I also had a cable from Duncan saying that he is still stuck in Singapore, poor chap. Tom is supposed to be arriving by boat pretty soon. God bless you and look after yourself. Thank you for being so tolerant and understanding. Love to David and Antony. All my love Ralph

An obviously loving letter from my mother prompts my father to write back immediately. It's the constant affirmation of their love that helps to keep it burning brightly through all the vicissitudes of wartime...........

Sunday, January 4th 1942

My darling

Thank you so much for your beautiful letter, and bless you for loving me so dearly. I love you too, so very much. Yes, we did have a good time didn't we? I really did enjoy it and I hope I behaved well! It was glorious to get into the country with you and to see some birds. Don't apologise for loving me – that's stupid. We must both go on loving each other more and more, as we do.

I have very little news, except a big hint from Brandon suggesting that when Tom gets back, I might have to go out in charge of the whole FAU section in the Middle East. I'm not sure it will come to anything, but it is flattering. I quite thought they would have found me out by now! At the moment I'm pretty busy as always, particularly as people are away - I think I mentioned that Barry is now on leave and Richard, following his bout of 'flu and rather down in the dumps, has gone away for the week-end.

The RAMC training course is over and seems to have been only a qualified success. They all enjoyed it and found it useful – except Barty who has been in a black mood of late, but they all doubted whether they had really learnt sufficient to make it worthwhile repeating the course with others.

I think all this joint action with America sounds most encouraging, and I really begin to feel that in the long run, victory is certain. Roger's brother, Geoffrey has returned from the Russian Embassy and will be talking at Friends House next week. Roger said that his brother thinks the Germans are now in more and more of a mess what with Russia turning into a disaster for them, and following Pearl Harbour, with America now also entering the war.

I saw Horace at FH about India on Wednesday and made some progress, though Olive is very ill. He told me that he had just seen an Iceland Gull on the Thames, which made me jealous! I think I might go and see if I can see it too before it flies off. I also saw Wilfred Littleboy (weighty f/Friend) the other day, who wanted to talk about how we could achieve more spiritual uplift in the Society after the war. I'm afraid that this was not top of things I have been thinking about recently, though I didn't say so! He was very grateful for the card we sent him.

I think that's all. Please give my love to the boys and tell David to take care of his trains. All my love always, Ralph.

PS 1. I stupidly left my Oxford book of English Verse behind, do you think you could kindly send it back to me. I am so sorry to bother you.

PS 2. I nearly lost my voice last week, but it seems to have come back now, thank God!

———

Here my father visits his old friend Jack Frazer at the Middlesex Hospital, both concerned about an uncertain future; and also visits Kew, a favourite haunt; tries to cope with 'the end of an era'; and has lunch with Geoffrey Wilson, who it transpires is less optimistic about the progress of the war than his brother, Roger had indicated..........

Monday, January 5th 1942 – London Hostel

Dearest Joan

I've just been to supper at the Middlesex, with Jack, and it was good to see him. He also kindly saw me part of the way back. He is feeling rather depressed at the moment, and wondering what the future will bring, as are we all. They are back from Cambridge now, having had quite a good time there.

Angela and I went over to Kew on Sunday afternoon, which was pleasant. It was a mild day with occasional sun and the trees were lovely. There were hardly any flowers except for some lovely cyclamen and begonias in one of the hot houses, but there were some semi-tame ducks on the pools, which were rather fun. It was so pleasant to get out into the country again and see grass and trees and birds. I so wished that you could have been there too, as it reminded me so of that glorious spring day in 1935, when we were at Kew that Jubilee year. Do you remember what a dream it was - hot sun, bluebells and the young beech trees and every flowering shrub in full glory. *"So sweet love seem'd that April morn"* as Robert Bridges[3] puts it, and how its promise has been fulfilled a hundred fold, my dearest. We must go there again sometime.

Life seems rather drab here at present with not much prospect of work. The old FAU relief section is ending, and the new Committee has not yet come into being. It is, as it were, the end of an epoch. An old order is passing and none of us much likes the look of the new.

Roger's brother, Geoffrey now back from Moscow, came into supper last night. He was less sanguine than Roger had led us to imagine. He said food is scarce there, but that only the homeless are actually starving. The Russians appear to have sufficient munitions, and the pace at which they are moving their factories to safer areas, is quite remarkable. He does think that the Germans, realising that they could not take Moscow, have been forced to retreat south rather faster than they had intended. But he also thinks the pace of the Russian advance is being somewhat exaggerated by the newspapers. On the other hand he thinks that it is possible that the Japanese and the Russians could be at war by the spring. The Japanese Ambassador has few friends in Kuibyshev* and is rather a lonely man.

[....] I can't think that there is any more news since I wrote on Sunday. I wonder if you have heard how LPA is. Give my love to David and Antony. I do hope they are both well and that you are not finding it too much of a strain without Edith. My voice has now come back thankfully, and my cold luckily doesn't seem to be developing.

God bless you my dear.
I send you all my love, Ralph

———

*See next page

Geoffrey Wilson back from Russia

"Roger's younger brother, Geoffrey is back from Moscow and came into supper. He's going to work at the FO in charge of the Russian Department"

Geoffrey Wilson (left) with Stafford Cripps. GW had been Cripps' right hand man in Moscow and worked closely with him till after the war.

He also later went with him to India where Cripps was very influential in advising the British government on Indian independence.

Photograph courtesy of Cripps family archives.

As my father writes above in a letter to my mother, Roger's brother, Geoffrey Wilson, returned from Moscow in January 1942, where he had been working with our Ambassador, Stafford Cripps in the Russian Embassy, which by then had moved to Kuybyshev in South West Russia, as the temporary capital of Russia during the German invasion.

As the Red Army withdrew behind the Dnieper and Dvina rivers, the Soviet high command turned its attention to evacuating as much of the western regions' industry as it could as well. Factories were dismantled and transported away from the front line for re-establishment in more remote areas such as the Ural Mountains, Caucasus or Central Asia.

Most civilians were left to make their own way east, with only industry-related workers evacuated with their equipment. Much of the population was left behind to the mercy of the invading forces, but by early December it became clear as my father has written, that the Wehrmacht did not have the strength to capture Moscow, and the attack was suspended.

So Marshal Shaposhnikov began his counter-attack, employing freshly mobilised reserves, as well as some well-trained Far-Eastern divisions transferred from the east, following intelligence that Japan would remain neutral. Hence Russia became one of the places the Unit were now considering for aid.

So despite my father's gloomy prognostications of no overseas work, openings did start to appear, as he writes here in his memoirs.........

Gradually overseas work did open up and with Russia now much in the news with the German invasion, when Geoffrey Wilson returned from the Russian Embassy in Moscow, people were talking of his success and the impressions Beaverbrook had made of the Russian's chances of survival.

Also ever since the Japanese invasion of China in 1937, there had been a growing response in this country to the suffering of the Chinese, and by 1940, when the Unit was scarcely a year old the obvious distress there evoked a wholehearted response, and a growing enthusiasm for a party to visit China.

Peter Gibson's original party were now working in the Middle East, building on the foundations laid by Ronald Joynes and members of the Finnish party, who had by now returned to the UK, following a period in Greece after the German invasion. And so all my close friends seemed to be going overseas. Peter Tennant was on his way to China, Dick Symonds and Horace to India and Richey Mounsey eventually to Ethiopia.

Soon after his return Geoffrey gave an interesting talk on his time in Russia at Friends House, and not long after, he was appointed to the Foreign Office in charge of the Russian department. Though he told me later - "department is a misleading term". "This so called department" he added "is GMW and one other", and "the salary, if you can call it such, is meagre"!

But on the strength of Geoffrey's account of Russia, Paul Sturge, (Secretary of the Friends Service Council), Roger (Wilson) and I went to the Russian Embassy to see the redoubtable Madame Agniya Maisky, the wife of the Russian Ambassador, Ivan Maisky. "Have you read Pushkin?" she asked us haughtily, and then continued bluntly that "What we need in Russia is supplies, not personnel."

The Russian Ambassador, Ivan Maisky and his wife Madam Agniya Maisky.
"She asked me if I had read Pushkin!"
Photograph National archives

It's early January and my father is still in charge and waiting for news of Tom's return, but generally feels refreshed after his Christmas break, and here writes a chatty letter home and can even make light of his friendship with Angela. But being who he is, there is still the odd twinge of conscience about having too comfortable a life in the FAU and has worries with still no definite forecast of a foreign trip......

Saturday, January 10th 1942 – London Hostel

My darling
Thank you so much for your very welcome parcel. It was a wonderful surprise; the shirt is admirable and the cigarettes and chocolates most welcome as always. [...] I told you that Horace had seen an Iceland Gull on the river at Hammersmith, well I am hoping to get down there and see if it's still there today.

I do think it is a good idea about you and David coming up to London. It would be so grand to see you and such fun to show David round the Zoo and take him on the underground. The only disadvantages that I can foresee are the lousy weather we are having and the possibility of further raids. Nevertheless, it's a great idea and when I see Millior – probably next week-end - I will discuss it with her and see if we can borrow her flat. If so, I really hope you will come, it would be so splendid.

On Thursday Michael Hacking invited me, as well as Millior and Alfred out to supper with his wife. He heads the Joint Quartermasterring Department, in charge of feeding us all and for training cooks. I must say they are very pleasant people. He took us to a Chinese Restaurant near here, and we had a good meal, though I hadn't a clue what I was eating! The only drawbacks were that it was very noisy and the Chinese seem to have little inclination to serve patrons with any promptness, so we waited a fearful time for our food. Millior, bless her, can make some rather silly remarks sometimes, and I'm afraid I wasn't the best conversationalist as I was rather sleepy.

Barty Knight has been here this week, and in very good form. And no, in case you ask, I haven't been out with Angela this week, though I gather she has been out with almost everyone else! We wrote her a strong note the other day, about meeting a strange man in the Regent Palace Hotel. Tomorrow Dick and I thought we would go walking in Epping Forest.

Though I often get a bit depressed with the futility of things and the wrongness of my comfortable life, wondering why we should be so comfortable and smug, when there is such a terrible lot of suffering everywhere, on the whole I have been more cheerful since returning from leave. It did me a lot of good, thanks to you. And don't worry, I haven't been asked to go out to the Middle East. It's still only a suggestion as yet. We still have no word from Tom, but presume he is on the high seas heading home.

I've been trying to have a tidiness and efficiency drive in the Hostel this week, in the absence on leave, of John Burtt. He is a delightful chap, but not an awfully good Warden. Perhaps I'm being rather hard on him.

Nothings else to add for the moment – except to thank you again for all the things you have sent me.
My dear love, Ralph
PS. Thank you so much for sending the Oxford Book of verse back. I do love to read it so.

Michael Hacking (centre back) trains up young successors to replace cooks going abroad.
Photograph from Friends House Library

With Tom still not back, there is ever more pressure on my father to sort out foreign trips, which in the pervading climate is far from easy. How understandable, therefore, to fall behind in letter writing and to fail to comment on one of us having an attack of bronchitis, all of which occasions the old anxiety in my mother, that my father was wrapped up in the Unit, while she was left to cope. A distraught phone call naturally upsets my father, and as so often, events get blown out of proportion. Another of the inevitabilities of wartime separation, not made easier by the ever growing prospect that his name is continually being mentioned as one who will soon have to go abroad………

Monday, January 19th 1942 – London Hostel

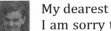 My dearest
I am sorry to have delayed writing for so long, and please will you give Antony very many happy returns of his first birthday. Congratulations to you my darling for achieving him and for all you do looking after both children.

Dear one, I know my job is not easy, but I know yours is far harder. You often have a dull, narrow and monotonous round, and I realise how sickening it must all be sometimes. You have all my love and sympathy and admiration. I love you so much and so much. The thought of our love and marriage is the solid rock of comfort on which I can always fall back. My dear loving wife, what should I do without you. Bless you a thousand times.

The weather is perfectly lousy and I hope to see Millior at the weekend and ask her about you and D coming up. I think it's a very good idea, and hope you will be able to manage it. But I do think it would be wise to wait until the weather improves.

We still have no news of Tom, but expect him almost any time now. Duncan's party were fortunately able to get out of Singapore and have now arrived at Rangoon and I'm sure they will be glad to get going.

Later the same day ....

I am really sorry sweetheart. You were so angry with me on the phone. Honestly dearest I don't deserve it. I have written to thee regularly. There was only the briefest reference to Antony having bronchitis in your last letter and no implication that it might be serious. I am not getting bound up with new friends and excluding you. I like them all, some very much. But I love you and you are my wife. Dear heart how could I not love you, my Joan, my own darling wife. Please my dear, do not be so doubting. How can I assure you of my love? You promised at Christmas that you would not doubt me, and I thought I had assured you that you are all the world to me.

I have friends and a life here, but my real life is with you, and all I want is to be with you again. Please dearest, believe that this is so. Don't be so hard on me. You did hurt me this evening and honestly I don't think I deserve it. I am sorry for all I may do wrong, but bear me no malice. You have no cause, for you must know that you are my only love. Oh this damned war. What sadness and ruin it brings in its wake. But someday, believe me dearest, it will all end, and you and I will be home again, with a house and a garden and books and flowers. And it all will be as it was, and you will know that I love you and always have loved you. Why you have forgotten it I don't know. But have courage dear one and life will be whole again.

Tomorrow I am going to see the High Commissioner for India on the possibility of a party going out to India. We have also had cables telling us to expect a request for 40 reinforcements for the Middle East. We are wondering who to send. Dick is very undecided, but I think would like to go, if his wife agrees. I shall not go as a member of the party, but if I were offered command of all the FAU Middle East, and if I felt there was a job and one I could do, I should, of course discuss it pretty seriously with you. Really everything depends on Tom. Indeed he may want to go himself.

I went with Dick to Epping on Sunday, and it was wonderful to get out into the fresh air and see the country. How I wish you could have been with me. On Monday, can you believe, we had an 8½ hour Executive Meeting, choosing a provisional list for the Egypt party. We had to decide amongst other things, whether to offer any Ethiopians over here, a chance to go. Jack would prefer Ethiopia to Egypt. Bless him, he likes me and would love me to go with him. It's strange how one or two people seem to quite like me. In fact a lot of people have been saying quite nice things about me, but I take them all with a pinch of salt. I know I've made a hell of a lot of mistakes, and I haven't done anything like as well as Tom, but I have not made a complete hash of things. There are actually one or two things that might make you proud of me. Now I am being conceited.

The chocolate and cigarettes were very welcome and the shirt is admirable – it looks very nice too and fits well. Thank you so much. Give David my love and say I hope to be playing trains with him again in a week or two. I do hope Antony is better now and give him a birthday kiss. Also please my love to your mother.

Now just remember, I love you and I am not deserting you for anyone, nor ever will.

Bless you always my very dear wife.
Ralph

———

Russia never really developed as an opening for foreign aid, but India did. During the Second World War India was still under British control, holding large territories throughout India. Though there were already the stirrings of demands for independence from Ghandi and the Congress party and even those like Chandra Bose who tried to form an alliance with Germany, most were still loyal to the UK and British India officially declared war on Germany in September 1939. Through Geoffrey Wilson, my father was already having talks with Stafford Cripps as well as with his old friend and mentor, Horace Alexander, himself a friend of Gandhi who knew the country well, and who was the ideal person to head a Unit deputation there.

The British Raj, as part of the allied nations, sent over two and a half million soldiers to fight under British command against the Axis powers. Their contribution was immense, including lending the British government billions of pounds to help finance the war, and India also provided a base for American operations in support of China in the China/Burma/India theatre.

Indians fought with great distinction throughout the world, including in the European theatre against Germany, in North Africa against Germany and Italy, in the South Asian region defending India against the Japanese and fighting the Japanese in Burma. Towards the end of the war, India also contributed greatly in liberating the British colonies such as Singapore and Hong Kong after the Japanese surrender in August 1945. Over 87,000 Indian soldiers, including those from modern day Pakistan, Nepal and Bangladesh died in World War II. In fact Field Marshal Sir Claude Auchinleck, C-in-C of the Indian Army from 1942, stated that the British "could not have come through the war if they hadn't had the Indian Army."

Horace Alexander with Ghandi and members of his Ashram
Gandhi is leaning on the shoulder of Abha, his daughter-in-law and granddaughter Sita.
Next to HGA is R V Shastri, Editor of the Mahatma's journal Harijan.
Photograph courtesy late Geoffrey Carnall and Edinburgh University Press

[Textual: Long before the days of computers, in the days when people still wrote letters, it would often be the case that absent-mindedly, people so used to writing the old year, would often date letters or cheques written in the early days of a new year, as still being in the old year. Here my father does exactly that, dating this letter as 1941, when it is patently 1942. Horace's wife, Olive Alexander died on January 14th 1942 and Tom Tanner got back from America in late January 1942.]

Although my father has been trying to persuade Horace to lead a unit of the FAU to go out to India for some time, it would have been impossible while his wife Olive was so ill. Suffering from MS, she had been gradually deteriorating in health and dies on January 14th 1942. Here my father comes to Birmingham for her memorial service at Woodbrooke. There is also further talk of an overseas posting for my father………

Wednesday, January 21st 1942 – London Hostel

My dearest

It was so good to see you and the children at the weekend, even though it was for so short a time. Please thank Win for putting me up and your mother for mending some clothes. How I wish I could have stayed with you for longer. But apart from the joy of seeing you and the children, I was glad I came up for Horace's sake. The memorial service for Olive was very moving, with some fine tributes. She was a person whom everybody loved and respected, and I was privileged to have known her. He will miss her terribly.

I had quite a good journey back, and fortunately it was nothing like as cold as in Birmingham, though today it has been snowing heavily again, and the streets are filthy and slushy. I have been caught up in a great deal of work since getting back, as these last few days have been extraordinarily busy, trying to choose personnel to be go abroad. It was decided that Jack Frazer would lead a group to India with Dick Symonds and Glan Davies as Sergeants.

There is still no decision on a team to go out to the Middle East, though they persist in talking about me leading a team out there. But this must wait until Tom returns from America, and we still have no news of him, though we expect him almost any moment. I rather think I ought to go if asked. Oh God, wouldn't it be wonderful to be out of this dreadful war and back at home, working in the Estate Office again. I feel now as though I could run the Trust standing on my head! Just to be back home, away from so many people, with my dear wife, in our own home and our own possessions, would be pure heaven. How I pray for that time to come, and it will come sometime, and perhaps, who knows, I shall be better for all this experience. Please give my love to David and I will try and send him a postcard very soon. All my love. May God keep you my dearest one, Ralph.

Realising the enormous extra responsibility it would place on my mother, my father has obviously discussed with her how she would feel if he had to go abroad. As always with my mother she accepted it with enormous grace……

Thursday, January 22nd 1942 – London Hostel

My dearest

I do want to thank you for your dear letter. You are simply the best wife that any man could ever have. I think your attitude over this foreign business is beyond praise. God, I am so proud of you. We can't reach any decision until Tom returns, and even then I don't know. I feel more and more that the job is too big for me, and that I ought to have enough strength of mind to say so this time, instead of taking on work I am not qualified to do. But I do thank you with all my heart for your ready sympathy and understanding. To have such a wife is a great privilege.

Brandon and I saw the Red Cross today, who were very friendly and seemed anxious for us to send reinforcements out. There is a very slight outside chance that we might be able to send a few women too. We have had a lot of hard work choosing the party. It's a thankless job and one which I do not relish. I went out to supper with Dick and Angela last night, which made a very pleasant change from the Hostel.

This evening I met John (brother) and we went for dinner at the Spanish Restaurant, which was excellent. Cadburys have suggested that he should try for another job[4], which he said he was going to do, as he has heard of one or two, at least one of which would offer him extra money. I'm also hoping to go and see Millior at the week-end.

I was so glad that you were able to go and see so many people on Sunday, and I know you would have looked nice, as you always do, so I am sure you deserved all the compliments that you received. All my dearest love, Ralph

With Olive's funeral over, Horace is once more down in London, and my father, as probably his closest friend, approaches him again on his thoughts about going out to India. As he comments on the service, and what he considers the sometimes indulgent fulsomeness of Friends, he talks of how he is ever conscious of her presence………

Sunday, January 25th 1942 – London Hostel

My dearest
I have been thinking of you so much. Often I feel that I have so much the best of life and it is so unfair. I will try and make it up to you after the war. How are the children? Please give them my love. I will send David a post card soon. How is he getting on at school?

Horace spent last night here, which was very nice. We wanted to talk to him about India and as he was in London for a conference over the week-end anyway, I asked him to stay here. In fact he has only just gone. He is being really rather wonderful about Olive. He says he is surprised that he feels so cheerful about it, but he has a great sense of his nearness to her. Just as her spirit triumphed over her body, so it is still alive and near him. I think that it is wonderful that he wants to continue to live in the same house and do the same things as she would wish him to do. It is immensely encouraging that he should feel like that.

He said he thought the memorial service was too occupied with tributes to her memory, and that some more silence and a sense of eternity, of God's grace and man's nothingness, would have been more appropriate and more helpful, and I agree. Friends talk too much and the continual praise was superfluous. He felt that Olive's comment would have been 'Tut, Tut', and he especially appreciated Richard Symond's tribute to her keen mind, common sense and humour. I suppose we should all feel this sense of nearness and have the same desire to carry on. Her last words to him were "We can never be separated." Don't pass any of this on. He is a lovely guest to have around and I think we made him comfortable.

On Friday Angela and I went to a French film at Studio One, *La Femme du Boulanger,* directed by Marcel Pagnol[5] with Raimu. He plays the French baker in a small village whose wife leaves him for another man and then is persuaded by the other villagers to return. The film is full of little details, that just give one a perfect sense of village life, and is in fact one of the finest films I've ever seen. In some ways almost Shakespearian, but in others more like a Russian novel. It was so true to life – men being sinful and cruel to each other, yet who remain essentially neighbourly and kindly and forgiving. It is a wonderful picture of a French village, and the acting is magnificent. I so wish you could have seen it.

Otherwise, we are still in the throes of the amalgamation with FWVRC and picking people for the foreign convoy. Acceptances are coming in gradually and I expect we shall soon have the party complete. Still no sign of Tom.

We now have quite a few women who have joined the unit, but my goodness they are a fairly dud lot to look at, and to speak to. Apart from a few such as Jean Cottle, who has been with the Unit as a nurse for a long time, Annette Cooper (later Caulkin), Gwendie Knight (Barty Knight's sister) and Angela, who are all excellent people and stand apart. But the rest....Ummm!

What a life I lead! All those 150 plus people to look after, and trying to get them to do things, and see that they are kept working, and then try to establish some sort of long term policy, and get it through committees and passed into action. You will perhaps understand what keeps me so busy.

Thank God it has at last started to get warmer, and the snow has gone this morning, and it is rather lovely. In fact I may go out for a walk with Richard later on. I shall miss him when he goes to India. How are you my dear? May God keep you safe my darling. I love you so dearly.
All my love, Ralph.

[Textual: Another undated letter, just marked 'Thursday'. But he refers to the Ethiopian government requesting 40 men. The agreement to send men out there was signed at the end of January '42, and they finally sailed in May. He also mentions India, and my father first seriously discussed the possibility of Horace leading a group going to India, within a week of his wife Olive dying, which was on January 14th '42. Finally, talks about an Officer being charge of the Middle East, was first mooted with my father as early as January '42 as well. So this short letter is most probably Thursday, January 29th.]

With permission at last coming through for further overseas work – Ethiopia, India and the Middle East - discussions with HGA progress and my father talks of a visit to Birmingham to see him and staying at Wolverhampton as well as talking more about his own posting........

Possibly a Thursday (eg 29th) in late January 1942

My dearest
Very many thanks for your letter. [......] I too wish more than I can say, that I could see more of the children. But a little of my anxiety is mitigated in the knowledge of how beautifully you look after them.

Everything is suddenly boiling up. The Ethiopian Government has asked definitely for 40 men, and there is also a distinct possibility of our being able to send a small party to India. I am expecting to be coming up to Birmingham again this weekend, in the hope of discussing the project further with Horace. I will confirm as soon as I can, but I'll probably come to Wolverhampton on Saturday evening, then go over to see HGA on Sunday, and return Monday morning. Will this be alright with all at Lea Road?

The Executive Committee have suggested that I should go out as Officer in Charge of the Middle East (OCME) together with the Abyssinian group. That is spend a little time in Addis, then go off from there to Egypt. Of course, I want to discuss all this with you. It may all come to nothing, because of the constant change of plans, or because there is no shipping. But we must talk it over in case. I am sorry to spring all this on you, but we have known it has been in the wind. I do know how difficult it all is for you and you are more than ever in my thoughts. I do love you so dearly and all this is so damned hard. I do pray that God will help us, my peerless, perfect wife. Dearest love Ralph

[Textual: This next letter is again dated only 'Thursday', but he mentions that Tom isn't back yet, so it's before the February 1st letter, by when he is back. Also the Liverpool section under Robin Whitworth first went up there in October 1941, but raids began again in Liverpool in January 1942, and the Ethiopia/Abyssinia party was hanging around waiting to go in January 1942, so Jan '42 seems the most likely date.]

Having run out of official headed paper, this letter is written on the nearest piece of paper to hand, hence the allusion to 'bog paper' in the first line! Reinforcements go off to Liverpool, whilst my father and Richard go visiting the rest centres around the country before Tom returns…….

Thursday, January 30th 1942 – London Hostel

My dearest

This is not bog paper, although it may look like it!!

We have had some really pleasant weather these last few days and the stars have been so clear. I have just got back from a Rest Centre meeting at the Middlesex hospital, and at 11.30 Orion is just coming up in the East. I really thought I might have had a few minutes to write to you before going to bed, but one of the chaps has just been in to see me. It seems one can never get away in this place.

We have sent a new section off to Liverpool to join Robin's group, as it looks as if there is going to be considerable work to do there, now that raids have started again with a vengeance. I wonder if you had a warning as well last night or the night before? The Abyssinian visit is really no further forward I'm afraid, though we are keeping the party together in the hope that they may be able to go soon. We had a Council meeting on Wednesday, but very few were there. Paul was really very pleasant - for once!

You may remember when I was still with the Trust, I was engaged on some research into future housing developments of the Estate – or at least I helped with it. The results have now been published as 'When We Build Again' (see p 499), and it turns out to have been rather popular and received some praise. I will let you see it when I come home next.

I have been feeling pretty glum and tired this week, but today I have cheered up somewhat. Perhaps because it has been a busy day and I haven't had time to dwell on missing you. I have literally been working from 9.0 in the morning till 10.0 at night.

Next week Richard Symonds and I hope to travel up to Birmingham by road to visit and harangue the Camp, then visit Keith and perhaps Kingsmead and Barnsley Hall near Bromsgrove. We shall probably sleep at Camp and then go on by road to visit Gloucester. I want to get to some of the Hospital sections while Tom is still away, and there are various reasons for my wanting to go to Gloucester. I am afraid I shan't manage to see you this visit as I really must stick entirely to a business schedule this time.

I must go to bed now……

Later…..The Egypt party seem to be getting on quite well and finding some work, and though overseas work is now opening up, it is often difficult to firm up details such as shipping etc.

I hope David's cold is better and that it has not made him too poorly. Give him my love. Also to your mother and thank her for all the mending that she did so beautifully. Millior rang this morning and I shall try and see her next week.

I don't think there is any more news. I do love you so and it was really grand being with you. God keep you my own incomparable wife.

Dear love Ralph.

Here my father writes of Tom's return and the difficulty of remembering that he is not number one anymore..........

By late January 1941 Tom had returned from America, bringing back, I recall, quite a lot of cigarettes and silk stockings with him. His journey home had apparently been terrible. They travelled in a small 3000 ton ship, which had taken over three weeks, and at one time he told me, there had been four inches of snow on deck with ice inside the cabins. Brandon and I went down to meet him at the family home in Failand, near Bristol, where his parents lived, to whom he is devoted. Despite the journey, he still looked as fit and well as ever. He is a big man Tom, no doubt about it! And I was soon made aware of it.

Forgetting that he was the Chairman now and back in action, I with my new found authority, told him that we had two jobs for him, as Officer in Command, Middle East and as Chairman of the newly combined FWRS Committee! He was I thought, rather non-committal, pausing only to say – "actually I've been asked by American Friends to go to clear things up in China." When one has been boss, it's strange to have to take second place, and I couldn't quite adjust myself! It was odd having him back; he often made me feel very small, and incompetent. I hoped I should behave properly. In his absence we might have forgotten a little of what manner of man he was; but his power and ascendancy soon made themselves felt again.

[Textual: This is again dated only by the word 'Sunday', nonetheless, internal evidence mentions Tom's return from America, which as we learn above was the end of January, so a surmise at the nearest 'Sunday' –viz February 1st - is probably not far wrong.]

Here he tells my mother of the embarrassment of blithely informing Tom of the tasks they had lined up for him. Only to be put back in his place! Then more discussion about Linden Road......

Sunday, February 1st 1942

My darling Joan
Thank you for your letter. Firstly, as to the position here. I'm afraid I rather embarrassed myself. Having been Deputy Director, it's all a bit difficult getting used to Tom being back. I started by telling him what we wanted him to do, before he told me what to do! But I expect I shall get used to it and settle down alright!

He has not made up his mind yet, but I think the idea of a visit to China quite attracts him. If he does that, I suppose I will stay here. On the other hand, I don't feel that he should really be spared from here. If he stays, I might then be asked to go to Egypt. In any case, the whole position is left in abeyance until Ronald Joynes returns from Egypt. He will then be in a position to say what is needed and might even be sent back as OC himself. I am afraid, therefore, that the whole matter cannot be decided for a few weeks. So whether I go or not, we shall not know for some time.

Now, about the Linden Road house. I feel that you must decide, because your happiness and peace of mind is the most important thing. The advantages seem to be:
1. To be back in your own home, would be a comfort for you, as I know how tired you are of living in other people's houses.
2. It will probably also be better for the children.
3. It will be pleasanter surroundings.
4. It will be much nicer for me on leave – (a purely selfish reason!)
5. You will be back with your neighbours' acquaintance and friends.
6. Away from the slightly deadening atmosphere of 31 Lea Road.

The disadvantages:
1. You would be lonely, unless you could find someone to share the house. Might this be possible? Maybe some other mother and child? Your mother wouldn't return would she?
2. You would be frightfully busy. Even with a nurse, you would be pretty busy. Could you get one? It would be no good until you can.
3. There would be considerable extra responsibility on you to have sole care of the children and a house to run.
4. A risk of air raids, though that seems to be considerably less now, I think.
5. Expense. We should lose the rent from Tritsch, and my extra salary would all go on home help, so we would not be any better off.

I am afraid this is not very helpful, but once again, I fear it is thee my little one, who should decide finally, as you will initially bear the brunt of having to cope. My own view is, I think, that if you could find a Nurse, you would find in the long run, that you would be happier back in your own home, and I should like you to go. But if you feel the upheaval and responsibility and loneliness to be too great, then I think you should stay where you are. I shall quite understand whichever you do. Please write again when you have read this, and I will then write to Cousin Dorothy and you can do likewise. I have tried to explain my mind and I hope it may be of some assistance to you. May God help you my dear.

Just when you think the weather has cleared up, as it did some days ago, the snow starts all over again and this week has been consistently foul. Hopefully it will clear soon, and depending, I will try to take either next week-end or the one after off. I will let you know when events and the weather are clearer.

This week seems to have been as busy as ever, and I have been a bit depressed, but I feel more cheerful now. Richard and Angela and I walked in the park yesterday afternoon, but it was so cold that we went into the National Gallery instead and looked at the War Artists exhibition and the Rembrandts.

American Friends have come in on the China expedition and are largely financing it. They are not at all happy about the leadership of it and want Tom and John Rich to go out and clear things up. The leader of the party - over Peter Tennant - is a man called Bob Mclure, whose ideas do not appear to be extremely Quakerly. Oh dear! This might turn out badly.

I am so interested that David can write already. He really is making good progress. Give him my love. I hope he got my card. I seem to have a perpetual cold, though it's not a really bad one. I am so sorry that you are getting one too. I hope it clears up soon.

You are always in my thoughts my dearest. May God keep you and bless you and help you to a right decision. I will see you before very long.
Dearest love Ralph

Instead of Tom going out to the Middle East, as it transpired, it was my father that was appointed OCME and perhaps a chance to prove himself.......

As it turned out, it was me who was asked to go out to the Middle East! I was appointed as Officer in Charge of the Middle East, or OCME, as it came to be known. I was to co-ordinate all the various sections at work there, to set up an HQ in Cairo, to visit and report and to look into Relief possibilities. Tom had even given me a letter of appointment, and everybody said (mistakenly I am sure) that it was a job that only I could do. Peter Gibson in particular was pressing for me to take it. I have often had cause to express my doubts about the value of our work in the Unit. Was it too easy, I wondered? Was I living too privileged a life? But here finally, was the opportunity to prove myself.

However, even with pressure from Peter G and others, and though I felt I ought to go, it was still no easy decision. I had many doubts, especially as to whether or not it was right to leave Joan and the children. Of course, she was marvellous, as knowing her, one would expect. She told me that I should do what I thought was right.

But as a member of the Friends Ambulance Unit, the decision to go or not to go, was one of the most difficult that we would be called on to make. In the army a soldier's decision is made for him. For us in the Unit, there was rarely a completely clear cut case, especially when people told you no-one else could do the job. So, though in many ways it was an attractive offer, it was with a heavy heart, and some reluctance that I eventually decided it was a job I had to do, and that I did indeed have to go.

[Textual: There's very little content to place this letter anywhere. It is written on FAU London Hostel paper, so probably early February 1942]

Although a decision has now been taken for my father to go out to the Middle East, as Officer in charge, the statistical problems of getting a team together and waiting for a suitable boat to take them out there, would take several months. Meanwhile life continued for both my parents much as before, with a week-end visit in the offing......

c. Friday, 6th February 1942 – London Hostel

My dearest

I was very sorry to hear that you were so miserable last night. I am afraid that you must have had a rotten time with the children, and I am sorry. I think of you so much dear heart. Try and cheer up. We shall be together next week-end, and I am looking forward to my leave very much. It will be so grand to be with you again. I will try to behave – honest I will!

You do realise don't you my darling, how enormously I admire the way that you carry on and look after the children in such an uncomplaining way. I am so very grateful and bless you for it. I have been looking for little gifts to bring up, but I'm afraid I have only got rather a dull book for you, though I did find a little Bear book for David. Otherwise I fear I haven't been able to get much else. I will probably get a train up next Thursday evening and will most likely return on the following Tuesday afternoon, if that's all right with W&L.

This week has been rather hectic, and we have a Staff meeting this Sunday. Considering all the mistakes I have made, I might get thrown off the Executive with any luck. I wouldn't mind, as I hate making silly mistakes. Besides I'm tired as I haven't had a real day off since you were here. Last Sunday was half a day, but not enough to really count, and I have had only two evenings out.

All the Executive come up early when there is a meeting, and I had breakfast with Arnold Rowntree yesterday at his Hotel, The Westway. He was very fond of my parents and by extension seems fond of me, and I like him. He is a nice old chap, though, dare I say - he can get rather boring at times! Paul also, of course, was here in good time and wanted to talk, talk, talk! Sometimes he can be really unbearable!

I am glad that David is enjoying school so much and that his first report is a good one. Please thank him for his drawing and tell him how pleased I am about his report. I am so pleased that you and my mother are now getting on so well. Who would have thought it?! I must stop now. You are always in my thoughts. All my love Ralph.

PS. I do hope LPA will pull through all right. Let me know if you hear any news.

FAU Executive Gordon Square 1941
Back Row: FRB, Peter Gibson, Freddy Temple, Dick Symonds
Front Row: Richey Mounsey, Peter Hume, Tom Tanner, Brandon Cadbury, John Bailey
Photograph Friends House Library

[Textual: Another undated letter, but it is clearly written later than the February 1st letter, with its references to Cos Dorothy, (who gave them Linden Road on their marriage) regarding what my mother should do regarding staying at Wolverhampton or moving back to Birmingham. There is also reference to 'waiting for Ronald Joynes to get back' which definitely places it still in February, as he got back in March.]

As so often plans get changed, which means my mother has to fit around the new arrangements, but she seems to take it all in her stride. Delayed mail from the Middle East means, when reading a letter from Nik Alderson, that until Ronald Joynes returns in March, they had not yet heard of Nik Alderson's death on February 14th. And another particularly bad 'black dog' period for my father............

Probably c. Wednesday, 11th February 1942 – London Hostel

My dearest

Thank you for your letters. I am sure yours is the right decision about Wolverhampton, if you feel as you do. Your letter to Cousin Dorothy must have been a good one, and her reply does not seem to need a reply at present.

I am so sorry, but my plans are now all altered, as Liverpool seems rather urgent just at the moment. So I am, going to have go up there this Saturday, returning Sunday. I think that I shall now go up to Birmingham on Thursday of next week and spend the night with Keith, then go to Camp on Friday and see the Egyptian party in training. I might perhaps go in and see LPA as well and then come on to you on Friday. I am so glad you were able to put off your dance. I hope it didn't put you in an awkward spot.

It was so good to speak to you on the phone the other night, and I really hope that you are better by now and that the children's colds are not too bad. God bless you all.

I have been asked to speak at Meeting for Sufferings tomorrow about the new set up. I am not looking forward to it. Things here are not much clearer than they were. Tom I think has decided to stay in this country for the time being, but for the moment there has been a hitch in the shipping for the Egyptian party, which may delay them indefinitely. It is most disappointing.

We are still waiting for Ronald Joynes to return from Egypt. A letter has come from Nik Alderson of the Hadfield Spears party, emphasising "the need for Tom or Ralph or someone of such standing to go out to the Middle East to co-ordinate everything." It's nice to know I am of 'some standing'! Well, well! Perhaps I'm not as incompetent after all!

I don't quite know what has been the matter with me these last few days, but I have been in a bottomless pit of despair and always sinking. Everything seemed as bleak and depressing as it could be, and there seemed no hope or light anywhere. It was at its worst yesterday morning, but I managed to climb a little way out yesterday midday, and then I dropped back. This evening I have managed to climb further up out of the pit, and hope the worst is over.

I am afflicted this way at times, partly I think it is due to being over tired, when everything seems bigger than it is. What with the breaking up of the sections and Dick almost certainly going off to India, as well as uncertainty about the future and the war itself, not to mention the weather! As always one is walking on the edge of the pit, and whilst mostly one manages not to fall in, when one does, it's perfectly bloody.

Tom is feeling down too. 'Why didn't I stay in America?' he says. 'No wife and children (with me) and the future fills me with gloom. I've been married for over five years and I don't like not having a woman in my life.' In addition his 'girlfriend' Ann Channer is about to go off to Stockholm. Poor old Tom!

Dick's wife was down here last night. She is upset at his going and feels afraid that they will drift apart. Dick is also apprehensive on the same count. What a tragedy this war is, and what personal tragedies this war creates too.

One thing I do know thank God, is that tragic and heart-breaking as a separation would be, we would not drift apart. Our love and marriage ties are so strong, that we would pick up where we left off. Of that I am absolutely certain. God bless you, my dearest.

Millior and Alfred came into supper the other night. It was very pleasant to see them. They said that when the weather improves, they would be very glad to have you and David to stay.

I am glad you and Win enjoyed the concert with the Birmingham Symphony under Sargent, though, as you know, I am tone deaf and would almost certainly not have appreciated it! I think it must come from the old Quaker tendency to frown on music, as, apart from hymns there was none in our house. My loss I know.

Dearest love Ralph

As it turned out, my father had to wait until June 1942 before he finally sets sail for the Middle East, and the next few months were anxious ones, not knowing from one day to the next, exactly when he would depart. Meanwhile he had to carry on as normally as possible with visits to Wolverhampton as and when they could be fitted in.

[Textual: This next letter has no first page. He mentions that Tom is now back so probably mid/late February, and he also talks about not sending women to Egypt, both mentioned back in January.]

A hint that much as he respects Tom, being number two isn't always easy.........

Last page of a letter sometime in mid/late February 1942 – London Hostel

(Dearest) [......] It's been bloody cold again, with frost and snow everywhere. I can't wait for it to get warmer. [.......] It seems rather doubtful now if we shall be sending any of our women to Egypt, as the Red Cross want to send some of theirs, which is rather unfortunate for us.

[.....] I'm glad you are enjoying *The Gay Galliard.* I should like to read it too when you have finished, as I usually enjoy Margaret Irwin's books. Is this one of her historical novels? How good that you have got the Boots subscription to buy some books.

[.....] My dearest one, may God watch over you and help you in your difficult job. Please think of me too, now that Tom has returned, which isn't going to be altogether easy, good as he is. Dear love, forever Ralph

My mother has been to visit their house in Linden Road, which stirs many memories for both of them as well as thoughts of what lies ahead. People come and go........

Thursday, February 27th 1942 – Students Hostel, London

Dearest Joan

Thank you so much for your long letter, which I was thrilled to get. I am glad that you were able to visit the Linden Road home and to do so much. How I wish we could be back there again. What a dear house it is and what good times we had there. Like you, I recall so many special moments: with friends, making the garden together, our neighbours. How special our love and life together has been. When will such times come back? If you see the Keens, please give them my very kind regards. I feel so sorry for them, as such upheaval in their late years, must be so disturbing. I will write to Mr Appleton about getting the main fence mended, but I think Mr Tritsch will have to take care of the emergency exit himself.

Not too much more news. We are still in the thick of the amalgamation with War Vics. It appears that it's going to save quite a lot of money, as all the WV staff, who get maintenance allowances earn quite a shocking amount of money, which at this time, we can ill afford. Christopher Taylor was here today discussing it with me. As usual, considerable comings and goings: Barry (Barratt Brown) has gone off for a week to tour South Wales with the mobile Citizens Advice Bureau, after which he is going to Newcastle for a few days, to see about setting up an Emergency Relief there too, along the lines of Birmingham and Liverpool.

While Richard is still waiting to go to India, he is coming back into the section on Monday pro tem, and going to do some mechanics training. It will be good to see him. Tom had an American man in to supper last night, who is over here studying British Air Raid Precautions (ARP). He is fairly high up in the American Civil Defence, and was such a nice person.

I am hoping to go and see Millior and John tomorrow, and will find out how long John is staying in London, so that hopefully we can arrange for you to come up to town. God bless you my dear heart. I do love you so, and how destitute I should be without you. Thank you for bearing everything with such equanimity. Love to the children. Dearest love, Ralph

With Tom back in the ascendancy, my father had the difficult task of continuing as Relief Officer, whilst at the same time kicking his heels awaiting for shipping to be available, and preparing with my mother for the inevitable parting..........

Women members of the FAU

Angela da Renzi Martin
(later Sinclair-Loutit)

Tessa Rowntree - later Cadbury

Photographs courtesy of Jessica Sinclair-Loutit and Jack Cadbury Library

Annette Caulkin – in later life she became Michael Barratt Brown's partner
Photograph Friends House Library

Chapter 15
Long Months of Waiting
March and April 1942

My father writes movingly in his memoirs of the time preceding his departure........

The decision to go overseas was not easy. On the one hand, one of my doubts was whether or not it was right to leave Joan. She of course, as knowing her, you would expect, was marvellous and said that I must do as I thought right. The decision in the Unit to go or not to go, is one of the most difficult we can be called upon to make; the army decides for a soldier. But rarely is ours such a clear cut case, when no-one else could do the job.

On the other hand all my friends seemed to be leaving, with Jack Frazer off to Ethiopia, and especially Richard and Horace going to India. In fact I nearly went instead of Horace, as so soon after his wife Olive's death and his commitments at Woodbrooke, it was not an easy decision for him to make. After the amalgamation of FWVR and FRCRS, and the resulting new FWRS now running relief, made such work for the FAU have an uncertain future. But there was a job as Officer Commanding the Middle East (OCME). I was to co-ordinate the sections already out there, to set up an HQ in Cairo, to visit and report, and to look into relief possibilities. Tom gave me a letter of appointment and said everyone concurred that it was a job that only I could do.....mistakenly, I am sure. Indeed Paul Cadbury was urgently pressing for me to go as well.

I had often felt that despite difficulties and hard work, my war service had been too easy, and that it was our duty, if we were called upon, to go abroad if we could. In many ways I was attracted and felt that I ought to go, but I went with a heavy heart. And the next few months hung heavy on us, as we awaited the final go ahead and the availability of room aboard a troopship. Meanwhile, I carried on as best I could with my relief work, while making what preparations I could to travel, and propping up Joan for our inevitable long time apart from each other.

[Textual: Another letter that my father also dates as being 1941 – forgivable in January, but hardly in March!! Although the eclipse of the moon, to which he refers, did take place on Tuesday, March 3rd, as he correctly writes, it was in the year 1942 not 1941! (In 1941 the eclipse was Thursday, March 13th!)]

Still very busy and still waiting around for the shipping situation to resolve itself, my father here fills a letter home with thoughts on books – Vera Brittain [1] was hugely popular at the time – as well as the eternal task of sorting out foreign trips including his own.......

Tuesday, March 3rd 1942 – London Student's Hostel

My dearest
I must apologise for not writing yesterday as I intended, but Christopher Taylor was staying at the hostel for the evening, and I had to entertain him. Did you see the eclipse of the moon which was complete about 12.20 this morning? It was really rather spectacular.

Thank you so much for your long letter, which I have just received. It was a splendid letter and full of interesting things. I always love to hear what you have been up to and I'm so happy, that with all you have to do looking after the children, you have still found time to read. I'm really pleased you enjoyed Vera Brittain's *Testament of Youth* as much as I did. It does of course speak very much to the Quaker condition and is most movingly written I think.

I have heard a lot about Hasel Mundy's[2] *A Thousand shall Fall*, which you mention, but have not yet read it. I wonder how many readers would recognise the origin of the title from the psalms... *"A thousand shall fall at thy side, and ten thousand at thy right hand; but it shall not come nigh thee..."* Because you believe in the Lord and follow his ways, he will protect you. I doubt many have that degree of faith these days. I'm pretty sure I don't, sinner that I am, though I'm sure my parents did!

Yes, I too love the *Rubaiyat*, [3] mainly because it sounds so grand, but I think its philosophy is rather simple and obvious – 'eat, drink and be merry for tomorrow we shall be one with yesterday's seven thousand years'! But it is good stuff and sounds terrific. [.......]

I am afraid I never took to Julian Bell[4] greatly. Even at Leighton Park he was a curious youth, and no-one ever expected him to do much. Perhaps, as he was a pacifist, I should try and like him more, though that in itself is, of course, no guarantee of likeability! His death in Spain was very sad too, but I always found his younger brother Quentin[5], who was also at LP with me, much more likeable.

You ask what I do in my spare time. Well, I worked pretty much all day on Saturday, which is not unusual. The truth is, I don't seem to have much spare time, and what I do have I usually spend reading or talking to people. Save for Sunday, I haven't been out for ages. Even this Sunday I mostly worked and read, but in the evening Angela had a birthday party at the Café Royal – she and Richard Symonds, Arnold Curtis and me. It was a good supper and altogether a very pleasant evening. I gave her a book as a present. Richard had just got back from Dunster, where he had been on holiday with his wife, which they much enjoyed, except for the cold.

We are now getting some work abroad, but it's really sickening that they are not able to get away, but with the demands for shipping army divisions half way across the world, a handful of pacifists does not rank that high in the shipping priorities, I fear. Despite all the problems we are still desperately hoping for more useful work we can do, to prevent us all feeling so useless and futile.

I had been hoping to go to see Millior and Alfred last week-end, but was too busy to get away, so I am afraid I haven't seen either of them or John, who is staying with them. I am hoping to have a bit of leave before long, and intend to come up for a weekend and then perhaps you and David could come to London and we could have a little time together. I am so much looking forward to seeing you my dear and long only to be with you and the children. All my love, as ever, Ralph.

A period of kicking his heels – carrying on carrying on. Endless committees, everyday business, meeting people – a visit to the dentist an ingrowing toenail and a boil...........

Friday, March 7th 1942 - Students' Hostel

My dearest

Thank you so much for your letter and for writing to me so often. [....] I seem to be very busy with various things – mostly lots and lots of committees, about the new FWRS, about trouble with ex War Vics, who don't like working with the Unit, reducing numbers in the section and so on and so on. I get pretty fed up with it all. God, it will be nice to have some warmer weather again too. [.....] I am so glad that Antony is getting on well, though God knows it's a grim world for him to grow up in.

Tomorrow Tom and I are going off for the day to visit one or two hospitals and 'War Vics hostels'. If it were a decent day, it might be quite pleasant, but if this wind continues, it will be pretty bloody. I apologise for my writing – it seems to be getting ruder!

You will be pleased to hear that I have been to the dentist - a nice, fat, talkative person with rooms in Wimpole Street. Can you believe he was in the Unit in the last war and now kindly looks after us FAU chaps on the cheap! He said I had good strong teeth and that the work of my previous dentist was first class. It's amusing to have a new dentist. He said that the cavity - you will remember my filling came out at Christmas – was enormous and that it was extraordinary that it hadn't given me pain. He has put a temporary filling in, and I am to go back soon for a permanent one.

Barry is back from a trip in South Wales with the mobile CAB. He says he has made some 20 speeches in 5 days. Arnold (Curtis) should be in Newcastle, but has a bad cold; Richard (Symonds) is off to do some mechanics training - he has given up his flat and is looking for another. It's nice to have him about, though he is feeling in rather low water just at present. Tom is, of course, full of energy as ever, though he professes he 'finds life totally bloody'. But one can't help liking Tom, even though he is overpowering at times, and one gets annoyed with him.

John Bailey is depressed about his wife working too hard and has now apparently lost the tenants who were living in his flat. Angela has got over the flu but on the whole is still rather low. She is also taking a part time mechanics course, and so has difficulty getting through all my work. But altogether we get on well and are a cheerful crowd. If only we could find new work or see some definite prospect of some. I do think my job is by way of being one of the lousiest in the Unit. To begin with it was the biggest, but now it is cutting back and cutting back, trying hard to justify what remains, and working hard to keep people up to the mark, when it all seems so futile.

On top of everything, my bad toenail and the boil are still bothering me and so I am feeling very sorry for myself! But I mustn't complain, as I know I am lucky in many ways. I have my health and comfort with plenty to do and good friends. And of course, as I said before, most importantly I have you and the children. I can't ask for more.

When we get together we can be a talkative lot and help to sustain each other. Gossiping about the Unit – who's in and who's out, who's misbehaving! Serious topics – Religion of course, and Quakerism. Culture – books we've read or films we've seen. Politics – how the war's going and how the Unit is doing. Much the same as chaps anywhere I guess. It all helps to keep the mind active and off more troublesome thoughts.

Arnold Curtis, who is in charge of Rest Centres, is getting married on March 28th up in Leeds, though there has been fierce opposition from his family. We could tell him something of that I think! Apparently he walked into a lamp post the other night and broke his glasses and he's as blind as bat without them.

I took a little time off to see Millior for a short while at Friends House the other day, which was very nice, and I saw John as well. But now that Tom is back I am doing a day a week's Medical Orderly duty again, and if I take any time off, the work just piles up. There is a Woodbrooke Council meeting on Friday, for instance, but I simply shan't be able to go. I was up at 5.0am on Friday to do an Orderly until 1.0pm, before I had to go off to the Dentist. I then went on to Gordon Square, followed by a meeting with the War Vics until 7.15. After that, I tried to finish some work, before I finally packed it in and went off for a drink with Richard. I'm not sure if it's all worth it, but it has to be done. Poor old me! Just remember how much I love you. God take care of you. All my love, Ralph

PS I enclose my ration book, so that you can use some of my coupons. Please return it when you have finished with it.

[Textual: Another letter dated 1941 instead of 1942 – my father must have been distracted! It has to be 1942 and not 1941, as Ronald Joynes arrived back at Gordon Square in '42 and Raymond Alderson was killed in February '42.]

A weekend leave coming up, a day out with Tom, visitors come and go, and news of 'Nik' Alderson's death........

Wednesday, March 11th 1942 - London Hostel

My darling

I am so looking forward to seeing you on Friday. I'll let you know what time the train gets in, but don't feel you have to meet me. I'm afraid it is not a particularly convenient week- end, as I am really hellish busy. But the following two week-ends are even more impossible, so it's the best at the moment. However, I have to have lunch with Robin Whitworth on Monday and present a report to the Executive, so that I rather fear that I may have to catch a very early train back. Quite why I am so busy, I don't really know, but I have been working very late all this week and tomorrow I am on Orderly duty again.

Tom and I had a very good day last Sunday. We started at 8.0am and went first to Petersfield and saw the FWRS scheme and the workers there. Then we went to Winchester, had a sandwich lunch on the way and a pint in Winchester. From there we went on to Salisbury and visited the hospital section there. Thence we went to see some friends of Tom's nearby – a Major and his wife, evacuated from London. They are in a perfectly lovely cottage in a beautiful village. He was billeted nearby and comes home every week-end. She was very charming.

Then we went home. It was a glorious day of sun and wonderful country. We had a beautiful drive, with good roads, fairly empty, so we were able to go at a fair speed from Salisbury to London and covered the 85 miles to Hyde Park corner in 2 hours, driving half of the distance each. Tom had invited Jean Cottle to join us and we all had a very pleasant day together. I wished so much you could have been with us.

Last night I went to the cinema with Dick. I hadn't planned to go but he was feeling pretty down and miserable, so I thought it might cheer him up. I worked late afterwards. The other day we finally managed to get a further 6 people off to China, so things are moving, if slowly. In the last few days, lots of chums have come into see me, which greatly cheered me up: John Terry came over for lunch today, who is working for NCSS*3 in Bristol; Ronald Joynes, now back from the Middle East, popped in yesterday, and it was really good to see him again; and Jack Eglon came in the other evening, though I thought he seemed to be in rather a bad way. Sadly, Ronnie brought news that Raymond 'Nik' Alderson had been killed by enemy bombing in the hospital at Tobruk, right back on February 14th. Nik was the real genius of the section out there, and he'll be greatly missed. Mike Rowntree has taken over from him as leader, with Pat Barr as second-in-command.

I'm sorry that you feel so fed up, but be patient, my dear, we have this next week-end coming up and that will be lovely for both of is. Let's try and get out while I am at home, perhaps to Belvide and perhaps to the theatre. I am so glad you are still finding time to read so many books. Huxley's[6] *Grey Eminence* sounds most interesting, though I'm not sure about *Greek Verse,* as I am always a bit shy of translations. You are always in my thoughts. Give my love to David and Antony – I am so glad that they are getting on so well together. All my love, Ralph.

PS Please excuse my writing, but I have worked all day and it's now 9.45 and I must be up at 5.0am. A CO's life is never done!!

---

*3 National Council of Social Service

[Textual: Slightly difficult to pin some of these letters down. As in a jigsaw, you fit one fact in with something in another letter, and then find that another bit doesn't fit at all. Where things are out of joint, I have done my best to keep them sequential, but have sometimes taken the liberty of cutting items that just make little sense date wise. Mostly these are family matters or things of small consequence, so it does not spoil the narrative to cut them. But of all the Sundays at this time (which FRB states it is) March 15 seems the nearest to a correct dating.]

The problem of Angela continues to niggle, despite her now going out with Dick Symonds; news of my mother's brother, Reg Barber being posted to Ireland and problems in both China and Egypt looming, which will soon crystallise in both Tom and my father being posted overseas........

Sunday, March 15th 1942 – London Hostel

My dear wife

Thank you so much for sending me that book. It was a kind thought and I really appreciated. It was a delightful surprise. Many, many thanks for that and also for your two letters.

I'm glad that you enjoyed the week-end as much as I did, though I resent your suggestion that I left early last Monday so that I could have lunch with Angela. Your assumption is entirely incorrect!

[.....] I didn't see the review of Edith Sitwell's poetry, but as a rule I don't much enjoy her writing. I have enjoyed reading *The Gay Galliard*[7] however, and think it is good. Thank you so much for giving it to me. Bless you too for Frazer Darling's *Birds of Scotland*. It is excellent, and I am delighted to have it.

I was sorry to hear about Reg being posted to Northern Ireland. How rotten for him. Vera will miss him a lot. I had supper with Duncan's friend Ralph Pugh on Thursday. We went to a place off Shaftesbury Avenue called 'Chez Victor' where we had a rather good meal. Ralph works in the Dominion Office and I thought he was a nice man. We got off to a rather sticky start, but soon found we had lots in common and got on well. He knows Duncan's 'fiancée', whose name is Katharine, and is Scottish. Apparently Duncan met her when he was studying French in Nancy. She is now teaching at Westfield College in Hampstead.

We have received rather disturbing news from both China and Egypt, suggesting that the FAU parties out there, are not as happy as they might be. Tom is rather worried I think, and it is quite possible that someone will have to go out to both Egypt and China. The best solution is that of Tom's, that he and I should fly out together via Egypt, leaving me there while he goes on to China and then pick me up on the way back. It may be quite impracticable, but we'll see.

It was lovely to talk to you last night: you sounded so much more cheerful, despite having a bad cold. I do hope that will clear up soon. God look after you my dear.

I don't think there is any more news, except that I love you and only you.

All my love
Ralph.

PS I am at last hoping to have lunch with Millior this week, and I'll mention you staying with them.

Reg Barber

Reg Barber, my mother's brother in his RAF Uniform about 1940

Reg and Vera Barber with their eldest son Graham 1940/41.
"How rotten for Reg being posted to Ireland."
Photographs by courtesy of Chris Barber

Reg had wanted to join the FAU, but having married in 1935, and with a son born 1936, he was concerned as to whether he would be able to support them on a tiny salary or even none. As it was, Cadburys paid half salary, and Reg always thought his slow promotion after the war, reflected his wartime decision not to be a pacifist, even though he was not engaged in fighting.

———

Once again the Angela question rumbles on, like an itch that needs scratching. How many service men and women must have found themselves in a similar position. Alone with her thoughts, my mother is naturally a little jealous; for my father she is good company and lightens the burdens of a long day. But coming from his strict evangelical background, and as the most senior person in the FAU, my father would never have allowed it to go further and here asserts as much – again.

It is interesting to note at this point, that Angela's daughter Jessica, recently gave me a letter from my mother to Angela after my father's death and her separation from her husband, written in the most loving of terms and inviting her to stay.

The shipping situation is still bad, and he is no further ahead in knowing whether he will be going abroad or when. All of which brings more 'black dog' depression..........

Monday, March 16th 1942 – London Hostel

My darling

Thank you so much for a lovely week-end. I did enjoy it so much. I do love coming home to see you all. But I was considerably upset by your attitude on Sunday night. The more I think about it, the more I can say with absolute certainty that you have got it all wrong. I love you as much and even more than I ever did. That is absolutely true. Please dear heart, believe me that is so. I like all these people, but you have all of me in your hands. I love you. I can't say more, except ask you to believe that I am speaking the truth. Have just a little faith in me. I find it rather sad you have not more. But I'll forgive you. I'd forgive you anything.

Life here is pretty bloody. I wish to God I could cheer up, but somehow at present I can't get a lift anyhow. All the prospects seem so black. The Egyptian shipping is pretty erratic, which means that their sailing day is quite indefinite. It seems quite probable now that I shan't go. But the situation changes daily. Some American money is being cut off, which means a reduction in relief work, and there seems absolutely no fresh line of work that we can follow. This means more and more people will have to work in hospitals. You will understand, therefore, that I find life excessively gloomy at present.

[.....] There is very little more news I fear, since I saw you at the week-end. Please thank Win very much for putting me up, and also thank mother for looking after the children. Dear love Ralph.

Maybe both my parents felt the need for some 'togetherness', which resulted in my mother sending some flowers, and my father finding a reason to suddenly go up to Birmingham for the day to meet my mother. Whatever the reason, peace seems to have broken out..........

Sunday, March 22nd 1942 – London Hostel

My dearest

Thank you a thousand times for the lovely bunch of flowers – carnations and narcissus, which look absolutely beautiful. You are an extravagant child, but they are a joy in this office. Thank you for thinking of sending them.

I did enjoy seeing you on Friday. Sometime things are good and some just ordinary. But occasionally they are lit up by a gleam of special pleasure or enjoyment, and sometimes something even more intangible. Friday was just such an occasion. Perfect in every way. Unexpected flowers and a book, a pleasant place, a splendid lunch and you my dearest. Thank you for everything. I had a good journey back and after I had finished some work, I started on the 'The Epic of America'. It is a fascinating book and I am delighted to have it. Thank you so much. James T Adams is a highly respected historian, and apparently he coined the phrase 'the American Dream'!

I have been extremely occupied since I got back, working until about 1.30 on Friday night, with meetings all yesterday and work all this morning. Because of various meetings, we have had lots of people over here this week-end including Robin Whitworth, Keith Linney and Arnold Curtis, which in itself has made for a lot of extra work. Then our regular Staff meeting, which was about as stupid as usual, going on and on, and reaching no very definite conclusion. I even managed to persuade them all of the virtues of FWRS without any difficulty! In addition we have a further party of 9 leaving for China any minute.

It seems to be never ending, as this coming week is just as bad, being as fearfully busy as ever. But I think I could probably meet you in Birmingham on Friday evening, then go to the theatre and return to Wolverhampton with you, and come back here on Saturday. Let me know if this fits in and is alright with Win and Llew.

I am very sorry to hear about Aunt Lou's death.***4** She was a dear soul, and an institution, who led a life full of thoughtfulness for others. I am afraid mother will feel it very much. I have written to her and to Uncle Ernest.

I don't think there is any more news. Thanks again for the flowers. Love to David and all my love Ralph

My father – for once – feeling cheerful! A meeting with Mrs Sieff, and a trip taking her to see both the London shelters, as well as my father old haunts at Wood Ditton, Cheveley and Banstead Manor - and a reunion with the famous Mrs M........

Sunday March 29th 1942 – London Hostel

 My dearest
Thank you for your cards – a poor substitute for a letter I must say! But I'll forgive you, as today, for no particularly good reason, I feel somewhat more cheerful. I do hope you are not too tired. Bear up my angel.

I am thinking of you so much, and wondering if you are finding life any more tolerable now. I am really sorry about your difficulties, and so wish I could be of more help to you. I do love you so much and long only to see you again. Let me know when it would be best for me to next come to Wolverhampton.

I haven't very much news since I last wrote. Tom and I had a day showing Mrs Sieff - a friend of Tom's - round various places. Mrs Sieff is the wife of Israel Sieff and is, as you might imagine, a member of the chosen race, and just happens to own Marks and Spencer! I suppose they are millionaires – at any rate they own a huge flat in Park Lane, where we met up.

She is fiftyish, very vital and enthusiastic, very knowledgeable and likeable. She is I understand, a keen Zionist. How Tom knows her, I have no idea, but he has a vast list of miscellaneous acquaintances. She is a great admirer of what Tom has done for the FAU in the East End and also wanted to see the evacuation work we had done. She is genuinely interested, but as she is shortly going off to America, she wants to speak about it there. So Tom, of course, is anxious to oblige, because he likes her, and because he hopes she will raise some much needed funds for the Unit too.

We took her to our holiday camp at Flaunden in the Chilterns, where young people from our shelters go down for a week-end, or maybe a week. David Tod and his wife are in charge there and have their two children with them. They seem to be doing a wonderful job. David is a delightful person, and a great loss to the rest of the Unit. His wife is good looking, and very capable I should imagine. They say their children have settled down pretty well. Then we went on to Newmarket and visited Wood Ditton, Highfield, Cheveley and Banstead Manor. I felt pretty cheered by them, the women and children seemed happy and clean, and it must benefit their living an orderly life with good well-cooked meals. In some ways I felt Cheveley was the least successful, unfortunately, largely because of the Edmunds, who simply haven't worked out. The Tod's will probably replace them soon, and then they should do extremely well.

---

*4 Aunt Louisa (aka Aunt Lou'), the sister of FRB's mother, married to Ernest Hutchinson, who lived in Carlisle.

Fund-raising with Mrs Sieff

Above - FRB (left) with Tom Tanner.
(Photo Friends House Library)

Together they showed Rebecca Sieff round the relief shelters in London and elsewhere, as she was greatly impressed by the work of the FAU and helped to raise money in America for the Unit's work.

Rebecca Sieff was the wife of M&S chief Israel Sieff.

Photograph courtesy of Women's International Zionist Organisation

The Rectory looks much as it always did, and the garden for which I bought so many bedding plants, is doing wonders, and the neglected front patch which I had dug, has a fine crop of potatoes. That is one of the few achievements I have to my credit - a few hundred yards of land under potatoes! Very gratifying. Oh yes, and a lot of lettuces in the garden at the Manor. These are about the only two worthwhile things I have done I think! Mrs M was very happy to see me, and it was good to see her again too. She asked after you. I got a curious feeling going back, as I had become very attached to the place and have many vivid memories. But already it seems a long time ago. I must have been in a very receptive mood when I was there!

The run back home was rather lovely – the flat open country with wide views from the low hills and the great skies, was very beautiful. Otherwise, I have been pretty occupied. Last night I went round some of the London shelters, although at the moment there are not that many people sleeping there. It is difficult to see how we can be best employed, whether in social work, for which there are so few facilities, or in medical work, which is not much needed at present. We are trying to institute morning gym classes in the hostels, though it is not proving to be very popular. Still someday it will all be over, and you and I in God's good time, will be back home. How grand that will be. It's all I live for. All my love to David and Antony and please thank mother for all she is doing helping you with the children. I'll write again very soon. Dearest love, Ralph

PS Tell Win and Llew that they are welcome to some of the apples from Linden Road, if they wish.

[Textual: This next - undated letter - could be early April 1942, but could in fact be almost any time following a week-end leave. I'm assuming that pending his posting abroad, he took an extra leave as and when he could, which only prompts him to plan a longer leave quite soon. (Easter Sunday was April 5th)]

A general letter of pleasantries – another visit to the dentist, and places for their holiday prior to leaving to go abroad...........

Tuesday, April 2nd 1942 – London Hostel

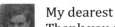 My dearest

Thank you so much for sending the book and for your lovely note. Thank thee too for being so nice to me over the week-end, though I know I was rather poor company. It was lovely to be with you and the children, and you are an angel to be so good and uncomplaining. I do think you are wonderful the way you carry on. I am sorry that I was not at my best, being amazingly tired, which I still am. But I will try and do better next time.

I had a very easy journey back, and the country looked so lovely. We had yet another Executive Committee on Monday, which as always leaves me prostrate. No doubt I shall cheer up soon. Please thank your mother for all the mending which she kindly did for me. How you both do spoil me and think of me. I am most grateful for the book and the card. Thank you so very much. [......] Please thank David for his card too.

There is not much news since I saw you. Just working and attending meetings. It seems as though I haven't been out or done anything for ages. I did go to the Dentist this morning and very much hope, this is now the end of my treatment. I am going to see Millior on Saturday and will see if anything can be fixed for you to come down and stay. I'll write on Sunday and let you know.

I felt terribly down this morning, but suddenly there is a real feeling of Spring in the air today, which has cheered me up no end, though the lovely weather makes it all the more heart-breaking that one is cooped up here in London. I think I will really try and get out somewhere this Sunday and see some flowers and hear some birds.

I was talking with Roger Wilson recently about places to stay on leave, and he told me of two places – one near Matlock in the Peak District, and the other in the Lakes, where FWRS have had offers to take workers in need of a rest. He is kindly writing off for particulars for me. Meanwhile, perhaps you could you ask my mother if she has anywhere to suggest. I simply must have some long leave soon, and I think sometime in May would probably be the best. I love you so much and just must see you – I must, I must. God bless you my dearest, Ralph

A welcome phone call means that most news has already been exchanged – so he indulges in some self-criticism that Easter is going to pass without due observance; plus a visit to the cinema and attempts to settle a date for a future meeting...........

Saturday, April 4th 1942 – London Hostel

My dearest

It was so good to speak to you on the phone last night, except of course, it means I have no news for a letter; only to say that I love you very dearly, and more and more and more each day. God keep you and bless you. And good wishes for this strange Easter, that doesn't seem like an Easter at all. I fear I have not done anything at all appropriate, save to read the Crucifixion story from St Matthew after breakfast yesterday. Tom, Barry (MBB) and I went out for lunch yesterday and had a good and reasonably cheap meal at St Stephen's Tavern near the Houses of Parliament.

Then Tom said he was in need of a whisky, so we had to go on to another Pub. I should point out that I was very abstemious, as my total consumption was 1 Pint! By this time it was raining and we abandoned our project of walking in the Park and went to a movie instead. It was called *Ball of Fire* with Gary Cooper and Barbara Stanwyck. It was very funny and damned good. It's about a group of retired Professors who are writing an Encyclopaedia, but after 9 years have only reached the letter S! Do see if you can get it.

I told you on the phone about Millior's close friend Gwen (Bevington-Smith) who is expecting, and staying pro tem with them, which makes your staying there difficult. So I am I'm not yet sure, but maybe Dick's flat will be free, if I can fix it, and both you and David could come to stay. But also think about our holiday together.

We are still no nearer getting people off abroad. I will write again very soon, my own dear wife. God keep you and bless you. Dearest love,
Ralph

My father seems to have had a good Easter, sharing it firstly with FAU friends subsidised unwittingly by Tom, and then a day out with Angela getting half way to Epping and ending up in Cambridge! But some strong assertions that it is all definitely platonic.........

Monday, April 6th 1942 – London Hostel

 My darling
You may be pleased to hear that for once I am in quite good form. I've really enjoyed myself over the week-end. This always makes me feel rather selfish, as you probably haven't and taken by and large, I have more opportunities than you. But I have my full share of depression and I don't think you'd begrudge me a few comparatively bright moments. No doubt I shall soon be back down in the pit again!

Saturday was quite fun. The joke was that after a bit, Tom found that he was paying for everything. I had lent my last £1 to Barry (MBB) for Friday, and he had already spent it all. So poor Tom had rather an expensive afternoon!

Sunday turned out to be a good day, though again I feel rather a pig, being without you. I had determined to go into the country and as a last thought, asked Angela, who surprisingly enough wasn't going out with anyone else.

Now please do not get upset about this. Firstly I am not in love with Angela. In fact far from it. I like her and that's all. Secondly, I am in love with you and only you. More than anything or anyone, I love you, and all the time I wished you could have been there. I tell you so that you can at least share in my enjoyment. I always tell you. Who else can I tell, and who else would be interested? There is absolutely nothing to be jealous about, except that you weren't with me, and that I regret quite as much as you. Sorry for all this long explanation, but I do want to make this very clear, and I know you will understand. I LOVE YOU AND ONLY YOU.

We got on a bus to Epping Forest, intending to walk, and indeed were walking quietly along, when she suddenly said "I think I'd rather go to Cambridge." Quite mad. Now you could say that Epping is vaguely *en route* for Cambridge, but it's still bloody miles away. However, believe it or not, we found there was a bus, but when it eventually turned up, it was full.

So we had another crazy thought – that we would try and hitch hike. And amazingly it worked! At least in stages. First an army lorry took us about a mile, then an airman in an Austin 7 drove us another 5 miles, and another private car a further 6 miles. Lastly, by great good fortune we were picked up by a fast empty lorry going through Cambridge, which took us the last 35 miles. People seem to give lifts to women much more readily than to men out of uniform.

We eventually got there by 2.0pm and had a much needed late lunch. Angela then wanted to collect some books of hers from Kings College, but for some reason it wasn't possible, so we took a boat on the river.

This was my first visit, and the 'backs' are so lovely, where the green lawns of the colleges run down to the river, spanned by the stone bridge. The colours all seemed at their brightest: the sky was clear blue, the clouds snow white, the grass a brilliant green, and the daffodils and crocuses bright yellow and orange, with all around the Blackbirds singing gloriously. Little wonder that Rupert Brooke loved it so. God, I wish you could have been there.

Afterwards we had a meal and caught a train back. It was a really lovely day out and to crown it all, I saw a party of Sand Martins. Oh, dear heart this spring weather goes to my head, and makes me long for you. Why are we not together? I must see you and go out with you, and hear the birds and see all the spring flowers. You and the spring are all one for me.

We got back about 8.30 and I went up to read. I was joined later by Tom, Barry, Keith and Dick, who were all in terrific form, due either to the spring or the beer. Both I suspect! I was completely unalcoholic, having not had a drop all day. Dick seems to have got himself involved in a promise to take an Irish nurse to a dance, together with two more 'unmarried' men – Barry (Barratt Brown) and one other I think. It all seemed an awful mess, though his wife was very amused and insisted on joining the party!

Tom had been out dining with Cousin Anna[8] – he really does know everybody! Barry had been to some music hall. Then Arnold came in fresh from his honeymoon. "Now I know why all you chaps are so keen on marriage" he announced proudly. "I used to have a passion for that striptease artist Phyllis Dixey. But do you know what? I've quite lost interest in Phyllis now!" Tom had sent him a wire saying "About time too!" The atmosphere of smoke in my room, when they had gone was appalling!

Ah well, I suppose it all sounds great fun and rather riotous, but only occasionally does it reach such heights of abandon. But after all the boredom and monotony, we require some compensation! Indeed, as you will know from my normal rather poor letters, I don't find life that interesting, so that a night out here and there is acceptable.
All my love dearest, Ralph

———

[Textual: As my father talks about going with Horace to various high level meetings regarding the FAU's forthcoming visit, April seems about the correct dating for this undated letter. Horace eventually left for India in early May 1942]

My mother has to go for an interview about call-up – and points out to the authorities, that she has two children and is exempt; supper with M&A one day and Richard the next..........

Thursday, April 9th 1942 (approximately) – London Hostel

 My dearest

Thank you so much for your letter. I am glad that your interview went off so easily. What a shame that David has been so poorly. I do hope he is getting better now. Please give him my love. We had a letter from Duncan somewhere on the high seas. They seem to making progress.

There is very little to tell you since my last letter. To quote Hamlet, life is rather "weary, stale, flat, and unprofitable" at the moment. What we are doing at present seems rather useless, and it makes me feel generally pretty fed up. How long will it all go on? Must I spend the rest of the war doing this damn job in Whitechapel?

Horace and I went to the Foreign Office yesterday to see the Under Secretary of State for Foreign Affairs, Richard Law. Horace had an introduction to him through Rab Butler, the previous Under Secretary, whom he had known in India when Butler was Under Secretary of State for India. I was keen to talk about a group to go out to Abyssinia, but they wanted to talk about India and other things. The Minister was rather reserved, and as a result, we didn't get anywhere much.

Yesterday I had supper with Millior and Alfred, who both seemed well. There were two other people there as well – Millior's doctor and a William Hazelton, who was quite pleasant, if a little dull. On Sunday I had supper with Richard Symonds and his wife. She is quite attractive and I believe very clever. Their flat is rather poky and the supper, while adequate, was poorly served. I think even I could have done better! I don't think I shall be free before the weekend of the 17th, but it will be lovely to see you then. All my love, Ralph

April 9th continued...........

I am sorry this letter – started yesterday – is so delayed. But after a terrifically long, all day meeting on relief work, I was pretty exhausted yesterday as a result. I don't know if we achieved anything at the meeting. We talk and talk, and then wonder what we've decided!

Thank thee again for your letter, and once again for the lovely present you gave me. I am so pleased with it.

I won't write much now as I shall be seeing you next week. I am so looking forward to it. Just let me know what time you will be coming on the Friday and I will meet you. Dick says he is happy to lend us his flat for the Saturday and Sunday nights. Friday, I think you'll have to sleep here. I am so looking forward to seeing you. I will come and meet you.

I will ring Millior and see what she proposes for the week-end – perhaps we can all meet up.

Excuse more now. All love to you and to David.
Dearest love
Ralph
PS Please excuse pencil, but I lent Barry (MBB) my pen and he's still got it!

My mother's visit to London has obviously been a happy one, which without my brother and me to worry about, meant my parents would be able to enjoy each other's company unencumbered………

Tuesday, April 21ˢᵗ 1942 – London Hostel

My dearest

I am so sorry not to have written sooner, and even this will be only a scrawl. First let me thank you for such a happy week-end. It was, as always, lovely just to be with you. I enjoyed it more than I can say. Thank you for everything and for the lovely book. Secondly, I can't say how much I admired your nobility in allowing me to go abroad. I know how much more difficult it is for you than for me, and how it must look so different from your point of view. I do feel it right for me to accept, but I know how wretched it is for you. You are wonderful and I thank God that I have such a wife.

There is no news yet about the Abyssinian party sailing, and we are still busy picking our Indian party. Everyone seems to think that Horace must go, and I saw the Quaker MP Edmund Harvey, who had been a friend of father's, at the House about it yesterday.

Dear love to the children, and many thanks to your mother too for all she does. In haste. Much love Ralph

My mother has a chance to meet my father's friends and colleagues and to see where he works, which gives her a better understanding of his life in the Unit. But it also increases the sense of impending sadness as parting draws ever closer. Lamenting the prospect of having to cope alone is not something either relishes..........

Continued.........Wednesday, April 22ⁿᵈ

My very dear........I can't help thinking about just how perfect the week-end was. It was so lovely and peaceful and domestic. I enjoyed every minute of it intensely. Kew was a dream of beauty. Some days are quiet and peaceful, ecstatic even, but patchy and sometimes rank bad, and you feel how every minute is passing. Last week-end however, felt good all through. Peaceful and harmonious and lovely.

I don't honestly know how I am going to face being without you. I don't want to dwell on it and it won't make it easy to talk about it, but I must say just once that I dread the prospect most terribly. I feel that I must go, but the wrench and the parting and the weary months without being near you, will be so awful and makes me very miserable. I am not sure how I will cope. I love you so desperately my dear. I do know however that we shall always be the same to each other, and that I think when I come back it will be the last lap.

Since you left, time has been full. Horace is still undecided, but the party now comprises Linney, Symonds, Griffin, Cottle and Banhart. Horace has seen Cripps' right hand Geoffrey Wilson again, who is very keen for us to go, and says India is waiting for us, and that six will only be an advance party. But he says Horace must now check with the Secretary of State, Leo Amery. If Horace doesn't lead the party, it might be Roger or it might be me, but I still prefer the idea of the Middle East, though the prospect of Dick's company is a counter attraction. I wish I knew which way it was going.

Dick and his wife were very appreciative of the way the flat was left. He said it was beautifully tidy and that he appreciated the primroses very much.

Thank you so much for making me so happy. Now that you have met all my friends, I hope you don't feel out of it. There is absolutely no need, as you are the only person for me, and you can hold your own with all of them.

Never think that you are losing me to other friends. Surely you must see that I need you as much if not more than ever. Are you so blind that you didn't feel it too, over the week-end? I daren't give way, or I should make a fool of myself. I could so easily break down and cry, but it would only make us both worse.

I have just received your letter, and I know how down you feel as I feel the same. I think you are magnificent to be so uncomplaining, and above all I admire your bravery. I know it is hell for you and you have all my love and prayers and sympathy. May God keep you safe always my dearest one.

Forgive me repeating myself, but thank you with all my heart for a very special week-end. How either of us is going to cope, I don't know, but we shall and with God's help, we shall come through. I know this all sounds a little incoherent, but understand that you are always in my thoughts and prayers. You know that I love you so terribly and shall miss you more than I can say.
Always in my thoughts, dearest love, Ralph

Indecision and more indecision combined with endless travel problems makes each day a trial.......

Thursday, April 23rd 1942 – London Hostel

 My darling
I have been thinking of you so continually and hoping that life may seem a little more tolerable. Though why it should do, I can't quite see. I must say that at present I don't see much purpose or object in life. No definite decisions, yet the prospect of being parted we know not when. I suppose all we can do is to hang on and hope. I'm feeling pretty blue at the moment, I must say.

Still no nearer a decision at this end I'm afraid. Horace is coming up again tomorrow, and then after seeing Leo Amery, he must decide. If he decides against, and as Roger has refused, it will come back on me, though I can't say I feel very happy about it. We have almost got an air passage for next week, which is for Dick. The boat passages are for some time in May. I've rarely felt so depressed.

The only consolation I have is that I think I have made the right decision to go, though what right means in this crazy world, I don't really know! Right to follow a selfish whim and sacrifice you? Is it my duty or is it selfishness? Yes, I do think it is right, and I suppose we must face this intolerably hard way, and when we come through, as we shall, we can be proud of ourselves. As it is you know you have all my love and that I need you.

Poor Richard. He's in a fearful rush. I feel so sorry for him and for his wife. In their case, it's almost worse than for us. We at least do know where we stand and will be able to pick up from where we left off and that our love will always be there. I'm not sure Richard is so lucky.

I am sorry this is not very cheerful! It's just to let you know that I am thinking of you and loving you and praying for you. God keep you safe.
All my love
Always yours
Ralph

——

Horace has finally decided to commit to India, but has to square it with Woodbrooke first. It looked at one point as if my father would join Horace, but Tom is definite that my father is the man for the Middle East and will be the next most senior post in the Unit. A medical passes him fit and he is measured for a uniform. In the knowledge of the security of their love, they learn to come to terms with being parted.........

Sunday, April 26 1942 – London Hostel

My dearest wife

Richard's flight to India is now postponed for a week or so. In a way I'm glad because it will give him more time to get things prepared. Horace came up on Friday and I met him at Paddington and then took him on to Gordon Square. We then went on to the India Office with Tom to see the Secretary of State, Leo Amery. We had quite a satisfactory interview and we came away with Horace having made up his mind that he would go to India, as long as he could square Woodbrooke. On this count he was going to approach Carl Heath (former Secretary of the Peace Council) to facilitate his leaving.

Before that I had fully expected to go as well, as even Richard was very anxious for me to go and I thought on Friday morning that I might, but Tom and Brandon feel that the claims of the Middle East are greater. So unless by chance Horace falls through, I shall not be going to India. This is a shame, as I have become keener on India than I was, and I am quite sure that there is a tremendous job to do there, and it would be most interesting. Also there is nothing I should like more than to go with Richard and if Horace went too, that would make a grand party. But on balance I am more drawn to the Middle East, and from the Unit's point of view, I think it is more important. Also if were to go to India in mid-May, that would bugger my leave and be a fearful rush. So on the whole I am glad both for me and you, as it would have been hellish for you.

The India party now comprises Richard and Horace with Keith Linney, Jean Cottle, Pamela Bankart and Ken Griffin. Linney, poor man has had a most difficult time deciding between his wife and the Unit. It is the same damnable, insoluble problem we all have. I am very sorry for him. What a shocking contrary world this is, with so many men leaving their wives. It has quite got me down this week. Just the thought of you and I being parted is bad enough, but also Keith and his wife, Richard and his wife, Angela feeling Dick's going, and missing her brother, Barty hopelessly in love with Bunty, who is married, Tom's wife in America.

What a mess of people's lives and for what purpose? Just this I suppose - that we <u>must</u> do what we see to be our job as far as we can, and keep up our courage and hope to come through. As Masefield puts it - "But tomorrow, by the living God, we'll try the game again!" Poor comfort for you and poor comfort for me.

My dear, in all this, I am so thankful that our relationship is secure. We are one and mean so much to each other and shall never be parted in spirit, for our love is like a rock. You need have no fear of my friends, for our relationship will survive all. We have been in love for nigh on ten years, and we can weather these storms safely dear heart. My dearest, may God keep you safe.

I have had a medical and am passed fit, save for varicose veins and some slight skin disease, both of which they are going to treat. I have also been measured for my uniform. It's been a difficult week and I have been up late nearly every night – both Thursday and Friday till nearly 2.0 talking about India. Not just wasting time, but doing my best to fill myself in on the background from Dick, just in case I should have to go.

I am going to Westminster Meeting on Sunday. I regret to say it will be my first meeting for months. Don't tell mother! I am then going to have lunch with Millior and Alfred and mother afterwards and probably stay over with them. I shall return on Monday, when I thought I might be going to India.

I'm still living off the joy of our week-end together. It was all perfect. I loved it, every bit as much as you did and I shall never forget Kew. Thank you for being such a darling. My heart bleeds for you dearest. May God help you. How inadequate that sounds, but what else can I say? It is so grand of you to let me go and wonderful to have such a brave wife. Keep going dearest, don't go under. You are too good and fine and courageous for that. Keep fighting. I am with you.

I had lunch with Mr Tritsch and have increased the rent. He was very apologetic about the clock and the wardrobe. One can't help liking him, even though he is an old rogue.

I must stop now. My love and thoughts are with you continuously. My love to the children.
Dear love, Ralph
PS Do be careful about our overdraft dear one, it is now quite high.

At last a definite decision that my father is not going to India, though the Middle East is now confirmed.....but with still no date.........

Monday, April 27th 1942 – London Hostel

My darling
Thank you so much for your dear letter. I am so sorry that you are still so terribly depressed. Try and cheer up sweetheart. At least I am definitely not going to India now, but I still have no knowledge of when the likely date of my sailing is likely to be. Probably not until June, which will suit me best. Horace is now definitely going and is coming up tomorrow to get on with his arrangements.

Dearest, you must keep your spirits up and see it through, and I know that you will. I rely on you so much for help and support and know that I shall get it. Please give my love to David.

I enclose a note from LPA (at the Trust) regarding my salary. It is very good of the Trustees to raise it, so with this and the extra rent, we ought to manage. If only the overdraft was not so big!

The uniform they are fitting me with, will be something like an officer's, so that I will mix in better on a troopship. Exactly how long I shall be away, I don't really know, but probably 18 months would be a fair estimate.

There is really very little news since I last wrote. My injection is beginning to take I think. I still have to go again about my varicose veins, because they don't know what to do with them. I am hoping to have the yellow fever injection tomorrow.

Always remember dearest, that you are forever in my thoughts and prayers and that I love you very much and admire you and depend on you.
God bless and I will write again before the week-end.
Dear love Ralph

———

As days and weeks draw nearer, the idea of being apart grows more real and more difficult to contemplate...........

Thursday, April 30th 1942 – London Hostel

 My darling

You are continually in my thoughts and I was miserable to find you still so unhappy. My dear one, I do understand, as I feel exactly the same about being parted from you. I shall miss you unbearably, as you mean so much to me. I pray that God will watch over you and give you strength, courage and endurance.

I know it's worse for you than for me and I do so appreciate all you have to bear. Please remember that I love you as you love me. Never doubt that, my own dear wife.

I have no news since we spoke last night. Dick and I met Horace at Paddington this morning, and he is still hoping that he may be able to fly out to India. Dick is now off on leave from this afternoon.

I think I told you that Tom has told Sir John Kennedy of the Red Cross that I shall be going out to the Middle East, and Sir John appeared to think this a good idea. I shall go out as a Commissioner though that makes it sound more like the Salvation Army to me!

It's all rather distracting trying to carry on with this job, as well as getting on with all the new arrangements. I don't seem to be doing either properly. Also I'm so worried about you. If I don't go grey it will be a wonder.

I've now had my yellow fever injection and my smallpox. I've got three more to go and also to have my varicose veins attended to. I hope it won't take too long.

The last few days have been perfect weather. I will write again on Sunday.
All my love dear one as ever, Ralph.

Plans at last seem to be firming up, and with the India party leaving shortly, my father can concentrate on preparations for his own leave-taking to the Middle East.

———

Chapter 16
Still Waiting to Leave
May and June 1942

Knowing that a long separation will happen any time soon, but not knowing exactly when, made life traumatic for them both. But as preparations, such as having various injections, went ahead, it brought a full awareness of the imminent parting, ever closer. This starts to affect them more and more deeply, as my father writes movingly in his memoirs......

I shall always look back on the time preceding my departure as among the most unpleasant that I have ever spent, and many people faced with the prospect of going overseas for an indefinite period must have felt the same way. At the end of May I had a few days leave due, and spent a rather agonised week-end at Wolverhampton, saying good bye to Joan, who had now moved there completely, to be with her sister Winifred and family. She was wonderful as always, but I returned back to London, totally dejected, awaiting my departure, whilst deputising temporarily for Michael Barratt Brown who was also on leave.

With the shipping situation so uncertain, and waiting for news of departure, the days seemed to drag on forever.

[Textual: There is no date of any sort on this letter. But as he mentions some upcoming leave on May 15 or 16, the beginning of May is a possible date.]

This letter reflects both their states of mind, trying to keep both of their spirits up.....

Friday, May 1st 1942 – London Hostel

 My dearest

I am more worried than I can say about your letter. What can I do or think sweetheart? How can I best help you? If only I could do something. We must see this through together, and it will demand courage and endurance from both of us. I know that's easily said my darling, but it's all that there is left. We must keep going somehow dear one. I pray for you every day and you remain always in my thoughts.

I know life is hell just at present. But it's not good for either of us. It's just as terrible for me as it is for you. We've just got to face it and make the best of it, or we shan't get through at all. I promise to take care of myself, and I promise to come back to you and life will be as it was. We love each other so much, and that's what will get us through. Please try and be brave, for if you fail, I don't think I shall be able to keep going either.

I expect to have leave May 15th or 16th for about ten days. I have no sailing date yet, but probably the end of May or early June. There will be a lot to do between now and then – equipment, more injections and heaps of clearing up.

Think of me my darling and pray for me in my new job. How I wish you could come too,

I will try and ring you tonight. There is no more for now, but will write again at the weekend. Probably Sunday, when there should be more news.

Dear love
Ralph

News of fellow Unit men, here and there. Then, in the first paragraph and several subsequent passages, almost deliberate attempts at lightheartedness by my father to distract my mother from her worries – as in 'did I tell you the one about...?' This is then followed by a summation of my father's familiar progression from apprehension of a new job, to familiarity and fondness, ending with sadness at leaving....followed by a new apprehension for the next new one.........

Sunday, May 3rd 1942 – London Hostel

My darling

[.......] Did I tell you about sending six of our men under Keith Linney to help deal with the homeless in Norwich? Unfortunately they arrived rather too late, did a little work in Rest Centres and then got landed with looking after 70 homeless, over 80 year olds in Rest Centres! The thought of Keith getting stuck doing this is most pleasing! But I have no doubt he did very well. Barry (Barratt Brown) and Roger went up there today to relieve them.

The mobile CAB is still in Bath, manned by the Terry brothers – Douglas and John - along with John Gough, and seems to be doing a very good job. I hear, however, that Bath has been rather badly damaged. There is also a fair amount of damage in York, and I gather that the windows at Bootham School were broken, but I don't think either they or The Mount was severely damaged. Tessa Rowntree is up in Yorkshire with Gwendy Knight, setting up training camps for women in one of the Quaker houses known as 'Barmoor'*, which is out on the moors, but so far they are the only ones of ours in that area. There were also some bombs dropped in the North East, but according to Arnold Rowntree, little damage was done there either. (*see further description on p 197)

Richard is still away and we don't know when he will be going. Horace is trying hard for an air passage. Although the party is an FAU venture, Meeting for Sufferings have taken very kindly to it, which is good news.

My approaching departure from this job and this place is now all coming to be very sad. I recall how I hated it to begin with and now I regret losing it. What a life this is. One begins hating the job and the people and longing for any way out, and then gradually everything settles down and before you know where you are, you are building up an amenable life and are sorry to have to leave it. I would be only too happy to leave it and come home, but not to go abroad. Everything I take on seems a bit bigger and more frightening than the last. First Cheveley, then the Mechanics Camp which terrified me, then Relief which seemed insuperable, then Deputy Chairman, which seemed even worse and now Egypt.

Oh God, how frightening that sounds! The climate, meeting FAU people I don't know, who may resent my coming, having to make all sorts of difficult Army and BRCS contacts, the chance of contracting a serious illness, having to make big and quick decisions which I am bad at, the prospect of a long voyage possibly by myself, maybe with little congenial company, the absence from you, and from England and all the things I love, such as birds and flowers, parting not only from you but all my friends. It all fills me with apprehension and makes me wonder if I can make a success of it. Was I a fool to have accepted it? I shall want all the help you can give me my dearest.

There is a lovely new story of Barry's (MBB) from the other day. He was walking along a country lane and was suddenly challenged by a sentry, and he completely forgot the correct response (ie 'Friend'). He swallowed hard, took a deep breath, and said "Um, yes, well, um... my name is Barratt Brown", which if you have ever heard him answer the phone in his slightly pompous manner "My name is Barratt Brown", sounds exquisitely funny.

Another story of Barry's was about a Frenchman in Cambridge, who had no English, and asked the way to the station. His informant, understanding no French thinks he wants the library and takes him to the City's splendid new building. The Frenchman's comment was "C'est magnifique; mais ce n'est pas la gare."!*5

I am on Orderly duty in half an hour, and then I shall do some office work and perhaps go down to The Prospect this evening. Tom went to see *The Man Who Came to Dinner* yesterday and enjoyed it very much. The real life man depicted in the play, Alexander Woolcott, according to Tom, is 'a complete shit'! Tom went on and had dinner at The Savoy, which - he said – was, for once, a teetotal meal, and he remarked "It's surprising how much cheaper a dinner is without alcohol. It cuts one's overheads down no end!" The night before he'd been seeing a close friend off to America, and though not drunk, was nevertheless rather more the worse for wear than usual, which was not very edifying.

I'm sorry not to sound more cheerful, but I keep thinking of you. It was lovely to see you on Friday a little more cheerful, and I pray God may continue to give you strength and courage to endure till we come through. Hold on to the good things in life and you will triumph. In Henley's famous words "Out of the night that covers me......I thank whatever Gods may be, for my unconquerable soul." Just keep on as you are and you will win. All my love, Ralph

Horace and Richard Symonds at last able to leave for India; worries about JMB and a fitting for a uniform..........

Thursday, May 7th 1942 – London Hostel

My darling
I am sorry I sounded so lousy on the phone yesterday, but I was feeling really down and in a bad way. I feel a lot better and more cheerful today for having spoken with you, and I pray that you'll manage to keep your spirits up to at this difficult time.

Richard and Horace are leaving very shortly, but I don't think I shall be seeing them off after all. It will be good if it happens quite quickly, as Richard is having a difficult time. It's a mess: his wife is in an unhappy state and Angela will miss him terribly, though she is trying hard to be good about it. I really hope that all three will get through alright, but I am worried about them........But in truth I am much more worried about you dear heart, and know that you are suffering just as much and far more. The separation will be terrible and I feel as you do, but there will be an end to it and a better tomorrow. We have only our courage to hang on to and we shall need all of it. I am rather dreading the whole prospect, but we must give each other all the help we can. I really can't understand why we don't all have nervous breakdowns!

Yesterday I was fitted for my uniform. It's still in quite early stages, but I presume it will eventually be alright. I shall be quite terrified to put it on, and feel sure I shall do all sorts of awful things that are just not done! The whole prospect scares me stiff.

I will write again at the week-end. I'm thinking of you always and love you so much.

God keep you safe, Love Ralph

---

*5 Cf "C'est magnifique; mais ce n'est pas la guerre."!

A Training Camp for Women

'Barmoor' became a training centre for the women's section of the FAU

Lent by the Yorkshire Quaker T Edmund Harvey, it stood on the edge of the Yorkshire moors, overlooking the small village of Hutton-le-Hole.

In December 1941, Tessa Rowntree and Gwendy Knight became the first officers of what was initially the WFAU, and together with eleven women formed a camp at Barmoor along the lines already established at The Manor Farm. Eventually the W was dropped and everything came under the one organisation.

Photographs courtesy Barmoor Trust

My father rather at the end of his tether – injections, friends leaving for abroad and general worries...........

Mid May 1942 – London Hostel

 My dearest

I am afraid this will be a scrappy letter. I am feeling about rock bottom, which is probably as a result of all the injections I have had to go out to the Middle East. Yellow Fever, Tetanus, Typhoid, Varicose veins, Smallpox and Diptheria! They haven't made me feel ill, just depressed. Enough to make an Elephant depressed! At the same time the weather is glorious, when I should be out enjoying it, which makes me even more depressed. I'm sorry my dear one, but there are times when I am just about at the end of my tether, and this seems to be one of them.

Dick sails tomorrow for India and Horace with him. I might have to go and see him off after all. The rest of the party leaves shortly. It seems as though all my closest friends are being scattered to the four winds. I shall miss them. Today we've had more dreary meetings lasting all day, about the future of relief work, as usual with no very definite decisions!

But I think of you and all your difficulties and trouble so much. May you have the strength we both need. I do love you very dearly. Thank you for your lovely letter. I am so glad you are feeling better.

I will get this off to the post and it comes with all my love. I will give you a ring about my leave very soon.

Dear love Ralph.

Distress all round: as Richard leaves for India - upset at leaving his wife and Angela; Angela upset for both; FRB upset for everybody.........

Friday, May 8th 1942 – London Hostel

 My darling

I do apologise for getting you up so late last night, but I didn't have a very good day yesterday and needed to hear your voice. It was mainly for Richard's sake that I eventually decided to see him off. I am afraid he has had a difficult time, and it all made me feel very down. Nor was lunch with his wife as easy as it might have been, but as R had asked me, I couldn't refuse. Afterwards she went straight back to the Ministry. I fear she has not helped him much. The more I see of others, the more I realise how supremely and wonderfully fortunate I am to have a wife like you.

I am also considerably worried about Angela. Dick blames himself terribly, though Angela blames no-one, and is extremely brave, but is obviously feeling it very much. She would not have it differently, but prospects for her are pretty bleak at the moment. She is not that well either, and is going to take some leave, but has nowhere proper to go – her family is abroad and no friends immediately available. Of course they may have been foolish, but that doesn't help them now. She says she saw it coming and thought it worth it. I wish there was something we could do, but I don't think anyone can help much. She will get through, but it is hard going. If only you were here in London, you could help, as I know you would like each other.

But while I think of others, I have not forgotten you, me dearest. I know what a hard time you are having, and you are continually in my prayers. I think I love you more as the years go by, and realise what a wonderful thing our marriage and mutual understanding is.

We know that we can rely on each other for help and support, and we know that there is sympathy and understanding between us. [....] I constantly thank God for your love, which I rely on so much. I was thinking only the other day of how long we have known each other, and how happy we have been.

Dear heart, I know at times you are jealous of my friends, but sweet one, there really is no cause or need. If you could just understand how our marriage stands absolutely secure in this mad world, you would know that we are not two people, but one and shall be always. I know I may be thoughtless and careless at times, but I am yours and only yours. We love each other and what else matters? You must not be jealous of anything or anyone, as there is no possible reason, least of all of Angela or Richard or any of the others.

If you were about, we could help them better. I can't do much as I am a man and a bit of a fool in such matters, and anyway very busy. What Angela really needs is a woman friend to be there for her. None of us here can really help, but I know you could, and I know one day you will!

Thank you very much for your letter. I too wish so much that we could be together, but we soon shall be, and I am looking forward to my leave at the end of the month tremendously. I hope the farm will materialise as it sounds just perfect for us, and it will be so grand to be with you again. I am going to enjoy it tremendously.

My plans are no further forward. The BRCS cannot get me a passage, and we are going to try to go direct. My uniform is now being made and I hope to get my equipment this week. Tom, went up to Liverpool with Richard to see him off, though we are not yet certain exactly when he sails. Six reinforcements for the Hadfield Spears Unit are leaving any minute and the rest of the India party also, with Ethiopia at the end of the month. I will be able to tell you more of my probable addresses when we meet.

To answer your questions...Dick had a leaving party and he and I had lunch at The Prospect of Whitby. Angela is going on leave, though where I don't know, and is then coming back to work at Gordon Square in the foreign department. She should do well there I think when she gets over all this business and if her leave does her some good, as I hope it will. Our squad has now returned from Exeter. Barry (Barratt Brown) is away this week-end and goes on leave in June. His parents-in-law's house was very badly damaged by explosions from ammunition dumps caused by heath fires.

I am glad you had a good time at Beaconwood and mother says she enjoyed having you to stay too. Can you please send her letter back to me? Give my love to David and Antony and bless you for looking after them.
All my love as ever, Ralph.

—

[Textual: There is no 1st page to this next letter, and the internal evidence is not always clear. The letter is written on the reverse side of official FAU Memorandum paper, which is an old scrubbed out carbon copy memo dated April 1st 1942. So FRB's letter must be after that. It also mentions that nothing had been heard from Richard (Dick) Symonds or Horace Alexander, who had just left for India at the beginning of May. They didn't arrive until mid-June. He also said that the China party, who had retreated to Burma were on route to India to fly back to Kunming in China, which happened in early June. So I am placing this mid-May.]

For a change my father is in an up, and even quite light-hearted mood, joking about cumbersome Quaker procedures, and almost jesting about his own depression.........

About middle of May – c. 12th/13th 1942 – London Hostel

 (Dearest) [...] Everything here seems to be going on much as usual. No news from Dick or Horace yet. The China party in Burma are now out in India and hoping to fly back to China any minute.

I usually tell you how down I am, but for once you might like to know that things are good at present! I've been pretty up today, though I daresay as the week goes on, I shall gradually slip back down again! I believe I might keep on a more even keel if I could be with you again. I am so looking forward to my leave dear heart: just to be with you again in the country will be superb. I do like all these people here very much, and they are a good bunch, but the more I see of them, the more I long for you to be here with me.

We had another long Executive this afternoon with an interesting report from Ronald Joynes on the Middle East. We have now appointed another sub-committee to look into whether Tom should go out to China. I think if they could, they would appoint a sub-committee to appoint the sub-committee!

I have nearly finished Lin Yutang's[1] *Moment in Peking,* which is very good, if a bit sketchy in places, but the main character is very good and rings true. I am also thrilled with the book *Shearwaters* by Ronald Lockley[2] that you gave me. He is a great naturalist and his extensive studies of this lovely seabird are absolutely fascinating. Thank you so much.

I must say the big air raids of ours on Germany make me sick. I think they are quite horrific and horrible and only confirm that I made the right choice in joining the FAU.

No more news at the moment, except to say again that I love you, and thank you with all my heart for all you are and do for me. I can never speak enough, of how glad I am I married you, or tell you enough how grateful I am. If you only knew.

I will write again soon, but it's quite likely I'll be down and depressed again by then, so the letter may well be another tale of misery!
All my love to David and Antony
And my dearest love to you, Ralph

———

My father is here deciding what books to take with him to the Middle East; drawing up his will and spelling out his hopes for us children.........

Sunday, May 24th 1942 – London Students Hostel

My darling
I've really not a lot to say since my last note.
I'm, going over for my equipment shortly. The Unit seem to supply most things, but there will be a few things to buy over and above. I must also decide what books to take, and that won't be easy. Beyond the Bible and Shakespeare and the Oxford Book of Poetry, and some modern poetry, it is really going to be hard to choose. What would you take? If fiction, it should be long and sustaining, nothing light and quickly read like a detective story. Possibly Jane Austen, Trollope, Scott or Meredith, perhaps something Russian. A little history I think too – but what? I'm not sure about autobiography, but maybe something about the country and birds and one or two of the Oxford Books.

I shall ask Alfred, when I have tea with him this afternoon. I have also asked him to draw up my will again. Sorry to be gloomy, but it seems a necessary precaution. I shall leave everything to you, knowing that you will spend it wisely on yourself and the children.

The only thing I would say about the children is that if by hook or by crook it can be managed, I should like them to go to Oxford or Cambridge, and whatever they read I hope they will have a reasonable level of culture, and that they will appreciate good literature, poetry and painting, and know something about it. If they can also appreciate the country and gardens, so much the better. I hope you agree. We should also want them to be of the world, and not in too narrow a rut as I was as a boy, which I'm sure was a mistake. But I know you will do all these things. I'm sorry, as I am not in the least expecting to die, in fact I'm sure I won't, but I thought I ought to say these things at some point.

I am so looking forward to our holiday dearest one. It will be just grand to be with you. God bless you, Dearest love Ralph

Prior to leaving, my father had a break in Stottesdon in Shropshire with my mother and David, whilst my grandmother looked after me, as he writes here...........

At the end of May 1942 Joan and I and David went by bus from Wolverhampton via Bridgenorth to a small Shropshire village called Stottesdon. Joan with her customary efficiency had arranged it all. We stayed in two farms, one small, rather isolated from the village, where we ate and lived, and the other larger and just behind the church where we slept.

Shropshire has to be one of the loveliest of counties in England. During the day we didn't do much, but we went for long walks in the evening - once to Cleobury Mortimer where we found a pub selling some excellent sherry. On another day we got a taxi which took us to the foot of Clee, which we climbed, affording wonderful views out over Shropshire. The countryside in those May days was just glorious, and it proved a most wonderful holiday. And we coped as best we could, with the shadow of my departure rather brooding over it.

A view of Stottesdon and over to Clee
"The Shropshire countryside in those May days was just glorious."
Photo ARB

News of his departure arrives out of the blue and farewells have to be faced, as my father writes in his memoirs........

One morning while on orderly duty, I heard that we were due to leave the following Tuesday, and I suddenly had the sad task of making my final arrangements to depart. The parting from Joan in Wolverhampton had already been dreadful enough, and now the last farewell phone call, which I shall not easily forget, was even worse. Sorrow at parting and dread of the future.

The night before I left I had dinner with Tom, then went round the Hostel saying my final goodbyes, before Barry drove me across London to the Middlesex Hospital. I remember passing through Westminster and many familiar sites, and to the other sadnesses was added the sadness of leaving London, a city that I had now come to love so well.

Words to be said prior to leaving........

Wednesday, June 3rd 1942 – London Hostel

My darling Joan
I hope you had a good journey home and that David was not too tiring. I thought of you so much.

There are various things to be said:
Firstly, let me thank you for a lovely leave. I am afraid I was pretty quiet, but I did enjoy it so much and shall always remember how happy we were. Honestly dear heart, your cheerfulness made it what it was and I am most eternally grateful.

Secondly, I appreciate more than I can say all you do for me and the children. You are truly a wonderful wife and mother, brave and cheerful and efficient, and all that a man can require. God bless you for that.

Thirdly, can I say it often enough? I love you so very deeply....and if it's possible, even more than that! Of course I have made friends here, but please understand they make absolutely no difference to us. I should hate to leave you thinking that there was a problem between us. There is not. Even though you were quite mistaken over Angela, and I know that you now realise that you were, I do want to say that you behaved most generously over her, and that generosity in this matter is a great credit to you and goes further, if that is possible, to confirm my enormous love and admiration for you. You are truly a great person.

Angela asked me to tell you how much she enjoyed coming out with us. She has the highest opinion of both David and you. She and Barry liked your new photo very much. In fact Barry liked it much better than the other, which he thought made you look a bit grim! It was so good having you and David in London. He really is a good child and I am proud of him and you for bringing him up so well. God bless you both.

On my return, people actually seemed quite pleased to see me back would you believe! And it was good to see John and Barry again. Monday was all Executive Meetings – I got the extra Sergeant I needed – a man called Philip Sanford, who had been at one of the late Camps, and who is supposed to be rather good. Tuesday was the FWRS Executive. Our probable plan is to come to Northfield on June 16 for a week. [...] *next page missing*

———

A birthday present for my mother – June 17th - combined with a leaving present. A gift my mother treasured dearly all her life………

Thursday, June 4th 1942 - London Hostel

My own darling

Here with all my love is a birthday present and a leaving gift. It brings my love, thanks and undying devotion. Keep it and wear it in memory of me while I am away. It brings my love and best wishes for your birthday, and may you have many more happy ones. It is amethysts in gold and about 130 years old, and can be a brooch or pendant. If you don't like it, they will change it. But I really hope you do, as it gives me so much pleasure to give it to you.

I love you so much, my dear Joan. God bless, and dear love, Ralph.
PS Don't reciprocate – we have no money left!

A letter from JMB expressing her love of the brooch and now having met Angela, friendship has broken out, which remained for the rest of their lives; a certain emptiness back at HQ with people now abroad; and honing up on background to Egypt………

Sunday, June 7th 1942 – London Hostel

My darling wife

Thank you so much for your dear letter, and I am glad you liked the brooch pendant as much as I did. I took Angela with me, because I know so little about such things, and didn't want to buy rubbish. So we went up from Gordon Square one day after lunch to visit this shop, which is a very fine one, with quite a large selection of brooches, though not that cheap. But it was by far the nicest thing we saw and we both immediately fell for it. I do love buying things for you, and so hoped that you would like it as much as I did. So I am very happy that you did. We had such a happy leave, and I am pleased that you appreciated my letter. You know how much I love you and that I only wait for the time when we can be together again. Believe me dear, I am all yours, and miss you terribly.

You made a very good impression on Angela, who thought you were extremely nice and she was genuinely touched by your kindness in being so good to her. She also appreciates seeing people's families and getting to know something of their whole lives, instead of just by themselves. At first it was quite fun being back, except that it was such a wrench being without you, but I am feeling rather grim now. There is no Dick, and Angela is very busy at the Square, and I see little of anything of her, save that on Wednesday night we went out for supper at a small restaurant in Limehouse. MBB has now gone on leave, but there are still John and Tom, though it's not the same as it was.

On Wednesday I went out to supper with MBB and his wife, who are enjoying Michael's leave, staying in one of those very nice old houses in Chester Place, overlooking Regent's Park, lent to them by David Astor[3]. Michael said the Astors let them have it rent free as long they acted as fire-watchers! Before the war, Astor spent a huge sum doing it up to his own design, and although it is only sparsely furnished it is a delightful house, finished throughout in cream. It has been well thought out with beautiful built-in cupboards, hidden lights, palatial bathrooms and Aga cookers. I wish you could have seen it. MBB's wife, Frances Lloyd[4] that was, gave us an excellent supper and afterwards we all went for a walk in a part of the Park I didn't know, which was really lovely, where there was a pool full of Irises, a rock garden, rose beds and flowering shrubs.

We had a cable yesterday morning from Dick and Horace, saying that they had now reached Lagos, which makes me very glad. Poor Barty however, is still anxiously waiting to go, so yesterday evening I went for a stroll with him round Wapping to take his mind off things. Happily the very hot weather had cooled off a bit by the evening, so we had a pleasant evening.

We still have no sailing date yet, and it is possible we may not come to Northfield after all, and may have to go somewhere nearer London. I will, of course, let you know. I now have all my equipment sorted and our arrangements seem to be proceeding alright.

I have been busy attending meetings and checking out all things Egyptian as well as deputising for MBB, who is doing great things, but really has too much on. They have had a gas week in the Hostel, training for what to do in an emergency. A small amount of tear gas was released, which is most unpleasant if there are large quantities of it.

Tom took me out to tea yesterday with some friends of his in South Kensington – a mother and daughter, both charming - who he had known when he was living in Scotland. I spent the evening reading yet more about Egypt and I think I've read enough for the present! Everything appears to be in hand, and thank you for all you have done too. Of course I will certainly come home for a week-end before I go. I'm sorry that you were so depressed about Linden Road. It upset me too.

I've had some nice letters, which I'm enclosing – one from mother, which I'd like back. Another from John Saunders, which was most pleasant and unexpected. He was under me as Shelter Assistant and Warden of Poplar, and is now in Liverpool. In fact if you could keep all these for me, I'd be grateful.

Thank you for sending Enid's letter, which I am returning. It was kind of her to write. It's a good letter, but I feel tempted to say - "She can turn it on when she wants to"! But perhaps that is uncharitable. If one could accept the truth of what she says, it might be a comfort. I don't mean that she is being insincere. I am sure she isn't, but is what she says true? Is ambulance work character building? Is being 'worthwhile in 5 years' time' sufficient justification for hardship now? And shall we be? I don't feel particularly fine. In fact I daresay I am a less good person now than I was. But I do agree entirely in what she says about you making the greater sacrifice, and doing the bigger job, and being the finer person. That is the only absolutely certain true thing that she says. And by the way, I don't think it is Jesus who got us into trouble. The bloody war has done that. Our trouble is separation, and that would have come even if I had not been a CO. Still it is a nice letter and I appreciate her writing.

I don't think there is any more news at the moment. I do know and understand what hell it will be for you, and you have all my love and sympathy. Remember always that I love you so much.
I will write again very soon. Dearest love Ralph
PS Did you manage to speak to Ronald Joynes? I do hope you enjoy meeting him.

———

My father and Tom host a luncheon for the Ethiopian Princess Tenagne prior to her return home to Ethiopia from exile in this country. An FAU party under Richard Mounsey and Jack Frazer was already out there and later my father would make a supervisory trip there..........

Wednesday, June 10th 1942 – London Hostel

 My darling

Thank you so much for your nice long letter, and I am sorry to have taken so long writing back. This will probably be a lousy letter as I feel so depressed today. My dear I would do anything to be with you and see some future for us together.

The Ethiopian party have left for a third time and I do hope, after so many false starts, that they really will leave this time. We gave a lunch to Haile Selassie's daughter, HRH Princess Tenagne at the Middlesex in honour of their going. Unfortunately the time was changed at the last moment and most of them had gone, but there were still 20 remaining there and together with a number of people from Gordon Square, it made for quite an impressive gathering.

She is a nice person, very small and was probably not quite as shy as she looked. Tom made a speech, and she replied in Amharic. She is the daughter of Selassie and the widow of Ras Desta, who the Italians killed, and has children who have been educated in this country. Our cooking department put on an excellent meal and though several things nearly went wrong, in the end we narrowly escaped disaster and the whole event was, I think, a success.

We of course, are still waiting for a date to leave and as soon as I know, I will keep you in the picture, and whether or not we shall be coming to Northfield for a pre departure get together. I have to say this place is unutterably dull now that so many are away – no Dick or Arnold or Barry and Barty, and Angela busy, busy. We did both manage however to go down to Greenwich Park on Sunday afternoon, and the river looked lovely and the park a joy, but otherwise she is out so much I hardly see her. She has very kindly been marking all my equipment and I think I am more or less ready to start now. In some ways I want to go – that is to say, I don't want to hang about – but for every other reason I hate the thought of going. Oh, isn't life bloody?

Dear one, always remember how much I love you and will deeply miss you. Always in my thoughts, my dearest wife. How can I tell you how much? You are so good to let me go abroad.

I am so glad you had a pleasant day in Birmingham....Ronald (Joynes) gave me your message. I am very glad you were able to speak to Jack's fiancée. It would be nice for her if you could see something of her from time to time. Jack is such a good friend of mine. Tom too has been very kind in suggesting that I should have extra money for expenses when I am in Egypt.

I'm sending you a letter from Michael Bagenal, who is an odd and very likeable lad, but who now feels he must leave the Unit. Tom wants me to go out to a party with him on Saturday, but I shan't if I can help it!

I don't think there is any more news.
Dearest love my sweetheart, Ralph
PS Love to David

Princess Tenagne meets FAU members

(Left) Princess Tenagne arriving for lunch with the FAU, prior to returning home from exile in Britain.

The Princess was the eldest child of Emperor Haile Selassie and Empress Menen Asfaw.

In 1935, following the invasion of Ethiopia by Italy, the imperial family was forced into exile, and came to live in Bath.

In 1941, with British assistance, Emperor Haile Selassie was restored to his throne.

Later in 1943 FRB joined an FAU group out there, including Selby Clewer helping to supervise the reconstruction of the country.

Both photographs Friends House Library

Princess Tenagne meets some of the Ethiopian section before they left to go out there, with FRB centre in his new uniform.

Up till now my mother's voice has only been present as a ghost in my father's letters, as sadly these have been lost. But now she speaks for herself in the first of many letters; a voice of love and devotion and longing, which will increasingly come to be seen as the voice from home, as my father moves to far away countries.......

Tuesday, June 16 1942 – Wolverhampton

Darling Ralph

Thank you for your sweet letter which arrived this morning. I was overjoyed to receive it. Thank you too for all the nice things you say, though God knows I am not wonderful at all. But I am so proud of you and treasure the picture of you in your uniform with me and the two boys. I could not wish for a better husband. In the months that come, you will know I am thinking and praying for you and loving you with all my heart and soul. I wish you everything you hope to achieve in your new work and I know and am absolutely sure in my heart that you will make good in the task that lies ahead of you. In this as in everything else you have tackled, you will succeed beyond all your hopes and dreams. You are always so thorough and conscientious and you have – one of the best things about you – a great sense of humour, which will help to carry you through.

I know how hard you always work, but try also to relax and enjoy this new experience as much as you possibly can, as in many ways, though it takes us apart, it is a wonderful opportunity for you. I only long to be with you and live for the day when we are together again. I think of all the glorious times we have shared when you have made me so happy. I just thank God I was fortunate enough to win your love. I am so much the poorer without you, but I will try to be all you expect of me and to bring up the boys as you would wish me to. They are darlings and I love them for what they are and because they are yours. David loves you so very dearly and asked me if God would look after you all the way on the boat. I assured him that he would!

This comes with all our love for your birthday and I enclose some introductions which I typed out for you last night, which I hope will be of help when you are in the Lebanon. I'm sure Jack Turtle will give you more introductions to the University. I also enclose some cigarettes as a birthday present. God bless you and keep you safe until we meet again. Ever yours Joan

---

A letter from Peter Gibson in Cairo to my father just prior to leaving London:

22nd June 1942

My dear Ralph.....

.....You are about to take on the <u>most important job</u> in the Unit....and I assure you, you will be welcomed with open arms. Of course, after 12 months of freedom, it is possible that I shan't take kindly to discipline from above.....so you will have to be brutal rather than gentle, and if I get too obstreperous, you can always wave this letter in my face, or send me to the desert out of harms way! I shall naturally call you Sir in public, to salute and curtsy to you on every possible occasion – in fact treat you as 'the greatest thing that happened in the Middle East since Wavell' But seriously, Ralph, it's going to be great seeing you and the boys and I shall be counting the days.

Yours ever

Chapter 17
Overseas – Round the Cape to Durban
June 1942

My father writes in his memoirs of the reasons for his posting and his eventual sailing.........

It had become increasingly clear, as Unit sections were now working with the British and French Armies as well as in Syria, and while another section was due for Ethiopia, that a senior Unit officer was urgently needed in the Middle East, who would be responsible for the whole field. Already there had been difficulties in arranging loans or transfers of personnel between the Hadfield Spears Hospital and the British Army work. The Syria clinics were expanding and further workers would have to be transferred to them. In general, with possibilities of further work afoot, there would be great advantages in pursuing a correlated policy. So it was agreed that a senior officer should be sent out. The choice fell on me, who was then in charge of the Relief work in London as well as Deputy Chairman of the Executive.

So arrangements were made for me to set sail, along with thirty three other men, on the long journey round the Cape to Cairo, as the Mediterranean was by then too dangerous. The shipping position was then at its very worst and there were long delays, with our party being assembled, disbanded, then reassembled. And with each new crisis in the Middle East, the question was raised whether it could really be justified for the Unit to send yet more hostages to an uncertain future. But then quite suddenly in the middle of June, the party set sail.

It was emphasized to all members of the group, however, that they should have no illusions as to what might or might not be in store for them. They had to be prepared for anything. Having left England in June, for instance, it could transpire when we finally arrived in Cairo in September, after the long voyage round the Cape, that the situation was completely different. Indeed, the war news being what it was, there might be no Egypt for them at all. *As Tegla Davies writes....*

> "In an army organized for total war it was not easy to incorporate a pacifist unit, which insisted on retaining its identity, which had to pick and choose what jobs it could and could not do, and which claimed the final authority over the disposition of its members. Success depended largely on patience and understanding on both sides; failure came when insistence on the letter crushed the spirit. Senior army officers who handled men by the thousand and ten thousand would, with very few exceptions, do their utmost to accommodate a group of men with whose views they completely disagreed even if they understood them. To them, as much as to anyone, did members of the Unit owe what success they achieved in their work with armies in the field."

Much might be written, and has been written by members of the Unit, on their experiences on board troop ships. For a party of thirty odd CO's to live with the Army in such close contact for a period of five weeks, is something of an experience, and is liable to be a great risk. But I was immensely impressed by the way in which Unit members fitted in, and officers on board paid a very well deserved tribute to their standard. Settling such a party in, seems a continual progression from one ship's official to another in search of small decisions or necessaries, and in the early days I seemed to spend my time wandering about the ship apparently with no results. Altogether it was quite a remarkable experience. We were on the Orion, a luxury liner, still maintaining a prewar standard of living, very different to the later period of the war.

[Textual: In reading the following correspondence, it should be borne in mind that due to the exigencies of wartime postal services to and from the far corners of the world, let alone from on board ship, the time gaps were often enormous. In such circumstances, therefore, one letter did not necessarily follow another, and several letters might arrive at once. But I have tried, for the sake of contrast, to alternate my parents' letters, at the same time as giving them some sort of sequential sense, even though the dates may sometimes be out of kilter. Inevitably, on occasions there is some miss-match, but that is also how it would have seemed to them. He also starts to number his letters, but as some are very long I have broken them up, so I have only numbered the letters when it is relevant, as in when my mother refers to a particular number.]

The rest of the journey to Durban over five weeks is most vividly conveyed through my parent's letters to each other, sometimes divided by extracts from my father's memoirs or my mother's diaries, which are in quotation marks. Otherwise I will leave them to tell their own eloquent tale, with only the occasional interruption......starting with a note from my mother..........

June 1942 – Wolverhampton

 Darling mine

This is just an extra letter to wish you very many happy returns of your birthday next month and to tell you again that I love you and am thinking of you this very minute.

I wonder what you are doing on the high seas and do long to give you my birthday greetings with a kiss. I hope you will spend it quietly enjoying the sea breezes in the warm sunshine, or perhaps reading in a deck chair, if there is room!

I hope you have found some pleasant officers for company. I know it isn't easy for you darling and I pray for help in your difficult task. But I know you will be liked and respected by everyone. You are so humble and so very nice! May your next birthday bring you nearer home to me where I shall be waiting for you with open arms, to love you and share your life with you, without any more long separations. Always remember I love you, adore you, and worship you, now and forever. God bless thee. Ever thy Joan Mary.

"Having left London early, we arrived in Liverpool by midday, and though our embarkation went fairly smoothly, it took forever and the delays were exasperating. The ship was a fine big, pre-war luxury liner, very well appointed, and I shared a double cabin with some chap in civilian clothes. For two days we just lay in the Mersey, though just watching the port had its own fascination, with tugs and boats of all sorts and sizes passing to and fro in the evening sun."

Saturday, 20th June 1942 – On board RMS Orion, posted before departure (No 1)

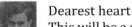 Dearest heart

This will be a short letter as I am exhausted after a long day. [.....] Now thank God, we are at last on board. I am writing this in the Officer's lounge, which is now crowded with officers of every rank and many different regiments. In fact conditions for officers really leave very little to be desired, whereas those for the men, though tolerable, are not anything like as good. The inequalities seem most unfair.

But what can I really tell you? It is so difficult to write any news while we are still waiting to leave. Also I have to be extra careful in what I do say, as I am acting as the censor to the whole party, and must try not to transgress myself. I find it so sad having to censor the men's letters: there are a few who are obviously enjoying it just for the travel, but most write home to friends or sweethearts, and of course their one and only wish is to be with them again. It's tragic, the more so as I am overwhelmed with longing for you. I have David's photograph out and at times can hardly bear to look at it.

I was talking to one of the party this afternoon, who had only been engaged for three weeks, poor man. Most of them think they are doing the right thing, and are most grateful to their wives and girlfriends for letting them go and for supporting them. I also feel I am doing right, thank God, but I am much more than grateful to you. I know how different it must all appear to you, and how difficult it will be for you. Believe me I am so grateful for your wonderful support and pray for you always.

I am not really sure what I believe, but I derive strength from somewhere to do a difficult job and I believe it comes from faith. Whether my prayers help you, I don't know, but I think they do and I believe yours help me. I always feel so close to you at evening time, and this evening I have felt certain that the day will come when we shall be together again and pray that we shall be able to take up where we left off. We are so close in spirit and we need each other now more than ever. May God keep you safe my dearest one and remember how much I love you. My undying love, Ralph

PS 1 On the train coming here, Paul Cadbury promised to see that if anything were to happen to me, you and the children's education would be alright and taken care of.

PS 2 Please tell me you still love me and that you are not angry with me for leaving you

"All that you may have seen and read about the fascination of convoys is true. These troopships were amazing – the troops fairly typical of the working classes, the Officers pretty typical of the middle and upper – every type represented. On board, the life was pretty busy, getting things sorted and fixed up, and everyone was very kind, considering that we were neither one thing nor another; neither army nor civilian. But the men all behaved very well."

Monday, 22nd June 1942 – In transit

Dearest one, my darling Joan

At last, the boat is moving, but I expect we are only going a short way out. The weather is beautiful and this evening very warm. On the whole we have done fairly well so far, though there have been a few irritating hitches, as we have not yet got all our baggage out, most of which is still deep in the hold. But the bar is open and the stewards are serving vast quantities of cheap alcohol, with cigarettes and tobacco at absurdly low prices – 20 for 8d! And the food is really excellent. Four course meals with such things as butter and fruit in plentiful supply on an entirely pre-war standard.

For some time now these sections of England have been going abroad to all the theatres of war. Yet, see the scene now in the evening sun, with troops lying around on the decks. Some Officers walking up and down, though most sitting or standing, talking and drinking, reading or playing cards and writing in the lounge. And outside, just sea and sky and night coming on. So much brilliance and apparent gaiety, yet death so near and the future so uncertain.

Today the sea and sky have been especially lovely; the sea so blue with white horses and the scudding clouds gilded by the sun, that one comes to realise that whatever stupidities and sillinesses man is capable of, nature – the sea and the sky, the clouds, sun and rain – remain unchanged and unchangeable – I thank God at least for that, and if it were peace time and we were just off on a cruise, it would be the most enjoyable experience.

I do wonder how you and the children are and what you are doing. I think of you taking David to school and putting the children to bed; of you brushing your hair or putting on your favourite brooch. I just live for the day when I will return and resume our life together. I don't know when you will receive my letters, but hopefully I can post at our next port of call. I must close now. I think of you all so often. I send all my love.

God Bless, Ralph

The RMS Orion was launched in 1934 and used as a troopship from 1940 -1945.
"We are on this fine, big ship, which is a luxury liner, and I must say, is very nicely appointed."
Photo National archives

"I have thought of Ralph so constantly these last few days and wished so much I knew exactly what he was doing."

June 1942 – Wolverhampton

My darling Ralph

How I long to hear your voice again. It already seems years since you were here, and yet it is only a short time. I don't know when this will get posted or whether you'll ever receive it, as Brandon (Cadbury) hasn't yet sent me particulars of your addresses. But thank you so much for your dear letter.

From all accounts you had a wonderful send off from everyone at Gordon Square. Millior wrote me a very nice letter telling me how smart you looked and all who were there to bid you farewell. Angela also wrote to me too, as you had requested, giving me all the particulars, so I could picture it all. I'm so glad the men are such a fine group, and that you are so proud of them. I can imagine that the London Hospital will be a dismal place now without you, and Richard and Barry will miss you a great deal, as of course, will Tom.

Reading the weekly newsletter from Gordon Square, they seem to have had a very heated staff meeting in your absence. No doubt they missed your quiet way of keeping order and smoothing over difficulties. The recent news makes me wonder whether you will end up in India after all.

I have written to your mother and passed on some of the letters you have had from people on your departure. I know she will be as pleased to see them as I was. We are all so proud of you, dearest. In fact I'm expecting your mother here for the day next Thursday, and hope the weather will stay as lovely as it's been the last few days. David and I are all the time thinking of you and talking of thee continually, praying for thy safe journey and that God may help and guide thee in the difficult work that lies ahead. David has been so sweet since you went; he is very sensitive to one's mood and has been most affectionate, calling me his 'precious mummy' and his 'sweet darling'. He says "Tell Daddy I am taking great care of Mummy while he is away."

I think I must hasten and post this and I am sorry for the delay, but I have been in bed for a week with a bladder infection – not very nice – and I can't throw it off. With Llew away, I had to call in Dr Fitzgerald, and poor mother had to look after me and the children and the house, and she is quite worn out. But I am already feeling better, so not to worry. I do so long to get another letter from you. As each day goes by I miss you more and more. Life is so empty without you. Remember dear heart how much we love you and miss you, and may God bless you and keep you safe. David and Antony send you kisses and love too.

Ever your own loving, Joan

Here my father writes in his memoirs of the changes he has already experienced since the war began......

"By the time I left England, what changes I had experienced already in the war. So many different people met, so many different societies, from AFS to camp, from Poplar Hospital and Hostel to Cheveley and back to camp again. Visits to Beaconwood and Wolverhampton, and then on board ship and out to South Africa and Egypt. By this time I was just anxious to settle down for a little."

Thursday, 25th June 1942 – In transit

 My very dearest Joan

I now have my baggage and have been able to dress for dinner this evening and feel slightly more respectable.

It's been so busy the last few days, with hardly a minute to write. But now at last I have a small gap and can settle down and write again, though I'm afraid this method of writing a little every day is all very well, but it produces a very rambling and disjointed letter. But life goes on and everything seems reasonably all right. It seems there is always so much to do, and I have started a note book; so far my entries include Devotional services (we hope to get a room soon), blood donors (we are to help if necessary), physical training, cinema and injections – in fact a whole set of new things I've got to learn. I chatted with the Padre yesterday, who asked most politely if he could join our French classes. I'm most impressed how polite everyone is to us.

Today is another beautiful day and I must admit life is reasonably comfortable. All my essentials are now unpacked I'm glad to say, and all my books arranged on a little shelf by my bunk. The chaps are also beginning to settle down now, either joining in classes, or doing PT, or just reading quietly and letter writing. John Gough has kindly let us use his cabin as a centre, which is proving invaluable, as I seem to be kept pretty busy just fixing things or trying to do what's best for everyone. Most of the time this seems to involve my seeing dozens of people, most of whom I can't find. The rest of the time I'm simply talking to the chaps and making contacts with Army Officers. The Army C in C has asked me to give a talk on the Unit, and John Gough is busy lecturing on First Aid to various groups. Both John G and Philip Sanford really are a great asset to have around.

Well, we seem to continue making excellent progress through a wonderfully blue sea, and there is a nice Scots Captain, who is interested in birds and keeps asking if I've seen any, but sadly there are no birds to see. How I wish I could give you some more details of this strange life, but it is almost impossible, with censorship.

Try not to worry and know only that I think of you all every day.

All Love Ralph

"I often felt rather depressed and as each day went by, I seemed to miss Joan more. It was as if I were among the foothills of an enormous range of mountains, which I had to climb with no turning back. It is a mountain of time unknown, of responsibility inescapable, and travel eternal. And all this time a loneliness and separation."

Friday, 26th June 1942 – In transit

My dearest wife

Yesterday evening we had a showing of the film "Next of Kin", with Jack Hawkins. It was so good to see a film again, even though it is a tragic tale and rather gruesome towards the end, but I think it is extraordinarily well done.

I do miss you terribly, but somehow I know that you and I together will surmount it if we pray hard enough. In a way, of course, life is tolerable, but there is always a sense of being an intruder. I met a very helpful Major yesterday, who is most co-operative, but however nice the military are – and they are nice – there is a feeling of not belonging, of being rather odd, and a fear that sooner or later something may go terribly wrong. It often seems as if we are living on the edge of a precipice. I write all this to you as I know you will understand as I understand you. And this above all, my dearest, is at the heart of our truth; that though we may be parted in the flesh, we are very near spiritually. Take courage my dear in this at least, that come what may, we have loved, we do love and we shall love.

Life is pretty busy getting things fixed up, with everybody being very kind, considering we are neither one thing nor another. The chaps are all behaving well and are busy settling in. The Scots Captain and I actually saw some birds today – Puffin, Kittiwake, Guillemot and Gannets – most satisfying.

The news of the fall of Tobruk is most disturbing and what we shall find when we get to Egypt is anyone's guess. I wonder where we shall go and what we shall be able to do. Still it's no good worrying.

We continue to make steady progress through a really very calm sea – to be honest we have never really felt the sea at all yet. But it does get hotter and hotter, and tonight it is especially close and sticky. Otherwise it is a most glorious evening; a clear sky with a few stars and a great moon rising. There are some pleasant people on board and my cabin partner is very likeable. The boat deck is full of army and naval Officers standing about or just walking up and down, and I happened to meet an Officer who was at school with Dick Holding. Small world!

In a few days we shall be at our first port of call and I hope to be able to post this letter to you. I need hardly say how devoutly thankful I shall be to get off this boat for a while. I probably exaggerate, as life could be a lot worse, but I do find the responsibility a considerable strain and a respite, however brief, would be welcome.

We seem to have been gone an eternity already, but it was only last week we were still together. What a wonderful weekend we had and how kind you were to me. I shall always remember that time.

All my love Ralph

FRB considers his choice of reading on the voyage – "On the whole I was very satisfied with the books that I took with me. Shakespeare is an ideal companion. *Othello* is a good play for a sea voyage; and between Karachi and Basra, Falstaff and Prince Hal were welcome additions to the passenger list!"

"How I longed to get news of Ralph and whether he had arrived safely in South Africa."

Beginning of July 1942 – Wolverhampton (Airmail postcard)

 Dearest,

A brief PC just to say that you are so much in my thoughts and I long to get news of you. We are all well and the children full of energy. David asks after you every day and says I am to tell you his tricycle is going fine!

I have heard from several people at Gordon Square what a good lot of men you all looked and I hope everything has gone well during the last months. You will be glad to settle for a while and I do hope your arrangements will go satisfactorily. Went to see "Ball of Fire"[1] today, but it was very disappointing I thought!

Very dearest love from David, Antony and JMB

"Our first port of call was Freetown and I had hoped to be able to post some mail to Joan, but we only took on supplies, which was frustrating to say the least."

Sunday, June 28th 1942 – In transit

My dearest Joan

I do hope you received the letter I posted before we left. Following on yesterday's letter, I had really hoped to be able to send you a cable from our next port of call, and I am most disappointed to find out that this won't be so after all, as we are not going to land and I am really very cross about that. We will probably just take on supplies, which will at least be a break in the monotony.

This evening there is another brilliant sunset, though before one can really take it in, in no time at all the sun has sunk into the sea. Yesterday was cloudy with a strong wind blowing, but today it has cleared and the breeze is cooler, and although the sun is out it is really quite tolerable. Indeed everyone has changed into drill outfit today: men in shorts, stockings and shirts; Officers much the same for day wear, but drill slacks and tunics for the evening. The navy look very dashing in their white jackets and shorts. Mine look quite well too, I think!

It's Sunday today and it somehow feels very Sunday-ish indeed, with some of the chaps having a bathe in the swimming bath! We have now been given a room for religious services and we are going to have a part Quaker meeting (Devotional) after lunch. I spent a large part of the morning trying to find something suitable I could say or read. Eventually I decided on "Ye are the salt of the earth", and to prevent them feeling too smug, the beginning of the next chapter of Matthew, about 'doing good in private'! Then to show how a challenge could be met, I read from Luke, Christ's "Father, if thou be willing, remove this cup from me: not my will, but thine, be done." And finally, just to show what a poor lot we really are, Peter's denial of Christ.

My readings effectively killed the whole meeting, and no one else had anything to say! But I do think that there are a few essentials of our beliefs that we must try to hang on to at such difficult times and I feel it my duty to uphold them. We must try and adhere to our faith especially at this particular place and moment, and not to fret too much about what may come. Actually, it made me feel quite good again, though I confess I'm not sure I have discovered any deeper understanding of life.

Well, preparing for meeting, collecting the week's cigarettes and overseeing the chaps in the swimming bath took up most of the morning. Then the meeting itself after lunch and in the afternoon, I prepared the talk on the Unit which I have been asked to give to the servicemen.

All for now, my love Ralph

"There were good days and bad. Often one felt tired and depressed having accomplished seemingly very little. Then with disturbing news from Egypt, one wondered whether there would be an Egypt there at all when we finally arrived, and what if anything we should be able to do. But there was little that worrying would do."

June 29ᵗʰ 1942 – In transit

Dear Joan

Not a good day really. [......] I was talking to quite a nice lieutenant in the lounge yesterday, who seems to know several people back in the UK who know me. He is also very well read, which makes a change. He asked me whether I felt out of place amongst all the military. I replied "Yes, on the whole I do." He seemed rather surprised. So I said "I might feel slightly better if knew more people." But the truth is, I've really felt decidedly out of place ever since the war began. I get so tired of being labelled a 'conchie'.

However, I have no complaints at all about personnel, and the whole party is generally bearing up wonderfully well in rather trying conditions. But we are looked after well and on the whole our food is still excellent, including plenty of fruit – apples, oranges or pears after dinner and grapefruit for breakfast – which is essential, even so we have had some minor epidemics of diarrhoea and some constipation, plus some skin trouble. Happily, so far, I have managed to keep very fit.

This evening we are to be given a talk by the army Padre, though I'm afraid I don't take to him much. Perhaps I am misjudging him.

Please tell anyone who is interested that I am well, especially mother and give her my love. Also, of course, all my love to all at Wolverhampton and David and Antony and you my dearest Joan.

I think often of all our life together, especially that last happy holiday before I left, which I remember vividly and was so special. Remember my love, I think of you always, and particularly now as I go to bed. Pray for me and for our speedy reunion. I shall hand this in tomorrow and hopefully it won't be too long before you receive it.

God keep you till we meet again, always your loving Ralph

My mother expresses her need to talk to my father.........

"Sometimes I just had to sit down and write to Ralph, even though I had no letter to answer. I so wanted to talk to him and this was the only way of doing it."

Early July 1942 – Lea Road, Wolverhampton

My dearest one

[.....] You are always in my thoughts and I miss you more and more as the days slip by. I cannot seem to get my balance or settle to things. I know it will come in time and I must be patient. But my life is so built around you and with you and for you and I have a terrible longing for you. On top of which I haven't been well, although Llew says there is nothing to worry about, and has given me something like the M&B pills I had before, to clear up the germ I have. It will soon go away he says. Unfortunately it tends to make me depressed. God knows, I don't need tablets to do that!

Antony is growing up so fast now, and getting to be quite a young monkey. He is so active and can put down the sides of his cot and even climb out of it. He really does need continual watching. But he is growing into quite a round, plump and jolly little boy, and is a darling.

D talks to you all the time and asks me every day 'how far in the sea is Daddy?' He loves you so dearly. He told the hairdresser that you had gone abroad for two months. How I wish it could be for so short a time! Each night he asks God to watch over you in his prayers, adding that 'Mummy doesn't always have time, as she has so much washing to do'! He is busy writing you a letter today for your birthday. You are so much in all our thoughts at this time, and this brings all of our loves for you that day.

David's report this term is very good, saying *"He shows liveliness and enthusiasm in his work and is a helpful member of the playroom. He has a good vocabulary and is quick in grasping new work. He has wide interests in all directions and a love of books. He is a happy member of his group. He will be ready next term to join the Upper Class."* He longs to get your letters.

I wrote to Ronald Joynes recently and asked for any news of you, and he wrote back an extremely charming note, which cheered me up a little. I do so ache for news of you. How are you fitting in with your men and what are the other officers like? I long to know how your time is taken up. Do you have much time for reading, talking and discussing things and mixing with the others?

I rang your mother the other night and said that I thought I would go over to Selly Oak Meeting on Sunday next, and wondered whether she would like to come with me and spend the day together. I said that perhaps we could have a quiet lunch and tea together, and she seemed very cheered by the thought. I think it is quite a good idea, especially while the days are still long. My, how we shall talk of our beloved one!

I read this the other day: "How pitifully feeble is any description of a person one loves." And how I agree. I can describe your career, or estimate your intellectual talents. I can tell the colour of your hair and eyes. But the thousand bonds that unite us; the chance remarks, the jokes that we share and the laughter; the common sympathies and antipathies; still more the games and the laughter, the days in the sun and wind and walking on the hills; the evenings before the fire. How can they be described? We've had some good times, dearest one and I thank God for our life together.

All my love my dearest Ralph, now and always Joan

"After we had been on the boat nearly a fortnight, I began to be heartily sick of it and would be devoutly thankful to be off it."

Friday, July 3rd – 14th – In transit

My darling Joan

Today, despite the heat, at least my time has been reasonably well filled. I spent the morning seeing our boys, writing to Gordon Square, censoring letters and thinking of what to say to the troops this afternoon about the Unit.

By the time for my talk came around, the heat had got progressively more overbearing, and the slightest exertion, even just sitting made one melt. We were on the lowest deck but one, but there too, just standing still, we all absolutely ran with sweat, My talk seemed to go down alright, and at least I wasn't heckled, though I doubt if they took in a word of what I was saying, which I imagine they thought very dull. All the same I can now claim to have spoken about Pacifism to both the Army and the FAU! As a quid pro quo, I've asked the Captain if in return he will ask one of his regiment to talk to the Unit on map reading.

Later I had to deal with money and supervised the handing out of funds from the Members Assistance Fund (MAF) together with the extra money we have managed to collect for those who have only MAF to live on. 6/- per week is not very much in these thirsty conditions and some will want more to spend if and when we get shore leave.

So we made a collection from those who could afford it. This, together with a very generous gift of £2.0 from the man who shares my cabin, provided an extra 15/- for those just on MAF, which I found very gratifying.

Then after tea I had a salt water bath, polished my shoes and buttons and am now writing to you in the lounge which is fairly empty at this hour of the late afternoon, as everyone is changing for the evening. Today, I have at last managed to get in some reading – *The Tempest* and *Measure for Measure* (not my favourite) and *All's Well That Ends Well*. I have also finished *Persuasion* and *Emma*. John Gough gave a poetry reading for some of our men and a few of the soldiers the other evening, and they later adjourned to one of the Sergeant's cabins and had a gramophone concert. Soldiers and Sergeants often seem to like to join in such events, with the Officers doing their utmost to keep their men amused.

Well, early this morning we sighted land, and we are now lying off the coast of Africa (Freetown). At midday we came in and docked and it is fascinating to watch all the shipping coming and going. The land is mountainous and the ground appears to be covered in a dense growth of vivid green, low bushes, surrounded by numerous taller trees, mostly Palms. The town is scattered up the side of the hill amongst the trees, and some of the larger white houses, look very pleasant. Altogether, with the busy roadstead, green slopes and fantastic mountain shapes behind, now covered in cloud, it makes for a most attractive picture. Out in the sea I can see some of the local African men fishing in their boats.

Nonetheless, I shall be very glad when we are able to get away, as night times are now really unbearable. All one can do is just sit and drip. At least during the day it is tolerable, thanks to a breeze and frequent heavy storms. In order to keep ourselves cool, one of the young lieutenants and I spent about an hour walking up and down the boat deck. We had a most interesting discussion: I told him about the Unit and he talked to me about the army. I fear most of it would fall foul of the censor, so I suppose I shouldn't repeat it here!

The news from Egypt gets daily more shocking – with us being out-fought and out-generalled by an enemy numerically inferior. It seems to be developing into one of the most disturbing parts of the whole war. We really are seriously beginning to wonder what we shall do when we arrive, but from here on board ship, it's no use our worrying. The only way to live, is to do one's bit each day and not to bother about the future – except for that great day, when we come home.

Today, I had to do some essential but rather boring tasks: a haircut, to make myself look half respectable; and some very necessary shopping – tooth paste, tooth brush, razor blades, and can you believe, a flannel, as some blighter pinched my sponge!   Afterwards I had some spare time, which I spent reading, first Milton's *Comus,* and then for a complete change, *Pride and Prejudice.*

This evening we had a ship's concert party in the lounge, which all things considered, was quite good. Some pleasant cracks about the army as well as our lot. It is good to find that we can all laugh at ourselves. So much I could say if it were not for the censor. I am afraid we are still in dock, but mercifully, thanks to heavy cloud and frequent rain, it is now not quite so hot. I must say there is so much I object to on this boat. I am not enamoured of sweating humanity, or going into a room full of strangers. I'm not very keen on having to make conversation with a lot of people I don't know or am not interested in, but I have 30 of them with me! I dislike having to tell people what to do. In fact I don't think I much like responsibility. But, hey ho, I am saddled with it. Perhaps it's all good for me, though above all I hate being away from you. All love for now, Ralph

"At last I received a letter from Ralph, and it was so comforting to know that he was safe."

July – Wolverhampton

Dearest, I'm, so happy.
A note from thee at last. It's the one you wrote about three weeks ago on board. It's the first that I've had and it's acted like a tonic already. I'm so glad to have news of you and to know that you are safe and comfortable and that life on board is tolerable. I hope you have got over your depression at the length of the journey. With your lovely letter, I am at last beginning to feel better and see things in a more balanced way. As you say, we shall pick ourselves up and put on a brave face and go through with it. You know that I will always do my best while you are away, and try and bring up the boys as you would wish. But oh, how I miss you, and your help and advice.

I heard this silly story the other day, which made me laugh. I wonder if it's yet reached South Africa. A group of Officers of different nationalities, were talking together. "Are you married?" said one. "Oh yes", he replied. "Have you any children?" "Oh no, my wife is unbearable." Another Officer chipped in – "Surely you mean impregnable?" A third said "No, no, the word is inconceivable." Ha! Ha!

How I long to have you here with me to share laughter together. I just feel so empty when you are not here, as you make my life worthwhile. But I know time will pass and that one day we will be reunited. May it come quickly. I will say goodbye now my dearest one and write again soon. This brings all my love. As always, Joan

"I'm not very good with heat at the best of times, on board ship I found it almost unbearable."

Wednesday, July 15th 1942 – in transit

My dearest Joan
Today again the heat is something terrific, quite the hottest yet; everyone is absolutely dripping. To compound matters, water is unfortunately in short supply, and washing is very restricted. It's 10.15 in the evening and I have just come down from the troop deck and my goodness it's stifling. The heat on the lower decks must be fearful. My own cabin is unbearable enough, the best place being the deck.

The sky is bright with stars and the clouds of the day practically gone. The funnel and masts tower black against the night; the officers walking quietly up and down; the hills dim against the night sky; a few lights in the houses. Searchlights on moving launches scan the water, while the lights of the smaller ships gleam in the black sea. On our own ship, the decks are crowded with troops, hundreds of cigarettes glowing in the dark, dim shafts of light from doors lighting here a man's face or legs, and there a crowd of faces: all singing sentimental songs, while someone's strumming on a guitar and all around the tropic night and above the bright stars.

I saw the Officer Commanding troops this morning with various suggestions for improving the organisation in the library. I've also fixed up for a lecture on map-reading from a Major, and a lecture from the Senior Medical officer. The food continues to be good, with grapefruit for breakfast instead of prunes and we get excellent apples after dinner.

The party are still pretty fit, thank goodness, save for some who continue to suffer from diarrhoea and skin diseases. Also we are in pretty good heart, which is a great credit to them, as life on a troopship is no picnic. It's like trying to run a training camp with innumerable obstacles added just to make it difficult – heat, crowds, regulations, lack of space etc. However, we are surviving.

Yesterday we passed through shoals of flying fish. They leap out of the water and glide for 20 or 30 yards and then drop back in again; they appear dark, above the sea below. They spread their broad side fins in flight and appear not to flap at all, but only to glide, so I presume they must use the air currents. They can also turn in the air, though often it looks as if they had been blown out of their course rather than that they turned by design.

I seem to spend most of my time asking people to do things for us. The cheek of the Unit is staggering! To travel on a troopship in the first place; to expect and get all the army resources of food, fruit and so on; to get lecture spaces and desk space: in fact to expect to be treated as normal human beings instead of the outcasts we are ! However, it seems to work, although it's a bit worrying for the master!

I am reading and much enjoying Gibbon's autobiography which mother lent me; also a variety of thrillers of doubtful worth. Last night the sea was luminous again and really rather striking. I have just finished reading *Black Mischief* by Evelyn Waugh[1], which is very amusing and really rather good.

I've spent all morning censoring letters – a boring occupation. The refrain behind all the letters is 'Someday (and the sooner the better) this will be over and then heaven will begin.' In everyone's mind is this 'looking forward to the future' – congenial work, freedom and reunion. I know, as it's about the only thing that really interests me at present too. Is it wise to build ones hopes up so much? Yes, I think it is all we live for – it is the natural way of living that we want back again. Good God, how we want it ! All for now dearest. Love Ralph

"The period of waiting for news goes so slowly and I ache for a letter."

Mid July 1942 – Wolverhampton (Airgraph)

 My dearest

I hope very much this letter will be waiting for you when you arrive at your destination, and I eagerly await a cable from you to say you have arrived. You'll be pleased to learn that I have recovered from the infection that I had and both D and A are flourishing and full of fun. David finishes school at the end of this month and next term I shall send him every morning.

As I mentioned in my last note, I went to Selly Oak Meeting last Sunday with your mother and then spent the day with her. She is well and sends her love. The gardens around Weoley Hill are beautiful now with masses of roses everywhere and all the herbaceous flowers imaginable.

We all send love, and kisses from the children, Joan

"We seemed to be stuck at our port of call for ever, and we all just longed to move on. Every day I was kept busy organizing things to occupy the chaps' time. Lectures on tropical diseases, religious services, games and just making sure everyone behaved themselves!"

Thursday, July 16th 1942 – in transit (No 5)

My dear Joan

We are still stuck here and we would all be very glad if we could move on, though I did see a Petrel yesterday in the harbour as well as one or two lovely butterflies flying past, which cheered me up. But generally it looks like another uneventful day. My friend the Captain wants me to tell him about Quakerism, so I have been reading it up. I am quite glad I brought my copy of Elizabeth Emmott on Quakerism (a distant cousin) with me; it'll give me some inspiration.

After breakfast, I drew the week's cigarettes for the men, and saw various people about various things, including setting up further lectures; and went to Divine Service. There were some good hymns, and really lovely prayers: many of the Anglican prayers are so beautiful. The sermon though was, I'm afraid, very mediocre! We then had a full Quaker meeting, which was an entirely silent one.

Later we all attended a mechanics class, after which I had a little spare time and managed to finish Emmott and read some of the book of Quaker Discipline, before re-reading one of my favourite books, Dorothy Sayer's *Gaudy Night*. To my shame, the first two books for only the second time, the last for about the fifth! That shows my priorities!

Later....... Thank God! At last we're moving and we are all very pleased. I've just come down from the boat deck, which was the only cool spot, but now thanks to some fairly heavy rain and a breeze, it is at last a little cooler. There are still a few places where it is fearfully hot, but I just hope in a few days it really will be generally much cooler.

As we got going this evening, we had a very good lecture from a lady doctor on tropical diseases and another on control of mosquitoes. What a lot of terrible things you can get, but hundreds of people seem to live quite happily in the tropics, so why shouldn't we? Otherwise there is really no news. If you have room, my dear, and you can bear to, it might be worth keeping these letters, as they could be of interest after the war.

It's so good to be on the way again, although we are still in the hot latitudes, but generally speaking it is much cooler. The sea-water baths have been cleaned, and now we are at sea again, I had a lovely bathe before dinner. The voyage continues uneventfully through calm and sunny seas, and last night the stars were clear and wonderful, with the Great Bear and the Pole star right on the horizon and my very first sight of the Southern Cross.

Another few days and we will have been on this boat for nearly three weeks and when we shall make land we do not know. One day is much like the next. Yesterday the Major I mentioned came to talk to us on map-reading, and he was actually quite good. There was also yet another lecture on tropical diseases, which I really hope is the last! The lady doctor who gives them is a specialist and certainly knows her subject. Last night she dealt in length with malaria, lecturing with immense pride and describing the loathsome disease with great relish! As someone said, she is rather like a female version of my brother-in-law, Dr Rutter in her lecturing.

This morning we had a free French Officer to our French class and he talked for an hour. One or two of our group are quite good French scholars, who were able to talk to him fairly fluently, but the bulk of the class were rather tongue-tied.

This afternoon I prepared some notes for a talk I am giving on the Unit's work in the Middle East to our chaps; also some cautionary notes about behaviour when eventually we get shore leave. All for now.......I'll write more tomorrow. Love Ralph

"Another of the events that stands out in my memory of our sea journey to Durban, is the boxing match somewhere in the middle of the Atlantic. Not a sport I care much for, but this was quite an event as I wrote to Joan."

Later ......July 17th [......] This morning I censored letters for about an hour, superintended the PT class and watched some of the boxing semi-finals on the top deck, which were rather scrappy, I thought. But what do I know about boxing? However, later they held the finals on A deck and I thought I would like to see it, so I secured a seat. That makes the first time I've watched boxing on a Sunday, or for that matter watched any amount of boxing at all.

The scene was actually rather striking – a perfect day with a cloudless sky and warm sun, the sea so blue and flecked with white, other ships ploughing steadily on around us; a ring set up on deck surrounded by sitting rows of men in khaki, sailors in white and blue and on one side, Officers, military and naval, the latter dazzling white, giving contrast to the khaki on the other; tables for judges and referees; a megaphone, and seconds in each corner fanning and sponging their men.

Not a very high standard of skill, but very plucky fighting. The winner of the heavyweight was a giant, with a tremendous physique who knocked his man cold in a few minutes. I don't know quite what I think about professional boxing, but amateur boxing of this sort, where the men do it because they want to, seems a good thing.

In between we held a devotional: very silent – it always is, unless I speak, and even if I had something to say, which I haven't, I can't speak every time. Last night, with the notes I prepared earlier, I spoke to the men – firstly about their behaviour when we reach our first port of call, and secondly in some detail on the work we may be doing if and when we get to Egypt.

It's quite cold and windy today and there's a bit of a sea, though not much. Last night there was a concert in the lounge, one item being a competition between ten army officers and ten navy officers as to which side could drink ten pints of beer quickest, each man drinking after the man before him had finished and put his glass down. The army won, having consumed their ten pints in about 5 seconds each! Not something I suspect for the Quaker annals!

A complete change in the weather today. In fact it's a glorious day – wind and waves, white horses and flying clouds. Some birds too, kinds which I don't know but I can more or less place the families. Another lecture on Tropical Diseases last night. We've had just about enough from the good lady. (Later same day: Our lectures have finally finished!)

I'm reading Henry Nevinson's[2] *Fire of Life*, which mother sent me. It is an abridged version of his three volumes of autobiography. Father knew him, as he had helped found the FAU in WW1, along with Philip Noel Baker and Corder Catchpool. He was an excellent war correspondent and journalist, who died last year. It's a very good book, and well worth reading.

I have now developed a sore throat – I do hope it won't get worse. I saw a film this afternoon - *The Follies* with James Stewart, Lew Ayres and Joan Crawford. I needn't have bothered – it was one of the worst films I have ever seen, with a very stupid story. The best thing in it was the skating, which reminded me of the two of us skating together one midnight on the yachting pool behind Woodbrooke long ago – how good that was.

I'll close for now.
All my love Ralph

———

A Boxing Match on board The Orion
Somewhere in the Atlantic

"Another of the events that stand out in my memory is the boxing match somewhere in the middle of the Atlantic, set up on A deck with tables for the referees and judges all around."
Photograph IWM

"In all my letters, I tried to keep several objectives in mind. To let Joan know what was happening; to let her know that I was well and how I felt and of course to tell her of my undying love."

Saturday, July 18th 1942 – in transit

Dearest Joan

[.......] I have been trying to write a little each day, which I will try to keep up, though it may not always be possible. I was going to keep this letter, but there seems some vague chance that I may get ashore and be able to post it, so that you might receive it in about 4 weeks! I so wish I had been able to have cabled you, but soon perhaps. Please pass on my news to my family. I do hope my letters will give you an idea of how things are going.

You mustn't think that I am incurably miserable, but away from home I can't pretend to be joyously happy either. I'm not in the pit of despair, just suspended rather nearer the lower than the higher end! I know you would rather have the truth than false cheerfulness. But don't worry about me. I have some good men here with me and we support each other. So I will survive and I hold fast to the day when we are reunited.

I told you what Paul Cadbury had said about looking after you and the children if anything happened to me, but I forgot to add that he said I could have all I want in expenses within reason, while I am abroad and that the Trustees have made me a gift of £25 to spend how I like in Egypt – if we ever get there! That is really most generous of him.

Once again, all my love,
Ralph

"I had to try and be patient, but I so longed for Ralph to get settled, so that news would start to come through regularly."

July 1942 – Lea Road Wolverhampton

My dearest Ralph

I have just sent off an Airgraph and an Airmail post card, but as one can't say much on either, I thought I would write you a longer letter. It is now nearly six weeks since I heard from you. It seems an eternity. There's so much I want to know. Life is hellish with you being away, and with no news of you either, I am plunged into the depths of misery and depression.

I was very relieved to hear through Gordon Square of your safe arrival in Durban. I wonder how long you will stay there. I do hope I get a letter soon. At least I get the weekly Newsletter from Gordon Square, which keeps me somewhat up to date, but otherwise the Unit would be a closed book to me! Sometimes I feel so isolated and cut off from everyone, which makes life seem so narrow and dull. I often wish there were more of our friends nearby who I could visit. Of course the children are wonderful and they keep me very busy, and I spend any spare time reading or gardening, and mother and I make occasional visits to the theatre. I mustn't complain!

In fact I went with mother to the Repertory Theatre here, which has been giving a little Shakespeare Festival this week with all proceeds going to the Red Cross. They did several scenes from plays, which of course, isn't nearly as interesting as a full play, but it was an experiment and was most successful. Next week they are doing three short plays by Shaw for the same cause. The main theatre is closed and the productions are being given in the Civic Hall for a fortnight. It is a lovely building, somewhat similar to the Stratford Theatre, only the seats are all on the same level, which is a bit of a drawback for us short ones!

I saw quite a good film the other day called *Remember the Day* with Claudette Colbert. It takes place during the Great War and though very good, it is almost too heartbreaking and close to what's going on in the world right now. I wonder if you have had any films or shows on board ship. The war news is very grim at the moment, and I wish so much we could do more to help Russia; they are suffering so and must be feeling the strain terribly. It is wonderful news that all the FAU men in the Middle East are safe, as they must have had a pretty tough time. I do wonder if Peter Gibson has been able to do any more about helping Polish refugees in Iran and Russia yet.

I had a letter from Mr Appleton (LPA) this week with the monthly cheque, saying that the Trustees had decided in certain cases, to increase the rates of pay to married men who have children, and who are serving in the forces or the FAU. So in future your cheque will be £35.17.0 pm instead of £26.18.6. This is excellent news and certainly most generous of the Trustees. I have written and thanked LPA and asked him to pass on thanks to the Trustees on your behalf.

David breaks up from School on Wednesday next and I do hope we shall have some good weather, so that he and Antony can play out in the garden. It makes things so much simpler to manage if they can be outside. He loves playing in the sandpit and will play by himself quite happily if David is out there too. Both the children are well except that A has been cutting teeth and so hasn't quite such a large appetite as usual. I hope you will like David's letter, he writes very well now and he is always drawing things for you, especially aeroplanes and buses.

Your mother is coming over for the day on Thursday. I think she misses the children and longs to see them. Antony is developing very quickly now, changing from week to week. He talks quite a lot and increases his vocabulary daily. Your mother keeps amazingly well and seems to go out quite a lot and have people in. It is a blessing that she still has Lydia to help her. She is going away at the beginning of August to stay with Millior and Alfred, who have just returned from their holiday and are both well.

I see in the paper that the Earl of Lytton, whose eldest son Antony, after whom our Antony was named, died in a flying accident some years ago, has just lost his other son, Alexander in action in the Middle East. It is tragic how that family has suffered. I wonder if you have heard from any Unit people here. Fancy Horace and Duncan meeting up in India. I wonder how Dick is liking being out there. I do long to hear from you and all the news. Ever your loving Joan.

———

It is interesting that in a letter of his mother's when my father was quite young, she writes "Ralph would never have done that....he was far too shy." Here, writing in his memoirs for us, his children, he is self-aware enough to know his limitations, and in a way his FAU career is all the more remarkable in my view, as his undoubted capability and success story, is achieved at the personal cost of having to overcome his shyness and his lack of belief in himself.

"I often wished that I did the job better. But I'm too reserved and shy and didn't find it easy to make friends. Though Johnnie Gough did say to me the other day "Stop putting yourself down Ralph. You are much loved and respected by the men, who all think you are the best," which was nice to hear!"

Wednesday, July 22nd 1942 – in transit

Dearest Joan

I hope my letters aren't too dull, but one day is very much like another, and censorship forbids me saying too much. The only compensation for all the bloodiness of this life, is that I do feel rather more at ease with myself and my conscience. I do feel at last that I am doing what I ought, which is some comfort. And much as I like and respect all the army people, my objections to war and all its implications are more strengthened than ever.

Standing on the deck the other day during one of our interminable boat drills, I lost my service cap. It blew away in a sudden gust of wind, damn it! Maybe as a result of standing around and the ever changing weather, I have developed a bit of a sore throat. I really hope it won't get any worse. I'll pause for a while – till later

Continued in transit - Friday, July 24th 1942

My dearest

My throat seems to have cleared up, I'm glad to say, which is just as well as it has turned out to be really quite a busy day for me. This morning, I saw various people, after which followed the usual inspections and boat drill. In the afternoon, we had a good two-hour lecture from the Senior Medical Officer on the jolly subject of VD.

It's now evening and quite glorious, with a wonderful blazing sky and a tiny crescent moon. The sea appears calm enough on the surface, but below there is a great swell rolling, making the ship pitch rhythmically. There are birds all around us now and in the dying light they glide and plane over the swell. The season here is, of course, now winter and the light has that peculiar thin clarity which winter sunshine often has.

After the lecture from the Senior MO, the two of us had tea together. You won't credit it, but it turned out that he had been at Hillstone Prep school near Malvern, which used to play us at rugger when I was at The Downs School in Colwall. As we were both at school about the same time, it is quite possible that some 18 years ago we may have played each other! Oh the whirligig of time, as Feste says!

I get so weary of arranging these lectures for the men and fixing up a room and then saying a few words of introduction. I worry whether the speaker will turn up, and then whether he will be any good and whether the chaps will get bored. Then as they are drawing to a close you worry whether there will be any intelligent questions. Well I suppose that's what I'm here for.

I am discovering that Other Ranks and NCOs seem to be able to do little without an Officer to help them, and it is sometimes difficult not to be filled with a quite mistaken sense of one's own importance – so much 'Sir –ing' and saluting all the time. I must say I am very fortunate in having John Gough as a Sergeant. I like him so much and find him a kindred spirit. He is hard working, very fair and good. He is I think really the only member of the party with whom I feel a real affinity. I wonder if there will be anyone like him in Egypt.

We had a most civilized evening yesterday talking civilized things together – about what makes life worth living and 'all the lovely things of home.' His family come from Shropshire, though he has lived for a long time in Tewkesbury. We talked of mutual friends, of the Malvern Festival and Barry Jackson[3]; of the Birmingham Rep and plays we had enjoyed; of English cathedrals; of Ludlow – do you remember that snowy April we went there? – of little Stretton – do you recall that Easter? – and of Wenlock Edge. We talked of wives and friends and of 'things we have loved' as Rupert Brook puts it. Such a pleasant evening.

There is now a strong wind and heavy rain and the incipient swell earlier on has now become surging waves, with the ship rolling and pitching quite strongly. If this were earlier in the voyage, there would undoubtedly be a lot of sickness but it seems that people are now acclimatised to it. I've just had a bath and I had a child's amusement watching the water tipping to and fro and backwards and forwards. It really is rather dramatic, with dark clouds, a grey sea, and great waves rolling and blowing spray every which way. Then quite suddenly there are patches of blue sky and dazzling light on the water. Happily, I seem to have found my sea legs and feel perfectly all right.

As we are now nearing our destination, I've spent most of my time getting our instructions for shore leave. I think it is about time this letter drew to a close and another one started tomorrow. So I will finish and post it and hope that you will have heard from me via the Square long before you get this. My dear love to D&A and of course to you my dearest.
As ever Ralph

A letter brings joy at home at last – in Othello's words "If after every tempest comes such calms.....'twere now to be most happy."

Late in July 1942 – Wolverhampton

 My dearest

Oh, my dear, a letter at last! I am beside myself with joy – and even if it was written five weeks ago, I am delighted to get news of you. After weeks of wondering and anxiety, to see your handwriting at long last and to be able to picture your life on board ship, has brought you so much closer to me. But the ache in my heart is terrible.

As it happened your mother was over for the day, so I was able to read it to her, and she was delighted to hear your news too. She said she had written a long letter to you and would write again after her visit here. My darling, she is so proud of you. She says you are just the right one to go out in command – which is perfectly true – being a teetotaller and setting such a good example, which is less true!!! Little does she know her son! Bless you, I know too thou art the right one for this special job and I know you will always do the right thing and I trust thee absolutely. I too am very proud of you. Your mother also said that she had seen Paul (Cadbury) at the Essay Meeting[4] last week and he told her "Your son Ralph is such a great man". So you see what you have to live up to and I know you will.

Your mother seems well, and manages to get about a great deal seeing people. She is devoted to the children and David shows a great deal of affection, which is so nice and Antony was very friendly too. She is going away a week today to Chipping Camden for a fortnight. I hope she will have a peaceful time there.

There have been raids in the Midlands again this last week, though they are not as bad as formerly. Here in Wolverhampton, we have had such a long peaceful period without raids, that it was odd to hear the siren again the other night and listen to the gunfire. It was a full moon and such a beautiful night, as mother and I got the children down under the stairs for safety. Antony slept while David lay quiet: both were angels.

Your wonderful description of the days and nights at sea brings back such vivid memories of my journey to Egypt. I think the long journey will probably have done you a deal of good, with the excellent food and so much sun. I picture you in your cabin reading in bed and I wish I could be with you. There is so much I want to know, so many details.

I am writing this in bed, sitting up with the reading lamp on by the bedside table. David is sleeping peacefully beside me, bless him, and your dear photograph looks down from above the bed. I wonder what you are doing just at this moment. Talking with some Officer I expect, or reading or admiring the sea. I'm glad you were able to see some interesting birds and discovered the nice Scottish Captain who shares your interest. They all sound a decent crowd. I'm so pleased that John Gough and Philip Sanford have been so co-operative, which must be such a help to you. I wish I could have heard your lecture on the FAU.

David finished school yesterday and had a very good report. Miss Parsons says he is exceptionally bright and advanced for his age. His imagination is amazing and his memory excellent. He really is a joy and great fun these days. Antony is talking quite a lot now, mostly single words. He has a delicious sense of humour and laughs his way through life at present. How I wish you were here to share them with me. We all miss you so. David asked me last night about the passage from Mark's gospel – "What does 'Master, carest thou not that we perish' mean?" He then proceeded to tell me in Biblical language the story of Christ and the disciples caught in a storm and how Christ stilled the waves! We talk of you every day and he is writing to you again. He thought he ought to clean his tricycle after your letter and so got out his cloths this morning!

Today has been a glorious summer's day; brilliant sunshine, with just a slight breeze. The first lovely day for some time. The lime trees have been smelling so sweet this last week when I went to fetch David from school, and it always reminds me of the Green at Bournville and the days when David and I used to meet you from work. The roses, carnations and the scabious are all so beautiful now and your mother sweetly brought a glorious bunch here today, so the drawing room is very gay, and on my dressing table I have arranged a little vase of pink carnations and red roses which smell heavenly.

I haven't read a great deal of late, though I have just got H G Well's[5] *You Can't Be Too Careful*, out, which I didn't like at all. It's about a working man's life from childhood to manhood, but I found it very crude, especially in his attitude to sex. A much better read is L P Jacks'[6] autobiography, which my mother brought in, called *Confessions of an Octogenarian.* I haven't finished it yet, but I think you would enjoy it. He was of course minister at the Unitarian Church in Broad Street, and was a great admirer of Friends such as the Cadburys, Lloyds and Wilsons. He comes across as a fine man.

Sweets and chocolates are now rationed and we are allowed just 2 ounces a week this month, possibly increased next month. After so many months of being allowed nothing, it is nice to see the confectioners' shops with a variety of sweets in their windows again. Barrows Stores say they can no longer supply us with groceries out at Wolverhampton, as we are too far from Birmingham, so we have changed to a local man, who is one of Llew's patients. This week we were lucky enough to get a lovely piece of ham, which is still unrationed, and your mother was able to share it with us for lunch today. There are a lot of privations with rationing, but when one reads of countries such as Russia, we must count our blessings. It is mostly fruit that we miss, though Antony gets blackcurrant juice, which he is entitled to.

I do wonder how you are feeling. Are you managing to keep cheerful? I am trying hard, but the best I can manage is 'fairly cheerful', especially as the war news is anything but cheerful. Everything seems grim at the moment. Oh, my dearest, when shall we meet again? If you close your eyes for a moment – I am by your side with my arms around you, holding you so that you will never go, and telling you of my love. I'll end now my dear. May God watch over you and bring you safely back home to us. Your ever loving Joan

An exhibition of paintings on board ship, from all ranks, and Jack Eglon from the Unit wins first prize for landscape......

Jack Eglon

"We had an exhibition of pictures done on board....and I was very pleased that Jack Eglon, a talented painter, who will be our Chief Liaison Officer with the Red Cross in Cairo, had entered three water colours he'd made of our first port of call, and got 1st prize for landscape.

Photo – Friends House Library

Saturday, July 25th 1942 – in transit

 Dearest Joan

Here is another letter bringing all my thoughts and love to you and the children. I do so hope all is well, as letters take so long to reach us. I'm told they are taking up to five weeks.

Today, there was an exhibition of pictures that had been done by all on board. It was a very good idea, I thought, as it was open to all ranks to compete. I was very pleased that Jack Eglon, a talented painter, who will be our Chief Liaison Officer with the Red Cross in Cairo, had entered three water colours he'd made of our first port of call, and got 1st prize for landscape. There was a professional on board who did not compete, but showed some of his own work independently, of men playing cards, standing and lying in groups, and they were very good indeed. He'd also done paintings of parts of the ship, the lifeboats, the rear gun, and the swimming bath. All most effective and giving such a good idea. The sea and sky, with ships and crowds of people offer such wonderful subjects for painting.

It had all been organised by a Lt Col, who showed me some of his own pictures, which comprised some really excellent portraits along with a very fine water-colour of the boat deck, showing a sentry with men lying in the sun and soaring above, the funnel and superstructure. It is a part of the boat I particularly like, so the picture had a special appeal for me. The Lt Col was kind enough to compliment me on Eglon's work! So I congratulated him on his men's work, but also on his own pictures. He was a very nice man indeed, and most generously offered to give our people more paper for further drawing if they needed it.

This afternoon, we had a Devotional Service. The sun was streaming in through the portholes, the waves breaking outside and light reflected from the water, played on the ceiling. I spoke, very badly, about what a Friend's Meeting might be, compared with what our Devotionals usually were. One or two other people spoke as well for a change, and it was better than some times.

It won't surprise you to know that I have been trying to reckon up all the birds I have seen since leaving England! I wish I had a book on African birds, as there are so many I can't identify. But so far I have definitely seen Lesser Black-backed, Herring, Common and Black-headed Gulls, Kittiwakes, Razorbills, Guillemots, Puffins and Gannets. Then except for a stormy Petrel or two, nothing much, until we reached our first call, when I am fairly sure that I saw a Black Kite and I think an Egyptian Vulture. That is all I can be certain of. I'm beginning to think I will also have to find a book on sea birds, as for the last four or five days, we have been seeing a great number which are quite new to me and I'll just have to look them up.

I have no idea when this will arrive, but it may come before or after the next two anniversaries. Firstly, of course, it will be after the 6th anniversary of our wedding, a day I think so often of, and how lovely you looked. Do you remember you nearly tripped as you smiled at me! It is the best thing I have ever done; I couldn't have had a more perfect wife and life companion. May we soon be re-united. Also, before very long it will be David's birthday. Please tell him how much he is in my thoughts and that I will write to him and hope that it arrives in time for the day. Now I shall close
With all my love to you, Ralph

"How I wished I could speak to Ralph on the telephone and hear his voice again."

August 1942 – Lea Road, Wolverhampton

My dearest Ralph

It was so lovely to receive your third letter so soon after the first. It seems so long since you were here. You are never out of my thoughts, especially in the evening when I remember all the happy times we have spent together. I was thinking yesterday of the holiday we had in Switzerland and remembered particularly when we were at Grindelwald looking out of our window first thing in the morning and seeing the wonderful light on the mountains. There are many such precious memories I love to dwell on; our honeymoon in the Lakes, making our garden together, our nights in the theatre, our suppers out, and our last holiday in Shropshire. So many wonderful memories.

I am sitting in the window seat in the drawing room, while the children are having their afternoon rest and all is peace and quiet. This is the one hour in the day when I can relax and read or write to you. I am wearing the lovely brooch you gave me, which is so pretty especially when it catches the light and sparkles.

Everyone seems to be getting jobs. How I wish I could be out meeting interesting people too, and perhaps earning a little money to help out. Life can be a little narrow and dull sometimes. I'm not grumbling and of course I have the children who are a bright spot and great comfort, but I long to go travelling again with you and doing lots of interesting things. Maybe once the war is over things will change. We have been having heavy raids again recently which came unpleasantly close one night last week. We all went down into the shelter. Win and Llew were Fire watching and urged us to go in. We seem to have given Germany heavy raids too recently. What a hellish world it is.

By the way, I have at last got glasses for reading. My eyes have been aching so much recently. Llew made an appointment with an eye specialist here and I have now got them and they certainly seem to ease my eyes as I have been able to read Winifred Fortescue's[7] *Trampled Lillies* and already I feel the difference. The book is her account of the fall of France, in which she tells of the tragedy of the wounded soldiers after Dunkirk, stranded in this country, with no news of their families; nearly driven mad when the Germans were over-running their country. It doesn't bear thinking about. The thousands of homes broken up. Pray God they be reunited one day not too distant.

I have also been reading Bernard Shaw's[8] plays, which I borrowed from friends of Win's and have just finished *The Doctor's Dilemma*, which you thought I would like. It is a curious play and Louis Dubedat is a very difficult character to understand. Was the love between Louis and Jennifer the perfect love, or only one-sided? She loved him and was either ignorant or blind to his faults, but there is something in the idea of 'the flame forever burning'.

I think this must have been the part you wished me to read, when Jennifer tells the story of her early days in Cornwall and how they lit the first fire of the winter and on looking out of the window, saw the flames dancing in a bush in the garden – Louis replies: *"Such a colour! Garnet colour. Waving like silk. A liquid, lovely flame, flowing up through the bay leaves and yet not burning them. Well, I shall be a flame like that....the last of me shall be the flame in the burning bush. Whenever you see the flame Jennifer, that will be me."*

Then Jennifer says: *"Oh, if I might be with you, Louis."*
Louis replies: *"No, you must always be in the garden when the bush flames. You are my hold on the world, you are my immortality."*
Jennifer: *"I shall not forget. You know that I promise."*

Later Louis says: *"I'll tell you a secret. I used to think that our marriage was all an affectation, and that I'd break loose and run away one day. But now that I'm going to be broken loose whether I like it or not, I'm perfectly fond of you, and perfectly satisfied because I'm going to live as part of you and not as my troublesome self."*

I suppose we do, and must, live on in each other. When two people marry they absorb so much of each other and so much of the one lives in the other person. You have enriched and made my life much fuller than it could ever have been without you. I have so much to thank you for. I think now I either live in the past or look to the future. Life now is grim and one must just meet each day as it comes and pray for courage to do the right thing. We have had so many changes since the war began and the last year has in many ways been the worst.

It has certainly been the most miserable for me and I was already nearly at the end of my tether with the thought of you going away. I only thank God I didn't collapse before you went. I am quite recovered now. One can face anything with good health, but without you everything becomes unbearable. I've never felt as I did the two weeks after you left. To feel so ill and to lose you at the same time, was something I hope never to go through again. I can talk about it now I am well and have got my balance again. But it was a nightmarish hell at the time.

Later same evening........It is now 9.0pm and I am thinking of you so much tonight. How I long to hear from you again. I know you have a difficult job in front of you and I know you will do it well. I have great faith in you and am so very proud of all you do. All at 31 Lea Road send their love, especially my mother and the children. Ever your devoted Joan

"I tried to write a bit to Ralph each day."

Friday, August 7th 1942

My dearest
I'm now starting a new letter. It is now 10.30pm and I am lying in bed and thinking so much of you. Oh, how I miss you. My love for you never changeth; come what may, you will always be my one dear love. What a joyful six years of marriage we have had and our two boys are so dear and like you. A is great fun now. I wish you could see him. I'm sure you would love him. Antony looks so charming at 18 months and has such a glorious sense of humour.

I try to picture you and wonder if you have reached your destination yet. I so look forward to a cable from you to say that you are well and safe. Your mother went up to the Manor for lunch with cousin Elsie and told me that Tom Tanner had spoken well at Yearly Meeting and read extracts from one of your letters. He is good at talking about the Unit, and I gather that his parents are lending their home 'Failands' for the Mechanics Training Camp. I do wonder what all your friends are doing now, as I haven't heard a word from anyone, except Ronald Joynes, since the day you sailed. Perhaps they didn't think much of me!

D has asked me so many times if he can go to the Park near the school, so yesterday we journeyed forth, while A stayed at home with mother. It would have made quite a nice day, as though it was cloudy it was quite warm. But when we arrived there, being Bank holiday, it seemed as though the whole of Wolverhampton was there as well, and it was rather unpleasantly crowded.

D really wanted to find the stream and the pool, to see the children sailing their boats, but there were just too many people. Happily, after a while we met up with the Walker family and very kindly they took us back to their home and we were able to enjoy their lovely garden, which was altogether nicer. D had a great time making paper boats and sailing them in a huge zinc bath on the lawn. They have invited us there for tea next week, A included.

Mother and I went to the theatre last night to see a new comedy called *Once a Crook* by Evadne Price and Ken Attiwill about honour between thieves, which was quite amusing in parts and very well done.

At last a cable from my father announcing that the Unit had arrived safely in Durban......
Monday, August 10th 1942 – Wolverhampton Airgraph

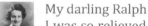

My darling Ralph

I was so relieved to get your cable saying that you had arrived. I do wonder if my letters are getting through, as this is the third Airgraph I have sent. I hope all your plans are going well and that they gave you a good welcome on your arrival. My dear I do pray your task won't be too difficult, but I know that everyone respects you and looks up to you, and I also know that you will do well. Remember my great, great love for you my dearest.

I do hope you will find my letters waiting for you at Cairo when you get there. We are all very well indeed – the children are fine. I am taking the children to the Walkers to tea today. David loves going there to play with their four girls. Next Thursday I'm taking David to Margaret Brockbank's. My darling I think of you every day and all day, and long for you to return...that is all I live for now...for the day when we meet again. I will write a long Airmail letter very soon with all news, but just to tell you that you are forever in my thoughts and prayers.

David sends much love and kisses from all of us. Joan

Chapter 18
Durban at Last – 'The Kindness of Strangers'
July and August 1942

In this chapter my father's use of terms such as 'Negro' or 'coloured' must be understood as being of the time and are not in any way used in a pejorative sense. I have not, therefore, made any attempt to edit them out or alter them.

Quoting from my father's memoirs, he here describes the Unit's arrival in Durban and the hospitality of Durban Friends along with the joys – or not of camping!

Eventually after five long weeks at sea, we arrived in Durban, where we were to remain for another five equally long weeks in a transit camp, which we shared with the army. We had some absolutely glorious moonlit nights, making the lines of tents look quite ghostly as the sun came gently up over the hills. For all that, I can't deny that a bed and modern plumbing would have been most appreciated! I do love camping, as you know, but............!

I was sharing a tent with John Gough, and I must confess that I felt that I never wanted to go camping again. No-one could pretend it was very comfortable, and living with all one's belongings in a series of bags is trying to say the least. Things had a habit of disappearing all by themselves, and only after a long search, did one find them again – inevitably at the bottom of some bag or other, which you could have sworn you'd already searched.

I remember John coming in on certain particularly bad nights, or perhaps when water was trickling into the tent from the outside, right over one's sleeping bag, and saying – "This is really too bloody much. I just can't take any more." However, in reality, it was a comparatively mild hardship, and there were many compensations. I remember, for instance, walking along the beach and seeing miles and miles of sand-dunes and a vast stretch of blue sea with a seemingly unending line of waves breaking in dazzling foam, rushing up the sand, and where there were rocks, spray rising into the air, sparkling in the evening sun.

Finding sufficient occupation to keep the men busy was the difficult thing, as I soon realised that endless route marches and stretcher drills would soon pall. However, we were very fortunate, as with the help of South African Friends, we were soon able to arrange work in the King Edward VII Hospital.

But there were many times, when we seemed to be waiting for ever for a ship to take us on to Cairo. The needs of a bunch of CO's must have featured low on the Army's list of priorities, and it often seemed to me quite possible that our particular section of the Friends Ambulance Unit might well be spending the rest of the war in a transit camp in Durban! The thought did not make me overjoyed! I wrote to Joan as soon as I could..........

July 22nd 1942 – Durban

My dearest Joan

As usual it is difficult to know how much I can say. However, at last we have docked and here we are in Durban and the weather seems set fair. It was nearly nightfall by the time I went ashore and left the huge ship behind, towering above the quay, showing grey in the moonlight. It was a cloudless, starry night with a brilliant moon, throwing patches of light over the black shadows.

The town seems pleasant enough, with some fine buildings and wide streets lined by trees of all sorts, giving off delicious sweet smells. Somehow I managed to find a telephone, and rang the local Durban Friends to let them know we were here. They were most kind and immediately offered to do all they could to help us.

Disembarking, entraining and getting in, was rather hectic, and excellent as the Sergeants are (both of them, quite invaluable), I could have done with a second Officer. John Gough is perfectly capable of doing the work, but dressed only in a Sergeant's uniform, he just doesn't have the status, and keeps saying "I think I'm probably going to need your help with this" or "It's just possible I may have to ask you to go and talk to so and so", when what was needed was a sharp order.

Anyway, here we are, near a railway, rows and rows of tents, surrounded by miles and miles of sand. The chaps are in four tents, and now that we have expelled a swarm of bees from a fifth, I thought I would have one to myself, but it looks as if John G is going to be moving in – though having a Sergeant in an Officer's tent is most irregular – but, hell, there we are. Anyway it's a very nice tent and it contains a lot of very nice sand, and not much else! We wash in adjoining open tin huts, though trying to keep one's uniform tidy and polished, is a job of a complexity all its own.

I mess a quarter of a mile away with the Officers, while the chaps mess just below their tents. I superintended all their first meals, which I thought were very fair. Generally the food is good with plenty of fruit – oranges, tangerines, apples and bananas. Later I made an inspection of all the tents and then we had a route march, which turned out quite well. We operate in units, so that we can please ourselves whether we do it or not and can decide how far we go. I shall make sure we do though, as it's good for us. I'm afraid one has to be fairly autocratic in such matters. Then from 1 o'clock till midnight they can get leave, as long as they have a pass, which I have to sign on behalf of our boys. They are all busy making plans to do all things they have been promising themselves for so long on the journey out, such as having a good meal and a hair-cut and going out to a concert or film.

We don't seem to get any of our news direct, and as we are just a small Unit, neither 'fish nor fowl', I have to go round gathering it in bits. But generally people are very good and the Officers of one regiment from the Colonel down, seem to have quite adopted me, and the kindness of local Friends is really overwhelming. They regularly have 12 or 15 of the group out every day, taking us on rides, giving us meals and baths, or even lending us a car. And their obvious enjoyment of our coming is humbling. We (John G and I) had a meeting with a group of local Friends about the possibility of forming a branch of the FAU out here, and they started the meeting with a Minute expressing their sense of spiritual renewal arising from our visit here.

It's rather wearing, disciplining the lads in the morning, playing the Camp Commandant, then in the afternoon and evening discussing Quaker matters and being the weighty Friend! However, we had a good meeting, making some progress in our discussions and I said I would write fully to Gordon Square[1] about the possibility of a local branch. After all, it could be very useful, firstly as an advance base, secondly for supplies and lastly as a base for a small number of personnel. We decided to send a joint message of greeting to London Yearly Meeting. You didn't know just how weighty a Friend your husband is, did you?!

This morning I marched the Company into Camp, with everyone saluting me. I must have taken at least 15 salutes. I only salute senior Officers, but if they salute me, I generally return it as a matter of courtesy, which can be most wearing! In between everything, I managed to do some shopping, and then have a much needed shower to wash all the sand off. A cold shower. Damn cold! But the sun is nice and hot and one soon warms up, though I seem to have chosen this of all times to catch a cold.

Later in the evening I introduced all our chaps to the local Friends over supper

Route Marches

Route marching in South Africa
Top photo - FRB front in army style cap. Bottom photo – right front of the picture in beret.
"Finding sufficient occupation to keep the men busy was the difficult thing, and I soon realized
that organizing endless route marches and stretcher drills would soon pall."
Photographs Friends House Library

The country itself is hard to describe, but inland there are what appear to be bare hills, just lightly covered with thick scrub. The town is mostly rather flashy new build, but everywhere there are trees and shrubs, which are mostly unknown to me. It's actually very beautiful, and I should like to see much more of it. The weather is mid-wintery with a clear sky and a line of fleecy clouds on the horizon, but by midday, even at this time of year, the sun is almost too hot. There hasn't been much time for birding, and I haven't yet been able to get a book on local species. So far I have seen Swifts and Swallows, some white Egrets, a possible Crag Martin, probably flown in from Europe, and a starling-like bird, possibly a Mina, which has a rather floppy flight and displays a lot of white plumage underneath. But that's all to date.

I've managed to fix the chaps up with doctors, dentists and oculists etc, and they seem to be enjoying themselves – I think. Philip Sanford, John G and I take it in turns to stay in Camp and today was my day, hence my letter-writing this afternoon, writing to you and to Gordon Square (aka 'The Square'). I then had to check all the tents while our three other guards had tea. Finally, I went to the mess to relax for a bit, had a sherry and managed to catch up with some reading. Later on one of the Adjutants came in from a regiment which was on our ship, and we had dinner together. He seemed a nice chap and as so often, I found he knew a man I was at school with. It gets dark here by 6.0, so I came back to the lines, talked to the chaps for a bit, rang up various people, scrounged half a candle, and am now in bed writing by its light.

There's a clear sky and a wonderful moon, glinting on the long, silent lines of tents. In the distance, the dim rumble of a train in the valley, and beyond the dark outline of hills. I'm in my sleeping bag, with an improvised pillow propped against a pile of boxes. The small candle is beside me perched on John G's typewriter box, throwing shadows of my clothes on to the tent walls. Outside, the night is just visible through the opening flap. It's all quite cosy and fun, but with my bad cold, give me a proper bed any time! I'm lying here, just waiting for John to come back, who has been out to supper and to a concert, before I turn in for the night.

I hope you may have received my previous four letters plus an Airgraph by now, as well as hopefully some news of me via the Square. Dear love to D & A, and to all at Wolverhampton and to you my dear. All love Ralph

JMB finally hears of my father's arrival in Durban, and writes of how relieved and happy she was to get his cable telling her that he was well, and that he and all the team were safe. She cabled back immediately, and wrote this letter........

July 1942 – Lea Road, Wolverhampton

My dearest one

Sorry, I haven't written any more for three days, but I have sent you an Air Mail Post Card, which I posted this morning, as soon as I got your cable. I hope my cable in return, was waiting for you on your arrival and that my letters have started to get through. I shall anxiously await a letter from you to let me know how things are going in South Africa. How profoundly thankful you must be to be there at last after such a long journey. However nice people are, one gets tired of being cooped up in a limited space.

As I mentioned the Walkers, a Quaker family from Wolverhampton, invited us to tea the other day, and yesterday was the day. D had a very happy afternoon with their white pony and even managed to ride her quite well. A was very good running about on the grass, and he took a great liking to a doll's pram and kept taking the doll out and putting it back in again and pushing it around the lawn.

After tea we all got to talking about education for the children after the war. They are thinking of The Mount² or Sidcot for their daughters and if they had boys, without hesitation they said they would like to send them to Oundle³. Mr Walker went there himself, and still knows several of the masters and thought it an ideal school. He said it was run on modern lines, with plenty of equipment and that they turned out useful citizens with plenty of interests, not just helpless little gentlemen! I wonder where we should send D & A? Are you for a Friends education and boarding school? I don't know. Of course we want to give them the very best we can afford, as I am sure that a good education is the best thing we can give our children. Perhaps all schools will be State schools after the war and maybe if they are good, we should opt for that. If there were State schools for everyone, people would see they were of the best. Do let me know your thoughts.

I seem to have been reading a lot of war books recently, and really must try and read something else to take my mind off it. They were all excellent reads – Somerset Maugham's book *Strictly Personal* about the last months he spent in France before the French collapse, and his journey home on two cargo boats that later became known as the 'hell boats' – fascinating, though I can't say I take to him as a man; [......] also Howard Smith's⁴ *Last Train from Berlin* which I'm very much looking forward to; but a good thriller would make a change! I wonder what you are reading now. Is there a good library nearby?

How grim the news is. India is particularly disturbing and I do wonder how Dick and Horace and party are getting on. Have you yet had any letters from them or from Gordon Square? Reg is still in Ireland and rather fed up. We are all well and just living each day as it comes. Oh, God, when shall we see each other again? Mother sends her love and very dear love from the children and from me. Ever your loving and devoted Joan.

———

"One of the lasting memories of Durban will be the wonderful hospitality of Durban Friends. No-one who experienced their embracing friendship can ever forget it. They invited us into their homes, gave us meals, lent us cars, took us out into the country to such local landmarks as the Valley of the Thousand Hills, familiar to all who have passed through this city, and just offered help whenever it was needed. I tried to express some of this in my letters to Joan" This is well illustrated in a letter from SA Friend Maurice Webb to my mother (see full letter in tributes at the end):

"Dear Joan, Last Monday evening a voice on the telephone said 'You don't know me, but I am with the FAU...' and I said: "You are Ralph Barlow", having been prepared by a cable from Gordon Square. Ten minutes later Ralph was in our home, and I hope that he felt at home. We were certainly very glad to meet him."

July 1942 – Durban

Dearest Joan
I didn't get much written yesterday, as I got involved helping the nice regiment billeted with us to pack up. Sadly they are departing and I'm really going to miss them. Their officers were so friendly, and I had some excellent long talks with them. There was one Major in particular who came from a well-known family of Scotch brewers, who was a very likeable, decent sort of fellow. I told him all about the Unit and being a CO, and about what we were going to do in the Middle East - when we finally get there. He was most interested, and as we parted he shook hands and wished me luck. So I thanked him for all his help and he replied "Not at all, old boy. I was only glad to do what I could. Fine organization your lot. Full of admiration and all that." He was particularly impressed at how well behaved we were on board.

Then, if you please, while we were holding our parade, their Colonel – a noble Lord no less, a regular army chap – came up, shook hands with me and wished me luck too. So naturally I thanked him in return. He said "Damn good lot your chaps. I wish they were my regiment. Very bad for us, you know!"

It may mean something or nothing, but it pleased me. It means the chaps, by just being themselves, created a good impression. So I'm feeling cheered. My cold is much better, I've bought a new cap and my spirits are up! As a result, we had a most pleasant route march this afternoon, and I even saw some decent bird life including a Woodchat, a Heron, some Finches and an Ibis, as well as along the road some quite lovely and brilliantly coloured flowering shrubs.

Helping the regiment to pack up yesterday, I realised just how time consuming the business of tidying up can be, which sooner or later we'll have to face ourselves, when we do finally leave. Even day to day, just washing and putting stuff away, polishing ones boots and buttons, organizing the tent, killing the wretched white ants, all seems to take forever. But how good it is to change out of battle dress and into an ordinary service uniform.

It was a day of doing things that I'd been putting off for too long. After the route march, I went off to have a much-needed haircut and shampoo, to smarten myself up a bit; saw one or two officers who were on our boat, who I had been meaning to catch up with, on small points of order; and finally to the Post Office to catch the post to send off some parcels, two for you including some rather lovely brocade I hope you will like, and one for David. I trust they won't take too long to reach you. By then it was time for a much needed tea, including – sheer gluttony – two meringues!

In the evening I met up with a local Friend, Maurice Webb[5], the Clerk of South Africa Yearly Meeting, to have some discussions about the possibility of forming a South African FAU. Finally, I went over to see another SA Friend, Florence Bayman[6], who had invited me for supper. She was so kind, letting me have a bath, which made me feel a hundred times better. I know I've said it before, but I cannot express often enough how kind local Friends are here, in welcoming us into their homes and lives. Not only do they let us have baths but give us meals and take us on trips into the country. It's quite wonderful.

As I left Florence's home, it was already dark with a brilliantly clear moon. Nearing the camp I bumped into a Dutch CO, who was clearly having some personal problems and we had a long talk, with me trying to help as best I could. He seemed most grateful, though I'm not sure whether I was really much use. At long last I settled into my tent, censored a few more letters, read a bit and fell sleep. All for now, Ralph

Continued………Another day. All the usual things – a parade, talks, censoring letters. I also sent off an airgraph to you. I do so wish we could now be moved on to Cairo, as time creeps on. However, a lovely change this afternoon, as Maurice Webb kindly lent me his car, and I and a couple of others took a wonderful drive out to a place called the Valley of a Thousand Hills. The road winds endlessly uphill through town and scattered suburbs, all apparently unplanned. A few poor scattered hovels here, and some stately houses with manicured gardens there, all with wonderful views down across the town and out to the blue sea beyond.

Every now and then we would come across banana fields, with all around us the splendid sub-tropical vegetation of palms, gums, mangoes and eucalyptus trees. And though it's winter here, there is still much in flower. And what flowers. Brilliant red ones, growing straight out of a tree's bare-barked branches, a hundred different shades of bougainvillea; peach blossom, azaleas and bright yellow flowers I didn't even know. All along the road were fruit stalls, loaded with oranges, bananas, apples and tangerines.

It was a perfect, cloudless afternoon, a bright hot sun, and the air fresh and bracing. As we climbed higher and higher, the trees dwindled and the ground became broken into hills and valleys, unlike any other scenery I'd ever seen. Then to our right a great stretch of country, vanishing into a mass of hazy blue hills and valleys, covered all over with coarse thin grass. A magnificent sight. The birds were exciting too, but very baffling. I saw a very bright yellow bird, another with a long, stubby black beak, and a Kingfisher with a brilliant red head. I really must find a book on these local birds.

When we got back home, I called on Dr Herbert Standing[7] and his wife Lucy, who are now living out here. Do you remember them? My mother would of course, as they are from my parents' generation, both now over 85, very frail, though their minds are still very active. For many years they were Quaker missionaries in Madagascar and he had also been the Headmaster of a Friends' school out there, for all of which body of work, Woodbrooke honoured him with a Fellowship. They had a Jenny Orde Brown living with them, who had known Win and Llew in Broumana, and said how well they had done and how much they were still missed. The Standings seemed genuinely pleased to see me and keen to hear news of Friends from Woodbrooke.

Half of Britain's Quakerdom seems to be either living out here or on a visit! Another recent arrival is Alfred's cousin, Fred Braithwaite's youngest son, Francis[8] and his wife, Elsie. I had never met him before, but as I know the family and was at school with Francis' brother Arthur, I called on spec last night. They were out of course, but neighbours asked me to wait, and luckily it wasn't long before they returned. I would have picked Francis out anywhere, as he is the spit and image of his brother. He and Elsie were both very pleasant and friendly and I liked them a lot.

They had recently been out in Australia in Darwin when the Japanese attacked the port during two very heavy raids, and so they were evacuated first to Sydney and thence on here. He was previously working for Qantas but is now employed by BOAC. They made me stay to supper and wanted to know all about 'Sheredes,' their family home, where Millior has been living recently to escape the Blitz. The neighbours joined us later and Fred's wife Elsie was relieved to see I drank Sherry! "You never know with Friends," she said! It made a pleasant change from most Quaker hospitality, which can often, shall we say, be a trifle 'weighty'! Do pass this on to my sister, as she may like to tell the family....at least about 'Sheredes', not the sherry!

Later that evening we had a Quaker Meeting at Maurice Webb's house, with about 18 of us and some 10 local Friends. I spoke, rather on the lines of what I once said long ago at Selly Oak Meeting, based on that quote from Revelations on 'the things that remain' – you'll remember it: *"Strengthen the things that remain before they die, for I find that what you have done is not yet perfect in the sight of God."*

I'm afraid that the change to this richer food is causing a considerable amount of stomach trouble – poor old Johnnie Gould is continually rushing off! He just manages to save himself by taking chlorodyne (diarrhoea treatment!). I am writing this now after lunch in the Webb's house, from which I have a splendid view out over the garden to the skyscrapers that rise along the front and the sea beyond. Their main garden contains many different trees, from exotic pears and palms, to mangoes and bananas; whilst in the kitchen garden they grow dwarf beans, tomatoes, peas, carrots and various vegetables I can't even identify. I had better stop now as I have been asked to write a message for the South African Friends' Bulletin, which I haven't even started yet. God keep you, my very dear wife, Love Ralph

Friends in South Africa

Florence Bayman, 2nd left with Alan Paton, far right, and Edgar Brookes, (others unknown).

"Florence is most extraordinarily helpful and good to me [.....] Kind, slightly motherly and sympathetic."

"Edgar Brookes is one of the four white representatives of the black and coloured people in the South African Senate." EB was a Liberal South African senator, who gave talks on race relations to the FAU.

Alan Paton, author of 'Cry the Beloved Country'

Photo: courtesy of Alan Paton Centre, South Africa

Maurice Webb
"A really good friend. I can't say enough about how good Maurice has been to us."

Photograph courtesy of Campbell Collections, South Africa

Durban Life

Durban sea front 1942

On a pc sent home from Durban, my father writes: "I have a splendid view out over the garden from the Webb's house, to the skyscrapers that rise along the front and the sea beyond."

"I've just received a cable from Ralph and we are all so happy."

July 1942 (Air pc) from Lea Road, Wolverhampton

Darling

I am sending this Air pc off straight away just so that you know I received your cable safely and that we are all so very happy to know you are safe and well. I could shout for joy. Dearest, you are forever in our thoughts and we think of you always. How glad you must be to have reached the end of your long journey. We are all very well here. Just now the children are in the garden and fit and full of life and energy. Antony is talking quite a lot now and is very jolly, whilst David talks about you all the time, and is writing you another letter. Your mother is well and presently away in Chipping Camden for two weeks.

All my dearest love and thoughts. I will write more later.
Joan

"After a while we settled down to a regular routine of marches, hospital work and various courses, though it was quite a strain finding enough things for the chaps to do all the time. Also the constant round of keeping an eye on everyone, maintaining morale, trying to learn when, if ever, we might move on could be tiring. I inevitably missed Joan terribly and tried to write as often as I could, though it often took forever for letters to get through."

July 1942 – Durban

Dearest Joan

Today was not a good day. I don't quite know why. I have felt pretty miserable, maybe because I am tired, maybe the aftermath of my cold, maybe I'm just missing you. But also I am very anxious to find out when there might be some more positive news about our departure, as we have been here nearly a week already. I failed, so I still don't know when we will go, and really wish I did.

I also needed to do the accounts, and as a result I didn't go on the route march this morning. When I'd finished all that, I changed and went into town to buy a few odds and ends, and also went to the Museum to try and identify some of the birds I've seen. I then went over to see Maurice Webb again, who is now our new best friend. He is such a kind man, a type of liberal Friend, who likes to busy himself with a hundred good causes before breakfast! But he is genuinely anxious about what's happening in South Africa, and is concerned that Friends come and live out here, not as missionaries, but to take a job.

He is a well-connected Friend, and very sound I think. I thoroughly approve of him. He took me a run round on his way to collect his wife from one of the University Colleges, where she is taking a course. On the way back we visited one of the parks on the outskirts of town, from where you get a splendid view of the broken, hilly country inland on the one side, and over to the sea on the other. We saw a number of monkeys and some birds called Honey Suckers, which are gaily coloured, yellow, black and blue, about the size of wrens.

We ended up going back to his place for supper, and while I do not as a rule like vegetarian meals, theirs was very good. Oranges, apples and bananas to begin with, then a paw-paw, which has a curious taste, somewhere between a melon and a pumpkin, followed by macaroni cheese with sweet potato and peas. All very delicious.

We had a long discussion about the racial problem out here. He told me how, when Gandhi was here as a young lawyer early in the century, he was refused entrance in quick succession, to a 1st class train compartment, and to a church where he was going to hear the Missionary teacher C F Andrews speak. The result, like St Paul on the road to Damascus, completely changed his life, from being a successful, rising young lawyer to the Gandhi we've come to know. In fact the more one stays here, the more one is aware that this country bristles with problems, but the racial problem is uppermost.

The imposition of the colour bar is really terrible, preventing any consorting between natives and Europeans. The whites say that the towns are only for Europeans; but as they need native black labour, they expect them to come in just for a limited period to work, and then return to their families. While they are here they have to live in barracks, as they are not allowed to own property or rent, and their wages are a pittance and much lower than those paid to whites. There is very little housing for them anyway, and what there is, is very poor, and of course they couldn't afford the rent in any case. I'm just a visitor here and don't yet feel I know enough to make a fuss, but it really is a fearsome problem and all so terribly wrong.

They leave their villages for up to three to six months at a time to earn money, but what they earn is hardly enough to pay their taxes let alone the increased expenditure of having to live in town. Meanwhile, their wives back home are scarcely able to keep their land properly cultivated. In addition there is a large Indian population, politically unrepresented, even though some of them are quite wealthy. Maurice is much involved with helping native clubs and trying to assist the black people to cope with such housing difficulties, and he says the churches are also doing their best.

There is an unspoken racial cloud, which lingers constantly at the back of one's mind. It hovers as yet unheeded, but one day it will surely engulf this nation. Durban is essentially a European town, with its fine marine parade, broad streets and splendid shops, and though, of course, there are a number of well-educated black people, but I am afraid they are mostly kept in the background as road sweepers, servants or just general labourers. Terrible. After supper we all went to the French club together, and now I'm back and writing to you in the Officer's mess.

———

"With Maurice's introduction, I went to the large local hospital and was able to fix up for 12 of our chaps to work there, while we were still waiting for our onward journey. There still appeared to be no immediate hope of a quick solution. But the work proved to be useful for everyone and in fact turned out to be quite a success.....as I wrote home to Joan."

Tuesday 28th July 1942 – Durban

My dearest
[.......] We now have some work in a civil hospital, but it has a military section too, with a Lt Col as the medical super-intendant. The Matron has a most forbidding exterior, but after we got off to a slightly grim start, she proved to be quite friendly. It is a fine, quite newish hospital, which was opened on the day of the abdication and called after the abdicating monarch. They told me that when the Earl of Athlone came to open it, he couldn't remember which numbered King Edward it was and he named the hospital after Edward VII instead of VIII. One hopes that didn't get back to Buckingham Palace!

The rest of the day I returned to Camp as it is my turn to stay in. Nonetheless, I have had quite a useful time, doing a bit of public relations over a pint of beer, getting to know the Assistant Adjutant. Nothing special came of it, but at least I know him a bit better now, which is always useful. He is a regular army man, who has been in the Middle East for several years and knows it well, but he had no concept of pacifism – "Just won't work old man", he said. [....]

Last night, the moon was full and brilliant in the West, and over in the East there was a really brilliant planet, though which one, I'm not sure. The nights are mostly quite cool here, with heavy dew making all our clothes and bedding damp, though come morning, they quickly dry in the hot sun. As I woke up, the sky was lemon coloured, with the beginnings of dawn in the east, while night still lingered in the west. The valley was full of mist, but one could just make out the hills in the distance. Light comes quickly here, and soon the sun was rising over the hill giving colour and shape to everything.

I have been keen to see more of the city and Maurice kindly showed me round a little, including over the University campus, on to some fine old churches and mosques, though somehow it was all a little flashy, like an American film, seeming to lack soul and belonging nowhere. But along the way we did see a few examples of good modern architecture, all quite sober with clean brickwork and not at all flamboyant.

The more I see of the town, however, the more I see a basically provincial city; beautifully situated, of course, with a pleasant environment, but rather dull with not much culture or entertainment. This could be because it is so far from anywhere else, though the war must have brought much fresh life and certainly a lot of money to the town. But despite all that, what stands out is the kindness of residents to visiting troops and units such as ours, which is a great tribute, when one remembers how many have gone through here.

Yesterday I did not write – perhaps it was as well, as I had a rotten night, waking continually with back ache, and consequently I felt rotten all day. The morning was a very profitless one, with my trying yet again to get information on our onward movement. As usual I failed completely, and felt singularly depressed. However, the day gradually improved and in the end I was quite busy. I went over to the Webb's and made use of a spare office to write letters to Tom, Richey and Peter.

I then went in to the Office of the Daily News to see Florence Bayman, who is the librarian there. She is a Friend, between 45 and 50, a widow with one daughter Cynthia, out in Denmark. She is very pleasant, sensible and sympathetic, with a slightly motherly air, even perhaps a bit lonely. But she is very brave, very thoughtful and very kind. I think I am going to like her! She very sweetly offered to send a cable to you, my dearest one, which I hope may get through quickly, as I am so worried about the German raids and do hope and pray that you are safe. Bless her heart, Florence had decided that I looked rather miserable (miserable. Me?!) and that something must be done to cheer me up! So we agreed to meet up later with John Gould and Philip Sanford and see a film.

Meanwhile, I went back to the hospital with Maurice Webb to pick up the boys, who seemed to be enjoying themselves and getting plenty to do. So I am very glad I organized this (and rather congratulate myself). The boys complain that the hospital is understaffed, and that those who are there, do not care too much about their patients. However, I'm sure they are getting some good experience, especially in tropical diseases, which will stand them in good stead later. Maurice and I talked a bit more about starting an FAU branch here, though I am not sure we are getting anywhere. Then at his request, I went to meet a Social Services woman who had been at Woodbrooke in 1923/4 and wanted to hear news all about it, and I tried my best to tell her the whereabouts of people who I knew of.

I then went on to meet Philip Sanford and John Gould for dinner. This was the meal that Philip and John have been promising themselves for some while, and as Florence had been so kind, we invited her along as our guest, and then we all went on to the cinema to 'cheer me up'! We saw a film called 'Listen to Britain' with scenes and sounds of Britain at war. This was good and somewhat nostalgic with its shots of London. So altogether we all had a most pleasant evening and I was indeed 'cheered up'! By this time, I was pretty tired and, thank God, had a really good night for a change. I'm now off to wash some clothes before going to tidy the tent up, not to mention myself, preparatory to dinner. I must try and get a bath this afternoon, as washing in the open with cold water is all very well, but doesn't get one very clean. I never even manage to get a good shave in cold water. Much love for now, Ralph

———

Durban Views

The Valley of a Thousand Hills, near Durban

Durban harbour 1942 with Troopships in dock.
Photographs Durban City archives

As usual my father's mood swings go from elation to gloom, depending on how events are progressing........and how a mere suggestion by Peter Gibson of FRB going ahead to Cairo, soon becomes a fact in my mother's mind........

Sunday, 2nd August 1942 – Durban

Dearest Joan

For a change I had a very good night's sleep. Thank God I am sleeping better now and I've managed to make the tent a little more comfortable. Last night I had another excellent supper with Florence, and afterwards on to see a film called *Tortilla Flat* based on the novel by John Steinbeck[9]. It was an unusual and almost very good film.

I seem to have let Maurice Webb talk me into giving a lecture on housing next week, to some Social Study students at the University. That's if we are still here. This afternoon I have been frantically trying to think what I am going to say. I'm shortly going down to Maurice's house for supper and will ask him if what I have in mind, is the sort of thing he wants. I also want to ask him various points about our next week's programme, again depending on whether we are still here. How I do wish with every bit of me that we could get away now.

Later......... Well I had a very pleasant evening with Maurice. We made further plans, in case we find that we do have to stay even longer, such as more hospital work, some lectures and the possibility of a visit at the weekend to Adams College, the large native school here, with which Maurice is involved. I was determined to get back early after supper, and left at 7.45 only to find there was no train until 9.0pm. It actually came in at 8.30 and I got in and despite all the noise, just fell asleep, not waking up till we arrived. By then I wasn't in the best of tempers, especially when I found that I had to walk home in driving rain!

I arrived back at camp soaking wet in an even worse mood. The more I thought about our situation, and the more I tried to sort matters out in my head, the more worried I became. I began to blame myself for our lack of progress, and wondered what more I could do. Peter Gibson wants me to leave the others here and fly to Cairo on my own, but I couldn't leave the chaps here on their own. That would be the worst of all options.

Sometimes, I must admit, the strain is more than I can take. But as John often says, when he is going to bed in the dark and finds the sand has got into his sleeping bag, and he has lost something absolutely vital, or has diarrhoea, or treads on a hot candle in his bare feet: "Really this is too much. I simply can't go on. I give up," and when one is in that state, life is perfectly beastly. But there's nothing to do but simply laugh, and over and over again we ask ourselves, 'why on earth did we come here?'

Excuse my writing, but it gets dark so early here, and I am in bed and doing it all by candlelight.

I must stop now and go to sleep. I'll close for now.
Always my love, Ralph

———

Oh, the confusions that arise when the post can take several weeks, and when what turns out to be only a possibility, is relayed to my mother as firm fact! As mentioned in my father's previous letter, Peter Gibson had suggested that with shipping so unpredictable, my father fly ahead to Cairo. To my mother's consternation, this had already reached her as fact via Gordon Square. And in this letter JMB thinks that my father is in Cape Town preparing to fly to Cairo.......

Early August 1942 – Wolverhampton

My dearest Ralph

It is now after 11.0 O'clock at night, but I do want to start another letter to you. I so long to receive news of you. It is nine weeks since you were here with me, and oh how the weeks have dragged by and only two letters from you so far. I gather from Gordon Square that you are now in Cape Town, and I wonder whether you are now any nearer your ultimate destination. I am sure you too will be wanting news of me, and I trust that when you arrive you will find a whole batch of letters waiting for you.

Continued from yesterday.........I am sorry my pen ran dry last night, so I had to stop. I have come to bed a little earlier tonight – it's 10.15, so that I can write for a while, before settling off to sleep. My dearest, how I miss you, and how my love grows ever stronger, and I now send it winging across the sea to you with all our prayers that God may guide you in your difficult task. I have been feeling rather cross with Gordon Square as no-one ever lets me have news of you. I shouldn't have known you were in Cape Town, if I hadn't bumped into Freddie Royal, who said that they had received a cable from you about flying on to Cairo. Surely someone in the overseas department at GS could keep wives informed of news of their husbands; even a typist could drop me a line now and then! No-one has been in touch since the day you left. I wrote a nice but firm letter to Ronald Joynes, asking for news, so perhaps in the morning I may get a reply. It's all I have to live on these days. End of moan!

We have been sitting in the garden this afternoon and even had tea under the pear tree, which is heavily loaded with fruit this year. David looks for fallen pears every morning when he goes into the garden. He thought it fun having a picnic and Antony thoroughly enjoyed the tomato sandwiches.

We tasted some of the pears the other day and they really are delicious. Win picked the first plums to night, which aren't quite ripe yet, but how wonderful it is to have some fruit again. The smell of fruit reminds me so much of late summer evenings, when we used to garden and you would light a bonfire, and then last thing before going up to bed, we would wander arm in arm down the garden to see if it was still burning. The smell was always so good. Oh, those golden days, what happy memories.

Win and Llew had several people in for Fire Practice this evening and David was so excited as Llew let him work the Stirrup Pump himself, which he managed quite well to begin with, but later succeeded in giving Win a soaking! A is growing up fast and is developing quite a hero worship for David. He runs up to David and puts his arms round him and says "Oh Dadid" with such adoration. He spent most of the morning on the swing and David pushed him quite high, while A held on laughing and singing with joy. It is such a sweet sight to see them playing so well together in the sunshine.

Antony runs and climbs everywhere and copies what D does. He insisted on helping me mow the lawn yesterday and walked up and down with me, trying to push the mower and wouldn't even let go to let me turn it round. David has written half a letter to you and will finish it tomorrow. He loves to write to you and is always talking of you and what you and he are going to do at Linden Road after the war. Bless him.

Both the children have been having quite a lot of ice cream recently, which they both adore. We've discovered a shop where the ice cream tastes just like pre–war, so creamy and good. So we're trying to enjoy it to the full while it lasts, as it ceases for the duration after the end of September.   No more for tonight. Goodnight my dearest and may God bless you and keep you safe. All my love dearest, Joan

A little later, my mother hears from Ronald Joynes that my father hadn't flown to Cape Town after all --- it was just another of many possibilities.........

August 1942 – Lea Road, Wolverhampton –

My dearest Ralph

I had a nice letter from Ronald Joynes today, saying he was very sorry they hadn't let me know particulars of your cable and that you were still at Durban and hadn't been in Cape Town at all as they had at first thought. What a muddle. So I quickly sent a cable off to Durban today and I do so hope you may get it soon, before you move off again. I do wonder if you have been able to occupy the men during your stay in Durban; it must be quite a nightmare for you.

David has finished his letter now and I'll enclose it with mine. Antony had his first diphtheria injection last week and will need a second in another three weeks. I shall be glad when that is completed. I have at last got the watch which mother gave me for my 21st back from the repairers now – nearly eight months. Still they only charged 2/6d !!

I gave the Keens a small snap of the family and they send you their love. Your mother is enjoying her holiday, and Millior sent me a card saying that she had heard from Tom that you were still in Durban! I sent Roger 2/- for his birthday and he wrote and thanked me with a sweet little drawing of an aeroplane for David. I see Jack Cadbury and Tessa Rowntree were finally married last Saturday, which you had predicted would happen.

I noticed that there is a new poetry book out, called *Poetry in Wartime*, which was quite well reviewed in the Birmingham Post. I wondered if you'd like it.   Dear love, Joan

Here my father writes in his memoirs about the future of housing development in Durban......

During my stay in Durban, the man in charge of the Housing Department, showed me round. It was interesting to see their plans and fun to talk housing again. The lay-out, at least of the prosperous parts, seemed fair. But although there is quite a bit planned, very little has so far been done, especially for native dwellers and Indians.

The main problem is a complete absence of suitably level sites. The land is so hilly, making it quite unsuitable, especially as the soil is mostly sand and shale, which easily washes away. The other problems are the multiplicity of ownerships and the high price of land. He showed me some of the native quarters in the so-called shanty towns, well outside the town, with hundreds living in appalling conditions, mostly in tiny tin shacks, which are squalid and overcrowded. There are no nearby services and the conditions unbelievably bad.

I have never seen anything quite like it. Disease, particularly TB, VD and enteric dysentery, are rife; and everything is very disorderly and unpoliced. White Durban shows a brave public face and pleasant enough front, this shows another story entirely, which few people see. The Housing Officer told me that the Council was now alive to the situation and prepared to spend money, but I was not entirely convinced. He really has a huge job on his hands.

The Indian districts are also pretty bad, though better than the shanty towns. Back in the town centre the roads are 100 foot across, wide enough in the olden days for the ox trains to turn around in, and there are fine parks, sky scrapers, hotels, clubs, cafes and shops. But the unplanned, squalid suburbs along with the Negro barracks and Indian settlements were some of the most depressing sites I have ever seen.

––––

"The long delay in awaiting our onward journey often got me down, with the feeling that it was all my fault. But local Friends were very supportive, especially Florence Bayman and Maurice Webb, whose help in finding opportunities to keep the men occupied, was invaluable. And much as I enjoy camping, after several weeks its joys can begin to pall!"

Wednesday, 5th August 1942 – Durban

 My darling,

I was very low yesterday, but today I am more cheerful, and starting a new letter to you. The camp, sand, heat, soldiers, homesickness, responsibility and a feeling of not being good enough, were all getting me down. But Florence and Maurice are very supportive and tell me how well I am doing! So perhaps I am not a total failure!

No one can say that living in a tent is very comfortable, or that living in and out of sleeping bags can be anything other than difficult and maddening. You put something down and five minutes later it's disappeared. After ten minutes of fruitless and frustrating search, you find it at the bottom of the sleeping bag, inevitably! God knows how it got there! Then even everyday chores, just keeping oneself clean and tidy and polished, or simply trying to ensure the tent is tidy, and that the clothes are properly aired and dried, can be nearly a full time job. This morning, for instance, I did little else but change, air my bedding and valise and put it all back again. It's amazing how it holds the heat – my pyjamas and blankets are still warm.

Then there's the whole lay out of the camp. If you decide to go down to the mess, it's a very long walk, and if you happen to forget to take a vital book or a notepad with you, it's another very long walk back again! Getting into Durban is not too bad, though the train journey back can be tiresome, as it's nearly always crowded, often with noisy drunks. Today I got a train and went to a place whose name I am not sure I can even spell, let alone pronounce, but it's something like Amanzimtote, and one of the other stations on the line was called Umbogintwini (believe it or not!).

The latter is a charming small holiday resort on the coast, and I continually thought of you and David, wishing so much you could have been here with me. There are endless miles of sand dunes here, with brush-covered cliffs rising inexorably behind a great stretch of blue sea, and lines of waves breaking in dazzling foam, rushing up the sand, as the spray rises into the air, all sparkling in the afternoon sun. The day was cloudless, under a hot sun, with a gentle breeze at my back. Ahead were rock pools, full of crystal clear water, just rippled by the wind, containing curiously marked tiny fishes, like those we saw at the zoo once – do you remember?

Occasionally, I could hear small Plovers, rather like Ringed Plovers, but without their especial ring marking, calling softly, as they ran and bobbed up and down on the beach or glided gracefully over the sea. Many another sea bird flew past too, like the ubiquitous Black-headed Gull, whilst on the rocks a couple of white Herons stood gracefully, or else walked about with absolute dignity, save occasionally when splashed by a disrespectful wave.

There was scarcely a person on the beach, and as Wordsworth puts it, "Dull would he be of soul who could pass by a sight so touching in its majesty."[10] Here was a clean, fresh pure world, which just lit up the human spirit, and as so often, I thought if only Joan could be here to share this with me. How I miss your company.

I seemed to get completely away for once. I then struck inland up a river estuary, through fields of sugar cane with brush covered hills beyond, down to the next station, a pleasant holiday place called Isipingo, where I got some welcome tea and caught the next train home.

All for now dearest, Ralph

August 1942 – Lea Road, Wolverhampton (Air pc)

 Darling

[....] I see in today's Newsletter, that Bob Cook's party has reached Addis Ababa. I wonder if you have met up with Richey Mounsey yet? My dearest, I know how you must be feeling, but perhaps by now your plans are going better.

All my thoughts and prayers are with you, my dear. I hope my cable to Durban reached you safely. We are all very well, except for the usual colds. The boys are at this moment playing in the garden and I can hear shrieks of laughter as they swing together. They are darlings and I do wish you could see them. Antony is growing quickly and talking a lot now. He is so adorable. David is always talking of you.
All our love, Joan.

––––

"I tried to write to Joan a little bit every day. Sometimes these were brief aircards, sometimes air letters that stretched on for several days. I hope I was able to convey something of the life and the company and the Friends I met, which might be of interest to our children."

Sunday, 2nd August 1942 – Durban

 Dearest Joan

Yesterday the clocks went back an hour, so we now get up and go to bed by candlelight. Talking of which, I don't know if I mentioned that the other day I bought two lovely coloured candles, which cast a soft gentle glow inside the tent.

I sent you an airgraph this morning as well as ones to Paul Cadbury and to Leonard Appleton. At the moment I am writing at the back of Gilbert Reynold's eye shop, as I am later going out to supper with him. I have also written a post card to David, which I hope he will get soon. I am very worried to hear of the air raids and do hope and pray that you are alright. It is an added worry for you and I long to hear that you are safe.

I wonder so often what you are doing, or wearing; whether you have seen any plays or films and hope you are managing to get out a little. It seems sometimes almost futile writing when one has no idea when or if they will arrive. But I do enjoy writing to you, as it seems to bring us closer together.

In the afternoon, I went over to the Webbs' house, as I was really anxious to see if your cable had arrived. Sadly I found out that it hadn't. I do so hope mine got through to you. Whilst I was there I also interviewed their two daughters as possible members of a future South African FAU. Then back to see Florence, who had sweetly asked John, Philip and me over for supper.

249

I meant to tell you that at last I have secured a book on South African birds and very soon I'll make out a list of those I have seen, and send them to you. Florence really is most kind and we had a delicious meal. Altogether it was an interesting evening, as there was also a Major there from the South African army and his charming wife. He had been all through the Abyssinian campaign and was later out in Libya as well. He told us some fascinating details about both.

In Abyssinia he had been with one of the columns which had advanced up from the south, where the Italians had constructed one or two really first class roads. The central highlands of the country, he said, were incredibly beautiful and full of wonderful wild game. "The people on the other hand", he said "are uncivilized and filthy to a degree;" adding that "the conditions away from the cities, are very dangerous indeed, even though the Italians are damned poor fighters." Then somewhat alarmingly he remarked "Nonetheless, it was a most enjoyable campaign." But by comparison, he said, "in Libya the conditions are bloody unpleasant."

We also talked a lot about South Africa: the country, its weather and the wild life. These colonial officers seem generally more liberal minded and freer than many of ours, and they have a critical attitude towards Imperial policy generally, which is hardly surprising.

Later, as I mentioned I had supper with Gilbert Reynolds, which was quite delicious. As well as being Clerk of Natal Monthly Meeting, he is a very well-known botanist out here, and a brilliant eye specialist, and guess what - we talked birds of all things, on which he is also knowledgeable, and he filled me in on a lot more that I didn't know, so one way and another, I'll soon be an expert!

I've recently been spending some pleasant evenings re-reading *Emma*, that is when I've not been censoring letters or sewing on buttons. There can be few better ways of passing the time. I think I'll close now and post this letter in the hope that it will not be too many weeks in reaching you. How I wish you could be here and share all this with me.

But this brings all love to you and to D&A. Always your own, Ralph

Gilbert Reynolds, Clerk of Natal Monthly Meeting, who sent the letter (right) to all Friends on the FAU's visit. He was also a well-known botanist, who wrote many studies on the Aloe plant.
Photo SA Friends Library

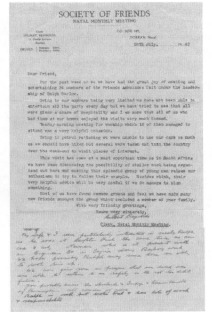

Dear Friend
For the past week or so, we have had the great joy of meeting and entertaining 34 members of the FAU under the leadership of Ralph Barlow......

My wife and I were particularly interested in meeting Ralph, as he was at Leighton Park at the same time as our own son, Norman, who is at present with an Engineers Co in Syria, working on the railways, and we hope possibly Ralph may some time be able to look him up.

Isipengo and Umbogintwini

A post card from Isipingo
"I walked down to the next station called Isipingo & got some refreshment at the Tea Rooms."

Umbogintwini beach
"There are endless miles of sand dunes here, with brush-covered cliffs rising inexorably
behind a great stretch of blue sea and lines of waves breaking.....and rushing up the
sand........I wished so much you could have been here"
Photo South Africa Tourist Board

My father writes in his memoirs about sharing the mess with the army.....

"On the whole our hardships were slight, and it was after all, what we had come for, and there were, of course, some really pleasant people in the mess, but generally one saw little of them, and as we are only there a short time, it seemed hardly worth making any great effort to get to know them, especially as most of the time the initials FAU meant little to them, as I told Joan...."

Wednesday 5th August - Durban

My dearest Joan [......] I sometimes get into conversations with the army, which can become fruitless and repetitive. Only rarely does one meet someone to whom the initials 'FAU' or even 'Quakers' mean anything, or perhaps I have been unlucky.

A typical conversation will usually go: "Excuse me Sir, which regiment are you with?", followed by my ever so slightly aloof reply: "We are a detachment of the Friends' Ambulance Unit, wearing Red Cross uniform – loosely connected with the Society of Friends, you know", which inevitably produces a complete blank. Once or twice you sense the word Quaker might just be stirring a chord, as you sense a glimmer of recognition behind the furrowed brow. But more often than not it's wide of the mark, as in yesterday's query: "You have something to do with kindness to animals, don't you Sir?"

Well, if there's time, and I'm feeling in the mood, I might gently try and explain. And sometimes when you think you have really got through, the next question makes it quite apparent that you haven't, as they usually finish up by asking: "Well, what's your rank, Sir?" I reply as patiently as I can: "Something like Major or Squadron Leader" and there the matter usually rests and they depart, believing us to be some branch of the services they've never heard of.

Just once in a while, one comes across someone who has heard of Quakers and is a little more aware, such as the rather jolly Lt Colonel in our lines the other day, who thought what we were doing was "a damned good show."

Well, I'm off into town now and then on to supper with Florence. All my love Ralph

———

"It really seems ages since I heard from Ralph. The weeks slip by without any news at all...."

August 1942 – Lea Road, Wolverhampton

My dearest Ralph

[.....] I do so hope I shall get a letter soon. I hear there is now an Aigraph Service from South Africa, so perhaps when I do start to get news, several letters will come at once. You are so much in my thoughts and I try to picture all you are doing and wonder whether you are still in Durban. I do hope you got the cable I sent to you there. It would be so wonderful if I could start to get regular letters from you. It really does seem years since I last saw you and I seem so out of touch and far away. I expect you feel just the same, only you are busy and I just live to get your letters. The ache is sometimes more than I can bear.

I do hope the stay in Durban was interesting. Are you still pleased with the men? I am glad that John Gough and Philip Sandford have proved so satisfactory. Have you met any nice people? What was Durban like? Is it a pleasant town? So many questions. I expect the climate is mild. At least you will have missed some of the worst of the Middle East heat. I do hope you are keeping well, my dearest. We are all very well, except Antony and mother, who have had heavy colds. But we have had a pretty bad summer with little sun.

D and A are a great joy and comfort to me. I only wish you could be here to see them. D is so sensible and affectionate and I can really talk to him and explain a little how I'm feeling and we often talk about you. He asks me so many questions about you, and will never settle off to sleep without saying his prayers and asking God to watch over you and keep you safe, "so that we can all soon be together in 26 Linden Road." Bless him, he loves you so dearly.

Antony too is adorable. His hair has grown a great deal recently and curls round his neck. He is very bonny and quite charming to look at, full of the joy of life, always laughing and happy. He is beginning to talk much more now too, He and David have great times together and he worships D. I will try and take some more snaps of them and send to you, if I can get a film, which is very difficult now.

Each day seems much the same here, what with being kept busy with the children and housework and mending. The children are in the garden every day, but I also try and take them a walk most afternoons. They both love to get ice-creams from a shop at the bus terminus. Your mother said she enjoyed her holiday and says she feels much better for the rest, and I believe she has written to you and also sent you a book of Henry Nevinson's.

Do you have much time to read, as I should like to send you some books, but it is so hard to know what is best to send, as I don't want to be sending you ones you have read before? Do tell me anything you'd particularly like. I have nearly finished *Last Train from Berlin* by Howard Smith, which is interesting as he was in Germany right up to the time when America entered the war. Llewellyn has now got Douglas Reed's[11] latest, *All Our Tomorrows*, which has been very well reviewed. I think next time I visit the Library I might try and get something lighter out. I seem to have read nothing but war books and politics recently, which, of course, is necessary, but we do need relaxation too!

Lots more questions! Where are you staying in Durban? Were you in a private house or staying with Friends? Everyone tells me how kind South African Friends have been looking after the FAU and how much they are helping you all. But I know however pleasant they make it, you will long to get down to real work and be doing a job. It must be rather sickening for you to be held up so long. All my thoughts and prayers are with you.

I know in an earlier letter I complained that I hadn't heard much from anybody, well suddenly things are looking up, as I've had a phone call from Honor (Cadbury) to see how we were getting on; a card from Jeph and Margaret (Gillett) who have been on holiday in Barmouth and want to come and visit. They both sent their love to you.

On Saturday I am taking David to stay with your mother for a short weekend, coming back on Monday. I hope there won't be any raids, as ever since we have been having incendiaries, D has been getting quite nervous of the house being burnt. Last night when the siren went off, he woke and at once said "I think we should go in the shelter mummy". We went down under the stairs, but I didn't take A down, as there wasn't anything nearby. I'm sorry D is getting nervous, but I suppose as he gets older, he realises more too.

Last Saturday Wolverhampton Quaker Meeting was invited to The Woodlands Home[12] to see the old people and I took the children with Win and Llew. We all took contributions such as scones and cakes, and joined together to have tea in the garden. It was a lovely afternoon and I enjoyed seeing round. David went off with young Tommy Brockbank and had a glorious time exploring the grounds. It really is a most pleasant house with magnificent grounds and lawns, all beautifully kept, and the greenhouses full of luscious looking grapes and tomatoes.

I was told that at one of the committee meetings they had discussed what should be done with the grapes and no-one, neither staff nor committee, had thought about asking the old people themselves. Really! Some folk have no imagination – or perhaps they thought as it was a Quaker home, they were all teetotal!

The Walker family have gone to Stottesdon in Shropshire for a fortnight, camping in the fields opposite the links. Do you remember our lovely holiday there? Such a beautiful stretch of heavenly English countryside with its green fields and rolling hills.

If I close my eyes, I can still see the view of the lane where we used to stand and watch the old bull. I hope they enjoy it as much as we did. Dearest heart, I do so long for the day when we can enjoy such wonderful times together again. Goodnight for now my dearest and God bless you always. D and A send their love too, and my mother sends special love as well.

Your ever loving Joan

———

"During our time in Durban, Maurice Webb, our wonderful South African Friend took us out to Adams College, one of the largest native colleges in SA and of which he is Chairman of the Governors."

Saturday, 8th August 1942 – Durban

Dearest one
Today we had Meeting for worship, which was quite well attended and very good, for a change. So often an inspiring meeting really does help one to cope. Afterwards we had a section meeting in the Webb's garden, when I explained my various proposals to everyone. Maurice then kindly provided lunch, before taking me back to Camp so that I could go and visit two of our boys who are ill in hospital.

Having seen the boys, who both seemed to be on the mend, Maurice took four of us out to Adams College, where he is Chairman of the Governors. The drive took us on a pleasant run, first along the high road close by the sea, then slowly climbing inland into rather broken country, with groups of trees and rough grass and magnificent views inland to miles and miles of the same. Rough grassy hills, jumbled with steep-sided valleys in between, brown and green as far as the eye can see. Here and there, round straw native huts as well as the occasional rather pretentious modern concrete building.

Adams College is certainly very impressive and owns 500 acres of land with the college buildings and staff bungalows scattered about like an American University campus. The buildings are nothing very much, but the grounds are lovely. Quite hilly, covered in places with bush and lines of eucalyptus trees with all sorts of flowering shrubs, all framed by glorious views out to the sea some ten miles away, and so many birds, that I've already lost count.

The staff, who come from all over the world, live in very pleasant bungalows with verandahs. I met two of them, one a German refugee, another an American. All very friendly. Originally it was an American Mission College, but is now administered by South Africans themselves. There are about 400 students, varying in ages from 14 to 25 and they come for one, two or three years, learning to be teachers, or to study agriculture on the College's own farm, or learning any one of a variety of trades. I found it very interesting indeed.

Yesterday I thought I would try something different with the boys, and decided to march them up to the little village I had visited earlier called Isipengo. Once there, I broke off and let them find their own way home.

It was a dull morning, but it came out beautifully sunny with a high wind from the sea. I came back almost immediately – it was rather lovely walking back through the cane fields, the leaves rustling in the wind and the eucalyptus trees along the broad swaying in the wind. In places they were cutting the cane (which is higher than a man) and it lay all over the ground in a thick carpet. Negroes stood in groups, and there were acres uncut; beyond were hills and above blue sky.

I got back to Camp by train after walking about ten miles; changed hurriedly, polished everything, and then back into town to Maurice and thence to the Natal University College, where I addressed 25 or 30 students from mixed backgrounds on social science and economic Housing courses. I spoke for an hour and answered questions for an hour. I remembered more than I expected, and they actually seemed interested. [.........] all for now Ralph

Adams College as it was pre 1947
The college was founded in 1853 by an American missionary.
Sadly much of the old school burnt down in 1947.
Photo Adams College archive

Adams College, Durban

Adams College was originally a missionary college. During the FAU's time in Durban it was run by Edgar Brookes, whose objective was to improve the lot of native Africans, and the school became one of the most important schools for black education.

Left: Philip Sanford, John Gough and Ralph Barlow in the grounds of Adams College.

Below left:
Edgar Brookes giving a talk on race relations – my father Ralph, sitting attentively at the front.
Photographs Friends House Library

My father meets Dr Gumede, virtually the only black doctor in the neighbourhood, who turns out to have been trained in Birmingham.......

Monday, 10ᵗʰ August 1942 – Durban (No 10)

My dearest

[.......] Today, a usual morning. I left Camp early, as I went as Maurice's guest to a Rotary luncheon. I always find Rotary rather amusing. Guests are always introduced so publicly: "May I introduce Mr Barlow, leader of the Friends Ambulance Unit," followed by a scattering of friendly applause.

There was an excellent speech on Race Relations and the War by a Prof Hörule, making a very eloquent plea for a more enlightened native policy. He said that if South Africa did not think again on this subject, she would find herself left far behind as a nation. The native troops, he said, are even now fighting so well, that white soldiers are beginning to realise their worth, and that after the war they must be given proper treatment. He illustrated this part of his talk with stories of praise told by white soldiers of their native colleagues.

Hörule is here as chairman of the Commission on Indian Education, and is a most likeable person and was making fun of Maurice for appearing before the Commission in three separate capacities. Professor Hörule said "I don't wish to be irreverent, but if I ever have any difficulty in understanding the Holy Trinity, I'll think of Maurice Webb appearing before the Commission as President of one Society, Chairman of another and Secretary of a third; and always Maurice Webb!"

Then I went to see a Doctor Innes Gumede, a local black Doctor who was connected to McCord Hospital, where some of our chaps were working. Such a coincidence, as I discovered he had trained in Birmingham between 1923 and 29 and was, I believe, only the second black African medical doctor to qualify. Not only did he train in Birmingham, but would you believe, he had lived near us in Selly Oak at Kingsmead Methodist College. "Barlow" he said, "Barlow is a well-known name in Birmingham; I knew your mother, Mabel. Very fine lady". He seemed genuinely glad to see me and hear news of the Colleges, where he had discovered a spiritual home.

He later opened up a practice at Inanda, a township a few miles outside Durban, which he said was where Gandhi had lived during his time in South Africa. But the good doctor felt somewhat aggrieved at the way he'd been treated in his home land, as he had been refused any financial assistance to help in providing accommodation for his patients. He was in fact virtually the only doctor for the native population, many of whom would often travel long distances in order to see him. Not much has changed I fear since the Mahatma's time. Dr Gumede's difficulties are sadly symptomatic of this whole country. The prejudice against the coloured population is really terrible and the country is riven with such problems, but both Maurice and Dr Gumede, somehow remain optimistic, saying much the same thing, that they still love the country despite its many problems, simply because it is so fierce and young. Maurice was quite eloquent about this on Sunday.

After I had seen Dr Gumede, I visited the South African Red Cross to see if there was any work they could offer our chaps, and they were optimistic....though quite likely the work will come up just as we are about to move on! On the way home I paid my outstanding dentist's bill, and ended up having supper with the engineer I'd shared my cabin with on the boat.

One of the first black African Doctors
Doctor Innes Balintine Gumede

""Then I went to see a Doctor Innes Gumede, a local black Doctor [....] Such a coincidence, as I discovered not only had he trained in Birmingham but lived near us in Selly Oak. [....]

He was only the second qualified black African doctor in South Africa.....the prejudice he received made him aggrieved....but native people came from miles around to be treated by him. Despite its problems, he says he still loves such a fierce, young country."

Photo courtesy of Dr Gumede's grandson Mr Samvu Gumede

Now at last I am back in my tent and able to write to you by the light of my candle. I'm hoping the weather will stay calm tonight, as yesterday, just after I'd settled down, there was one hell of a thunder storm with vivid lightening, each flash making the whole place as light as day, and torrential rain, which after a time came pouring through our tents and we had to lift all our stuff off the ground and start digging trenches. I really don't mind if I never ever go camping again!

I miss you terribly already, and wonder how on earth I am going to manage for months without you. I can only pray that it won't be too long before we all meet again. I know I have responsibility for the men here, and then I think on that and just take hold and shake myself up and get on with it. But it is a struggle without you here and all the time aching for news of you. I suppose it's these sort of times which are the acid test of character. The long waiting, the forced inactivity, rather than the rush and press of work and action. Well, I know I must try. Keep me in your thoughts, my dearest.

———

"Suddenly I received two letters together from Ralph, which made my day…" **August 1942 – Lea Road, Wolverhampton**

My darling

I could shout for joy! Two Airgraph letters received this morning. AG 1&2. I am so happy to get news through at last. They have come fairly quickly – the one only taking just over three weeks and the other a little more than a month. I expect I shall get the Air Mail letters soon now.

So glad you have had an interesting stay in Durban and that Friends have been so kind. Glad you have found lots of birds. Have you found anyone who could help you over them? Your mother was overjoyed to get a letter today. I rang her up to give your news. How good of you to send parcels. I do hope they get through safely. I don't think I remember the Standings.

Oh, it is lovely to get letters from you, it has quite altered my outlook on life. I know how much you are wanting my letters, but when you reach your destination, you will find a large number waiting for you, dear one. Remember, I think of you always and love you more and more each day. God bless you dearest mine. All love Joan

"….and I read and re-read them….."

August 1942 – Wolverhampton

My dearest Ralph

I have read and re-read your two Airgraphs received last Tuesday. I was so grateful to get them after so many weeks without any news. So now I have had three letters and 2 cables and 2 Airgraphs. I do so hope your other letters will start coming through soon, as I long to know so many details of all you are doing. Nearly every other minute I think of you. You are always so near me.

I do wonder whether you are still in camp, and how you are occupying your time, are you doing hospital work and I wonder when you will be moving on. Oh hundreds of questions and I imagine all my letters piling up somewhere and hope that you will get them all one day. What a time you will have wading through them one day.

David looks each morning for a letter for him as he so longs for one from you. I am enclosing his latest to you. He adores writing to you and would happily go on for pages if I had the time to help him with the spelling. He wanted to put on the bottom of his letter, that he had much more to tell you, but I said it could go on the next letter, which he is already saying he will start tomorrow! I think he is writing very well now as he isn't yet five.

He had a heavenly time last Friday. I took him and Antony to the Fitzgeralds for tea. It was a gloriously hot sunny day and it wasn't too far to go, so I was able to manage it alright. Mrs F promised David he could help her David, who is a medical student, pick some of the fruit. So he had a grand time climbing the ladder and putting the pears and apples in the baskets. We had tea in the garden and we enjoyed the change.

Antony can be rather a handful as he is so very active and needs constant watching. Everyone seems charmed with the children and I feel very proud of them, but I do miss your help in training them. David has such a strong personality and needs careful training just now. He is so sensitive and imaginative and I know I am far from being the perfect mother. I need so much more patience than I possess! He definitely has charm and is very friendly and natural. He adores going out to tea and I'm afraid he is always inviting himself to different houses!

I overheard him asking the lady next door this morning, when he might go to tea with her. She said "Oh, tomorrow David if you would like." Whereupon he quietly said "You must ask mummy first you know. Ring up and invite me properly!"

He was sweet this morning. It is Llew's birthday today and very early when I was between sleeping and waking, D crept out of bed and ran to L's bedroom and presented him with some chocolate and an old purse he had! Then before breakfast he went to his own little garden and picked some stocks and nasturtiums and arranged them in a little vase and put them by L's plate at breakfast. He said "Daddy used to do that for Mummy's birthday." I could have wept. Just imagine his remembering. It is amazing what children remember. He told me the other evening when I was changing for the theatre, that I looked very fashionable and decorated! I'm sure I had the simplest frock on!

I'm sitting at the bureau in the drawing room and it's nearly dark, so I've just drawn the curtains. It seems that summer has gone and autumn is here already. W&L are out and mother is reading in the arm chair by the fire. Both the boys are in bed and asleep I hope, and all is quiet. I am wearing the blue dress trimmed with cherry that you liked, and which I wore on your last Sunday before you left. I wish you were here to see me in it again.

It will soon be the 17th and another wedding anniversary – our sixth – and I do so pray that we will be together to celebrate our 7th next year. Thank you for all the happy times that we have had, and I thank God for you and for all you are and have been to me. I love you so much and life seems so very empty without you. I send you my dearest love and a special kiss for the 17th. David goes back to school that day too, after 7 weeks holiday. He longs to go back, as he misses the other children I think. It's good that he likes school so much.

They announced on the wireless this week that all Christmas parcels for the Middle East should be posted this next week. So I must go and have a good look round Hatchards for some books that you might like. I wish I knew what to send you. Perhaps you'd like a poetry book. Do let me know. I love choosing things for you.

Next weekend David and I go to your mother for a short stay. I hope we shall have a peaceful time. I sent your mother an Airgraph form last week and explained to her how she should fill it in. I believe she sent it off straight away.

A woman from Holland has just been speaking on the wireless, in a special Dutch programme. She has recently escaped from Holland and gave a most moving account of what it feels like to live in your own country when it is occupied by the Germans. "Oh, do you all realise", she said "What it is to be free, or what your freedom and liberty mean to you?" Such accounts bring it all home to one.

David asked me today "Why are we sometimes afraid mummy?" I asked him what he was afraid of. He said "Oh, I'm only afraid sometimes – of – well just things!" I couldn't quite make out what he was afraid of, except he said "I used to be afraid of engine noise and smoke at the station, but I'm not now." I think he's a little afraid of the gunfire. More tomorrow my darling. Goodnight dearest one.

All love Joan

———

"Our stay in Durban seemed an eternity, and there were days when I thought we would never get away. I would get depressed, thinking that there must be more I could do about it. But I tried hard not to let it get me down, and to be positive for the boys sake and to keep their spirits up."

Thursday 13th August 1942 – Durban (10 contd)

My dearest Joan

Well, we are still here in Durban and I'm now getting very depressed about it. There is still no news and I wonder all the time if I ought to be doing more to get us moving, and yet being unable to do it. I just pray that we shall be moving soon. Movement Control naturally give us no information. I try hard to think positively though and on the whole, I suppose I have enjoyed my stay here. Well, perhaps enjoy is too strong a word, but it has been extremely interesting and we have received great kindness, such as I'll never forget.

Yesterday I went to see the city's Air Raid Precautions man, who was quite amiable. They all treated me as though I was an expert, God forgive me! I also called the South African Red Cross again and the British Red Cross, though they had nothing very positive to offer. In the evening I had supper with Maurice, and this time managed to catch the 8.0 o'clock train home with no problem.

By the way, I forgot to mention the supper party I had the other evening with Florence, with a most amusing collection of people. She had asked me earlier what I wanted to do, and feeling grumpy, I said 'I don't feel much like doing anything.' However, she twisted my arm and persuaded me to join her and some Jewish friends for supper later on. She is so good to me, I must say.

But I am glad I went, as they were so hospitable and such a collection of odd characters. The party included Florence, an Indian woman doctor, myself and the Jewish family. The husband was a well-to-do shopkeeper going up in the world, while his wife seemed to be content to remain as she was, but their daughter was definitely moving up. They were all very kind and were in great jubilation because their son was coming home after two years of being away in Egypt. They gave us a really wonderful meal.

Apart from the Jewish family there was also another girl there, who was quite good looking, whom I tried to engage in conversation. But 'Oh dear' when she opened her mouth, she turned out to be a rather vulgar, brainless, young typist – (nothing against typists, of course!) A little later that evening, the flat was invaded by a large crowd of their other Jewish friends, who had come to congratulate the family and we decided it was perhaps time to take our leave.

Saturday and Sunday had turned into a minor triumph, though I says it as shouldn't! Occasionally I can get permission for the lads to sleep out, so after I'd talked to Maurice the other day, I suggested that we should all march out to Adams College and spend the night there. I thought it would make a real change and be nice for us to get our own meals, while at the same time giving us good marching exercise. When the date was still some way off, everyone thought it a great idea. But naturally as the time came nearer, no-one wanted to go. "Damned bad idea. Whose idea was that?" However, as it was all fixed and the food ordered, I stuck firmly to my guns. We walked for about nine miles and then I marched the unwilling crowd another nine miles up hill, which afforded us sensational views out to sea and over the hill country beyond.

We were carrying all our own bedding and necessaries, and I was full of foreboding that the whole enterprise would turn into a disastrous and wretched week-end. But by the grace of God, it was a terrific success, and everyone enjoyed it. Our own two cooks had ordered extra food in addition to the rations we had carried with us from camp, and went on ahead to prepare it. So when we got back to the College, we all had an excellent meal awaiting us. We invited the Principal, as well as some of the coloured staff to be our guests. Then they invited us into the dining hall where some 400 black students of both sexes were assembled, who sang to us really beautifully. Somebody made a speech welcoming us, to which I replied at short notice, and then there was some more singing. Finally some of the white staff all put on another entertainment for us, after which, tired out, we all slept soundly on the floor in one of the empty class rooms.

More tomorrow,

Ralph

———

"How I longed for more news of Ralph and often rushed to the door like an eager schoolgirl to see if there was a letter. Perhaps today, I thought, I shall get a letter from Durban."

August – Lea Road, Wolverhampton

My dearest Ralph

Just a little extra tonight before I post this off to you tomorrow. There is always the hope that there maybe a letter from you tomorrow and I can tell you that I have received it. Antony has been a little upset today; nothing much I expect, but he was violently sick at tea-time. However, he seemed lively enough afterwards, if a little pale. When I eventually started to get their baths ready, I couldn't find him anywhere, until finally I found him in the lavatory, emptying the water from the bowl on to the floor with a tiny teapot! He is so mischievous now.

This morning I put the children in the garden, and as it was wet, I put them both in gum boots, but A's are rather large for him and he kept taking them off, and when I looked out of the window, he was running on the wet grass without socks or boots!! Three times I went out and put them on, and each time he took them off again. There is a large petrol can full of water at the back gate and he will go and play with it and get himself totally soaked and greasy!

Well my dear husband, I managed to buy three books for you and have posted them off to you today: one of Russian poetry and one a collection of modern poetry, plus a book on London with some lovely sketches in, which I hope you well like. I think of thee so much and all our prayers are with you. Everyone at 31 sends you their love. God bless, my dearest,

Ever thine Joan.

———

"I remember clearly one Sunday morning in August getting up early at 7.0am. Outside it was cool, clear and lovely, with the sun just coming up, drying the heavy dew. There was scarcely a person to be seen and for a whole hour I enjoyed a brief time quite alone, almost as though I was here on holiday. And for the first time I was aware that all around me were birds of such beauty - Red-winged Starlings, Orioles, Sunbirds, Doves, and Swallows. What an unexpected joy."

Sunday, 15th August 1942 – Durban (10 contd)

My dearest

[.....] I rose early this morning, had a leisurely breakfast and afterwards to church. It was rather a poor service, and save for some great old Zulu hymns quite beautifully sung, awfully dull. It was a Communion service, which made it last an hour and half! I am prepared to accept the value and meaning of Communion in an Anglican church, but here – badly conducted, with prayers and readings of no particular dignity or beauty, and with the wafer handed all around the congregation on tin plates, and the wine given out in little aluminium cups, it seemed a mockery.

Afterwards we were entertained by various people on the College staff, with a talk by their Principal, Senator Edgar Brookes, who is one of the four white representatives of the black and coloured peoples in the South African Senate. He talked well on race relations, and though it is of course, a very pressing issue out here, we do seem to have had rather a dose of it recently!

Anyway, we then had lunch, and our cooks really excelled themselves, as they have the whole stay. This morning for breakfast they gave us mealie porridge and scrambled eggs and for lunch, ham and salad with hollowed-out tomatoes stuffed with pineapple and banana, topped by generous helpings of mayonnaise, followed by fruit.

The weekend had gone so well, that I decided to postpone our scheduled departure and let people just amuse themselves for the afternoon. Johnnie Gough and four others meanwhile returned to Camp, just to ensure that nothing drastic had occurred in our absence, whilst I went around making sure we had all cleared up properly, before getting in another half hour of birding!

Before we left, we were beautifully looked after by Dr Wilkes, a German refugee Friend. He and his wife work here at the College and he is a most charming man; dignified, humble, friendly, understanding and sympathetic. One feels that even though he and his family have suffered much in life, miraculously they've managed not to become in any way embittered. Prior to moving here, he had previously lived many years in Switzerland and loved it there. But now they have a bungalow here, set quite high up, with a wonderful view of trees and hills and sea. In the front they have a rock garden, which he tends with obvious love and care, and I spent a peaceful thirty minutes, just looking out over the sun drenched country and chatting with him. He is a great bird lover as well as something of an artist, and it was a pleasure to share his company and erudition and to look at all his wonderful books and pictures.

They kindly gave us all tea, and afterwards we marched back home in the cool of the evening with the last half hour entirely by moonlight. It had been a very rewarding exercise, but a wearing one. What with making all the arrangements, then having to cope with some of the troops not wanting to go. And once we got there, being concerned that everyone should be on their best behaviour, and before we left wanting to be sure we had properly thanked everyone.

However, finally, they all said how much they had enjoyed it. And at the end, by collecting up the left-overs, including some bread I was able to scrounge from the Camp kitchen, there was enough to feed everybody again when we eventually arrived back at just after 9.0 o'clock. Quite a triumph in itself! Exhausting! I'm really quite tired now and long only for a place where "the wicked cease from troubling and the weary are at rest" as the poet Henry Milman puts it!

May God keep you my dear, all for now, Love Ralph

"After we'd been in Durban a while, we were eventually able to move to a distinctly better part of the camp, and oh the joy of having real sheets to sleep in, and a bedside lamp instead of candles."

Tuesday, August 18th 1942 – Durban (10 –final)

My dearest Joan

I hope you have received some of my letters by now as well as some cable and airgraphs, and that they are getting through better. It won't be long now till our wedding anniversary, which makes it six years we've been married and I give so much thanks for these wonderful years. Bless you dear Joan for all you are.

Dear Florence is being so good to me. Yesterday she invited me to go with her to supper with some friends of hers, Dr and Mrs Farren. If you have a moment you might write and thank her for mothering me so well!

They are Friends and Dr Farren is young, impetuous and very talkative, but most pleasant. He is having a conscience about whether or not he should pay taxes for war purposes. His wife is quite a bit older and also charming. They have a girl of about 2 as well as twins of 10 months, all fine children. I do get so jealous seeing other's children, longing so much as I do to see D & A. I happened to say how difficult it was to get children's things in England, and she said she would send some for you. They may be unsuitable, but if they arrive, they come with all our love.

We've now moved to a distinctly better part of the Camp with an infinitely superior type of tent, and I now have a table which we've scrounged, and instead of candles there is a bedside light and a proper bed with sheets. What bliss!

Yesterday I had some distinctly depressing news concerning our departure, which for a while made me think we should be delayed here indefinitely. But today it all sounds a lot more cheerful, though we still have no definite date, and God knows when we shall actually get on board. As usual, Maurice has been a really good friend to us, and has introduced me to yet another hospital, where I went today to fix up work for another section of our group, as I have to keep them busy while we are still here. He has also put us on to a room that we can use in town, which will be of great use. And with his help I am planning another week-end out. He really is quite tireless, wise, efficient and expeditious. All for now, as ever, Ralph

———

"It is nearly a fortnight since I received Ralph's two AGs, which I have read so many times…."

September 1942 - Wolverhampton (Air pc)

Dearest one

I think of you continually darling and long so much for a letter from you. We are mostly well, though Antony is rather poorly with a tummy upset, but I think he will soon be well again. David and I go to Swarthmore Rd tomorrow to stay with your mother.

I love you so dearly, my darling and miss you more and more. Your family are well. Millior is fine and your mother seems better for her holiday. I hope to take David to Selly Oak meeting on Sunday and perhaps might call on Heather if I have time. I wonder how things progress at Gordon Sq. Do you get much news through? Mother sends her love and D & A too…and all my love darling.
Ever your own Joan.

"Whenever I received a letter or Aircard from Joan, it had the power to raise my spirits, and the world seemed a hundred times better."

Friday, 28ᵗʰ August 1942

My dear Joan

All blessings - I got your cable today, which made me feel so much happier, and consequently already I feel over the worst of my depression. It is a great relief to know that you are alright. As an offering of thanks, I went and bought you a handbag which I hope you will like when it arrives. It comes with all my love and thankfulness that you are safe. Secondly, and far less significant, I had a haircut and shampoo and as I like having my haircut, that made me feel a whole lot better too!

Maurice is such a good friend to us, and we have now fixed up the room in town, which he found for us, and it will act as a centre and common-room, where people can go and write and read, and where we can have meetings, lectures etc. I have also fixed up another hospital section, for two people in a VD clinic and two in Casualty. That makes 19 of us in all now working in hospitals. Last night I had supper with Maurice, who said he had written to you, and I know Florence has also written. Both have really been most extraordinarily kind and helpful.

I can't think why, but everybody seems to think I need cheering up! So the night before, Johnnie arranged a party and a dance. He went with a girl he'd met called Pamela, though I understand she has a fiancé up north, to whom she claims she is very attached. Then there was her sister Zoë with her fiancé, and another friend called Dulcie. What names!

We had dinner at their home and then progressed on to another house for the dance. They were what would be described as 'easy to look at', and are, I suppose typical of middle-class Durban; that's to say very pleasant, with heaps of common sense, but coming from rather a narrow society, they appeared to have little or no culture, and not many ideas. However, they're nice enough, and quite amusing, and we all had a good time. Pamela is reasonably pretty and quite pleasant; Zoë is less pretty but at least has the dawnings of a mind, while her fiancé, a Lieutenant in the South African Air Force, seemed an exceedingly nice fellow; finally there was Dulcie, who was very pretty indeed and extremely lively. I don't expect I shall see any of them again, but it passed an evening, and it was actually quite a wrench having to get back, and we only just managed to catch the last train.

The more one talks to everyone here in Durban, the more one realises just how many people have friends and relations, killed or just missing following the carnage at Tobruk. It makes one wonder sometimes, if the game is worth the candle.

My love to all, ever yours Ralph

—

"I know I shouldn't, but I do get cross with Gordon Square for not keeping me in the loop. With no mail, I feel so much in the dark…"

Friday, September 4ᵗʰ 1942 – Swarthmore Road

My dearest one

It's 7.30 and I've just finished packing the boys off to bed. I'm afraid I am rather tired and irritable today. It's been a trying day, and little Antony is still poorly. It's either a chill on his tummy or more teeth; or else he's eaten something out of the garden! He's been very sick and miserable and although he did seem a little better, he has been whimpering all day and cried if I left him for a minute. It is so unusual for him to be like this, as he is always happy and full of fun. David is a little off colour too, but I think he's been eating too much fruit.

Tomorrow evening, or at least late afternoon, we're off to your mother's for two nights, returning Monday morning. I hope A won't be too difficult for my mother. We are taking D to Quaker meeting on Sunday. I hope he won't talk too much, as he does find it hard to be quiet for very long!

Your mother has been trying to decide what to send you for Christmas. I said I felt sure you'd rather have books than anything else. She was going to send you some socks, but I think I persuaded her against that. I said I was sure that you could buy socks in Cairo! Instead I think she is going to send you a book by J R Glover of essays about classical Greece instead, which was well reviewed in last week's Friend.

I heard from Millior that you had sent a cable to Gordon Square, saying that you were hoping to move on soon. I do so wish they would let me know? I did write to Ronald Joynes, but it doesn't seem to have made much difference. I seem so cut off from you. I do think they might let wives know any news. It does make me cross as I pine for a letter from you. I do miss you so. If only we could have an occasional talk on the telephone, it would bring you nearer. It is nearly three months since we talked together. I am sure you must be feeling the same way, with no letters from me, but you will have a lovely lot when you reach your destination. It will be so heavenly when letters start getting through regularly.

D has been collecting caterpillars again – he caught a beautiful one the other day and put it in a tall tin and left it in the garden. Alas, when he awakened from his mid-day rest, he rushed to the garden and found his caterpillar had crawled away. Poor boy, he was heart-broken and wept piteously. Today, he found several more and was happy again. Later he tried to cut A's hair at the front with his cutting-out scissors. Fortunately they are very blunt or I tremble to think what might have happened.

Mother and I went to theatre last night to see *The Silver Chord,* by Sidney Howard[13], which we thought a very exaggerated play. It's about a mother and two sons, with one son's wife and the other's fiancée. The mother has a very strong hold on the two boys and ruins one's life and very nearly wrecks the other. The mother was rather a stupid character and said such silly things, but I suppose the moral of the play was, have children and give them your love, but let them go and be themselves. How very true, I must say.

Did you manage to see any good plays or films in Durban? I do long to hear news of your life and what you are doing. How I would love for you to be here, sitting on the settee together, with you reading poetry to me. How glorious that would be. How many years, or dare I say months before we meet again? Shall I be more dull and old when you return? I'll try not to be.

No more tonight. I must hurry and finish a baby coat for Millior and read my library book. David is so excited at the thought of visiting your mother tomorrow at Swarthmore Road. I shall wear my blue costume and mauve blouse and the lovely brooch you gave me, which is so nice. David's going to wear his brown hat and coat in which he looks quite grown up.

David's last words at night are always "God bless Daddy and keep him safe, because we love him so dearly." Antony can also say 'Daddy' now and often goes to your photo and points to it saying 'Daddy, Daddy'. He says new words each day. So Goodnight my dear husband, with love and kisses from the children too. All love, Joan

At last the news came through for which they had all been waiting – a ship to Cairo.

Saturday, 5th September 1942 – Durban

 My dearest Joan

Great news today. Hallelujah, hallelujah, hallelujah! If all goes well, we might actually be off tomorrow. I heard midday yesterday and I was really happy – as happy as I can be that is! To be off at last is wonderful. I know that there are still many, many things that could still possibly stop us going, but it really is a weight off my mind. I've rarely made so few roots in a place as I have here.

I regretted the break-up of my training camp in Birmingham and the two other camps I ran, and even regretted Cheveley and Poplar, and I was torn in two and have hardly recovered from leaving you to go abroad. But I go from here rejoicing. At times, of course, it has been very pleasant with kind and lovely people. I like Florence very much, and I like Maurice a great deal: they have both become friends. But even so, I shall be glad to go. For reasons I'm not sure I can explain, I have had moments of intense depression as the weeks drew out. I felt so responsible, that the delays were all my fault and that I ought to be doing something. Well, thank God all that is over. Of course we don't know what bloodiness may lie ahead for us, but we are moving, and for that God be praised.

With a little time still left, Maurice took John, Philip and myself out for a drive. It was especially nice as we could relax a little, knowing we were at last moving on. It was a glorious afternoon, and we drove up inland through miles of sugar cane fields, up and up as far as the Valley of a Thousand Hills, which lay in front of us. There was a long valley with high hills on either side running out into fine bluffs and headlands, covered mostly with rough grass, with here and there stretches of bush or isolated clumps of trees. The view stretched away, line after line of hills, hazy in the afternoon sunshine.

We left the car and walked. The air was fresh and warm on our cheeks, and ahead of us the Valley stretched out on either side, down a little stream which ran over broad rocks, where native children paddled and women with enormous breasts washed their clothes. The stream eventually went over a great cliff into a deep narrow valley with high limestone cliffs on either side. The trees below the rocks were still winter bare, only just beginning to show a hint of green. It was all quite lovely, but made me aware of how much I missed England and its countryside.

I had originally intended that we should all march out to the Valley and sleep out, but now that we are leaving, we probably shan't. I saw a number of birds – several Hawks and as before, flocks of red-winged Starling, which are fine creatures about the size of a Mistle Thrush, with glorious red wings. I called on Innes Gumede (the black Doctor I mentioned), to say 'good-bye' in case I didn't see him again, and then when we got back, we went to supper with Maurice and with the aid of two typewriters, we produced instructions for our departure and wrote heaps of 'Thank you' letters. Finally we dropped in on Florence for a short while to say 'Good-bye'. She kindly agreed to send you a cable from me, in case I am unable to. I shall miss them both enormously.

Today we have been packing, and all our heavy luggage has already gone. I have had a shower, and am now sitting on my bed writing to you. There is a pleasant sense of completion and finality and 'last time-ness' quite unmarred by regrets. I meant to tell you about some of those who were on the last boat now that it no longer matters, but there has been such a gap that I almost forgot. Anyway, there were five, very pleasant young Officers going out to join their regiments, with whom I messed. They had no other people with them, and have had a wonderful time out here. Women, drink, bathing, golf, tennis – in fact a perfect holiday. They are also continuing on with us on the next boat.

My cabin companion, a Mr Tait, was one of five civilians on board. He was a working engineer, widely travelled with long experience in South America, most friendly and easy to live with and a thoroughly sound and well-connected fellow. There were two other pleasant Petty Officer engineers, plus a civil servant and his wife and child of six. He must have had some extra pull to be able to be able to get them on board. The child was charming and reminded me so much of David and made me very homesick.

Then there were two rather strange Catholic women, who seemed rather silly to me; two honest-to-goodness, sensible, plain and very nice "Soldiers' and Sailors' Homes" women; and sixteen, young, not especially good-looking and rather uninteresting WRENS Officers. Perhaps I'm being unfair, as I had very little to do with them. But as you may imagine, they had a marvellous time among 400 Officers. There was nearly a marriage and god knows what else!

The Officers varied strangely according to their regiments. One regiment I really didn't take to very much at all, while another I liked enormously, and yet another I found extremely pleasant. Altogether a mixed lot, but all in all, they were very good to us, and now I wonder what our next boat will be like. I'll end this long letter and send it off. Thinking of you always.

Love Ralph

A red winged starling
"Fine creatures, about the size of a Mistle Thrush"
Photo Birds of South Africa

Map of Africa

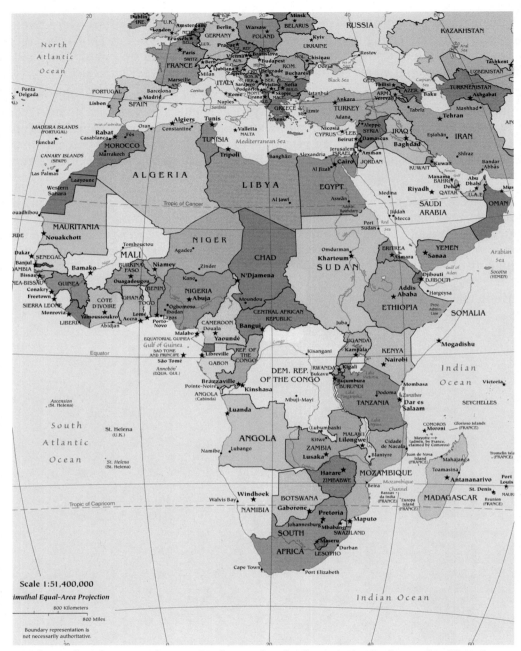

And so at last they were leaving Durban and embarking on the final stretch of their long journey from England, up the East coast of Africa through the Indian Ocean and so on up the Red Sea to Cairo.
Image World Atlas

Chapter 19
And so to Cairo
September 1942

In the previous chapter of my father's memoirs and letters, he relates in some detail the story of the journey from London to Durban with its ups and downs, shepherding a group of some 30 CO's on a troopship round the Cape. We saw how during the long five week trip, this involved maintaining morale, keeping the men occupied and preparing them for the tasks ahead.

Once in Durban, they encountered yet another hiatus as they waited for a boat to become available for the onward journey through the Indian Ocean and up the Red Sea to Suez. This period was also enormously frustrating, as all involved were only too anxious to get to the theatres of war and begin the ambulance work for which they had been trained when they originally joined the FAU.

Throughout the trying long weeks in Durban my father had to find work to occupy the Unit's time yet again, but through the extraordinary kindness of South African Friends, he had been able to provide the men with hospital training, where they gained valuable experience of tropical diseases, which would eventually stand them in good stead. They had also been royally looked after by local Friends and been able to see something of the country.

After five weeks in the city, they were at last able to embark on the final stage of their journey and make their way to Cairo. Because of the freer atmosphere on this Dutch boat, my father felt able to leave his Unit members to entertain themselves with a minimum of supervision.

[Textual: Since he received no correspondence on board ship, my mother's letters won't start again until they arrive in Cairo, where at long last he found a pile awaiting him.]

Here my father describes the rather miserable journey from Durban to Cairo......

"What can I say of the trip from Durban? What I remember chiefly is the great heat, a terrible stomach disorder which swept the whole of the ship, including even our own party and the members of the Ethiopian party who were on the same ship, and which reduced us to a state of complete collapse, making me feel like death by the day we disembarked, as I wrote to Joan..."

September 6th 1942 – In transit

Dearest Joan

It's exactly five weeks since we first docked here in South Africa, and now at long last we are on our way. Eager to board the boat, we woke early at about 5.0 this morning. The moon was still bright, but as it went down, everything became black night again, lit only by a few brilliant stars, including Orion standing on his head, which was still bright in the morning sky. Gradually a faint gleam of dawn appeared on the horizon about 6.30, and after an early breakfast we moved off towards the boat about 7.0am and by 7.30 we were all aboard.

Once we had embarked, nothing much else happened for some while, and as I write we are still lying in harbour under a glorious full moon, feeling fearfully hot in the blacked-out ship. But I am just so glad to be leaving, as I'm dreadfully tired and really hope we shall soon be off and away. When we do finally leave, I shall indeed say 'Nunc Dimitis', even though I know when we do eventually get to Cairo, there will be a much bigger and more difficult job ahead of me.

But this whole journey I regard as a job all on its own, and I shall be really thankful to finally get the boys to Cairo. Just before we left, Philip Holding's[1] boat came in (Dick's brother), who was on his way home I believe. Some of the others in the party saw him, and I was really hoping to catch up with him as well, but somehow we missed each other. Curious that he should be getting in now just as the Abyssinian party were going through, as I believe he once contemplated applying to join this group himself. I expect he will be back home before this letter even reaches you.

I've no idea how busy I will be when we finally get to Cairo, but I rather doubt if I shall be able to write quite such full letters, though I will try. I wonder how many letters you have received from me. Did you get a pair of stockings, a parcel of food, some cosmetics and a handbag, plus a book for David? And did you get a parcel of baby things from Florence? I do so wonder if things are getting through. I so look forward to getting to Cairo and finding all your letters.

I don't suppose I'm allowed to tell you what our boat is like, (though I don't think I'll be giving much away if say she is very big!) and it's such a contrast to our last boat. For one thing, instead of being all army, there is quite a mixture, of RAF, American ambulance as well as Army; in fact all sorts of odds and ends. She is thus much less strictly run than the previous boat, and a great deal more free and easy. The boys have come on board as Warrant Officers instead of Other Ranks and while their sleeping arrangements are none too wonderful, at least they have first class meals, sitting in the first class saloon, and so far they have the use of the first class lounge as well. It is certainly more tolerable for them than the previous boat.

I don't think I'll get into too much trouble if I also tell you that this is a Dutch boat and must once have been very fine, though it's now looking distinctly down at heel. I have actually been most fortunate, as I have been allocated a very nice double cabin with bathroom attached, while some of the other Officers are in much more crowded accommodation. The strangest thing ever, is that I discovered Richey Mounsey and his party including Barty Knight, are also on board, having got on at the Cape (en route for Ethiopia). It really is very good to see them both.

Later......... Today has been uneventful, and I am considerably exercised as to whether or not I should arrange anything to keep the men occupied, as some of them are likely to get terribly bored. But as they are travelling in second, it seems best to let them amuse themselves. While it is very nice that they are allowed to use the 1st class lounge, generally we have very little space, and time is short. The atmosphere is strangely informal, with the Americans and ourselves, some women, and a sprinkling of civilians. It's beginning to get very, very hot and I really wish the chaps had better sleeping accommodation.

I had quite a talk with Richey this morning about the prospects for his men out in Ethiopia. Apparently their boat broke down 34 times on the way out. I must say it's good to have Barty about too, and I have been talking with him and Gordon most of the evening about books and plays. What a queer world of coincidences this life can be! Barty and I always seem to be bumping into each other. First we met up at the Northfield Camp, then again in the London HQ, and now here we are on a troopship together out in the Indian Ocean.

There are also a number of officers with us, who I have gradually got to know and it's curious to have so many people one knows in the lounge after being on one's own for so long. In some ways this is the most peaceful part of the whole trip, and although there is a lot of vibration, the sea is perfectly calm.

Yesterday, unfortunately, something went badly wrong with the food, and I should think 75% of the first and second class passengers have had food poisoning, with continual diarrhoea and sickness, as well as in some cases, spasms of great pain. Practically all the party going to Abyssinia were tossing on their beds in misery, and six or seven of our lads were down too, including my own cabin companion, who was in a really bad way.

Altogether there were only about 20 people on the whole boat who turned up to the third sitting for dinner. Today, people are just beginning to stagger about a little. Luckily I just had slight pains and the occasional sick feeling, but I really had nothing to complain of, and I have been eating all my meals and otherwise carrying on as normal.

I think we must now be going at a fair speed as the ship is vibrating a lot, so I'm sorry about my writing. I think we are probably in an area of considerable danger, though with such a fast boat we are probably safe enough. By the standards of peacetime, I suppose there would be much to complain of, what with poisoned food and poor service (both much below the other boat, incidentally), little water in the cabins and some rather surly stewards – but by war-time standards I actually think myself pretty comfortable.

There seem to be quite a decent lot on board this boat, with six very pleasant captains at table, and a jolly little Free French Lieutenant. It's odd how so many people seem to know somebody who knows somebody! For instance, I was chatting to one of the Captains who was for a time in the same regiment as Alan Cadbury[2], and spoke most highly of him, saying what a first class officer he was. Yet another chap was at the same school as John Gough, whilst my cabin companion is a friend of the Fox family, and is now seconded from the Ministry of Labour to the Colonial Office to go and establish a Department of Labour in Palestine.

One day just follows another. We don't know where we are, nor when we shall arrive. The heat is so overwhelming that sometimes one really begins to wonder what we are doing here. This morning our cabin temperature was 84°, which simply isn't funny. During the day, the lounge is just about tolerable, but at night it's simply terrific. I really do dislike hot weather. The boat deck is like a flaming hot cooker, but even so one or two indefatigable people are out playing deck games, all wearing their solar topees and now burned brown all over. I did have a game of table tennis myself this morning, but I am very much out of practice since my frequent games at the Fire Station.

I have had some chats with the American Ambulance men. They are all so typically American – well why wouldn't they be? But I cannot discover that they have any common philosophical basis between them, as we are supposed to have. They have come straight from college and been sent overseas with scarcely any training. They are all civilians who are going to drive ambulances, and there are already several hundred of them spread all over Egypt. One wonders how such a chance collection of men, without any common background, training, tradition or discipline, will succeed.

For all our oddities and shortcomings, we do derive some benefit from our Unit tradition and loyalty, as well as our Christian foundation. And I'm quite sure we are better trained especially on the medical side. The Officers don't quite know what to make of them – or us, for that matter. It's actually rather an anxious business letting our chaps loose in the lounge, but thankfully so far, all is well. I insist on them all changing for dinner, though tonight I have said that they may wear shorts instead of slacks. With a bit of luck, I think we should be in the Red Sea tomorrow. Good night for now, my darling and God rest you. Love Ralph

Even my father finally succumbed to the plague, lying in his cabin hoping it would pass.......

Thursday, September 10th 1942

Dearest one

I didn't write yesterday, as I'm afraid I too, finally succumbed to the plague, with a general nausea, diarrhoea and stomach ache. So I just lay in my cabin all afternoon and all night. I probably wasn't that ill in truth, but as there is no air in the cabin, except from the blowers and fan, one is afraid of getting a chill, especially when you are already wringing wet with sweat. Quite soon I shall run out of clean clothes. But everything is comparative I suppose. In peace one would have said the atmosphere, the heat and the noise were intolerable; but in war-time it is relative luxury and I think of the many worse situations one might be in.

I'm sitting here smoking a really foul tobacco, as we coast up the Red Sea in flaming heat. We are ahead of schedule and so now going quite slowly. It is over 90° in the cabins, and I don't even attempt to go on deck much before 4.0 o'clock. But even so one just lies and drips away and each morning the sheets and pyjamas are wet through. Everyone is just going about in sweat-soaked shirts. I was getting so short of clean clothes that I had to wash a lot of things through this morning in what little water there was. I do try to set a good example and have changed every night for dinner, though last night, because of the heat, I only changed into another pair of shorts and shirt. We shall all be very thankful to get in, though I fear the getting ashore will be pretty unpleasant.

This evening, I was talking to one of the Americans on board, who it turns out is a Quaker. He is a very nice fellow from Moorestown[3]; a town-planner and landscape architect, who has been in Japan studying Japanese gardens, in the hope of picking up some ideas which he could develop for a new style of garden for a new type of house. Since then he has been out in Florida, working on a housing scheme there. We found quite a lot to talk about, and he was particularly interested in my account of the way the Trust uses trees in our planning schemes. It was really pleasant to be talking of Cherry trees, and Poplars and Maples instead of the war. I can't remember his name, though I think it might have been Collins – Leslie Collins maybe.

You may remember my cousin Helen Peile, though I'm not sure you ever met her. I believe she gave us a cream jug for our wedding. But mother, Millior and I stayed with her in 1924 and 1925 and we had a very happy time. She had a brother, Sir Harry Peile, I think, living quite near, who had two sons Haswell and George. We used to see quite a lot of George, who was about my age. Well there is a Captain aboard, who is in the Royal Artillery, whose face was vaguely familiar, and when I spoke to him, it turned out to be George, whom I hadn't seen since '25. He was very pleasant, and remembered us and asked after mother and Millior. He said that cousin Helen is still alive but now completely bedridden. Curiously enough there was a Captain on our last boat, who came from their part of the world, and told me that Haswell was a Major out in the Middle East, but George told me that sadly he had been captured at Tobruk.

We should be in in about two days now, and I have just distributed what is, I hope, our final landing instructions. I do fervently hope that all goes well and that we find that Peter Gibson is there to meet us. Last night, it was so hot, I slept on the 1st class deck and there must have been at least half of the first class passengers of both sexes who were there too. Even then I was still hot, but at least there was a warm breeze blowing, and though the deck was hard to lie on, it was preferable to being in my cabin. Actually it was rather pleasant, lying and looking at the stars and the waning moon, and gradually a whole flood of light as the sun came up.

There is one relic of the former splendor of this ship, which is beautifully air-conditioned and which must be at least 20° cooler than all the rest of the boat, and that's the hairdressing saloon. I was in there yesterday having a trim, and had about half an hour's wait, before I was attended to, and it was positively chilly. Johnnie Gough maintains that spending even a short period in there, helps one regain one's sanity and contemplate life more calmly. I really think that it if I had to live forever in such heat, I should either fall apart, or go mad – or possibly both!

Since we left Durban, I have managed to do a fair amount of reading. I re-read *Northanger Abbey,* which despite much that is delightful, I find the least appealing of Austen's books. Nevertheless, JA is always wonderful reading, and even more so in these conditions. Since starting out, I've read *P&P, Emma* and *Persuasion* as well. What a delightful, sheltered life they all lead – such comparatively small problems to contend with – 'should I go for a walk this morning?'; 'Is he really in love with me?' No nonsense about the heat and the tropics, or the sweat and the luggage!

I've also re-read *Antony and Cleopatra,* which I persist in thinking one of the most magnificent of all Shakespeare's plays: it is royal and colourful and full of splendor. But then I love both parts of *Henry IV* almost more than any. Falstaff is such an exquisite creation, that I could read it over and over again. How he pooh-poohed 'honour and duty' and how he would have railed at the foolishness of leaving home and comforts to waste one's time travelling in the tropics!

I managed to finish Gibbon Vol 1 as well, which goes from Augustus to Constantine, and enjoyed it very much. He has such style, all so well arranged, with good perspective and forward movement, and in such a stately fashion. In Gibbon's world, for all that he depicts decline, ruin, murder and disaster, you feel a certain safety and security. His orderly mind reduces the Roman panorama to the stately order of the 18th century and it is almost as if one were looking at the pageant passing on the stage, while one sits in the stalls.

I think I'll end this long letter and seal it up ready for post when we arrive. Tell my mother that I think of her and Millior and send them all my love. I do hope D has received some of my letters to him and I will write again soon.
Dear love, always your own Ralph.

At long last, nearly three months after they left England, they finally arrive in Cairo and slowly begin the task of settling in to another new country.........but not before my father sends greetings for his sixth wedding anniversary.......

Saturday, September 19th 1942 - Cairo

Darling Joan
I am afraid this must be brief as I have so much to sort out. Two days ago was our sixth wedding anniversary and I do hope you received some letters from me as well as a cable, which Florence kindly said she would send, in case I was still at sea. I know this will arrive weeks after the day, but it brings my thanks for all you are to me and have done. It was indeed a happy day and a most triumphantly right decision. I could not have been more blessed. Bless you my dear.

Well, we got up at an unearthly hour this morning and for some awful reason I had a frightful stomach again with diarrhoea and felt like death. I staggered about and doped myself and slowly began to feel better. After the usual delays we got our instructions and after still further delays got ashore in a lighter. We ate our rations on the quay and then formed up – ourselves, Richey Mounsey and his Abyssinian group and a few other army odds and ends - and marched up to the Camp (think of me marching the army about!).

Children waiting at home

"David and Antony send their love, and kisses from all of us."

David and Antony
"Looking after one another"

Chapter 20
Cairo and Alexandria
September – October 1942

Having finally reached Cairo, my father, now a much relieved 'Officer in charge', describes his first impressions........

On our arrival in Cairo, frankly none of us was feeling at our best and our place of disembarkation was hot, sandy and smelly, and seemed altogether about the last place God ever made, only redeemed by seeing the welcoming faces of Peter Gibson and John Bailey driving toward us in the staff car.

Saturday, September 19th 1942 - Cairo

My dear Joan
Well we've arrived and despite not feeling my best, it is actually really rather exciting to be here in a fresh country – and to see Peter and John Bailey again and exchange news, and to find that we have a car and best of all to discover a pile of letters and airgraphs from you and also some missives from Gordon Square. It is amazing how such a little euphoria can triumph in a wonderful way over physical tiredness and lack of food in such situations. Though I have had no food from dinner on Saturday to tea on Sunday - save an egg, an orange, and some water - I seem to have survived! We did eventually have a little tea at some Club or other, which looked out over the canal, and so at last I have time to read through your letters and cables, which cheered me up no end. God bless you: how I've missed you.

Then we were up and off again to see about our baggage, which had still not come ashore; back once more to Camp for meetings and yet more meetings, first to explain the whole situation to Peter G, and then to talk about the plan for the future. Finally, Michael Vaizey and Richey Mounsey joined with us for a much-needed supper in the Mess and an equally needed pint of beer to quench a raging thirst!

Afterwards we again went down to see about the baggage to find Philip Sanford, Barty Knight and the baggage party only just getting ashore, with the baggage still not unloaded. Poor souls, they fully expected that they would all end up having to sleep on the dockside, to prevent everything from being stolen, left unguarded.

We slept in Camp, which was warm, and not too oppressive and above us a sky of bright, wonderful stars and all the old constellations keeping us company. By the end of the day, I was really rather elated: we had managed to get here, we were feeling well – fairly well anyway - and we had all managed to meet up. A new country and new conditions.
Dear love for now, Ralph

—

As he described, on arrival my father collected a whole lot of my mother's letters, which were awaiting him in the Cairo office, some sent while he was in Durban and some while he was on the boat to Cairo. I have grouped a number of them together, much as he would have found them. Though many of them would undoubtedly have arrived much later, I have put them in the date order in which they were written, to give them a sequential sense in relation to the time line of my father's, and I hope will add to their relevance in the story. They really speak for themselves, so I won't add any further commentary......

Thursday, September 10th 1942 – Wolverhampton (Airgraph)

My darling

I am so delighted to hear this morning from Gordon Square, of your safe arrival in Egypt. It is wonderful news and I am very relieved and happy to get it after so many weeks. Also your Airgraph from Durban arrived this morning, but still no proper letter since I received three letters weeks ago. I shall probably receive the Egypt letters before the others! I do hope darling that you found lots of my letters waiting for you on arrival.

I have written every week with several Airgraphs and Airmail postcards in addition. We are all well and David sends special love. David and I spent this last weekend with your mother, who seems well, but rather tired, and I saw the Keens and Heather, who all asked after you. I took David to meeting and he behaved very well.

I am sure you will have received a great welcome from Peter Gibson and Barty. I hope you are well, my dearest and reasonably happy. I think of you always and love you very dearly. All our fondest love, ever yours Joan.

Saturday, September 12th 1942 – Wolverhampton (Airgraph)

Darling

I am thinking of you so much and picture you at last at your new destination. How thankful you must be after so many weeks of travel. I do hope it isn't too hot and uncomfortable. I very much wonder if you have set up headquarters yet, and where you are living and whether your address is the same.

Winifred and Llewellyn go away on the 16th to Criccieth for a week and David starts school again on the 17th. He is so eager to go back. We're all well, and the children have been able to play a good deal in the garden, as we've had some lovely days recently – brilliant sun, but not too hot. I know how hot Cairo can be, and wonder if you are able to bathe at all?

How are the men faring? Are they all a good lot of chaps? I do hope you will be able to smooth out the difficulties. But I know you will do your job well, as I always have so much faith in you. So many questions!

Dear love, Joan.

Monday, September 14th 1942 – Wolverhampton (Airletter)

Dear darling

Thank you so much for the cable, received this morning, saying that you had got my letters and sending special love for the 17th. I do wonder how many letters from me you received, and really hope that they all got through. I have pictured you plodding through them all, and trust you haven't got too bored with them. But anyway, you will know how dearly I love you and that I am thinking of you every minute of the day.

Darling you know that I shall be thinking of you especially on the 17th and our 6 years of wonderful happiness. I do want to thank you sweetheart for making me so happy and for our two dear children. You have been a perfect husband and I love you more now than ever and you must know I only live for our reunion. Oh God speed that happy day.

Dear heart, how I long to hear your news. So far none of your long letters have arrived. Perhaps before many days I shall get a letter from Egypt. I do hope the books I've sent you for Xmas will get through all right. I'm longing to know what you have sent us in your parcels from Durban.

I wonder if you are now down to the real work of the purpose of your long journey. I am sure they will be pleased to see you, and no doubt you are relieved to be there after all the hold ups. Oh, it's so annoying not getting your letters, as there is so much I long to know about everything you are doing and thinking. All your first impressions; if you are feeling the heat; if you are well and not too tired; if you are enjoying the company and the country. Do write and tell me everything my dear.

Well, life here goes on much the same. The boys are amazingly well and full of fun and energy. I hope sometime to get a film for my camera, so that I can take some photographs of them, as they look so jolly. Do send me a photograph of you if you have any snaps taken.

I hope all will be quiet while Win and Llew are away. Your mother is very good sending chocolates and sweets for the boys. I think maybe she is even a little fond of me these days. In a way your being away has drawn us closer together, though I do wish she wouldn't sign herself MCB! She sent me a letter from Millior for me to read, who says she is very well and still fairly energetic. She is coming up to stay with your mother on the 3rd or 4th of October. I'm struggling to finish two little coats for the baby.

Apparently your mother and Lydia[1] had a row (if that is possible!) and Lydia threatened to leave, as now that Mrs Fisher cannot go in, Lydia has additional work. However, it seems to have blown over and all is well again at the moment. Lydia has quite an easy time really, although your mother can of course, be very particular and quite demanding. But I did feel rather sorry for your mother, as she is getting old now, and is very worried over Millior and I'm sure she will be glad when M's baby arrives.

My mother is well and keeps up her job, although her feet ache a great deal from so much standing around in the shop. Antony adores her and David too, of course.

Norman Birkett[2] was speaking at Bournville Meeting last week about his visit to America. I would have liked to have gone. Afterwards he went on to the Manor where Cousin Elsie was entertaining about 1000 Home Guards and their wives!!

By the way I wrote a note to Mr Appleton and told him you had arrived, as I thought he would like to know. I will write some more tomorrow as I want to write a quick note to your mother and thank her for the letter she sent.

Good night dearest husband. God bless thee and keep thee safe always. I do love you so dearly. As ever Joan

Wednesday, September 16th 1942 – Wolverhampton (Air Pc)

Dearest....I don't think I told you much about our visit to your mother, so I will start another letter tonight or tomorrow about it. But just to say that we had such a nice visit there, and the time has simply flown past since. David has already packed up a Christmas parcel for you, of tooth brush and paste, before going to bed and has even written a little note to wish you a happy Christmas. We are both starting back to Wolverhampton in about an hour's time, so I must go and pack up our things.

So all my loving thoughts and prayers.

Ever thine, Joan

This next long letter describes my mother's visit to see her mother-in-law – taking David to Quaker meeting, wrapping parcels to send to our father and visiting friends and relatives – and longing for more news from Cairo.......

Saturday, September 19th 1942 – Wolverhampton

My dearest One

I just wanted to write again and tell you a little bit more of our visit to your mother's. David and I started from here about 5 pm on the Saturday, after I had put Antony to bed. He was still rather poorly when I left, but when we got back I found him quite well and jolly. We had rather a ghastly journey over to Selly Oak, as all the buses were so crowded and I had so many parcels as well as trying to nurse David as well! I took a basket of pears and our rations in addition to the ordinary luggage, and your mother seemed pleased to see us. She gave us a nice tea and I put David to bed, but both nights he found difficulty in getting off to sleep until about 10.30. I think he might have been rather frightened of all the fresh noises like the trams, or even a little nervous since we've been having all these air raids, so I now leave the bedroom door ajar, showing a little light. But fortunately the raids have been less for the last few nights and so the nights have been quieter.

On Sunday we all went to meeting with D looking very nice in his new coat and talking politely to everyone. He went into the children's class and wasn't the least shy, but they all came back in at 11.40, which was really too early for the youngest. Ernest Sawdon[3] went to sleep and Mary Mason got up to pray at 7 minutes past 12, so poor David sighed rather audibly "Oh mummy, I'm so tired. When is it going to finish?"

After meeting I went round to the Keens to see if I could borrow their ladder to pick some apples. They gave me a great welcome and asked after you and sent their love. I thought they had aged considerably since I saw them last. Our Polish refugees, the Tritsch's have gone away to the seaside for two weeks. I must say they get about a lot! I also went round to see Heather (Cadbury) and little Andrew, and they seemed well. She said she had a guilty conscience, having not written or phoned and was quite pleased to see me I think. She has been lucky having Mickey quite near, being at camp for so long.

When I got back Enid had cycled round to see your mother. Apparently Roger had gone on his own to stay with Alfred and Millior for the weekend. Your mother told me later, that she thought J&E were spoiling Roger too much, waiting on him all the time. Your brother so adores him that he can do no wrong.

I am going through a tricky stage with David. He needs very careful training and I find him rather difficult at times. He isn't as obedient as he should be. Oh, how I miss you and your help and advice. I find it increasingly difficult living in someone else's house and I do wish we could be at home all together again. I'm missing so many things just now and life seems very complicated.

We left your mother on Monday morning and she kindly came to Selly Oak and saw us on to the bus, which was a great help. We arrived home in time for lunch and Antony gave us a great welcome. He is such a darling now, though full of mischief. Your mother helped David pack a parcel for you. It was only toothpaste and a brush, but he loved getting it wrapped up and posted. I do hope you will receive it safely. I believe this week is the last week for sending parcels if they are to arrive for Christmas.

There are quite a few new Penguin books out recently, and I wonder if you would like any. I'm afraid you will soon come to the end of your reading matter. I am going into Wolverhampton tomorrow and I'll see if I can see something that you might like. I notice in Horace's journal, he bemoaned the lack of books out in India, and I do hope you have enough. Do please let me know if there is something special you'd like me to send.

I wonder if you have seen Horace's journal letter, written en-route (from Lagos?). It was most interesting and he said how much he liked Richard Symonds and if he hadn't been there, he would have gone mad! Millior told me that 8 or 9 more people are hoping to go out to India. I do wonder who they will choose.

Oh darling, I do miss you so much, and the longing doesn't seem to ease with the months. Just remember that you have all my love for always and always, in this life and beyond. I just long for the blessed day when we are united together again.

Every morning I rush downstairs, hoping to find a letter from you, as I want to know so many things. It's now nearly three months since I heard from you, which seems an eternity.

How thankful you must be to have reached your destination and how pleased Peter Gibson and party must be to have you with them at last. I think these past weeks must have been very trying and difficult for you and I hope and pray for you continually, darling one. I know you will have handled every difficult job with thought and care and I am very proud of thee dear.

I wonder if Tom Tanner will pay you a visit before long? Do write and tell me the details of all you are doing and thinking. I long so much for every scrap of news. I will try and send an Airgraph towards the end of the week. Perhaps by then I shall have heard from you and can answer your letter.

David is now having his mid-day rest and Antony – the scamp – won't sleep today, so I have to put him in his cot to play while I finish this letter. David has just come down half-dressed and wants to add his love.

I must take the boys for a walk. It is so nice and sunny. I do hope it won't be too hot for you now darling. Reg (brother) is at last a Leading Air Craftsman and is rather pleased. He so longs for his commission, but I don't know if it will come. He is still in Ireland.

Goodbye for now my own darling, my dearest husband. I am thinking of you always. God bless and watch over you.
Your own Joan.

—

This is obviously quite a difficult period for my mother, longing for the receipt of letters which is her only link to my father, finding coping with two children very demanding and missing a father's wisdom and advice; and longing for someone to share her thoughts with and to be able to talk about books and plays as they used to. She ends with one of their favourite poems.........

Monday, September 21st 1942 – Wolverhampton

My dearest Ralph

I am so miserable with my longing for a letter. I have still had none from South Africa. Perhaps I shall soon get one now that you are settled. [.....] Life is very lonely without you and your letters do cheer me so. [....] However, I am at least happy that you are receiving my letters all right. [....] I miss you too with the children - most terribly. I'm finding David is going through quite a difficult time just now. I know that I probably don't deal with him always in the right way. Do pray for me dear that I might have more patience and understanding. Antony is a darling, but so very active and full of mischief, that at the end of the day I'm very tired. I've been busy all this week with W & L away, there is more work to do and mother is out every afternoon and all day Saturday.

David is at school each morning this term and loving it. He learns quickly and is very intelligent and bright. He is a dear child really, but he is certainly going through a problematic stage, and it isn't easy to get to the root of the trouble always. He is very nervous of being left in the dark now since the raids, and insists on having the door wide open and a light on the landing. I try to be understanding as I can over this, especially as I know I was sometimnes afraid as a child too. I do so often wish you were here to help me darling. Each day is like any other – filled with routine jobs. I take the children walks in the afternoons, and in the evenings I usually sit mending, knititng or reading and sometimes listening to the wireless. Last night Max Beerbohm[4] was on, and was most amusing talking about advertisements, saying how most of them were so hideous and badly displayed. If it is published in The Listener, I will try and send it to you.

As I mentioned the other day, I am reading *A Leaf in the Storm* by Lin Yutang, which is good as novels go and certainly his are more worthwhile than most. It contains recent accounts of the Chinese war with Japan and a bit about the guerrilla fighting. I have a huge list of books to get through, but there just isn't enough time. I do try and read in bed as well, especially poetry. I see the biography of Octavia Hill[5] has just been published. I'd love to get hold of it.

I am wearing my new brown costume today with a blue blouse, which I am very pleased with as it has a good cut. I wish you could see me in it! David has started another letter to you, but I'm afraid it must wait to go with the next week's letter, as it takes him quite a time to write it.

My dearest darling husband, you are forever in my thoughts and prayers. I do so wonder how you are spending each day and I try to picture you busy in your work, Have you heard any news from Dick Symonds and Horace? They seem to be finding plenty of work to do, and to be in touch with many groups and parties. I think they are having an interesting time. Is there any news from Duncan yet?

I see they are holding another Camp at the Manor in October. I wonder who will run it. I believe Michael Cadbury did well with the last. Do you hear from Tom Tanner? I don't hear anything from Gordon Square or the Hostel. [....] Life is narrow these days - inevitably so - I don't grumble, thousands of wives are in the same boat, but I do wish sometimes I could get out and see more people and hear lectures or music. However, the children are my big job at present and I try to bring them up as you would wish, though I know how I lack much that I ought to have.

Darling, remember always my faith in you dear heart. You are my inspiration. Everything in you I admire and adore. You have all I want and look for in a man. All that is fine and noble and good. I am indeed lucky in having such a husband. How I miss you now. Do you remember Elizabeth Barrett Browning's wonderful 'Sonnet from the Portuguese'? It expresses my every thought for thee dear one............

> How do I love thee? Let me count the ways
> I love thee to the depth and breadth and height
> My soul can reach, when feeling out of sight
> For the ends of being and ideal grace.
> I love thee to the level of every day's
> Most quiet need, by sun and candle-light.
> I love thee freely, as men strive for right.
> I love thee purely, as they turn from praise.
> I love thee with the passion put to use
> In my old griefs, and with my childhood's faith.
> I love thee with a love I seemed to lose
> With my lost saints. I love thee with the breath,
> Smiles, tears, of all my life; and, if God choose, I
> shall but love thee better after death.

Right now the children are playing in the Nursery and all is quiet, except for their laughter coming down to me. I must soon take them out while it is still fine, as today, though warm has been showery. I so wish you could see Antony. He is growing up so fast and is now a sturdy young boy and such fun. He is talking a good deal, though can't yet put sentences together. The other day I found him in the bath, turning the taps on. He worships David.

I do hope you are keeping well dear heart and I trust you won't get that germ that's forever flying around Egypt. No doubt everyone is giving you plenty of advice on everything under the sun! I wonder when you will go to Syria and Ethiopia – not yet I expect, as it will take you time to investigate and clear up some of the things in Egypt.

I hope you are settling down now and still feeling glad you accepted the job. I am sure you will find it interesting, and in years to come, no doubt, you will be pleased you went, and I like to think you are seeing some of the places I visited and the friends I made.

Darling, I am so proud of you. Write often my sweetheart. David sends his love to you and kisses from us all. You are ever in my thoughts. God bless you and watch over you always.

Ever you loving and adoring Joan.
PS Mother sends love to you too. Another Airgraph later in the week.

———

Now that my father and the Unit had at last arrived in Cairo, the work for which they had come began in earnest. My father had been appointed Officer Commanding Middle East to co-ordinate the ever increasing number of Unit sections that were now operating in the Middle East, from the Red Cross and St John's, to Hadfield Spears and the British Army Medical Corps. His function was to develop a unified policy based on an assessment of the value of the work that was being done in various fields, to balance conflicting claims for extra personnel that might be available, to pay regular visits to sections, to represent the FAU to military HQ, and to keep the executive Committee at home abreast of any developments of new work in his area. Here my father explains..............

In the Middle East at that time, the Unit had some thirty men with the 8th Army, which was increased to over sixty by the arrival of our party, and there were some on-site clinics in Syria such as the Hadfield Spears Mobile Units[6], which served with the Fighting French throughout the Syrian, Middle East and North African campaigns, and which relied on a section of the FAU for its transport and medical work. These were separate sections and before Middle East HQ were set up in Cairo, there was little co-ordination between them.

We arrived straight into a first class row between the War Office and voluntary bodies such as British Red Cross Society and the FAU, regarding difficulties over the newly concluded 'Agreement' from the War Office, in which the rights of FAU men were to be circumscribed and were unacceptable to the Unit. I was to spend much of my early weeks in Egypt trying to sort this tricky situation out, as it went to the very heart of the ability of pacifists to work alongside the military. I wrote home to Joan in a note of some exasperation........

Monday, September 21st 1942 - Cairo

My dearest Joan

My first task on arriving here has been to sort out a huge row between the War Office and the voluntary bodies such as ourselves and the British Red Cross Society, regarding our difficulties over the so-called 'Agreement' with the WO which would deprive us of much of our independence. It is certain that if Queen Mary had 'Calais' written on her heart, I will have 'Agreement' written on mine!

I can't go into it all here, but it is threatening to rather overwhelm me. Yesterday afternoon proved to be the most hectic yet, as I tried to sort matters out. I spent the whole day doing the rounds visiting the BRCS Commissioner and his assistant, the Directorate of Medical Services and his assistant and many others and their assistants! As well as all these meetings, I paid a visit to Camp and had long talks with Mike Rowntree.

Eventually, at the end of a long day, I slept in a *pension* in Cairo, where the Unit is now staying, with both Elliott Burgess Smith and Douglas McKenzie as part of the section. They are a fine lot and it was really good to see them all again and regain some sense of sanity, after so many sensitive disagreements. [.....]

All my love, Ralph

—

To set the background to the Middle East campaign and the situation the FAU found themselves in, perhaps a little history is needed. Britain had taken control of Egypt as far back as 1882, making it almost a de facto colony. And although the British had granted Egypt its independence in 1922, they still continued to station troops there and support the royal government, first under King Faoud and later King Farouk. They thus retained both political influence as well as military control. The battle for North Africa in 1940 therefore, was largely a struggle to retain control of the Suez Canal and to gain access to vitally needed oil from the Middle East and raw materials from Asia.

Oil especially, had become the most important strategic commodity, due to the increased mechanization of modern armies. Britain, which by this time had a completely mechanized army, was particularly dependent on Middle Eastern oil. In addition, the Canal provided Britain with a link to her overseas territories, which was part of a lifeline that ran through the Mediterranean. Thus, the North African campaign and the naval campaign for the Mediterranean were extensions of each other.

So, although the Egyptian forces actually played no role in the War, the Suez Canal certainly did, and whilst the British owned it, the Axis forces, especially Italy under Mussolini, wanted it. With the increasing importance of North Africa, the Royal Navy moved its Mediterranean war Headquarters from Malta to Alexandria, and with the importance of Suez in mind, Britain made Alexandria and Cairo their military bases. British and French naval power, which had previously been dominant in the Mediterranean, suddenly found after the fall of France, that the military balance had radically changed. Not only was Britain now alone, but Italy with a powerful fleet and with army forces in neighbouring Libya, declared war. This brought the campaign to the borders of Egypt, and in 1940 the Italian dictator Mussolini, ordered the Italian Army, then based in Libya, to invade Egypt.

By the beginning of 1941 however, the British had driven them back and then proceeded to drive into Libya themselves, taking Tobruk and seemed poised to take Bengazzi, when Hitler dispatched Rommel to North Africa with his German force, the infamous Afrika Korps. There then followed a see-saw battle in the Western Desert, which only after General Montgomery was appointed to take charge of the 8th Army and, helped by generous American supplies, did the superior British forces achieve victory at El Alamain in October 1942. This was basically the political situation that the FAU found themselves in when they arrived in Cairo in 1942 and a major part of the FAU's operations during the war was undertaken in North Africa and the Middle East, working alongside the British and French armies. Importantly, as Tegla Davies wrote, this also became .....

".....a test of whether pacifists could serve alongside their fellows in the Army without on the one hand feeling aloof, nor on the other that they were violating the integrity of their conscience."

So far the understanding between the Unit and the Army had been on an informal basis. General Orders were agreed from time to time to meet particular situations, such as the Unit being allowed Army rations, and petrol and oil for its vehicles. But now, in an attempt to regularize the status of all voluntary bodies, the War Office in London produced a very formal and detailed 'Agreement', in which the position and rights of FAU men were clearly delineated. All too clearly for most people, as it made the Unit part of 'the core military establishment', which meant that all Unit members working with the Army would be considered part of the military strength, and would once again raise the critical question as to whether the Unit was being too closely absorbed into the military.

Under this new 'Agreement' the War Office would take over responsibility for such matters as accommodation of Unit members, previously carried out by the Red Cross, which could mean military barracks, thus depriving the Unit of its own headquarters. Discussions ensued for weeks with my father to-ing and fro-ing between the two camps, in an attempt to determine a formula which would prove satisfactory to both sides and would clearly delineate where ultimate responsibility lay. Eventually, a solution was agreed, which finally ensured that the Unit would remain completely independent of both the Army and the Red Cross, and the FAU agreed to pay all its own bills for its own accommodation and its own Headquarters.

Before long my father was installed in a flat at Bab el Louk in downtown Cairo, as Officer in charge, where he was joined by Peter Gibson, responsible for British Army work, Michael Rowntree for the Hadfield Spears Hospital section, John Gough for work with the Syria Clinics, and Eric Green for finance.

Some doubts still remained about 'the Agreement' which continued to lurk in people's minds and there were members of the Unit who wondered whether they had worried about individual points that didn't really matter, and perhaps under the stress of war and desert life, were seeing the issues out of proportion. But Tegla Davies insists that this was not the case.......

"The issues were not unimportant; they were all part of the mental and spiritual struggle of the pacifist in determining how far he could correlate his anxiety to serve the wounded, with his determination to maintain certain principles which were of vital importance to him. The great majority of members would say that it was worth it; that the work itself was also worth it, and that if pacifist witness meant anything, it stands out in far greater relief when troublesome problems arise to which an answer must be found.

On the field of battle the pacifist is at least conspicuous, though he may sometime fail to live up to his beliefs. On the individual member of the Unit the effect was two-fold. It made him more conscious of his pacifism, because he was so often up against things which were a challenge to it. On the other hand, many felt that, with one small compromise after another, their faith was losing its freshness; their pacifism was in danger of being acclimatized to war."

So now with this troublesome problem largely settled, the Unit could begin to concentrate on the tasks for which they came. Once they were truly settled in, the Unit would divide its time between Cairo and Alexandria, but the problem of accommodation was still crucial. Before the 'Agreement' was even contemplated, Peter Gibson who had led the first Unit party to the Middle East a year previously, had stumbled upon Daly's House in Alexandria, a large and comfortable place on the sea front, presided over by the wonderful Madame Haddad. In anticipation of increased numbers, he had taken over the whole of the house as well as a villa next door.

However, it was also clear that premises would soon be needed in Cairo as well, which was a far more convenient centre than Alexandria, and so arrangements were made to take over a fourth floor flat next door to Bab el Louk station – not the most salubrious part of Cairo – but convenient. Here my father gives a picturesque description of the Cairo flat in a report to Gordon Square......

In the street outside there is a gharry-stand, which is a sort of horse-drawn taxi service, and it's always a pleasure to watch the Cairo gharry drivers as they look after their horses so well. Down the street opposite was a market and a roller-skating rink from which, from a certain hour in the morning until late at night, we could hear the raucous sound of records played over a loudspeaker. The best thing about the flat is that we have four wonderful Egyptian servants, who we got by great luck from an American Archeological Mission. They are perfectly trained, and cook, wait and clear everything away beautifully. It all seems slightly immoral, but it does mean that we can all get on with our work. There are some twenty people here, but with Egyptian servants and a ménage run most ably by Eric Green, it all seems to work out well. Never before, or ever again I expect, shall I be so well looked after.

—

And here in a letter home, he writes a description for my mother..........

Wednesday September 23rd 1942 - Cairo

My dearest

Well here we are here at last, and now settling in to our new Cairo Headquarters, in a down town area known as Bab el Louk. The flat is really quite noteworthy. It's on the top floor and quite large with several airy bedrooms, a dining room and lounge, set round a central court with a nice-sized roomy office and a balcony which runs along the front providing a good view onto the street below.

To the left is the station, which before was only used by electric trains, and was comparatively innocuous, but since it has been lengthened to take steam trains, has become something of a nuisance, as black smoke now invades the bathrooms, and the vibration causes the tiles on the walls to fall down. I have spent most of today trying to sort such matters out.

I have driven a lot today, as I must get used to it. It is all right hand, and as far as I can see, sheer luck if you don't crash into someone. I have written quite a lot of letters to day - to the Square and to you. And now I'm off back to the camp as the lads seem all rather unhappy and depressed. So I shall have to do my best to cheer them up.

I had tea yesterday with Douglas Allen and his wife, they are friends of mother's and knew her when she was a girl, saying how lovely she was. They asked to be remembered tell her.

Love for now Ralph

PS. Tell David I've sent him a special letter for his birthday with all my love for a great day.

The Gharry stand outside the FAU office in Bab el Louk, Cairo
"All day there is incessant noise, with a line of two-horse-cabs, known as gharrys, drawn up in the centre of the street."
Photo Cairo History Society

The Mediterranean Area during World War II

Friends House Library

Friday, 25th September 1942 – Cairo

Dearest Joan

I rose at 6.30 this morning, and was able to read your letters. It was wonderful to hear from you again and to see your writing. I am so sorry that you have been ill. Please do take care of yourself. I have so much rushing about to do today; sorting out new premises and the like, but I will answer them properly later.

I had thought most of our troubles regarding the 'Agreement' were over, but sadly, the crisis still rages, with all sides digging in. For instance, yesterday I had the stickiest of interviews with the Red Cross, and yet another in prospect this morning. But on the other hand, when I visited the Army Medical Services today, everything went smoothly, as happily I seem to be on very good terms with them.

Then again, when later I made yet another trip out to see Hadfield-Spears, things there were still very tricky. So as you will gather, just at present we are working about twelve hours a day, and it's difficult to grasp all the new problems without getting very tired; so please excuse these somewhat incoherent letters. The good news is that the weather though hot, is thankfully not too oppressive, and is really very lovely, so instead of uniforms we can wear shirts and shorts all day.

All my love for now

Ralph

My father is gradually finding his feet, and generally getting accustomed to being in Cairo and to driving on the right hand side, and negotiating the donkeys and camels, as he writes………

Saturday, 26th September 1942

Dearest Joan

Well we've now been in Cairo for a few days, but it's really too early to express my feelings about it. I love the clear sky and the sun, which is hot but not over much. I like the curious mixture of people here, from our Army and Airforce, to the local Egyptians both Arabs and Muslims. Then for a while, the ever present camels and donkeys are fascinating. But on the other hand the city is ugly and dirty and smelly and noisy and full of beggars. As I mentioned before, the driving is on the right-hand side of the road, but no-one has the slightest road sense and possesses even less manners. I have driven a lot today, and am slowly getting accustomed to it.

Today I saw Mike Rowntree and discussed Richey Mounsey's progress out here and it seems that all is going satisfactorily in that direction. Later I had still further discussions with the Red Cross regarding negotiations with the Army, which was not so satisfactory. Somehow, in between I have managed to squeeze a few moments to write some letters and a brief airgraph to you, but then it was on to Camp to give a short talk to the lads, who at the moment are all rather disgruntled and jaded.

I had a brief lunch in camp in the Officers' mess, before making a call to Richey following my talks with Mike, and then driving out to see Hadfield Spears Unit, who are stationed under the Pyramids. But don't ask for my opinion on this crisis, as with matters still bubbling up all the time, I'm not sure I can form one yet. Thus the days continue in a hectic blur of activity, with talks with the men, back to the office to sign the lease for our new Unit Headquarters here, and then on to see the Red Cross.

When eventually I got back to our Unit flat, David de Renzy-Martin called in to see me. He's Angela's brother and is out here as part of the 8th army. He seems much younger than Angela, though they are actually twins, but very likeable and I chatted to him for about three quarters of an hour. I hope to see him again on Thursday.
Ever my love, Ralph

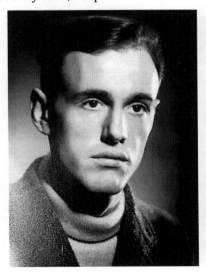 

David de Renzy-Martin and his twin sister Angela.
David joined up and was in the 8th Army, while Angela joined the FAU in 1941, initially working in the office, but later going out to Egypt and then in Yugoslavia helping refugees.
Photos courtesy of Jessica Sinclair Loutit

My father's reports to Gordon Square describe well the offices in the two cities.......

Our great lack in the early days was not having a regular typist, and so long as I was in Cairo we never had more than one, and even though he was an extremely efficient man, who came in for an hour between six and seven, we still have to do a good deal of typing ourselves, which in my case is not especially good. With Unit premises in both Alexandria and Cairo, I have become very familiar with the desert road between the two cities, often driving with Peter Gibson at the wheel, which is an education in itself !

After Cairo, the magnificent sea-front at Alexandria was always a pleasant change. And of course, there was Daly's House. To begin with accommodation for the Unit had been hard to find there, with the men sleeping in a rather dubious hotel or in transit billets at Mustapha Barracks, where they were bitten to bits by the mosquitos, which left everyone very irritable. But by chance Peter Gibson discovered Daly's House, a large and very comfortable place right on the sea front, presided over by the redoubtable Madame Haddad, who was in her element looking after 'her boys' as she called us, and provided us with the semblance of civilization, away from the trials of the desert.

Tegla Davies expands:

"Meanwhile at Daly's, though it was not their home, there was always a warm welcome. The delightful and motherly French-Syrian, Madame Haddad had adopted them as her own; she was always sad to see any of them go and continued to offer them the use of her *pension* as a club. Ther were ping-pong tables and cheap food, with armchairs and a gramophone and wireless; and Madame darned their socks. Daly's had come to stay. "

Daly's 'where there was always a warm welcome from Madame Haddad.'
Photgraph Friends House Library

September was a special month for my parents, being the month they got married and my mother kept every note my father sent her on such days all through their married life........

Wednesday, September 16th - Wolverhampton

Dearest Ralph

[.......] I keep hoping there will be news from you as I long to hear all your doings while you were in S Africa. Perhaps I shall get a letter from Egypt first. I do hope so. It is lovely to think you had my letters when you reached Cairo.

I have just finished washing up the dinner things. Mother is out, David is asleep, Antony is in his pram in the garden, and I am sitting in the kitchen writing to you, wearing my sherry coloured summer frock with white spots, which you like.

Last night mother and I went to the theatre to see *Jam Today* – a modern comedy. We both thought it rather a poor play. I am reading Lin Yutang's latest book *A Leaf in the Storm* set in Peking during the Japanese occupation, before the American's entered the war, which I am enjoying, and am also starting to read Douglas Reed's *All Our Tomorrows,* a picture of our history and looking into the future. I do wonder if you are finding time to read and if so what you are reading just now. I must hurry and post this darling, and I will send an AG at the end of the week. Goodbye my dearest dear. All my love and kisses from the children, ever your devoted Joan.

Thursday, September 17th 1942 – Wolverhampton (Airgraph)

My darling

Many happy returns of our special day, my dearest! I am thinking of you so much. Thank you a thousand times for making me so happy and for the six years spent together. Truly the happiest of my life. God bless you darling, and keep you safe always and may we meet again soon. Oh, yes, please soon, as I miss you so much my dear one.

I am so longing for you news of you, dearest. I wonder how you are spending each day and where you are settled, and if you have any spare time and what you do? You are never out of my thoughts. [....] Always remember that I have such faith in you. I know you will do this big job wonderfully well, and I am very proud of you.

David started school again today and is now resting. Antony is playing here by me while I write. We all send our dear love. God bless you. Your ever loving Joan.

My father writes to the Square of his life in Egypt and the difficulties of life in the desert..........

The trials of the desert are all very real, with the heat and its endless tedium, not to mention the sheer physical weariness which can so quickly come over one, whether fighting on the front line or working as a pacifist. I was constantly making trips into the desert to visit Unit Sections working with the Royal Army Medical Corps, the longest journey being when John Bailey and I went up to Fort Capuzzo, and on from there to see a Friends Service Unit at Tobruk and on again as far as Martuba in eastern Libya. This was a particularly harrowing trip, being quite soon after the British advance from Alamein, with German vehicles scattered in various stages of wreckage along the road, and our own transport travelling up in a continual stream. On the whole, our car behaved itself, only completely breaking down once. This rather disastrous situation was saved by some wonderful mechanics from an Indian Ambulance Company, who arrived apparently out of nowhere and came to our rescue. I have felt great empathy for all Indians ever since!

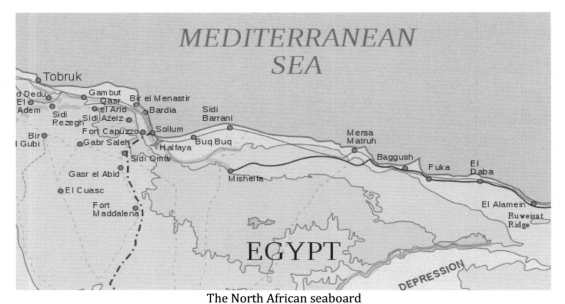

The North African seaboard
This shows the route followed by FRB and John Bailey from El Alamein to Tobruk,
Image World Atlas

Letters from Horace about India and from Duncan on the worrying situation in China, which in the near future will draw my father into a visit there to sort it out………

Tuesday, 29th September 1942

My dear Joan

I've just had a letter from Horace, in which he talked again about Olive's death, which is not unexpected, as I know it upset him greatly. I think India will be good for him, and help to take his mind off that, but I worry that he is getting drawn too much into Indian politics. But he did say that he and Dick Symonds are getting on very well, which is encouraging.

I also had a long letter from Duncan, who says he has received 4 of my letters. Apparently they are up against enormous difficulties in China. Bob Mclure, the Canadian doctor who is supposed to be leading the party, isn't going down at all well with the Unit. On top of which there seems to be a lack of petrol, plus two members of the party have been attacked by bandits. It seems they may have bitten off more than they can chew, and have insufficient central control. Duncan is having to deputise while Peter Tennant is in Burma, and is doing some very good work in his stead.

I don't think I told you that I had a very pleasant dinner with Douglas Mackenzie the other day. He took me to the Anglo-Egyptian Union, of which he is a member. It is a very big place with nice empty lounges and we were able to have supper in the garden, which was quiet and peaceful. We later went together out to the pyramids at Giza, which was an amazing experience, of which more later.

Our new lady secretary came in yesterday and is undoubtedly most efficient – or at least she appears to be: we must see how the letters turn out. She speaks almost perfect English, and takes dictation extremely quickly. It's not the same as having someone who can file and run the office, but at least it's better than nothing. I may have to try and do some typing myself. I received some letters from The Square saying that they want me to go up to Syria as soon as possible, so I'm going to have to sort that out on top of everything else. Also had airgraphs from Millior and mother. Please thank them for me. All for tonight, sleep well. Ralph

Airgraphs Explained

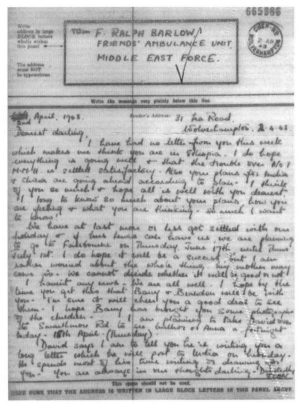

In the early months of World War II, the Ministry of Transport in Great Britain was faced with serious problems in maintaining a postal service for forces stationed in the Middle East. After the French surrender to Germany in May of 1940, and with Italy a key Axis member, the western and central Mediterranean were under Axis control, with key parts of North Africa also Axis-dominated, thus closing the short route to the Atlantic. The preferred alternative was to send mail by air, but space for mail by air was extremely limited, so letters to and from the Near and Far East were taking 3 to 6 months to reach their destination by the only method remaining - via ship around the southern tip of Africa.

The British Post Office realised that the solution could lie in the Kodak microfilm system that had already been used for record-keeping by banks and other businesses since the early 1930's.

By 1940, things had changed and almost anything that could aid the war effort seemed worth trying. Thus the "Airgraph" was born, the word becoming a registered trademark of Kodak Ltd., who controlled the process. The concept was simple: letters were photographed on the sending end, then the negatives were sent by air to the destination end, where they were printed and delivered. The volume and weight of the film were less than one fiftieth of the volume and weight of the letters, so a large number of letters could be transported quickly at a relatively small cost.

The Kodak office in Cairo already had the equipment required to photograph the letters, and was able to start processing almost at once. Airgraph service started from Cairo on April 21, 1941, arriving in London May 13.

Left - Airgraphs between my parents 1943

At last relief for my mother, as some letters have arrived from Cairo and even one from South Africa, and she immediately writes back elated.........

Wednesday 23rd September 1942 – Wolverhampton (Airgraph)

Darling, darling Ralph

Hurrah! Hurrah! At long last two letters from you this afternoon, and the one posted 18th September took only five days to get here (the long Airmail one) and the AM letter card, a little longer, but isn't it wonderful to come so quickly? It has made me so happy dearest. The earlier letters have still not reached me yet, so imagine how pleased I was to receive these and hear something of your life and all you are doing. I do hope all the others will eventually come through, as your journey and story in SA is mostly still a closed book to me.

I hope you are feeling fit again my dearest – your life sounds absolutely hectic, but it is much better to be busy and occupied. I do hope all the many difficulties are getting smoothed out by now. Oh, I am so proud of you. I phoned your mother and let her have news of you. [....] All love from me and the children. We are well. Ever thine, Joan

Friday, September 25th 1942 – Wolverhampton (Air pc)

Dearest mine

I've just written an AG off to you, but one cannot say much on that, so here is a little more. I do want to thank you again for your very interesting letter telling of your visits to the Red Cross, to Alex and also to the Allens. The descriptions bring back so vividly my visits to Egypt and I can picture all you are doing. Oh darling, it has cheered me up so much to hear from you at last and to think it was only posted on the 18th Sept and took only five days to reach me, brings you so near to me. The little card arrived at the same time, and I do hope letters 4 – 11 will arrive in time. I seem to have missed so much of your time in SA and your journey. We are all well and David is back at school and happy. I'm sitting up in bed writing this as I do want to post it first thing in the morning. I do post all my letters Air Mail, so do not know why they are taking so long. All my v.d.l. - Joan.

Friday, September 25th 1942 – Wolverhampton (Air pc)

My own darling

I am now about to write a long letter, but I must quickly let you know that I am very happy because I have received your lovely long and very interesting letter telling me much of your life in Camp in SA, and of your visits to Adam's College, the Rotary Club etc. I hope you are not so down and depressed now. I think you must have left almost immediately after you wrote that letter (Aug 18th). How profoundly thankful you must be to have reached your destination at last dear heart. [....]

Every morning I rush down to see if there is any post, and this week I have been lucky for a change. Oh God! How it cheers me up to hear from you. I have been in the depths of misery with no news for so long. Thank you so much for sending me a handbag. I shall love it, I'm sure. Bless you my dearest one.

David sends xxx and love and all my v.d.l. too.
I love you so much Joan.

A Birthday letter to David and the Pyramids

My father writes to David for his 5th birthday from Cairo.
"There are camels and thousands of donkeys that 'ee-aw' at all hours."

People on camels and donkeys at the Ancient Egyptian Pyramids of Giza
"Every now and then we would meet men with their camels, accompanied by
their children riding on donkeys."
Photo Egyptian History Society

My father gives a vivid description of the contrasts of life from stunning scenery to abject squalor.........

Wednesday, 30th September 1942

Dearest Joan

Peter and I with John Gould came down to Alexandria yesterday, driving by the desert road. It's good to be by the sea, which smells quite wonderful and looks so beautiful in the sun, whilst overhead float glorious clouds. The front itself is a long line of sky scrapers stretching for miles and miles and is quite impressive, if you like that sort of thing. But the city itself strikes one as squalid.

The tempo of life here does not seem to be decreasing much as we are trying to settle the boys in, and I have already visited two sections, one in the delta and one in the desert. I can't really describe the desert, though I suspect you may have seen it when you were out in the Lebanon. Surprisingly it's not very flat and it's not very sandy, but it does stretch for miles on miles and is glaring white in the morning sun, while the evenings are gloriously cool and lovely. Where we were was rocky, with broken and crumbly limestone.

Army units are scattered everywhere, with their vehicles raising clouds of dust as they drive to and fro. Every now and then a Bedouin family with their goods loaded on two or three supercilious camels thread their way between them, and not far away is the blue Mediterranean. We fed here in Alex in the Officer's mess, who seem a pleasant crowd of chaps, and tried to find out about how our boys were doing. Afterwards we called on various Colonels and Brigadiers with whom we have contact, and who were genuinely appreciative of the work the Unit was doing and then at long last, after a tiring day, we found a spare, empty tent and enjoyed a good night's rest.

The next morning we continued on to the delta. Such a contrast, with the road leading along a canal in which the traditional wooden sailing boats with their enormous sails, known as feluccas, were sailing with the wind or being towed along by their crews. On either side of the canal, the land stretched far away completely flat, with every tiniest corner cultivated and covered with cotton and all sorts of crops that I couldn't even identify. Every now and then we would meet men with their camels, accompanied by their children riding on donkeys, and the women driving flocks of goats or cows with curiously small heads, and dragging great water buffaloes on a rope behind them.

Along the roadside were occasional villages made of mud houses huddled together, unutterably squalid, with people, animals and herds of cattle all crowded into small bare rooms with flies, smells and children playing among the heaps of manure. In the larger villages and small towns, crowds of white-robed natives were gathered, talking and sitting in the streets. Every now and then you came across a water wheel being turned by some blindfold beast*6 walking round and round in seemingly endless circles, or a man ladling water out of a stream into a bucket. The whole sad scene lit up by the evening sun, looking nice enough from a car, all colourful, eastern and picturesque; but close to, smelly, fly-ridden and rotten with disease. It was somehow such a cruel and extreme poverty. Our camp here is also nothing much, being flat and rather damp, with frogs in the tents and crickets, beetles, mosquitoes and every other sort of creepy crawly thing in the beds. We had to sleep under nets but even they did not stop us getting bitten to bits.

As always in a new job, I feel absolutely oppressed by it and totally inadequate.
Thinking of you so much, and send you and the children all my love, Ralph

---

*6 To prevent them getting giddy

Drawings of Local Life in Cairo and Alexandria
by Ralph Barlow in letters to my brother David, then 5 years old

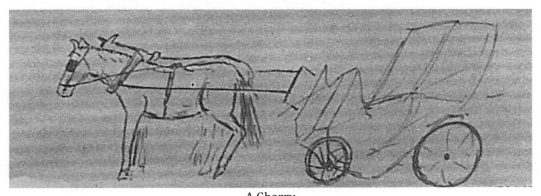

A Gharry
"A two horse cart which plies for trade like a taxi, and there is a stand just below my office."

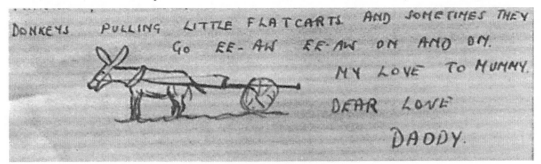

A Donkey – "pulling a little flat cart. They go 'ee-aw' on and on"

Buffaloes –"with long curved backs which pull ploughs and turn water wheels."

Camels seen in the country
"Last Sunday in the country, I saw camels and lots of Egrets"

Life on the Nile

Feluccas on the Nile
"Traditional wooden sailing boats with their enormous sails…..moving with the wind."
Photos Egyptian Historical Society

"Every now and then you came across a water wheel being turned by some blindfolded
beast walking round and round in seemingly endless circles."

With the post speeding up a little, the gap between posting and receipt was not quite so long and so these letters from my mother are able to comment on my father's early days in Cairo. Being a very astute person, she is also gently able to encourage him from afar when he gets downhearted, but above all she details the essentials of family life and what everyone is up to, which keeps my father in touch as nothing else can.........

Friday, September 25th 1942 – Wolverhampton (No 12)

My dearest darling Ralph

These last three days I have been so happy, having received Airmail letter No.12, and letter card on Wednesday and then this morning came your lovely, long and very interesting letter No 10, completed on the 18th August, and telling me so much of your doings in SA. You cannot imagine how they have cheered me up! I am a different person. Tuesday I was as miserable as could be, absolutely in the depths, as I hadn't had any news of you for weeks and weeks. I think now, perhaps, I shall start getting more regular news from you, as you are more or less settled for a while.

Thank you sweetheart, for such long and interesting letters. It has brought you so near to me – bless you my darling. I hope my letters are also getting through to you quickly as well. I send one Airmail every week, also an Airgraph and Airmail postcard. I try never to send them ordinary mail as I know how long it can take to reach to you. I think it was wonderful that your letter No 12 got through in 5 days – almost quicker than pre-war. My, didn't I shout for joy!! I was beside myself with happiness.

Dear heart, I do sympathise and pray for you in your very difficult task. It must have been ghastly arriving right bang in the middle of the crisis over 'the agreement', but I am sure you have succeeded in dealing with it by now in your usual tactful way. There couldn't be a better person for such a sensitive job. I know how you hate new work and fresh responsibilities, but they will right themselves in time, so don't get too down-hearted and dispirited my darling. Everyone realises your great capabilities, tact and charm, and I know from friends how much you are respected and liked by everyone. I am so very, very proud of thee. I do so wish I could be with you to encourage you. [....] Always remember that when you are lonesome and discouraged, I am here, loving and praying for you.

I really wish I could have been with you in Durban and have met Florence Bayman and Maurice Webb, and all the others and seen something of the country and interesting places. I will certainly write to Florence if you will give me her address. Is she Miss or Mrs? How kind of her to look after you so well and give you some of the little comforts you were needing. I am so grateful to her. How I wish I could have heard you speak to both the Rotary Club and the University as well. I should have felt so proud of you. [....] It was a kind thought to send the clothes. I will certainly pass them on to Millior if they are no use to the boys.

Oh, the complications of distance! When I got your cable saying "All well and safe" it had taken much longer than it should for some reason, so I thought when it arrived here that you must have already moved on. This is why I foolishly thought that you must have already reached your destination, and why I sent my answer to Cairo. Anyway I am glad my cable did eventually reach you in Durban, even if rather circuitously! If I'd realised you were still in SA I could have written there, but I am glad that you found them on your arrival in Cairo, even though there are probably rather a lot to read all at once, but at least you will get an idea of what we've all been up to.

I wonder if you hear much from Gordon Square or from the Hostel? I have felt quite annoyed with Gordon Square, as if I didn't read the Newsletter, I wouldn't know anything. Millior and Alfred seem to pick up all sorts of bits of news that they pass on, which I had never heard before at all. I did get one letter from Angela which was good of her.

Is Maurice Webb married? So far I don't know much about your SA friends, as quite a lot of your letters haven't yet arrived. I do hope they will come through soon. It was so sweet of you to buy me a handbag dear, and I can't wait for it to arrive. I know I shall like it. I wish I could send you more. Would you like more books? Do let me know what you would like. I love buying things for you. I think I had better start numbering my letters as you do, as it will be easier then to see if they are all getting through. I'll call this letter number 12.

I think I must take the children for a walk now, and I will add to this tonight, when they are in bed. David wants to write to you too.

Later the same evening.......

The children are safely tucked up in bed now, so I will try and write a little more. That is if I can concentrate, as the family is listening to a programme on the wireless called "Britain to America". The other evening I sat alone after everyone had gone to bed and listened to a programme of old love songs. I felt thoroughly sentimental and found the tears running down my face.

If I could only see you and talk to you about all the little difficulties that arise, which can look so silly when written down on paper. I miss your advice so much with the children. I expect you wish you could see them too. Only when you were in London, I always had someone to confide in and talk to. Here I have my family, but that is different. I don't confide many of my innermost thoughts to them. There is no-one I can really talk to here and I am often very lonely without you. God speed the day when you return to me.

I've just put the children into warmer clothes, as it has turned very autumnal, although at the beginning of September we had some wonderful sunshine with a little frost in the air. W&L returned from their holiday on Wednesday; they enjoyed their stay in Criccieth, but the weather wasn't very good. I was kept very busy while they were away with all the shopping, taking D to school and getting mother's evening meal after I had put the children to bed. Life seems very full at the present, without much free time for personal things and writing letters. I must try and type a few copies of your letters and pass them round the family. I always phone your mother immediately I hear from you. So many people ask after you and are quite anxious to know how you are getting on.

I'm taking David over to your mother's on Sunday, as I want to call in to Linden Road for some old clothes of David's which I think might do for Antony. Also I want to see if we might have a few apples. Only it will mean going over with suitcases, which will be heavy to carry. Millior comes to Swarthmore Road next Saturday, October 3rd until she goes into the QE to have the baby. Then she is returning to your mother and taking the monthly nurse who looked after me, back to London for a while. Millior has kept very well and is quite cheerful about it all.

Mother and I went to see three one act plays done by amateurs at the Civic Hall last Wednesday. Apart from one or two of the company, they weren't very well done. Last night we went to the Rep here to see *Pygmalion*[7]. It was very well done, and although I have seen it many times, I thoroughly enjoyed it again. I would really love to do some more acting - it would be such fun.

299

I am glad you had an enjoyable visit to the Allens. I gave your mother their message. Do call and see my friends in Syria. I wonder if you are on your way there by now. I liked John Gough's letter and will put it with the collection. You are so well liked by everyone darling. I am so proud of thee. Do take care of yourself dear heart. I do hope you won't get any more tummy upsets with awful diarrhoea. I know how ghastly that can be. I've never felt so much like death as when I was ill in Cairo. The Edward Cadburys got me pints of grape juice, and I remember how much I blessed them.

It must have been rather exciting seeing Peter and John coming down to meet you when you arrived in Cairo. As you say, you arrived there with all the company intact, which is no small accomplishment after all your difficulties and hold ups. How I wish I could have been there to greet you. I look forward my darling to the day when we shall meet you and welcome you home.

I know how you will enjoy driving again, even if it is on the right hand side! I wonder if you will go by car to Syria. I doubt it, but the run along the coast from Palestine to Syria is such glorious scenery. I am glad you are being so well looked after and having good food. That is splendid. It must be nice for you to be waited on for a change and not continually having to think of the others every minute of the day. It's getting late and I am tired now, so I'll finish and go to bed.

My darling I always think of thee so much, especially last thing at night, when you seem so near to me [....]. David is always talking of you and asking me what you are doing. He does love you dearly. Mother sends love and W&L too.

Goodnight and God bless you. Ever your loving Joan

Monday, September 28th 1942 – Wolverhampton (No 13)

My dearest, darling husband

I feel I must start another letter to you to night as you are so near me and I feel so much in need of your love tonight. Dearest one, I love you so desperately and you are always in my thoughts and prayers. I am constantly saying to myself "What is Ralph doing now? Perhaps visiting the Red Cross, or discussing something with Peter or Mike Rowntree; maybe on his way to Syria, or smoking his pipe and relaxing for five minutes, perhaps lying awake thinking of me (only you never did lie awake for long!!); perhaps you are driving and getting used to the left-hand drive, or maybe you are writing to me. I try and picture all you are doing, and having seen something of Egypt and Syria, I can now do that a little. How long ago all that seems.

I hope soon for another letter from you. Perhaps some of the later SA ones will turn up soon. I just live for your letters dearest. I closed my eyes and I can see your dear face so well. I know just the way your hair falls, every mark and line on your brow and your beloved blue eyes and just the way you laugh. [....]

There are times I long for you so much, I fear my heart must break. You have so much of me, that without you I am weak. I need your love, but I also need you for so many things: you have brought so much into my life and taught me to appreciate so much and I feebly hang on everything in your absence, but I continually need your help and thoughts and prayers as you need mine.

Darling, take courage, don't get downhearted. You are doing your job well, you are giving the very best of yourself, and you are doing the right thing. I feel it so definitively and surely in my heart.

You have all my thoughts, and all my prayers are for you, dearest husband. I am sure with God's help and guidance, you will get through and feel that all is well. May God give you the necessary strength and courage that you need. Bless you dearest. I wish I could help more. I am sitting up in bed in a pink nightdress and a blue bed jacket and writing by the light of the little bedside lamp. (I do not have my curlers in!!) David is peacefully sleeping in the other bed – bless him.

It is quite autumnal now and gets cold at night and first thing in the morning. We've had some lovely days – mellow and sunny. The gardens and flower shops are full of Michaelmas Daisies of every shade of blue, mauve and pink and Chrysanths and Dahlias. How I wish I could send you a bunch of English flowers.

Yesterday, David and I went to Swarthmore Road for the day, but as it's late I'll write of this tomorrow and put the light out now and cuddle down and think of you while I gradually fade into sleep. Goodnight darling of my heart. A kiss goodnight. Joan

Wednesday, September 30th

Dearest one......I'm afraid I didn't have time yesterday to add any more as I was rather tired when I went to bed.

But such excitement this morning when the handbag you sent me arrived. I was just delighted to receive it and it's taken less than five weeks to come. Dearest I am thrilled to have it and I like it so very much indeed. It was sweet of you to buy it for me and I shall use it all the time and think of thee. Bless you for getting it. None of the other things have yet arrived and no more letters either, but David was very pleased to have the South African stamps and we have now stuck them in his book.

Now for news of last weekend at Swarthmore Road. We spent Sunday with your mother, but did not go to meeting, as it is rather a rush for me to get over to Selly Oak by 11.0am. We had an early lunch and then D and your mother had a rest and I went over to Linden Road to get one or two of D's old clothes which I wanted for Antony. It was a glorious autumn day, with bright sunshine and a clear, blue sky and our darling garden was looking quite gay with Michaelmas Daisies, some late Roses and the Hydrangea a mass of bloom, as well as Heleniums both golden and orange. There is quite a good show of apples too, and we are hoping to have a few later on. I collected quite a few things stored away in your wardrobe, but I was very annoyed to see they had forced the lock of your desk and I don't know where the key has been put. However, I suppose it's no good worrying too much.

When I got back to David and your mother, they had been having a fine time hunting for frogs on the rockery. D was delighted because he had found several baby ones and held one, but it had hopped off!

Your mother gave us a good tea and also some eggs to bring back for the children. She is very kind to them. I was laden with every kind of parcel imaginable, but we had a fairly comfortable journey back. I thought your mother seemed very well except for rheumatism. I read your three letters to her and she enjoyed hearing all your news. Millior comes to her on Saturday next and expects the baby about October 18th I think.

Winifred has gone to the Women's Luncheon Club this afternoon, at which the Editor of The Observer is speaking. I wish I could have gone too, but it just isn't possible at the moment, as there is no-one with whom I can leave the children. I don't think I'll be able to get to the National Council of Women's luncheon either.

Never mind, there will be chances later on. I've just started reading E Phillips Oppenheim's memoirs called *Pool of Memory,* which I am finding most interesting. Have you read any of his adventure stories? I don't think I have.

The children are now playing in the garden and I must soon take them out for a walk, but I must try and finish this and take it to the post this afternoon. I will send an AM card today too, to let you know the handbag arrived safely. I do hope my letters are getting through quickly.

So many people have been asking about you and are thinking of you my darling. Mrs Carter came over to Swarthmore Road when I was there and asked for your address and I believe has already written to you. There is an article in today's Birmingham Post by Horace (Alexander) on Indian birds, which I'll cut out and send you.

David is writing another letter to you – he is very proud of his first attempt at doing small letters, and I'll post it off in the next few days. His teacher told me the other day how good he is at arithmetic! He really is doing very well at school.

I must finish now dearest. Remember you are with me always, [....] and long for a sight of your dear face. [....] May God be with you and watch over you always. Mother sends her love, as do all the family.

I kiss you my dearest, and remember that I have great faith in
you. My dearest love, Joan

Wednesday, September 30th 1942 – Wolverhampton (Air pc)

Dearest one
This is just a short pc to specially thank you so much for the lovely handbag which I received this morning. I am so delighted to have it and shall use it and treasure it always. It took just five weeks to come. Have written you a long letter and posted it today. No more news from you as yet. I am always thinking of you darling and long for another letter. I will send another AG on Friday or Saturday. I hope they are getting through quickly. I wonder if you are yet in Syria. If so, I expect you won't get letters for a while.

We are all well. D and A send love and kisses and all my v.d.l. Joan.

"The other evening I sat alone after everyone had gone to bed, and listened to a programme on the wireless of old love songs. I felt thoroughly sentimental and found the tears running down my face."
Photo National Archives

Meanwhile my father is continuing his travelling round the different sites, especially on the roads between Cairo and Alexandria, where they are particularly rough and the traffic in the cities seemingly chaotic. As always he is able to paint a picture of his daily life including its problems which can range from lack of typists to trying to keep up morale.....

Friday, October 2nd 1942 – Alexandria (No 13)

Dearest

We came back to Alexandria today after a very early start, and as we left the city behind, the salt lake looked lovely in the early light. We are now driving a Ford V8 with a new engine and she goes very nicely indeed, and we did the first half of the trip very fast; the second half, when I was driving, was much slower, owing to the traffic.

There is so much to do here, with many visits to make, and seeing among others Mike Rowntree and the Red Cross. The interview with the latter turned out to be much more friendly this time, thank God. This evening I had a meeting with Peter Tennant, John Bailey and Mike, and tomorrow there will be yet more visits, not to mention piles of letters to answer, with no secretary to help me again, as our lady left for another job.

The boys at Alexandria are still rather dissatisfied with things, feeling the work is not worthwhile and wishing they hadn't come. I'm afraid I've not much patience with them, but it all adds to the general worry. I'll finish now and begin again later, all my love Ralph

Continued.....Sunday, October 4th – (No 13 contd back in Cairo)

The office here in Cairo is really rather pleasant. It is a big, high room, with double glass doors and half-panelled walls, and we have a huge office desk, which we inherited. Outside, there is a balcony with a view over the roof tops and down on to a noisy, crowded street. All day there is incessant noise, with a line of two-horse-cabs, known as gharrys, drawn up in the centre of the street, plus the drone of the traffic and the shouting from a nearby market with its hens and geese.

The flat accommodates self, Peter and Eric Green, our accountant, who somehow manages to get flowers from the market and there is a lovely bunch on my desk just now as I write, which reminds me so much of you. The rest of the flat is pleasant enough as well, though I do miss even the small amount of privacy which I had in London. Here there is no single bedroom or quiet place to sit, which I must say I do find rather a disadvantage. However, on the plus side, the Egyptian servants I mentioned earlier are a tremendous asset.

There is no-one here I find terribly congenial, apart from Peter T and Douglas Mac, both of whom I like a lot. Peter has done a very good job out here and I'm going out to dinner with Douglas tonight. But there is no-one quite like Barry (Barratt Brown), Dick (Symonds) or Angela as there was back in London. However, I daresay I shall survive!

Cairo is heartily disliked by many of the men. The Nile of course is very grand, the father of all African rivers, and looks especially fine in the soft evening light. The city itself has some good shopping streets, and there is an interesting mixture of people, with women both veiled and un-veiled, beggars and street urchins, Arabs, rich Egyptians, and everywhere soldiers and officers of all nationalities. But on the other hand the streets are dirty and noisy, full of donkeys and camels as well as all the cars and lorries which hustle with the animals for a space to move, and with the very poor driving standards here, that is not a good recipe for healthy living. It's not that I object to it all, but just I suppose that I dislike living in a city, though I have been in many worse places.

But though driving in Cairo is bad enough, the main road into Alexandria is even more appalling. There trams run up the middle of the road, while cars wander every which way, and pedestrians walk about with sublime disregard for their own safety, jumping off the trams directly in front of you, while the mostly mule and donkey-drawn traffic swerves about anywhere between the middle and the wrong side of the road.

We sadly lost another of our original typists yesterday, but we have found a married Greek woman of uncertain age, who will come in and type for a short time each afternoon, which should be a great help. What we really need is a competent person who knows the FAU and could be an extra person in the office.

I think and hope that the worst of our difficulties with the Red Cross are at last over. It was most unfortunate that my arrival here should have coincided with the upset. I am preparing a longish report to Gordon Square on the matter, which I hope to dictate on Monday. I'm afraid that there is a good deal of dissatisfaction with the work here among some of the Unit members. They get upset by the long lulls between stretches of work, but more seriously they feel it doesn't give them sufficient responsibility, and being so close to the army, they feel that they are too much swamped by them. However, I think that the more sober elements are reasonably well satisfied, though it does rather add to one's general worries.

The last ten days really have been pretty full. I've slept in seven different places, seen I don't know how many of our Unit chaps and tried to listen to their problems and talk them round, which I hate having to do. I've seen heaps of army people, been in a seemingly never ending crisis, and worked all day. I probably exaggerate, and I suppose I'm lucky to be busy, as living on one's work is a distraction from missing you and the boys. But as I found in London, you never seem to get away from it. I feel as though I have bitten off too much, but again I expect I shall survive. Much love for now, Ralph

—

Meanwhile, post reaching Wolverhampton was often erratic, with some from Cairo getting through before that from South Africa, but with my father constantly on the move it was not always easy to get letters posted.......

Saturday, October 3rd 1942 – Wolverhampton (Airgraph)

Dearest Darling
I had hoped for a letter this week, but sadly there is no more news from you. I'm beginning to think that maybe none of the SA letters or the first parcels will come through now. I suppose it's still possible that they may come later. I do hope you received my AM card saying I had received the handbag. I was so happy to get it my dear.

I do wonder where you are now and long to know more news. The children are well but I have a foul cold. I hope you are keeping fit. Millior is coming to stay with your Mother today, and she seems fit and well. I posted letter 13 off to you this week and will write another and post it early next week.

My darling there is not a great deal of space to say much here, but you know that you are always in my thoughts. [....] All my dearest love and lots of love from David too.

Ever you own Joan

Letters cross in mid-air, so very often they are both writing into a void, hoping that news will reach the other at some point...........

Tuesday, October 6th 1942

Dearest Joan

I wonder so much how you all are. I have all your photos out on my desk, and you look so good. I do love you all. Are you bearing up, with all the responsibility you have? I know the children must keep you so busy. I've just had a few letters from you, for which I am very grateful. I hope by now some of mine have begun to arrive. I had a good letter from the Trust the other day, saying that they have kindly offered to put my salary up, which is a great relief and will certainly help the Bank balance!

I seem to have got a touch of one of those filthy fevers now. Nothing too serious, except that it makes one feel rather lousy all the time. It gives you a headache and back ache and eye ache and stomach ache and every other ache imaginable. None of it is really bad, but all in all it's so debilitating and makes everything very tiring.

Sunday and yesterday I was in all day busy writing reports, etc. In the evening, the Quaker educationalist, Lettice Jowitt, came over to see us as she is passing through on her way home from Syria, and stayed to have supper with us. She is a very pleasant and interesting person, if rather typical of the elderly unmarried Friend!

Yesterday I thought that maybe I was slowly on the mend. But today the fever, or whatever it is, simply won't go away. I seem to have aches everywhere that it's possible to have an ache, and at present my side and my right shoulder are aching. I think I may have had a temperature, but I have resisted testing it with a thermometer for fear of the worst. I keep taking Veganin tablets which seem to do more good than anything. In a way it's more annoying than anything, stopping one from getting on with work. Don't worry: by the time you get this it will have been over long ago.

Yesterday we went to see a house someone offered us. A very nice modern villa in a garden on the island of Gezira in the Nile river, with fine big rooms and a wonderful balcony space. It was an exciting lay out, putting some Bournville houses to shame. Unfortunately, it's too good for us though, and anyway we are settled where we are for the next six months.

I am sorry that you have received so few of my letters from South Africa, and I do hope they arrive soon. I am sending little gifts for you and the children for Christmas in the hope that they at least may arrive in time. Tom Tanner wrote to me, telling me of various Unit movements – Peter Hume to go to America, Brandon to go to China and some reinforcements for India.

How I wish I could shake off this wretched germ. My aches and pains have mostly vanished and a day in bed did me good, but I still have a headache with apparently a slight temperature and Peter Tennant insists on my seeing a doctor. The whole business is most annoying and sickening. There is of course nothing like illness to bring people together, and in an amusing interview I had with the Red Cross Commissioner yesterday, we discovered that we both had the same disease! As a result it proved to be quite the most friendly discussion that we had yet had! I also had a very interesting talk with an official here whose job it is to look after the thousands and thousands of refugees coming through this part of the world. The ones he is dealing with are mostly destitute Polish women and children, coming down through Persia. I did think that there might be a job for us there, but I am not sure. He also told me how appalling the famine conditions are in Greece too. I was eventually persuaded to see the Doctor. You'll never guess his name: a Captain Barlow, would you believe!

His advice was to 'Go quietly!' so I did, and slept in all afternoon. But before I could stop them, Peter and Douglas had taken my temperature and found it to be 102°, and absolutely insisted that I go to the hospital. When I resisted, they treated me like a naughty schoolboy and summoned Dr Barlow again, who said I simply must do as I was told. So here I am in hospital!

There was no room in the officers' ward, so I am in an Other Ranks Ward for the moment, though I expect I shall soon be moved. I was given some of those blue trousers and jackets, patients wear when they get up; they really are a bit much. Actually it's quite pleasant as I am sleeping on a balcony, which overlooks the river with eucalyptus trees in the foreground. But it really is the most infernal nuisance and could hardly have come at a more inconvenient time, as I had planned to go to Syria in the next few days. What with one thing and another the beginning of my stay here has not been very auspicious.

I finally received some letter and airgraphs from you. Thank you for such newsy letters. I was pleased to see David's report and have written to him for his birthday. I so wish I could see him and Antony. Mother says you are so good with them.

How I long for England now. Rich, golden, mellow autumn sunshine, clear pale blue skies, yellow leaves falling, Michaelmas Daisies, Dahlias, Marigolds, late Antirrhinums, all red and gold and gracious in the sun. And here I am in a country flat and hot, fly-ridden, noisy and diseased. No, that's a bit unfair. It is of course, a fascinating country with a marvellous history and full of glorious monuments: a mixture of East and West. But give me England any time, especially at this time of year.

All for now, Ralph

My mother found out about my father being ill from the FAU Newsletter, long before his letter arrived giving more details.....

Friday, October 9th 1942 – Wolverhampton (Air pc)

My darling
[......] Your AG posted on Sept 8th has just arrived, for which many thanks. It has taken 5 weeks to get here, but I still have no real news of you. But I did see in the Newsletter that you have not been well, and I'm so very sorry my dearest. I do hope by now that you are quite well again. Do take care of yourself. I believe you may be in Syria by now. I wonder if you will see any of my friends. We have all had colds I'm afraid, but are mostly feeling better now, though David has been in bed with a temperature for a few days, but was well enough to commence school again today. I spoke to your mother who is well and has Millior staying with her now, and they both send their love.

Darling, you know I think of you all the time and so wish I could be with you. I suppose you won't get my letters while you are in Syria, but I expect you will receive a lot when you return. Reg is on leave from Ireland and he and Vera are coming to stay for two days next week.

Goodbye for now
All my dearest love, Joan.

Lettice Jowitt (1878-1962)

Lettice Jowitt was a remarkable Quaker, whose life was a vocation of service to the under-privileged, to social work, inter-racial relations and adult education. During the war she worked tirelessly for the Society of Friends in the Lebanon, South Africa, and East Africa.

She studied at Somerville College, Oxford which may well have inspired her life's work. In her younger days she had been a well-known educationalist and relief worker and the first warden of an extraordinary Quaker Educational Settlement in Gateshead, transforming a tranquil Quaker house into a vital, if controversial educational settlement.

For a while she ran the Friends school in Broumana, when many men Friends left for Palestine. She then went on to teach at the American University in Beirut and later in Africa during the Second World War, sometimes in primitive mud huts. She was still contributing well into her eighties to what she saw as her fight against the 'injustices and inequalities in the social system'.

Photo Friends School Broumana

My father in my memory, was never a good patient; never wanted to admit to being ill, and even when positively diagnosed as ill, never wanted to be told to stay in bed. But here he is in hospital under doctor's orders, though straining at the leash to get off to Syria and visit Unit groups elsewhere…………..

Saturday, 10th October 1942 - Cairo

Dearest one

Well, I have now been moved to another ward and am sharing a double room with a young and very pleasant Major of Hussars. He is a regular soldier who has been out here since 1938. So now instead of eating off a tin plate and drinking out of a tin bowl, in which one is presumably expected to wash oneself as well, I have been upgraded and now have a bed table and crockery and servants, and orderlies who say 'Yes, Sir', 'No, Sir'. All totally immoral, but naughtily rather pleasant. Douglas Mackenzie, who has just been to visit me, says 'Back again in your proper environment, eh Ralph?'

Well, I've now been examined by yet a third Doctor, who, wonder of wonders, turns out to be the same Doctor I had when I had measles in 1932, and what memories that recalls! He is now a Captain and came over on the same convoy as we did, though stupidly I can't remember his name.

Everyone seems to think I'm through the illness, whatever it was, but this Doctor wants me to stay in the hospital for several days more. It is absolutely exasperating, but with the Major moving out soon, I shall have the room to myself and I suppose I might as well make the best of misfortune and enjoy the luxury and quiet for a few days. It's so long since I've been in bed for any length of time, and it has given me time to catch up on some reading. I have just finished *Pride and Prejudice*, as well as a book called *The Skies of Europe* by the American novelist, Frederic Prokosch[8], which I think is really very good: it's a very well written account of the author's travels in Europe in the two years immediately preceding 1939. You would enjoy it.

I'm now re-reading some of my favourites, including Pepys' *Diaries* and *Henry V,* which is I believe more subtle than I had ever imagined. In one respect of course, it is a straightforward patriotic play and gloriously so, but in another respect, how empty it makes war seem, and how irresponsible Shakespeare makes the King and the Lords out to be. As he wrote his patriotic epic, Shakespeare must have witnessed the brutal side of war around him all the time. Doug Mackenzie has also lent me *The Root and the Flower* by L H Myers, which I think you said you had read. I am conscientiously ploughing through it, though I can't say I am enjoying it that much. Doug assures me it is a great novel, and I recall you did too. (Later: I have finished it: and yes, I believe you both. It is a fine piece of work!)

I was chatting with a guy in the next room this morning. He seems a pleasant man, and his wife and children were here for a while too, though they have now gone home. He told me he had been in Palestine during the troubles fostered by the Arab leadership of Mohammad al-Husayni, and then went through all the fighting in Libya including being in Wavell's campaign. It makes me feel colossally inexperienced by comparison.

The Major has now gone. He was such a nice man; a landowner with property in Somerset, running up on Exmoor, and was interested in farming and planting. After he left, somebody else came in for a brief while, but only stayed about half an hour and has now been moved on elsewhere, so I am alone at last.

I had my chest X-rayed this morning, with what results I don't know, a curious scene – the room completely darkened, patients standing in front of the screen with a dim light on them, and doctors in goggles, like some torture chamber. To be ill in a strange hospital, in an unfriendly country, with no friends around, with none of the familiar comforts of being ill at home, and worst of all no Joan to look after me. I know. I mustn't complain.

Actually, the truth is, I am being well looked after and friends do drop into see me, and I have time to relax and books to read. I don't expect the world will come to an end if I delay my Syrian visit by a week or so. Actually, it's quite nice to be on my own, which is probably the best way to look at it.

Indeed the great thing about this hospital is that they do leave you alone. Sister seldom if ever comes in, and then only to tidy up and take my temperature, while the orderlies bring in the meals. So mercifully it's pleasantly quiet. Matron pays us a daily state visit and without fail says, "And how are we today?" The first time you think, my goodness, she really means it, but by the fifth or sixth day you realise it's all a bit mechanical and means nothing at all. I think I really am beginning to feel better now, thank the Lord. All for now. More later, Love Ralph

As so often, the erratic nature of the post meant that a whole bunch of letters would frequently arrive together - and as he recovers, he once again plans to visit Syria............

Monday, 12ᵗʰ October 1942 Saturday - Cairo

My darling Joan

[.....] A whole batch of your letters have just arrived, dated August 15, which I am delighted to have. Thank you so much for them all. Please also thank David for his lovely letter and I hope he has had some of mine by now too. I am so pleased that he and Antony are getting on so well together. I am sorry for the confusion as to my whereabouts, but I am afraid Tom is not very good at passing on information. It seems to get stuck with him, either because he's too busy or forgets.

You should begin to hear more frequently from the Square now, as I am sending regular AGs and AMLCs to them every week, as well as letters every fortnight. I wrote an AG and an AMLC to you last week from Cairo, so I hope those will arrive soon. My Syria trip seems to be back on now that I am feeling better, and I'll probably go around Tuesday next. Let's pray I keep fit from now on.

Being better again, means a whole lot of work again, of course. Can't win! I've just had a great pile of minutes and reports from London to deal with, but inevitably they are a good deal out of date. There is also an interesting short account of Peter Tennant's remarkable escape from Japanese occupied Burma, where he had been sent to assess the medical needs, which I believe Tom Tanner did a broadcast about. I have also had a letter from Dick Symonds, who is now the moving spirit, together with Horace, behind the FAU in India. They are very short of men and asking for more to be sent out. He doesn't say very much more about his work besides what you probably know.

Anyway I'm up today and sitting up on the balcony. I think perhaps I must have been quite ill after all, as though I came out of hospital this morning, I still feel pretty shaky. However, I am most glad to be out and by this afternoon I will have begun to catch up with some rather necessary work. I still feel fairly mouldy, but I'm recovering gradually, and have done quite a lot of work today. I had a splendid long letter from Jack Frazer in Ethiopia and he and his group seem to be settling down fairly well. He has found the local people there very friendly and co-operative and he has been able to arrange for the men to have quite a lot of training.

This is the first day that I have really begun to feel my old self, and even I am beginning to think that I shall be well enough to go through with my Syria visit. I went round to see the Red Cross people this morning, but otherwise haven't over stretched myself. My new secretary came in yesterday and is undoubtedly most efficient, or at least she appears to be. We'll wait and see how the letters turn out. She speaks almost perfect English and takes letters extremely quickly. But it's not the same as having someone who can file and run the office. But it's better than nothing. Maybe I shall have to try and do some typing myself. Anyway, during the last few days I was in hospital and also since I've been out, I have managed to write quite a spate of airgraphs to such people as John and Enid (FRB's brother and wife), Jack Frazer, Edward Cadbury, Wilfred Littleboy[9], Paul Cadbury and John Burtt in India. So about a month hence, quite a lot of people may come up to you and say - "I've just heard from Ralph."!!

Two more long airmail letters have just come in from you, for which a thousand thanks. One contained a lovely picture of Antony, which I am delighted to have; my how quickly they grow up. I do so love to get your letters and to know how brave you are being amidst all the trials and difficulties of our life. I will stop and write again later, and post this off to you now. If this arrives about Christmas time, it brings many, many good wishes and much love. Love too to the boys and please don't worry about me. Love, and ever more love Ralph

New Zealand soldiers stand in front of the battle-scarred Fort Capuzzo in Libya, circa December 1941. The Italian frontier fort had fallen to the New Zealand forces.

"I went up to Fort Capuzzo, and then on to Tobruk and on again as far as Martuba in eastern Libya. This was a particularly harrowing trip, being quite soon after the British advance from Alamein, with German vehicles scattered in various stages of wreckage along the road, and our own transport travelling up in a continual stream."

Photograph Friends House Library

Ambulance Drivers in the Middle East

Ambulance Drivers in the Middle East ready to drive off.
Photograph Friends House Library

An Ambulance Driver by his vehicle.
Photograph Friends House Library

Chapter 21
Travelling to visit the Hadfield Spears clinics
October 1942

The Unit's life became the life of the desert
"They have a pleasant site [....] in tents all along the Mediterranean fringe of the desert."
Photograph Friends House Library

Here my father describes in his memoirs his many visits out to the Hadfield Spears Unit in Syria......

Amongst the pleasantest memories of my time in the Middle East are the frequent visits I paid to the Hadfiield Spears Units out there. In Syria, some twenty members of the Unit provided staff and organisation for the Spears' Mobile Clinics founded through the instrumentality of Lady Spears. The object of the HSU organisation was the provision of clinics amongst Arab villages in Syria and the Lebanon, to reduce the suffering of these people by curative and preventive medicines. Each clinic was staffed by a native doctor and nurse with two or three members of the FAU, serving as local organisers, dispensers, medical orderlies and driver mechanics. The most common ailments were malaria, dysentery, typhoid and pneumonia. They were working among people of many races and religions, to whom medical services were almost unknown and there was much suspicion and superstition to overcome. But health education was widely encouraged and gradually villagers began to travel to these clinics from miles around. Some 4,000 patients were examined every month and an average of fifty patients were admitted to the hospital at Tel Tamer for instance, which was the headquarters of the mobile clinics, and was partly supported by gifts from the Society of Friends.

There were five centres from which some eight to twelve villages were visited each week. Chtaura in the Bekaa Valley, just over the mountains behind Beirut, which was in a primarily agricultural district; Sedmayeh in the mountains near Damascus; Selemiyeh in the desert east of Homs and Hamas, where they were largely a desert people, settled in small mud villages among the Bedouin tribes; Tel Tamer in the north, in the Jezireh district on the Khabur river[1]; and from Latakia[2] on the coast in the north.

From each centre a doctor, and a couple of driver-medical-orderlies went out each day to the surrounding villages. The headman of the village made the most convenient room available, which was used for examinations, with medicines usually being dispensed in an adjoining room, while at the door, all particulars of the patients and their examination and treatment were entered on a card. The crowd gathered outside, comprising perhaps nervous old women with nothing really the matter with them, who merely wanted just to look at the doctor. But there were also many patients who did have serious eye diseases or chronic malaria, along with mothers with their children crying in their arms. A small charge was made, not because it materially affected the work but because the work was patently more valued if it had been paid for. Those who simply couldn't pay were always given free treatment.

Here my father writes home after one of his many visits to Alex, and talks of some of the distinguished people in the Unit at that time, including the actor Patrick Barr [3], to whom my father introduced David and me after the war on the many times we visited him back stage at the theatre, and the artist and landscape gardener Humphrey Waterfield [4] ......

Tuesday 10th & 11th October 1942 - Alexandria

My dearest Joan

We drove over to Alex before breakfast this a.m. It's a fairly straight road all the way through the desert, if rather narrow and not at all a good surface. But when you can get away from the traffic, our staff car will do a fairly steady 55/60 mph. It's actually rather a splendid drive in the fresh, early daylight, with the sea and dunes on one side, quite lovely in the morning sun, and on the other miles of lake and marsh, rather like the broads, dotted with punts and sailing boats. I should think it's an ornithological paradise. From time to time one comes across little villages, with their water wheels and date palms loaded with clusters of dates, but when we stopped off for a lunch break, proved to be actually incredibly squalid close to with the usual collection of donkeys and camels everywhere.

When we got to Alex, the boys seemed fairly happy, though they are still waiting for regular work. John Gough who is in charge of Clinics, already looks much better for his month here. We discussed various points while we were there and then after supper, Mike Rowntree brought me on to the Hadfield Spears Unit not far from Tobruk. I really enjoyed seeing the chaps in the HSU here, who are a most interesting bunch.

They include Pat Barr, Mike Rowntree's No 2, who is quite a distinguished actor and Humphrey Waterfield, a good artist and landscape gardener, whose talents are just rotting, thanks to the war. And there are a lot of other very good, solid and sometimes brilliant chaps as well; altogether a very fine lot and, with few exceptions, making up a happy and useful group, who stand in distinct contrast to Peter Tennant's lot, who appear quite ordinary by comparison.

But there are, of course, problems beneath the surface, arising particularly with those whose agreement was to come out for a year, which is now up and who want to go back. I feel pretty strongly that they ought to stay, but I do not see that we can hold them. That and various similar matters have been occupying us all day. However, generally I feel better today, and this is not an unpleasant spot, quite close to the Nile mouth, and is altogether much fresher than Cairo. On the other hand, the food here is generally very poor and shockingly served, with masses of flies everywhere, and even though I slept under a mosquito net last night, I was badly bitten.

The 'Capitaine' in charge invited Michael and Pat Barr and myself to dinner in the mess, so for once we had a much better and properly served meal. The French Officers out here all talk some English, but I wish I talked better French. The women drivers and nurses, known here as Lady Spears' 'girls', also feed in the mess, but the boys think it rather complicates matters for them, as the English won't allow women in front line areas, which makes hospital work quite difficult. But from my point of view, it's certainly pleasant to talk to some women for a change.

Most of the French doctors in the hospital had been out in Bir Hakeim in Libya, and had had quite a dangerous time getting out through the minefields, for which they have been given a special medal.

The FAU men from Alexandria, which comprise mostly my party, came over to play the Hadfield Spears lot at soccer this evening on a field of sand. I'm afraid HSU won 5-1! That's all for today.

I'll say 'Goodnight' now. Ralph

Humphrey Waterfield
Here with his painting of Regents Park
Photograph courtesy Paul Mellon collection

Patrick Barr
A well-known actor before and after the war
Photograph Friends House Library

My father describes his further choices of reading: "In the Middle East particularly, the Bible is excellent company. Driving through Beersheba, coming down the long slope into Hebron, or going through Bethlehem and looking out from the road to Jerusalem over the Red Sea to the mountains of Moab, one can understand why this country made so strong an impression on the Hebrew writers, why their work is so full of flocks and herds and vineyards, dawn and sunset, and the stars of night – '*Canst thou bind the sweet influences of the Pleiades, or loose the bands of Orion?*'"

Here my father writes of a hair-raising journey to Ismailia on the West bank of the Suez Canal, including a night at a very noisy NAAFI[5] and driving along a dangerous road in a thunderstorm with no car lights.......

Monday, October 12th – Haifa

My dear Joan

Yesterday was not an especially good day. We left Alex driving the first 30 miles in one hell of a thunderstorm, which meant our progress was snail-like. We grabbed a snack lunch in a NAAFI, until it had cleared, and at last then I was able to make reasonable headway. At this point we changed over and poor Mike had to drive most of the rest of the way to Cairo in a sandstorm.

We had two other Unit men with us, John Marley and Ian Scott-Kilvert, who were on their way to Syria for a bit of leave. They were both very pleasant young chaps, not long out of University and joined the Unit in '41. John is quiet, pleasant and very intelligent, whilst Ian is a knowledgeable and very interesting man, who came down from Cambridge with a first in English literature. He is most friendly and what's more a good ornithologist. He's also a first class driver; much better that I am, and is happy to share the driving, which helps us all.

We stopped for a short while in Cairo for some tea and did a few bits of business. Then on we went, and by dint of some hard driving, got well out of Cairo before it started to get dark. Inevitably, it was just at this point that the car lights failed, so we had to complete the remaining 40 miles into Ismailia in virtual darkness, which was a total nightmare. Mike and I shared the driving, though not without some near mishaps. I managed to graze a lorry which was hurtling towards me, and Mike just missed another by inches.

We had a break for supper about half way at a down-at-heel NAAFI before pressing on to Ismailia and our hotel. I think it must have been the noisiest hotel I've ever been in, with American sergeants partying downstairs and drunken natives singing raucously as they paraded up and down the streets. Doors and windows were banged regularly as though someone had been especially detailed to the task, while all around people were clanging anything that came to hand and cats noisily making love all night long. As you might imagine, we didn't have the best of night's sleep and woke early. But with some 300 miles still to cover, it was as well to get on our way. It was tiring, but with four of us taking turns, it wasn't too bad and the car went like a bird. But as we still had no lights, yesterday Mike had tried tailing a lorry quite successfully, and today I tried the same, only less successfully, missing an island by a thousandth of an inch!

The first 170 miles took us across the Sinai desert, with nothing but sand and dunes, and rough grass, with the occasional rocky hill in the blue distance. Just a few other cars on the road and occasional groups of Arab road workers. The road itself was rough and narrow, covered in a light tarmac, stretching straight for miles and miles only to make a sudden curve round the hills or dunes, before snaking on and on seemingly forever, black against the sand. Then gradually there was a change as we came into broken limestone country, with more frequent bushes springing out of dried up watercourses, and here and there a few camels, donkeys or the occasional herd of goats. There were Bedouins too, scratching the surface with primitive wooden ploughs drawn by disdainful camels, preparatory to the sowing of barley for the winter rains to bring on. We filled up at a solitary petrol pump, and continued on till we came to yet another NAAFI where we stopped for lunch. As we journeyed on, the ground became muddier and the country rolled away on either side as far as the eye could see.

As we came down into Beersheba[6] there was considerably more cultivation and the road was a much smoother surface, enabling us to make better speed. Here and there we came across the occasional house, with camels and donkeys in the streets and Arab horses tethered to gates. Gradually as we descended to the plain, there were more and more houses with orange groves scattered all around, and small mud Arab villages, with acres of land properly ploughed. Some of these little places were rather beautiful, but so often there was much that was not, especially as we neared Tel Aviv. How invariably squalid, untidy and unplanned man can so often be. Once upon a time in the age which produced the real English countryside, our country was an exception: now alas, she is as bad as any!

I feel really tired now after so much driving. So I'm off to bed! Ralph

It was obviously a real difficulty writing letters to each other, when they could only speculate as to what the other was doing and had no idea as to whether they have read your last letter or not....so you post them off on their long journey, hoping against hope that they'll arrive sooner or later and still make some sense. Here my mother has no real knowledge of how ill my father has been, or whether he is better and off travelling again........

Monday, October 12th 1942 – Wolverhampton (Airgraph)

My dearest darling

Probably you are now in Syria and you will not get my letters unless someone forwards them. I saw in the Newsletter that you had been ill, which worried me greatly. I do hope you are quite fit again by now my dear – do take care of yourself. I haven't had a letter for over three weeks, but perhaps I shall get several together.

We are all well now after our colds etc. I heard from your mother this morning, and she said Millior has been in bed with a cold too, but is better now and goes into the Queen Elizabeth hospital on Thursday to have the baby.

David is having a small party on his birthday and is very excited about it. I wish you were here to celebrate with us my darling. You are so much in my thoughts and prayers, and I do so hope all your difficulties are over and everything is now running smoothly.

Goodbye my dearest and many kisses and love from the three of us. Joan.

Sunday, October 16th 1942 – Wolverhampton (Air pc)

My darling

I received one AM letter card[7] yesterday and another AM card and Airgraph[8] this morning. So far I haven't received another long letter. I am very worried knowing that you have been so ill in hospital. I do wish I could get more news of you – why doesn't Gordon Square give me more news? I expect you are up in Syria now. Do take care of yourself dearest one, and don't over-do things. How I wish I could see you. Reg and Vera have been here for two days and Reg returns tonight. Vera went back to Canterbury this afternoon. They are well. It was really lovely to see them again. Millior has now gone into the Queen Elizabeth hospital, so perhaps we shall soon get news. [.....] I will send an Airgraph tomorrow and a long letter on Monday. D&A are well.

All my dear love darling, Joan.

Saturday, October 17th 1942 – Wolverhampton (Airgraph)

My own dearest darling

All of a sudden two AM letter cards and one Airgraph this week, which has cheered me up no end. Such a joy, as it's over three weeks since I received anything, except one short Aigraph, which had taken 5 weeks. Apart from the lovely handbag, which I am thrilled with, none of the other parcels or letters from South Africa have come through either. In fact I've only received three long letters since you left England! But I know it isn't your fault, but I do so long for news of you.

I posted an AM card yesterday and letter 15 this week. I expect you are still in Syria. My darling, I do hope you are quite better now. It was bad luck to be in hospital, but I'm thankful you were so well looked after dear. I think of you so much and long for more news of you. I miss you so terribly.

David and Antony are well and all send many, many kisses and our dear love.
Ever your loving Joan.
PS Your letter 5 has just arrived, which you started 4th July. I was so happy to get it. JMB

———

My father continues his journey into Lebanon, which is of course, familiar territory to my mother, as she spent some time out there when her sister Winifred and brother-in-law Llewellyn Rutter were living and working in Broumana in the early 30's........

October 14th 1942 – Beirut (No 14)

Dearest Joan

Mike Rowntree and I travelled on further, when the view was improved by sight of the Mediterranean to the west and the hills of Judea to the east, with a glorious sunset, bathing everything in rich colours. We are now at last in Beirut and for once staying in a reasonable hotel, and I have just had a much needed supper!

We had a lovely run up yesterday with a clear sky, and the blue sea dotted here and there with white-sailed barques. Jutting out into the sea one could plainly make out the grey walls of the historic cities of Acre, Tyre and Sidon, rising up from the sea, looking splendid in their ancient glory. The scrub-covered limestone hills ran down from inland to the coast, and between the road and the sea, the railway, now just a single track, somehow managed to squeeze itself in, though with scarcely an inch of room for the line, let alone a train. I imagine come the winter storms, it could so easily be washed away.

We are staying with the British Quakers, Roger Soltau and his wife. He is Professor of History here at the University of Beirut, and they both have vivid memories of your sister Winifred and Llewellyn, when he was the Doctor out in Broumana, and never stopped telling me how charming you were!

I must say they really have been most hospitable, and it is very restful just to be still for a day. Roger and his wife paint a rather gloomy picture of the state of the country at the moment, with so many people – even amongst the best – appearing to have lost their respectability and principles under the stress of war. Everyone is buying goods and hoarding them for re-sale at a profit, in a few weeks or months or whenever. There are shortages, but no rationing, and everyone grabs what they can regardless of legislation.

They also commented on the situation of Vichy France[9] and the Free French officials and officers, regaling us with the scandals concerning the French Governor, Henri Dentz[10] and his wife, but I think censorship must exclude all this from my letter. Both however confirmed the view expressed to me by Lettice Jowitt, that the future of Quakerism here is very uncertain.

I had a letter from Duncan written from China, saying that he thought the country seemed to him like he imagined England was in the eighteenth century and Roger Soltau thinks the Lebanon and much of the Middle East, at least 200 years behind England and much of Europe. Little public conscience or morality, and no respect for law whatsoever. He puts it down to climate, disease, religion and years and years of foreign rule. I expect Llewellyn will have views on this.

I must say having now travelled so many thousands of miles and seen so many different countries, that I find the world extremely depressing right at this moment. Won't future historians look back on this as a particularly dark age? Everywhere one looks one sees exploitation: be it capitalist exploitation, or the ruinous native exploitation of natural resources; be it war and starvation, or ugliness and squalor. And only just the merest veneer of twentieth century civilization with its flashy ugliness everywhere, to mask the true horror lying beneath.

Perhaps you would say that that is a shallow view, and that there are seeds of many better things to be found, such as improvements in public health and housing, advances in medicine, and any amount of fine constructive effort, not to mention heroic examples of courage, idealism and goodwill. And of course, you would be right. But on the whole, I can't help feeling the view from the stalls is resolutely black.

But when things look depressing, I often try to remember the simpleton shepherd Corin's enlightening words from *As You Like It*, *"that a great cause of the night is lack of the sun!"* And indeed there is much 'sun' to be seen, especially with all the constructive good going on here amongst the Hadfield Spears Units. This afternoon Mike and I spent time talking to the Clinics with Michael Shewell, who is the FAU man in charge of the Headquarter's staff here, looking after the HSU and their essential services.

The Hadfield Spears Unit has already acquired a large circle of friends here, and Mike Shewell has been taking us round, endowing us almost with the status of weighty Friends (may we be forgiven!) But I have to tell you that our warm welcome here has nothing whatsoever to do with me or my position, nor to Mike or his standing, nor even to the Friends Ambulance Unit and its reputation. It simply devolves from the fact that I am your husband and brother-in-law to Winifred and Llewellyn Rutter! I am, as it were simply basking in all your reflected glory. You certainly did make an impression when you were out here. So what with such receptions for Barlow and Rowntree united, as well as for the FAU, it's made for a busy day!

We had supper with Emile Cortas[11], who, I seem to remember, stayed with us in Birmingham, didn't he? He was very friendly and hospitable, but now looks every inch the successful business man, and even though he says all their export trade has gone, they have managed to secure army contracts for jam and dried potatoes. He was with his wife Wadad, who is quite short, but very pretty, dark and lively and very likeable. She is Headmistress of a local girl's school and very capable, I'm told. They have one child of ten months. Emile's brother, Michel was also there and on the whole I like him better than Emile. He is unmarried and seemed simpler and more likeable, as though business had affected him less. He asked most especially after you and said he would try and send you some food.

Their sister, Najla and her husband Costi Zurayk, who has striking red hair, were there too with their daughter. Zurayk is a lecturer at the American University in Beirut. Najla is still most charming, and asked very affectionately after you. In fact the whole family came along, with old Mr and Mrs Cortas there too. Everyone was extremely friendly and kind, interested in all that was going on, and all asked most especially after you and Win and Llew and sent their love. Please tell W&L how much they are remembered out here and asked after.

Emile has a flat just above that of his parents near the American University, and he and his wife gave us a very good supper, after which we had a Quaker meeting, with all the family and some of the local Friends such as Marshall and Annie Fox[12], who are both nearly blind now and remember you fondly. Marshall spoke and prayed for our success and safety. How his style of address brings back memories of my father's generation of Quakers, sending poor old Mr Cortas to sleep! Barlow and Rowntree also managed to speak.

In the afternoon we drove up to Broumana, which is indeed a beautiful ride. The green Aleppo pines, the view of the sea, and the mountains stretching far away in front, are breathtaking. The British have made Broumana High School[13] their military headquarters for a year and part of it is being used as a hospital.

But despite the war, the school has somehow managed to stay open, though the staff including John Turtle and his wife Dorothy, now Principals, are living in a house below. Jack Turtle is much the same as ever, perhaps even more precise than before; and Anna Fox, who I also saw, has had a difficult time nursing typhoid cases. Both Jack and Anna sent their love to you. We had a long and interesting talk with them all about the future of the clinics and about Friends' work generally. Both feel that there is little hope for Quakerism in Syria at the moment, at any rate from local Friends, and they also feel that Syrians themselves should support the work that they have been spoon-fed for too long. They think the clinics are useful, but only if the Government follows their example and eventually takes them over. But they are even more despondent about the Broumana hospital, and rather doubt if there will ever be a need for the hospital again.

Despite the war and all the difficulties, the school is nonetheless very full, as there is a great desire among the Syrians to learn English, so that they can get work with the army. A cousin of Hilda Ransome's, David Stafford Allen[14], who is in the army, was there too. We drove back down again as the sun was sinking into the sea, and the evening light just catching the mountains. It surely is a most beautiful place. No wonder you loved it. When we got back to Beirut, we had lunch with the Leavitts, who you will doubtless recall along with their two daughters, who are another family who also remember Win and Llew very well. I liked both Mr and Mrs Leavitt though I think her judgment is less good than his. But I must say everyone has been most hospitable to the Unit since we got here.

It's lovely to come to somewhere you have been and to know that you can see in your mind's eye what I am writing about. Tell your mother that the Cortas family and the Turtles all asked after her. How I wish you were here so that we could share it together.

It's late now and I must get some sleep.

Yours forever, Ralph

———

Friends in Syria

Roger Soltau - British Quaker, Professor of history at the American University of Beirut in the 1930s and 1940's

Mary Borden, Lady Spears – who supervised the Hadfield Spears mobile units in the Mididle East.

Sydney and Joice Loch
"Two charming people who were deeply humanist - Quakers in doctrine - and came to volunteer their free help to the refugees in Greece, Poland and Syria."
Photographs courtesy of John Murray

Broumana Hospital and High School

Dr Llewellyn Rutter and his wife Winifred centre back with hospital staff.
They went out there directly after their marriage in 1932 and returned home in 1936
Photograph courtesy of the Rutter family

John and Dorothy Turtle (centre) with members of the Junior school.
The Turtles had a long connection with the school. They were Principals during the war.
Photograph courtesy of FSC

Sir Edward and Lady Spears in the Lebanon 1942

Lady Spears (centre) with her husband Sir Edward Spears (behind left)
December 1942 in the Lebanon on the steps of their residence.
Photo Hadfield Spears archive

Centre back, to the right of Sir Edward, stands Henry Hopkinson, private secretary to the Permanent Under-Secretary of State for Foreign Affairs; to the right of Lady Spears is Richard Casey, Minister Resident in the Middle East, with Mrs Ethel Casey to her left.

Emile Cortas   Michel Cortas

The Cortas brothers, from an old Lebanese family, became good friends of my parents.
Photos courtesy of the Cortas family

View of Broumana

View from Broumana
"We drove back down again as the sun was sinking into the sea, and the evening light just catching the trees and the mountains. It is a most beautiful place. No wonder you loved it."
Photo Lebanese Tourist Board

Letters bring great joy to both my parents, but the sudden arrival of five letters from my father from South Africa and the boat journey, fills my mother with great happiness and begins to inform her of a whole section of the time my father had been away, and gives her a picture of his life, albeit in retrospect!

My mother in return, writes details of her everyday life, especially with news of my brother and his 5th birthday party, as well as other family members, particularly my father's mother, brother and sister and close friends. She also talks of the problems of coping with two growing children missing a father figure, while doing her best to keep them aware of him and getting my elder brother to write to him, which he loves to do.............

Monday, October 19th 1942 – Wolverhampton (Air pc)

My darling
Hurrah! Today I received 5 letters from you – 3 written on the boat and 2 in SA and David had two letters to himself, and I also had another (No 4) written on the boat on Saturday. So you can imagine what a wonderful time I have had living through the last four months with you. Oh darling, it has made me so happy and feel so near to you. David was delighted with his picture one and the birthday one with so many lovely drawings. I thank you a thousand times for them all. Just the kind of letters I love to receive from you. Wasn't it nice that D's should arrive just a day or two before his birthday? Millior had a daughter on the 18th October. Your Mother is so happy and Mill and the baby are progressing well.

Dearest love from the three of us, Joan.

Monday, October 19th 1942 – Wolverhampton (No 16)

My dearest darling Ralph

It is nearly midnight and I am very tired as I have had a busy day, but I'm so happy and you are so near me tonight, that I must write to you a little. Dear heart, I had 5 wonderful, lovely letters from you this morning, David had two from SA and I also had a letter from Maurice Webb and Gil Reynolds, saying such fine things about you. Oh darling, I have felt such a sudden warmth surrounding me today and here, tonight, as I sit up in bed writing to you, I feel you so close to me.

I love you so much and realise how lucky I am to have such a fine husband. I have always known you were the dearest and most wonderful man I have ever met, but I am coming to realise more and more how much other people value your worth too. Dearest, I am so proud of you, and this is truly said from the depths of my heart. Don't ever dare to get down hearted or depressed over yourself and your capabilities. You are doing a grand job and all I can say is that the FAU is jolly fortunate in having Ralph Barlow as its Commandant in the Middle East. I will go into more detail over all the letters tomorrow, as it is late now.

Continued Tuesday morning, October 20th

How I wish I could have been with you in SA to have seen all the interesting things and met the people you mention. You have written such vivid descriptions of everything that I can easily picture it all and your impressions are intensely fascinating darling. The heat on the boat at times must have been terrific and how thankful you were to finish travelling and land safely in Egypt. But now, after a very brief stay, you are off again to Syria and then I suppose to Ethiopia. This last week has been a full one. Last Wednesday Reg and Vera arrived for two days and I went with the Inglis family – some friends of Win & Llew's – to hear the London Philharmonic Orchestra, which was so wonderful and I greatly enjoyed it.

On Thursday mother and I went to the theatre to see *Milestones*. Do you remember reading it at Selly Oak? It's a play about three generations of a family of shipbuilders. It's quite a good play I think, and we all enjoyed it. Friday, mother and I set forth to see the film *Mrs Miniver,* but it was raining slightly and unfortunately there was a queue when we arrived and after waiting ¾ of an hour, we realised that we shouldn't get in for the beginning of the film, so we came home again!! However, we went again tonight and finally got in, and we both greatly enjoyed it. It is a fine film, starring Walter Pidgeon and Greer Garson, showing how the life of an unassuming British housewife in rural England is touched by the war.

It starts just before the war and then moves into the early years of the war. The change from the happy carefree life of summer 1939 to the grim days of the war is very cleverly done. So much of it reminded me of you and me. They were so happy in their married family life. The little everyday things they liked, with the wife shopping and buying a smart new hat and very carefully concealing it until the right moment when the husband was happy and tender and loving and then appearing in it when he was in bed! Then the husband buys a new car and does the same, both of them rather extravagant and liking nice things. It also shows how the war affects the children. It has little touches of humour too, as when they are in the air raid shelter, and having some coffee they have made after the maid has left, and the husband, says how much better their coffee is than any the maid ever did.

A scene with two men from the village, talking of the annual Flower Show on the day war is declared, and the one saying to the other "Looks as if there isn't going to be a Flower Show now. What'll happen to those fine roses you were going to show? There probably won't be any roses soon." The other replied "Don't be stupid man, there will always be roses." A human and lovely thought and so true.

Sorry to go into it in such detail, but it brought you so near to me, and made me miss you even more. I do pray to God to bring you back to me very soon. I had great difficulty in doing any work this afternoon, or in getting D to school as your lovely letters gave me so much to read! This afternoon, after washing up the lunch things, I settle down to an afternoon of baking for David's party tomorrow. He has invited 7 children from school, so I set to work making ginger biscuits and little cakes, and Win made a nice birthday cake and iced it, and then we decorated it with 5 candles.

He is very excited at the thought of it. When I returned from the cinema, I laid the table ready in the dining room to save time tomorrow. I managed to buy some fancy hats and crackers too, I think he will have a happy day. I am giving him a book on birds written by Enid Blyton and also a kangaroo with a baby one in its pocket, which he specially asked for months ago. Mother is giving him a bus conductor's set, which will probably give him more pleasure than anything else. I have had such fun arranging things and tying up the parcels, which is something I love doing. I so wish you could be here tomorrow to share in his birthday, but I know you will be thinking of him.

Today has been so warm and sunny, a lovely day in fact, so mellow and soft. We really have had a glorious autumn and I do wish I could get into the country to enjoy it all. One day I hope not too far distant, you and I will go for a walk together to see the beauties of England again, hand in hand. The leaves are nearly all down nearby, but the Dahlias are still lovely as well as the Michaelmas daisies and Chrysanths.

We have a nice bowl of pink Chrysanths and Scabious in the drawing room. Do you remember what lovely flowers we had at our "At Home" days after we were married? I shall always remember the rust-coloured Chrysanths in the hall. I want to say so much to you tonight. I just want to talk to you, but it is 12.30 and I am dropping asleep, so any more must wait till tomorrow. Dearest husband, how I wish you were now with me, so that I could kiss you good night. My own darling Ralph. Goodnight sweetheart.

Continued Tuesday evening 11.0pm, October 20th ....

I am not much earlier to bed tonight than last night, as I have been clearing up after the party. It has been a very happy day and David has had a wonderful and memorable time! He was so pleased early this morning to open his presents. He has been playing conductors all day! W&L gave him 'Snakes and Ladders' and other children brought books. He had invited 7 children to tea, mostly from his school. I bought crackers and fancy hats and funny animal masks, which caused great fun and a very hilarious tea party.

We managed a really pre-war tea. I made oat cakes and ginger biscuits and Winifred had made a birthday cake and iced it and written DAVID on it. I made tomato sandwiches and jellies and bought some scones and a few small cakes from Pattisons, and also found some chocolate biscuits. So they all did well..! I wish you could have seen it all. It was such a happy picture with the children seated at the table and the cake lighted and gay with red crackers and paper hats. After tea we had a kind of treasure hunt. I had wrapped up a little parcel of sweets for each child and hid them in the garden. Unfortunately, one of the children couldn't find theirs and I thought I had hidden them in such easy places! So I had to quickly produce another! Now it is pouring with rain, so wherever it is, it will be properly soaked.

Everybody was most generous: your mother very kindly sent a pencil box with pencils and a rubber as well as a block of chocolate and John and Enid sent a very nice paint box. He certainly was very fortunate and has had a happy day. He has been very good and helpful too. Everyone at school was amazed that he was only 5 today, as they all thought he was at least 6, as he is so sensible! The greatest thrill of all for him, has been his paying his own ½d fare on the bus!

He is progressing so well at school too. Miss Riddlesworth says he almost has to be kept back, because he is so bright. She remarked upon his very good imagination. Are the early school days anything to go by I wonder? I think one of the best things about D, is his aliveness to everything and his great sense of humour and his gaiety. He is such a jolly child.

I wrote you a letter a little while back, saying I was having a difficult time with him. I am so sorry I worried you with that my darling. I now feel rather ashamed to think I poured it all out to you like that. [........] I think I was very tired at the time and consequently rather irritable and losing patience. I often feel how much I fail in coping with difficulties and realise at times that maybe I am not a very good parent. I try hard to improve myself and I certainly read enough on child guidance and psychology. But I like to talk over difficulties with you, but I'm sorry if I made you worried. Of course, by the time you read about it, it has blown over. I do have difficulties, of course – but what mother doesn't? But on the whole I am very lucky with our two boys. David is liked very much and everyone has a soft spot for him. He creeps into everyone's heart!

I phoned your mother tonight. She was tired as she had been to see Millior and little Anna Millior (do you like the names?). Millior is progressing well and happy at the QE, where she is being well looked after and seems to like her lady doctor. Your mother is so happy to have a granddaughter. I sent you an Air Mail card yesterday telling you the news about Mill. I am green with envy at her having a daughter – so hurry back so that I can get even!! The baby is supposed to be like Millior some say, and Mill said "I didn't know I was so plain!" But neither your mother nor Millior see any likeness! Hardly any new born babes are pretty, but happily they improve!

Your mother has written to you today. She was delighted to hear I had news from you and especially pleased about the Webb's and Reynold's letters. We are doting females, your mother and I! She asked if she could be allowed to read parts of your letters, but I am not sure I should, as some of them have a good sprinkling of mentions of sherry and beer. I'll have to read them all through carefully! Can't have you in trouble!!

All for now…more tomorrow, when I will try and finish this and get it to the post. I do so love all your dear letters, they bring you so near to me. God bless you and help you always and may he send you back to me soon, soon. Goodnight. I send you all my tender love. David sends you kisses too and wishes he could send you a slice of his birthday cake!

Wednesday 21st …continued…….I meant to say that Winifred has been in bed most of today and unfortunately her cold has left her an awful, irritating and hacking cough, making her feel rotten. I do hope it doesn't spread to the children. I won't stop for more now, or I shall never get this to the post. I will start another tonight, when I have read all of your letters again. There is so much I could say. I do hope you are well now and quite recovered. You are never out of my thoughts.
God bless.
Always your adoring and loving Joan.

Meanwhile, my father continues his journey round the Middle East, especially the Lebanon, so beloved to my mother, and he is able to talk of people and places she knows..............

Friday, October 16th 1942 – Cairo (15)

My dearest wife

I managed to send letter No 14 off from here yesterday and hope very much that you will soon get it, as it contains news of so many people you will remember. This afternoon we had tea with the University President, David Dodge, whose family have close links to the American University here. What a beautiful site the University has, with lovely grounds and such glorious trees everywhere, and a fantastic view of the sea and the anti-Lebanon mountains behind!

The Rutter memory continues everywhere out here, and please tell Llewellyn that his introductions to the University President were most helpful. David, who is now Chairman of the clinic Committee, remembered them both very well and he has been most welcoming and friendly to us, though I'm not sure I took to him that much. I wasn't entirely convinced that his overly cordial manner was totally sincere and his eyes never seemed to smile.

Then we went on to see Lady Spears and had quite a pleasant meeting, talking about the whole future of Hadfield Spears. She is very conscious of being Lady Spears, with a real love of power, who knows everyone, and always goes straight to the top to get her way. She has a profound interest in her reputation and her own publicity, but nonetheless maintains a real and genuine interest in good causes. If you ask me to describe her....well, she's a sort of cross between Mrs Morris of Cheveley fame, who thought herself a lady, and Cousin Elsie (Cadbury)[8], who as you know, can be very grand! I think she's probably cleverer than both. I quite liked her, though no doubt I was meant to!

She is quite plain and heavily made up, and can be extremely difficult and a bit of a so and so. I've seen LPA manage one of her species, and in the end, I coped well enough with Mrs M, so I dare say with a little practice, I'll be able to handle her Ladyship. (All probably censorable, so keep to yourself!) She had just been on a tour of all the clinics, and was quite frank in her criticisms, but also very appreciative of the work our boys are doing. We in the FAU are obviously very determined to uphold the quality of the work we do out here; and so in her way is she, but she is more interested in the propaganda value it may have than we are.

But then of course, she holds all the trump cards, having both the money and the influence, as her husband, Sir Edward is liaison officer for the Free French forces and is now our British Agent in Syria and Lebanon.

Good bye for now, my dearest.
Love Ralph

———

American University Beirut campus

A view of the American University campus in Beirut
Photographs American University archive

"*FRB writes*

"This afternoon we had tea with David Dodge (left), whose family have had close links with the American University for generations.

"What a beautiful site the University has, with lovely grounds and such glorious trees everywhere, and a fantastic view of the sea and the anti-Lebanon mountains behind!"

David Dodge came from a prominent American family, closely involved with Lebanon and the American University for well over a century. Born in Beirut in 1922, Mr. Dodge was the son of former AUB President Bayard Dodge and the great-grandson of Daniel Bliss, who founded AUB in 1866.

And so on along the Damascus road into eastern Lebanon.........................

Tuesday, October 20th 1942 – (15 contd)

Today we have driven up over the mountains along the Damascus road and down into the Bekaa Valley in eastern Lebanon, running between Mount Lebanon in the West and the Anti-Lebanon Mountains in the east. It's about 20 miles from Beirut and you would no doubt have travelled this way yourself, along its broad flat bottom, with Arab villages scattered everywhere, all white in the evening light. Just now it looks quite lovely with the long line of grey mountains hemming us in on each side, and white clouds scudding across the blue sky making deep purple shadows, which drift gracefully across the hills. And everywhere Arabs can be seen in their white headdresses, surrounded by donkeys, camels, horses, bullocks and yet more donkeys, some ploughing the fertile soil, some carrying huge paniers and all the time sun, cloud and the distant mountains.

The first clinic we saw is in a low-roofed room with just a bare table for examinations and a few medicine bottles. There are only two FAU men and a doctor here, with crowds of women and children waiting outside to be seen. The second clinic was in quite a clean mud house, overseen by a venerable grey-bearded Druse dressed in his white robes and carrying a young child. Many of the people here suffer from trachoma[15] and right now there is an epidemic of malaria. These clinics are just too small to begin to touch the real problem of mosquito control, or health education, or even public health. I'm afraid they only just scratch at the surface, but I think they do some good. They have some 300 or 400 patients per week, and boast many recoveries. In the afternoon we drove on through bare, limestone, mountains with thin soil and fine outcrops of rock against a clear blue sky all the way to Damascus, which afforded us fine views of the distant mountains.

I'm not sure if I told you, but Peter Thornton, who was in the Fire Service with me at Poplar, has joined me on this journey. We decided that we'd be better off if we left our rather small staff car behind in Beirut for someone else to take back, so that we could continue on in an open Bedford buggy. This is a much bigger and stronger vehicle with a more powerful engine, and a great deal more space for the stores, which Michael Shewell is delivering round to the clinics. Also having an open vehicle in this weather, makes life much more pleasant. Later that evening we dropped Michael off as he had to pick up an ambulance, so unfortunately we didn't have time to see much of Damascus. But we did manage to have a good meal at about 7.30pm, before we continued on with the two vehicles to the next clinic, which is about another 30 miles up in the hills, which seemed a very long climb in the dark. By the morning the weather was crystal clear, almost like being in Switzerland, with bare mountains all round us. The soil here is very stony and almost orange in colour with only arid patches of rather miserable cultivation everywhere.

The next village we came to was Greek Orthodox Christian, and the clinic is in a largish stone-built house where the team, including a doctor and nurse, all live and eat together. The conditions here are squalid, with dirt and ignorance everywhere and terrible poverty, so inevitably they are prone to all the usual problems: too many sickly children, women prematurely aged and men too weak or lazy to work. Depressed by what we had seen, nonetheless we pressed on and were rewarded by a simply glorious run back to Damascus, lifting our spirits as we drove down through a narrow valley with fine gorges and a rushing stream in its lower reaches, which was such a welcome sight after the barren hilltop. Here instead was terraced cultivation with many sorts of trees, especially fine tall, straight poplars.

Damascus stands on the plain with hills all around, well-watered and surrounded by the welcome sight of fresh green cultivated land and beautiful trees. It is the most eastern city I have been to and at first glance is a great, untidy sprawl; trams weaving amongst a few cars, the inevitable donkeys laden and ridden everywhere, horses, mule carts and camel trains. It's fascinating to see so many small individual trades, with here a tinsmith making all sorts of things out of old petrol tins, or there a wheelwright working away in his tiny shop. There are fruit-sellers strewn along the pavements selling grapes and quinces, apples and bananas, all covered with flies. And just around the corner one can find bazaars: long, covered, ramshackle arcades selling anything from hand-crafted shoes, to fine woven carpets, from detailed leather work and beautiful silks to junk from places like Birmingham! An odd amalgam of filthy tinkers next to an immaculate European-clad tailor. I saw a few items which I bought for you. I hope you will like them, if they ever arrive; they're not especially useful, but one can't always give useful presents!

Then we continued on for about 130 miles through hills and plain to a small mud village. As yesterday, the hills are bare, with fine outcrops of limestone and here and there a few birds, mostly Wheatears and Larks, but also two splendid big Eagles and my very first sighting of a flock of Bee-Eaters. From time to time we came across more mud villages, often at considerable distances apart, and then gradually the nearer hills fell away, revealing a high range of purple mountains. The sun was slowly sinking behind a broad bank of dark clouds almost obscured in a golden mist, whilst to the right, another bank of clouds seemed to come towards us like snow-capped mountains.

It began to get cold in the open buggy, so we pulled the hood up and put on some warmer clothes. As we continued on our way, the nearer hills fell away, revealing a high range in the distance. The sun was slowly sinking behind a broad bank of dark clouds, against a clear lake of pale blue sky with the occasional line of white. The mountains were dark purple, and then as the sun came out of the clouds, almost obscured in a golden mist. To the right another bank of clouds suddenly appeared like snow-capped mountains.

Michael Shewell – Photo FHL

By this time we were running through a wide barren plain and on into Homs, where we turned east, and Michael Shewell took over the driving for the next two hours or so. It was completely dark by now and the road became a rough, very bumpy track, often disappearing altogether, as we drove over several fords, where I had to get out and probe with a spade to sound out its depth. Tell David that in one such ford I found a small tortoise.

Then suddenly out of the dark, a string of camels or a double mule cart would appear as if from nowhere, blowing the dust over everything and everybody, including poor Mike Rowntree sitting in the back, who was soon covered and smothered by it. When we finally arrived at nearly midnight, we got a very welcome meal, as we had not eaten since 1.0pm, before thankfully and gratefully trying to get some sleep, though the first night we lay on the floor, while tonight is at least on a stretcher! All my love for now Ralph

Meanwhile, my mother was still enjoying reading and re-reading the batch of letters and catching up on my father's time in South Africa…………

Friday, October 23rd 1942 – Wolverhampton (Air pc)

Darling Ralph

I am still enjoying the lovely batch of letters that arrived last Monday. It was grand to get so many and I especially enjoyed reading about Durban and the friends you made there. I am writing today to Maurice Webb and Gil Reynolds as they wrote such fine letters of appreciation of your work and leadership. I sent off an airmail letter (16) on Wednesday the 21st, telling you all news of D's birthday. I do hope you are well and enjoying life as much as possible. I wonder where you are now. In Syria or on your way back to Cairo by now? I only live for your return after and our life together after the war. Wasn't it strange you should meet Dr Geddye in the hospital? Nice to see someone from Selly Oak I should think. I will send a long letter in a day or two. We are all well. All my love Joan

Wednesday, October 28th 1942 – Wolverhampton (Air pc)

Dearest mine

Your book to David on South Africa arrived yesterday to his delight. He is writing a letter especially to thank you (below). He was most excited to receive it and has taken it to school. I have also started reading it and find it most enlightening. Strange to relate, I very nearly sent the same book to you!! I am eagerly awaiting more letters from Egypt, as I have only received one long one since you arrived, but the AM letter cards and Airgraphs are coming through, taking only about 3 weeks. Your Airgraph of 2nd October arrived 2 days ago. I do so hope you are quite well now, my darling. Perhaps you are returned from Syria. I do long to hear more news of all your doings. I expect all the men are very busy now and will be more so as the weeks go by. I posted Airmail letter 17 on Oct 26.

All my love darling, Joan.

My brother David's letter to his father on October 26 & 27 1942

Dear Daddy
Thank you very much for the barley sugars, they are very good.

I posted mummy's letter today and went quite by myself to the post office.

Your lovely book arrived today. I do like the pictures of South Africa. I have a Kangaroo with a baby in its pocket.
Lots of love David

My mother has written over David's letter, the two dates on which it was written.

331

Friday, October 30th 1942 – Wolverhampton (Airgraph)

 My dearest darling

I wrote one Airgraph to you this morning, but now cannot find it. May have dropped it or left it somewhere. Someone may pick it up, in which case you may receive two! It was to thank you very much for the stockings, received two days ago. It was kind of you to send them. I had the SA Friends' News Bulletin this morning with an article in by you and other letters and news. My darling, I do stand before you in admiration. It is wonderful to hear the praise and affection from every side. You know how proud I am of you.

We are well except for colds. God bless you. I love you with all my heart and soul.

Kisses from me and the children.

Ever your loving Joan.

From each centre a doctor, a nurse and a couple of driver-medical-orderlies went out each day to the surrounding villages.
Photograph Friends House Library

From the Lebanon my father went on into the desert and an amazing encounter with a Bedouin tribe, which he said he would never forget.

The Life of the Desert

Edward Bawden's wonderful painting of Shaikh Raisan al-Gassid, made during his time as a war artist in the Middle East, might have been commissioned to illustrate my father's tale of dining with Oulad Bou Sbaa and his Bedouin tribe. (Chapter 22)

© By kind permission of the Imperial War Museum (Art.IWM LD 1048)

The Unit's life became the life of the desert – pitching camp wherever possible.

Photograph Friends House Library

Chapter 22
The desert and Bedouin tribes
October 1942

Here my father writes in his memoirs of meeting Sydney and Joice Loch [1] and a very unusual meal with a Sheikh in a Bedouin tent.........

Going round Beirut with Michael Rowntree was a remarkable experience, as was an Arab meal taken with a Sheikh when we were visiting the clinic at Selemiah. Under the direction of John Gough, the clinics have established and strengthened themselves enormously in the past two years. My visits to Syria necessitated passing through Palestine, and I shall always think of it as one of the loveliest countries which I have visited. I liked Jerusalem particularly, where I called on Sydney and Joice Loch, Australian humanitarian workers several times. They have a small house in the Russian garden of Gethsemane, let to them by the Nuns who lived in the convent grounds next to the Russian church. They had a view which looked straight across to the terraced slopes of the old city. They took me to see the work which they were doing amongst the Polish refugees.

Thursday, 29th October 1942 – Syria (No 16)

Dearest Joan

I'm sorry if this seems somewhat sketchy, but it's difficult to find the time and opportunity to write, as we are on the go most of the time.

We have been in this place for a day now. There is one FAU man, two Army Fire Service (AFS) men, a doctor and one Field Security man. They appear to have quite a comfortable mess. The AFS man is stationed on his own, as his job is to keep a look out for German agents, which must be a very lonely job I imagine. Mike Rowntree and I went on to a Bedouin Clinic this morning. The tribe was moving east for the winter, and there would be no more clinics this year. But as Mike and I were there, we were handsomely entertained. We arrived at about 11.0 in the morning, and were taken to the reception tent, which was very long and made of black material, open on one side. All around us were other low, black tents, as well as large flocks of sheep and camels. The tribe was called Oulad Bou Sbaa – Father of the Lions – and we were entertained by their chief, Sheik Rakaan. It is a large tribe and he proudly claimed that he has 20,000 men, 5,000 camels and, even more proudly, stated that he owns three cars!

He was a fine-looking man, richly dressed, and with a grand manner. Carpets were laid out for us, and cushions – from which I'm still scratching! We sat opposite each other and we talked through the doctor as an interpreter. He asked us about the war, and we talked uneasily and with some difficulty for quite a time. Meanwhile, at the far end of the tent, eight or ten other men were squatting. They all wore long garments, with sheepskin coats and headdresses, and rather worryingly, all sported belts with revolvers and cartridges. Soon someone lit a dung fire in a hole in the middle, and boiled up a large pot of water, while another beat roasted coffee beans with a pestle in a copper bowl. Eventually, coffee was made and we were each allowed three sips from the same cup. Meanwhile, in another corner a goat had just been killed.

Gradually our conversation began to die, and we started shifting from foot to foot like small boys wanting to go out, and kept looking at our watches, fidgeting all the while. But it was no good, as we soon realised that time meant absolutely nothing to them, and that we were just stupid Westerners. In another corner there were some women taking down a tent and loading it onto the Sheik's lorry, ready for their coming move up east. But still we waited, as in yet another part of the tent, a doctor started to operate on one of the tribe who had a gangrenous hand. And still more time passed.

At long last at about a quarter past two, a great plate appeared, piled high with rice and topped by portions of the slain goat. We were each given enormous sheets of Arab bread and sat round as best we could while we began to eat with our right hands. The Sheik of course got on fine, spitting continually as did they all, whilst I managed to spill half of it on my knees and down my chin, with my hand getting ever messier and messier, as I scooped up the rice. All our gnawed left-over bones went back into the dish and as we got up, some Negroes, who appeared to be servants, came over and poured water over our hands. The plate was passed over to the retainers, who all sat close round like vultures, and in no time at all, had reduced it to a pile of clean bones.

We later counted the diseases we might have caught from the spitting and the dirt and the vermin, guessing at anything from TB and dysentery to VD! At last the end came and through our interpreter we made solemn speeches of thanks, and the Sheikh pledged us 'the friendship of all Arab peoples', and 'hoped earnestly for an Allied victory'. It was, dare I say, quite an occasion, and certainly one I can dine out on for the rest of my life! But once, I suspect, is enough!

We drove off with our thoughts, pondering on our visit, through the limestone waste with just the occasional green patch and a few scattered villages comprising beehive houses as there was no wood to make rafters. Each village was surrounded by a protective wall, as the Bedouins still raid and fight each other, despite the French.

The next village we came to was very squalid indeed, a real apology for a Clinic. It was just a tiny bedroom, where the landlord, a rather odious young man, was drinking Arack, the local alcoholic drink made from rice and sugar, which he shared with some of the other men. The people were all dirty, debilitated and so relatively primitive, and the men just idled about as the women did all the work. Somewhat depressed, we left and drove home in a lovely, soft evening light, with far away to the East, the clear outline of the Lebanon, and in the West a glorious sunset.

Good night my darling.

You are always in my thoughts. Ralph

FAU mobile ambulances in the Middle East
Photograph Friends House Library

Chapter 23
Further journeys into Syria

In a report for Gordon Square my father writes of the frequent problems he encountered visiting the many clinics in the Middle East, mostly due to fear and superstition, but also, of the successes and for all the difficulties, of the undoubted good that they did........

During its time in the Middle East, the FAU helped to establish a system of medical services among two underdeveloped nations: Syria and Ethiopia. In both countries the same obstacles were encountered, of superstition and fear and prejudice; confidence was only established very slowly. Constant work in lonely outposts among illiterate peoples was often a strain, which demanded resources not only of technical skill but also of character.

In both countries, too, the Unit eventually came face to face with an inevitable problem which arose from its very nature as an emergency wartime organization. Clinical medicine, itself a palliative, led on to Public Health, and Public Health to Education as the only ultimate solution to disease and suffering. Sooner or later the time was bound to come when the Unit itself would have to leave, and then the question would arise, what was to follow?

Perhaps we rushed in too readily into work which involved the many chronic health problems of the Middle East and Africa: perhaps with the impatience of youth we expected results in two or three years which maybe twenty or even a hundred years would barely achieve. But in both countries a great deal of very valuable work was done; many lives were saved and many men, women and children were rescued from crippling illnesses. It is doubtful whether a temporary body such as the FAU had the right to expect any more. In both countries we did leave a legacy, more perhaps in Syria than in Ethiopia, and in neither as much as anyone would have wished. But no one who served with the Unit in those countries would say that the work should never have been begun.

Many members of the Unit chose to serve in Syria or Ethiopia in preference to work with the armies in the field, not because the life of a Syrian or Ethiopian peasant was more valuable than that of a British or French soldier, but because they felt that among civilians, particularly those whose needs were forgotten when a war had broken out, that there would be opportunities for pioneering work, and for service of a more abiding value.

———

The next paragraphs are taken from a letter written by my father to Tegla Davies, much of which was incorporated into Tegla's history of the FAU, published in 1947, and provides an overview of my father's time in Syria visiting the many clinics there, often travelling many hundreds of miles a day into the desert, to inspect the work that had been carried out by Unit members. The correspondence to my mother, which follows, offers a more personal account by my father of his day to day life, and the people he met, in his stream of letters home, fleshing out the bones of his official account. First my father's letter to Tegla:

My dear Tegla
[.....] Down near the sea in Beirut, between the American University and the Pigeon Rocks, stands a tall house on the slope of a hill running down to the water. The slope is so steep that on the lower side there is an extra storey, half-tunnelled into the ground. In front stands a balcony in full view of the sea, and behind, to the east, rises the mass of Lebanon. This flat was the Head-quarters of the FAU in Syria and the Lebanon. Elsewhere in Beirut, beyond the University, an office and two or three storerooms full of drugs and medical supplies completed the Unit's quarters.

There were never more than some twenty Unit members at work in Syria at any one time, but they were widely scattered, and during 1942 I had occasion to visit all of them. I would drive from Beirut on the Damascus road, climbing steadily up the slopes of Lebanon, crossing the top of the pass before descending steeply down the eastern slopes towards the flat and very fertile Bekaa Valley. Facing one, down the valley, are the Anti-Lebanon mountains and Mount Hermon towering away to the right, with traces of last winter's snow still lingering in its crevices.

Before one reaches the floor of the valley, you come to the first clinic in the large village of Chtaura, which is a popular resort for summer holidays, and a favourite meeting place for the politicians of Beirut and Damascus. But despite its civilized appearance, it is just one of many villages round about, which are as primitive as any to be found in this most inaccessible region of Syria. Further on, in another small village called Jdita, I came to the house where three Unit men were living along with the Druse[1] Dr Hamdan, who runs the clinics in this area with them.

From Chtaura I carry on to Anti-Lebanon, over the mountain pass and into the oasis of Damascus. Skirting the town itself, I would take a turn north into the eastern foot-hills of Anti-Lebanon and eventually pull up in the village of Sednaya. This is built tier on tier up the side of a hill, which is crowned by a Greek Orthodox convent, a favourite place of pilgrimage, dating as far back as the time of Justinian[2]. It is mainly a Christian town, both Greek Orthodox and Catholic, with a small Muslim minority. In the cramped quarters of a native house, flat-roofed like the rest, and approached up steep and narrow steps, one finds another section with three more Unit men, also with a Druse doctor, Dr Najjar, and a nurse, Marie, who lives with the nuns in a convent up on the hilltop.

I would usually stay a night at Sednaya as a guest-of the convent, as often there was no room in the Unit's quarters. Then the next day I made for the north through Homs[3] and Hama, the Hamath of the Old Testament, with its vast water-wheels that churn the waters of the Orontes. Turning eastwards one soon entered the country of the Ismailia, a sect which broke away from Islam and regards the Aga Khan as its spiritual head. They are mostly of Arab stock and until the last century lived in the Alouite mountains of the north. In a country which has been rescued from the desert by irrigation, they have built some fifteen villages, with the town of Selemieh as its centre. There are some fourteen thousand inhabitants of the town, with perhaps another fifteen thousand in the surrounding villages.

In these villages served by the Selemieh section, there are three Unit men working with a young Lebanese doctor Fuad Mu'akessah. They all live in a comfortable and spacious house on the Hama road out of the town. From Selemieh comes the longest drive of all, on towards the north until after some hours of hard driving under a cruel sun, you reach Aleppo; the very name of which conjures up pictures of caravans and wealthy merchandise, Oriental spices and filigree silver and exquisite brocade.

But that is only the first stage. From Aleppo you follow the road on east to the Euphrates, striking the river where it bends round from running south to running south-east. Somewhere on this stretch of the Euphrates, one supposes Abraham's servant must have crossed on his way to Haram when he found Rebecca, or Jacob on his journey to find Rachel. The road deteriorates as it continues along the south bank, through Raqqa to Deir-ez-Zor, where a suspension bridge carries it across the river.

From there the way travels over open desert, with the bewildering possibility of several different tracks, of which the driver may take his choice. One can travel for mile upon mile without seeing a soul, except the occasional Bedouin on his horse, or a herd of goats or flock of sheep following their shepherd or grazing on the withered desert scrub, which looks as if it could not keep any creature alive.

Sometimes you might meet a small caravan of camels, or alternatively some rich Bedouin's herd of several hundreds of camels grazing on the scrub. After about four hours of such terrain, the track leads on to the river Khabur at Hassetche, which signals that one has reached that part of Syria called the Jezireh. In this remote land along the Khabur river from Hassetche to Ras-el-Ain on the Turkish frontier, stands a string of villages about a mile or two apart, with houses of familiar beehive fashion, constructed of mud and brick, with each room having its own rounded cupola.

Here dwell the Assyrians, a race of Christians, who, after repeated persecutions, moved from their mountain homes in Turkey, migrated to Iraq, and were finally settled here by the League of Nations. Now, like the other inhabitants of the Jezireh, they depend on agriculture for their living. But they have not taken kindly to the life of the plain, and many still regard the villages on the Khabur as only a temporary home.

The Jezireh is sparsely populated perhaps by about two hundred thousand people in all; among them are Bedouin, Syrians, Kurds, Armenians, Circassians[4] and Assyrians. In the largest of the Assyrian villages, Tel Tamer, there was a hospital of fifteen beds before the war, opened by the League of Nations, and here another Unit section has been established. This has now grown to five Unit men, with the Armenian Dr. Shirajian and an assistant, together with a Syrian nurse. The small Syrian Government hospital at Hassetche and the larger Missionary Hospital in Deir-ez-Zor are largely specialized for the inhabitants of the upper Jezireh, as travel is so difficult and expensive, and the clinics based on Tel Tamer provide virtually the only medical service for the whole of the Khabbur Valley.

After a stay of two nights in the Unit's cupolaed mud-brick house at Tel Tamer, we take to the road again, back across the desert to Aleppo. Now, instead of turning south from the bend of the Euphrates towards Hama, it keeps straight on across the Orontes, traverses the mountain passes, and strikes the sea north of Beirut, at Latakia. There, in a flat on the roof of the American Presbyterian Girls' School, lives another section, running clinics for the villagers who live in the Alouite Mountains north and north-east from Latakia towards the Turkish border, with the help of a large and genial doctor, Dr. Mina.

Finally, from Latakia the road bears along the coast, back to Beirut. In all it has been a round trip of 1,500 miles to visit the five centres from which clinics are operated. To the casual observer, it might sound a trip full of glamour and excitement, but one only had to be in a clinic centre for a few days to see below the surface colour and witness the hard and wretched conditions of poverty, and ignorance, and disease which harass any attempt to seriously improve the health standards of the Middle and Near East. Working on the clinics required as much stamina and inner resources of the spirit, as any work which the Unit undertook. It still held a fascination, but it was the fascination of a hard job that obviously needed to be done, under the inspiration of an all too clear need, rather than the facile appeal of the gorgeous and mysterious East.

All my best wishes, Ralph

Images of Syria in 1942

A view of Damascus in 1942 - "Damascus stands on the plain with hills all around."

Photos Syrian Historical Society

Typical beehive-shaped homes to be found in Syria.

And now here is my father's letter to my mother......

Sunday 1st November 1942 – Hama (No 17)

Dearest Joan

I'm afraid I've managed to miss two days, but life is so hectic at the moment. On Friday we had an early breakfast at the hotel, and were away by 7.0am managing to cover 30 miles of pretty rough track into Hama, a city which is supposed to be one of the oldest inhabited cities in the world. Standing right on the banks of the Orontes River, bordered with tall tropical trees and lush gardens, it is acclaimed as one of the most unspoiled Eastern cities in this part of the world.

Sadly, we didn't have much time to look around, but in many ways it is the usual agglomeration of narrow streets and over-hanging houses, little open stores, crowded with shoppers, and everywhere the familiar assemblage of donkeys, horses and camels. Right by the edge of the river are enormous 30ft high wooden water-wheels, which lift the water up, and all day long and throughout the night, you can hear them groaning away. From Hama we journeyed on to Aleppo, driving through a rolling, partly-cultivated country, with here and there farmers ploughing their fields. Under the burning sun, the soil seemed to have turned a rainbow of colours, from dark browns and russet to deep yellows and greens, while the purple shadows of clouds played on the distant mountain slopes.

As we approached Aleppo, to the north and west was farmland, covered in light green olive and pistachio trees, whilst to the east are the parched lands of the Syrian Desert. Here at last, the birds began to be more interesting with black and red Kites, Buntings and Hen Harriers, red-footed Falcons and a glorious Cream-coloured Courser, very much a bird of the desert. We all sat in the front and drove an hour and a half at a time. The buggy went beautifully, reliable and sturdy, and seemed to manage every terrain we encountered, and though not very fast, did at least a good 35-40 mph. On arrival at Aleppo we had only a little time, scarcely enough to take in this old city with its ancient citadel, but just time enough for a good lunch, before moving on again, surrounded by flat mud desert for miles and miles.

It's curious how many different deserts there are; some flat for miles, all sand and dunes, some mud and stone, still others strewn with boulders. After a time we dropped down into the Euphrates valley, driving till dark, only stopping when we neared the river. We then pulled off the road, made a fire of sand and petrol and heated up some tins. Finally, we had a much needed sleep, some lying on the ground, others in the buggy. In the morning we added camel dung to the fire, which burns well when dry. On either side of us was just desert for yet more miles and miles.

In the morning Michael Shewell got breakfast, while Mike Rowntree and I went down to the river, where we saw Avocets and Herons right by the water's edge. I am so fortunate to have Mike with me, as he is really knowledgeable on many of the local birds such as Rollers and Bee-Eaters, as well as being a very good companion and friend. All morning we wandered along the burnt flat valley of the meandering river, or up on the cliffs of the adjacent desert. Just occasionally one would see nomads and mud villages with the odd sign of cultivation, but little of beauty save the many differing shades of russet and brown of the mud flats, the desert and the ever changing wide river.

Time and again we stopped the car in our search for birds, quite oblivious I fear of poor Shewell and the cooked breakfast he was preparing! But one always had the feeling one might see anything here as this is such an important migration route. If only we had had more time.

The marshes, not far off, looked thrillingly inviting, as we could see clouds of waders quite close, including a Bar Tailed Godwit and a Redshank, and Mike identified two new to me, a Marsh Sandpiper and a flock of Ruddy Sheldrake. It was all so specialized. But soon we heard the distant rumble of thunder and turned for home, just missing a terrific thunderstorm as we arrived back.

We ate a very doubtful looking lunch, filled up with petrol and set off again over the gravelly desert, just as flat as the sea. A line of telegraph wires showed us our direction, which was fortunate, as we could otherwise have taken any one of a number of possible tracks. But once we got going, you could just put your foot down and let the buggy go anywhere; a lighter car would not have coped, but the buggy, save for the occasional bump took it without a murmur. Another town, another river, a little cultivation and Bedouin villages and yet more beehive settlements, with fierce, barking dogs that rushed out us as we passed them in the dark.

Now here we are, some 700 miles from Beirut, with Stephen Verney and Freddy Temple, who run Clinics up here among the Arabs, Kurds, Circassians and the remnants of the Assyrian people – Christian Nestorians[5] – now a dying race, persecuted by the Arabs, who were settled here by the League of Nations. Stephen and Freddy live in two of the beehive buildings thrown into one. They have a doctor, a Security Officer and a servant here with them, and there is also a Canon out from Jerusalem, who is here to establish a school. He is a pleasant man, and very knowledgeable about the country, which is still a wild place, with much inter-tribal raiding and fighting. They live in a very basic peasant style, but what a difference birth and education can make. This ménage presided over by Stephen, is so different from the other places we have visited. It has some dignity about it and we sat down to a very good supper.

The following morning the Canon celebrated Communion in a tiny, little Nestorian church; a simple mud building, dark, with small windows and rich with the scent of candles and incense. There was a standing congregation of poverty-stricken old men and women with their children, and presiding over all, a richly-clad, bearded priest in the sanctuary, intoning, much as one imagines a medieval congregation must have looked and sounded. The six of us sat on two benches, while the women stood behind looking on. The Canon wearing priest's robes conducted the service beautifully, leaving a deep impression on all of us in that dim, candle-lit sanctuary. How wonderful it was to hear the stately seventeenth century English in this primitive but holy place – "Come unto me all ye that are heavy laden, and I will give you rest." It was a very special occasion.

Afterwards we awaited breakfast, having an odd hour to spare, while Freddy and Stephen went down to the small hospital which they now run in connection with the Clinics (tell Llewellyn that some of the medical instruments from the Broumana Hospital have been lent to the clinic here, which we brought up for them.)

Forgive me, as I fear this is becoming just a dull catalogue of events, but just at the moment I am driving all day and by nightfall I am pretty tired. Even then there are people to see, arrangements to make and when I finally settle down to write, there is little or no light.

Whenever I see something – a place or building or a view – I think – I must remember to tell Joan that when I write. My dear you are always with me.
Love, always, Ralph

———

Sights of the Middle East

A Water Wheel on the Orontes
"Enormous 30ft high wooden water-wheels, which lift the water up, and all day long and throughout the night, you can hear them groaning away."

The ancient Citadel at Aleppo
The large medieval, fortified palace in the centre of of Aleppo in Northern Syria.
Photos Syrian Historical Society

A Nestorian Church and FAU members

A Nestorian Church
The remains of a "tiny, little Nestorian church; a simple mud building, dark, with small
windows and rich with the scent of candles and incense."
Photo Syrian Historical Society

Stephen Verney   John Bailey
Photographs Friends House Library

As ever, the post is as erratic as usual, and often several weeks behind, hence my mother, longing for ever more news, can only write into the blue beyond, telling my father about the children and the wider family, and what they have been doing as well as having just the first thoughts of what the world might be like after the war. But her letters conjure up perfectly an idea of what life was like in 1940s war-torn Britain…………

Tuesday, November 3rd 1942 – Wolverhampton (No 18)

My own darling

I'm afraid I have missed one or two days, but I did send off an Airgraph on Friday. Life seems very, very busy at the moment – taking and fetching David to and from school, as well as the washing, mending and shopping, which all completely fill my mornings. In the afternoon I often have ironing to do, and then taking the children for a walk. In the evenings I have been struggling to finish the baby coat for Millior's little Anna, plus a pullover for David, by which time I feel rather too tired to start a letter. The children occupy my time a good deal just now, but I have to say they are very good. I try and get some reading in as well, but fitting in everything is increasingly difficult.

Darling mine, I had hoped for another long letter from Egypt since you arrived there. I do hope you are sending them Airmail, as otherwise they take so long. I think you must be back from your visit to Syria by now, and I long to know what you thought of it all. I wonder whether you got to see Jack Turtle, the Cortas's or Blanche when you were in the Lebanon. Or if you managed to visit Broumana? Oh, dearest, how I wish I could have been with you. What glorious fun it would have been to have shown you around, though I don't expect you had much time for sight-seeing, as you had such scattered sections to visit.

Oh, do write often darling, I feel so terribly cut off from you, and there is so much I want to know and most of all to hear if you are quite well again. I miss you so much and it gets worse instead of better. I miss you in hundreds of ways – talking things over with you, your sound advice and your gay laughter, your tenderness towards me, your loving caresses, and your help with the children. The last six years have been so wonderful. You deserve all the best my dear one and I do pray that you will be happy. Please, for my sake always take great care of yourself.

The poor children have had such awful colds and their coughs are a long time going. The weather has been pretty beastly – cold and foggy. However, yesterday, was the most perfect late autumn day – bright, clear sunshine, making the trees a glorious show of browns and oranges with the last leaves still just clinging on and I even heard a robin and a thrush singing from a neighbouring bush.

I made a real effort to take the boys out today, and we went over to the Park near the school. David's school friend, little Selma Walker came with us as well, and she and David had a grand time looking for Horse Chestnuts and acorns and watching the Mallards and Swans. They also had races on their tricycles, while Antony ran about completely happy.

I was amazed to find such a variety of flowers still out – chrysanthemums, dahlias, fuschias, Michaelmas daisies and Poulsen roses. Do you remember the flower shop where you bought the beautiful bunch of flowers for me the day you left? Their shop looked so lovely this morning, and I so wished I could send you some, even just the smallest bunch of violets. Instead I am enclosing two little primula Wandas, which I found in the garden, bravely showing themselves, in spite of the cold.

———

I wonder if Tom Tanner has yet fixed a time for his visit to the East. I believe they have had a difficult time deciding who should accompany him. I heard a rumour that Robin Whitworth might now be going. You will no doubt have heard more than I have through your many correspondents at Gordon Square.

Thank you again a thousand times for the parcels – the barley sugar and the book for David's birthday, the handbag and the stockings. It was so sweet of you to send them. Just a tiny point, but if you should send some again…I'm size 9½ not 8½ !! I do hope you will receive the books I and the rest of the family have sent you. I had a book token given me the other day, so I went to Hatchard's this morning to try and buy one I might like.

They have the shop well laid out for Christmas and I found it difficult to decide in a hurry. I could have done with a whole morning to look around, which is, of course, impossible. There is an amazingly good variety of children's books at the moment, and the standard of these has improved enormously of late. David is now collecting quite a library. Your 'British Birds' is still coming regularly. I think I'll try and forward some on to you, as you may like to read them.

I think I told you I was going to hear the Liverpool Philharmonic last Wednesday. It was a most enjoyable evening; a fine orchestra with Malcolm Sargent conducting and they played Beethoven's 'Emperor' Piano concerto with Benno Moiseiwitsch[6] at the piano. I did enjoy it. I'm coming to enjoy good music more and more, and Wolverhampton has some really good concerts at the Civic Hall, which is a fine concert venue.

On Thursday mother and I went to the Rep theatre to see a play called *Billeted* by Tennyson Jesse, written in the last war and now brought up to date a little. It was amusing in parts but rather improbable and not a very good play I thought. The Birmingham Rep, can you imagine, is producing *Hamlet* in two parts! The first half this week and the second half next. I hear it is quite a good production, but it seems a silly idea to me to split it, as it would destroy the whole tension of the play. Just when one is getting into the spirit of the drama, it would break off. T C Kemp writes in The Birmingham Post "Hamlet should sweep along the high road of tragedy, which it must cover at one stretch if the procession of events is to be comprehended as a whole." I agree!

I was most interested in the Friends' News Bulletin from South Africa that Maurice Webb kindly sent me. I feel extremely proud when I see your name at the end of such a fine article. You have certainly made a name for yourself in Durban my dearest. As I said in my Airgraph "I stand humbly before you, very proud, worshipping and adoring." I know I am not fit to breathe the same air!! I must gently tease you a little, but truly I do think you are doing a wonderful job dear heart and I only wish I could be more worthy of you.

I've just bought a book to give Winifred for Christmas called *The USA at work and play*. I have scanned through it and it seems to give one a very good idea of America today, what it is thinking and doing. It was well reviewed. I do wonder what you are reading these days. Do tell me if you would like any special books. I have bought a book to send you, but I am reading it myself first! It's Hilaire Belloc's collected essays, called *Places*. I am enjoying them immensely, and I hope you will like them too when I send them on to you.

We have been very worried this last weekend over Vera and the children, as Canterbury had a big daylight raid. We haven't heard any details, only a wire saying 'Safe'. I wish they could move from Canterbury as it is such a nerve racking experience for her with the two little boys and a great worry for Reg too.

Margaret (Gillett) and Heather (Cadbury) both rang up last Friday! M to see if she could come over soon, and H to ask if I could go over for the day on Saturday, which proved impossible. But Margaret is coming over here for the day on the 20th November, which will be nice. Heather is expecting another baby in May, though it's all very secret at the moment, so don't say a word. They are very pleased. I should like a little girl, wouldn't you?

Bobbie (sister) is coming over for the day tomorrow. We haven't seen her for months – last June I think, just after you went away! I know she is kept very busy with the pigs and fowl, and of course there is baby Susan now, so it will be good to see her. Barbara's going to the High school now and likes it very much [.....]

The children are fine. I took David and Antony to a birthday party last Saturday and they hugely enjoyed themselves. They are due for another one next week! I do hope you will find them boys to be proud of when you return my dear. David is a dear and growing up fast. He is very affectionate and companionable. Antony is adorable, talking more and more. He is very round, jolly and such fun. I think he will be good looking!

I wonder how you feel the war is going. What are we to make of the war and what sort of world can we expect after the war? Sometimes all the cruelty of war frightens me and I find it difficult to sort out my beliefs and know what my religion means to me. What am I to teach the children, when I don't know exactly what I believe myself? I pray, though often with difficulty and I try to live a decent life, but what do we want for our children after the war? I wish I knew more what I believe and want for the future. One thing I am sure of is that I desperately need you here to help and encourage me. I am so much better and nicer when you are near me. Pray for me darling, I do love you so. God bless you always. Everyone sends their love.

Ever your living Joan.

Thursday, November 5th 1942 – Wolverhampton (Air pc)

Darling

I am sitting on the bus, off to see your mother and Millior. I had so hoped for more news of you this week [....] I do so long for a good letter telling me all you have been doing and your impressions. I wonder whether you are back from Syria yet. Good news from Libya this morning. I expect your men are very busy. I hear this morning that Tom and Peter Hume are hoping to see you all before long. What an interesting trip!

We are all well. I've just taken David to school and one of the other children is seeing him home. He can now read small words and seems to be making excellent progress. Antony is fine and so jolly. I wish your mother could see the children more often. She so enjoys having them.

From MCB (my father's mother) at Sunnybrae

I am finishing this card off, as Joan left it behind yesterday. We greatly enjoyed her visit and hearing of all your delightful letters.

Much love from Millior and mother

The next letter is very much a repeat of the previous letter, my mother not realising that MCB had found the letter she lost and sent it off for her!

Friday, November 6th 1942 – Wolverhampton (Air pc)

Darling

No letter from you for ages. The post seems to get worse and worse, and slower and slower! I expect you are back from Syria now and I do long for news of your trip and your impressions. I've only had one long letter (No. 12) since you reached Cairo. News from Egypt is brighter, but I expect you are very busy and I hear you will be seeing Tom and Peter H soon.

Yesterday I spent the day at Swarthmore Road and saw Millior and Anna. They seem fine and your mother is bearing up wonderfully well. Anna is getting on well – very like Alfred at the moment! Your mother says she is a real Braithwaite, but Enid thinks she is getting to be like Mill now. Anyway, she is very sweet. I had an awful journey home. It poured down in torrents all day. I will write a long letter over the week-end.

Maurice Webb and his wife sent me a parcel of dried apricots and sultanas in "appreciation of Ralph's visit". Wasn't it kind of them?
Dearest love Joan.

The Khabbur River,
"We all went for a walk up the Khabbur River, which here is a broad, deep and swift-flowing stream running through a flat plain, and with the distant mountains, makes a most attractive setting."
Photo Syrian Tourist Board

———

In these next two letters, my father continues on his journey near the Turkish frontier, with walks up the Khabbur River, the largest tributary of the Euphrates in Syria, and gradually visiting all the clinics en route, and of course seeing some exotic birds……………

Monday, 2nd November 1942 (No 18)

My dearest Joan

We are now only about 20 miles from the Turkish frontier here, and some 220 miles from Russia. Yesterday we had a long talk with Stephen and Freddy about the Clinics and how it was all progressing. After lunch we all went for a walk up the Khabbur River, which here is a broad, deep and swift-flowing stream running through a flat plain, and with the distant mountains makes a most attractive setting, though now in a rather sad autumnal way. The cumulus clouds were glorious and it soon cleared into a beautiful golden evening. Flocks of black and white sheep came down to water, and we watched as a herd of cattle – black, white and brown – along with some grey donkeys, were all being driven in for the evening.

This trip has been a good one for birds, with a great many going through on migration, and often we've seen parties of Swallows steadily working their way south. We have also seen some seventy varieties of species during our few days here, including Red and European Kingfishers and Black Tern and Nightjars. In the evening we had a Quaker meeting and Barlow and Rowntree ministered. I must say that I have, on the whole, appreciated the value of meeting much more since I have been away. It seems to mean so much more in these times of difficulty, stress and separation. I felt likewise that the service in the morning in the tiny Nestorian church, was the most moving Anglican service I had ever attended.

The people here live in constant terror of being raided. Indeed only last night a woman had one of her cows stolen by a Bedouin tribe. The Canon I mentioned earlier, who seems to know about everything out here, told us a lot of the history. Most of these people came down from Turkey in the last war and settled in Iraq and the men folk joined up with the British forces. But then after the removal of British power in Iraq, the Iraqis disliked the part played by the Assyrians with the British forces and massacred many of them, while the remnants were moved over here by the League of Nations. The following morning we visited a Clinic and in the afternoon, the hospital; tomorrow we leave.

It is just possible, if you have time, and can bear to type some of my letters out, that parts of them – (please be discreet) – might be of interest to Tom Tanner. I know how busy you are darling, so only if you find time. All for now, dear love Ralph

Thursday, 5th November 1942 – Syria (18 contd)

Dearest Joan

We left Freddy and Stephen soon after breakfast on Monday. There was a thick mist which gradually cleared. We took the Canon with us on our way back, as far as Aleppo. It was an uneventful day driving over the same road as we had come up, stopping about 5.0pm while Mike and I went off and had a wonderful hour's birding on a muddy pool by the Euphrates. It was sheer paradise with Pintail, two sorts of Sheldrake, Teal, Wigeon, Mallard, crowds of waders, including Black-winged Stilt, Greenshank, Dusky Redshank, and Great White and Buff-backed Heron. We got ourselves very muddy, but very happy.

In our absence the Canon and Michael Shewell had prepared a supper for us of bully beef and beans. By this time there was a glorious moon and we pushed on till 10.0pm, and despite the rough road, there was enough light to make a fair speed. We pulled off the road somewhere in the desert and slept beside the truck. We went to sleep with the moon going down behind the truck and the brilliant stars above. I woke just once to see a donkey being led by two men and followed by two camels going silently down the road, silhouetted against the sky.

The Canon, who never stops talking, was talking away quite happily as I fell asleep, and was still talking when I awoke at first light! As the sun rose in full glory, he and I went off to collect dung for the fire. Dung-collecting, with a Canon of the English Church, now there's an experience to go down in the annals!

Friday 6th November– (18 – final)

I fear this letter has been shamefully interrupted. It is now Friday night, and I take up where I left off. We arrived in Aleppo in good time and went to a hotel for a wash. It was really good to have a hot bath in a proper bathroom. One gets so tired of scratching about in inadequate cold washing facilities, and even more tired of totally inadequate lavatory conditions. Still, I suppose men in the western Desert have much worse to put up with. The Canon treated us to coffee and bequeathed me a box of matches and a half-used toilet roll! He was very talkative, but also very knowledgeable and a great worker. I liked him and we parted cordially.

From Aleppo, which is as I said on our journey out, a land of lovely soft colourings and comparative fertility. But gradually it starts to get hilly, with olive groves and fruit orchards covering the slopes, and then bare mountains, grey and stony, like parts of Scotland or the Pennines. Then eventually we travelled back down to the Orontes valley; the river in the bottom of this wide valley, surrounded by grey mountains, heavy clouds, driving mist, and rare patches of blue sky. I am prepared to think kindly of any place that reminds me of home, and it was wonderful to be among mountains again, and see the grey clouds and shafts of sunlight; to smell the wet earth and see the pine trees, birches and scrub all wet with recent falls of rain, and the river now in muddy spate, and to feel the freshness of it. To forget the people and the war and to think for just a brief moment that it was some special mountain place one had once known and loved. In Stephenson's words[7] – "Where about the graves of martyrs, the whaups (curlews) are crying, My heart remembers how!" After such nostalgia, it was perhaps healthy that we were engulfed in a terrific downpour and got soaked!

Latakia is the largest costal town in northern Syria, and the last of any importance before the Turkish frontier is reached. The Clinic here is on the top floor of an American Mission, but there was no room for us. So we ate at the hotel, looking out over the sea, but in some ways how lucky we are. In peace time, one would pay pounds to be here! These Clinics are up in the pleasant pine-clad hill country to the North of the town. It was a lovely run up with glorious views of mountains across to the Turkish frontier. They were just opening a new clinic, with great crowds of eager people, all prepared to pay just to see a doctor, rather than because they were necessarily ill. The afternoon and evening were rather blotted out as far as I was concerned, by a sudden and devastating attack of gippy tummy, which completely bowled me over, but thank God by this morning I felt more or less all right again.

Peter Gibson and John Bailey have just turned up, having come up from Egypt to see me, where all sorts of problems seem to have arisen, of which more later. Anyway we came down to Beirut today. It was a beautiful run down the coast, always the blue, blue Mediterranean to the West with occasional white-sailed barques. To the East the blue-grey mountains of Lebanon. It was wonderfully clear and fine, and the grey rocks by the sea, the stone houses, seemed soaked and mellow in the sunshine. My dear one, I seem to have spent all day trying to sort out the problems here, talking to the Soltaus and anybody else I can think of; and then with a gippy tummy on top of everything and being sick earlier on, I'm worn out and it's now 11.40pm, so forgive me, but I must now go to sleep. As always at this time, I am thinking of you and send you and the children all my love, Ralph

Having been away for some time, more problems have arisen back in Cairo, which prompts my father to hasten back to Egypt.........

Sunday, November 8th – Nazareth 1942 (19)

My dearest

As usual, Beirut was hectic. John Bailey and Peter Gibson had come up to discuss arrangements for future work. John had also apparently lost the confidence of the chaps and had been asked to resign by them. He feels it badly, but I see no option but to accept, though I don't like the way it has been handled. It is in fact rather difficult, but then it may come to all of us. Later Mike Rowntree and I had a very useful Committee meeting along with President Dodge of the University and Lady Spears.

We later met up with the Soltaus again, who have been most hospitable, and had invited the Kenneth Olivers to lunch. I liked them. They have the poorest opinion of the Lebanon. He also has a very low opinion of the Clinics. But I think he's mistaken and generally the Clinics are doing some very useful work for the war, though of course, they are the merest scratch on the surface of an enormous problem which must be tackled at the roots. These involve the over-riding problems of health-education, nourishment, birth control, mosquito control, better agriculture and, as Kenneth Oliver said, a proper body of responsible doctors.

After a further talk with Michael Shewell, we were ready to leave, especially as I was worried about being away from Egypt for so long. But I am sure it was a useful and worthwhile visit, besides being by far the most interesting trip so far, with two very pleasant companions. As we left, we heard that the great military push was on, and we all had the usual horrible sinking feeling when great events happen, and an overwhelming desire to be back on the spot. How often in the last few years has one had that feeling?

It was a most glorious run up over the mountains on to the Damascus road, with Peter and I in the staff car, while Mike Rowntree and John went another route in the buggy. On we went into the Bekaa valley turning south west on to the Jerusalem road. To the South East of us the great mass of Mount Hermon rose up before us, with the colour gradually fading and just a few clouds circling round the top; whilst to the West the sunset glow was slowly dying behind the mountain. Soon the light had completely disappeared, and as we rounded Mount Hermon, the moon rose among the angry low clouds, which gradually cleared as we swung up into a clear sky, giving us a full light for driving. It was one of those curious moments when you can get out of one world and into a totally different one, however temporarily, and forget all the worries and tumults and stupidities. Then, wonder of wonders, after no time at all we dropped down into Galilee.

We stopped by the lake for a few moments in perfect quiet. The moon was now high in the sky and there was just a faint path of light rippling across the water. All around, the hills stood silent, reflected in the lake. The sky, mountain and water were full of perfectly indescribably beautiful colour. It could not have been more lovely or more moving, and a scene we could never forget. If only you could have been here too to make the moment complete.

We ran on to Tiberias and had supper in a decent hotel, then on again, reaching our hotel at Nazareth by 11.0pm. From our balcony we looked out over the cypresses and silent town, the clear sky all moonlit, and Orion rising over the hill. We were up again by 5.45 and off to Jerusalem by 6.45. We had a lovely run in the early morning, through grey hilly country, little mud villages, terraces, rich, orange soil and brilliant leaves on the vines just turning colour and fruit trees contrasted with the silvery grey of the olives.

In Jerusalem we just missed seeing the Lochs, whom we had come all this way to see about Polish refugee Relief, which was a disappointment. But by then there was scarcely time to see much of the town and we set off hard for home. For all of this long journey we have been hurrying the staff car along between 50 and 60 mph all day, and it has really gone beautifully. We covered the last 94 miles in two hours, driving in turns, with only brief pauses for lunch and tea and petrol, and we are fairly exhausted after a total of some 410 miles. Mike and John in the buggy, who started earlier, actually got in about the same time as we did.

We arrived back in Egypt in full face of a brilliant sunset, filling the sky and burning on the water, against which felucca sails and palms stood in lovely silhouette. It has been a most memorable trip, despite in some ways being too far and too quick; covering some 2,700 miles in just 17 days, seeing and talking to so many people and assimilating so many facts, it could not be described as a honeymoon. But it has been as enjoyable as anything can be without you. Syria is a lovely country, even the desert in sunshine has its beauty, and Lebanon as we both know, is amazing too. It is a fascinating part of the world both historically and racially, and the people have been wonderfully kind to us too. And on top of it all Mike and I think we probably saw well over 100 birds between us, and I counted 12 species that I've never seen before.

Now here we are back again, full of work to do: reports to write to the Square, a new set up to get used to, the John Bailey problem to deal with, Polish refugees to look after, and a new car. All that and the Red Cross agreement to cope with again! No peace for the wicked!

I fear I haven't written much to David of late, but I know you will pass my thoughts and love on to both the children. Peter has just brought me a new lot of your letters, and I am thrilled and can't wait to read them. I will answer on my next letter. How maddening that my letters are not getting through. I take some trouble over them, including ones to David with lots of drawings. I do hope they turn up. I will try and post the present I bought for you in Damascus, which I do hope you will like. I showed it to Stephen and Freddy and they thought it lovely as did the Canon. So I hope very much it arrives in time for Christmas. Send my love to my mother and Millior. Meanwhile, all my love. Ralph

"We stopped by the lake of Galilee in perfect quiet. The moon was high in the sky and there was just a faint path of light rippling across the water."

Photo Syrian Tourist Board

Back in Cairo, my father spent time writing a report on his visit to the clinics for Gordon Square.......

Wednesday, November 11th – Cairo (19 final)

My darling Joan

Since we got back on Monday, I have been occupied the whole time. A whole pile of correspondence to deal with, and a repoprt on Syria to write (see below). I have dictated to my Greek secretary solidly for 1½ hours each night. I have sent off my Syrian report and am quite pleased with it. I gave a full account of the position, pointed out that we are only scratching the surface and that a fundamental approach is needed: I said that on the whole I was against trying to carry on after the war, but that we should do it as well as possible now.

I've also posted a long letter to you about my Syrian trip so I hope this and the one I sent from Beirut arrive soon. I do long for the time when you and I and the children can all be together again, in our own home and garden, sharing holidays and life together. I know it will be so wonderful and pray for such days to come again soon. God bless, Ralph.

An extract from my father's report on Syria to Gordon Square, which clearly outlines the extent of the FAU and Spears work in the area, as well as its many problems.........

The life of the clinic worker is not easy. For the most part they live roughly and simply in remote country districts. The work is hard, continuous, responsible and often frustrating. Sometimes a case which has been progressing nicely goes right back, from carelessness or neglect. Patients whose recovery depends on regular treatment, do not come back. Often the people are too uneducated to fully grasp the medical directions, and 'a table-spoonful, three times a day' for instance, needs careful explanation which, as often as not, is not understood.

The overcoming of apathy and superstition and the building up of confidence are among the greatest problems. Harmful traditional cures have to be discarded, and faith evoked in, what may be to them, un-heard of treatments, by doctors whose reputations can be made by the success of a lucky cure or lost as quickly by a single unlucky accident. It is often difficult to persuade a patient to return to the clinic or to continue treatment, when the most obvious symptoms have subsided. Payment in advance provides a partial solution to the problem, as it has been found that confidence in a treatment increases proportionately with its cost. A charge is always made, except in cases of the most extreme poverty.

There is, I think, little doubt that the static clinic, though it may cover a smaller area and perhaps treat fewer patients than the mobile clinic, does a much more thorough job. Patients can be seen daily, treatments can be followed with some degree of regularity, and when a patient can be brought into a hospital, proper care can be exercised. This fact is well illustrated by the Syrian clinics at Tel Tamer, where the work is centred on an Assyrian village. This unfortunate people, after wanderings and massacres during and since the last war, were settled by the League of Nations, who built a small hospital here. On the outbreak of war, this fell into disuse, but has since been brought into service again by the Spears mobile clinics, whose clinic workers are using both the wards and the operating theatre. It is primitive, bedding is absent, relatives are expected to bring food, but even so, recovery is more likely in hospital than if the patients were to return to their over-crowded and dirty homes. This hospital does, I feel sure, make the clinic one of the most worthwhile of the ones which are being run in Syria. For the most part, however, they do not touch the fundamental problem.

Ill-health has its roots in malnutrition, lack of all knowledge of hygiene, absence of birth control and prevalence of malarious mosquitoes, and until these problems are tackled on a full scale, no major improvement can be expected. Education in a small way is, however, possible though progress will take a long time. Villagers can be encouraged to clean drains on their land and prevent stagnant water. They can be encouraged to cover their food and excrement from flies. But the urge to action of this sort, dies very rapidly, unless there is some powerful and continuous outside stimulus. There is enormous scope for child welfare workers; so many of the children suffer from troubles, which a little maternal care and knowledge could avert. In addition to curative treatment, the clinics should be a centre of health education.

A very obvious and necessary way of progress is to train certain of the native population. For instance in Syria, certain people have been instructed how to carry on the bathing treatment for certain eye complaints. In Tel Tamer, there is an Anglican school, where the school master, working in close co-operation with the clinics, can do invaluable hygiene teaching among the growing generation. However, I think, with all their disadvantages and shortcomings, there is no doubt that these clinics have some considerable value. Health education, as suggested above, can be carried out, with many lives saved, and ease from suffering given to many. They have a valuable place too, in meeting epidemics. For instance, the Syrian clinics have done much to inoculate large numbers of the inhabitants against small pox. In addition, they are gathering a vast mass of knowledge and experience and it is on this that the future of health services of these countries must be based in future.

Muslim, Druze, Ismaili, Christian and Bedouin Arabs, Turks, Assyrian, Circassian, Armenian and Kurdish people are all treated on the same footing. The extent of the work is small, but the FAU and the Spears Mission hope that the workers in these clinics, may play a part in increasing the mutual respect and understanding between the people of the West and the people of Syria and Lebanon, by living and working amongst them; and that the close contacts thus formed may help to ensure appreciation of each other's point of view. The future of the clinic work is difficult to forecast and the chances of it being taken over by an official body of the Syrian or Lebanese governments, seems very unlikely indeed I think.

A patient in a Syrian mobile clinic
Photo Friends House Library

Clinic work in Syria

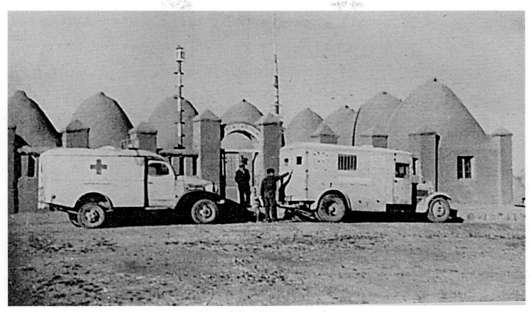

A mobile clinic at work
"It is often primitive, and bedding is absent, with relatives expected to bring food."
Photograph Friends House Library

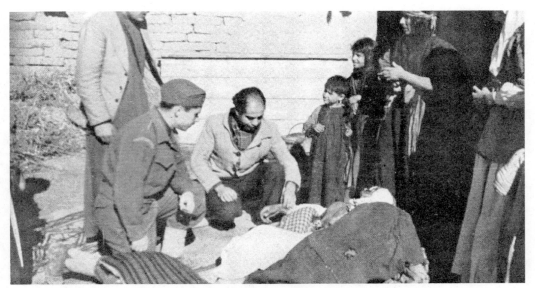

The hospital at Tel Tamer in north eastern Syria
Tel Tamer was the headquarters of the mobile clinics, and was partly supported by gifts
from the Society of Friends.
Photograph Friends House Library

At last my mother has received some letters from Syria, which cheer her up, plus David writes wishing our father a Happy Christmas........

Thursday, November 12th 1942 – Wolverhampton (Airgraph)

My dearest one

I posted letter 19 on Monday, having received your AM letter card written 26th October, also letter 11. I was so pleased to hear your Syrian news. What an interesting visit you had and you certainly travelled and saw a good deal of the country. I am longing to get letters 14 and 15. I hope you are keeping well now and not too tired. Isn't the news of Alamein yesterday splendid? We are all feeling so much more cheerful! I expect you are very busy right now.

We are all very fit – also your family. Millior and Anna return to London next Monday, Nov 16th with the nurse. Alfred is up in Birmingham for the Woodbrooke Council and will travel back with them.

My love for you is stronger than ever. David and Antony send their love And all my dearest love too. God bless you, ever yours Joan.

Tuesday, November 17th 1942 – Wolverhampton (Airgraph)

My darling

I sent off letter No 20 yesterday with two photographs of the children – I do hope you will like them. They are part of my Christmas present to you and come with all our dearest love. A very happy Christmas to you darling and I hope you won't be too lonely. We shall be thinking of you and longing for your dear company. David sent you a card for Christmas today – he wrote it himself (see top of p356). Your mother and my Mother both sent AGs yesterday too.

I long for more letters from you. Millior and family returned to London yesterday. On Thursday next I am meeting Jeph and Margaret for lunch, and then they are taking me to see 'The Desert Song'!! I haven't seen them for over 18 months.

Reg has been over and settled Vera and family back in their own house once again, which I think is better. How are you darling? I miss you and feel so lonely, my heart aches so much for you. Oh so much. God bless you and watch over you always. Dearest love, Joan.

Antony (left) and David and Antony 1944
"I've sent you two photographs of the children."

Tuesday, November 17th 1942 – Wolverhampton (Air pc)

Dear Daddy

A very happy Christmas. I am in bed with a cold, but I am not very poorly. I have been writing on my blackboard and doing numbers up to 100. Lots of love David xx

Friday, November 20th 1942 – Wolverhampton (Air pc)

Darling Ralph

I've not had any long letters from you for over a fortnight. I feel so cut off when I don't hear anything, and wonder if anything has happened to you. I know you do write often, and I'm sure it's just the slow post, but I do so long for your letters.

Yesterday I met Margaret and Jeph in Birmingham. M & I had lunch at Barrows Stores[8], then J, M and I went to the theatre to see 'The Desert Song'! [9] We then had tea before I caught the train back home. It's the first time I've been taken out since you went away. More of this anon. I did enjoy it immensely. They are both well and send love to you. They are still trying for a family. D & A both have awful colds, and D has been in bed for several days, but I hope he will be able to return to school on Monday.

Only one long letter has come through since you reached Cairo – letter 12 was the last. How I do long to hear all your news. I wonder if you are hearing from me. I try and send cards and AG's every week and a long letter weekly. God bless you dearest one. All my love and xx from the children. Joan

Tuesday, November 24th 1942 – Wolverhampton (No 21)

My own darling husband

At last my darling, I received a most welcome Air Mail letter card, saying you were sending a parcel by a friend of John's. Bless you for sending that. It is sweet of you, and I shall love to have it. I expect you have told me more about it in previous letters, which as yet still haven't come through. I do so long for a letter – a really long one! I haven't had the one you wrote before leaving Syria yet. I love to get your letters so, as it's all we have now and it does mean so much to get regular news from each other. I do hope mine are getting through well.

All the parcels from South Africa have come except the cosmetics and the parcel from Florence. By the way I had a very nice letter from her yesterday. It does make me so happy and proud to hear all these fine things about you. She says how much they all loved you and they felt "such a spiritual uplift" from your visit, and how happy they were to welcome you in their homes.

Really darling, your charm and powers as a leader seem to have overflowed in all directions. You certainly made a 'hit'!! And then you are so stupid to say you are no good. What rot! Blah, blah!! Truly it makes me very, very happy to receive all these letters. I wrote off immediately to Florence and thanked her for all her kindnesses in looking after you and for sending all the cables and parcels. I also said that when you return home, I shall bring out these letters and never let you get dissatisfied with yourself again! I told her you had a very poor opinion of yourself! She sounds very nice.

Your mother was wondering what we could send to the Webb's as a small gift for all they had done for you. She was talking to Cousin Elsie about the book on Housing that the Trust brought out and they thought it might be a good idea to send a copy to Maurice and also a copy for Adam's College Library. I think they will like that don't you?

Also your mother thinks she can get hold of some nice old lace to send Mrs Webb. We can never repay all these kind Friends enough, but perhaps one day we shall have the opportunity of entertaining them in our own dear home. By the way I sent Florence the family snap taken just before you left. I thought she might like a copy. I hope you will receive the photos of the children soon. I also posted yesterday the Hilaire Belloc book I mentioned before. I do hope you''ll like it my dear. It comes with very dear love.

It's your mother's birthday tomorrow. I wish I could call in and see her, but I am sending a note and David is writing a card as well.

The milk position here is critical here now. We're only allowed 1½ pints a week for Adults. Antony gets a pint a day and David now only gets ½ a pint a day, as he also gets some at school. I think it's very hard on children who are just 5, as they don't get the full meat ration or any extra eggs now. I wonder what will happen on the school holidays when he isn't getting school milk. I must phone the Food Office I think. Compared with many countries we are very lucky I suppose, but I am anxious for the children. What must conditions be like in Greece and Norway? That is tragic.

The shops are all Christmassy now, though there is little to buy. Toys are a terrible price and mostly rubbish. Books seem the best things to get. I do wonder what you are reading. I've just got the biography of the American politician Cordell Hull which looks interesting. Also a book on Russian children. I've just bought Mary Webb's 'Spring of Joy. A Little Book of Healing'[10] with a book token which I had given me. I've always wanted a copy.

There was a very interesting account of your visit to Adam's College in last week's 'Chronicle' by Gordon Cox. There was also a good article on the journey to Addis Ababa. What a relief it must be that they have all arrived at last.

We've had several lovely frosty sunny days. How I long for a good walk in the country. I take the children out, but not very far. The thrushes are singing so beautifully right now, it might almost be spring! There are not many flowers about except Chrysanths and one or two late roses. The shops have Violets and Anemones, but the trees are quite bare now. What is the weather like with you? I think it must be rather nice at this time. Not too hot but pleasant sunshine. I have a feeling that great things are going to happen next year. God, I do long for the end to come. I'm missing you so and the longing is sometimes unbearable.

David is back at school now, but his cold hasn't entirely gone. Antony has a chest cold with a horrid cough, but he is cutting the last back teeth. He is cheerful and such a darling, so lively and full of fun, talking all day. David is growing up very much and I think he is going to be quite tall. He still has a wonderful imagination. He's eating a little better now and has a knife and fork which makes him feel very grand. He can now read a little too.

I'm afraid my letters must be very dull, but there is no news. Each days is much the same as the last and I'm steadily stagnating. It is inevitable I'm afraid. I get so tired. Mother and I do go to the theatre occasionally, but that is all and now the buses stop at 9.0pm it makes even that difficult. As I told you in my last note, Jeph and Margaret took me to the theatre last Thursday. It was a real change for me and I thoroughly enjoyed it.

I met Margaret for lunch at Barrows Stores and then we met Jeph at the Theatre Royal after and saw *The Desert Song*, which was delightful. We just had time for a cup of tea after before the train left. They both seem very well and happy. But they long for their own home and privacy again. I think they are rather tired of living in a community every day and of course they are rather cut off at Barnt Green.

Mother is very busy at the bookshop and I suppose they will get busier every day now with Christmas nearly upon us. She stands up to it remarkably well, but understandably she gets tired at the end of the day. [......]

I say what a terrific trip you had through Syria, Michael Rowntree says you covered 3000 miles. You will have seen much more than I did or W&L. I'm glad you liked it so much, but I knew you would. I think the land nearer the coast is the loveliest of all, with the mountains rising up suddenly ahead of one and pine trees growing everywhere. I wonder if you were able to see the famous cedars of Lebanon.

I'm reading Henry Williamson's *The Beautiful Years*, which is the first book of the four part novel [11]. I found it most enjoyable, and he certainly has a deep love of the country, with a special understanding of a child's mind, which he describes in the most wonderful way. Have you read any of his books, they are well worth it?

W&L sent an Airgraph off to you at the weekend. I hope you will receive it for Christmas. We are always thinking of you and longing for you. My heart aches so for you and your companionship, and to see your dear face again and feel you close to me. I do love you so very dearly my sweetheart and long for your return.

No more for now my darling, dearest, sweetest Ralph. I long to hold you again in my arms and to kiss you once more.

All my love, my dearest.
Your ever loving Joan

And so one period of travel ends and another begins.

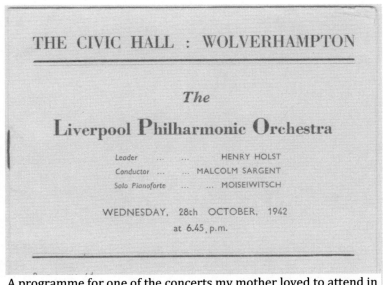

A programme for one of the concerts my mother loved to attend in Wolverhampton (see page 345)

"It was a most enjoyable evening; a fine orchestra with Malcolm Sargent conducting and they played Beethoven's 'Emperor' Piano concerto with Benno Moiseiwitsch at the piano. I did enjoy it."

Working alongside the Army

Eric Green really runs our HQ very well.

The food is extremely well served, and the servants are the best you will find anywhere. They are called Bishir, Mohammed, Achmet and Hadad, and were previously with the American Archeological Mission. They are perfectly trained, and cook, wait and clear everything away beautifully. It all seems slightly immoral, but it does mean we can get on with our work !

Unit members liaising with the army

Photographs Friends House Library

Chapter 24
The Military Hospital and Blood Transfusion

For some 30 months the FAU worked in association with the Blood Transfusion service, first in Alexandria and later in Cairo and Tripoli. They helped with the supply of blood and other fluids for field units, the bottling and storing and testing of blood as well as the manufacture of blood serum. Unit men worked closely with field Blood Transfusion Units attached to light surgical units and field ambulances behind the lines. They drove and maintained vehicles and refrigerators, acted as medical orderlies and carried out transfusions under the direction of an RAMC officer. Their service helped save many lives from Cairo to Tunisia.

Meanwhile my father is experiencing many problems, from relations with the RAMC and the Red Cross to dealing with his own ranks.........

Wednesday, November 11th – 1942 Alexandria (20)

My dearest Joan

[.....] Life continues pretty frantically. We are sending John Gough up to take charge of the administration in Beirut, and I may drive him up there to show him around. I have been to see the British Red Cross several times and to talk to various Officers at GHQ in Alexandria, from where I am now writing. There has also been the Bailey affair to deal with, which has not been easy. The lack of confidence in him as an Officer seems general and I think I must accept his resignation. It's very hard on him, though he is behaving very well, and as a man he is still very much liked.

During these last few busy days up here in Alex, hurrying from place to place in the heat, one realises just how calming amidst the pressure, the sea can be, looking at its most beautiful right now in the heat. Here am I rushing about seeing people about this and that, settling points with Peter Gibson before he goes off to join his new section, working closely with the Military Hospital, and arranging if I can, to go Teheran fairly soon, yet the sea ebbs and flows reassuringly in its own sweet way, quite unperturbed by all our hustle and bustle!

I sometimes feel this is an impossible job. Dealing with the outside world, which can be hard enough God knows. But on top of that, there are all the internal Unit troubles and crises, not to mention the criticisms and having to be nice to people all the time. I often wonder if I am the right person for the job, though people seem to have confidence in me. So much to do and so little time in which to do it. I've just had a very full day at Daly's with Peter, before we went to visit the Unit at the Military hospital, to which we hope to be moving, talking with some of our chaps who are already there and then having a rather difficult interview with the Colonel who is their Commanding Officer. I can see that it is going to be a ticklish business settling the men in, as I don't think the Colonel really appreciates how the Unit works or what it is trying to achieve. His sole priority is the success of his hospital, and he isn't prepared to have an independent group mixed in with it, which isn't under his control. Without a second Officer in Peter's party, we are going to be pretty busy.

How long one can keep this up I don't know. More of this later, as I now need to make arrangements to go to Teheran, to see if there's any possibility of Unit members helping with all the Polish refugees, who are pouring down through Iran at this very moment. There is heavy fighting in progress all around us, and we can just hear the thud of the distant guns, but little news gets through. From what we can gather though, things seem to be moving rather slowly. More tomorrow. Ralph

Despite the 'abhorrence of anything that crawls' my father has acquired a deep love of the country and understands the Bible so much clearer, especially the psalms, and why Christ illustrated everything with parables, surmising that in essence it is probably largely unchanged in millennia..................

Sunday, November 15th – 1942 Cairo (20 contd)

Dearest Joan

It has been a hectic visit to Alex and now I am back in Cairo, where there is a pile of work waiting for me. I had quite a pleasant journey back here with one of Lady Spears 'girls', as she was coming this way in one of the staff cars. She seemed to have been stationed all over the place with the Spears set up, even spending time in Bordeaux, where she saw quite a lot of the war in Europe.

On arriving back here, I got talking to John Marley, one of the two men who we'd taken with us on their way to Syria for a bit of leave as we left Alex. They'd just returned from their leave, where they seem to have had a fascinating time. They both shared my love of this extraordinarily beautiful country, and concurred with my natural abhorrence of anything that crawls, especially scorpions and beetles or mosquitoes and earwigs, all of which proliferate out here!

But the pluses greatly outweigh the minuses, and it is surely no surprise that the Old Testament writers were so filled with such a sense of the beauty of the world, so evident all around one here. Each day they saw the sun rise and set in glory as we have, saw the sun shine after rain, and glorious clouds circle the mountains in the purple distance. They saw olive trees and vines against the sun-soaked grey rocks, and sailed at night on Galilee under a full moon as we did, or lay out to sleep in the silent hills as Orion strode across the sky.

No wonder the Bible is full of the wonders of nature and the Psalmist could write – *"When I consider thy heavens, the work of thy fingers, the moon and the stars, which thou hast ordained; what is man, that thou art mindful of him; and the son of man, that thou visitest him?"* Or even just – *"I will lift up mine eyes unto the hills..."* Being here, one understands exactly why Jesus illustrated his parables with such vividness. It is surely likely that the flocks of black goats, the herds of camels and even the miserable Bedouin tents are little changed from the time of Abraham. And I'm told that if you compare the writings of Saudi Arabia's founder, Ibn Saud[1] and the book of David, there is a remarkable resemblance in character. I don't care a damn for historic spots of dubious validity, such as in Jerusalem, where the children come up and say "You like to visit tomb of Virgin Mary?" which is nauseating. But I do care for places which have atmosphere and association.

Thank you for all your lovely letters, which have cheered me up no end. I am only sorry that so many of mine have not yet arrived – especially since I have taken some trouble with them! It is lovely to hear news of the children and I know what a responsibility it is for you, but know that I have absolute confidence in you. I'm sure D is growing up so much now, and I wish I could be there to help. I hope that he will grow up to have a love of nature and beauty, literature and poetry. His letters are so well written; what an angel he must be. How I miss both the children. Now I am back, there seems more to do than ever. So please excuse any more for now. I send you my love. Ralph.

PS Mike and I haven't yet made out our final list of birds for the trip, but after looking certain things up in the books, it appears that we saw over 100 different species between us, which included 12 new to me.

In this letter my father tries to describe the many faces of Cairo, part Western with its posh hotels and trams, and part primitive with its cacophony and filthy smells…………

Monday, 16th November 1942, Cairo (20 contd)

My dearest wife

Now that I'm back in Cairo, I really feel quite worried about our whole situation. There is plenty of rumour but little solid news, besides what we read in the newspapers, which will be the same as you get. But from what little one does hear, the battle seems to be going well enough and according to the papers our forces are well beyond El Daba, and I fully expect all our Units will begin to follow them up soon.

There is little else to say at the moment. I am beginning to get a bit more on top of things now, having spent the whole week in the office writing letters. I do wish though that my typist could arrive before 7.0pm, as it means working on so late into the night. I've also spent a lot of time seeing various persons about this and that, but whether I achieved anything is less sure. For instance, I had a long and rather unsatisfactory meeting with the Red Cross this morning, but quite a satisfactory one with GHQ. So on the whole, the day finished about equal.

It was all quite useful, but I think I ought to be travelling again soon, as I don't think this is really a job in which to sit still for too long. So I shall make a flying visit with John Gough up into Syria, and then after a short interval, I'll probably try and make a round of our desert units, before going on to Persia, by which time I'm supposing Tom Tanner will be here. The weather is really excellent now, with beautiful clear skies and sun all day, but happily not too hot. We are still wearing shorts and shirts, but it's beginning now to get quite cold at night and I expect we shall change into warmer wear soon.

Cairo is a strange city. I can't say I like it very much, but it has its fascination. There is continual noise, which I don't like: noise of cars, horse's hooves, crowing cocks, braying donkeys, tram bells, raucous and monotonous street cries, street vendors ringing bells, and mewing Kites, which all go to make an unending background of sound. In many ways, though, it's a Western city with its smart shops and Shepheards Hotel, its cars and trams. But then again it isn't. The groups gathered outside the cafés talking interminably aren't Western; no more are the sudden street quarrels, nor the innumerable craftsmen from tinsmiths to leather workers carrying on their trades on the pavement, shoeing horses in the middle of the street, or brushing a carpet in the road.

I hate the dirty beggars, the diseased children, the touts selling cap badges, socks, papers or lottery tickets; the filthy fruit stalls, covered with flies with a vendor as dirty as his wares; and the diseased women selling roasted corn cobs. Neither am I very enamoured of the smells: horse dung, petrol, sewage and filthy garbage.

On the other hand again, the crowds are interesting; so mixed, from the dirtiest and lowest to the fat, respectable, wealthy Egyptian in his fez. And I love to see the carpenters crafting good, sensible furniture in workshops opening onto the street. The white-clothed police are amusing, though totally ineffective, and everywhere troops of all nationalities and varieties fill the streets. Soldiers, sailors and airmen from Britain, New Zealand and South Africa, and from France, Greece and Poland.

All of them a complete mix: from really untidy soldiers to subalterns conscious of their uniform, from rising captains to Senior Officers, some fat and fierce, others rude and vulgar, some kindly and refined. There are even nurses and women of the Auxiliary Territorial Service. Yes, it is a fascinating mixture.

The shops are all well filled with splendid cloth and leather goods, with a seemingly unending supply of food and a cornucopia of fruit, from dates and bananas to guavas, oranges and grapefruit. If you were to be let loose in Cairo now my dear, you would soon spend all you had, I think. Talking of which you might send me the state of our overdraft at the Bank!

Thank you for sending me the books, though I don't seem to have as much time as I used to for reading, though I hope that will change soon. And I was delighted to hear of you taking David to Selly Oak Meeting. Fancy our son now old enough to go to Quaker meeting! How much that meeting and the Adult School has meant to us over the years.

I shall not be able to get Christmas presents off to you this year, but please count the gifts from South Africa as presents and can you buy something suitable for the boys from me with all my love. How I wish you were here now, and how I wish I could be with you this Christmas.

I must close now, my love, as I am going out to supper with Douglas Mackenzie this evening.   Lots of love, Ralph

And an afterthought – he forgot to mention the Nile..........

Wednesday, November 18th 1942 continued – Cairo (20 final)

My dearest
How could I forget the Nile? In my eloquent account of Cairo above, I somehow seem to have forgotten the great river, which really is rather imposing. The broad, muddy, swift flood of its onward rush has a grandeur all its own, and the huge-sailed feluccas, congregating in large numbers waiting for the bridges to open, make a splendid sight, even though they're a nuisance when you are waiting to cross. And all along the bay, the palm trees are truly splendid.

Douglas and I had a very pleasant evening yesterday. A lot of the conversation centred on women, or the lack of them! Douglas said that on the whole, he was resigned to being celibate for the duration, but that he did sometimes dream that he'd wake up one night and find a dream woman beside him. But then added "Of course, I would think I was dreaming, and in unbelief roll over and go to sleep again!" How wonderful it would be though, if I could wake up and find you beside me.

I seem to be covered in bites, probably from the gharry we took to the restaurant! We went to a new restaurant, where there was good service and good food, and Douglas and I had excellent conversation. We walked back through the streets under a brilliant starry sky and looked in briefly at Shepheards, where everyone was dancing under the trees all decked out with hanging lights. The stars, the lighted windows, the food – how I wish you were to see it. Oh what a waste without you.

Eric Green really runs our HQ very well, and now we have more furniture, it makes a very pleasant dwelling. The food – army food – is extremely well served, and the servants are the best you will find anywhere. They are called Bishir, Mohammed, Achmet and Hadad, and were previously with the American Archeological Mission. Eric is trying to learn Arabic, but they speak pretty good English. They don't have to be told what to do and they work well and unobtrusively, dusting and polishing, even buffing up my buttons! Never as long as I have lived or shall live, will I have better, quieter, more efficient servants. We are lucky!

I have just written a long letter to Duncan in China. How I wish I could see him. I also wrote to Dick in India, and I would love to see him too. Well, I'm off to the post and hope you get this before too long. Dearest love, Ralph

Air Post Cards seem to get through, though longer letters continue to take for ever, much to my mother's frustration, as she longs for detailed news of my father's time in Syria and the Lebanon.......

Wednesday, November 25th 1942 – Wolverhampton (Air pc)

My darling Ralph

Thank you very much for your AG received this morning, also one for David and W&L posted 7th Nov, so they came through very well. I posted letter 21 yesterday. Longing to get some more long letters though.....the last I received is still number 12.

We are all well, except that the children haven't quite lost their colds and coughs yet. I wish you could see Antony at this minute. I am writing this in the bedroom, having just returned from taking D to school. Antony keeps taking up your photograph and kissing it and saying "Daddy, Daddy – nice"! I told him I was writing to you. He is growing up fast, and is now definitely a boy and no longer a baby. He talks all day.

Millior is safely settled at Gower Street again with the nurse still there for a week or so. The baby thrives well. Your mother seems well too, but is feeling tired now after all she has done during the past weeks. I think she is hoping to go to Millior and Alfred in December. How I wish I was coming up to London to see you. It seems such an eternity since last May.I do long for you so much and pray we may soon see the end of this ghastly war. We all send dearest love.   Ever your loving Joan

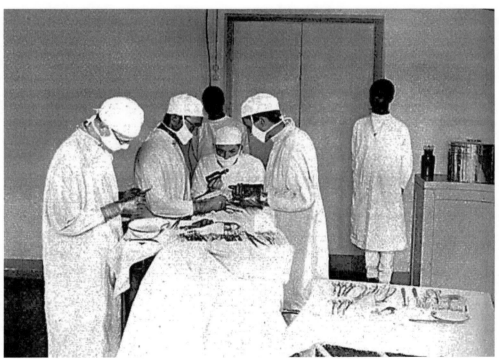

Operations and Blood Transfusion in Colonel Buttle's Unit
"We of the FAU felt quite proud to be able to play a small part in this great achievement."
Photograph courtesy of John Blake Publishing

Buttle's Bottled Blood

Lieutenant-Colonel G A H Buttle
"A huge chuckling bulk of a man….imperturbable, adored by his junior officers, he lit
his organization with such a flame of enthusiasm that no demand on the resources of
the blood transfusion service became too great or impossible to surmount."
Photograph courtesy Holly Aylett

Undoubtedly the most successfully sustained chapter in the Unit's work with the British Army was its Blood Transfusion work. Lieutenant-Colonel G A H Buttle, who was in charge of the Blood Transfusion work was full of enthusiasm to build up the unit and keen to use FAU men where there were no Army personnel to cover the work. This led to the FAU feeling that they were making an important contribution to a job that might otherwise have remained undone.

In the diaries of Stanley Aylett's 'Surgeon at War', edited by his daughter Holly, he describes Buttle as follows – "A huge chuckling bulk of a man….imperturbable, adored by his junior officers, he lit his organization with such a flame of enthusiasm that no demand on the resources of the blood transfusion service became too great or impossible to surmount." As work progressed, further men were added, some in Alex and some in small Field Transfusion Units in the desert, where they established as close a working relationship as could be wished.

The 15th Scottish Blood Department under Colonel Buttle, known as No 1 Base Transfusion Unit, was the only source of blood-grouping serum and plasma in the Middle East, in which the Unit played a significant role in supplying all the 8th Army area with blood.

In Alexandria, though less blood was collected for sending to the desert, the team nonetheless had the advantage of clinical work and working with the Hospital's own transfusions. My father reported back from men working in blood transfusion "that members of the FAU are now working together and share a considerable responsibility for the bottling, classifying and issuing of all blood-grouping serum. They produce all the blood serum used for transfusion, and all the blood taken for transfusion passes through their hands in order that the bottles may be capped under sterile conditions. 'Buttle's bottled blood' soon became a by-word in the Middle East!"

There was bound to be an increased demand for blood during a military 'push', but this latest 'push' was in excess of anything previously dealt with. So a mobile unit went to areas of potential donors and on one memorable day, some 400 bottles were filled and despatched to the desert fighting area. Douglas Mackenzie, who was a qualified bio-chemist and dealt with all such requirements of the hospital, soon became responsible for the whole work of the department under Colonel Buttle.

He said later that "We of the FAU felt quite proud to be able to play a small part in this great achievement." Colonel Buttle himself wrote to the Unit some time after they had departed: "So now that the last of the FAU have departed personal regrets are felt by both sides. There are points of view in which the FAU and the military folk do not see eye to eye, and in this I feel that a commendable tolerance was shown by all. It is gratifying that a great degree of working co-operation has been achieved despite academic difficulties, and that a great deal of very good work was done."

Encouraging military news from Alamein; cheering news of the men pulling out the stops; and heartening news of the men beginning to settle in. Here my father describes in a letter home, a visit to the Colonel's flat.........

Monday, November 23rd 1942, Cairo (21)

My dear Joan

The news from Alamein[2] is cheering. It almost makes one begin to hope. But that would probably be rash. Yesterday evening Douglas Mackenzie and I went to the flat of Colonel Buttle who is in charge of the Blood Bank, where our people are working. It's known as Buttle's bottled blood! He is in charge of all ME blood, and is an absolutely delightful fellow.

I'm often amazed at how situations draw qualities out of a person one never even suspected existed. Take Douglas, for instance, who is a very private man and if anything a bit of a dilettante, but he has really managed to get on so well with the people out here. He has qualifications in chemistry which hardly anyone else out here has, and although he's not an Officer, he commands respect in the Lab, simply because he possesses such a firm and competent grasp of a difficult and specialized job.

After we'd had some refreshments Buttle, Douglas and I went on to the Anglo Egyptian Union for dinner, where there was an exhibition of drawings by the war artist, Edward Ardizzone. I remember being very impressed when I first saw his work in London, especially those done aboard troopships. But I feel this is rather less good, or maybe his particular tricks and style pall after a time. Altogether we all had a very pleasant evening. I've decided I really must try and get out and meet more people: you never know when such contacts may be useful.

Peter Gibson came up on a flying visit from Alex on Saturday. I drove one of the ambulances down to meet him, though it really is a nightmare driving through Cairo at night. He says the boys have settled into the new Unit, so I do hope things will start to go well now. Afterwards I had an interview with the Deputy Censor, a Colonel and a most charming man. I must say the army, with one or two exceptions, are so good to us, which is heartening, as though we must very often be a pain in their side, hopefully they also think we are making a valid contribution. People really are beginning to get very excited about the military developments. I'm not sure about bringing the Free French into the war, but if it finishes Rommel off and clears the Mediterranean, it will surely be tremendous. Then Italy? Greece? Perhaps things are moving, or is it only a false dawn?

I haven't had a day off for ages and have worked all morning. Ah well, perhaps some fine day not too far away, all will give way to being at home with you again with week ends with the children. It can't be good living on the job like this. I wrote some Christmas cards yesterday to my mother and sister and your mother and David, with an airgraph to you. I'm afraid I haven't written a card to you, as we are only allowed four. I know you will understand, though I am afraid they are not very nice ones anyway.

All my love for now
God bless, Ralph

The Free French – who'd refused to sign up to the Vichy Government – began as just a limited rebel faction of the French Army, made up of volunteers from metropolitan France and the French colonies, but gradually evolved into a full scale army after it was joined by recruits from the French resistance and then merged with the 'Army of Africa', led by General Henri Giraud. The 'Army of Africa' was largely made up of European settlers and indigenous colonial forces from France's extensive empire and was mainly equipped by the United States through a lend-lease scheme. Eventually the US Army supplied both the Free French forces and Army of Africa with Sherman tanks and hundreds of US-built aircraft, plus vehicles and artillery, helmets, uniforms and firearms, as well as fuel and rations, for many thousands of troops. They soon became a vital element in the allied victory.

———

My father further contemplates his reading: "I have just read the history of the Crusades. It is a fascinating story of action, of devotion, of fantastic bravery and endurance, ruined by ignorance, stupidity, jealousy and faction. As one sees British army lorries on a road near Acre, one remembers that over seven hundred years ago Richard Coeur de Lion stormed and took this town. For how long now have British troops fought for Christianity, or for what they believed to be right? As Shakespeare's *Henry IV* says: *'Therefore, friends, As far as to the sepulchre of Christ – Whose soldier now, under whose blessed cross, We are impressed and engag'd to fight in those holy fields, Over whose acres walk'd those blessed feet, Which fourteen hundred years ago were nailed, For our advantage on the bitter cross.'*

Edward Ardizzone – Boarding a Troopship

Edward Ardizzone (1900-1979), after a short spell in an anti-aircraft unit, worked as a full-time, official war artist, assigned to the War Office by the War Artist's Advisory Committee. This one above, which my father had particularly admired at The Bloomsbury Gallery in 1939, is titled 'The Dock Operating Company Boarding a Steamer to Unload It.'

Reproduced by kind permission of the Imperial War Museum

At last my father sets of with Johnnie Gough to introduce him to some of the people he'll be working with in Beirut. It's a long journey of nearly 400 miles on to Tel Aviv, but is somewhat beset by engine failure. He finally catches up with the Lochs in Jerusalem.........

Thursday, 26th November 1942 – Tel Aviv

Dearest Joan

We started out from Cairo for Tel Aviv at 6.0am yesterday. The early morning was quite lovely, with a clear blue sky and the rising sun just catching the tops of the trees and the felucca sails as they gradually appeared out of the mist, still lingering on the canals and round the bases of the date palms. There were peasants starting work, geese babbling, donkeys, horses, and buffaloes waiting to cross at ferry points, while parties of Egrets could be dimly seen in the mist standing by the pools.

Our journey however, was less calm, being fraught with bad luck, beginning with the old engine completely dying on us. By good luck, rather than good management, we had just arrived in Ismailia, and by a stroke of yet more luck, managed to find a garage able to help us. While our 'new good friends' the engineers fitted a new engine for us, we took the opportunity to have some breakfast. In just a couple of hours, we were on our way again, only to find a little further on, that the road had been totally washed away, incurring even longer hold ups.

It was not to be our day, as with the new engine just installed, we took the desert run very slowly, so as not to risk further trouble, and the journey took forever, which meant it was already dark when we limped into the city of Beersheba at about 5.15, with our lights hardly working. Then by some miracle things improved. With a little tinkering, the lights came back up again; the new engine seemed to have settled down; and by pushing on somewhat faster, we arrived in Gaza in time for supper. Finally, after several more hours of driving, we arrived here in Tel Aviv by about 11.0pm, having driven some 380 miles.

Having missed Sydney and Joice Loch on my last visit, I was determined to see them on my short stay here this time, and made the journey over to Jerusalem to call on them. They are middle-aged Friends, who are the fortunate occupants of a small house in the Russian garden of Gethsemane, which looks straight across to the terraced slopes of the old city and the walls beyond. They seem to have spent a life time in relief work and later took me to see some of the work which they are doing among Polish refugees here in Haifa. This will be very helpful to me if I manage to go to Teheran, to see if the Unit can assist the Polish refugees, who are now pouring down from Russia through Iran, as I mentioned earlier.

The two of them had joined the Friends Relief Service in 1940 specifically to help the Polish refugees who were then fleeing Nazi persecution into Romania. I admire them tremendously. Almost single-handedly they had organized the evacuation of thousands of these refugees, taking them on by ship, all the way through heavily mined waters across to Haifa. They are typical of many Quaker relief workers: prying into things, getting round obstacles, winning respect, and doing so much 'little good' that the whole is a great achievement. But why, Oh why, do all women Friends look just the same? Go to Monthly Meeting and you'll see Mrs Loch all around the room!

But they are both very nice, and I have the greatest respect for such people. They have just rented part of the old Russian Orthodox Church of Saint Tabitha, near Jaffa some 60 miles West of Jerusalem, as a school and home for women and children. It is built on the site of St Tabitha's tomb, among orange groves and mulberry trees. It is a lovely place and just now the trees are loaded with oranges. You may remember that St Peter raised Tabitha from the dead; unfortunately he wasn't available the second time!

I liked Tel Aviv better than I expected to. It is not an Eastern city. In fact it's much more like a new European suburb. Modern, flashy, with some of the poorer buildings showing signs of fading and cracking, as so many modern buildings do, and all rather soulless. But some of the better buildings are well designed, with real feeling and imagination.

There is hardly an Arab to be seen; only a few beggars, and a great air of purpose and business, which is unusual out here. Everywhere, there are unveiled women, playing a full part in the life of the town, which is so refreshing after Cairo. I actually saw a man offer his seat to a woman on a bus. I was so surprised that before I knew what I was doing, I offered mine to another! Usually the Arab rides on the donkey while the woman walks behind. Yesterday we saw a donkey walking, a woman carrying the load on her head, and kicking the donkey along at the same time!

It was a lovely day, and we had a pleasant run into Haifa where we had lunch. Just recently it's been a succession of coincidences. In the middle of the Sinai desert, I met a Greek Field Officer who had been in Durban with us, and yesterday, just as we got out of the car, I bumped into the man I had shared a cabin with on the Amsterdam from Durban to Cairo, who is now Labour Officer here. I will close for now, my dearest. My love as always, Ralph

And then they drove back again to Beirut to introduce John Gough to as many people as possible, as he takes up his new position as head of the FAU admin there.......

Saturday, 28th November 1942 – From Beirut (No 22)

Dearest Joan

The run from Haifa to Beirut was a dream of beauty. It was a glorious afternoon, bright sun but not too hot, and clear with the clarity of winter sun light. The sea, a deep, dark blue as far as the horizon, was calm with tiny waves breaking on the shore, and two-masted barques bobbing gently along. It was a cloudless, blue sky, and everything was quiet, pin sharp and bright in the sun. The road was bordered with stone walls and cypress trees, but further on we came past grey hills and orange groves, and across rivers, held up at one point on a bridge, while two camels crossed, with a man riding the first, towering high above the car as he passed us by. Then as evening came on, the light got fuller and richer, and more mellow, like autumn sunshine; but autumn sunshine mixed with the glory of evening light.

Since we arrived in Beirut we have been enjoying the almost overwhelming hospitality of the Leavitts[3] who really are most kind. They have two sons away in America and two daughters, Marga and Hayan here. Marga is 16, a sensible, quiet girl and quite good to look at, while Hayan is only 12.

I want to take John Gough on a round of calls here and introduce him to as many people as I can, before leaving on Saturday. So this morning we went to see President David Dodge at the American University, where the grounds were looking at their very best, with Bougainevillea on the walls, and a blazing bed of red Chrysanthemums, and beyond that the unbelievable sea and the grey mountains. Later I took him up to Broumana, which was looking as lovely as usual, with the heather in full bloom all over the slopes, as I wanted to see about the Clinics and also to introduce John to the Turtles, but poor Dorothy Turtle had run a piece of glass into her hand and the doctors have so far failed to dig it out, making her partially lose its use. Then in the evening we called in on the Spears Mission, so that John could meet the staff there. Beirut must, I think, be the worst town that I have ever driven in. For some unknown reason the trams suddenly come at you on the wrong side of the road, and the on-coming cars all follow them, so if you don't follow onto the wrong side yourself, you've had it.

We are all desperately wanting to know what is happening in North Africa, as one hears so many versions. I do wonder by the way, if Lord Dillon has gone back to North Africa, since he knew the terrain so well. Roger Soltau, who I bumped into at the University, thinks that with General Eisenhower doing a deal with François Darlan, after collaborating with the Germans at Vichy, he has completely done for General de Gaulle. All for now, Ralph

Continued....Sunday 29th November – Jerusalem (No 22 contd)

The Leavitts really have been kindness itself. They pressed me to stay, but as I couldn't, laid on an early meal for me instead. I left John, having introduced him all round as much as possible, feeling rather down, I fear. It was a very pleasant visit, especially being able to stay in the Leavitts home. Having someone look after you and feeding you and really bothering, was rather splendid in itself.

I left about 12.30 on my own. I like my own company, but on these long distances with possibilities of breakdown, and having to re-fuel and re-water, it's much better and nicer to have a companion. Also I don't much care for night driving, especially with indifferent lights on unknown mountainous roads.

However, I covered the 200 miles without mishap in about 6¼ hours. The staff car behaved like a perfect lady, save for a slight roughness at low speed, and we cruised along at 50-55mph to our mutual satisfaction. I came across several soldiers hitching a lift along the way, so happily gave them a lift, which gave me some company too. The last stretch by moonlight, through the hills from Ramallah was most beautiful. I parked the car and set off to find a hotel, and was directed to a veritable palace; very extravagant I know, but so nice and I'm alone! I had a good bed and a good meal, then went out for a stroll, and now I'm very tired - and so to bed, as Pepys would say.

I did enjoy my solitude in a luxury hotel. Such peace and calm. I collected the car and went off to find the Lochs. I must say, I like the new Jerusalem: it's spacious, clean and with some really fine new buildings. I could only glimpse the walls of the old town. The Lochs have a bungalow in the garden of Gethsemane. Do you remember that view? Behind the Mount of Olives, with the gilded domes of the Russian Church towering above one. In front, the Church of All Nations, then the Kidron valley and the terraced slopes covered with olive groves, and on top the walls of the old city. Sidney Loch pointed out the supposed site of the Agony, the ride to Jerusalem, the Via Doloroso, and took me through the Garden of Gethsemane.

Despite the many churches that crowd the historic sites, it still retains a sort of beauty. The grey stone of the hillside, reflected in the grey of the buildings and the silver grey olive trees, is set against the dark of the cypresses, and the brilliant blue of the sky. I don't really mind whether the disciples slept on that rock or this, or if Christ passed over this slab on his triumphal ride, but it is inspiring to be in a place where great events have happened. Is this really the stone slab where the disciples slept? How often today one sees Arabs similarly asleep. Are they tired? Ill? Bored? Lazy? Perhaps all of these. Yet of those typical natives, Christ made men who set the world on fire. No mean task.

Roger Soltau's wife Irene, was telling John and me that the only way Christ could get his point home to a poor and illiterate people would have been through simple stories, hence his use of parables. And here are crowds of just such simple people, surrounding the supposed tomb of the Virgin Mary, now all bathed with incense and lights. What pomp there is here now over the imagined grave of a poor peasant woman.

Sometimes I feel we Quakers lose out with our lack of ceremony, but at other times, I begin to wonder. Yet here there are still worshippers of magic and the unknown, and even amongst the most rational and civilized of us, still those who believe in the supernatural. And who dare criticise or say it is wrong, or old fashioned? Certainly not I!

Every day one sees yet another horror that brings one up short. Yesterday I met a Greek woman, oppressed by the tragedy of what had befallen her family, having lost five children in the fighting back home in Greece. Here the tragedy of the Poles, with parents seeing their children die of disease and starvation in front of them, or women being shot by firing squads. Sometimes it is almost too much to bear. Yet what can one do? Oh Lord, how long?

I'll stop now and write more tomorrow.

All love Ralph

Leslie and Margaret Leavitt
"The Leavitts really have been kindness itself."
Photograph courtesy of International College Beirut

The Garden of Gethsemane in Jerusalem &
The Church of St Tabitha near Jaffa

The Russian Orthodox Church in the garden of Gethsemane with the Mount of Olives

The old Russian church of Saint Tabitha
"Sydney and Joice rented part as a care home for Polish girls and women."
Photos Jerusalem Tourist Board

My father was taken by the Lochs up 'an alpine steep track' to see the work they were doing with the Polish refugees, then back to Jerusalem and eventually home to Cairo........

Monday, November 30th 1942 – (No 22 final)

Yesterday the Lochs took us to see the work they were doing with the Polish refugees. We drove on through the ancient village of Ain Karim, still just in the Jerusalem District, set amidst that beautiful grey, terraced beauty of Palestine, with its vines, olives and cypresses. It is reputed to be the birth place of St John the Baptist and the scene described in Luke, of Mary's Magnificat.

We continued on up a hill which Sidney said had just been repaired. "Quite alright for a car", he said jauntily! Had I known what he was letting me in for, I assuredly would not have driven the car up there. It was alpine steep, full of sharp stones and so narrow that we scraped the car as we rounded a particularly foul corner. However, we made it and the car, bless her, did it without a murmur. There in Jaffa about 65 miles from Jerusalem, was the old Russian Orthodox Church of Saint Tabitha that I mentioned earlier, which Sydney and Joice have partly rented as a care home for Polish girls and women. The Poles have now taken over the running themselves, and they are all beginning to recover and are apparently well and happy. It is no mean achievement.

Then we returned down to Jerusalem again. I packed up my luggage, re-fuelled, and was off by 2.0pm, intending to spend the night on the east side of the desert. It was a good road, hilly, but with a fairly good surface. The day was fine and the car behaved just perfectly, climbing up the steepest hills, taking corners and hairpin bends without any trouble at all. So with everything going well, I made the desert frontier by 4.0pm and with no problems from the border guards, I went quickly across, re-fuelled and drove straight off into the sunset.

Ahead was miles of desert and miles of a blazing sky; quite beautiful, but very trying to the eyes. Then as evening came on, in that half-light in which one's vehicle lights are useless, the dying day no help either, and the rising moon powerless, I stopped at a police check and tucked into some bully beef and biscuits. I got chatting to an ex-Seaforth Highlander Military Policeman, who kindly brought me a cup of tea and told me how he had narrowly escaped after Dunkirk. He made even Othello's *"hair-breadth 'scapes"* pale by comparison!

I felt much refreshed, and better able to carry on. Driving by moonlight, I made good progress and before too long saw the lights of the canal in the distance, and after over 170 miles of mostly desert road, I crept slowly down to the ferry, stopping only once to eat an orange, put in some extra petrol and have a pee. Everywhere was eerily silent, with just the waning moon and the stars. By the time I crossed the ferry, I estimated it would be gone 1.0am. The question was, should I do the extra 100 miles, or stay the night here? Of course, being me, I went on! This long distance driving is all very well, but it can become addictive. Once you have started, something makes you go on and on, but it is nervously exhausting. However, I made Cairo safely by exactly 1.0am, having driven in all some 350 miles in a total of 11 hours and from 4.30pm all in the dark.

When I got in, I found a splendid batch of letters from you. Thank you so much, I do appreciate it that you write so much and I love to hear all the news. I am glad D is getting on well at school. Don't worry too much about his being afraid of the dark. I was at his age tell him. Have also heard from brother John and my mother. It's so good that you are getting on well with my mother.

So all my love, and may God keep you safe. Ralph

Being apart is often almost unbearable, and my mother imagines scenarios when the door will open and there will be my father. As another Christmas approaches without my father, thoughts inevitably stray to wishing they could all be together again soon.............

Monday, November 30th 1942 – Wolverhampton (No 22)

Darling heart

It seems to be my turn to write into the blue this time as I am without news of you since I received letters 11 & 12 weeks ago. I do hope you are alright. Thank you for the Airgraph to David and me and W&L, wishing us good things for Christmas. David is writing to you – he so loves to get your letters, especially the ones with drawings.

It is half past two and I have just finished washing up, and both the boys are sleeping (I hope) and I am in the kitchen, where it is fairly warm. Oh, dearest how I wish I could ring you up and talk to you. Sometimes you seem so far away and cut off from me, and I long to have you near. My love just gets stronger every day and sometimes I feel I can't exist another day without seeing you. I know I have to, but how I long to put my arms round you and hold you so that you can never go. [....]

Bless you for being so lovable and precious, for being so fine and noble and all I ever wanted in a husband. Sometimes I allow myself to daydream about the days when I know you are on the way back to me. Beloved, you will never step off the train at Wolverhampton, because I shall come and meet you off the ship!!! I shall have our home ready, and the drawing room will be gay with flowers and the boys all eager and excited to welcome you home. It is good to allow ourselves occasionally to dwell on such things. I often do this at night when I am lying awake and wish I had you here to tease a little bit.

Your mother rang last night, but I was out. Mother said she seemed depressed. I expect she is missing Millior and she says John and Enid are so busy, so I'm afraid she must find life lonely. I must ring her up and try and cheer her a little. David and I wrote to her for her birthday. Florence's parcel arrived on Friday and I immediately posted most of them off to Millior. I wished very much I had a little daughter to wear the charming dress and other dainty things. It was so kind of her and I've written her a second letter saying they have now arrived. I hope Millior will like them. By the way I'm enclosing two of Millior's letters, which your mother thought you might like to see.

Last night I was invited to the Inglis' for a musical evening. They have quite a good collection of gramophone records and we listened to Schumann and Tchaikovsky, and then we had coffee and biscuits. There was a very nice young Dutch boy there from South Africa, and I enjoyed the evening. It was spoilt a bit, however, as when I came home at 10.30pm, it was pouring with rain and as the buses stop at 9.0pm, I had a long walk home. As it happened, of course it was also a very dark night and my torch gave out!

Do you remember someone of the name of Dick Webster at The Downs and LP? He is Mrs Inglis' brother-in-law, and a cousin of the Fox's in Birmingham. I believe he is very keen on birds. I was at the Walkers this morning – they have some lovely Peter Scott paintings of birds, which look grand in their sitting room on the cream wall. They all have wonderful colours and reflections. The Walkers were out at Belvide yesterday, but saw only Shovelers – no waders.

Mother and I saw a good play by A J Cronin at the theatre last Thursday, called *Jupiter Laughs*. It's about a young Doctor whose selfish concentration on his research work, results in the death of a missionary worker whom he loves. I thought it the best play they have done this season. It will soon be Pantomime time again.....and I know how much you will miss it this year!!! Winifred has two friends coming to tea today and also a baby. It is quite a business finding enough milk to entertain at the moment.

I wonder if you heard Churchill's speech last night, which was rather aimed at Italy. I had been feeling more cheerful about things, but his speech didn't give me much to hope for, except a final victory in the far distant future. But it looks better on all fronts at the moment and I do believe the tide has really begun to turn at last. I do so wonder how your men are getting on at the front in the hospitals. I'm sure they must be kept very busy. I see John Gough is now in charge in Syria.

Yesterday when I went out with the children, there was such a chorus of birdsong – mostly Thrushes and Robins; but I can't recall hearing birds singing so at this time of year. Mother has been feeling very tired recently as they are getting busier and busier at the shop in the lead up to Christmas, and she finds her legs ache. I also find her such a help here in the mornings. I don't know how she keeps going at 64. She is wonderful. I wonder if you have written to her for Christmas.

What can I tell you about the children this week? Their colds are slow going and Antony is cutting more teeth, but otherwise they are well and happy. David is getting to be a great help, as he can do so much for himself now: dressing, washing, cleaning his teeth, changing his shoes, brushing his hair and he is very good at going to the Post Office for me and bringing back the right change. He and Antony are getting to be good companions. On Saturday morning they played for about 2½ hours together, making a house and sweeping up leaves. Antony works to D's orders at the moment! A is talking all day and is so jolly and such fun.

Did I tell you that sometime ago I was telling D off, and he turned round and said "You will make me have a broken heart"! He always says "Don't tell Daddy I've been naughty, will you?" Oh, and he told me to tell you that he now eats with a knife and fork and not a spoon! Or if he has done something I praise him for, he says "You will tell that to Daddy, won't you?"

He so often talks of you, and even A says 'Daddy' now, and if I post a letter he says 'for Daddy'. I was busy in the kitchen this morning and gave Antony a box of dead matches to play with. It kept him happy for an hour, as he took them in and out of the box. I shall have to get D some new clothes soon, as he is fast growing out of all his ones.

Darling, do tell me what you are doing every day, what you are reading and what you do in your spare time – if you have any. Is there anyone of the group who you like specially? Doug Mackenzie or John Bailey, I wonder. I do so love to hear your news, so that I can picture you in your various tasks.

Win has just been in for two cups of tea, as someone has fainted and the friend with her too! Llewellyn is fairly busy, especially with maternity cases – every other person seems to be pregnant!

Dearest darling of my heart, I must go now and get the children up and change into my blue costume. I am afraid I am smoking too much. I think I'd better give it up. [....] You are ever near my heart, and we all send love and kisses. God bless you. Ever your own Joan.
PS. By the way, I have sent the books off to Maurice Webb and Adams College.

Meetings and yet more meetings, the death of Ray 'Nik' Alderson, and after having his ears syringed....my father can hear again with extra clarity........

Tuesday, December 1st 1942 – Cairo (No 23)

 My dearest Joan

At last my pen is mended and I can write in ink again, so you might be able to read my writing better. Last night Doug Mackenzie and I had dinner at the Anglo-Egyptian Union with the writer Robin Fedden, who is a friend of Tom Tanner's, though quite unlike him. He speaks excellent Arabic and for a while was closely involved with setting up the Spears Mobile Clinics with a guy called Raymond Alderson. But he left the Unit and now lectures at the University here, and has a most charming Greek wife.

He has a sister who's in the HSU, and has had to go into the 15th Scottish Hospital here, as the poor girl seems to be losing the sight of one eye. He wrote an excellent book on Egypt called 'Land of the Valley', which Tom gave me just before I left the UK, and says he hopes to write another soon on Syria. But it was Raymond Alderson, known to us all as Nik, who was the real inspiration behind the Mobile units in Syria. Doug has just told me that he was tragically killed a while back by a German bomb which hit the trench where he was sheltering in the Western Desert. He will be greatly missed. Nik's death makes the second Unit casualty out here, as we lost James Tonks in July when he went over the edge on a difficult road on his way to Jerusalem.

My time at the moment seems to be taken up with meetings here there and everywhere. Yesterday I went to see a man at the ministry of State about the possibilities of relief for the Polish refugees, and I am quite hopeful that something may come out of this. Today I have been to the Censor about trying to send information, which we collected from the Poles in Palestine, back home for them. I also managed to see Lady Spears for a short time about this and that, including, of course Nik's death, which has hit her especially hard.

Then finally I went to the 15th General Scottish Hospital to see a Research Doctor, a Major in the Army Medical Corps, about a new typhus serum. This was absolutely fascinating. He showed me how they are trying to produce this by breeding the virus in guinea pigs, inoculating fertile eggs, partially incubating them and then extracting some substance which, mixed with other compounds, makes the serum. It will, I'm sure, soon be in great demand. This evening, my Greek secretary and his wife came in to supper. He is such a nice chap, speaks about four languages, and is a very good typist into the bargain.

I went into the Scottish Hospital in Cairo myself this morning, and had my ears washed out as I was gradually going deaf. I now hear everything with double extra clarity! I've had the most God awful cold, which is making me feel like death, on top of which my stomach is playing up. But it's no good moaning. One just has to get on. Anyway, hopefully the worst is over. Goodnight and God bless you for mow.
All my love, Ralph

———

Feeling a lot better, he drives again to Alex, but once again by night, which he really doesn't enjoy.......

Thursday, 3rd December 1942 – Alexandria (24)

My dearest

I am actually feeling a bit better now. Today, well this evening, I came down here to Alex. I seem fated to drive at night, but really it's my own fault, for not starting earlier, so don't pity me. The trouble is it gets dark so early, but since it is now December, that is hardly surprising, I suppose! At least there was a moon, which made it better than it might have been, but there was a great deal of sand blowing on the desert road, which makes driving very exhausting, and I was tired out by the time I arrived.

However, I have recovered and feel far better, and I am going on to the Hadfield Spears Unit after lunch. There appears to be some hold-up in the mail, as I have had nothing from the Square for weeks and I haven't heard from you since last Monday, and probably I won't get any more until I get back to Cairo in about ten days or a fortnight.

The trouble with all this travelling is the frightening rate at which I keep losing things. Every journey I make, something seems to get left behind. I left my cigarette case in the NAAFI at one end of the Sinai desert, and my razor and some clothes at the other. By some miracle I recovered my cigarette case, but I've had to buy a new razor, pullover and pair of slippers.

I'll continue later.....all for now
Love Ralph

The sea at Alexandria

"Here am I rushing about seeing people about this and that.......yet the sea ebbs and flows reassuringly in its own sweet way, quite unperturbed by all our hustle and bustle!!

Photo Egyptian Tourist Board

Unit men working on the front line

Eric Green outside local clinic

Unit men outside mobile hospital tents near Alamein
Photos Friends House Library

Chapter 25
Thoughts of a Quaker CO at War - 'An Exacting Mistress'

Throughout his correspondence home, my father is constantly questioning his pacifism and whether the CO's witness makes any difference. As quoted previously, he expressed his doubts from the very beginning - "I have never been a very rabid pacifist, yet I was a Quaker, born of many generations, strictly brought up, and I could not believe that for me war was right. I believed war to be so utterly wrong that even though short term results seemed to justify it, it would be wrong in the long term. So I registered as a CO and though I have learnt much, I do not regret it."

Then again in the early days in London, he writes: "I was still very homesick and my conscience was troubling me. Was I doing the right thing?" And out in the Middle East he writes: "Along with many other Friends I have often had cause to wonder how far the Unit overseas succeeds in making any pacifist witness..."

Now in Alexandria he returns to the subject and tries to set out the principles by which he lives, using the phrase that gives this book its title. In the end, as in his previous debates with himself, he states that his conclusion is that pacifism is not only a valid option, but that it also makes a difference. "I have come to the conclusion," he writes, "that the Unit does make a very real witness. However infinitesimal, comparatively speaking, the Unit's achievements may be, it is impressive that a band of young and largely inexperienced young men, holding unpopular views, has been able to build up the work it has." Below too, he concludes that on the whole "he is more of a pacifist now than ever" and how the sea is a great calming influence.........

Saturday, December 5th 1942 – Alexandria (24 contd)

My dearest Joan

It's a curious life out here, and the Unit is an exacting mistress. The great thing is to try never to let oneself get an idea of one's own importance, and to remember how inadequate one's own contribution is. How pitifully inadequate, compared with the vast scale of the task before us. Then when one thinks of the enormity of the war and the sacrifices of the forces that are in conflict, how insignificant a thing the Unit seems. Yet what we do calls for much effort too. But is it worthwhile, and what does it mean in the long run? Do we actually stand for anything positive and if so, does our contribution have any effect, or are we so hopelessly compromised, being neither quite in nor quite out?

It is I suppose, one's own life that is the real question, or partly at least, and I'm only too aware of mine own inadequacies. One tries so hard to testify against war, but here am I sharing in other manifestations and activities of the army life and the society which produces it. We are outside the army, but we have many of its privileges and some extra ones as well, especially for me as an officer. And liking the good things of life, it's all too easy to take the occasional perk. Ah, well, perhaps it's no good being too introspective, but I often have my moments of doubt, wondering if it's all worth it; so much effort and expense, so much trouble to others and so little to show for it. And yet the more I see and know of war, the worse it seems, and I think I am more of a pacifist now than ever. We have chosen our way, and we are here to make the very best of it that we can.

I had a long talk to a man this morning, who asked me what I thought was the spiritual level of the life in the Unit. I said I thought on the whole, it was very low. Probably, this may be inevitable, as those of us who are Quakers in the Unit, are possibly not a group of sufficient strength of purpose to offer spiritual leadership.

By which I mean, we are all young and have little experience to draw on. This man said he had been in a pit of depression for some time back and had not found anyone who could help him. I think it is very difficult to help someone who is genuinely depressed or enduring so much suffering. Of course you can give sympathy and understanding, but I think in the end it amounts to very little.

It all set me to wondering just what it is that I do believe and hold important. I suppose, it comes down to something roughly along the following lines:

- A belief in something we call God, interpreted partly by Jesus, partly by Art, Nature and Beauty; and a faith in those things which go beyond reason, and certain principles implied by the above, such as:
- Giving service to others, though not just service by itself, but a service rooted in faith.
- Honesty - especially being honest with oneself, which must involve a realization of how little success is due to one's own effort, and how often one could have avoided mistakes.
- Never to say "Well, it wasn't my fault".
- The courage to carry on, and the courage and honesty to review one's own life and see how far short it falls.

George Fox passed through the valley of deep shadow and found no-one who could speak to his condition save Jesus Christ. I do not feel that with quite such a blinding flash as he did, but those things I have listed do help to get me some distance.

But how far, I wonder? I'm only 32, and have seen comparatively little of life's hardships. I've experienced great worry, often unbearable separation, severe depression, and quite onerous responsibility. Yes, all of these in some measure. But compared to the lives of many I've worked amongst out here or in the East End, they are little to their often terrible hardships, thank God.

Our links with each other my dearest, are fast and unbreakable, but suppose our link with life should break? What then is the future? Despite all our sad partings, how fortunate in many ways we still are. We are still a privileged class. We still have food and shelter, a certain position, some privilege and money to spend. Meanwhile many Greeks are starving. Thousands of Poles are homeless and stricken with disease. Yugoslavia is devastated, and our own people are being bombed out of their homes. If we can hold together, you and I can still hope for an existence after all this, which gives us something tangible to live for. I pray that it will. And I do believe that it will.

And then another disjointed thought. How brief and fleeting is the present! It flies past, and is gone in a moment, often meaning so little. A shaft of sunshine as we walk up the street. An hour or evening of perfection with you. The holidays we had in the Lakes or in Switzerland. Our years of happiness together. Our past is ever real. Yet the past is also made by the present and was the present. Perhaps we should see the past, present and future more as one whole. As Eliot says in Burnt Norton, "Time present and time past / Are both perhaps present in time future/ And Time future contained in time past."

Ah well! I mustn't get too despondent, but when I do, as happens quite often, I've found that the sea is a wonderfully recuperative presence, especially here in Alex, and it never fails to cheer me up. There must be fifteen or twenty miles of shore line here, with the sea an ever changing kaleidoscope of colour, from deep green and the occasional dark streaks, where the shadows of the white clouds fall, to the white, flecked waves breaking on the sandy beaches. It always lifts my spirits and completely restores my sense of perspective and gives me a saner and calmer view of life.

I met up with Mike (Rowntree) briefly yesterday as we had a quite a lot to talk about having not seen each other for a while. We also managed to fit in about half an hour looking for birds, though we didn't see very much of note. We had lunch in the Officer's Mess today, and I was introduced to the Officer in charge, who was Pierre Vernier, brother of Philippe, the French pacifist. He is a charming man and I liked him a lot. I also met Lady S's deputy who I thought a very nice person. I didn't dare ask her how she coped with her boss!

It's very odd, but for two nights running now, I have dreamt that I was home on leave. The first time it seemed as though I was home for several days, and I saw you, but you were living next door with the Keens! The second time it was only a very short visit and I only saw Tom Tanner. Most peculiar. It just illustrates how I long to be back home. Though much as I like the Keens, I'd prefer it if you weren't living with them, and much as I respect Tom, I'd rather just see you! I must go to bed early tonight – and hope I don't dream again!
All my love dearest, Ralph

Meanwhile in Wolverhampton thoughts are turning towards a Christmas without Daddy.........

Wednesday, December 2nd 1942 – Wolverhampton (Air pc)

Darling Ralph
I received your AM letter card of Nov 18 yesterday, for which many thanks. I'm glad you had such an interesting time again in Syria, and how fortunate you had a car to do all these long journeys. How I wish I could have been with you.

Life here is very dull by comparison. But we are all well and busy with everyday things and beginning to think of Christmas, with shops now in full swing, or at least as much as they can be in war time. Here it is now very cold and frosty; how we long for some of your warm sun.

I also noticed this morning that some of them were selling Christmas trees, and I will see if I can get a small one for us later on. I still have last year's baubles we can use to decorate it with, along with a few crackers. David is already quite excited at the thought of it, and he finishes school in a fortnight for five weeks holiday. I do wonder how you will be celebrating this year.

The letters are still very slow in getting through, and I am so miserable without hearing your news. Lots of people are asking after you – Frank Westlake, for one, wrote enquiring about you - and wondered if we might meet in town, but I doubt it's going to be possible, with so much going on. I do hope all is well with you, as I worry so much.

David and I went in to Birmingham yesterday by train. D enjoyed himself so much and is writing to you all about it. Both the boys are well, except A has no appetite as he is cutting teeth at the moment. I think you will soon be meeting Tom and Peter Hume, so I presume you will be hearing much more news about the Hostel and Gordon Sq. The Airgraph letter service opens here next Monday, so I will try and send one off to you.

I think I told you that Florence's parcel had arrived, and I sent the baby things she'd sent, on to Millior, who was delighted to receive them. Your mother tells me that she is going to spend Christmas with Millior.

I do hope your cold is better, and always remember how dear you are to me.
Very dear love from us all, Joan.

Life continues as usual in Wolverhampton for my mother.......trips with David into Birmingham, to the theatre with her mother and reading - books of all sorts, especially biographies, but time is inevitably more restricted as we children grow up..........

Monday, December 7th 1942 – Wolverhampton (AM)

Dearest darling Ralph

This is the first day for sending these AM letter cards from here, so I will post these today and send my long letter tomorrow or Wednesday. Still no more news of you. There must be several letters piling up in the post for me. I expect these AM letters will get through quicker than the ordinary mail.

Last Wednesday I went with Mrs Carhart, a teacher from David's school, to see some Indian Ballet dancing with Indian music and instruments. It was very colourful and most graceful. I'm sure English people or any European for that matter, couldn't be as graceful or light and quick as these Indian girls. But I don't think our ears – or certainly mine - are trained or attuned to appreciate their music. It is perhaps a little monotonous to our ears, but I am glad to have seen it. They were working in conjunction with CEMA*7.

As I mentioned before, David and I went into Birmingham on Thursday. We had lunch at Pattisons in Wolverhampton first, and then went by train into Birmingham. D did enjoy himself and was so good and happy. He bought some violets for mother and a little car for Antony and clutched them tightly till we got home. When I was putting him to bed, he suddenly put his arms round me and said "Thank you <u>so</u> much mummy for a lovely day. It was all most enjoyable." He and Antony play so well together now. A adores D and copies all he does. A is putting short sentences together now. David asked him something in bed this morning and he answered 'No, David', to which David replied. "Oh, Antony you mustn't say that, it's untruthing." When putting him to bed one night, he said "I love Mrs Carhart so much, I shall give her a penny!"

The other evening mother and I went to see Priestley's *Dangerous Corner*. It's a curious play about truth and how much it is good or wise to probe into people's past lives? Sometimes too much can come to the surface and everyone's life is torn apart and all are miserable and wretched. Is this true? I like to think we should know all about each other.

I have now ordered a Christmas tree for the children and shall get it in a day or two. D is very excited at the thought of it all. How I wish you could be here my darling. We shall miss you so terribly. There are no little things in the shops to buy for the tree and stockings this year, but we'll make do with last years, which I kept. I do wonder what sort of Christmas you will be having. You know that wherever you are, I shall be thinking of you and loving you dearly. Life is so empty without you.

I am now reading Ashley Dukes'1 book *The Scene is Changed* about drama here and in Europe since the last war. He is married to the dancer Marie Rambert and owns The Mercury Theatre in London. You may remember that he wrote *The Man with a Load of Mischief.*

This morning I have been busy cleaning the hair brushes you gave me; they are so lovely and you couldn't have given me a nicer present. I absolutely love them. David spent yesterday helping Llew prune the fruit trees. He thought it great fun climbing the ladder. He is such a dear child. Your mother rang to say she had received your Airgraph for her birthday, and was thrilled to hear from you....so you'll be in her good books!

All my love, Joan

---

*7 Council for the Encouragement of Music and the Arts. A forerunner of the Arts Council.

Letter cards from my father arrive with some regularity, but longer, newsy letters are taking up to five weeks, which was obviously frustrating for my mother. A talk by Joyce Cadbury (the wife of Laurence Cadbury) on women's rights and an offer to drive David to school....and a first look at a radical new social document - the Beveridge report............

Wednesday, December 9th 1942 – Wolverhampton (No 23)

My darling husband

I posted off an Air Mail letter card to you on Monday (7th December). I hope it gets through fairly quickly. Your Air Mail letter card of November 1st arrived yesterday, giving dates of previous letters, Airgraphs etc. The last letter I received was the one you wrote on September 8th. I suppose they will arrive some day, but in the meantime I am pining away with no real news of you!

We've had rather a hectic two days, as Joyce Cadbury came here yesterday to speak to the Forum, (with Dr Grant, the Assistant Medical Officer for Wolverhampton) on Women's Rights. They both spoke well. Joyce talked about women being more independent after the war, and that for that to happen, there should be better education for them so that they could get better jobs and have money to call their own. At the moment, Dr Grant said the lot of the working man's wife, was still largely one of drudgery and that with so many women helping the war effort at home and abroad, this would have to change after the war, as women would demand better.

It was interesting and I feel sure they are right. With women serving in the army – and the FAU of course – and taking over many men's jobs back home, they won't willingly relinquish that post war. There was a lively and interesting discussion afterwards. We enjoyed having her and she fitted in very well. She was very taken with David, and said he was most charming and friendly, and most good looking! She also said to me that if the children went to Edgbaston High School after the war, she would happily take them in her car! She did, of course, add that Julian and Adrian were both at Eton and were loving it, and she thought that it had developed them and made them more independent. Alright if you can afford it, but if D and A don't go to Edgbaston High, I'd prefer them to go to a Quaker school, wouldn't you?

Mrs Carhart at the school is full of praise for David. She says she has never known a child with such a wonderful memory, or who learns so quickly and talks so intelligently. She thinks he is a good companion to be with as he has such a lively sense of fun. The other day I was reading him *How the Whale Got his Throat* from *The Just So Stories* [2], and he was very amused about the mariner and his suspenders and loved the sound of the words. You will remember how it repeats several times "And do not forget the suspenders" and he wondered why men wore suspenders. I told him that Daddy was very naughty because he wouldn't wear any and let his stockings come down to his ankles. That amused him very much!!

Llewellyn has bought the Beveridge report today, which is a pretty solid thing to absorb, but there are two main sections, which put over the important ideas. Llew thinks it a radical new approach, and I'm sure he's right. Beveridge very much wants to ensure that there will be an acceptable minimum standard of living for everyone in Britain after the war, below which nobody should fall, and that in return for a weekly contribution from everyone, the unemployed would receive benefits and there would be good health care for the sick, which particularly interested Llew. Let's see how it all works out. Perhaps 'a brave new world.'

The Beveridge Report – "A brave new world."

Sir William Beveridge presented his now famous report in November 1942 and many households including that of my Uncle, Doctor Rutter read it with interest, as did my mother.......'perhaps 'a brave new world'."

It was one of the most radical changes to living standards in generations. It provided a summary of principles necessary to banish poverty and 'want' from Britain, indeed his mantra throughout the report was 'abolition of want'.

He insisted that the war provided an opportunity to make life better, proposing a system of social security which would be operated by the state, to be implemented at the end of the war. In Beveridge's words:

'Now, when the war is abolishing landmarks of every kind, is the opportunity for using experience in a clear field. A revolutionary moment in the world's history is a time for revolutions, not for patching.'

There always seems to be a pile of mending to do not to mention the washing too, but I do try to make time for reading. And if it's not books, there's always the New Statesman and the Post and The Friend to catch up with. I wonder if you saw the article in The News Review about the FAU in Abyssinia? It was most interesting and good publicity. I will cut it out and send it when I get time. There is also a cutting on birds from The Post, which you might like to see.

I bought Masefield's new poem *Landworkers* today and Charles Morgan's[3] poems *Ode to France.* I wonder if you would like them. I also see that Marjorie Rawlings[4] has just published another book called *Cross Creek*. It will be interesting to see if it's as enjoyable as *The Yearling* was. Do tell me what you are reading. Would you like more books to read? If so please tell me if there is anything in particular.

Win and I have been doing quite a lot of cooking these last two days, as we've had a run of visitors. We had to save up the fat for some time, as we are also hoping to make a Christmas cake. I made some mince pies, which were very good – oh, and also a fruit cake.

It was mother's 65th birthday yesterday, and we opened a tin of fruit to celebrate. I gave her *Mrs Miniver* [5] and some handkerchiefs. She also received several books and some money. I think she is amazing for 65 as she is still so energetic.

I can hear Antony crying – I put him to sleep after lunch, but he is so lively today, he has just been playing instead!! He is a darling, absolutely bubbling over with fun and the joy of living. I'm knitting a balaclava helmet for David for the cold weather, and some more trousers for Antony, but it is difficult to get pure wool now as most of it has cotton mixed in with it.

I must stop soon and take the children for a walk, as it so mild and nice at the moment. How I ache to be able to drive out into the country with you my dearest. Oh, speed the day when we shall be together again. I miss you in everything I do: in walks, in reading, in going to the theatre, in sleeping. Oh, in every way I miss you terribly. I just want to know so much of what you are doing and thinking.

My mother discusses in these next letters and at some length not only how much she misses my father, but how, of necessity she has almost got used to it, having to rely on her own resources, which in a way she thinks may strengthen them. But it's after the war that they long for and look forward to, when they can resume a life interrupted and enjoy once more everything they hold dear – the children, and each other, and to enjoy doing things together again such as the garden, reading and the theatre.......

Later – 10pm........

I'm now in bed – early you'll say - but I get rather tired and I like to come up early and read a little or write to you. You know in some ways I have got used to being without you, because I have to, but it's such a queer sort of life. I am not at all myself and I'm just not used to being without you, and each day I am alone, I miss you more. I am flung back increasingly on myself, so to speak, when what I need is you to confide in and lean on. [....] I want you to join in the joy of the children as they grow up. I want you to talk with and discuss and read with. I am in such a narrow groove. We used to think our life somewhat narrow before the war, but it's ten times more so now.

Perhaps in some strange way it is all good for us, and will strengthen us, but I am not in the least myself. It isn't in the wider sense a 'full life' of course, it cannot be, and it's a very one-sided life for the children. It isn't our real home life as I can only give the children a very limited amount without you. I think war does teach us to search ourselves. I know a little more now, I think of what I want and value in life. Most of all I want you home with the children and I want the children to have the very best education we can give them. I want us all to be able to spend as much time as possible out in the country, to have leisure time for our garden, for reading and music and the theatre. I want us both to be able to give the best of ourselves to the children. I want to be able to live a good life without being 'goody', but to help the children to be good citizens, good husbands and above all to give the best to the world and receive and appreciate the best. I want our home to have a certain atmosphere, where there is love and understanding, true joy and happiness.

One thing stressed in last night's Forum meeting, was that husband and wife should have the same sense of values, but not necessarily exactly the same interests, which is a good point. I think you and I have the same sense of values and some of the same interests and some different...just as it should be!

I am sitting propped up with several pillows, in a pink nightie, blue and pink bed jacket...and a hairnet on...for which I humbly apologise and beg your forgiveness! I would, of course, take it off if you were here!

———

David is in dreamland right now, bless him. He told me today that he was going to marry a girl from school called Katherine. I said she may not want to marry him, to which he replied "Well, I shall make her and you mustn't laugh Mummy"!

I've just read in a Government pamphlet which I bought, about the stand the Norwegian teachers have made against the Nazi threat to run all the schools on their lines. People are so brave when they really believe in a thing and have a burning desire not to have it crushed. Theirs is truly a democratic country, and the account in the pamphlet is a fine testament to their courage and high-mindedness.

Darling I do apologise for my bad letters. Tell me if they are too dull or badly written, or if there is something that you especially want to hear. Do I tell you enough about the children and what we are doing, and about outside things? Please tell me how I can improve them. I'm enclosing a letter from David. It's not one of his best, but he so loves to write to you, and I encourage it.

I hear that Enid has had bronchitis. Do you ever hear from J & E? I am told that Millior's little Anna flourishes and is putting on regular weight. I expect Tom and Peter will soon be with you. My goodness! How your tongues will wag, as you hear all the gossip from Gordon Square and the Hostel. I am completely out of touch with everything, as no-one ever writes. I do get some news via the Newsletter, but that's all. I wonder what news gets through to you.

Well, darling, this must be all for now. It's time I had some sleep. Goodnight my sweetheart. You will just have to imagine I'm kissing you goodnight, and telling you of my love.

Ever yours, Joan

Saturday, December 12th 1942 – Wolverhampton (Airgraph)

 My darling

I am so longing for more news of you. I sent a cable off to you on Thursday, 10th December, and I do hope it reaches you in time for Christmas. I sincerely hope my letters are getting through better than yours. [......] I know so little about your work, or what you are doing and thinking, which makes me depressed.

We are all very well. The children are in the garden playing this morning – they have built a house and are having a grand time. We have now got our little Christmas tree and we are hoping to be decorating it this week. David is very excited about it all. I enclosed a letter from him in my last letter. I am thinking of you at this moment and wishing you were here to join with me in Christmas celebrations for the children. Very many thanks for your cable received yesterday. I feel so near to you darling and send much love and greetings for a happier New Year.

David and I have been decorating the Nursery today and it looks so gay. I think so much of last year, when you were here. Your mother is better and going to Millior on Monday. I hope you are well and fairly happy dear heart. God bless you, my darling husband.

All my dearest love
Joan and D & A.

Chapter 26
The Worst Job in the World
December 1942

The section that my father led out to the Middle East all had to be assimilated and new work found for them. It had been decided that the best answer would be a much larger section working under its own officers, who would in turn be responsible to the Army officers concerned, but the army had other ideas.

It was the same problem that they had experienced with the 'Agreement' in Cairo: the degree to which they were prepared to compromise with the military. The arrangement that had been concluded with the Directorate of Medical services was that the Unit would provide thirty-six drivers for the No. 1 Mobile Military Hospital, which was commanded by Lt Col Croft. And the Unit section would be led by Peter Gibson, whose enthusiasm for making a success of working with the Army, was undiminished. It was a challenge he accepted gladly.

Unfortunately, things went wrong from the start. The Colonel's first concern was, of course, the success of his hospital and he found it difficult to appreciate what the Unit was trying to achieve. He was not prepared to have an independent group such as the FAU, which was not under his personal control. From the very first day matters got off on the wrong foot, as when the first twelve Unit men arrived on GHQ instructions, they found themselves totally unexpected and quite superfluous, as no adjustments had been made in Army numbers to accommodate them. And though Peter had been appointed to take charge of the Unit section, the Hospital authorities refused to accept him, as there had been no official posting for him, and from the Colonel's point of view, his presence was unnecessary. This small dribble of incidents soon became a downpour, some of which was the Unit's fault, with inexperienced drivers having unfortunate accidents on the poor roads, and some down to the bloody mindedness of the Army top brass, insisting on treating the Unit members as Army officers.

My father had arrived from Cairo just in time to try and sort matters out, and gradually the tensions did begin to ease, as the Unit settled down to regular work. Friendly relations were eventually established, and by Christmas there were parties and carols. Here, however, he writes home to my mother in despondent mood...........

Tuesday, 8th December 1942 – Cairo (No 25)

Dearest Joan

I must say life is about as bad as it can be right now, and things in our Unit here in Cairo, are going very badly. The Colonel in charge here, a Lt Col Croft, not I think with any particular ill intent, is not co-operating with Peter G, and all the boys are very unhappy about it. Naturally, Peter himself is having some of the most difficult weeks of his life. I have already had three long sessions with the Col as well as several talks with the boys, but so far with little success. My head is in a complete whirl, and I am mentally exhausted and filled with a sense of my own failure. This sort of thing always wears me out.

Sometimes I feel that I am a very lucky person, but in times like this, I think I've got the worst job in the world. I just wish I could see a way out. The Col. obviously regards us as a nuisance and pretty odd sort of creatures. In some ways, I suppose, I can't blame him. Well, no one said this was going to be an easy, sheltered existence, and undoubtedly I shall pick myself up.

Monday morning was beautiful and clear and stayed that way the whole day, as we drove all the way up the desert road. It was a monotonous journey, beset with heavy traffic and took us right across the battlefield. All along the road on either side, were ruined, burnt-out vehicles. Sometimes there was just one on its own, sometimes they were in little groups; some were the right way up, some were on their sides; some were upside down and some had their noses buried in the ground. At one point there was a prostrate steam roller, which looked sadly out of place! Further along were abandoned petrol tins, exploded shells and all sorts and sizes of blown-out tyres. The airfields were strewn with ruined aeroplanes and the road was pitted with bomb craters and crossed by bomb-damaged bridges. But through all this mayhem, our transport vehicles rolled on unceasingly. God, how I hate war.

Our own car had behaved well for most of the journey, when all of a sudden she died on us. Luckily we got a tow by some Indian ambulance men, who were passing by us in a lorry and who kindly took us to their camp. They proved to be more than Good Samaritans. Two of their mechanics nobly slaved away on the car until late at night and again the next morning, while their CO, a captain, gave us dinner, and afterwards an ambulance to sleep in. Next morning the car still wouldn't go, and I was just arranging to go on alone, leaving John Gough to cope with it, when suddenly, praise be, it started and mercifully hasn't looked back since! I often think I would like to command an Indian company, as they are generous spirited and helpful. If you look after them well, they give very loyal service in return. Thereafter, we made good headway and reached our chaps well before lunch.

I left this morning after a good night, to re-visit another section and am now about eight miles from Tobruk. I suddenly realised that it's over a fortnight now since I left for Syria and that I've nearly covered 1800 miles, of which I have driven at least two-thirds myself. I wouldn't mind if I felt I was doing some good, but I'm not sure that I am.

My love to you, my dearest and to the children…..more later
Always, your loving Ralph

"All along the road on either side, were ruined, burnt-out vehicles……….some were on their sides; some were upside down and some had their noses buried in the ground. […..] a landscape of desolation, just an incredible mass of tangled wire."

Photographs courtesy Imperial War Museum

My father journeys on to Tobruk to visit another transfusion unit and meets up with Colonel Buttle again, encountering along the way, the sad detritus of battle, not to mention a lot of looted items, which my father describes as 'maybe one of the sad by-products of war'................

Thursday, December 10th 1942 – Tobruk (25 contd)

Dear Joan

I meant to add yesterday, that I had just finished dinner in the Officer's Mess, when a doctor walked in from a neighbouring Unit and recognising me, greeted me as a long lost friend. It turned out he had been at Leighton Park with me, though I'm afraid I couldn't place him. Well, I haven't seen him since, and it must be nearly sixteen or so years ago. He was a very pleasant chap and cheered me up somewhat.

The Officer in charge of our boys who make up a small Transfusion Unit here, took me to supper in the Chief of Staff's mess, to which they are attached. I must say they were very friendly and the food was excellent. Everywhere one looked around, there seemed to be enemy loot, from German petrol cans, known as jerry-tins, which are much better than ours, to tyres and all varieties of food. This particular mess had acquired large supplies of oatmeal, and we had some excellent porridge for breakfast! But also they confessed to having large supplies of mineral water, fresh meat and even the odd bottle of Chianti, though sadly that had finished! Should one be shocked, or treat it as a sad by-product of war?

We left there this morning and carried straight on towards Tobruk, through a landscape of desolation, just an incredible mass of tangled wire and mud, damaged vehicles and bombed buildings. The harbour too is badly destroyed and full of sunken ships. How indescribably awful are the results of war.

We carried on driving west till midday, with the country getting ever greener and at last we reached a stretch of pleasant uplands with stone outcrops covered in green grass. We must be at least 550 miles from Alex now. Here I was able to talk to one of our men with the Transfusion Unit, and Colonel Buttle, the Officer in charge, who I knew already of course, and was keen to consult about our difficulties back at base. He took me to lunch in his mess and we had a long talk, which proved to be very helpful indeed, and I am really glad I was able to have this meeting.

I had also hoped to see the Brigadier before nightfall, but before we could, we met Peter's Unit moving up and just turning off the road for the night. So we pulled off too, blacked out the car and had a meal with the men. Talking to them, you find that most of them have experienced some pretty ghastly things. One Unit was almost caught up with our military tank force, clearing up pockets of resistance, while another witnessed a jeep blown up by a mine just in front of them.

I'll close now and start again tomorrow.

My father encounters along the way the terrible aftermath of war – the signs of death along the road and the inhumanity of war which turns men into mere pawns.........

Sunday, 13th December 1942 contd – Tobruk (No 25 final)

We had a good night sleeping out and in the morning I was able to find the Brigadier. He turned out to be a most charming man, and by coincidence had worked with the Unit in the last war. He readily agreed to do what he could to ease the situation. I had been slightly dreading this interview, but actually it went well and cheered me up a good deal, though we are not quite out of the wood yet.

After our meeting, we pushed on to Tobruk, but the journey was just one continual procession of passing streams of military vehicles, all going up and down the coast road. Large tanks, guns, and thousands of lorries on their way up, and then thousands of empty lorries coming back again. The road is too narrow for two streams of traffic, which means dangerous driving on the verge, letting the army vehicles pass, and then a stretch of open road for a while, before yet another stream comes past.

We constantly had to make diversions round obstacles and broken bridges, often over stony desert where the crawling vehicles raised clouds of dust, so thick that you could hardly see. Eventually we made Tobruk, together with the blood serum which we'd collected from one of the aerodromes and brought up with us, and handed it over to the Transfusion Unit. It has been fascinating to see the Transfusion Service close to, especially as we have so many of our chaps working for it. The Officers in charge are all an exceptionally nice lot, and it's been interesting getting to know the various medical and surgical Units, as well as some of the personalities. Altogether it has been a most useful trip and I learnt a great deal.

After depositing the blood, we bought two tins of peaches from a small market stall to eat with our supper and began the long journey home, which was a most monotonous run. We stopped by the roadside somewhere for supper, made a fire and heated up some tinned stuff. There is so much war detritus lying about that you can pick up almost anything along the road, such as petrol tins which make passable kettles, or wood from old petrol-tin containers and sand-soaked petrol, which help make a fire in next to no time. Actually our meals have been quite good, mostly heated up tinned food, but once we had four eggs, which we had exchanged for tea and sugar from some Bedouins selling by the roadside. They are always the first looters after a battle, probably profiting pretty well from the different passing armies.

After supper we drove on in the dark for about two hours, with only one stop for a punctured tyre, which John Bailey and I managed to change successfully. The car really has done wonderfully well. The drive is nothing special here, save for the descent from the escarpment above the village of Sollum, where the bay and blue Mediterranean are really rather lovely. Soon we decided to stop for the night and cleared a small area where we could sleep out. Our sleeping bags are very warm, so that sleeping outside makes a most pleasant change, and while you are awake you can lie and watch the stars. Then in the early morning when you awake, the dawn is just lighting the east, slowly catching the clouds and turning them yellow, orange or salmon pink, while gradually the light grows, and then suddenly the sun is up. It reminds me of the opening of Fitzgerald's translation of the Rubaiyat:

> *Awake! For Morning in the Bowl of Night,*
> *Has flung the Stone that puts the Stars to Flight,*
> *And Lo! the Hunter of the East has caught*
> *The Sultan's Turret in a Noose of Light.*

Of course, if it rains you awake in a puddle, which is less poetical! It may all sound fairly rough and ready, but I can't honestly say that I have really tasted the hardships of desert life. I haven't seen much of the real desert or spent weeks and months of boredom, living with endless sand and monotonous food in uncomfortable conditions. I do admire those who have and who can take it, but I can't truthfully claim to be one of them. On the other hand, this trip has been a very tiring and wearing one, and I was so glad I took John Bailey with me as co-driver, as he was not only excellent company but prevented me getting over tired whilst driving what must have been over 1000 miles in five days.

Like all such long trips, it has also been quite emotionally exhausting, not only seeing the desperately ill and wounded in the transfusion Unit, but all the signs of death along the road. Oh how I hate the inhumanity of war and the way it hardens our feelings till a man becomes just a pawn in the chess game that is being played out. Each man is surely still a son of God, whatever that may mean, and is someone's nearest and dearest.

As we drove back from Tobruk, we encountered all along the road, pitiful little groups of crosses as well as more pretentious cemeteries, with stones inscribed with 'Gefallen für Führer' or 'For King and Country', while elsewhere one would come across some poor Italians lying there forgotten by all but their families. It has to be wrong, wrong, wrong.

Each country is involved in such feverish activity, such ingenuity, and all to kill a few more of the other side. I may be sensitive and soft, but I know it's wrong. I don't deny the heroism, the devotion to a cause or people's duty. I don't deny the courage, the humour and the unselfishness. I don't deny the real care of most officers for their men or the thoughtfulness of the high command. The human spirit shows well here and often finely in these circumstances too. But surely man was born for better things, for life and beauty, creative endeavour, home and loves. These are the things I honour.

The last miles into Alex were rather lovely, with dazzling white sand dunes, groups of late palms, fig orchards bare of their leaves, shining silver-grey in the evening sun, and above us the blue sky, behind the blue sea. No sooner had I bathed and changed, than I heard that Michael Rowntree had been taken ill. Of course, I had to go and see him, even though it meant driving another 30 miles to the main hospital at Buselli. But I'm glad I did as he really has been poorly, with a very bad appendix and twisted bowel, but happily he seems to have come through it all right.

I spent the night at Buselli, and although Michael is getting on well, he is likely to be some long time yet convalescing. I had lunch in the Officer's Mess, and I must say they really have an exceedingly nice lot of Officers there, and the Commandant is perfectly charming. After lunch I came back down to Alex, but I'd only gone about 15 miles when a spring broke, throwing us right across the road. I managed to crawl up to a Military Field Phone post and rang up John Bailey, who came out and fetched us. It was all a great nuisance.

I'll end this now and send you all my love.
I do miss you all so much, Ralph.

My father, in typical down-playing mood, tells my mother off for making him out to be something special – "I'm just an ordinary fallible mortal" – but of course, it is just such constant praise that keeps him going.........

Monday, December 14th 1942 – Cairo (No 26)

My dearest Joan

I came back to Cairo from Alex yesterday, but as the staff car was not ready, I came back in one of our ambulances, which shakes like an old farm cart. They won't go more than 40 mph and manage to find every bump and pothole in the road. But it was a lovely day, clear and sunny. The sea in the early morning was calm and streaked with incredible colour, with the buildings on the front looking almost ethereal. Of course, as always, the last hour I did in the dark!

Last night we had a very nice American, Lester Collins, a Friend, in to dinner. He was in the AFS and had been one of the party on our boat coming up. He has been up in the desert and is now in the AFS Headquarters at GHQ. It's always useful to know someone like that and to be able to compare their circumstances to ours.

They definitely score because they have their own ambulances, much more money and being American, they have no stigma regarding conscientious objection. Douglas came with his new lady friend – she's in the Women's African Service – who seems very sweet. He said he had forgotten what it was like to have someone's arms around him. Aaah! And so say all of us!

Thank you so much for all your letters which have suddenly arrived, which I always love to read to learn about what you and the children have been doing. I do so appreciate your love and faith in me of course, which is a tremendous help and inspiration to me. But you mustn't build me up into being a great hero. Really I'm just a very ordinary, fallible mortal like any other. Don't get too exaggerated an idea of your poor husband. I just try and do my best, often in the most trying and awful of circumstances. But if things were to go seriously wrong with the new Unit set up, who knows I might lose the confidence of the men as happened with poor old John Bailey. Then I might feel duty bound to offer my resignation.

I say this, not because I haven't tried. I have, but I too have made mistakes, and you may discover that your 'plaster saint' husband is as much a failure as the next man. I know you would bear it along with all the other privations you've had to put up with, and I bless you for all your loving thoughts and prayers, which I value so much, but I'm really very ordinary and full of human faults, like any other person, who makes mistakes and is rather unsure of himself. We must love each other just as we are.

I've also had a number of Airgraphs and letters from the Square and it seems as if it's general post there. Barratt Brown says he is leaving the Unit to join the Middle East Relief and Refugee Administration, Annette Caulkin[1] is leaving to have a baby, William Barnes is going to China, Dick Symonds is in India and heaps of bloody new faces. It will be a sorry shadow of its former days, with the glory utterly departed. Even my old office 115 has been closed down. I liked Annette and William so much. Her husband, David is of course in the army still, and likely to be tied up for some time yet. She desperately wonders when they will both be able to make a home together, as do we all.

You mustn't be too hard on the Square, my dear, they are run off their feet. They can't send every scrap of news to all the relatives, and so much often gets stuck with Tom, who is very busy, and scarcely has time to pass it on or even write to people like me.

I was sent a number of copies of 'The Friend' the other day and I've been looking through them. It is still the same old paper: rather an odd journal in fact. Little trouble has been taken over the reporting, many of the news items are so badly written, and there is a poor selection of articles and reviews. It remains inbred and rather priggish. The personal columns always make me smile too, with the inevitable CO whose been granted total exemption, advertising for a job! There was an item too about Arthur Massey having been sent to prison, as he had declined to either join the Unit or do any alternative work. Well who shall say which of us is right? Certainly not I.

I was speaking to an Intelligence Officer over supper last night, who says he expects the war will all be over by Christmas. Hmph! What a hope! In fact there seems to be a whole wave of false optimism and optimistic speeches suddenly, but I don't think one ought to begin to hope yet. The great thing about the PM is that he doesn't make cheerful forecasts. He sticks to his promise of 'blood, toil, tears and sweat'. Probably better than building up our hopes. Just see what's happening in Tunisia. It's just like last winter in Russia, with tremendous advances claimed, yet they are still fighting outside Stalingrad; and the position at Rzhev has been static for months.

I don't expect this will arrive before Christmas, but hopefully it might get to you for A's second birthday. Please wish him a very happy day. Bless you for going to so much trouble for David's birthday; he did seem to have had a wonderful time. How I wish I could have been there too. I do appreciate all you do and I know what a strain it must often be. I hope you are bearing up. You mustn't shrink from telling me all your troubles, or think I don't want to hear them. That's what I'm here for. I do understand all you are going through right now, and one day will make it up to you. You say a daughter. Yes that would be splendid wouldn't it? I have sent you a cable for Christmas, which I dearly hope you will get very soon. It brings all my love and wishes that you will be able to have as happy a time as possible. I am so glad that the handbag I bought has got through at last. I wonder if any of the other little gifts I have sent will arrive in due course.

As it approaches that time of year, I begin to feel so terribly homesick. Christmas is a time for all the family and here we are so many thousands of miles apart. I've just had a PC from David, which is so nice and I have put it up beside his photo. Please thank him for it.

You are always in my thoughts, and this brings all my love. Ralph

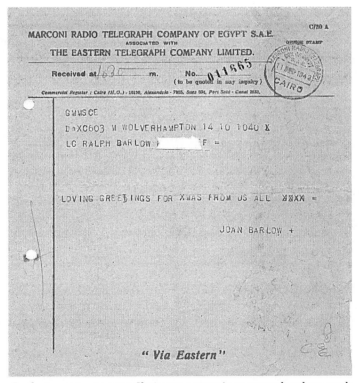

Both my parents sent Christmas greetings to each other, such as this one from my mother and all at Lea Road to my father in Cairo. A censor has cut out my father's Identity number.

At last some long letters from the Middle East are getting through and causing my mother great delight, and my father's vivid depiction of all the places he visits not only summon up places my mother would have known, but also giving her a better picture of my father's day to day life. She also comments on books read and her hopes for David's possible education at Oxford…………

Wednesday, December 16th 1942 – Wolverhampton (24)

My darling husband

I am more than delighted and happy to have your two letters (15&16) which arrived yesterday. I immediately posted off an AM letter card to you thanking you and giving you a little news too. No 15 was such a wonderful letter my dear heart and though I have read it twice, I still feel there is so much in it, that I must read it many more times. Bless you for writing such dear letters and spending so much time on them. I do appreciate them and so love to receive them. I am quite a different person since I had news of you. I was getting so depressed and felt so out of touch. Now I can clearly picture you in your work and sympathise with your many worries and difficulties.

It is grand to hear news of Syria and all the people I used to know. I do hope letters 13 and 14 will arrive before too long. It makes me so long to be with you. How splendid to have both Mike Rowntree and Mike Shewell with you. Your descriptions of the country are so very vivid and it certainly brings back many memories, although of course you will have seen so much more than I ever did. It is amazing that you saw so many birds, which made Win and Llew surprised as in Broumana the people tended to kill them for food! I expect as you say, you would see more by the Euphrates, where the migrating birds were passing through. I can just imagine your joy and happiness.

Darling, I am sure you are managing everything splendidly. You have such a wonderful way of getting on with people and smoothing out difficulties. I do so admire your courage and fine spirit over everything. Take heart my dear husband – you are ever in my thoughts and prayers.

Lady Spears sounds a real terror, but I've no doubt about the success you will achieve with her. After all you have had much experience during the past three years, what with Mrs M and Lady Dillon in Cheveley. You have always come out with flying colours, and I know you will again my darling.

What enormous distances you covered, though I can quite realise how tired you would get from so much driving. But what a store of experiences you will carry with you in your memory. You will have so much to talk about when we meet. I always thought Syria beautiful, although I only saw a small part of it, but the coast and the mountains behind are especially lovely, where the colourings are so beautiful.

I am very interested in your accounts of the clinics. I should imagine the problems are tremendous, and as you say, you can only hope to touch the surface, as the internal problems are so often at the root of all troubles. Have the French really tackled it in the past? I do think the clinics are so well worth while at this dangerous time, and from what you say, the people are very grateful.

I should think John Gough will be a great help in charge out there. Will he be stationed in Beirut? I can imagine your joy at the thought of Barry coming out to join you. You will soon be your old London crowd again, apart from Richard. Have you heard any recent news from him or Horace? Or indeed from the Hostel or Gordon Square?

I am absolutely aching to see the brocade you have sent me. You are a dear, darling husband to spoil me so. I wonder when it will arrive. Many, many thanks my darling. I have another book for you, which I will post after Christmas. It's Harold Massingham's[2] *The English Countryman*, which I thought you might find interesting and remind you of home. How are you off for books? Can you get any from a Library or borrow from the other men? Do let me know.

I am now reading quite a fascinating book in its way. It's about an RAF pilot who was at Oxford before the war and he gives a very good account of pre-war Oxford. He was eventually shot down and very badly burned. But he gives a thrilling account of the flying and the life in the RAF. Most of the pilots are very young and with their youth, feel so deeply about things. Just one part about Oxford, I'd like to quote:

"Had the war not broken out, I fear I should have made a poor showing in my finals. This did not particularly worry me, as a degree seemed to me the least important of the University's offerings. Had I not been chained to my oar, I should undoubtedly have read more, though not, I think for my degree. As it was, I read fairly widely, and more importantly, learned a certain savoir-faire. I learned how much I could drink, how not to be gauche with women, how to talk to people without being aggressive or embarrassed, and gained a measure of confidence which would have been impossible for me under any other form of education."

I wonder if this is a fair all-round description of an Oxford education, whether many other people would say the same thing. If David goes to Oxford, what do we want him to gain from such an education? I certainly think it does give a person a certain savoir-faire.'

Thursday, December 17th continued.....

I fully intended to finish this last night, but I was busy and rather tired. I'm sorry to be a day late in posting this week, but I sent an AM letter card on Tuesday and posted another this morning, after receiving your snorty one! Don't get cross with me. I certainly wasn't grumbling at you my darling, only it did seem weeks (2 months) since I had a long letter from you and I was beginning to feel so isolated and so 'at sea' about your work. However, I have been lucky in having two (15 and 16) this week and I am very happy to have them. Thank you again for giving so much of your busy time to them. I am grateful and do appreciate them.

I have been reading your letters again. How vividly you write of the scenery in Syria. I think so much of your letters, which would I feel sure make an excellent book. They are intensely interesting and I will type some copies for your family and for Gordon Square. It is just finding enough time to get down to it. Your descriptions of eastern life in the villages and your impressions of everything are absolutely fascinating. Freya Stark[3] has just published *Syrian Letters*, which I am giving Winifred for Christmas. Many of them were written from Broumana and Damascus and as she stayed with the Foxes some of the time, and mentions so many people we knew, they will be of great interest to her I think.

I am glad you met the Soltaus, and Kenneth Oliver, also President Dodge. Contrary to you, I must say I liked the Dodge family very much indeed, but perhaps you are better at summing up people than I am.

What a unique and thrilling time you had with the Bedouins. You were frightfully honoured to be feted in such a way. But their having no sense of time is absolutely right, but must have been trying when you had so much to do. You wrote it so well, that I can see it all actually happening. Darling, I am grateful to you for writing at such length.

The Canon sounds an interesting man. I was also interested to hear of the tiny hospital up in the north, where Stephen Verney is working. W & L were fascinated to learn that the medical instruments from Broumana Hospital had gone up there! I wonder when you are thinking of going to Teheran and Ethiopia. My darling, you are certainly having a very interesting, if very busy and worrying time. You are leading a full life and you will have gained much from all these years, and what interest it will be in later years when you can think back on it all. You will have seen so much of the world.

I am sorry you had gippy tummy and were so sick. I do sympathise. Do take care of yourself. You are so precious to me. I hear Mike Rowntree has been ill too, but I gather he is recuperating in Syria. I expect you wish you could join him for a real rest. Will you get some leave in the spring and where will you go?

David finished school yesterday and has a good report. I will send you a copy of it. Everyone seems charmed with him. Your mother met Joyce Cadbury, who was full of praise for his charm, friendliness and good looks. I hope he will never lose his ease of manner.

Win and Llew have so much enjoyed hearing news of Syria and we all look forward to receiving letters 13 and 14. Mother has gone into Birmingham to meet Bobbie, though it is a dreadful day and pouring with rain. They all seem well at Sutton and Barbara is enjoying the High School. Reg is still in Ireland and Vera and the boys are back in their home at Swalecliffe. Did I tell you that W & L had a letter from Noel Hunnybun the other day? It was to do with the children in America. I wonder if she is enjoying her new work helping with the British children in America?

It is a real job to get sweets and chocolate now. The ration is still only 3 ounces a week, but most of the shops haven't anything in at all. Do you manage to get anything in Egypt I wonder? I hope to secure some for Christmas, or perhaps if we can find a little spare sugar, which is difficult, I shall make some fudge, although only A likes it…David definitely not!

My own dearest one, how I long for all this business to end. I do so admire you, and all you are doing. God bless you always and watch over you and guide you. May he give you strength and courage to face all the difficulties and problems and may the New Year bring happiness and hope to us all.

Mother and the children and W&L all send love and kisses.
Dearest love, your devoted Joan.

Here my mother gives a lovely description of the excitement and joy of Christmas day, especially for David and me, of stockings and presents and a Christmas lunch and a routine that remained substantially unchanged throughout our childhood. She also talks ***of her favourite verses………***

Monday, December 28th 1942 – Wolverhampton (Long letter)

My darling, darling Ralph
Your letter Number 20 of December 14th has just arrived. It is wonderful to get it so soon. I hope by now you have received my three Air Mail letter cards, which I posted last week. I'm afraid I didn't get my long letter posted – the first I've missed – but with Christmas Day coming on the Friday, I was too busy with the children and all the preparations.

I posted an AM Letter card on Christmas Day, telling you something of how we spent the day. The children have had a marvellous time and I have longed again and again that you could have seen them so jolly and happy. Christmas Eve D was terribly excited and I thought he would never settle off to sleep. He had written a letter to Father Christmas and pinned it on the bedroom door and his and Antony's stockings were hung up on the wardrobe door. He so badly wanted a Gollywog*8 and I'm pleased to say the good Santa left one!

It was fun on Christmas morning, as I had both the children in my bed and it was such a squash with all the toys and the two boys jumping up and down, shouting and laughing. Antony was so pleased to discover chocolate and lumps of sugar in his stocking! After a breakfast of tongue, we went into the drawing room, where the presents were in a huge basket. D distributed them all and got quite mad with excitement watching his pile get bigger every minute. A was struggling with lots of paper and string to find his presents and a bit overwhelmed with so much, but he obviously enjoyed it all and both he and David did very well.

We made the Nursery and Hall very gay with paper decorations and a tree in the drawing room, and they both enjoyed having the tree lit with candles. We all had a good Xmas dinner of chicken and pork and a Christmas pudding that Mother had made. One does rather miss the usual Xmas dessert, but all the same we did very well. Win had made a very good fruit cake, which we had for tea, and I so wish I could send you a slice, knowing your fondness for such things. I made a nice cake for the children and iced and decorated it with things left over from last year. So thanks to everybody chipping in, it was a great success.

I played Snakes and Ladders with D after tea and later when the boys were tucked up in bed, we spent a very quiet evening reading and eating fudge which Win and I had made on Xmas eve. I do so wonder how you spent the day, and long for a letter giving me the details of what you did. I have missed you more than you can ever realise and pray that next year, may see our family united once again. Oh, dare I hope for such happiness?

I expect you had some kind of celebrations, and I hope you were able to be as happy and as gay as it is possible to be away from your loved ones. The bells were rung on Christmas morning, but with so much excitement for the children, I'm afraid I didn't hear them. The rest of the time has been spent very quietly, except for yesterday when Dr and Mrs Rutter came over for the day. I read part of your Syrian letter to them and they were most interested and thought what wonderful letters you wrote, so very descriptive and vivid.

Your mother sent me £1.1.0*9 and odds and ends for the boys. She is always very generous and has now put £50 in the Bank for David, which is so good of her. Millior and Alfred also sent me £1.0 and a book for David and a white toy lamb for Antony, which was so beautifully made. My mother has given the children money, which I have put in the Post Office Savings Bank. Win and Llew gave me a lovely pair of stockings and I had several other small gifts too, though no books unfortunately this year.

I wonder if you got all the many books the family sent out to you? And The Countryman from Win and Llew? I hope they are all what you like. I have rather a lot of books on the go at the moment. Pearl Buck's[4] *Dragon Seed*, which is about the Sino-Japanese war and the conflict of characters caught up in it, which is quite interesting though rather violent in places.

---

*8 Times change!!

*9 1 Guinea is approx. £60 in 2020

I don't think it's as good as *The Earth*. I'm also reading another book about America; I shall be well up in the subject soon! I have a book on Dunkirk by Philip Gibbs[5] and *The Scarlet Fish* by Joan Grant[6], who wrote the *Winged Pharaoh,* to read as well. Those should keep me going for a while yet. I'm glad you managed to read *The Root and the Flower* [7], you ought to read the sequel called *The Pool of Vishnu*, which is also very good and rather deeper than some modern novels.

Thank you again for number 13 letter, which arrived Christmas Day. I am so happy to have it my dear one, and I can at last piece together your life in the Middle East. It has been so difficult to imagine just where and how you were living, as the letters are so slow in getting through, and as I received 15 and 16 first, there was quite a lot in between that I didn't know. With the arrival of 13, the jigsaw is now more complete! I now can't wait for number 14 to arrive! I do want to thank you dear heart for writing at such length. It is marvellous to get these lovely letters and they make me suddenly feel so near to you. Bless you for them and all the nice things you write about me.

It must have been sickening for you to be so ill, especially with so many worries and difficulties for you to solve and not being able to get down and do them. I do sympathise dearest and pray and hope you are now really fit again. I can quite realise that the strain must be terrific. You are ever in my prayers, and I know you will be given strength to see it all through. I am so proud of you. I am indeed lucky. [....] Oh, dearest love. The lovely words from Herrick's[8] poem *To Anthea* always come back to me as they echo so well my feelings:

Thou art my life, my love, my heart,
The very eyes of me,
And hast command of every part,
To live and die for thee.

I've just been reading Siegfried Sassoon's[9] poem *When I'm Alone*, which I rather like:

"When I'm alone" — the words tripped off his tongue
As though to be alone were nothing strange.
"When I was young", he said; "when I was young.
I thought of age, and loneliness, and change.
I thought how strange we grow when we're alone,
And how unlike the selves that meet and talk,
And blow the candles out, and say good-night
Alone . . . The word is life endured and known.
It is the stillness where our spirits walk
And all but inmost faith is overthrown."

I do love the Albatross book of verse you gave me. I've just started to read *The Sun is my Undoing* by Marguerite Steen[10]. It's a very long book of 884 pages about the slave trade – a second *Gone With The Wind* - and supposed to be even better I believe. I'll let you know!
Later...
I'm now in bed at 11.20, and I'm steadily freezing! I hope you appreciate my martyrdom! Up till now this winter has been so mild, but tonight there's a frightful wind. I took the children to a Christmas Party today and they had such a good time. D is so friendly and natural. I do hope he will never lose it, as I am so afraid he might. D was so pleased you liked his letter and sat down to write you another. I do hope my books (and mother's) have now reached you, as we sent them off months ago. I'm also posting Massingham's *The English Countryman* to you tomorrow. I'm so longing for the brocade to arrive. I can hardly wait to see it. It is so sweet of you, my darling.

By the way, with my Christmas money I've just bought Tolstoy's *War and Peace*, as I feel my education is sadly lacking until I have read it. The Brains Trust claimed the other day that it is the greatest novel ever written. I think you have read it more than once. How long ago did you last read it? Oh dear, for more time in which to read.

I went into town this morning to change my library book (I've now got *Mission to Moscow*) – you've no idea how knowledgeable I'm getting about Russia, America and China, from the books I've read recently. I also booked a seat for myself for next Sunday, 3rd January to hear The Hallé Orchestra at the Civic Hall with Malcolm Sargent conducting. I'm looking forward to it. I'm getting used to going to things alone, though I would rather I had a companion.

Thank you for A's birthday wishes. Good heavens is it 2 years already since that awful snowy January at Beaconwood, when you ploughed through the snow to see your second son and wife, and brought me such lovely flowers? I shall never forget the joy and happiness when you suddenly appeared round the door and I sat on the bed so proud of my dear family. Such moments are stored up pearls, gathered together as the years go by, and I am so thankful for them, so that now I have so much to think on and be happy for.

To come to earth, my hand is nearly frozen stiff and I think I must curl up and go to sleep with sweet thoughts and longings for you. Poor mother has scalded her foot tonight as she was filling her hot water bottle. I do hope it isn't bad. In last week's Brains Trust (Radio programme) there was an open question given – 'What 5 things would you bestow on a girl when she is born, if you were a Fairy Godmother and had the power to do so?' You may be amused at some of the answers:

Professor Joad: Good temper, a degree of plainness, impersonal interest and conformity!
Commander A B Campbell: Health, a sense of humour, poise, and understanding of the opposite sex.

Professor Gould: Common sense, tolerance, unselfishness and a sense of humour.
Julian Huxley: Health in body and mind, charm, good nature, beauty, sensitivity and intelligence, good taste and a love of beauty.

I think with this I must end and wish you good night and a Happy New Year. Oh, my darling, darling Ralph, I send my dear love to you now and forever and may you come back home to me soon….as Alice Meynell[11] puts it so well:

> But it must never, never come in sight;
> I must stop short of thee the whole day long. But
> when sleep comes to close each difficult day,
> When night gives pause to the long watch I keep,
> And all my bonds I needs must loose apart,
> Must doff my will as raiment laid away,
> With the first dream that comes with the first sleep
> I run, I run, I am gather'd to thy heart.

God bless and keep you and watch over you always and forever. I do love thee more than all else and shall do so to the end of eternity. Ever your loving and adoring wife, Joan
PS1. We're still eating the remains of our Christmas chicken!* Pretty good going to last four days!!!
PS2. Thank you so much for Airgraphs received yesterday and for letter 20 posted on the 14th December, telling me of your departure for Teheran. I wonder if you flew and whether you will be there for Christmas. It is difficult to piece things together sometimes, as letters arrive in such an odd order.
(* Ed: I well remember in my childhood how my Uncle Llew could carve a chicken so economically that it lasted for days. Obviously learnt during wartime rationing!)

Shepheards Hotel, Cairo

Shepheard's Hotel, seen here about late 1930's was the leading hotel in Cairo and often the central meeting place in town. It was one of the most celebrated hotels in the world from the middle of the 19th century until it was burned down in 1952. A new hotel was built nearby with the same name in 1957.

It had been established in 1841 by Samuel Shepheard under the name 'Hotel des Anglais' but was later named "Shepheard's Hotel". Shepheard was himself an Englishman from Northamptonshire and the Hotel was famed for its grandeur and opulence. It was renowned for its opulence, with stained glass, Persian carpets, gardens, terraces, and tall granite pillars resembling those of the Ancient Egyptian temples. Its American Bar was frequented not only by Americans but also by French and British officers. There were nightly dances at which men appeared in military uniform and women in evening gowns.

Photo Shepheard Hotel archives

Chapter 27
To Teheran and back
December 1942

My father paid a short visit to Teheran at the end of 1942 to investigate the possibility of Unit members helping with the Polish refugees who were at the time pouring down from Russia to Iran. His task was to assess the value of the work and to balance conflicting claims for extra personnel that might be available. As soon as a flight became available he was off in mid-December 1942. "It was an extremely interesting visit" he writes, "though I cannot feel, from a Unit point of view, that much, if anything, was achieved." I shall let this account of his visit stand on its own, without my mother's letters, as it is of a piece, and while he was in Teheran he wasn't able to post letters and in the lead up to Christmas, post was getting through even less regularly than usual......

Thursday, 14th December 1942 (No 26 contd)

Dearest Joan

There has always been a slight possibility that I might go to Teheran to look into the problem of the Polish refugees. It is beginning to seem more likely, though the flight situation doesn't appear too good right now. I do have quite high priority, but apparently it is not always high enough to command a flight!

Later....... It now seems to be a definite, and I have just had a phone call to say that I may have clearance after all, so am frantically rushing around getting fixed up and ready to go, probably at some god awful hour in the morning. I got my passage as predicted, and left this morning at 5.15am from outside Shepheards Hotel. Eric Green kindly took me down by truck to the airport, which was rather dramatic, with the dark night sky behind us and the fading stars, while in the immediate foreground stood our plane, lit by a floodlight. In the distance, one could make out the dark shapes of other planes on the aerodrome silhouetted against an amazing yellow dawn sky just appearing. Once aboard, we got away without much palaver.

"A wonderful view of the mountains, no great soaring peaks, but a splendid conical shape and covered in deep, deep snow."
Photo National Geographical

You may wonder how I like flying. Well, of course, to begin with it's quite exciting, but inevitably with familiarity comes a certain routineness. It was quite cold and I was very glad I had my great coat on. People often say planes are very noisy, but actually I didn't find the noise that bad. It was also very steady in flight, but the landing plays absolute hell with my ears, which are still aching, making me half deaf. From the air one gets a curious view of the desert, which looks as though it might have been moulded by hand.

We were soon across the canal, and in two hours we made Lydda, where I should have met Sydney Loch, but to my great disappointment he was not there, which does very much detract from the value of my visit. I suppose I ought to be pleased with life, but I am not. I know it's partly because I'm tired, but Sydney not being here is just another reason I'm fed up.

We were a mixed group - a couple of very pleasant Officers and some civilians, one of whom, believe it or not, had been at Bootham School. We crossed Jordan leaving the Dead Sea on the south, and made for our next stop, the RAF base at Habbaniya just west of Baghdad. It's curious to fly in a little closed box in the full sun so high above the earth. Most things don't look at all as you might expect, but the ground from the air is exactly as it should be.

Our final hop to Teheran was undoubtedly the most dramatic. As we took off over Lake Habbaniya, we climbed steeply, leaving the rather barren hill slopes and tiny scattered villages, far behind. Then suddenly we soared even higher as right in front of us was a range of rugged snow-capped mountains, not grand like the Alps, but well over 12,000 feet. You know how I love mountains, and here they stretch as far as the eye can reach, and as the sun began to go down it caught the snow-covered rocks, and turned a sea of white fleecy clouds to a glory of lemon-coloured radiance.

Lake Habbaniya at sunset
"As the sun began to go down it caught the snow-covered rocks, and turned a sea of white fleecy clouds to a glory of lemon-coloured radiance."
Photo National Geographic

Eventually we dropped down to a brightly lit Teheran, just to the left of the mountains, now dim in the dusk, and in front the darkening night. It was quite lovely, and should have been a great experience. And in a way it was, but everything suddenly seemed against me. The airline had given us quite a good packed breakfast and lunch, but I was just aware that my ears were hurting and I was very tired. I was cross at missing the Lochs, I didn't know where I was going to stay in Teheran, and I began to wonder if I should ever get back to Cairo. But the ridiculous can always break in and change the mood. I noticed a lavatory on board which said "Please don't use except in emergency". No-one it seemed was prepared to be the first to declare a state of emergency!

I soon found a place to stay of course, and am writing this from my Hotel in Teheran. But I find it's never good being on my own for long, as I just start to question what I'm doing. I get so tired of arriving in new places after dark, and feeling quite useless and stupid. I had that new place feeling, and suddenly everything seemed more than I could cope with. Is it all going to be just an extravagant wild goose chase? What was I doing here? Why had I come? What could I achieve, if anything? All my usual self-doubts!

In reality, I ought to be pleased, and sometimes think I have an inbuilt depressive nature. But it passes and then when both my ears and my depression are forgotten, I shall remember that wonderful vast expanse of sunlit beauty and all will be well again. How I wish you were here to reassure me. I do miss you so much.

I have now been here for a day already. Teheran is not like so many towns in these parts. It has a flavour all of its own, but at 4,000ft is rather bleak and dusty at this time of year. The buildings are mostly two stories high, built of brick and often adorned with coloured tiles. Some of the public buildings are quite impressive with the odd open space, though the shops are mainly small and rather squalid with no big stores that I could see. The streets are the familiar mixture of cars and donkeys plus the occasional horse, so thin that one wonders how it could stand at all. I have no idea what there is to do here. I passed a couple of rather miserable looking cinemas and a museum, but it gets dark by 5.0 o'clock and there's a curfew at 8.0.

From the end of one of the main streets there is a wonderful view of the mountains, no great soaring peaks, but a splendid conical shape and covered in deep, deep snow. Their beauty catches you by the throat and shakes you as does the almost alpine beauty, whether they are sparkling clear in the morning sun, or ghostly white above a sea of haze, just catching the sunset glow. It would be splendid if I could have a chance to climb some way up. I must leave off now. Love Ralph

Joice Loch in her autobiography 'A Fringe of Blue', writes.....

"Poles could never forget the main issue, which was to them the preservation of their race and civilization. They were proud of being Poles and determined, wherever they might find themselves, to succeed, and to keep themselves as a group entity. Their time was all taken up in planning courses which would help them to live wherever they might find themselves."

This sums up so well the spirit of the Polish refugees and the determination not to be cowed by the horrors they were experiencing. While making their way to freedom from various parts of the Soviet Union, Polish refugees travelled from Turkmenistan across the Caspian Sea to reach Anzali Port on the coast of Iran. In 1942, the port became the gateway to liberty for thousands of Poles, being the first stop on their journey, where people, notably the British began to take care of the starving exiles.

As a result of an agreement with the Soviet authorities, Anzali became the destination for thousands of Polish refugees, from where they were transported to evacuation camps in Teheran and other Iranian cities.

Thanks to the personal intervention of Colonel Alexander Ross, the representative of the Middle East Relief and Refugee Administration (MERRA), Polish and British bases of evacuation were established in Teheran and Anzali in 1942, capable of receiving some 2500 refugees a day from the Soviet Union. With the co-operation of Polish and American Red Cross organizations, and the inspiration of people such as Joice and Sydney Loch, the lives of thousands of men and women and above all children, were saved.

My father writes in his memoirs ....

I was impressed by the standard in the refugee camps and full of admiration for the tremendous courage of those who had suffered and lost so much. But it was also clear that they had learned very little. They were still thinking and planning for a future in which they imagined Poland would be a great military power again and in which they would be able to serve on equal terms with Germany and Russia.

December 16th 1942 – Teheran

My dearest Joan

Well what have I done here, you may ask? I saw Robert Hankey, widely known as Robin at the Legation, who is one of the principal officials here, the first Secretary in fact. He is the son of Lord Hankey, Lloyd George's right hand man during the last war and very pleasant. I have also seen Colonel Alexander Ross, who is dealing with the refugee issue out here, who seems rather glum, but is willing to be co-operative I think.

Certainly there seems to be a job to be done, and I may know more tomorrow. I think I've managed to fix my passage back, which is a weight off my mind. But it looks as though I will have to stay for a week, which is a bore as there is not enough to do, whereas in Cairo, there is more than enough. However, I suppose I should be glad of the chance of some peace and rest. But somehow that's not me. I get restless, unable to be still.

God give me the gift of tranquility and doing nothing gracefully! I was thinking about that again last night and came to the conclusion that I must be a shallow creature, always busying myself doing things. I don't seem able to take pleasure in just sitting quiet. To always be busy may sometimes be a virtue, but in me it is nearly a vice! Perhaps that's why I was so restless when I was last on leave. Forgive your restless husband!

Last night there was a slight frost, though the day had been cloudless with a warm sun. In fact I had a very pleasant walk through Teheran, and there are some really splendid views to be found. One spot in particular gives a magnificent view of Mount Damavend, an extinct cone-shaped snow-covered volcano, which must be well over 18,000ft.

I spent this morning with Col Ross, and together we had talks with the Polish man who is helping with the refugees. Ross is multi-lingual, speaking Polish, Russian and French. How I wish I had better French! Instead we discoursed in a mixture of my poor French and Ross speaking both French and Polish. It appears that it's not medical personnel that they need, but practical help in setting up homes for the old and infirm. I'm not sure whether we will be able to help, but it's definitely worth looking into.

In the afternoon his secretary took me to two Camps for mothers and children, both able to hold up to 8,000. By peace-time standards, of course they are not good. There is much overcrowding, no privacy, no beds and no space to do anything. But then again, by war-time standards it is comparatively good.

There is shelter and food and medical care, water and latrines and a surprising standard of cleanliness. It's terribly difficult to judge, but on the whole I was impressed. The people were clothed, looked personally well-fed, including the children who were all playing cheerfully. In fact, though deep down they must be unhappy, that was not the dominant impression given.

The Poles carry out the administration themselves, and we were shown round by a very capable seeming Polish doctor. The sick rooms are very clean, with plenty of nurses, and they say they have a sufficient supply of drugs. The doctor told me that malaria was rife, but that there was very little typhus. There is, of course, limited accommodation, but as far as space allows, the children are taught by Polish teachers. The boys and the men all go into the army, and many girls are nurses or in the ATS [1].

After all the clinic tours I have made, and after some of the appalling conditions I've seen in Egyptian villages, the apparent good health and cleanliness here were astonishing. Relatively, the conditions are bad, of course, but so much better than they might be. I felt a reasonable standard had been achieved, and though much is lacking, that is largely because it is impossible to supply. They had come down out of Russia, almost all in pretty bad shape, but due to good organisation and determination, they have greatly improved, and gradually they are being moved to East Africa. Something really cheering for a change.

After our visit to the first Camp, we visited another, high above the city and up towards the mountains. I wish you could have seen the view. The sky was absolutely clear and blue, save in the west where there were bars of clouds masking the sinking sun. Behind us were the snow-capped mountains, picking up colour from the sun, and away in the east Mt Damavend itself, seemingly floating on a sea of haze. Away to the south lay a vast plain sloping up to the mountains behind us and to the east and away on the horizon to more distant blue hills. All around us the barren soil was rich in colour, and one could just see some of the buildings of Teheran caught by the sun, with the city's smoke hanging in the still air. All was rich in the glory of the setting sun. Near the camp were Plane and Ash trees, bare of leaves, silver barked and full of colour as only bare winter trees can be. The climate now is just wonderful, clear and fresh and bracing. My, it was lovely.
All for now, my dearest, Ralph

The occupation of Poland by Nazi Germany and the Soviet Union during the Second World War, began with the German-Soviet invasion of Poland in September 1939, in accordance with the secret Molotov-Ribbentrop pact against Poland. By this agreement, apart from Poland, the Soviet Union annexed Lithuania, Estonia, Finland and Romania, most of which remained with the USSR even after the end of WW2.

Throughout the entire course of the foreign occupation, the territory of Poland was divided between Germany and the Soviet Union with the intention of eradicating Polish culture and subjugating its people by the occupying German and Soviet powers. Both occupying powers were equally hostile to the existence of a sovereign Poland, Polish people or Polish culture. The Soviet Ministry of the Interior rounded up and deported between 320,000 to 1 million Polish nationals to the eastern parts of the USSR, the Urals, and Siberia. Waves of deportations of entire families including women, children, and the elderly were put aboard freight trains and sent primarily to Kazakhstan. About 6 million Polish citizens, which amounts to nearly 20% of Poland's population died between 1939 and 1945 as a result of the occupation, half of whom were Polish Jews.

After the collapse of the Nazi pact, an agreement was reached with the Soviets to allow the evacuation of thousands of Polish citizens from parts of the Soviet Union. There were some remarkable people, like the Polish General, Wladyslaw Anders, who had been captured and later released by the Soviets, and were able to organise the evacuation of a sizeable contingent of Polish civilians, who had been deported to the Soviet Union. Well over 100,000 Poles including 36,000 women and children were enabled to leave with many of the men forming the basis of a Polish fighting force who joined the allied army in the North African campaign. Of the other refugees, they mostly ended up in Iran, India, Palestine, or British Africa. Among those who remained in the Soviet Union about 150,000 Poles perished before the end of the war.

The evacuation of the Polish people from the USSR lasted from March 24, until the beginning of September 1942, and over 30,000 military personnel, and about 11,000 children left Krasnovodsk crossing the Caspian Sea to Iran. It was in British occupied Iran, then under Mohammad Reza Pahlavi, the last Shah of Iran, that my father visited Teheran to see what possibilities there were of the FAU helping with the ever growing refugee problem...........

Thursday, December 17th 1942 – Teheran (No 27)

My dearest Joan

We came back down to the city and everyone kept telling me how the late Shah had spent much time improving this city. And certainly I came across some really good modern buildings, mostly by German and French architects, and the roads are wide and well-surfaced, with trees close-planted on either side, running through the town.

This morning I dictated some notes to Col Ross' secretary, and later I invited the Colonel himself to have lunch with me, along with two other Colonels plus the Polish guy who had kindly showed us round.

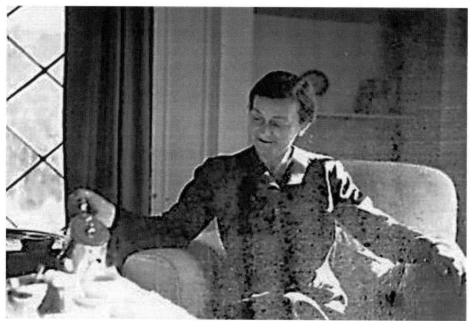

Mrs Sheehan.......a charming woman

"The wife of a high-up British Bank official....She provided us with a real English afternoon tea in a most pleasant English home."

Photo courtesy the Sheehan family

Afterwards we visited two more hospitals as well as another Camp. Then another officer, a nice man, Colonel Drummond, took me out to tea with Mary Sheehen, the wife of a high-up British Bank official here. She has been out in Persia for a number of years and has had a lot to do with helping Polish refugees here, who seem to be rather at sixes and sevens as far as I can tell. In fact there are so many conflicting ideas being thrown around, that it is quite difficult to keep pace with them all.

I suspect that the two Colonels, Drummond and Ross do not see eye to eye. But Mrs Sheehan seemed a charming woman and provided us with a real English afternoon tea in a most pleasant English home.

I am staying at the best hotel in town, but I doubt if there's room elsewhere. It may be extravagant, but work is helped by comfort and good service, and one must have room to write. It's very central, and one can invite people out and arrange to meet people here, as it is an address people know. "Where are you staying?" they ask. "I'm at the Ferdowsi[2]," I reply. "Oh, excellent. I'll call for you there," or "I'll be having dinner at the Ferdowsi. I'll see you there for coffee afterwards." In fact Col Ross said to me only yesterday "So and so is staying there, you are bound to see him. Let's all meet in the bar later." In fact I am supposed to be dining there tonight with the Polish Red Cross delegate. So I think I can justify it! It's also happens to be very comfortable and clean, with big stoves warming the rooms, Persian carpets everywhere, private baths, a very fair cuisine and a much frequented, very expensive bar. Reasons enough!

I get the distinct impression that conditions in Persia are pretty bad at the moment, and there were riots here recently, due to shortage of bread, I believe. We know what Marie Antoinette would have said to that! But actually there is no rationing and seemingly plenty of other food. The riots were soon quelled, I am told, when a famous Scotch regiment marched through the main streets with bagpipes playing, and everything has been very quiet since. There's a lesson for everyone! All my love for now dearest, Ralph

The Ferdowsi Hotel – the best in town
"Where are you staying?" they ask. "Oh, I'm at the Ferdowsi," I reply.

Photo courtesy Ferdowsi Hotel

My father continues his tour of the camps, impressed by the dedication of the military, and perhaps also the unpredictability of the Poles.....

Friday, December 18th 1942 - Teheran

Dearest Joan

Today is counted as Sunday here, and to make it even more so, everyone who has not a special pass is confined to their houses while bread cards are distributed. It's been a really dead city all day. Last night I had an interesting talk with a Polish man by the name of Mr Colat, who is extremely pleasant and seems wise and humorous. He is primarily concerned with getting information through to the Poles still in Russia and has good contacts there. Today he and Colonel Drummond took me round, showing me the Polish Red Cross stores where they keep large supplies of vegetable oil and fats as well as clothing, which is transported through to Russia. I didn't have a pass, but it didn't seem to matter. The stores are all near the station, which is a modern German building, with a fine hall, decorated with white Swastikas all over the ceiling. Most of the trains, however appear to be English locomotives.

I was then taken on to a laboratory where all the people from the Camp, suspected of malaria, are given blood tests, and I am full of admiration for the thorough treatment they are given. It seems to me that Col Drummond, who is the Military Liaison Officer, is doing a very fine job. We talked about providing further relief work, but at the moment, it would seem that the army is managing. We continued our visits to Camps 1 and 3 as well as a convalescent home, and my first impression persists, that within the limits of the possible, they are good and well managed.

Afterwards, Mr Colat took us all out to lunch at a big hotel, which is a newish building built by the late Shah, situated at the end of a long new road, right at the foot of the mountains, only spoilt by its ugly grounds. Later I was able to spend a glorious half hour walking up in the mountains at the back. How I wished it could have been more! It is fairly barren and rocky, with just a few trees down in the valley, but further up are clear mountain streams, which are oh so lovely. I should adore to go up and see over the other side, which is thickly forested and then down to the shores of the Caspian. To the south-east of Teheran is another group of mountains, and the afternoon sun cast a wonderful pattern of light and shadow on them. I thank God that I have been able to see such mountains and snow and streams; they are glorious indeed. As ever I so wish you were here to share these splendid views, and how you would love the sheepskin coats the people wear and I wish I could buy one for Christmas, but they are so expensive and I doubt I could get it back.

I do wonder what you are all doing for Christmas, and so wish I could be with you. I am sure somehow you will manage to give the children a happy and lovely time. Please give the children all my love and to all at Wolverhampton. I had some drinks with a group of the Polish men last evening, which are generally rather expensive. One of the popular tipples here is Vodka and Vermouth, though not for me. But the Beer is good and somewhat cheaper.

The majority opinion amongst the British here seems to be that the Poles are a charming people, though rather touchy and unpredictable, and occasionally liable to behave like children. There doesn't seem to be a consensus of opinion about the Persians, except that all the Cabinet is corrupt, and there is absolutely no love for the Russians. Say what you will, and I know we have our faults, but I often feel there is a great deal to be said for our own countrymen! I'll stop now....all love, Ralph

Here my father discusses the fickleness of human nature; learning more about Persian history as well as everyday life in Teheran………

Saturday, December 19th 1942 – Teheran (No 28)

My dearest

I saw Colonel Ross again this morning, and the Polish delegate and tried to draft my report, though I wish I knew what we ought to do. I believe that if there was somebody here with money to finance an old people's home, they could do a really good job. This afternoon I was able to have a very interesting talk with the American Red Cross representative, who is a Mennonite[3], and very nearly a CO. He is helping to distribute supplies to the Poles on a large scale, but didn't have a very high opinion of the Poles who are in charge here, which others have also confirmed to me. The Poles are our allies, so I suppose I ought not to repeat the stories here.

On the other hand he speaks in equal disapproval of the Persian ruling classes. In fact wherever you go through the Middle East, it seems to be the same story. On the one hand, a rapacious, money-making, moneyed class, callous and indifferent to the people. On the other, an ignorant people, stricken with poverty and disease. All equally dishonest. Everywhere one goes there is a shortage of many articles and commodities, and consequently hoarding, profiteering, and high prices. Then there are the allied troops all buying up limited supplies too, so that prices soar even higher. Sometimes I think there is not much to be said for mankind. The Poles appear to be very religious, with chapels and crosses and religious postcards in their rooms. And everywhere you go there are patriotic slogans saying - 'We shall win', 'We shall return', 'We shall have power' – as though training their people for the next war. What a world! We learn so little from our misfortunes!

Sunday, December 20th 1942 – (No 28 contd)

I seem by nature condemned always to worry about something. I now wonder if I shall get a seat on the plane back, or be compelled to spend Christmas here. What a dismal prospect that would be! It now really is Sunday and I don't think the army is working. The Legation works Sunday, but takes Friday off, though the majority of Teheran works as usual. Last night I went out to supper at a very nice French restaurant with the Polish soldier who had taken us round the Camp, along with his wife, who was rather over made up with awful, bright red talons, but otherwise perfectly charming. Before the war he had been a journalist. They were living in Warsaw at the beginning of the siege, and then left with the Government; he to produce the newspaper, whilst she listened to the radio and supplied him with news. He said they were bombed over seventy times on their journey to the new seat of Government. The paper only lasted a week and eventually they got out into Russia, with she contracting typhus and he forced to do heavy manual work in the camp.

It's strange isn't it how quickly we revert to type. One has a picture of all refugees being destitute, or if they do have any money, one supposes that perhaps they will share or save it. But we aren't like that. I make no condemnations. I should probably do the same. Here are these same Polish families, newly escaped from the terrible Russian camps, quickly reasserting old habits. Now living in decent lodgings, and earning money again, they buy clothes, books and jewellery; they dress well, wave their hair, paint their nails and go out and eat in fine restaurants. And why not? Were we refugees with money, would we deny ourselves pleasures and comfort any more than we do now? Human nature and desires are pretty fundamental; probably rightly so. But it makes you think.

The Pole who I mentioned above lent me a recently published book called 'Borderline Russia' by Foster Anderson. Do read it, if you possibly can. It's well written, and most interesting. The author knew Russia, especially the Baltic States, and was responsible for Polish Relief in Lithuania, while there still was a Lithuania that is. I've also managed to borrow, and am reading Sir Arnold Wilson's[4] book on Persia (*The Persian Gulf*). It's rather uncritical, but none the less informative for that. They are an interesting race, with an ancient history. So I felt a lot better informed when I was at last able to visit the Museum for a short while today. It's well done, with new, spacious halls, plain distempered walls, pleasantly tiled floors, show cases with well-spaced exhibits, and no over-crowding. There was some really exquisite pottery and beautifully designed old carpets; many richly coloured tiles and beautiful inlay work. An old tradition of a high standard. In fact just what a Museum should be. I wish I had had more time there.

I've misjudged this town in several respects. Firstly, I think I spoke too highly of it. The general impression, save for a lot of really good buildings, is rather drab and characterless. On the other hand, the shops are better than I thought. There is a main shopping street that I hadn't seen before, with some small, but quite good shops, and many jewellery and antique dealers with splendid stuff in the widows. This afternoon it was full of people with a sprinkling of Tommies[5] and RAF men, and a few Officers. There was also the Persian army: their Privates in rough coats and Officers in narrow–waisted greatcoats. There were helmeted and stupid-looking Persian Police; there were heavily built, solid, grey-coated Russian soldiers; and two delightfully homely and reassuring-looking British military police. There were the usual collection of beggars, fruit-sellers and droshkies[6], with desperately thin horses only just managing to totter along. There were crowds of Poles, women and children, and soldiers with their wives and girlfriends, and a few Americans.

At night this quarter is brightly lit and crowded, and it seems quite strange to be in a city where all the street lamps are ablaze. The cinema was rather bare and drab but comfortable enough. They were showing a British news-reel with Persian commentary – pretty poor I thought. Then there was a Russian news-reel with Russian commentary – also pretty poor I thought. Finally, a news-reel with a French commentary – hmm, fair I thought. Finally came the film *Break of Hearts* with Charles Boyer and Katherine Hepburn, which is my first movie since I landed in Egypt. An old, old story, well-acted, but pretty thin. He is good. She I hadn't seen before and she acts well, but the camera had to work hard I thought, to make her beautiful. I find cinemas strangely nostalgic, as they bring back so much. Then there is that flat, disappointed feeling when it is all over, a feeling one doesn't get with a good play, which has the contrary, stimulating effect.

The people here are a pleasant bunch – the Area Commander who is a full Colonel; my Colonel Ross who seems to come in with a fresh girl every day; his secretary, a very charming American girl; the American Red Cross guy; the Reuter's man; the Polish Red Cross representative; and numerous Americans men and officers. The bar is always crowded, and the amount they must spend on drinks is terrifying, but they are a friendly lot. I talk to them all, but I wish I was a better mixer - or do I? I get on, at least I think I do, but somehow I don't feel the part. I might if I were here longer. Then again, do I want to? It's not really my world, though what exactly my world is, I'm not quite sure.

The view of the mountains today was particularly glorious. All dazzling white after a fresh fall of snow, and a thin band of cloud just along the snow line, all against a clear sky. Perfect....now that's my world! I managed after all to buy you a sheepskin jacket. I think it's very nice and hope you will like it. I do so wonder if the brocade I bought you will ever arrive, as it was rather special and I know you'll love it too. All my love, Ralph

The Beauty and the Squalor
Mount Damavend and the plight of Refugees

"Mount Damavand, seemingly floating on a sea of haze"
(c.18,400 feet tall) in the Alborz mountain range, north of Teheran, Iran.

Photo National Geographic

A large numbers of Polish refugees gather in Teheran camp.
This picture shows some of the children about Christmas time. They are orphans first deported
by the Soviets to Siberia in 1939, and then evacuated from the Soviet Union to Persia and
Palestine with the main body of the future 2nd Polish Corps.

© Photo IWM

412

As usual my father worries about getting back to Cairo and, finding that he has been struck off the list, whether he will be able to get a plane back……..

Monday, December 21st 1942 - Teheran

My dearest

A terrible shock this morning, and my heart completely turned over and has still not returned to normal. I went over to the Airways office merely to check that my flight was still OK, and they said my name had been struck off the list. Was I scared?! What with so much work waiting for me to do in Cairo, the prospect of spending Christmas here all on my own, does not fill me with delight. I went straight up to Robin Hankey who soon got me on again, but I shan't feel safe till I'm actually sitting on that plane.

Colonel Drummond took me to tea at Mrs Sheehan's again, where there were Mr. Colat, who is an absolute dear and the American Red Cross man, and a visiting Brigadier. Mrs S is one if those delightful women who provide an English house in these foreign wildernesses, who are worth their weight in gold. She sweetly asked me in to Christmas dinner if I am still here.

I had a very interesting talk with Mr Colat this evening, in the Hotel bar. He is a big ship-owner, who somehow managed to get nearly all his boats out of Poland just in time. He says, further to my remarks about refugees, that many of them have seen so much suffering and death that they have become almost callous; life has sadly come to mean nothing. They have seen too many die – often their nearest and dearest – that they have no sensitiveness left. "Only when you are in comfort and civilization can you really value life" he said. That is one of the tragic things about fighting. You can't fight without losing the feeling that there is sanctity in human life. What will the world be afterwards, after three four or five years of treating life so lightly?

I had rather a pleasant time this evening. Colonel Drummond, who has been so nice and helpful, and whom I like a lot, asked me out to dinner at the Teheran English Club. He also invited an American gentleman, a Mr Wiens, who is also very pleasant, Mr Colat and Mr and Mrs Sheehan. The Club is good with first class food, and good conversation. I really enjoyed myself.

I wish it were tomorrow and that I was certain that I still had that seat. It's been such a day of suspense, not knowing whether I will be able to go or not. God grant I can leave. Till tomorrow…..Ralph

Great relief all round – he still has a seat on the next flight…….maybe!

Tuesday, December 22nd 1942 – contd

My darling

Well it **is** tomorrow, and I think I still have it! Hoorah! I've paid my Hotel bill and am busy saying my good-byes. I now have a little time, and I even paid a courtesy visit on the Polish Minister, who seems to think the war is nearly over – I wonder. When I left the Minister, I managed to do a bit of shopping, and I now have no money left, so I hope to God I get back soon!

But the plane wouldn't start – back to the Hotel and another fit of nerves……

Wednesday, December 23rd 1942 – contd

More dramas! As we left the hotel early this morning, the mountains looked extraordinarily lovely, and I just prayed all would be well. Well, I actually got on the wretched plane and with a seat, but would you believe, the damned thing wouldn't start? Isn't that bloody typical? I suppose the engine's cold or something. So we all went back to lunch at the Hotel, only to learn that the flight had been postponed till the next day.

By now I was having another attack of the jitters, and quite certain that either I should lose my seat again or else that it still wouldn't start. On top of everything, I had lost my nice room and had to sleep in a great empty dormitory.

During the afternoon I had a long talk with Mr Colat. My, how these Poles do hate the Russians. As he remarked, there are at present two evil forces in the world, Hitler and Stalin. And when we've finished with Hitler, he says, we shall have to deal with Stalin. He hopes it will be a chance for men of goodwill to bring a peaceful reconciliation.

I wonder if we English even begin to understand the continent. The Poles may have themselves to thank, and they may be foolish, but my God, they have suffered. A people, as I said previously, who have lost all feeling, having seen so much suffering. A people whose women have been forced to sell themselves simply to acquire bread; women who have seen their husbands shot and their children die of starvation; and women who are now forced to work as waitresses or God knows what. Is it to be wondered at, that they have such a visceral hate?

The Ferdowsi Hotel is staffed almost entirely by Polish girls who worked as waitresses, or barmaids. They were jolly girls, all used to better things, but glad of anything. When not on duty they would sit in the lounge and talk to the officers, or go out to tea with them. It was rather a pleasant, informal atmosphere. I had dinner with a nice chap there, who is fighting locusts out here. Before the war he had spent seven months poling up the Niger with a group of ten natives. In the afternoon I had nothing much to do, so I went out and bought *The Sowers* by Seton Merriman[7], and I also managed to borrow Dickens' *Hard Times*, which I finished but didn't enjoy as much as his other books. Perhaps I'm old fashioned!

Well I think I'll end this now and seal up ready for the post in Cairo. Always I seem to say the same thing, which I know must get hackneyed and lack variety, but you know that it is none the less heartfelt. So as ever my dearest, I send all love to you and the children and pray that events may bring us together before too long. I shall be thinking of you on A's birthday. As ever, Ralph

Miraculously the plane starts, and with an odd assortment of fellow travellers, he arrives back in Cairo in time for Christmas and Christmas dinner and a Christmas service in the cathedral...........

Thursday, December 24th 1942 – Cairo (No 29)

My dearest Joan

I think I concluded my last letter waiting in the Hotel for the next aeroplane to Teheran. This morning I got up in the blackest of moods, feeling quite certain that Christmas would see me still stuck in Teheran. But no, miracle of miracles, the thing started and we got off with a full load, pretty well on time. Nine hours in the air is a long time and quite a strain for some, especially the children, as the journey is boring and tiring, but that's air travel. At least I had *The Sowers,* which filled the journey nicely, and for what it is, made for a good read.

As we went over the mountains, there was actually frost inside the plane, and the poor souls who had insufficient clothes, including me, were really cold. But everybody offered each other gloves and pullovers, and I was soon beautifully warm. There were some people who found considerable difficulty in breathing at 16,000ft, but a kindly, capable-looking American, busied himself looking after everyone. Whenever he didn't catch a remark, he would say "Sir". Rather surprising, till you realised he meant "I beg your pardon!"

We were quite an odd collection. There was a Diplomat in a fur coat, travelling with his manservant, who had brought a whole cold chicken with him; a somewhat comic Jew with a caricature of a nose, wearing a tiny trilby hat, and carrying all his belongings in a red-spotted handkerchief, feeling very sick; a charming Russian girl with a nice looking husband and two children, one aged about a year old, who she fed quite unconcernedly, whilst the elder, aged about 3, was sick most of the time; an Englishmen, a Colonel with an eye-glass, quite good looking, and behaving much as you'd expect an English Colonel to behave, obviously thinking that all these people were not quite the sort he usually travelled with, and seemingly under the mistaken impression that I was the only proper person on board! He shared some dried dates with me and I gave him an orange!

Well I am back and can hardly believe I have really made it. Inevitably there were piles of letters to answer and work to do, though no major disasters, and some rather better news of Peter Tennant. It is now Christmas Day and I send all my love and thoughts to you on this day of all days, and pray that next year we will be together again.

I've had a few Christmas cards; from the Webbs and Florence in South Africa, the latter with a handkerchief (!); and some letters dated October from you, which as ever were most welcome. I do wonder if the food I sent from SA – marmalade and dried fruit – together with some stockings, ever arrived. I really think the brocade is most likely now lying in many feet of water, which is a really great shame as it was such lovely material, and I'm sure you would have loved it. Another casualty of war.

Douglas McKenzie took me to a Christmas party at the hospital, where I saw the British journalist George Gedye and various others. We had an excellent Christmas dinner, and a really pleasant time. In order to catch up, I have worked most of Christmas Day and will also on Boxing Day, but I did go to Church this morning. The Cathedral was absolutely packed, with many people standing. It was a really good service and I enjoyed it.

Well Happy Christmas and God bless you my dearest, Ralph

"Cairo Cathedral – on a memorable Christmas day"

Chapter 28
The deaths of Tom Tanner and Peter Hume and the aftermath
December 1942

SS Ceramic torpedoed in the North Atlantic on December 6th 1942
Tom Tanner and Peter Hume were among 655 casualties, with 1 survivor.
Photo Naval archives

In the course of 1942 it had become obvious that a visit by the Chairman, Tom Tanner to China would be of immense benefit to both China and London. Communications from so far away were bad, often up to several months, with the problems detailed, solved long before the letters arrived. The section out in China was also having its own difficulties, so by the autumn, plans went ahead for a visit by Tom with Peter Hume chosen to accompany him. They set off in November on SS Ceramic and were expected to be away about nine months.

These were among the darkest days of the war with the U-boat campaign at its height. By December with their arrival long overdue, news came in on the 29th that the Ceramic had been torpedoed on December 6th, sunk off the Azores in the mid-Atlantic, with only one survivor. It was one of the biggest single disasters of the war at sea and for the Unit the cruellest of blows.

The name of Peter Hume, was not as well-known as that of Tom's, though his record was distinguished, holding several crucial posts including the delicate one of Recruiting Officer. He was also among the first appointed to the Executive, later becoming its full time Secretary. As John Bailey records "Peter's fine service with the Unit was one that commands our respect. We also grieve for the man, with his gay smile and mischievous twinkle; his gifts were rare and to be treasured." His many fine qualities made him an ideal companion to share the China trip with Tom.

The loss of both men was terrible, but Tom's death marked the end of an era. As Tegla Davies remarks in his history of the FAU – "From his appointment as Chairman of the Executive in December 1940, the reign of TLT had been inaugurated." In every way he had been the architect of the Unit thus far, and in the words of my father "From the first meeting with Tom, it was apparent that here was someone out of the ordinary. In Tom's loss, the Unit suffered an irreparable blow, and those of us who knew him well, have lost a friend, whom we shall never forget."

My father once more became Deputy Director and was asked to take over Tom's mission to China, which he did in June 1943........

Tuesday, December 29th 1942 – Cairo (No 30)

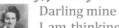

My dearest Joan

I've neglected you this week, partly as I've been so busy, and partly as I've have been away, but mainly as I've been so depressed since I learnt that Tom and Peter were missing in the North Atlantic. Everything has been overshadowed by the news. For some while we still had hope that they may have been picked up. But our hopes were soon dashed. They were torpedoed in the Atlantic, which has made me very down and want to go away and cry. It was only by chance that I read it in the Palestine Post, and it came as a terrible shock.

Now two days later, it seems even more of a blow for the Unit, and a truly dreadful loss. As you know I had profound respect and a sincere liking for him. He was a great man and the Unit owes him an incalculable debt. He really is irreplaceable. Tom made the Unit what it is. Even though he often annoyed me, one could not help but like him. Likewise, though I criticized Peter quite severely at times, he was also immensely likeable. This tour to China was of great importance to everybody, and we had all been greatly looking forward to their visit.

There was so much I wanted to discuss with them both. Today I have been going through their mail and one is even more aware how tragic a loss it is. So you can imagine it has not been a very cheerful day. To read of thousands dying in Russia is of course tragic, but when it's two of one's friends dying, it brings it much nearer home. My darling I thank God for you and for our love. You have been so strong and steadfast through all these difficult times, and I feel so lucky. May I be worthy of you.

Love and more love Ralph

My mother, now apprised of Tom and Peter's tragic death, commiserates with my father. But with their deaths, comes notification of more responsibilities for my father, and the possibility of him travelling to both India and China to complete what Tom had intended to do. My mother muses on the toughness of war, and the hard decisions that have to be made, often excluding the feelings of those left at home. Back in Wolverhampton, however, life carries on........

Monday, January 4th 1943 - Wolverhampton

Darling mine

I am thinking of you so very much at this time, knowing how the tragic news of the death of Tom and Peter will have upset you a great deal, as well as bringing so many problems in its wake. [.....] And I fear you will now have even more responsibility thrust on you. I so wonder how it will affect everything and whether you will have more travelling again, as I see from today's Newsletter that you could be asked to go to China for several months, possibly with Brandon Cadbury, and to join an American, John Rich out there. It also mentions that you may be asked to include India in your tour as well. With all these new cares, you are even more in my thoughts than ever.

[.....] The more I read and hear about my clever husband, the more my heart swells with pride, and the more I realise how fortunate I am. But it is with very mixed feelings that I view the whole of the future plans. You will seem so very far away, and letters will probably be even scarcer than they are now. Ah! Well! I know that will be a wonderful experience for you, my dear one. My goodness, you will have travelled almost round the world before you return to us. Evidently, some people thought you should be asked to return home now, to fill Tom's place, but I gather that has been turned down – at any rate for the present.

In a way I'm quite glad of this, as I feel you are doing such a valuable job out there, and for me the strain of your being on the sea again for a long journey would be almost too much! However, I do understand that the exigencies of war must often supercede the desires and needs of a wife and family. Sadly, these often count for little in wartime, when big decisions are being made, and we must necessarily take a back seat! I do try and accept this, but my goodness, it's so hard on the "wives left poor behind" as the soldier says in *Henry V.*

The Newsletter says "It seems to us that the Middle East needs a man of Ralph's calibre, but it may be felt that he must be spared to visit China for three or four months following Tom's death." Darling, I do realise beyond doubt, that you are now more than ever, the number one man in the Unit!

I know you must be feeling the very heavy responsibility upon your shoulders, and I do appreciate all your difficulties, when I know that deep down, all you really want, is to be back with us at peace. I am afraid you will never be free from responsibility. You are too capable, and such men as you are very rare. I fear in comparison, my capabilities are very small and limited, but I am so happy to be your wife, and being at home and bringing up the children is the best thing I do right now, and passing your love on to them. As I said before, maybe I wouldn't rate too highly in the league of women's rights!!

The children are fine and this afternoon David is going out to tea again. He seems very much in demand, and just loves being allowed to go on his own. He is a very sensible boy and very helpful with Antony, often helping him to dress, so I am more than happy to give him responsibility now, in a small way. I always feel parents shouldn't tie themselves too much to their children. He is a dear child, and Antony is becoming a charming and most amusing child. We are indeed blessed with two lovely children, and I hope you will be proud of them.

Your mother seems to have much enjoyed staying in London with Millior. She said baby Anna is making wonderful progress and putting on almost too much weight. Milli seems easily able to feed her and is herself now well and strong again. Unfortunately, when your mother returned home, she found Lydia quite poorly, and she consigned her to bed to get some rest, and was caring for her herself. But it turned into pneumonia and so she is now in hospital. So with your mother now on her own, I am going with the two boys after all, to stay there next week, and we expect to stay two days and nights. I only pray that the weather will be kind to us, as I don't much look forward to doing the journey alone. Fortunately A sleeps in a bed now, so that eases things considerably.

I managed to post letter 26 (see p 428) off to you yesterday and an Airgraph last Friday. I hope that some at least of my letters are getting through. I am still hoping that your letter 14 will turn up one of these fine days. [....] I so hope you are now quite better, and haven't had any more trouble with gippy tummy making you feel wretched. Here, happily, we are all pretty well – and despite the sudden very cold weather and snow, the children are fit.

I sent some extracts of your wonderful Syrian journal off to Gordon Square, as I felt it only right to share parts of it with others who might be interested. I copied ten pages out by hand!!! Gosh did my hand ache! When they return it, I will send it round to one or two others as everyone thinks it to be one of your best letters ever. I still long to hear about your visit to Teheran, a letter I haven't as yet received. I so hope that was successful and interesting for you.

Some people are saying that the Unit is currently rather short of real leaders, though I hear that Brian Taylor is joining. At least that should be good news for the Unit, as being a doctor, there will be many openings for him, and they will surely have need of him abroad. I wrote to Jack's fiancée at Christmas, but I am now not certain whether I wrote to the right person. Have you heard anything from him I wonder?

Many people have told me that they were so happy to get Airgraphs from you at Christmas. It was good of you to write to so many people, and much appreciated. I haven't been able to get hold of any AML cards for some time, I suppose because of the Christmas rush, but today at last, the Post Office had some more in. I shall be interested to know if they reach you any quicker, as I can write more on these than on an AG.

It is suddenly so cold, that I just can't keep warm at the moment. I'm actually wearing my lambskin snow boots in the house, to keep warm. We are trying hard to economise, and unless one keeps moving around the house fairly quickly, it is easy to freeze! My bedroom, where I am now writing is like an ice box. The Nursery doesn't seem much warmer either. In fact the only warm room is the Kitchen, where we mostly live, except in the evenings when we have a good fire in the drawing room. It has been so mild up until Christmas, but now winter has come with a vengeance.

As always, my darling you are in my thoughts, and I pray that 1943 will see the end of all this misery and suffering – in Europe at least. And how soon I wonder, shall I see you, my dearest? I long for you so terribly. This comes with all my love to you and with kisses from the boys and good wishes from all at Lea Road.
Very devotedly, your own Joan.

————

But as my father writes, they all have to carry on as 'Tom would have expected us to do".
And so my father and Eric Green drove over to Jerusalem to meet John Bailey, and the
beauty of the old city strengthens his faith, and makes him certain that he is right to be a
pacifist. All correspondence, however, seem to get permanently stuck and so they are
both writing off into the blue, hoping against hope that all is well on both sides..........

Wednesday, December 31st 1942 - Cairo

Dear love
Amidst the gloom of the news, we had to carry on, as of course Tom would have expected us to. So today we drove over to Jerusalem, which must be nearly 400 miles. But the car behaved well, and we got up there in under ten hours. I took Eric Green with me, to share the driving, as though I have done the round trip alone, it's really too much.

The journey from Beersheba onwards was lovely. The sun and cloud, the purple distances, the barley incredibly green in the sun; the beautiful grey fig trees; the olives grey and green; and the almond blossom. You remember in Ecclesiastes it says *"when men fear the heights and dangers of the road, when the almond tree blossoms, then man goes to his eternal home."*

When we got to Jerusalem we met up with John Bailey, who'd arranged for us to stay at a nice hotel, with good beds and good food. It was so nice to see him again. He is such a stimulating person, and one respects him for being so sincerely religious and not being ashamed of it. He is an Anglo-Catholic, while Eric is a Catholic, and on Sunday evening they both had a go at me about being a Quaker. We talked for about two hours covering everything from religion to pacifism.

We had a very pleasant time in Jerusalem, which is a city I like, especially the new part of the city. Of course I love the old city too with its winding streets and bazaars; and the mount-of-olives with its view of the city walls and its terraces of grey olives. I do not really object to the commercialism, or even the religious strife, or the pomp and circumstance; because I still feel that Christ lives there.

It gives me great comfort and I feel my faith to be stronger, so that despite all my doubts, I have a deeper conviction, that I did the right thing being a pacifist. Maybe my pacifism is not resisting the evil of Nazism, but at least I am doing no evil in return, and I do not believe that it really pays to do evil that good may come from it. Is the pacifist witness an effective one? Who shall say? But I believe even more strongly now, that there should be some who say 'No'. It is such a help to me, that of all people, you understand my mind and way of thinking. Bless you for that.

I'm afraid both our letters are not getting through just now, or are taking for ever. It's a while now since I heard from you and I do trust all is well. I did have a long letter from the Square, though it didn't contain much news. They did say that Barry may be coming out here, and I do very much hope so.

Apparently Angela was turned down for India on account of her medical examination. Poor lady, it will be a disappointment for her. I had dinner with Douglas last night at the Anglo-Egyptian Union. It was a really very nice meal in a quiet and peaceful atmosphere. We chatted for hours about this and that. I kept saying that ever since I left home I seem to have been only half alive without you and home, and everything that means something to me. Flowers and birds, gardens and trees, the countryside and plays and home and the children. Life is so empty without all these.

And now the loss of good friends too. How bloody life can be. Well, you know how you are all in my thoughts, and so I send you all my love. As ever Ralph.

———

And here is my mother's first letter of the New Year, in which she hopes against hope that 1943 may bring them together again. In one of her down moments she tries to describe the ache of missing the physicallity of my father's love. The love of us children, the love of the family are all fine and necessary, but pale in comparison. At one point she says "think of me", almost as though she were on the phone, forgetting that her letter won't be answered for weeks.........

Friday, January 8th 1943 – Wolverhampton (26)

 My dearest

Well, we are now into a New Year, and I pray 1943 may bring you home to me. I long – oh how I long - for you my sweet dear Ralph. I seem to spend a good deal of my time letter writing! This afternoon I sent out copies of your very interesting Syrian tour to Gordon Square. I felt it only right to share extracts with others who might be interested and when they have finished with it, I shall send it round to John and Enid and one or two others. I sent most of it to your mother, who read it to Millior and Alfred.

It really is a fine piece of work and I have enjoyed reading it many times. I also sent it to Ronald Joynes, as I know him slightly, and asked him only to show it to the few who would be especially interested and perhaps they might like to put it in the Chronicle.

I'm feeling rather sad and depressed tonight – I don't know quite why. It will pass, no doubt, in time – It's just that I miss so terribly being loved. I have the children's love, which is very sweet and of course I have the family's, but that, although deep in a way, is very matter of fact. One can jog along with this, but all that makes life sweet, full and lovely is missing, and only the rather dull path remains. The same, no doubt for thousands and thousands. And I have so much to be thankful for – but I do ache for the fuller life with thee.

I have just come up to bed, after staying up rather late to hear some poetry readings. Six people were chosen from an audition, and then read quite beautifully, poems they themselves had chosen. Three Shakespeare sonnets, two of Keats, Rupert Brooke's 'Heaven', one poem each by Byron and Hilaire Belloc's and one of W H Auden's. I enjoyed it so much. I'm afraid I behaved rather badly though, by making W&L listen for nearly half an hour too!! There seem to be so many things I want to listen to but no-one else enjoys!

Yesterday, I went to hear the Hallé Orchestra. It was a treat for me – I was alone, but didn't mind that. It was a packed hall, holding about 1300 I should think. It was a fine concert with Handel's 'Music for the Royal Fireworks' suite, Haydn's 'Clock Symphony' Stravinsky's suite of his ballet 'The Firebird' and Brahms' 'Symphony No 4 in E Minor'. I greatly enjoyed it. I had a very good seat yesterday, and it was interesting to be near enough to watch Malcolm Sargent – he gives every ounce of himself and appears fairly exhausted at the end, tho' obviously happy! The Inglis's have just kindly phoned to see if I would join them for The London Philharmonic concert on January 27th. They are so kind to me.

It's freezing cold now and I'm afraid we may be in for a good fall of snow. It was very slippery out yesterday and when I took the children out in the morning, both D & A fell over several times. I'm sitting up in my bed jacket with the nice rose-pink dressing gown you like, wrapped round my shoulders, but I'm still nearly frozen. The order is no heat upstairs, except in the nursery – quite right - but one must become very spartan and move quickly or else curl up into bed with only a lick and a promise. You would be horrified if you knew how little I wash these cold nights!! I like to think I'm still fairly sweet smelling though. I do pray so!"

I think your mother's visit to London was a success and she enjoyed seeing the baby and some of the men from the Unit – Sandy Parnis and Freddy Royal, I believe – came in to tea. They are all feeling the shock about Tom and Peter Hume. It is tragic and has made me terribly depressed. I am only doubly thankful that you arrived safely.

I told you that I am taking the boys to your mother for two days and nights on the 13th of Jan. I rather dread the adventure on my own – at least the journey part. I hope the weather will be fine. [.....] I hope all goes well – think of me. Oh, I forgot - it will be too late by the time you get this letter! Sometimes while writing I feel as though I were just talking to you - you feel so close!

[.....] We had quite a fright the other evening. The catch on the door of the Nursery hasn't been right for some time and we got a carpenter up to see to it. He took the thing to an Ironmongers (I believe) and when it came back it seemed stiff, but alright. Later in the day I found it stuck a little, but I thought it would work easier later. After tea D&A were playing in the Nursery and I went up them and couldn't open the door.

The catch wouldn't spring back for me to open and so I couldn't get in. D was very good, but after a while when nothing seemed to do the trick A began to cry and he fairly worked himself up, Llew was in the surgery, but came up eventually and thought he'd better take the ladder and get in through the window! I explained to D to put the light out, and unscrew the window, so that L could get in, but he couldn't manage it and got frightened. Finally, mother and I forced the door and all was well. Apparently, the thing had been put in upside down and so didn't spring back properly! What a to-do!

I was amused at David's conversation when the young boy came to see about the latch.
D: "What is your name?"
Boy: "Horace"
D: "Are you any good at this sort of job?"
Finally, when the boy was going, D said "Come up again soon, Carpenter Horace. Goodbye. Horace!"

He has got very interested in making things and trying to help with jobs. He very much wants to help you with carpentry when you return and has several times told me all he is going to make with you. He is always talking of you and writing things for you – when he was resting today, he wrote a curious jumble of French songs and bits of conversation. I don't think I'd better send it, as it looks so curious. The Censor might think it's something written in code! D loves you very dearly. Tonight he kissed me goodnight and said "Bless your heart – don't ever die will you mummy!"

I'm so cold, I must finish for tonight, as it's already midnight. Goodnight darling of my heart. More tomorrow. I kiss you very lovingly.

With heat rationing and the icy weather outside, the only warm place is in bed..........

Continued....Saturday afternoon.....January 9th

We hardly know how to get warm at the moment. [....] However do the Russians put up with such intense cold? They must be very tough. Here we think our winter is pretty terrible, but it's nothing like theirs. David went out with Win to help her clear away the snow from the steps and the passage. He enjoyed it up to a point, but soon came in saying his feet were cold! I made him a hot drink and he was soon alright again!

Both the boys are resting. Antony usually has a good sleep, but David only rests quietly now and looks at a book or writes. I can't really expect him to sleep now he is over five, but I insist on him resting, if only so that I can a moment of quiet too!

I have written a note to Barry, who is now up at the Manor with the Hadley Spears reinforcements, saying I knew you would be delighted he was going out and wishing him luck, also asking him to bring you my very dear love. I hope that it wasn't stupid of me?

I do hope you have received my books by now as I posted them back in September. I hope they'll be acceptable. It's a little difficult to know what books are really worth sending, especially as I don't know if you have access to any library in the ME. I suppose you can always borrow them from the other chaps if they have anything decent to read.

I thought I would try and post part of your long Syrian letter to Miss James[5]. I feel sure she would be interested to see the part about the many birds you saw. Perhaps when Gordon Square return it, I will send extracts to her as well. [......] Also Cousin Dorothy kindly sent me your Aigraph to read, which was very thoughtful of her. She and Cousin Edward had spent Christmas at Winds Point – lucky people!

[.....] Your mother says Sandy Parnis thought that possibly you might be asked to go on and visit India since Tom's death. I wonder if you think that is likely? My darling, dearest Ralph, I do so love you and think of you continually. David and I are always talking of you and long for your return, so that we can all be together again in our dear house. Sometimes I'm foolish enough to think it may be in a year's time, but in my saner moments I'm very afraid it may be another two years, as I think it will be sometime after the war before you finally return to us.

What an eternity that seems. We're getting so much older and my hair is getting grey! I so often lie awake making absurd plans about all the things we are going to do when you return and I will make it all so lovely for you. Our garden will be gay again and our sitting room so charming and cosy; our bedroom pretty and inviting and I will put your pyjamas to warm and let you get into bed first, so that I have to open the windows and draw the curtains!! I will tuck you in and bring you a drink and chocolate biscuits. I will spoil you horribly! I will never let you go away for long without me again. You are so dear and precious. It's not very feminist sounding I'm afraid, but no matter!!

I just daily thank God for such a wonderful husband and I often wish that I was more worthy of you, my dear heart. I sometimes feel but a poor worm in comparison. But I have made several New Year resolutions to improve myself - and I really will try dearest.

I will send another Airgraph tomorrow. Wolverhampton is very short of Air Mail Letter Cards for some reason. I expect there was a great run on them for Christmas. One can't say much on an Airgraph, but they are just to let you know that I am thinking of you.

Darling of my heart, I hope you aren't getting too depressed about everything. Whatever you do, <u>never</u>, <u>never</u> lose faith in yourself and your capabilities. You <u>can</u> do it and you do it wonderfully well.

Cousin Dorothy said she had seen your Syrian report, and that it was so very wonderfully written and something to be proud of. I tell you, after all the praise I have heard from many, many parts, I will never, never let you get a poor opinion of yourself again.

I'm gradually making a wonderful collection of all the letters about you, and when you return I shall frame them round your study or file them and continually bring them out for your inspection. I'll say "Letter X, written by Y, says such and such; now remember what a high opinion he/she has of you; and you will not dare to get miserable ever again!"

Sweet darling, I must finish this and write several other letters. God bless you and keep you safe and watch over you always. [....] David and Antony send love and kisses and the family send much love too. All my dearest love.
Devotedly yours, Joan

PS I'm glad Christmas is over and 1942 behind us as it is at least another milestone reached.

—

Meanwhile in Jerusalem, my father calls on the Lochs and discusses the Polish refugee situation that he saw in Teheran. He looks forward to being back in Cairo, especially to collect some mail from home, as he hasn't heard from my mother for a long time during his various journeys.........

Saturday, January 2nd 1943 – Written back in Cairo

Dearest Joan

We met up with the Lochs in Jerusalem, who were as nice as always. Before the war they lived for twelve years in a castle in a remote part of Greece, and they have invited us to stay there after the war.

We stayed with them all morning in their tiny garden in Gethsemane. I told them of my trip to Teheran, and Sydney said how much he would love to go there too one day. They both confirm my observation from there, that there is a complete callousness to human life among those refugees who have suffered so much. Jerusalem really is an experience. God make me a better man; give me more charity and sympathy and understanding. Free me from pride or self-seeking or resentment.

Our return trip back was pleasant as well, with all the flowers just coming out. There were scarlet anemones, cyclamen, tiny marigolds, small irises, speedwell and geraniums: all chaste, pure, delicate and lovely, and I thought so much of you. We brought back three chaps who'd been on leave, so we were quite a car full. There were several delays along the way, what with carts with no lights, stationery lorries parked any old how, cars with glaring headlights and cyclists with no lights at all, but we still did it in just under 12 hours. The last 90 miles from Ismailia to Cairo I drove myself in the dark, which we did in about 2½ hours. Rather good going! Forgive my pride, but I think I drive pretty well!

Now I'm back in Cairo there will be plenty to do after such a long absence, and I long to hear news from you. The mail seems to have gone haywire again, with the last letter I received from you dated as long ago as October. I do pray all is well, and that my letters are getting through to you.
This brings all my love as always.
God bless.
Dearest love Ralph.

—

And indeed back in Cairo there is plenty of mail awaiting my father, though as yet no Christmas mail. So these next letters from my mother, written at this time, will not probably reach my father for another few months or so, and my mother wonders about whether she should continue sending letters to Egypt or to India instead, in the hope that he will collect them there......

Monday, January 11th – Wolverhampton (AMLC)

Dearest darling

I hope to get letter number 27 off (p426), either today or tomorrow, but I rather wonder about sending long letters to Egypt now, as I gather you will be moving to China later for several months. However, I will continue, until I hear further details from you. I hope to get an AG or AMLC soon and I do still hope your lost letter number 14, will arrive too one day, as I long to get it so much. I have now received your letter number 20, but numbers 17 to19 are still out there somewhere!

I told you that I had written a note to Barry (MBB), sending my best wishes for his journey out to the Middle East, and I had such a nice letter back this morning. He said how much he appreciated me writing, and how much he misses you. But he also said that he wasn't absolutely sure if he would be going now, as Tom's death seems to have thrown the Unit into a bit of a spin. He said they missed you so much when decisions had to be made, and that the time when he worked with you in London, was the happiest time in his life.

He very kindly asked if I could meet him and his wife in London sometime, which, of course I should love to do. But it's so difficult to get away at the moment, and it is tricky to ask my mother to look after the children too often, though I am sure she would. Life can sometimes get a bit humdrum in Wolverhampton, but there is nothing I should like more than a weekend in London. However, at the moment, I'm rather permanently glued to the spot - until happier days. I wonder who will be taking out the Hadfield Spears contingent now, if Barry's not going.

But how are you my sweet? I think of you so often, and wonder when I shall see you again. Not knowing the future, how can one look forward to something these days? I miss you so terribly and long more than words can tell, for the end of all this separation and misery. Life for you must be a strain too, I am sure. So many decisions to make and such heavy responsibility and continual travel [....] I do sympathise with you so, and wish I could be near you to help you at such a time. I wish I knew more of your future plans.

It isn't quite as cold here for the present, though cold enough for me. The children have slight colds, but nothing serious. Happily, I have kept wonderfully fit, except that I get tired like everyone else. Antony is talking all day long now and is great fun. He and David play well together. D is always talking about you and of the many things he is going to do together with you when you come home. But he says you mustn't come back until all the submarines have gone!

There was an official BBC broadcast from Cairo one night last week, giving a general picture of what it is like there now. It made me feel so near to you and gave one quite a vivid impression of the war out there. I long to hear of your visit to Teheran. I expect you had a very busy time. Were you there a few days - or weeks - I wonder? Did you fly there, and will you be flying to China? So many questions! I expect plans are still very much up in the air.

I wonder if you have read 'Mission to Moscow'? It is pretty solid reading, but very interesting, and I think you would enjoy it. It's written by the former American Ambassador to Moscow from 1936 –1938, Joseph Davies, just after you visited Russia. Try and get hold of a copy if you can.

I wrote to Tom's wife and parents, as I feel for them so much. So many people will miss Tom greatly I'm afraid. Though, of course, I know Peter's family and friends will miss him just as much too. It was in all the papers including The New Statesman. There was also quite a lot in this week's Friend about Tom and Peter. I will send it on to you, though heaven knows when you will receive it.

Dearest husband, I love you so much, and long to have you near me. When, oh when, will that be?

My darling – all my love, Joan.

PS It's now pouring with rain and I love to hear it beating on the window as I snuggle under the bedclothes, and I thank God for quiet nights and the luxury of a warm bed!

———

It's already seven months since my father left for the Middle East, and the ache of missing each other gets worse not better. But as she knows, one of the most important things my mother can do in her letters is to paint a picture for my father, of my brother and me as we grew up, so that he can picture us in his mind's eye. Consequently, however, she trusts the daily round of bringing us up, will not make her seem dull, by comparison with all the interesting things my father is doing and the places he has visited.......

Friday, January 11th – Wolverhampton (27)

Darling of my heart

Just seven months since you left England. What will this time next year bring? The end of all this? If it doesn't bring the end, I suppose we shall at least be nearer the day when we meet and settle again in our own house.

It is terribly difficult not to get into a complete rut, being with the same small group of people day in and day out, much as I love them all. But life can be narrow. I do miss you so much – to be able to talk to you and have fun with you, or just to tease you. The only way I keep myself at all alive is by continually reading, and I have to stay up late to do that, as there is so much else to do – mending and washing etc. I pray you won't find me dull and stupid when you come back. By contrast you have done so much and met so many interesting people.

I wonder how you view the next few months. Are you keen to visit China and India? I suppose it is all experience and you will have the chance to meet up with Dick, Horace and Duncan, which I know you will look forward to. It will never the less mean more responsibility, difficulties and worries. But I have such faith in you – in your capabilities and judgment, and your charm and personality - to win through against the odds.

I know you will succeed in all you undertake and when you return to me I shall be more proud than ever, and love you even more than I do now – if that is possible! [....] When I think of all you are doing, I feel a warm glow of happiness and pride. We are all so proud of you - your mother and family; my family, your friends and of course, the whole Unit.

[....] I do wonder what Cairo is like these days. Apart from all the crowds, is it still a pleasant city to live in? Here everything is now very wintry, though in fact today is slightly warmer and we have at least had some sun. But Saturday was bitterly cold, with a strong icy wind, while Thursday was a glorious day – still cold, but sunny and very frosty. I imagined how lovely the countryside must be just now – with the bare trees silhouetted against a pale winter sky, the grass crisp and sparkling with frost; the distance blue and mauve – all rather sad but nonetheless so very beautiful. I do miss getting out into the country so much, and pine for it as much as I know you do too, longing for just a glimpse of it.

Today, I bought a new pair of shoes, as my others are badly worn out – these are brown, suede ones, which are rather nice. Shoes are so difficult to get, and soon I hear, we may have to wear wooden ones! Imagine me in clogs! I've also managed to get one or two pairs for the boys, as children's shoes are a real problem at the moment. In fact most children's things are difficult to buy right now. I am so thankful I bought a few things in advance and have them fairly well set up for a while. David will probably want a coat later this year, and I think I shall need to get him a little grey flannel suit. His brown coat is still wearing well and Antony is now wearing many of D's old cast offs! I don't think I shall need anything new myself this summer, except possibly some underwear and a hat – well, that's an intriguing combination!! I do wonder how you manage for things. They said on the wireless that there is plenty of everything in Cairo, but at a very high price.

On the whole, we do very well for food, so we have much to be thankful for. There isn't a great deal of variety, but we can't complain about the quantity. Sadly, eggs have disappeared altogether, except for the dried egg variety from America, which is useful but not very nice! David is growing up splendidly now and Antony is quite a boy already, so jolly and amusing. He talks a lot and already puts whole sentences together. His appetite is quite amazing and he especially loves his porridge!

How I wish you could see them, romping about together, so noisy and energetic. They love me to play with them and I try to give up half an hour to them after tea. I give them pick-a-backs and play musical chairs or hiding something for them to find. Antony plays the games well and understands perfectly what he has to do. He can now put most of the endings to the Nursery rhymes.

David asks questions almost every minute and longs to go back to school. He asks me all sorts of embarrassing things as well! But I try, to the best of my ability, to answer them honestly. I think it's the best way, and I hope that by doing so, I shall gain his confidence for the future. He is a dear companion and so sensible. He is very disappointed that we cannot go and stay with your mother for two days, and he was sorry to hear Lydia was ill, and that your mother was now quite alone. He said "Isn't anyone going to see granny, to cheer her up?" He hates to think of anyone being at all lonely and unhappy. He is a little afraid of the dark still and going upstairs alone at night. I suppose we all go through that stage, I know I did.

I have very much enjoyed reading a book called 'The Last Enemy' by the fighter pilot Richard Hillary. I think I mentioned it before. Well I was very sad to see in the paper yesterday the sad announcement of his death - I imagine while flying. He had first been shot down during the battle of Britain and terribly badly burned. Then after months in and out of hospital for treatment, he had recently returned to flying, and I believe met his death during only his second flight. What a tragedy. A brave man and it's a very fine book; I think you'd enjoy reading it. I'm also very much enjoying 'The Silver Darlings' by Neil Gunn[1]. I believe your mother sent it to you. There are so many books I want to read, but not enough hours in the day!

Corder Catchpool[2] is coming here tomorrow to speak to the Forum, and will stay the night with us. We shall enjoy having him and David is delighted at the thought of a visitor. Did I tell you that D can now tell the time and is very quick at numbers, knowing them all up to one hundred? I am certain I was never as quick at the same age. He can read small words now too and is eager to read better so that he can tackle books himself. I always read to him when he is in bed at night.

David has just come down from his rest and brought me a magazine, which the postman has pushed through the letter box. He said –"This is all mummy – a mouldy post today – and nothing from Daddy."

Did I mention that I gave Freya Stark's book 'Letters from Syria' to Win? I haven't read it through myself yet, but I've glanced at it, and I think you would enjoy it. I'm afraid it doesn't speak very well of missionaries! She stayed in Broumana for three months in 1928 to learn Arabic and mentions so many people W&L and I knew. Cousin Dorothy had also read it and mentioned it to me.

I will try and finish this tomorrow. I'm afraid it is rather a dull letter, but there isn't any real news to tell you, except our day to day life, which is mostly the same! Forgive me my bad letters dear one: yours are so lovely and interesting. However, I do love you, and the main reason for writing is to tell you that I love you. I always shall and always will – for ever. My dearest Ralph, as always, I send you all my love.

Later 10.45pm – in bed.......

Hilda Ransome rang me up tonight. It was so nice to have a talk with her. She wondered if I had thought of taking the children away in the summer! And would I like to join her and her three children. I hadn't really thought about it, but it might be a good idea. I feel the children definitely need a change of air, and they haven't been away for some time.

She thought of trying to book us in somewhere in Wales - by the sea if possible. If we could find somewhere cheap and nice, I would certainly like that. What do you think? I'm very fond of Hilda and we get on well and it would be good for the children. I left it that Hilda would try and hunt for some places. Of course we don't yet know what the summer will bring, and so it isn't easy to make plans. And also I don't know if mother wants to do anything, but I rather feel she doesn't very much want to go away, though I'm quite sure she ought to have a holiday, as she works so hard and gets tired.

Dearest one, I wonder if you are in bed by now? I've almost forgotten what it is like to be a married woman! [....] I miss your love and tenderness, your good advice and teasing. I miss the way you comfort me. I miss walking in the country with you, going to the theatre and cinema with you. But most of all, I miss laughing and being gay, and having fun with you. I am, as it were, a shell, but all these many things are deep in my heart and when you return to me, I shall awake from my hibernation and be your gay Joan once again. I shall live and love again. I just plan for that blessed time, and wait only to welcome you with open arms never to lose you again.

Dearest, darling husband, I can see you now, this minute, so vividly - your dark hair slightly ruffled, your dear blue eyes and smiling lips. I can still see you so clearly that afternoon you parted from me, standing in the hall, looking down at me. You looked so fine and dear in your uniform, so handsome and splendid. Everything about you just right. And I wondered how I could possibly let you go from me, I loved you so much. [....] Always remember my love, and how much faith I have in you. Never forget that.

God bless you and watch over you and guide you in all you do, and may you soon come back to me and the children. I live for that day when we shall be together again. The boys send their love, and mother too, with every good wish for your new fields of adventure. This comes with all my love, my dearest.
Devotedly your own Joan XXX

Still very depressed about Tom's death my father looks ahead to life after Tom.........

Monday 4th January 1943 – Cairo (29)

Dearest Joan

When I got back to Cairo, there was at last quite a good lot of mail awaiting me, including some Airgraphs and an Airmail letter card, and I'm so glad that some of my letters have at last arrived with you too, including my Syrian ones, though I fear that the rather nice brocade which I sent you from South Africa, may be at the bottom of the sea, along with the marmalade and stockings, which were probably the wrong size anyway! It is really damnable, but if by some piece of luck they do arrive, let me know.

Your letter of November 3rd was most welcome and I am really happy that the children are so good and well behaved. You know that I have absolute confidence in you. I would really love to have seen some of the autumn flowers back home. Here there is not much variety in the shops and the blossoms are poor.

I haven't received any Christmas mail from you yet, but the excellently chosen books you sent me came in today, for which I thank you so much. The book on London is most welcome and the wonderful illustrations are a dear reminder of a city I came to love, which I shall enjoy greatly. The 'Auden and After' is good too and just the sort of book that will prevent my mind from going completely stagnant. The Russian poetry I haven't managed to look at yet, but bless you for all of them. I look forward to reading them all. Thank you a million.

I still can't get over the terrible news about Tom and Peter. I think I told you, that for some while we kept a forlorn hope alive that perhaps they had been picked up. But eventually after we'd had confirmation, we were suffused in gloom. I wonder if we shall ever hear the full details. I must write to Tom's father and his poor wife Dora; how they and the two children will miss their father. I must also write to Paul Cadbury, who will take Tom's loss very badly. So many letters to write, including to Peter's mother, who will be devastated. Now Tom and Peter are not coming out here, I may have to go to China myself quite soon.

It's been a fairly quiet week with Mike here finishing his convalescence. We had both hoped to go out to the oasis at Fayoun yesterday to look for birds, but unfortunately the car we had arranged to hire did not materialize. So after a vain search for another, we took a tram to a place up river and walked part of the way back. It was not very pleasant weather, but it was so nice being out with Mike again. The river was fine, but sadly we saw few birds. One of the big drawbacks of this place is that there is hardly anywhere to go, and getting out into the country seems impossible.

I have written quite a few letters in the last couple of days – to my mother and sister, to brother John and Enid, and to Florence in Durban, to LPA at the BVT. I feel that one must try and write to all these people, to keep them informed and so that one isn't totally forgotten. This threatens to be the shortest and most unsatisfactory letter yet. I think I have been so down since Tom's death and wondering as usual whether I am doing anything useful out here, that it has deprived me of inspiration. Also I haven't heard from you for a while, and I hope all is well. I do long for news.

Can you believe, I have had terrible rheumatism? Yes rheumatism in this climate! So I'm off to bed.
All love for now, Ralph

It's only when you read the stark facts, that you realise the gap in time taken for letters to arrive. It's now January, and my father has only just received a letter my mother wrote at the beginning of November. It must be almost like a parallel universe, where one is living in the present, whilst your loved one is living in a world several months behind, where Christmas hasn't yet happened! But here my father describes for the fist time the reality that he will be asked to go to China in Tom's place........

Thursday, January 7th 1943

 My dearest Joan
Your very welcome letter – No 19 – dated November 3rd (p354) has just got through, and I am so happy to hear news of you all and the children. It cheered me up no end, and fortunately my rheumatism has now disappeared as well.

I fear I have done remarkably little recently. Since Tom's death there has been more talk of me going to China in his place and I sent you a cable about it, so that you wouldn't hear first from the Square. It is worrying me a lot, but if the Unit want me to go, I think I really ought to.
I recall Tom saying to me before his trip, how he was dreading it, and I do not particularly want to go myself either. It will be very awkward for them here, but no doubt they will all manage. I had thought that maybe the Middle East would be my last trip, and now this has come up. Is there is no peace anywhere?

My cable also sent my love and good wishes for Antony's 2nd birthday. I shall be thinking of you so much on that day and wishing I could be with you. You really are my anchor, and your love and confidence encourages me so very much.

I had a rather sad letter from Horace yesterday, saying how lonely he feels, and is missing Olive more and more since her death, as well as their many old associations. He says he feels so old amongst so many young people. I'm sorry this is such a miserable letter. I'll be brighter when I hear more about China. This brings love to you all my dearest, Ralph

And now my father, having received a cable from Gordon Square, is able to tell my mother for sure that the Executive want him to go to China and India. He is worried about her reaction as it will mean him being away longer. True to his usual self, my father reacts at the prospect of a new job with his usual apprehension..........

Saturday, January 16th 1943 (Airgraph)

My darling wife

Excuse me typing this letter. I do not intend to type my letters as a rule, but just to show that I can type, if only with one finger! The chief purpose of this letter is put you completely in the picture. I have received a cable from Gordon Square saying that the Council and Executive unanimously hope that I will be able to go to India and China, as both are considered of paramount importance and this is the best way of providing some substitute for Tom and Peter. The idea is that Brandon Cadbury should join me here and then that we go out together. My view is that the Middle East can ill spare anyone, but if it is the Unit's need, then that should come first and we shall somehow cope here the best we can.

I should probably be away four months, and personally view it with extreme dread. I do not know enough about China and always vowed that I would try and keep out of that particular mess. I am tired of travelling and the thought of uprooting myself again does not fill me with delight. I feel so inadequate to be able to do the job properly and it is one that I do not deserve. However, I have just received a letter from Horace (Alexander) pressing me to go, which is a slight comfort and the knowledge that I shall see both Horace and Duncan is some compensation.

The news will I am afraid worry you a lot, and I so wish that before deciding I could have consulted you. But I know you will support me, if I felt that it was the right thing to do, as you always have done. I do not think that it need cause you extra worry, as I promise to take special care of myself. I was so afraid that you might get rumours of my trip before I could tell you, which is why I sent you a cable, and have asked Gordon Square to keep you especially informed of the trip. I will probably go about the end of March and get back in July or August.

I do realise, my dearest that you have gone through so much because of your husband, and are now being asked to bear even more. You have all my thoughts and prayers and may God give support you. It is such a strength to me to know that you support me and to know that you have such courage. Think of me too, and know that I do not go with any eagerness. I do so pray that we shall soon have some peace, my darling.

Please say something kind about my typing!
All my love to you and the children. Ralph

———

My mother has now received the cable confirming my father's forthcoming visit to India and China, but other mail is taking even longer and she feels starved of real news. As usual, she accepts the inevitable with grace and fortitude..........

Monday, January 18th 1943 - Wolverhampton (No 28)

Dearest precious husband

Thank you for your cable received this morning. I at once cabled back sending you all my loving prayers and thoughts for your journey to China. It won't be an easy job for you my darling. I know that, but I have great faith in you and know you will succeed. [....] Plans seem to change so suddenly and I feel so out of touch with you. News comes through very slowly. It is nearly a month now since I received any letter from you.

I think I told you I had received a lovely letter from Barry in response to mine, but saying that following Tom's death he wouldn't be going. Then by the next post I received a card saying that he and Brandon would be going out after all, and that he would happily take a message of love out to you from me. I only wish I had thought to get in touch with him before. I rang him, up at the Manor, and he told me more FAU news than I have heard since you went away. I realise, of course, that Gordon Square is very busy, but I do think they might just give me a little more news than they do.

I suppose they will be with you before long and then you will be off on your new adventures. What a travelled man you will be by the end of the war, and how I wish I could be with you to share it all. I wonder if I shall get any news of you once you start? Do send me cables or something that will arrive quickly to let me know that you are alright. Otherwise I shall feel so lonely without letters.

I believe there is some talk of you returning home in the Autumn to report on your visits, while Barry holds the fort in the Middle East. I don't know if that is a good plan....another sea journey. If you are to remain here, all well and good, but I don't feel I can go through another parting, with yet more months or years of separation.

I had a letter from Tom's father thanking me for writing and asking me to write to Tom's wife, though in fact I had already written to her. Mr Tanner said that Tom's wife had actually been most anxious that Tom shouldn't make that fateful journey, as she was very worried for his safety with all the torpedoes and submarines. I feel so sad for her, and there must be so many things she wants to know, and of course, there will never be an answer. It is a tragic loss.

I am still longing to hear of your visit to Teheran. Do you know yet whether you will be flying to India and China? How happy you will be to meet Dick and Horace and then Duncan. Do take great care of thyself darling – especially in China and try not to get ill my dearest one. I hope you don't find your wife too much of a burden, worrying about you at home! Don't feel like Prince Andrei in 'War and Peace', who says to his friend Pierre – "My dear fellow, do not marry till you have done everything in life that you care to do." I am enjoying the book so much, and cannot think why I haven't read it before. It is exciting and the characters so true to life. The BBC are now doing it on the Radio as a play, and it is so well done.

Corder Catchpool was here Tuesday and Wednesday of last week. He is a nice man, but rather lives up in the sky. He almost seems in another world at times. He very nearly missed his train, as we couldn't get him to realise that he only had a few minutes to get there. He spoke well on Germany, but spent too long telling us all the books we should read, when what we really wanted to hear were his own experiences. However, I am sure he is a fine man, even if he is an idealist!

I spent Thursday with your mother. It was a fairly successful visit, although she was rather glum and conversation was quite sticky! She can sometimes be two quite different people. I am afraid it must be very dull for her alone, and heaven knows when Lydia will be well enough to return to work. Life is often so difficult. The lady who helps Win both with the surgery and in the house, has let us down this week, and said she would have to give up coming to us, So Win and I are doing most of it ourselves at the moment which is tiring with the children as well. [....]

Do you get any news from South Africa of Florence Bayman or the Webbs? I hope they received my letters. Michael Edwards, the Editor of The Chronicle, wrote and asked me if I would allow parts of your Syrian diary to appear in it. I said yes. I hope you are in agreement. I feel sure that your letter number 14 is now at the bottom of the sea, though I hope against hope, as I am sure it contains news of so many people I knew from the time when I was in the Lebanon. Perhaps you could try and write some of it again for me and tell me about the friends you met and if they are well.

It's Antony's birthday tomorrow, and we are having two children in to tea – school friends of David's, including a little girl called Kay, of whom he is especially fond. I must now set to and make some jellies this afternoon. I have bought a little cart and a duck for him. It has been difficult to find anything suitable in the shops at all, just now. He is a dear darling, so full of fun and talking all the time; always so lively, never seeming to tire. He and David had some paints and a mug of water to play with this morning, while I went to have my hair done. When I returned they had practically painted the whole Nursery, with water and paint everywhere, including all over their faces, as well as the windows and the floor! David is longing to go back to school on Thursday, but I am afraid Antony will miss him very much.

It is quite mild again now, almost like early spring. The shoots are appearing on the shrubs and trees, and primroses are already out in the garden. I really feel spring can't be far away, and that will be another war winter behind us and bring you nearer to coming home. Oh, how I miss you my dearest Ralph. Just remember my deep love for you and my great faith in you. I know you are doing a fine job and I am so proud of you. I have a lot to live up to. You have all the virtues a man should have, and all I ever wanted in a man. You are just as dear and precious as when we first fell in love....no, ten times more. We all long to have you back with us.

[....] Forgive another rather dull letter, but in truth there is not a huge amount of news to tell you. Every day is spent doing much the same sort of things, so there is nothing much of shattering interest to tell you. But I know that it's news of the children you want most, and I try my best to give you that.

The postman has just brought a letter from Ruth Heynemann, Jack's fiancée, in answer to the Christmas card I sent her, so it did get through after all. She says she has very good news from Jack and that letters seem to come through reasonably regularly. I do so wish yours would come a bit quicker! I feel rather depressed when they don't come, but I expect I shall get several all at once one of these days.

David wants to enclose this letter which he wrote in bed during his rest this afternoon. It's not one of his very best, but he so loves to write and I know you like to hear from him. He is always talking of you and plans to do so much with you when you return.

We all miss you and love you and will write again very soon. All my dearest love my darling. Very devotedly, Joan

A Letter from David

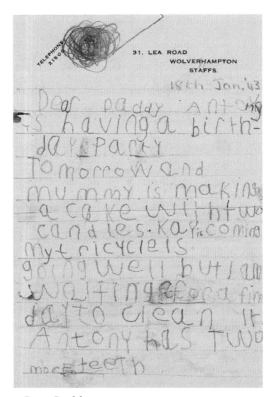

Dear Daddy
Antony is having a birthday party tomorrow and mummy is making a cake with two candles, (my friend) Kay is coming. My tricycle is going well, but I am waiting for a fine day to clean it. Antony has two teeth. I start school on Thursday. Much love David XXX

And........a Christmas Airmail 1942 from the Middle East to David and Antony from Daddy.

Chapter 29
Life in Cairo carries on as FRB goes down with Jaundice
January and February 1943

With still no definite news from Gordon Square regarding a date for my father's departure for India and China, life in Cairo carries on including a few moments of relaxation such as a visit to the Zoo, an outing to an ENSA [1] show at the Opera House, a dinner with Agatha Christie's husband, Max Mallowan - and the FAU's film star, Pat Barr gets married. Less happily, my father contracts jaundice, which lays him low and delays visits elsewhere for some while.............

Tuesday, January 19th 1942 - Cairo

My dearest Joan

On Sunday I had a most pleasant time visiting the zoo, which brought back many childhood memories. It's very well laid out, with lots of trees and bushes which makes it very restful. There are a fine lot of animals and do tell David that I saw lions and tigers, crocodiles and monkeys and many different varieties of deer. There were also many pools which were full of ducks of all kinds and even some flamingoes.

You will be amused to learn that our film star, Pat Barr has suddenly got married after a whirlwind romance to one of the young ladies from the Hadfield Spears Unit called Anne Williams, though everyone calls her Jean. This has, of course, set everybody gossiping! But she is a charming person, and he is delightful and both are mature people in their thirties, so I feel confident it will work out.

Last night John Rose, who is an architect by profession, invited three quite entertaining people in to dinner, and Eric put on an extremely good meal. Before the war John had done a lot of digging in Iraq and Syria, and his companion on the digs is now a Squadron Leader out here, and came with two friends. The SL's name is Max Mallowan, who is Agatha Christie's husband, and a very distinguished archeologist, having worked with Sir Leonard Wooley at Ur. Of the others, one was an authority on Ancient Egypt - the sort of man who reads Papyri at breakfast! Altogether a fascinating evening. Thinking today so much of Antony on this his birthday, and recalling that snowy day 2 years ago when I came to Beaconwood to see you both. No other news at the moment.
All my love Ralph

Back in Wolverhampton, my 2nd birthday party seems to have been a success, but lack of any mail from my father for a month, is now causing my mother concern ....

Wednesday, January 20th – Wolverhampton

My dearest Ralph

If I hadn't had your cable two days ago, I should be very worried about you, as I haven't heard any news of you for a month, when you were just off to Teheran. I hope you received my cable in answer to yours. I now gather from Gordon Square that you had a successful visit to Teheran and are now back in Cairo. It really is sickening that the news is so slow, as it makes me wonder if something has happened to you.

I expect you will now be making all sorts of preparations in readiness to go off to India and China. I know it will be a difficult job for you, but I think an interesting one too. I feel that you are moving ever farther away from me, with news likely to get through even slower than it does now. But all my blessings go with you my dearest, and I shall be thinking of you and wishing I could be alongside you to share all your experiences.

I do hope you aren't too depressed with too many worries or difficulties to cope with. I sympathise with you so much, but everyone has such faith in your capabilities, from Gordon Square to all your friends and of course your family. So never lose faith in yourself, my darling.

Yesterday, we had two children in for Antony's birthday. I can hardly believe it's already two years since that terrible snow-bound day up at Beaconwood, when you struggled up Monument lane on skis! What joys our son has brought us since.

For his party I baked a cake and iced it – with our last bit of icing sugar – and wrote 'Antony' on it, and decorated it with two candles. I also made some jellies in two colours and put them in pretty paper cases. The table looked very gay and both D & A were very excited. It was all great fun. In fact David woke several times during the night before, he was so excited. I do so wish you could have been here with us. A is a very charming boy now and so full of fun. David starts back at school tomorrow and is very keen to be there again. Both the children are well and have managed to keep very fit this autumn. A has two more double teeth, so now there are only two more to come through.

I wonder if you heard about the raid on London. Milli was all alone and twice had to take little Anna away to a shelter, but happily all was well, and I think it was mostly the noise from our own Ack-Ack guns. [....] Honor (Cadbury) phoned me last night to wish Antony a happy birthday and to say that she is expecting another baby in June – and Virginia will only be 14 months!

Your mother is still by herself, but Lydia is recovering in hospital and I hope will be back at Swarthmore Road before too long, which is good news. I wonder if Barry and Brandon have left to join you yet.

Always in our thoughts, we send all our love and kisses across the sea to you. Ever yours Joan

In his account my father wrote for his children, he describes an evening out - and falling sick:

One evening in Cairo, John Rose and I paid a visit to the old Cairo Opera House to see an ENSA company in a light comedy. The venue was built for the opening of the Suez Canal in a considerable hurry and is made entirely of wood. The auditorium is actually quite small and makes quite a cosy, intimate theatre, all decorated in white and gold. The play was well enough done but pretty poor! Not long afterwards, I managed along with various other Unit members to contract jaundice, one of the more depressing illnesses I had during my time in the FAU.

The old Khedival Opera House in Cairo

"Tonight John Rose and I went to the Opera House to see an ENSA company in 'Lovers Leap'."
Photo Opera House archives

In his letter to my mother, he describes the rather silly play at the opera house, but at last some news from Gordon Square and a cable from my mother. But like my mother hoping that she wasn't becoming dull, my father trusts that he won't have become unliveable with.........

Wednesday, 20th January 1943 - Cairo (No 30)

My dearest wife

Tonight John Rose and I decided to go and see a light comedy at the Opera House, performed by the visiting ENSA Company. There was a band, and a good audience mostly made up of service people, making for quite a pleasant evening in all. It was good to see real people on the stage again, but it was a supremely silly play, called 'Lovers' Leap', and though the company tried hard, why in God's name couldn't they have chosen a decent comedy?

However, a couple of days later, on top of everything else, I have been confined to bed again, this time with jaundice. It's a disease that everyone seems to get out here sooner or later. No-one really seems to know the cause or any prevention. I don't think I've got it very badly and I shall probably be up in a few days, but it's a bloody nuisance.

As it happens, I hadn't been feeling too well for some days and in a way it's quite a relief to be in bed and I am able to do quite a bit of work while I am here. They are looking after me very nicely and even one of the Indian servants, Bisha brought me some roses, bless him. My diet is very restricted and I have to eat a lot of fruit. Fortunately there is no shortage of that. Being ill, of course, I have as yet, no idea when I shall be going up East. So much love, Ralph

At last I've had some long reports in today from John Gough, who seems to be doing a good job with the clinics in Syria, where the staff has been enlarged to deal with the growing responsibilities. Every month someone has to come down from one of the four nearer clinics to collect their ration of drugs and to discuss Unit affairs and the clinics. This time it is Mike Shewell's turn and he's also taking a few days leave while he's here.

A cable has just arrived from you, for which so many thanks. I seem to get more and more homesick. Homesick for so much. For you and the children, for our home and for England. Someone here has had some editions of *Country Life* delivered, and there are articles on birds and trees, houses and farming. My God, how I miss it all.

I hope I won't have become unliveable with by the time I return home! I really can't say I'm over enamoured of this community life, though of course, it has its own attractions. There is pleasure in travel and of trying to do a job well undoubtedly, but I cannot pretend I am entirely happy. I miss you and home and all that England means; I miss having any really close friends; I often feel a sense of being inadequate and not having a sufficiently deep spirituality; and my innate shyness makes me loathe interviews and having to constantly ask for things. I suppose I am not really a community person and don't take easily to being a public figure, which inevitably I am in my position. So it all begins to add up, but I can carry on and shall of course. Though why I should be burdened with a trip to China on top of everything else, I don't know!

I've just realised that I have been out here for nearly five months, and eight months since I left home. How time passes, and how I long for it to be just you and me at home again, an old happily married couple! Dearest love for ever, Ralph

––––

My father, still sick in bed but being well looked after, is taking the chance to catch up on his reading and while lying in bed thinking, recalls their happy days together before the war............

Friday, 29th January 1943 - Cairo

My dearest Joan

Well I'm still in bed with the jaundice. In a way it's quite a relief to be in bed as I've no energy to do much besides lie and read. I am quite yellow, but I've no temperature to speak of. It's not all that serious, but one has to treat it with respect. Thank God I'm not in hospital. I'm comfortable and well looked after: Eric is very good in that way. I can eat a little of what I'm allowed. In fact I don't feel much like anything except fruit, and fortunately there is an abundance of oranges and bananas.

I've had heaps of visitors, too many really, but of course it's nice to see them. I've been able to read quite a lot too. Virginia Woolf's *Jacob's Room* and *Death of a Moth* [2], the latter posthumously published in collected essays; Antoine de St Exupéry's *Flight from Arras* [3], which is very good indeed; Balzac's *Short Stories,* rather pleasant; Chekhov's *Short Stories*, [4] which are terrific; and some criticism by T S Eliot [5].

While I'm lying in bed here, I keep remembering our wonderful holidays in Dunster and then in Ewyas Harold in Herefordshire. What glorious days those were, and how I long for such days again. Did I tell you that the BRCS (Red Cross) Commissioner has changed? Sir Duncan, with whom we had that awful row in September, has now gone. Though we had so many disagreements, I had grown to quite like the old boy. We now have Lt Gen Sir Bertram Sergison-Brooke, a distinguished, if ageing looking officer of the old school if ever there was one, but he seemed pleasant enough when I saw him this morning. I imagine he is a gentleman in the best sense. He has a rather fine face; the face of a man one would be glad to serve under. Otherwise nothing very much has happened. There has been no mail at all: it's quite exasperating. Not a letter card, nor airgraph.
All my love Ralph

For some reason, mail in both directions has been taking an inordinate length of time and both my father and mother are naturally concerned......

Sunday, January 31st 1943

Dearest one

I'm really quite concerned as there has been a dearth of mail here for some days now, nothing from you or Gordon Square. Allen Maw [6] has just been in to see me. He has been out in Egypt for two years, and is about to go further East. He now has the rank of Major, but is still much the same as ever, and asked after you.

As for me, I am afraid I'm still in bed, though I expect to get up later today. The Doctor thinks I ought to get away for some leave, but we shall see. On the whole I think I do feel better, and it's time I tried to become more active. I have managed to do a little work in bed, though lack of news from Gordon Square is really very frustrating.

I continue to read a lot, including three plays by Synge[7], which brought back memories of you and I going to see a production of *The Playboy of the Western World,* though I can't for the life of me remember where. I've also read a most interesting book on Louis Pasteur[8] by his son-in-law René Vallery-Radot, which illustrates just how important his discoveries have been for modern health. Somebody lent me *A Life of Jesus* by Conrad Noël, known as the 'Red Vicar' for his left wing views, but I cannot say in all honesty that I thought it very good. What else? Oh yes, Samuel Butler's *Erewhon*[9], which now seems a rather dated satire on Victorian society and frankly bored me. On the other hand, I really enjoyed Constance Holme's famous novel, *The Lonely Plough* [10], which is set in Westmoreland, a county I love as you know, and depicts the strong loyalties of the north-country character. It is quite sentimental, but I think there's something there besides that, which catches an old way of life very well.

But now I'm feeling tired: tired of reading and tired of bed, and a general desire to get up. The trouble is that when I do get up, I just don't feel like going anywhere or doing anything, which is absolutely no good at all. I must start to take hold of myself! I'll close now as I'm not in a good state to write.

I'll write more tomorrow. All love Ralph

A visit to a National Council of Women's meeting with her sister Win, has cheered my mother's spirits no end, especially as the speaker was so young.........

Wednesday, January 20th 1943 - Wolverhampton (Airmail letter)

Darling mine

I will only write a very little tonight as it is very late. I am in bed and have already posted an AG to you today. However, I feel I must write to you, as I feel so much more alive and very much refreshed, having been out this afternoon to a National Council of Women's meeting. The speaker was Marie Osland-Hill, the step-daughter of the American writer and journalist Nora Wain[11]. She talked about her time in Germany, and it was such a change to hear a young girl of 20 or 21 speak. She was so natural and refreshing, it did me a lot of good. Just to get out and meet other people was wonderful, and I almost feel a new person. I went with Win and felt rather guilty leaving both children with Mrs Morris, who comes in to help. However, it was only for two hours and all was well, though I think Antony had missed us being there and was a bit tearful. But I felt I had to get out of the house for a little change, otherwise I get so rusty and dull.

I wish I had more time for reading, as I have so many books to read. I'm still reading 'War and Peace', and have also started Dick Shepherd's life as well as Vera Brittain's latest, and a book your mother has lent me.

I do so wonder what you are up to and where you might be at any time of the day. Will you get any leave before you go off to China and India, I wonder? I feel quite strongly that you need to go somewhere, where you can rest, read and even see some birds. Is there any chance that this could be possible? I'm sure it would do you good.

I often feel this world is so rotten with so much unhappiness and suffering in it, but realise also that I have a great deal to be grateful for too – with a husband I am so proud of, two lovely children and friends and family. [.....] We all pray that your new mission to India and China will be a success and that you come back to us safely very soon. Goodnight now my dearest and I hope tomorrow may bring a letter from you.

All love from me and the children, Joan

Continued.....Saturday, January 23rd

It's now Saturday, and still no letter from you, which is so disappointing. But I think I must get this to the post this afternoon, as it'll just get more delayed. I'm not blaming you, as I know you write, but this time it has been especially long without any news.

Today is so lovely with brilliant sun. How I wish I could get out into the country somewhere. I've hardly been out of Wolverhampton since you left. It would be so lovely if I can take the children away with Hilda this summer. We'll see how things develop.

David and Antony were in the garden all morning and brought down some logs which filled up a large box in the yard, which will be enough to last a week at least. They were so happy. A is growing up fast and chatters away happily all day. I took some photos the other day, which I hope will turn out well, so that I can send you some.

I wonder how much longer I should send letters to Cairo? I suppose you will let me know when I should start writing to India or China, though I doubt there is an AMLC service to China. Maybe you know more about this at your end. I seem so out of touch just now and I don't know what you are doing or thinking. The wireless has just announced that Tripoli is now in our hands. What excitement there must be in the Middle East. I imagine some of the FAU men have been having a busy time, and should have quite a story to tell. Cousin Dorothy has returned your journal and thought it so good, and is going to write another letter to you very soon. I have now sent the journal on to Mr Appleton, who loves to hear your news,

Dearest heart, this brings all my love and the children's across the waves to wherever you are. Ever yours, Joan

---

FRB discusses reading *War and Peace*: "*War and Peace* is the perfect book for a long voyage, and lasted me from Suez to Bombay! It is one of those books that can be read incessantly with little fear of coming to an end. When one finishes one volume, there is always another of five hundred pages! How many people must have read it since the war began? I cannot say, however, that I entirely agree with Tolstoy's philosophy of war, which hardly seems applicable to this war. But I would certainly put him with Shakespeare, at the top of my list."

To much relief, a whole collection of Airletters from my mother arrive in Cairo, to my father's delight, which gets him to wondering what life might be like after the war, when they are together again. Finally, he is allowed up, but still no news about the China visit.......

Thursday, February 4th 1943 – Cairo (No 31)

My dearest Joan

I've just had a splendid lot of Air letters from you. Thank you so much and please thank David for his letter too. I do tremendously value your support and love; it is such a great strength to me. You tell me all the things I want to know and I am most grateful to you for writing in such detail, when I know you must be very busy.

I do wonder what our life will be like after the war. Neither of us will be quite the same and we shall have to readjust ourselves, and give time to the children and everything we so much hope for them, such as a love of the countryside and adventure, a full life with lots of interests, and a good education; helping them to make friends and being able to welcome them into our home too. I think and pray you will find me much the same. Quieter perhaps, wiser perhaps, older and with a greater awareness of myself....perhaps!

It really is sickening that so much of my correspondence hasn't arrived yet, as I have written and posted many airmails and letters at regular intervals. I also sent you a couple of essays on birds I have seen, which might very well be suitable for the Birmingham Post. Well I am up at last and doing some work, though I'm probably not supposed to. On the whole though I really do feel a lot better, but I don't know when I shall be fully fit to travel anywhere. I still have no news from Gordon Square, which is all very awkward as I desperately want to go to Addis and see what's happening there, and I want to see Peter Tennant. As it is I do not yet know when I am expected to go to China.

Two bizarre and scary true stories illustrate the rough and ready nature of Egypt and how unsafe the country still is.........

Friday, February 5th 1943 (No 31 contd)

I have at last been out today and yesterday, which makes a change. I'm still not allowed to eat fats of any kind, or eggs or cheese. But my taste for tobacco is returning and generally I am feeling much better.

Today a woman came in to see us, who is attached to the American School of Archeology at Gizah, the establishment that kindly loaned us our excellent servants. She had some unsettling accounts of how unsafe the country was, and Egyptians were frequently being murdered in the villages near the Pyramids. She related one rather macabre story which she swore was true, and I have no reason to doubt her. "Quite recently," she told us "a senior Police Official was patrolling nearby with a rookie Policeman, when the latter spotted a dead body on the roadside. The senior man said to his companion 'You stay here, while I go and get some officials to come and investigate.' So the young Policeman stood guard over the dead body, while the other officer went to get help. The Officer was away some time, and before long the young Policeman fell asleep. To his horror, when he woke up, he discovered that the body had disappeared."

This, however was not the end of the story. "The young Policeman," she continued "was very worried at what his boss might think when he came back, and discovered that due to his carelessness there was no body. So he decided that somehow he would have to produce a corpse. Before long he saw a man approaching on a donkey. 'Aha', he thought, 'here was his chance.' He hastily took out his gun and promptly shot the man, quickly laying his body in exactly the same position as the missing corpse.

"Eventually the senior Officer returned with some extra help and the young Policeman led them to the dead body. Unfortunately for him, the Senior Police Officer was sharper eyed than he had bargained for. "'Ere, 'ere young man,' he said sharply. 'What's going on? This isn't the same corpse I left you with this morning.' Under some pressure, the young Policeman had to own up." But even this was not the end of the tale. "They were all somewhat at a loss as to what on earth should be done next," she continued. "However, the senior Officer thought they might be able to identify corpse number two, if only they could find the donkey. So they all started looking around and didn't have to go very far before they came across the animal wandering about aimlessly a mile down the road.

Taking a look inside the donkey's panniers, to his shock, the Officer discovered the body of the first corpse, which the rider had removed while the policeman had been asleep. Thus by a roundabout coincidence" she concluded, "the murderer of the first corpse had received a sort of summary justice, unorthodox though it was!" I have to confess, in her telling, bizarre as the story was, it did make for a pretty hilarious, if unedifying tale.

I also read another pretty unedifying, but true story in the Cairo papers a day or two ago. This was about a peasant up from the country, who came to Cairo with his savings, some £80, which he wanted to invest. He got talking to a chance acquaintance he'd met in a café, who said 'I have just the proposition for you. Why don't you buy one of these trams,' pointing to a municipal tram as it passed by in its usual crowded state. The peasant was soon persuaded that buying the tram would be a very good investment for his £80, and would bring him in a fine return.

So he handed over his money to his new friend, and soon set about selecting a tram. He waited until a particularly full one came past, and then said I think this is a good one. His friend helped him on to the tram and discreetly told the Conductor not to pay the man any attention. Throughout the ride, the peasant man watched with pride as the crowds clambered on, and from time to time he would draw the Conductor's attention to children who were escaping without paying their fares.

At the end of the ride, he went to the Conductor and asked for his takings. 'What takings?' replied the Conductor. 'I bought this tram earlier today, and want my money' said the peasant. 'I'm afraid you've been swindled, my friend,' replied the Conductor. What a terrible story. But what a country!

I'm feeling quite tired now, and suspect that I've probably done too much too soon. I can't make out if I'm really better or not, but think I should probably go away for a few days recuperation. Michael Shewell has just come back from leave in Luxor, which he made sound so interesting, that I think I might well go there too. My love to the children and to your mother and mine, and of course to you.

Dearest love,
Ralph

———

At last some letters arrive from my father, including one for David which brings delight all round. But the ones to my mother cover Tom and Peter's death, which makes for sad reading, though the shared unhappiness somehow brings them closer.......

Wednesday, January 25th 1943 - Wolverhampton (29)

Dearest husband

I had really made up my mind never to write on Air Mail blue paper, as it is usually so difficult to read, but I bought this sometime ago, as it seems such nice smooth paper, so I hope you'll manage to read it alright.

After so long without any letters from you, I have just received two AMLC's today dated December 25th and January 6th, and David also had one, and he is absolutely thrilled. Your January letter made me weep and long to take you in my arms and comfort you and kiss away the misery and unhappiness. I can so clearly understand how you felt on hearing about Tom and Peter. You must have thought the bottom had completely fallen out of everything for the time being. I knew you would be utterly miserable and I felt unhappy with you and for you. It was such a shock. It seems Tom's life, although such a success in so many ways, was a tragedy.

How many will be feeling sad and wretched. I have written, but feel I would so much like to be in touch with Tom's wife, just to be friendly and kind and sympathetic to her. She must feel lonely. To be so far away, not knowing any Unit people, must be heart-breaking. I was glad I wrote and I hope she gets my letter. Tom's father asked me to write if I felt able to. Apparently, she had been very much against him making the journey.

Dearest, I feel so near you tonight. I want to fling my arms about you and comfort you so much and talk with you into the night. There is so much I want to say to you and so much I want to know. My love for you grows stronger by the day. The more I know, the more I admire you for the way you carry on and assume all these added responsibilities and perform them so well. I feel that I must say this to you, even though I've said it before, as I realise that my love for you is the best thing I have to give in life, and I remain so proud to be married to you, and the mother of your children. Please may God bring you home to me soon. Only when I am with you do I feel truly alive.

It is now 11.45. So goodnight my darling. May God bless you, always. More tomorrow.....

Tuesday....continued.

It seems as if I shall never finish this letter! I have been rather busy today and written several letters, all of which ought to have gone several days ago. I wrote a letter to Angela in answer to hers and I also wrote to Barry and asked him if he would kindly take the photographs of the children out to you. All letters are taking such ages to get through at present, everyone says, and I thought perhaps you wouldn't get them before you left for India and China. I only hope Barry and Brandon haven't departed already. The photos are lovely of both D & A. I do hope you will like them. You can tell how mild the weather has been for January, as the children have no coats on, as it is so warm and sunny.

It is amazing - just like March or early April and the birds are singing. The primulas have never ceased flowering and all the bulbs are about 2 inches high. I think the forsythia will flower early too. But the flowers in the shops are a terrible price – 5/- a bunch! I am so pleased to have the plant Cousin Dorothy sent me. It is a glorious sight now – a mass of lovely bright, cherry coloured flowers and it smells so sweet. I'm afraid I don't know what it's called. Your descriptions of Palestine and the wild flowers there, make me long to see it all again, but with you this time.

David has become terribly keen on making things with wood, although he hasn't any real tools, except what Llew is good enough to lend him. But he made a very good attempt at a boat over the weekend and nailed sails and guns on too! He is so alive to everything and anxious to help in all sorts of ways. He asked me the other day – "Mummy, do you think Father Christmas is a bachelor?" I'm afraid on the spur of the moment I said "Yes", but thought afterwards, how completely wrong I was! He bought another packet of seeds today – parsley this time. He really means to have the garden full of things in the summer.

We are feeling rather worried over Vera's mother, as it appears she is gradually dying from cancer and nothing can be done for her, as it has gone too far. She may live a while yet or only a few months. But it is a terrible worry for Vera with Reg away. Mrs Lunt is still up and about in her own home, but in great pain and Vera thinks she may have her mother to live with her, so that she can look after her. But it will be so difficult with the two children. Vera's younger sister Irene is getting married on Saturday.

Mother has been rather poorly with rheumatism, but seems a little better today. I'm afraid she gets rather tired these days.

While still completimg this letter, another long letter arrives from my father, and in response to Douglas Mackenzie's letter on fidelity, prompts thoughts from my mother on the ways men and women differ in this respect......

Wednesday....continued

I really must finish and get this to the post!! Three cheers! This morning's post has brought letter number 17, posted November 8th (p340)! What an age it has taken. But still no sign yet of number 14. You talk in your letter of our visit to Swarthmore Road and thank you for enclosing Douglas Mackenzie's letter to you. As you say – it delightfully sums things up. This matter of loyalty is interesting. I suppose for one who isn't attached and has no special person to be loyal to, it is more easy to get caught up in the romance of the place and the fascination of a woman. How many men – or women for that matter – can truly remain loyal, not only physically but mentally too?

For me, I want no other man but you. I love you and always will. I must admit I have no opportunity for mixing with others, but I also have no longing for the company of other men. I live for your return and miss you desperately. I don't think a man ever grows up in his attitude to women. They always attract him and he is constantly falling.

For a woman, it is rather different. When she is young, she loves men's company and likes a good time and lots of fun. But once she is married, provided she is still in love with her husband, children bring some kind of satisfaction and deep happiness that it is difficult to explain. For a man it is different – maybe children don't mean quite the same to him, not that he doesn't love them as much, but that they don't altogether complete his happiness. A man is always ready to respond to a girl's attractions and charm. I suppose physically men and women are so different. [....]

Douglas says how he "longs for those eternal moments when one can worship someone close, infinitely dear, warm and alive." However, I have never been able to think – "this will last me through life." I feel the more happiness we have together, the more I crave. I never feel I can have too much of you. I love you so dearly that I literally ache to catch up the threads of the past and weave some more.

———

It is a pity we women seem to age so much more quickly than a man. I quite realise that my young fresh charm – if ever I had any - has gone. I am 28, the mother of two children and already my hair is going grey! I don't think I should appeal to many men! A sad thought! When our youthful attraction has gone, do we gain something else? Does some other attraction take its place? I don't know. I just wonder. Youth always charms, and it is hard to grow older gracefully and attractively. I'm not fishing for compliments...I do mean it all.

Well, my dearest, I didn't mean to ramble on so. You haven't told me if you ever received the books that I sent to you. I do hope so. LPA (Appleton) has returned your Syrian Diary and asks me to forward it to Henry Cadbury as he feels sure he would be so interested to read it too. LPA so much enjoyed reading it he said.

Tonight I am joining up with the Inglis's to hear the London Philharmonic Orchestra, and I am so looking forward to it. They are having the actress Margaretta Scott to narrate Prokofiev's children's piece 'Peter and the Wolf', which I am sure will be fun.

Your mother very kindly sent me a parcel of various useful things, just household things, but most welcome – dusters and cloths and towels and some sweets and chocolate for the children. She is so kind. She has now opened an account for Antony and started him off with £10. They are lucky children. She also enclosed one of Millior's letters, writing of Anna's progress and how she is doing well and seems to have an enormous appetite like Antony. Milli has had her great friend Gwen Bebbington-Smith staying, along with her baby, George, for a few days, as they were up to see a specialist about the baby. Nothing serious fortunately.

The flower shops this morning were full of jonquils, snowdrops and violets. How I longed for a bunch, but I did buy mother a small bunch of snowdrops. They look so heavenly with their white and green buds just opening.

Your mother was pleased to get an Airgraph from you yesterday, dated January 5th. Lydia is still away but getting better I think and hopefully she will return before too long.

My darling I must close now. I take you in my arms and hug you close. Thinking of you so much, I do hope you get this before you go to India. Love from us all, Joan.

PS. Good news about the Casablanca Conference, which seems like a big step forward.

The Prime Minister visits the Middle East

Churchill in Tripoli 4ᵗʰ February 1943

The PM is greeting an officer of the 51st Highland Division during his visit to Tripoli, to thank the 8th Army for its success in the North African campaign.

The British Army, which had finally confronted Rommel, had been on the move since October. Now having driven the German forces out of Libya there was a pause for many of the units as they re-equipped. There was also time for a formal celebration for the men who had taken part in what was now recognised as a major victory from which the Axis forces in Africa could not recover. At home Britain had celebrated the victory at El Alamein with ringing church bells in November – church bells that had not rung since the threat of invasion had begun in 1940. Now there was time for a Victory parade in Tripoli.

Photo National Archives

Chapter 30
Leave in Aswan and Luxor
February 1943

In my father's notes for his children, he writes.........

After I had had jaundice in 1943, which has to be one of the more depressing diseases I contracted in the FAU, I went for a week to Aswan and Luxor to recuperate. I greatly enjoyed seeing all the antiquities in Luxor of course, but an abiding memory for me is the garden of the hotel at Aswan, which was bright with flowers, running right down to the shining black rocks which bordered the river, on which white-sailed yachts bobbed gently along. Beyond was an island covered with Palm trees and beyond that again were the sandy hills of the desert.

Monday, February 8th 1943 (No 32)

My dear love

This week I have received four Air Mail letters from you. Thank you so much; they have made me very happy. It is really good to get so much news from you. Quite why you have had none from me is a mystery. When you do get more of mine, remember they are written for you and the family, so be careful not to broadcast them too widely.

But you mustn't build me up to be too great a hero. I am really a very ordinary mortal, and one day I shall be found out! But it is wonderful to know that I have your support. It is a great help and strength to me.

I think I mentioned that Sir Basil Neild came in the other evening, the MP for Chester. He had travelled out to the Middle East in the Prime Minister's party when he visited the troops out here the other day. Neild disclosed privately that the PM had found the air trip out here very tiring, and was not relishing the flight home, especially as the weather looked pretty unpleasant. I don't know how the PM stands it.

But during the trip Neild had been able to spend about half an hour on his own with him, and reported that following Alamein, the PM seemed much more hopeful and upbeat, and quoted him as saying "It won't be very long now." Let's hope so for all our sakes. Much love Ralph

[NB. While on FAU business – all my father's travel, petrol, hotel bills etc – are covered by Unit expenses – including the odd 'expensive Hotel!]

So, my father finally decides to take a break, and contacts a travel agent for an all in package of a train down to Aswan and a hotel there. Here he describes the journey alongside the Nile, and relishes being on his own and enjoying the sites......and being in an expensive hotel! ....

Wednesday, February 10th 1943 – Aswan (No 32a)

Dearest Joan

Well, I decided after all that I would take some leave, as I was feeling fairly tired having done nearly a full week's work since my illness. It's quite difficult not to, when one lives on top of it, so I think it was sensible to come away, and I am now writing this from Aswan.

I left on the 7.50 night train from Cairo yesterday in a second class sleeper. But their sleeping cars are really good, with only two in a compartment and they are very comfortable and clean, with separate washing facilities. In fact I slept very well. The man I was sharing with got out at Luxor at 7.30 in the morning, and for the rest of the journey I had the compartment all to myself and a good breakfast on the train to boot. In fact, train travel as it should be, and I so wished you could have been there with me.

The railway runs along the Nile for most of the journey, and on either side the flat green stretches along the banks gradually narrow, as the desert cliffs and hills get nearer and nearer to the river. The country is pleasant enough but fairly uneventful. Closely cultivated green banks, groups of trees, mud villages with date palms towering above them, Doves flying up from the ground and Egrets standing in the fields, with the usual collection of donkeys, camels and water buffaloes.

My Hotel, called The Cataract, is a huge, ugly, palace of a place. But it's clean with excellent service and good food. The guests are mostly Officers and Queen Alexandra Sisters[1]. In peace time I suppose it would have attracted the travelling wealth of Europe. I got an Agency in Cairo to fix the trip up for me. I know it's expensive but as I shall do very little here but rest, read, sleep and eat, I am sure it will be worth it, and if I hadn't gone, there might not be another chance. I trust I shall get back twice the chap I was….some hope! Could you kindly ask Gordon Square to remit £15.00 to me in the usual way?

The Hotel stands on rocks directly over the river Nile and has a fine view of the river, which at this point is shallow and rocky, with sand spits and rocky islands. Here the desert hills are very close, and only further along the river is there much greenery. I'm actually very glad I came here, and I think I am going to like it. We'll see, but so far the weather is absolutely perfect; a clear hot sun and a cool breeze. In fact it's ideal for sitting in the garden, which is exceeding pleasant with petunias in full bloom, as well as snapdragons, marigolds and bougainvillea.

Also thank God, it's beautifully quiet, such a change from the racket in Cairo, which is sometimes intolerable. At one time I nearly came with Douglas Mackenzie, but it's actually good to get away completely on one's own. It's only a breathing space, but just what I needed before another fearful bout of activity. With a little more time on my hands, I was able to settle down and re-read Newman's *Apologia Pro Vita Sua* [2]. It is such a readable book, and very strange that ecclesiastical controversies of a hundred years ago can still be interesting. But he writes so well, that he gives the arguments continued life.

The Cataract Hotel
"My Hotel in Aswan is a huge, ugly, palace of a place."
Here viewed from the Nile; it was built in 1899 by Thomas Cook, to cater for European travellers.
Photo courtesy Cataract Hotel

The train journey from Cairo to Aswan

My father booked his trip to Aswan with a travel agent. This is an Egyptian train advertisement of the time.

See Egypt by train.....

"Egypt is fabulous, and Cairo one of the most fascinating cities in the world. There's no need to book a tour, it's easy to travel round Egypt independently. Egyptian Railways are easily the most comfortable way to travel between Cairo, Luxor, Aswan, Alexandria, Port Said & Suez. The views from the train can be wonderful, especially along the Nile amongst the fields and palm trees on the Cairo-Luxor-Aswan and Cairo-Alexandria routes. As so often, the train journeys give you an insight into the country."

Image Egyptian Travel Agency

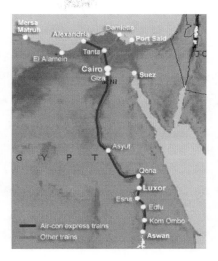

Thursday, February 11th 1943 – second day (No 32 contd)

I had the most amazing night last night. I went to sleep by 10.0pm and didn't wake again until 8.30. I've just had breakfast, and the meals here are really good. Well so they should be for the cost! I didn't enquire about separate prices when I booked, just paying the Agency an all in fee. But I see from the tariff, that the evening meal costs ten shillings (about £30 today)!

I am now sitting on some rocks in the hotel garden that juts out into the river. It's wonderfully clear and I can see for miles. On the far bank are sandy hills, and in the river, shiny black rocks. Way downstream is the palm-covered Elephantine Island, which was once used as a fort and has several ancient temple ruins on it. Further towards the north are hills, while on this side close in, the stream disappears as it bends to the west. The sky is forever cloudless with a gentle breeze blowing, filling the white sails of the yachts as they go up and down the river.

The water itself looks dirty and muddy, but takes a little reflected colour from the sun and sky. Behind me is the hotel garden, bright with flowers and I can hear Doves gently calling. Over the river swallows dip and dive, while the noisy Kites and Crows scream as they fly to and fro. I have not read at all. It was so quiet and peaceful that I just sat and watched. Later on, I moved back into the garden, and relaxed in the afternoon sun with only the buzz of insects, butterflies, and the scent of gay coloured flowers. If only you were here with me.

I wrote an article on the bird life here, which I enclose, (see appendix) and you might like to see if The Birmingham Post would like it. You can say your husband wrote it, but don't put my name, just put FRB. If by any chance they offer to pay, which I doubt, it will be a present from me.

The agency I booked with has supplied me with a dragoman (guide/interpreter), who I am convinced is an old rogue, but is nonetheless obliging. This afternoon he took me sailing round the islands.

Kitchener Island

Kitchener Island
"This has now been laid out as a glorious Botanical Garden. [.....] The sky is forever cloudless with a gentle breeze filling the white sails of the yachts as they go up and down the river."

Photo National Geographic

While we were waiting for the boat, the river looked at its best. Before us was a wide reach, with the wind causing little ripples and filling the white sails of the boats. From where we were standing, the islands looked impressive, rising steeply from the water, sometimes only mud and sand, but often huge fantastic black and grey water-worn granite boulders. Further still, to the south, a maze of rocky islets and sandy spits with the river flowing in between, and in the sunset they looked almost mysterious and unfriendly, like the entrance to an unknown land.

Just behind Elephantine Island is Kitchener Island, where the General once had his HQ, which has now been laid out as a glorious Botanical Garden. There are long walks of grass with huge palm trees everywhere, and flowering shrubs of every colour, from blues and pinks to yellows and oranges. Elsewhere are hedges of scarlet poinsettia and masses of petunia, marigold, scarlet salvia, and the brilliance of the evening sun. Some flowers need rain and clouds and sunshine to appear in their full beauty, but these seemed at their best in the sun-laden afternoon. And as if this was not colour enough, there were yet more blazing trails, covering the pergolas, and hedges of bougainvillea.

How I wished you could have been here to share it with me. This place is so lovely, but I am only half enjoying it without you. Perhaps my words will help to conjour for you something of what it's like. And when next you see a summer migrant, a Chiff Chaff, Willow Wren, Swallow or Redstart, remember that I saw it first here, and that when it reaches England it brings my love with it!

This morning I went to see the Aswan dam and the lake above. It was built around 1900 and is still, I believe, the largest dam in the world, providing storage of annual floodwater and regulating the flow, providing them with greater irrigation. It is impressive rather than beautiful.

It's a straight structure of granite, holding back the river and making a lake some 200 miles long. Out of the lake rise the tops of submerged hills, all rocky, barren and desert. Below, the water pours through the sluices into the rocky, river bed. Soon they will release the stored water for use, then the floods will come again in June and until October will pour through unchecked. When they are past, the sluices will be closed and the water stored again.

This afternoon I hired a sailing boat with a young lad, who took me right up to the lower end of the first cataract below the dam. The sun was hot, but there was just enough breeze for sailing, and it was glorious. To the east were cliffs, not that high, whilst to the west were sand-hills and all around a maze of rocky islets. Other yachts and native boats were crossing from village to village. And though some people might find it somewhat hard and unattractive, to me it has a beauty of its own, and I have greatly enjoyed these three days. There has been only myself to please, and no-one to talk to, save a New Zealand Captain I'd got to know slightly when he invited himself to have breakfast with me.

Early morning here is lovely, absolutely fresh and clear and calm; while the evening, as I had my tea on the balcony and watched the sun set behind the desert hills, was a perfect picture. What beauty there can be in a landscape. So many places I've visited alone and as well as those we've been to together, whether in England or Scotland, Switzerland, Syria or the Lebanon can overwhelm one with their beauty. Here this has a character all its own. Whether it's of the same beauty, I won't say, but it's extraordinarily attractive, strangely fantastic and infinitely worth seeing.

On my last day here, I spent a pleasant morning just quietly looking at the river and reflecting. What was I thinking? Yes of course, it is beautiful. The clear air and ever blue sky; the wide, silent river, with its black rocks, palm trees and white-sailed yachts. Then in the garden I looked down the central path, with great acacias behind me in whose shade I sat, and in front two lines of tall palms, bright flowers and butterflies, while on the left was a white wall covered with bougainvillea., and every now and then a bird flew past. What splendid beauty it all was.

So much so, it inspired me to write a second article on Syrian birds for the Post. When I'd finished the first one, I found that I'd rather enjoyed it. I am no judge whatever of their merit, but I think they may be just passable. If you're too busy, don't bother with them, but I had fun doing them. As usual this brings all my love, Ralph

———

Meanwhile, not aware as yet that my father has been to Aswan or Luxor, despite correspondence being so out of kilter, my mother writes religiously to keep my father in touch, in the hope that sometime they will catch up with him either in Cairo or in India……..

Monday, February 1st 1943 – Wolverhampton (Air Letter)

Dearest
I'm afraid I had to cut a piece off this, as David tore it by accident! You shall have another letter later in the week to make up for it! I was delighted to receive your lovely long letter (18) (p373) this morning, posted November 16th!

I wonder if you met up with Najla Cortas (now married) and the Rizak's or Blanche Lohéac while you were in the Lebanon; and I wonder if Michel Cortas ever got my letter, which I wrote very soon after you left.

Your description of your visit when you took John Gough up to Beirut (p369) are immensely interesting and how well you enable me to picture it all again. How splendid it would be to join with you in your travels. What an experience you are having and I hope it is giving you self-confidence, as you are doing it all so brilliantly. I feel so near when I think of you visiting lovely Broumana. God, what happy days I spent there! It would be ten times better if I could do it all again with you!

This morning it was simply pouring with rain and I got absolutely soaked fetching David from school. I only had a costume on and no mac or umbrella. We have had so much rain recently, but on the whole it has been a very mild winter, with hardly any frost and only a sprinkling of snow. Even the Thrushes are singing, just as though it were spring. I can hardly believe you have been away nearly eight months already. I wonder if I shall have you back home this time next year. If you do return to London, I think I shall try and get a flat nearby you, so that I can be with you!! I couldn't bear for you to be in England and separated from me again.

I've now sent the photographs I took of the boys off to Barry so that he can bring them out to you. If you have any more photos of yourself do let me have some copies.

Some letters still haven't arrived and neither has the brocade you so sweetly sent me, though I am sure one of these fine days, they will all arrive unexpectedly.

Your mother tells me that she is hoping Lydia will be with her this week, which will be a great relief for her.

One of D's class mates has the measles, but there is no sign of D getting it yet, touch wood.

All for now my dearest. All my love, Joan

FRB on a suitable reading contrast: "Could there be a greater reading contrast to Shakespeare and a history of the Crusades than *Pride and Prejudice* or *Persuasion?* Did those men of Jane Austen do anything but manage their estates through a bailiff, read, shoot, visit their friends or flirt? Why should they? It is true that some of them were in the Navy; and of them Jane Austen says through the mouth of Louise Musgrove, that 'she was convinced of sailors, having more worth and warmth than any other set of men in England; that only they knew how to love, and they only deserved to be respected and loved.' In comparison her soldiers are a poor lot, their job a sinecure.

What a secure and comfortable world it was! The working class never obtruded. It was Anne Elliott's opinion that with the Croft's 'the parish was sure of a good example, and the working class of the best attention and relief.' One reads of the villagers whom Lady Catherine de Burgh 'scolded into harmony and plenty.' There was a plentiful supply of male and female domestic servants, duly subservient. General Tilney 'was convinced that to a mind like Miss Morland's, a view of the accomodations and comforts by which the labours of her inferiors were softened, must always be gratifying.' And how much depended upon their housekeepers – 'a respectable-looking elderly woman' she says of one, 'much less fine and more civil than she had any notion of finding her.'

Yet it is not wholly escapist. Jane Austen does not hesitate to condemn her worthless characters and commend those who are 'sensible and gentlemanly'. If they have ten thousand a year, so much the better. Mrs Bennet is described as a woman of mean understanding, mean information and uncertain temper. And of Mr Elliott it is said 'she saw that there been bad habits.'"

The old Aswan Dam and Luxor hieroglyphs

The old Aswan dam built between 1899 and 1902, which still supports two hydroelectric plants.
It was eventually found to be too low and the new Aswan High dam was opened 1970.
"It is impressive rather than beautiful," writes FRB

Trees being transplanted from the land of Punt, near the Red Sea, back to Egypt, following an expedition by Hatsheput's soldiers.

One of the images of birds from the tomb of Hatsheput - an Ibis - that impressed my ornithological father.

All photos Egyptian Tourist Board

After three days in Aswan, my father travels back to Luxor, and meeting up with some other Unit men, visits the tombs, relishing the delicate carvings of the hieroglyphics, and its glimpse into the everyday life of three thousand years ago. Yet he concludes, despite all their skills and knowledge, they reached a certain pitch of artistic and scientific knowledge and then no further, remaining static for hundreds of years...............

Friday, February 12th 1943 – Luxor (No 33)
My dearest wife

After three blissful days in Aswan, I came on here to Luxor. Aswan was exactly what I wanted. Beauty, peace and solitude and a chance to try and find my own soul. Thank God I was able to enjoy it quietly without restlessness. I did as I pleased, though with a certain discipline. That's to say I read books other than novels and I did some writing. One does not fully realise, until one gets right away from it, just how much the Unit is always on top of one. Oh I know it's only a breathing space, just a part way up the mountain, but it was truly blessed.

It wasn't a particularly pleasant train journey up here, and then there were so many people on the station pestering you to take your luggage, show you the sights or find your hotel for you, that it is a wonder that anyone escapes unscathed. My hotel here seems alright, but it's nothing like as good as the last. The meals are all perfectly served, and we are excellently attended to by an efficient, and doubtless grossly underpaid, Nubian staff. But although it's quite good, the atmosphere is very different here. For instance the few poor 'other ranks' who found their way here, are seated in a completely separate part of the dining room, which I don't like.

When I got here, I discovered that a group of our chaps had also come here for a break, including Eric Green, our man in charge of finance and another friend of his. Douglas Mackenzie was supposed to join them, but like me, poor fellow, had contracted jaundice and stayed behind, so today I joined up with them.

I don't really like comparing places, but generally speaking, I think Luxor is more beautiful than Aswan. The river is very broad here and the fertile strip on either side is wide, with hills all along the desert edge. The Hotel garden, though having many of the same flowers as at Aswan is, I think, even more beautiful, especially the glowing sheets of bougainvillea. This evening after tea, the flowers looked especially lovely, and all along the river front, is a mud road with vivid coloured flower-beds down the center. The river itself was a wonderful shade of blue, and over on the other side green cultivated land, clumps of trees and the distant hills, all dappled light and shade in the evening light.

Today we spent sight-seeing the many antiquities here. I won't go into too much detail, but a bare catalogue of what we saw comprises four king's tombs, two nobles' tombs, three Queen's tombs and three Temples! To get there one has to take a boat across the river, a short ride on a donkey, then a car up into the hills. The hills are fine, but barren, with glaring limestone rocks, and precipices strewn with fallen boulders. Under cloud or rain they would be merely ugly and depressing, but in this glorious fresh air, against the incredibly clear blue sky, they are really very striking indeed. And wonder of wonders, they are not spoilt by tourism.

I won't describe the tombs, as I you will know them well by report. They are, of course, quite empty, but the interest lies in their depth and length and the wonderful wall carvings and paintings. We visited the tombs of the 18th, 19th and 20th dynasties. What can one say of Egyptian art? It is, of course, very stylised, and the figures are not accurate representations, but have symbolic purpose. Sometimes it is so beautiful, one wonders if it was designed just to serve a purpose?

The delicate relief carvings of the hieroglyphics, for instance, are breathtaking, and the colouring of the figures still clear and bright as new, after 3,000 years. Beautiful or not, they have a unique fascination. Not so much for their symbolism or the story of life after death - the passage through the underworld and the judgment of the animal-headed gods - but for the wonderful picture it gives of their everyday life. There is one tomb, which belonged to a chief gardener, which shows this beautifully. Here they are harvesting and ploughing, reaping the corn, picking the grapes and hunting the animals.

And it's not just people, but birds and wild life too. Easily recognizable are the beautifully cut Ibises, Teal and Pintail, all perfectly drawn and coloured, seen rising from the reed beds, while life-like Owls and rabbits inhabit the hunting scenes. And then there are the clothes too, with one I particularly remember, depicting a Queen's dress, all in white, which was so accurately drawn and coloured it seemed real. In another temple, one could follow the story of a great expedition to Somaliland, and the travellers bringing back new kinds of trees and animals to Egypt.

Behind it all is this intense preoccupation with death, with the preparation of tombs beginning long before death was expected. And all of it involving enormous labour, not just of the artists, but of the workmen who quarried them too. Some tombs – many, in fact – are unfinished, and on the walls can be seen the first freehand sketches for the final drawings, all ready for the artist to cut them out in recess or relief.

It is amazing, not only that they could produce such fine colours and such lasting colours, but that they could plaster so smoothly, and that the plaster has remained virtually undamaged over millennia. On the whole, I think it is impossible to avoid the conclusion that much of the beauty has to be intentional, or at the very least that it is inherent, in the fact that they were such fine craftsmen.

We also saw three funerary temples, remarkable chiefly for the rows of enormous columns, because of course, they were restricted through not knowing about the use of the arch. Instead buildings were tapered and roofed with slabs placed over the vast and heavy columns, impressive just for their size. Every stone is carved with war scenes, or hunting scenes and images of the gods. In one temple, one can still discern the remains of a blue colour on the columns and roof slabs, and looking down from above on a colonnade, with sunshine throwing shafts of light between the pillars, it is exceedingly fine. Interesting, impressive, and totally fascinating.

What a people! I really must read more, as I know so little about them. But what can one surmise? That they had amazing proficiency in the arts and were supremely capable artists; that they were fine potters and weavers, wearing elaborate clothes; that they had some knowledge of agriculture and were soldiers, administrators, colonists and explorers.

On the other hand, they were also polytheists, living on slave labour, and dedicating vast sums and thousands of lives to their own glorification and preparation for the next life. Yet with all this skill – yes, including mathematical knowledge – they were restricted. They reached a certain pitch of artistic and scientific knowledge and then no further. Think by comparison of the Greeks, and how far they carried human thought and knowledge forward. Egypt got so far and then remained static for hundreds of years. Strange.

Why do we go and see it? Because of its intricate beauty? Yes, partly. Because it shows how men lived and what their tools were; what they ate and wore; and how they passed their time? Yes, partly that as well. Because of an emotional attraction to artefacts 3,000 and more years old, with colours that have stood since the craftsmen first put them on; and sketches of work yet to do, left unfinished because of some accident or catastrophe and still unfinished? Yes, partly that too. Because we marvel that life could be so relatively civilized so long ago? Yes, and that too. Because we marvel at the first developments of craftsmanship, mensurations, agriculture and religion? Yes, for all these reasons. But what do we learn of the sort of men they were? Did they love and hate? Did they feel the beauty of the evening sunshine? Did they wonder and marvel at the world, did they wonder why, and did they wonder what it was all for? That one would love to know.

One gets a glimpse into their feelings with the statues of Queen Hatsheput, which were all mutilated by her stepson when he succeeded as Pharaoh. Well he must have hated her to do that. Then King Akhenaten worshipped the sun, so he must have understood its beauty, and the artist who painted those pintail, must surely have enjoyed his own work. Do you remember that poem – "To a Poet a Thousand Years Hence" by Elroy Flecker[3] - *I care not if you bridge the seas, or build consummate palaces, but have you wine and music still, and statues and a bright-eyed love, and foolish thoughts of good and ill, and prayers to them who sit above?*

We also saw the Colossus of Memnon[4], huge, disfigured and rather sinister, sitting alone among the crops! One can't help but think of Shelley's *Ozymandias – Look on my works ye mighty and despair....Round the decay of that colossal wreck, boundless and bare, the lone and level sands stretch far away."*

One more scene. We climbed to the top of a temple, and there standing in the sun, the breeze in our hair, we looked out over the country. Behind us, stood the bare mountains, bright in the sun against the sky. In front, as far as the eye could see, on either side was cultivated land, as level as a billiard table, in varying colours of green. And all about were mud villages surrounded by palms gently moving in the wind, while Swifts, Sand Martins and Swallows flew round us, and a pair of Kestrels screamed from a nearby ruin. Below us, white amongst the trees lay Luxor. Yes, Egypt is beautiful here.

It is touristy, of course, with shops full of bric-a-brac, children clamouring for baksheesh[5], men trying to sell you fake scarab beetle gems, carvings or pots, while the donkey-men fight over you for trade. Yet, miraculously it isn't spoilt. Agriculture goes on just the same as it always has, the roads are still made of mud, and primitive villages cluster round the ruins. Above all, the Valley of the Kings has been handled in a dignified manner, with no advertisements or ugly notices, no tea-shops and no men selling Luxor rock! All credit to the Egyptians!

I hope my descriptions will perhaps give you some idea of my stay here, as all day I have wished so much that you could have been here to share it with me. You would so love the sun and the flowers, the boats on the river, and the wonderful views. And how I'd love to have visited the tombs and the wall paintings with you.

This is my last afternoon, as tonight I have to go back. I can't tell you how that thought fills me with despair. I'm feeling rather tired now and I must change for dinner, so I'll close now and post this tomorrow.
God be with you, all love Ralph

Chapter 31
Back in Cairo to face another impasse with the Army
February 1943

Back from a restful few days in Aswan and Luxor, my father soon comes back down to earth with a bump, as he returns to yet another difficult impasse with the army, similar to that with 'The Agreement' that he encountered soon after he arrived in Cairo. Plus a trip to Tobruk to the Hadfield Spears Unit.........

Wednesday, February 17th 1943 – Cairo (No 34)

My dearest Joan

I am just back from my leave and feel completely recovered, thank God. I went up and came back by train, which was really quite easy, and altogether had a delightfully lazy time doing not very much. Now I am back in the middle of a hectic time catching up, though I have received a grand lot of Airmail letters from you, which has greatly cheered me up. I loved to read about your Christmas, and thank you for making the children so happy. How I would have loved to see them. Please thank David for his excellent letter too.

It's been a rather desperate week since my return. Peter Gibson came down from the desert and there looks like being another major crisis in our relations with the Army. It's the same problem we had before with the 'Agreement,' with the Unit getting too close to the Army, and being asked to do things which conflict with their principles. We've had some critical discussions, and I am afraid it looks as though we will have to withdraw from some of the army work, which will be a terribly difficult decision to make and one that will be even more difficult to carry through. People will never understand our motives for so doing. I must say I view the whole prospect with dread. We seem to move from crisis to crisis, and have no idea how I shall ever get away to China.

Peter's section have had an interesting if difficult time in Tripoli, where they are now working. They were only the second medical Unit there, but relations with the Army were still tense. I don't really know that censorship will allow my saying more. (Ed: Differences with Army Officers who insisted on being in charge.) It is tragic for Peter that this Unit should have turned out so badly, as no-one could have worked harder than he to ensure it ran smoothly. I'm sure he has made mistakes, especially in insisting on reinforcements being sent, but who hasn't? I feel so sorry for him and on top of everything, I fear he is not very well. It has made for a very hectic week, and feel I need another holiday!

It has rained really hard and blown up a storm all last night and all morning too, which is most unusual. The wind has brought down several large trees, especially the eucalyptus, and consequently the city looks very wet and dejected. [....] Douglas Mackenzie, who is recovering from jaundice, has rather frightened me by saying that Lt Colonels Pulvertaft and Buttle, (by the way the latter has just got an OBE), under whom Doug works, will not let him go back without two weeks sick leave. Further, that GHQ, Middle East has made an order that anyone who has jaundice twice must go home. I better make sure that I don't contract it again!

I've just had a letter from Tegla Davies at HQ, explaining proposed arrangements. He even suggested that I should return to take over as Chairman, though I trust that won't be taken up. I feel I have quite enough on my plate trying to sort out things here, not to mention visiting Ethiopia, and fulfilling Tom's itinerary in India and China. It seems to have been non-stop of late, and I am now feeling very tired. I probably came back from Luxor too soon, and I really hope to God I don't get a relapse, as I am just on the point of going up to Tobruk to see Michael. All my love for now, Ralph

Blood Transfusion Unit in Tripoli

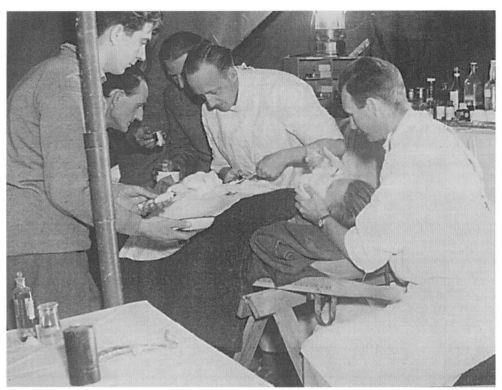

Operating on a wounded soldier in a field operating theatre in the Western Desert
Photograph courtesy Metro Publishing

Douglas Mackenzie
"A qualified bio-chemist."
Photograph Friends House Library

Lt Col Robert G Pulvertaft
"What we used to call quite a character.
 Photo; IWM

Sometimes, in juxtaposing letters of roughly the same date - because of the time gap in receipt - they often reflect a different state of affairs, and you get an unintended commentary on current events. Here my mother is responding with pleasure to a letter from my father from the previous November, in which she is pleased that a tense situation with the army has resolved itself. A few months later, however, it sounds an ironic note against quite another, yet similar disagreement! What goes around, comes around........

Monday, February 1st 1943 – Wolverhampton (30)

Dearest husband

What a wonderful letter number 18 is! (p 348) It arrived this morning and I am very, very happy to have it. You really ought to write a book! You write so vividly of the country as well as bringing a delightful freshness and charm to it that enables me to picture it all so very clearly. Also your descriptions of the people make me see them at once – and make me long to be with you and to share it all with you.

I wonder if you will find life rather tame when you return. Not that you won't love being home again with us all, and able to enjoy home life once more and tend our garden, with the leisure to do what you want and when you want, and not being tied down. But it is such a full life you are living now, meeting so many interesting people and broadening your outlook, that after the war, life is bound to be much tamer by comparison.

I hear such high praise of you from all directions, which must be gratifying to you. I know you have huge responsibility, but your standing commands such great respect, and I get a warm feeling when I learn how affectionately everyone speaks of you. I feel so proud to be your wife.

I am glad that the Army are now being so co-operative and friendly. This must make all the difference to your work with the Unit, helping it to go ahead that much more smoothly and not continually looking over your shoulder, in opposition with each other. How fortunate that you have a car in which to do all your travelling. I too remember the journey from Haifa to Beirut with great affection. It really is heavenly.

I am fascinated to read your descriptions and impressions of Tel Aviv, as I only had a glimpse of it when I was there. How wonderful it would be to see all these places again with you. It is ten years since I was there, when I was only 18, and I'm sure I should view it all so differently today. How changed I am in ten years! I wonder if you saw 'Roissee' in Broumana, the house where Win and Llew lived? It had such a wonderful position, looking down to Beirut and across to the mountains, with Mount Sannine capped with snow. I shall never forget the sunsets in Syria – the lovely red, purple and orange glow reflected on the mountains and then, suddenly, nothing but greyness as the sun sank below the horizon.

The Levitts sound charming people. You should really try and keep in touch with some of these people after the war. I always think it is a pity to let them go. I wonder if by chance you have bumped into Allen Maw, as I believe he was in Ismailia, and whether you have seen any more of Angela's brother, David?

I know - I want to know so much! I want to know whether this letter will reach you, and where will you be in three months' time? India or China? And I want to know where to send letters in future. I sometimes feel so cut off, especially when mail takes so long to come through, that I often think I'd like to go Gordon Square and read all your reports and learn about your future plans straight from the horse's mouth!

I sometimes feel as though my wings have been clipped, when in reality I long to fly away on great adventures!! If only I wasn't so glued to the spot. David said yesterday, he was making three pairs of wings for us all to fly away to be with you. How magical that would be!! David has just come downstairs with some ribbon pinned to his shoulders as imaginary wings! He is determined we should fly!

I must tell you some of the funny things David has said in the last few days. I asked him to post some letters for me and on his way back he saw the postman and ran after him and told him that the Airgraphs were not coming through – and what was he going to do about it? He came running in and said "I think he has now learned his lesson mummy. But that postman is rather a gruff fellow!"

He is very fond of a girl called Kay at his school, who is 9, and he told me that he was going to marry her. "I know she loves me, because this morning I was sitting on the stairs and she came up behind me and tapped me on the shoulder and said "Hello my little darling!"

At school they have been learning the Charles Wesley hymn 'Gentle Jesus, meek and mild', of which the 3rd line is - 'Pity my simplicity'. David piped up and asked the teacher what mice had to do with it! He is so friendly with anyone he meets. He found a soldier to bring him across the road the other day. He was so pleased and said "I've found another friend, mummy, and we talked a great deal. He was such a nice chap!" He is certainly very entertaining and great company. You would enjoy being with him so much now.

Antony is adorable too, though he can be quite a young rascal. When I went out to meet D from school on Friday, he had taken the soap from the washbasin, and made it into small pieces - for a tea party! Today he has scribbled red crayon all over the walls! But I have to say he is very charming with it and lovely to look at, with a sparkle all his own.

Well life goes on here much the same as usual. Each day much like the rest. Llew has been very busy recently, so much so that Win has been helping in the dispensary too. I'm afraid mother hasn't been too well of late, and Llew seems to think it is probably the result of the awful rheumatism she's had. But thankfully she seems to be quite a lot better now. Mercifully, I've managed to keep free from colds, though I too have had rheumatism. I think it must be partly due to this very damp weather we've been having, with such unusual quantities of rain.

I told you I was going to hear the London Philharmonic Orchestra last Thursday. Well, it was a wonderful concert; absolutely overflowing, with people standing and some sitting behind the orchestra. They played 'Peter and the Wolf' by Prokofiev, which is really written for children as an introduction to the various instruments, and the story was narrated by Margaretta Scott. It was delightful and I think David would have loved it. They also played Tchaikovsky's Piano Concerto No 1 in B flat, which is truly splendid and ended the evening with Vaughan Williams' 'Fantasia on a Theme by Thomas Tallis. It was a splendid programme and a great treat for me, getting me out of my rut for a few hours. The more I hear, the more I appreciate the beauty of such music, but I wish I understood more. I should have persevered and listened more in my youth!

On Thursday mother and I went to see Walt Disney's 'Bambi', the story of a deer, based on Felix Salter's charming book. It was a beautiful film and quite tearful at the end. You won't believe it, but your least favourite entertainment – the Christmas Pantomime - is still running! How I long to see a really good play. I read the other day that J B Priestley had written a new play called 'They Came to a City', which is set in a 'brave new world' after the war. It's had good reviews, so l hope it comes here before it goes to London. I'll try and write a little more later on, but I must take the boys out for a walk now, as it's stopped raining.

Later.....Henry and Lydia Cadbury have just returned your Syrian journal and said they so much enjoyed reading it and he also read it to Michael Crosfield and his father, when they were staying at Winds Point. I think it is an amazing piece of work and I have read it many times now. I will also try and copy out some of today's letter, as that is so interesting too.

I had an amusing note from your mother this morning. She wrote a really funny account of trying to buy some fish for John and Enid last week. Fish is almost impossible to get these days, so your mother thought she would have a go in Birmingham at the large market there. But even in town, there were long queues at every stall, but finally she spotted one stall with only two people waiting. So she walked over and saw some fish she'd never seen before. She wrote - "They were quite unknown to me, and I looked at them very dubiously. They were actually very pretty to look at, but totally strange, to me at least!"

So she said to the man at the stall- "These are curious fish. I've never seen them before. Are they nice?" "Oh yes, Ma'am, very sweet they are" he replied. So your mother asked if he thought they'd be suitable for a person ill in bed? "Oh yes, Ma'am, very sweet indeed," he replied again! Then she went on - "As I couldn't get even close to any of the other stalls, let alone catch so much as a sight of a fish's tail, I finally purchased two of these rather gaily-coloured, golden brown ones. I got them home and realised I hadn't the slightest idea how to cook them! But anyway, somehow with some parsley from the garden, I made a nice parsley sauce, and managed to make quite an attractive meal. I was quite pleased with my efforts and John and Enid seemed to enjoy them! So all was well!"

I say there are no fish, but recently we have been very lucky, and just occasionally managed to get some plaice and hake. I think Lord Woolton[1] (Minister of Food) has done an excellent job, and we certainly haven't starved, even if the diet is a bit monotonous. I've even had some eggs twice this week which are the first in about two months.

The news of the Russian forces is most welcoming. Indeed for once the news on all fronts is exciting. I expect Egypt has been celebrating these last weeks: the 8th Army has done wonders. I hope North Africa will be quite free very soon, Then what? We are all getting rather optimistic. Is that unwise? I'm sure there will still be some hard fighting during the next few months, but victory doesn't seem quite so remote. No more for now my dearest.

Later in the evening.....

Now the boys are safely tucked up in bed and I am sitting in an arm chair by the fire. The days are slowly drawing out and black-out time isn't until 6.20 now, which means we are able to have tea in the light, which is such a pleasant change, though the mornings are still pretty dark. If the weather keeps fine, we might go to your mother for half term.

I bought some wallflowers on Saturday. They <u>are</u> lovely with such a marvellous scent. Wolverhampton has had a 'Dig for Victory' exhibition this last week and many of the shops have had displays of seeds and vegetables etc. The large store in the town, Bakers, had a wonderful show of tomatoes and apples of almost every kind. It quite made my mouth water to see them. It's all to encourage the country to grow more fruit and vegetables. There has been an absolute glut of greens these last weeks.

David said his own prayers tonight. "Thank you God for my nice silver sixpence – and for the half crown, when I get it!" Hopeful! I promised him that when he had saved 30 pennies, I would give him 2/6d in a silver piece.

My dearest darling husband. You are so much in my thoughts and we all long for your return. All the family send love. All my love Joan.
PS. I've decided to send this to India, as I'm sure you'll be there in a few months.

My father was intent on visiting Tobruk where the Hadfield Spears Unit were stationed. Following the death of Nik Alderson in 1942, Michael Rowntreee became leader of the section with Pat Barr as second in command. But relations with the army were once again in crisis. On the surface relations were quiet, and appeared to be improving, but it was still very diificult. Some Unit members felt that they had to make a stand on grounds of conscience, whilst on both sides there was a lack of sympathy and a feeling that people were constantly on their guard, ready to pick faults, rather than combine readily into a working team. Here my father describes his trip to Tobruk - and back..........

Wednesday, February 24th 1943 Cairo (No 35)

Dear One

I am just back from Tobruk, having travelled over 1,000 miles in 3½ days, with a total cost to the FAU of 10/- (c £30.00).

A group of us left here in a Red Cross truck at midday on Wednesday last, and we made Alex about 5.30 after a fairly uneventful run. We had some tea there, before travelling on in the dark. The truck seemed to go much easier at night than the staff car, perhaps because it's slower and the lights are better. We spent that night at El Daba, a small village about 100 miles west of Alex, sleeping in the truck, which was none too comfortable. The next day we pushed on early, stopping briefly for breakfast at the seaport of Matruh, about 50 miles further on. We then drove all day and reached the Hadfield Spears Unit at about 7.0pm, which is about eight miles this side of Tobruk.

You would have enjoyed the run if only for the wonderful flowers all along the road. They were absolutely glorious. In places the ground was more like an English meadow in buttercup time, with sheets of yellow, mixed with dots of purple, pink and white flowers. When we got to Tobruk I had a chance to examine them all in some detail. I was completely out of my depth, of course, but Jocelyn Russell, one of the MTC girls, who is a keen and knowledgeable botanist, and an accomplished flower artist, knew them all.

The yellow appears to be a daisy with leaves like camomile and rich deep yellow flowers; the pink a night-scented stock, which grows everywhere. Then there is purple mallow, a glorious little pink geranium, more vivid than our herb robert, and scarlet red Flanders poppies. We also found an inconceivably lovely yellow anemone, with a delicate black centre; a tiny Iris, much smaller than reticulate; bright purple sea lavender, white daisies; vetches of all sorts; clovers, small purple toadflax; and an exquisite pink rock-rose, like the one we have on our bank at home. Jocelyn says she has found all together 190 different sorts.

In a Wadi [2] below the camp, the bare limestone sides were like an enormous rock garden, with rock roses, geraniums, clumps of spurge, drifts of yellow daisies and a stray growth of wild barley, all blowing gently in the wind. A lark tried to sing, a fine cock Redstart flew from bush to bush, the warblers called in the bushes in the valley bottom and a magnificent cock Stonechat flew off as we approached.

To find such beauty on this black, arid Continent; indeed to find a glory of flowers – that will live for ever in the memory, alongside those from Scotland or the Alps – set down here, where so few can ever have come, is miraculous. Here indeed are flowers which in Grey's[3] words are "born to blush unseen, and waste their sweetness on the desert air." To see them under fair blue skies with the glorious Mediterranean beyond; to see them growing unabashed round abandoned guns and burnt out tanks, makes one of those moments when the soul comes to rest and knows that for a few brief moments, it is at home where there are flowers and peace and God and beauty. Only you were missing. If only you could have been here to share it with me. How I missed you.

On the way to Tobruk

A group of FAU men with the truck on the way to Tobruk
"We left here in a Red Cross truck at midday Wednesday last, making Alex about 5.30pm."
Photograph Friends House Library

Hadfield Spears were in good form as usual. They have a pleasant site as sites go, set up in tents all along the Mediterranean fringe of the desert, where the ground is often covered by a carpet of flowers. Other buildings have been constructed too with great ingenuity, using a variety of material scoured from the desert, from stones to petrol tins filled with sand. There can't be another unit as odd in all the battlefronts of the war.

I had lunch in the Officer's mess, which was very friendly. The boys have built our young married couple, Jean and Pat Barr, a stone hut on the edge of the camp site. Mike took me over there for elevenses. It only has rough stone walls and a tin roof, with an improvised divan bed in one corner and a small table, which is covered with a chaos of cosmetics, and cigarettes! When we arrived, poor Jean was only just up, having been on night duty, but was soon busying herself dispensing tea, still dressed in her pyjamas, covered only by a mackintosh! After a bit Pat joined us in jovial mood. It was all rather refreshing. An English commanding officer would go crazy, of course, but it seems to work. They like each other, work hard, and get things done. They must be quite the happiest Unit section out here.

I might add that this was sandwiched between two long meetings. After lunch Mike and I had a walk, then went down into Tobruk to see about a train for my return, as Peter Gibson had gone ahead taking the truck. The town is incredibly knocked about after all the fighting, but oddly enough had a strange desolate beauty in the setting sun. I found there was a train going that night, which suited me fine. We walked back to the camp in time for dinner, after which we had another long Section meeting, which was useful. Mike then drove me down to catch the train, by which time it was pretty cold, though the sky was crystal clear and ablaze with stars.

War-torn Tobruk

War-torn Tobruk
"The town is incredibly knocked about after all the fighting, but oddly enough had a strange desolate beauty in the setting sun."
Photo Imperial War Museum

The Radio operator had told me there would be heaps of room in first class, but when I turned up there was hardly any, as a number of first class carriages had been invaded by Other Ranks. The Officer in charge sent a Colonel to find me a seat, who succeeded in getting us into an embarrassing diplomatic situation.

The Colonel belonged to the Self Defence Force and announced rather pompously that "The white Senussi Officer (Sufi) on board, will have to share with the two coloured Senussi Officers." That might normally have been alright, except that the white officer was an Indian Army Lieutenant, and the two Senussis were Commissioned Officers to the Viceroy, VCOs. The Colonel, who was actually quite a decent man, stupidly persisted with his impromptu diktat.

He went to the compartment containing the white Indian Army Officer and the two other British Officers, and said "Now look here, there's a British Officer on board without a seat. I'd like the Indian Army Officer over there" pointing to the white Officer, "to move in with his VCOs" pointing to the two coloured officers, "or even better to move out, all together and make room for this British Officer."

The white Indian Army Officer, who only had one pip, was very polite, but absolutely firm. "No, Sir," he said. "I am very, very, sorry, but I cannot go in with them." He even refused to move them into the corridor, saying "I would rather sleep in the corridor myself." All this was punctuated by apologetic mutterings from me in the background. But the Colonel remained equally firm.

"This is a very difficult situation" he said in his best Colonel voice. "In war time, we all have to share and make sacrifices. There's a British Officer here without a seat and he must be found one." Even more mutterings from me. Eventually, the Colonel recognised an impasse when he met it, and decided to retreat gracefully. We thanked him profusely and he discreetly returned to his carriage, having solved nothing and upset everybody. I should add, that despite the brouhaha, the two Indian VCOs somehow managed to keep the carriage all to themselves for the whole journey. Meanwhile the three other British Officers all squeezed up, and FRB settled in quite happily!

Well, sort of happily, though I can't pretend it made for a particularly pleasant journey. Four is definitely too many for a thirty hour journey, and sleeping sitting up is not much fun either. The train was absolutely packed, with chaps on leave and Units coming down the line. Outside it was desert all the way. However, it was an experience – of sorts!

We stopped at about 7.30am for an hour or so, while we all queued up for breakfast. We stopped again later for a very good lunch, with Officers and all ranks in the same queue. And we had two other stops: for tea and about 10.0pm for a late supper. We arrived in Cairo at 7.0 this morning. Some journey!

Thank goodness I had managed to borrow *When the Rains Came* by the American writer Louis Bromfield[4]. It is 500 pages and did me just fine. I think he has got something as a novelist, and on the whole I enjoyed it. I must stop now.

So this brings all my love to you and the children.
Dear love, Ralph

Hadfield Spears Unit
With the HSU Mobile Hospital in the Middle East

Photograph Friends House Library

My mother, now apprised of my father having been taken ill with jaundice back in January, commiserates, wishing she could be there to help. News of my father's forthcoming trip to China and India has been in the press, which brings a moment of pride as well as concern to my mother. Also decisions to be made about a move to Swarthmore Road when Granny Barlow moves to London. Several of the following letters cover much of the same ground, so I have incorporated them into one longer letter...........

Tuesday, February 9th – 15th 1943 – Wolverhampton (Air Letters) (Inc Nos 30 & 31)

My dearest husband
I've been so worried about you having jaundice, and I do hope you are being well looked after. How wretched for you to be ill again. I only hope you have plenty of books to read, and perhaps even some nice flowers to brighten your room. I wish so much I could look in and see you and bring you some daffodils or jonquils. Of course, by the time you receive this letter, you will probably have forgotten you ever had jaundice. Maybe by then you will be eating curry with Dick and Horace, or trying your best to use chopsticks to eat rice somewhere in the wilds of China with Duncan!

Not having had any recent news of you come through since your AMLC of January 6th, I am thinking of you so much and hope you are not too miserable with this jaundice. I wonder if you are in hospital, as I suppose there is no-one to look after you properly. I wonder if you got my cable, which I sent off as soon as I heard from Ronnie Joynes? I had a note from Barry saying that he hoped to be with you before long now, and would deliver the photographs of the boys when you meet up.

I must say it came as something of a thrill to see your name in all this morning's papers! "The London Headquarters of the FAU stated last night that Mr Ralph Barlow, its Deputy Chairman, and Mr Brandon Cadbury are going on a mission to China and India to organise the work of the Unit out there." And a bit more saying that you were already in the Middle East. I am so happy and proud to think the Unit entrusts such responsible work to you. [....] I do hope all your plans are going ahead alright. I realise that there must be so much to do in planning for the trip to India and China, as well as leaving the ME in good order, so that those left behind with Barry's help can carry on for you.

I received another AMLC written on December 28th, which arrived two days ago, for which so many thanks. I sent your extracts from your journal to the H G Woods[5] and had a letter from Mrs Wood this morning thanking me. She talked about all their children....Audrey has now been made Assistant Matron and Sister Tutor of a large maternity Hospital in Belfast; Ross is training to be a pilot and expecting to be sent to Canada or South Africa for six months training; Margaret and her husband are still farming; and she says Duncan's letters come through very slowly, so I'm not the only one waiting. The last letter they had was before Christmas, which was written in September. I know how pleased you will be to see him, when you get to China.

I saw an announcement in the Wolverhampton paper recently that Harold Thrift, who is in the FAU and is shortly going to the ME, had married the Art mistress from King Edward's School, Camp Hill. So I wrote to them and suggested that we should meet. I know - I do some mad things, but I thought it might be nice to meet up, as she was at Camp Hill where I was, and her husband is in the Unit where you are! Well, I had a reply yesterday from Harold, saying that he is expecting to leave quite soon and will call in and see me one day this week. He very much appreciated my writing and says his wife wants to meet me as soon as she gets a weekend off. He told me that the school has been evacuated to Lichfield. I do hope they turn out to be nice people after writing to them! But it seemed a kind thing to do, and I meet so few people nowadays.

I do think of you taking this long journey, with so much responsibility, and I hope you and Brandon enjoy each other's company. I trust you enjoy the journey too. It will be a wonderful experience for you, though I expect everybody will have told you that. What fun it would be to come along with you and see all these faraway places. How much you will have to discuss with everybody when you all finally meet up. Try not to do too much as you usually do and then get over tired and depressed!

I do pray that when you eventually arrive in India, that news of you will somehow get through to those back home, though I rather fear that I may be quite some months without any letters at all, and I shall be in the depths of misery. I understand from Ronald Joynes that I must send Airgraphs destined for China through India, who will then forward them on. So I'll send all letters to India from now on, until about May, then I will start again to address them to Cairo, as I suppose you will be returning there in August or thereabouts. I do wonder if I shall see you in the autumn. Wouldn't that be wonderful? Oh, joy of joys if it happened. Your letters continue to come in a peculiar order –I've had no 20, but not 19. I am posting letter number 31 today.

The children are well and happy. David is going into a higher form next term, although he isn't yet 6. He can read quite a bit now and is making quick progress. He is so interested in everything and full of the joy of living. Sometimes he and Antony make so much noise, I can hardly believe it is only coming from two children! How I wish you could see them dear one. They are quite adorable and such dear children. David has become such a charming companion and so sensible.

I think I mentioned that the BBC have been broadcasting 'War and Peace', and I have been reading it at the same time, trying to keep up. It really is a fine book. I don't think I've ever read a book where the characters are so alive. Tolstoy sees into their very minds and spirit too. He has the unique art of making you see every side of a person's make up and character, and how each different experience affects their lives and reacts upon them. It is quite glorious. It has been so enterprising of the BBC to do it at this time, and they really have made a wonderful job of it.

David was so pleased to get your two Airgraph letters with so many beautiful drawings. It is really worth framing, it's so good. The horses are so life like and look as if they might trot right out of the picture! It is a little masterpiece! I thought I might get lucky this morning with more mail from the Middle East. But no. Perhaps I shall be lucky tomorrow.

I had a long letter from your mother today. I'm afraid I haven't been in touch for some time. She has been in bed for a few days with a cold, but says she is better now, though Lydia still doesn't seem any too well unfortunately. She says she is definitely giving up the house in Swarthmore Road and going to live with Millior and Alfred when they buy a house this summer or autumn. She wants to know whether we would like Swarthmore Road and let Linden Road out. I don't know what to say. I leave it entirely to you. She says she has written to you about it. Of course, Swarthmore Road has its advantages – more modern, central heating, a garage and definitely easier to run. But Linden Road has a better view and is more attractive and prettier in many ways. I suppose the gardens are much the same, except that Linden Road has more possibilities and the fruit trees.

As far as schools for the children are concerned, there's not much in it. I think the King Edward's High School, will be best for both of them when we return – and Joyce Cadbury said she would take them in her car! It certainly needs thought. I wish you were here to discuss it with me. I don't really mind which it is. I should be sorry to leave Linden Road as we have known so much happiness there.

I think Swarthmore Rd is easier to run without help. It isn't that much bigger, but the rooms are a little larger. Linden Road is nearer the Estate Office. Oh dear, it is difficult to decide. <u>You</u> must decide! Your mother wants to know, as she must settle things soon. Perhaps you could reply by AML Card or Airgraph what you feel. I don't know what Cousins Edward and Dorothy would feel about our leaving Linden Road either.

The weather has been quite mild this winter, but Oh my Goodness, the rain we've had! Hardly a day has gone by without it. Last month there were terrific gales and floods in South East England. The Medway was a mile wide in places. But thank goodness spring will soon be here, and I know how much your thoughts will fly to England, thinking of fresh green grass, primroses, cowslips, beech trees and hedges all looking beautiful as only England knows. May God grant that you'll be home with us this time next year.

I long to hear how you are, and whether your jaundice has finally cleared up yet? I send all my love to you and long only to see you. Lots of love Joan.

PS. How sickening that Barry and Brandon are held up so long. Harold Thrift called in to see me on Friday. He seems a nice lad, though perhaps not quite our type!! I haven't yet met his wife. Do you remember him in the 11th camp?

—

My father back from Tobruk, is now anxious to get off to Ethiopia, before he eventually has to leave for India and go on to China. But his seniority doesn't always guarantee him a flight, and so he and Eric Green take some time off to visit the Pyramids at Sakkara. Meanwhile he has again been made Deputy Chairman.........

Monday, 8th March 1943 – FAU MEF Cairo (No 35)

My very dear wife

When I got back I found a pile of Airgraphs from Gordon Square, though not containing much news that you don't know already, except for one from Paul Cadbury making me Deputy Chairman again, God help them! There were also two lovely long air letters from you as well as an Airgraph dated February 2. Thank you so much. I do appreciate hearing all your news. I've been feeling so dissatisfied with myself of late, though I'm not sure quite why, and your confidence bucks me up no end.

The Airgraph from Paul managed to say almost nothing, except that he was very busy! Join the club! Since I got back, it seems to have been non-stop. But I did manage to post you a long letter last Friday as well as a letter card to David. I am really hanging in here, desperately hoping that I may be able to get down to Ethiopia, but I do not know how soon I shall get a place. My seniority isn't always enough to guarantee me priority.

The other night we entertained the Captain who deals with our people at the hospital. He turned out to be quite pleasant, and rather as an act of duty we took him to the cinema afterwards, to see *Gulliver's Travels*. It's not at all a bad film: indeed in parts it was really very good and made me laugh. And Veronica Lake[6] is really exquisitely lovely.

The next night Eric Green and I went out to dinner at the St James, which is by way of being one of the top restaurants in Cairo, and we had one of the best meals I have had since coming here. We then went to see an ENSA performance of Bernard Shaw's *The Devil's Disciple,* one of his I have never seen or read before. It acts well, and it was a remarkably good production.

The Hilaire Belloc book of essays, *Places* that you sent has arrived at last. Thank you so much for that. I do like his essays a lot. He has a real understanding of countryside and landscape, an appreciation of history and the place of man in the countryside, which I greatly value. He can write this sort of essay better than almost anyone.

The Pyramids at Sakkara

A view of the famous Step Pyramid at Sakkara.
"The oldest stone construction ever discovered......built over two and half thousand years ago."

Photo Egyptian Tourist Board

I have been working most of the morning and feel rather weary, so Eric and I decided that we would drive down to Sakkara to see the pyramids there. I will write more tonight when we get back.

Continued........

We're now back from Sakkara, where we had a most pleasant time. In the end we hired a taxi instead of driving and took a picnic lunch, which, of course, had been wonderfully prepared by Eric. It's only about 15 miles from Cairo, and the drive through the villages and valley country is quite beautiful in places. The crops are so green right now, the palms look lovely standing singly in groups, and the flax was beginning to come in to flower.

Sakkara itself is very interesting, but less exciting I felt than Luxor. It is supposed to be the oldest stone construction ever discovered, built over two and half thousand years ago. There are several Pyramids there, including the famous step pyramid from the third dynasty, as well as several tombs. The mural art, while very similar to the later periods such as those in Luxor, is much more alive, and though the perspective, for instance is often wrong, they have movement and vitality and experiment, whereas by the later dynasties, the art seems to have become quite stylised and static.

Well, I nearly got away to Ethiopia on a BOAC plane today, but as I predicted, my priority was not quite high enough. My only hope now is for the Americans to come to my rescue.

There is not a lot more news for the moment, so I will close for now.

All my love, Ralph

The Linden Road Home
The question of staying on there or moving was much debated

A sketch by Deryk Darlington of the front of my parents' first home at 26 Linden Road
Neighbours Mr and Mrs Keen's house is on the right

A photograph of the back of the Linden Road house

Chapter 32
Letter No 14 arrives at last and some postwar thoughts
February 1943

My mother is delighted that at last the longed for Syrian letter 14, has arrived describing my father's visit to all the places and people she would have known from when she was out there, especially Broumana. This next letter is also two letters contracted into one and brings up the subject of my parents' postwar plans and decisions to move house......

Friday, February 18th – 27th 1943 – Wolverhampton (32)

My darling dearest one,

You'll never believe it, but your long lost letter number 14 (p317) from the Lebanon, posted the beginning of October has just arrived! Where on earth could it have possibly have got to these last 4½ months? What a story it could tell! I am so delighted to get it, and be able at last to hear your first impressions of Broumana. I'm absolutely thrilled to know that you have been there too, and seen its beauty and met so many of my friends. I'm glad you met the Cortas's. I was very fond of Najla and Michel. I can see it all in my mind's eye so vividly again. Do try and see Blanche if you go there again. She would be so disappointed not to see you. How I would love to be there too.

You do write a great letter my sweetheart. Your last AMLC to me was January 6th and David had your Airgraph written on January 17th. I do hope you are now quite recovered from your jaundice. With the mail being so slow, I have been so worried about you. I wonder if mine take as long to reach you?

Extracts of your Syrian Diary have appeared in The Chronicle, published today. I'm sure you couldn't possibly object to it my dear, I have only included bits about the journey and descriptions of the country. Your Syrian journal is still going the rounds. The Watts much enjoyed reading it. Harold added a PS to his letter, saying that he had known Kenneth Oliver well, as he shared an office during the last war. He also said "The BVT will need to attract more birds to the Estate if Ralph is to settle down happily. He won't be content with Sparrows and Rooks!!"

Another very welcome AMLC arrived on Thursday written on January 31, which only took 2 or 3 days longer that the one written on January 7th. I was so pleased to get it. Fancy Allen Maw being a Major! He's done well for himself. I wonder if he has any more self-confidence nowadays! I'm glad he popped into see you; that was good of him.

I had a letter from Eleanor Sawdon, congratulating you on your appointment to India and China, but sympathising with me that you would now be away even longer. It was so nice of her to write. I also had a charming letter from Mickey Cadbury, giving me quite a bit of news and information from the Square. He says that now he is in the overseas section, he hopes to be able to keep me informed of all the happenings. It tickles me no end to think that Angela is now his secretary!

I shall post this letter to India today. It'll be the third I've addressed there. I do so hope that they will reach you one fine day in the not too distant future. It must be so frustrating that Brandon and Barry are held up. It'll mean that your trip will be more delayed as well.

There is a parents' meeting at the school, next Tuesday afternoon. I'm really hoping to go, as it is good to get out and meet people. I seem to get out so little these days, but Win has kindly promised to look after the children. They are both well and happy and David is doing so well at school. As it is half term, we are hoping to go to Swarthmore Road for a long weekend on March 6th with your mother. I do hope the weather will be fine, and that is a success.

I wonder if you have thought any more about the Linden Road house? There seems so much to discuss. How I wish you were here to talk it all over.

I do hope you are feeling better after your holiday. How long were you away? By now I expect you have been back some while and busy again with preparations for India/China visits. Do take care of yourself dearest one. I know how much responsibility you have and how many difficult decisions you have to take and I sympathise that you won't want to let anyone down. But don't get downhearted. You will come through and all will be well – I know!

Yesterday I had my hair permed and there was such a crowd, I was there from 9.30 till 2.30! But I must say I am glad to have it done at last. I fear our overdraft is still quite high, though I really am being very careful – in fact downright mean these days. I spend nothing except absolute necessities. I even sold an old frock to pay for my perm! I don't think I must plan to go away with Hilda – it will cost too much, and anyway we must see what the next few months bring. How lovely if we didn't always have to worry about finances. I am trying my best to be careful, my dearest. But it is difficult with the children growing up so fast and constantly needing new clothes.

I'm rather tired today, and I wish so much you were here, to cheer me up. I do hope you are not too worn down with all your responsibility. I know you must get weary and tired. I pray that God will watch over you in all these difficult tasks ahead of you.

With this mild weather and sunny days, I expect in just over a month the first Chiff-Chaff will be here. I pray so much that next year you may be back here in England and we can enjoy a lovely spring together. Everything is wonderfully spring like; in fact it has been such a mild winter this year that now everything is in flower with forsythia, primula wandas and primroses all adding glorious colour to the garden.

There is not much more news. But you know that you are always in my prayers and thoughts. The children both miss you, especially David. He really enjoyed staying at school for dinner, as you will see from his letter. He is so sensible and I forget that he is still only 5 years old.

I wrote out most of your last two letters and sent then to your family. My, did my arm, ache?!! But I know how your mother longs for news of you. Lydia is finally back now, and all at Innage Road (FRB's brother's family) are now recovering from their bout of 'flu. They do seem to be an unlucky family, getting anything that is around! Millior is well and Anna has already doubled her birth weight. I saw some pictures of Anna today, which are very jolly. She is a sweet looking child, and Alfred a very proud father!

The boys got shut in the Nursery again this morning. The wretched catch keeps getting stuck and we had to get the carpenter in again. The boys were so good and sensible and didn't get frightened in the least. David said "Carpenter Horace isn't much good, is he mummy?!!" He's very young, but I do hope Horace will finally get it fixed this time.

Luckily no other child has developed measles yet, which is fortunate. I really don't much want the children ill right now. Although, I suppose it is just as well to get these things over in early youth. D was most interested to hear that you had measles when you were young too. It is now Saturday afternoon, and both the boys are resting. I'm in the kitchen trying to get a few letters finished to various people. Win and Llew have gone to Llew's parents in Middle Park Road (Birmingham) for the weekend. All for now my darling. God bless you and be with you always. Mother and W&L all send dear love as do I. Ever your loving Joan.
PS. By the way, I paid the £15 into Gordon Square as you wanted.

Since their marriage, my parents had been living at 26 Linden Road, Bournville, a house gifted to them by Edward and Dorothy Cadbury, of which they were inordinately fond, especially of its glorious garden and fine view over Frankley Beeches[2]. In this next letter from my father there is quite a lot about decisions that will soon have to be taken, which will affect their life after the war. My mother has already referred to the idea that my grandmother was planning to move down to London to live with Alfred and Millior and Anna, just as soon as they find a suitable house, and that my parents and my brother and I should then move into her house at No 6 Swarthmore Road, instead and let their Linden Road house.

My Grandmother was by now aged 75 and had been widowed for nearly 20 years, since John Henry Barlow's death in 1924. After he died, she remained in the marital home - 'Sunnybrae' on the Bristol Road, just above Woodbrooke College, where she had lived since 1900 - until 1932. She then moved to a newly built house, not far away on the Bournville Estate, in then still leafy Swarthmore Road. After my grandfather died, my father and his siblings lived at 'Sunnybrae', and/or later at 6 Swarthmore Road, until they got married: my Uncle John in 1926, my father in 1936 and my Aunt Millior in 1939. So by the 1940's they were all wed with children of their own, and living in homes of their own.

Inevitably, therefore, there were a number of letters and Airgraphs to-and-fro, discussing the merits and demerits of the proposal, largely concerning the extra costs involved and the sadness of leaving their first home together. Initially neither of my parents were anxious to make the decision and each kept passing the final choice to the other!

After much debate, they decided to move to Swarthmore Road, which they did in late 1943, when my father was invalided out following a debilitating illness, and remained there happily for many years as two more children, Stephen and Rosemary were born in 1945 and '47 respectively. My father also passes on praise for my mother from Granny Barlow, which in light of her earlier opposition to the marriage, is a great achievement for my mother's charm and personality………

Sunday, March 14th 1943 - Cairo

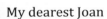

My dearest Joan

I have just received a long letter from you posted on January 4th, for which all thanks. It is such a good letter and so good to hear all about David and Antony. Please give them all my love. There was also a letter from my mother asking us about moving into No 6, Swarthmore Road.

I know that like me, you will hate to leave our beloved No 26, but maybe sooner or later, with two growing children and possibly more, and someone to help you, and visitors to stay, we would inevitably one day want more room. There will be more work for you and we must consider the extra costs and whether we can afford it after the war. I think on balance, we should probably take mother's offer, but I leave the final decision to you, and if you are too attached to 26, and can't face the extra housework and all that a move would involve, I will, of course, quite understand.

As well as our moving to Swarthmore Road, she talks more about her moving to London to live with Alfred and Millior. I have sent you a long Airgraph about it. I think on the whole it will be good for her to live with A and M, though of course it will be a cruel wrench for her and a huge upheaval. The final choice about our move must be with you, and I'll go along with whatever you think is best, as much of the burden will fall on your shoulders. Talking of houses and arrangements does make me terribly homesick. How I wish I could come home and be with you again.

Mother wrote to say you had taken the children to stay with her and writes: "Joan is so patient with her two sons and keeps so calm. I do admire her and she looks so very bonnie in such a pretty bright, charming red frock. David bewitches the heart….and Joan and I have got to know each other much more." Well, what a change and all due to you my dear. You have suffered much with wonderful patience, and at last the family knows what I knew all along, that you are a very special person. She also says the photo of the two boys is so good. I would really like a copy of that. Do thank her for her long letter to me, which is quite one of the most beautifully written I have received, though it's a little like mother on the telephone. Loving but very upright and Quakerly!

I hear that Brian Taylor and Brandon Cadbury are delayed in getting out here, and my visit to Addis is still very uncertain, which is most trying. So life continues to be frustrating and more and more complicated. The problems of travel seem almost insuperable. I think I may have to give up the whole idea of Ethiopia. Today is a Sunday and I have been working for 3 hours already, writing reports of my visits, for Tegla and Gordon Square generally, as well as letters to Horace in India and Maurice Webb in South Africa. I think that is quite enough!

I fear this is a poor letter. It's partly because there is little news and partly because I really am very busy and rather tired. I seem to work such long hours with so many letters to write, all of which are letters that take much thought and effort. I'm so sorry and I will try and write a better letter next time. Meanwhile you know you are ever in my thoughts, and I live only for the day of my return.
Ever your, Ralph

No 6 Swarthmore Road
My grandmother's house, into which our family moved in autumn of 1943.

Photo ARB

Chapter 33
Ethiopia
March – April 1943

Located in the Horn of Africa, Ethiopia, or as it is also called Abyssinia, shares its borders with Eritrea to the north, Somalia to the east, Sudan to the west and Kenya to the south, and is one of the most populous landlocked countries in the world. The capital, Addis Ababa, nestles in the foothills of Mount Entoto at a height of nearly 8,000 ft, which makes its climate mild for most of the year.

From 1889 until his death in 1913, the country was ruled by the Emperor, Menelik II, who began the modernisation of the country, building new roads, introducing electricity, reforming education and the construction of modern day Addis Ababa. Following Menelik's death, Haile Selassie assumed Imperial power and was given the title of Ras 'Tafari meaning chief (Ras) respected one (Tafari).

Long part of colonial Italy, the country initially gained its independence from them under Emperor Menelik II. But when Mussolini's fascist Italy invaded and occupied the country again in 1935, Haile Selassie was forced out. At the League of Nations in Geneva he delivered an impassioned appeal against the invasion, which made him a worldwide figure. But unable to return to his country, he fled to Britain, where he lived in exile in Bath for the next six years.

The occupation lasted until 1941, during which time Vittorio Emanuele III, Italy's king, assumed the title of Emperor. But Mussolini's declaration of war on Britain and France in June 1940, exposed the weakness of the Italian military, and a series of defeats soon followed in both North and East Africa. British forces, together with Ethiopian patriots, ousted the Italian army, and restored sovereignty to the country, paving the way for Selassie's return from exile in May 1942.

On his return he found his country ravaged by war, and the administration completely disrupted. In an effort to introduce reforms, establish social services and rebuild the national life, the Ethiopian Government accepted the offer of the FAU to send forty men to assist with medical work and the development of medical services. The first party, comprising seven doctors and thirty three others, arrived in 1941, and set about assisting with public health administration in hospitals, provincial clinics, and schools, as well as working in a leprosy camp, and supplying equipment and drugs.

My father's report that he wrote for Gordon Square and his account in his memoirs and in letters home moves seamlessly through, so I leave it as is, and as no letters were getting through from my mother, I'll start them again at the end of the chapter........

Addis Ababa bears little resemblance to a European's conception of a capital city. Beautifully situated on an open plain and surrounded by high hills, few of its streets suggest an important capital. There were a few large, mostly pre-Italian buildings, but many others were only half built, including a large opera house, which still stood gaunt and empty behind a network of scaffolding, their building rudely brought to an end by the war.

Otherwise the city resembled an enormous village, with miles of winding country lanes, and here and there Italian villas interspersed with corrugated iron shacks and tukuls or huts, of wattle and daub and thatch, in which the native Ethiopians lived. The streets were thronged with people, ranging in shades from the paler and proud Amhara, dressed in a white shirt and shamma with tight cotton jodhpurs, to the jet black of the Shankalla, considered by some Ethiopians a lower class.

Here and there an occasional touch of incongruity would be provided by the addition to the native garb, of Italian uniforms and trappings, boots and battered trilbies or sola topees. There were some Italian cars and lorries in various states of disrepair, but for the most part vehicles were drawn by small horses, and Jehu-driven[1] pony traps, which served everywhere as taxis. On all sides there was a profusion of lofty eucalyptus trees and the brilliant yellow daisy, which covers the rural areas so profusely after the rains, for this was just at the end of the monsoon season. Soon the ground would be caked and parched, but now it was green and carpeted with flowers and the climate was that of a pleasantly cool June day in England. For Addis, though nearer the equator than Berbera in Somalia or Massawa in Eritrea, manages to avoid the sticky stifling heat because of its height.

It is true that during the Italian occupation, they had built new buildings and brought in new transport, developed communications, with better roads, built industrial plants and opened mining operations. But on the down side were all the disintegrating effects of conquest, from imprisonment or execution of members of the resistance, to unemployment and poverty, along with the centuries old problems of ignorance, illiteracy, superstition and disease. The central government's authority was weak, especially in the remote provinces and there was no clear system of taxation to produce an adequate revenue. If the country was to be built on the Western pattern, which Haile Selassie had set his mind to achieve, then there would be need for assistance, for after the mayhem wreaked by the Italians, there would not be sufficient Ethiopians to carry out the government and social services for the country in the way the Emperor wished.

The Unit in Ethiopia works under the Ethiopian Medical Directorate, at the request of the Emperor. For the most part they are using old hospital buildings erected by the Italians and are operating these as clinic hospitals. There are some half dozen within a radius of eighty miles from Addis Ababa and more in the north. Most of the buildings were badly damaged during the fighting, with many hospitals found with no beds or bedding. But gradually, with help from the Unit in the form of drugs and implements and beds, hospitals were made functional again. In Ambo, west of Addis, for instance, a 35 bed hospital was soon established with an operating theatre. Still others had rooms that were able to be used, and on the whole the facilities, both in accommodation and equipment were far better than in Syria. Each morning they held an out patients session, which were attended by anything from sixty to a hundred patients, with complaints varying from fevers and tropical sores to eye diseases and VD.

Basically we are providing a skeletal medical service for the country, between the collapse of the Italian service and the time when the Emperor can employ foreign doctors and re-establish a proper service. There will obviously also be a considerable period after the war, before he can get such doctors and during which our members will wish to go home. Richey Mounsey is the Commandant out here, in whom I have every confidence, Jack Frazer is an excellent Deputy, along with help from Dr Michael Vaizey. Richey suggests that reinforcements should be sent from the UK, to tide over the transition period, with people who would be willing to stay for two or three years after the end of the war. I hope this may be possible, as we have entered in to commitments in the country, which we cannot lightly drop. Perhaps the Society might even consider finding Friends who would be interested in taking jobs under the Ethiopian Government. We await a report from Lady Barton into her welfare work, but I also think women interested in such work, would be very welcome here. I feel the Unit is doing a very necessary job in Ethiopia and doing it well.

Hospital in Ethiopia before and after

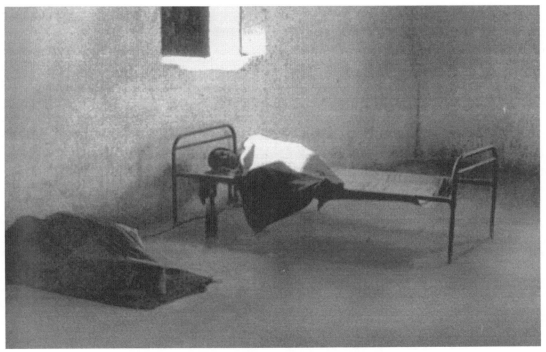

Many hospitals were found with no beds or bedding
Photograph Friends House Library

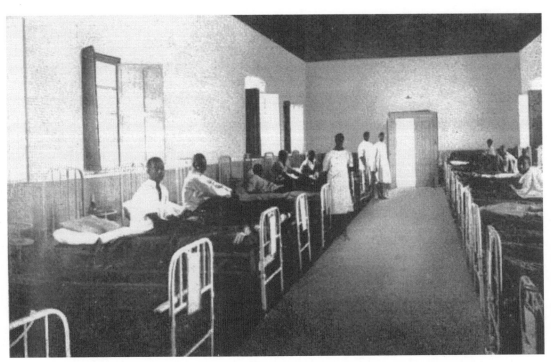

"But gradually, with help from the Unit, a 35 bed hospital was established."
Photograph Friends House Library

Pictures from Ethiopia

Standing left: Freddy Temple, Front seated: Jack Frazer as Deputy (left), Richard Mounsey as Commandant, FRB. Photo Friends House Library

Brigadier Daniel Sandford (left) with Haile Selassie in Ethiopia. Photograph Alamy

Sir Sydney and Lady Mary Barton outside the legation in Addis Ababa.

Sir Sidney had been HM Minister in Ethiopia, and after his retirement, he became adviser to Selassie, with his wife involved with welfare work out there.
Photo Alamy

North Africa

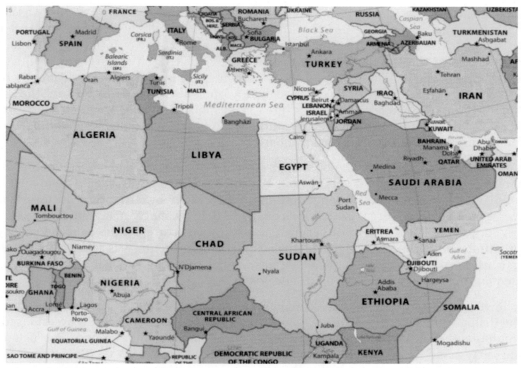

North Africa, showing the countries FRB visited during his time in charge of the Middle East. From Egypt, Libya and Syria on the Mediterranean coast to Eritrea and Ethiopia.
Image World Atlas

"In Highland Ethiopia, after the Monsoon rains, rural areas of the country bloom with the yellow daisy."
Photo courtesy 'Flowers of Ethiopia'

Here my father writes in his memoirs, of his assessment of the situation in Ethiopia........

It had been as far back as 1941 that the possibility of sending a party to Ethiopia was first mooted and discussed with the War Office. They had originally been given clearance to assist the British Army doctors in the larger towns and a party of forty was assembled from those with the most hospital experience. But the political situation changed with the withdrawal of the British Army and the hand over to Hailie Selassie. Consequently the Unit would be acting more or less independently, and with fewer Army doctors, the Unit themselves would have to bear far greater responsibility. Before their departure therefore, the men were given further training in tropical medicine, venereal diseases, and eye problems as well as in basic Amharic.

With the Italian defeat, the whole complex structure of hospitals and clinics, doctors and nurses had collapsed, and it was obvious that the Ethiopian government would have to build up its own medical administration from scratch by attracting doctors from overseas. A voluntary organisation such as the FAU, in a country many times the size of Britain, was no substitute for a permanent medical structure. So the advance party of forty Unit members arrived in the full realisation that its function was a limited one in the first instance, to fill a gap for maybe a year with a possible extension, while a more adequate and permanent service was developed.

Following a journey of disasters from Liverpool that sounds more like a Marx brothers' film than a wartime mission, during which they broke down on nearly 30 occasions, the Unit found themselves converging on Addis from all points of the compass. For instance one party came from Berbera, the port of British Somalia, across the Gulf from Aden, where the authorities were rather taken by surprise, when a garbled message had led them to expect ten Quaker women missionaries.

Such a prospect had naturally caused some alarm and consternation. The ten Quaker women, however, turned out to be six Quaker men in khaki Red Cross uniform, seeking transport to Addis Ababa. From Berbera they made their way by lorry through barren, sandy country along a rough road to Jijiga, winding through hill country and on to Dire Dawa, where they eventually caught a train to Addis.

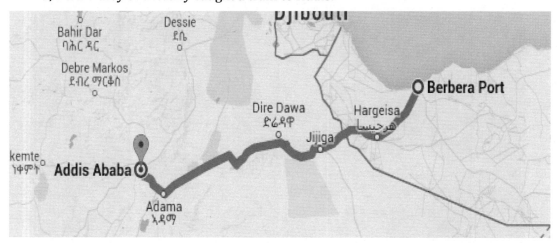

"A message saying 'ten Quaker women' would be arriving, turned out to be six Quaker men in khaki Red Cross uniform, seeking transport to Addis Ababa from Berbera."
Photo Ethiopian Maps

479

This was the situation I encountered when I arrived in early 1943 to assess the medical situation and the continuing needs of the country, and this group of Quakers were in fact the first contingent of forty members of the FAU on their way to Ethiopia, until by the end of 1942 they had all reached the city, and in this group were Richey Mounsey, the Commandant and Dr Michael Vaizey, the senior medical Officer, and Jack Frazer.........

Thursday, March 18th 1943 – FAU MEF In transit (No 36)

Dearest Joan,

Last night I finally got clearance for a flight to Ethiopia, praise the lord. I was up at 4.0am. Eric kindly got my breakfast and ran me down to Shepheards Hotel[2], and we were off at 6.30. It has been an uncomfortable, tiring and uneventful flight. Also, to one coming accoutred in battledress from winter in Egypt, unpleasantly hot. We flew above the clouds at first, but later when it cleared, we could see the Nile, villages, fields and more desert, and finally a long space by the Red Sea, and at last barren mountains. The plane pitched a great deal, and what with that, a sore throat, aching ears and general tiredness, I did not enjoy the flight very much.

Our first stop was Luxor, where once again I was able to see hundreds of white storks on migration through the Nile valley. When I first caught sight of them, they were resting, but when some noise disturbed them, they slowly rose as one, circled gracefully in the air, and then continued their journey north. We too continued on our journey to Addis, putting down again at Asmara, the capital of Eritrea. It is a pleasant town, well laid out, with good unpretentious modern buildings, wide streets, public gardens, quite good shops, which are fairly well-filled. There are plenty of people in the streets, some of whom are quite smartly dressed, especially the women, who for the most part are unveiled. We spent a short night there before completing our journey down to Addis, leaving very early while it was still dark.

It was a most wonderful clear very early morning, soft with a full moon, then as the light grew, white and cool, gradually turning gold in the east, and with a rush, the sun. It was a much more pleasant flight than the earlier one. We rose to 12 or 13,000 feet and it was cold but not unpleasantly so. Beneath, the country was most lovely, as the early sun cast long shadows and the earth was dappled with dark and light. The ground was not bare, but covered with what presumably was dry grass, with here and there patches of cultivation, woods and villages. In places it was broken up in to mountains with dramatic precipices and crags, fine but dwarfed from the air, and one could see the very skeleton of the earth, ridges and valleys, each stream course with its tributaries, and each stream joining its river. One could see watersheds for streams, watersheds for rivers, and watersheds for whole tracts of land. Then suddenly Lake Tana came into view, one of the sources of the Blue Nile.

On my arrival in Addis, I was met in a small Italian car by Harold Waller and a monkey. The monkey had inconsiderately made a mess on the driving seat, and I have always admired the way in which Harold just sat in it. He kindly brought me out to the Unit section in Addis, which occupies two blocks of double flats built by the Italians, in what was to have been their residential quarters. They are pleasant enough buildings, but shoddily constructed. Richey Mounsey is the Commandant here, working to the medical directorate with Dr Michael Vaizey and Jack Frazer. Richey is very good in his way, if rather unimaginative and stubborn, and I don't find him that easy to get on with. But it is lovely to see Jack again, though sadly he is not well, and is having a personal crisis, as do we all from time to time, as to whether he is in the right Unit section, or indeed whether he should still be in the Unit at all. He is such a fine person, so efficient, modest, hard-working and unassuming. I do like and respect him tremendously.

Tom Barnsley runs another Clinic with native help, based at the Hammanuel Hospital in the city, where he has sixty to seventy coming in daily with such illnesses as trachoma, syphilis, typhus, pneumonia or meningitis. In the afternoon he also runs a leper Clinic for some 270 patients. They are trying to separate the children from their parents, in order to give them a chance of not contracting the disease. It was started a while back by some Missionaries, and is quite well planned, but now that the Mission has gone, expelled by the Italians, they are neglected. I went out there this afternoon to see, and Barnsley is doing a good job, but it is so tragic to see these people rotting under this loathsome disease.

The town is wonderfully situated on a plateau 8,000ft up, amidst a forest of eucalyptus trees and rolling grass-covered country with fine hills, rising from it, and on all sides magnificent views. But the city itself is a mess. The Italians had just started on it, when they were forced out. There are wide streets half-finished and shoddy buildings still under construction. For the most part it is just a bewildering, squalid, unplanned collection of shacks and native huts. What problems!

The Emperor, one is told, is well educated and concerned, but the Council consists of aristocrats, mostly corrupt and inefficient. Large numbers of the educated intelligentsia were killed off by the Italians. There is no money, no supplies, no capable official class, no education and little hope of any of these until after the war. There is a Military mission training the army, and a few Englishmen struggling against a mountain – no, a whole mountain range - of difficulties. Everything from health and education to housing, has to be started from scratch, with so little from which to build up or plan. And the country is still desperately unsafe, with each man or woman for themselves.

The people are fine-looking, aquiline and light black. The men wear a shoulder-cloth, trousers, full round the thighs and tight on the legs, and some sort of headgear, either a cloth, or an old sola topee. The women wear a long robe caught at the waist, with their hair standing up in a sort of black fuzz or hanging in long rolls.

One thing the Italians did start was a good medical service, but now that is all gone, and the medical director has to improvise, with no doctors and no money. Otherwise Italian rule seems to have been a disaster and usually a brutal one, bringing ruin to Ethiopia and not even profit to themselves. The languages are Amharic, Gulla, Italian and French and we have people who speak bits of all four. There is certainly a job here for the FAU. We are filling a need, but it is so frustrating, trying to cope amongst such desolation. And what will happen when we go? All for now, Love Ralph

(No 36 Contd) Tuesday, March 23rd 1943.........Today I paid visits to the Director of Medical Services with whom we work, and the Educational Advisor. I feel the Unit could very well extend its work into teaching and helping with the organisation of schools and reformatories. The Educational Adviser is very charming and an enthusiastic man who would like more Friends to be working in his Department. He wants education to be practical, based more on hygiene and agriculture and not just academic.

We had tea at the Red Cross Hospital, and in the evening we had dinner with Brigadier Sandford and his wife, who live in one of those old fashioned English homes that one can still find hereabouts. He knows Ethiopia well, having been prominently concerned with the invasion, and is now an advisor to the Ministry of the Interior and one of the most influential Englishmen here. He is well informed, friendly and enthusiastic and has great faith in the future of the country. His wife, Christine is also out here with the two children, having come out about a year ago.

Like us they came out on a troopship to South Africa, but then came all the way up by land, which must have been a wonderful experience. They are a very pleasant family. Meeting all these people who are interested in the work the Unit is doing out here, and being polite to them all; taking notes from all our meetings and writing follow up letters; trying to weigh up the situation, and decide how we can best help; and coping with the height here, is all very tiring.

Yesterday, Jack Frazer and I caught the early train down the line to see another Clinic at Bishoftu, twenty five miles south east of Addis. The Clinic itself, though managing to cope, lacked firm guidance and was in danger of lapsing for lack of funds. But joy of joys, Bishoftu nestles among the hills near the lovely Lake Hora, a splendid natural habitat, and as we had a couple of hours to spare, you can imagine we spent it happily watching the many birds that abound here. And dear Joan, what birds! Just below us was a tree which contained Blue Starlings, whose wings are a most wonderful glossy metallic blue, Red-winged Starlings, Bulbuls, Mousebirds – curious looking things with long tails – Cormorants, Ibis, so beautiful in flight, white with dark along the back of the wing and black head and long curved beak.

We walked slowly round a section of the lake, and saw an extraordinary range of beautiful birds in the trees, from Bee-Eaters and Hornbills, to ring Doves. Then suddenly we saw a group of these huge birds on the water. What do you think? Pelicans, yes, real wild Pelicans! What a thrill. As we slowly returned, we sat, with the sun behind us, and just looked. There before us were brilliant Yellow Wagtails, two Redshanks, a Dunlin, a Bittern and a flock of Ibises flying past. A few minutes later a skein of Duck flew in including Pintail, Wigeon, Gargany and Tufted, their whites and yellows and chestnuts rich in the sunlight. Some Kestrels flew past just as a Vulture swung into view. Ravens and pied Crows, hopped among the stones, whilst all around there were Swallows and Sand Martins. Jack was an excellent guide, and I had perhaps the best birding of all my time out here.

After so much excitement, we walked slowly back to the station to catch the train home. It seems there are only two sorts of train on the line here, one a Diesel rail-car and the other a train of cattle trucks. Naturally, we caught the latter, where the guard's van is the only place to sit, normally reserved for the guard and his mate, and today the odd English person as well. The train trundled along through the darkening countryside, and at the station we were met by Barty Knight, who had come to meet us, to take us back to his home. He lives alone in a town of some 6,000 inhabitants, where he has a pleasant bungalow, with a kitchen, laboratory, bedroom, sitting room, and a stable for his horse next door. He seems very happy living alone, with two lads to look after him, and there by lamplight with pictures on the wall and Barty's books on the sideboard, three officers all from the 11th Camp sat down to supper together! Quite like old times.

I'll finish now and continue tomorrow.
All love Ralph

Scenes of Ethiopia
Lake Hora

Lake Hora, Ethiopia.
"Bishoftu nestles among the hills near this wonderful natural habitat."
Photo Ethiopian Tourist Board

A Mousebird
"Curious looking things with long tails."

Photo Birds of East Africa

FRB (centre) in Ethiopia
with Peter Gibson (left) and Jack Frazer (right)
David Tod (back right) and two others
Photo courtesy of Hilary Skelton J Frazer's daughter

Some time spent with Barty Knight, gives my father an insight into the work, influence and substantial change one able person can make in a short time, and gives him a new respect for BK..........

Friday, March 26th 1943 Addis Ababa (No 36 final)

We had a splendid evening with Barty and he looked after us well. Here he is in sole charge of a hospital of ten beds, and a big out-patients Clinic. He is in his element, and doing a first-class job to a high standard of skill, and his medical knowledge improves daily. He has six men under him to dress wounds, and all day a stream of people come in, with a whole litany of diseases needing treatment. Syphilis (masses of it), malaria, typhus, pneumonia, burns, cuts, tropical sores and eye diseases. He now has enough confidence and skill to perform minor operations as well, and it is absolutely fascinating to watch the people coming in to be treated. In the hospital there was a malaria case, a child with a badly burned face, a horrible tropical sore, pneumonia and a myriad other complaints, and his confidence is catching, as his influence in the town continues to grow.

He visits the school and tries to enforce hygiene. He visits the prison – a ghastly squalid hole – and if the Governor proves awkward, he shuts the hospital till he gets his way. He is quite alone in a town which is not at all safe, and often gets men and women coming in, suffering from gunshot wounds or knife injuries from daily brawls and fights. Still the same old Barty, intolerant, difficult both to others as well as himself, but absolutely in his element and doing great things.

This morning was market day, and natives came in from miles around, driving their herds of donkeys which carried their wares. The animals, donkeys, mules and horses were tethered in thousands in a great square. There too were flocks of long-horned cattle with their drivers, the handsome upstanding Amharas, down from the central highlands. The women, mostly very dark Somalis, with fuzzy hair, or the ethnic Galla women with hair in ringlets held in place by grease. And a few stray Greeks and Italians. All gathered in crowds round the wares laid out on the ground, from cloth, cheap silverware and rough agricultural implements to saddles, skins and piles of corn. A noisy cacophony, with smells and dust blowing everywhere. Probably a dangerous place, but no-one bothered us.

Waiting on the station to return to Addis, we saw a train go down, which is quite a social event here. Crowds come down on to the platform, with no intention of travelling. They just gather round the engine, trying to catch water from it, as the town supply has broken down. There are children here selling paw-paws, and a crowd of ineffective police, dressed in dirty wraps, close-fitting trousers and disreputable headgear. But everyone is good humoured.

We travelled back in the guards van, which doubled as a mail car. It was a lovely journey, and the countryside round here, where Barty lives, is my idea of Africa, with dry grass, scrub, hundreds of flat-topped trees, and distant mountains, purple and eternally lovely, as mountains always are. Then as you get higher and nearer to Addis, undulating dry grassland with groups of eucalyptus trees, and more mountains rising up from the plateau to ten or eleven thousand feet. It really is a fine country.

I hope this doesn't sound too dull a letter, but it is written in odd moments and brings nonetheless, all my love and longing to be together with you again. I know how difficult life must be for you and I am full of admiration for all you do. You remain a beacon for me and an anchor in all my wanderings out here. If only you were here too. All my dear love to you and the children. Ralph

A map of Ethiopia

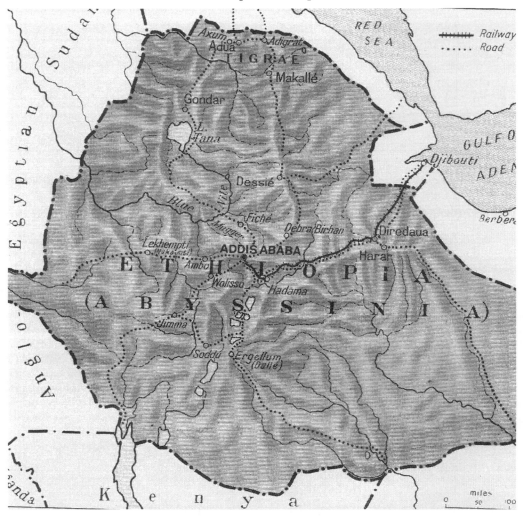

A map of Ethiopia in 1943, showing places visited by my father including not only Addis but
Debre Birhan, Ambo, Fiché, Hadama, the Blue Nile and Lake Tana.
Image Friends House Library

*My father, as always, is exhilarated to be high up in the mountains, here visiting the Clinic
at Debre Birhan.........*

Monday, March 29th 1943 Debre Birhan

My very dear Joan

I am writing this from a Clinic hospital at Debre Birhan, in central Ethiopia, north
of Addis, which is where we came up to yesterday. It is 1,500 feet higher than
Addis, which makes it about 10,000 feet, and very exhilarating. The country around here
is largely undulating grassland, still brown for the most part, save where it is near the
river which flows near it, or where teams of bullocks are lazily ploughing the distant hills.
The air is sparkling and clear, there is a strong breeze, and the bright sun and the clouds
throw purple shadows everywhere. Yesterday the sky had cleared completely, and we
walked down to a deep ravine into which the river plunges, and all this lovely upland lay
bathed in sun and wind. Just above the ravine there were "banks where the wild thyme
blows" in Shakespeare's words, and I spotted a single solitary wild rose in flower.

485

Ethiopia

I believe you could lose your heart to this high grass country, with its wide variety of truly different birds, including some sort of canary, a kind of Raven new to me, two species of Vulture, a Crow I've never seen before, and one bird that has me absolutely foxed. At any time of the day you can see Ravens and Kites, or perhaps a Harrier hanging in the wind, while higher up, a Vulture soars. There are flocks of yellow and black Canaries on the ground, and blue-headed Wagtails bobbing up and down amongst them.

There are two FAU men here in charge of the Hospital, where there are some twenty beds. Dr Michael Vaizey, now the senior Medical Officer, recently arrived from the London hospital, is out here with us and it is such a great help for these chaps to have occasional visits from him, as it is a heavy responsibility all on their own. During our visit, the patients in the hospital included two soldiers badly injured in a bomb explosion, a man with a deep knife wound, another man stunned by a stone thrown at him, cases of meningitis, pneumonia, syphilis and gonorrhoea, along with some women attacked by bandits and left with terrible burns all over their bodies.

The morning out-patients section was full of the usual collection of sorry and tragic cases. Syphilitic women and children come for injections, others with scabies and sores, ear trouble and bad eyes. There were wounded men from the army, and a man with an enormous distended stomach, and at 1.30pm, a man came in from a distant village with his hand blown off by a bomb he had found. I am full of such admiration for the way these chaps cope. They must make mistakes and wrong diagnoses from time to time, by the very nature of things, but they are infinitely better than nothing, and the great majority of their cases do get better. This particular afternoon was an especially heavy one for operations, with the hand having to be amputated, the distended stomach pierced, and with two more waiting to be treated.

Richey Mounsey and I have talked about various points, including finances which haven't come through, leaving some of the dressers unpaid, and how best to spread inadequate numbers to make the most effective impact on the vast demands. I think my visit has been worthwhile, giving me a clearer picture of the work being undertaken here, and giving him the chance to discuss problematic points with me. Afterwards we went for a walk, right out to the head of a magnificent canyon. Its course was not straight and here and there promontories of land jutted out, sometimes falling sheer in embattled rock with a tumble of boulders at the bottom, and sometimes running down in steep grass slopes. This great cleft disappeared in the far distance in a blue and purple haze. Behind us the sky was incredibly blue and trees and hills stood out clear. What a grand country this is.

I travelled back down on the back of the lorry and got very sunburnt, but it was a beautiful run. First the plateau - undulating is hardly the right word – as some of the slopes are too steep and there are ravines and knolls and distant mountains and great stretches of grass. Then as one gets nearer to Addis, there is another great slope of hills from the north, down to the vast plain all round Addis itself. Here the brown grass contrasts with the ploughed land and green stretches along the streams, with dotted here and there groups of acacias and eucalyptus, herds of cattle or horses grazing at intervals, with great cloud-shadows sweeping over all. To the north, a line of hills; to the south, nothing but plain to the horizon, save for the occasional magnificent mass of mountains. I did so long for your company to share the glory with you.

I'll stop now and write more tomorrow....my love for now, Ralph

Debre Birhan

Debre Birhan
"It is 1,500 feet higher than Addis, which makes it about 10,000 feet, and very exhilarating."
Photo National Geographical

A visit to see the Emperor, a journey to Fiché suffering a total of five punctures, some beautiful views, and FRB is tricked into becoming Doctor Barlow..........

Continued............Wednesday, March 31st 1943 – Debre Birhan

This morning I went to visit the orphans' school, as education has to be the key to any permanent development in the country. Bernard Fisher, one of the two headmasters out here is trying his best, but he has a colossal task. The buildings are bad and there is a totally inadequate staff for the 175 boys, but I think he is making some progress. Both he and Selby Clewer, who is the architect now attached to the Directorate, are already making huge improvements in the buildings as well as in general hygiene, which is encouraging to say the least.

In the afternoon Richey and I had an audience with the Emperor. He is a dignified man, and though only about 5 feet 4 inches tall, manages to convey an imposing presence with his bearded and dark-complexioned face and aquiline nose. He is quite pleasant, yet still maintains Shelley's 'sneer of cold command'. The Palace, or what we saw of it, is not large, but quite imposing, and we had a useful talk through an interpreter, about the work the Unit was doing, of which he seemed genuinely appreciative.

I later had a typhus injection, which made me feel lousy, but I picked up sufficiently to make a visit to another Clinic about 75 miles north at Fiché. The road was well engineered for a change, built by the Italians of course, but with such an execrable surface we suffered a total of five punctures en route. As we had insufficient spare tyres, only one badly patched up inner tube, and no pump, we rather wondered what we should do next. But before too long, we were lucky to encounter another lorry and flagged him down. It turned out to be the only other lorry between Fiché and Addis, which didn't have a pump on it either. But the driver was an angel, as he said he had a pump back at his home only a short distance off the road, and drove me there and back and stayed while we repaired the tyres. A gentleman.

Despite the punctures, it was in some ways the most beautiful run of any that we made during my stay here. The journey began with a terrific climb out of Addis, and then hill country all the way. Sometimes there were vast stretches of level grassland, bounded in the distance by mountains, with a few knolls or groups of trees, but for miles and miles it was just smooth turf, flat as a billiard table, dotted with hundreds of grazing cattle.

From time to time, we crossed hill ranges, where the road was steep and the ground rough and from the pass we were afforded views of endless rolling hill country and distant purple mountains. We passed villages standing among eucalyptus or giant cactus plants, men ploughing behind stubborn bullocks, and a continual stream of men driving herds of loaded donkeys, horses and mules. Sometimes someone of importance would ride past on a mule with a bevy of retainers behind him, carrying spears and guns. Occasionally we crossed a stream, now reduced to a mere trickle on a rocky bed. At last we approached a range of hills and suddenly in front of us was an enormous gorge, where the road turned away down a side valley, and then climbing the flank of the hills for some miles, swung back towards the gorge.

On the slope of a hill, a short distance from the huddle of native huts and Italian shacks, is a stone house that looks for all the world like a Cotswold farmhouse. Here lives Ken Tipper, the able FAU man, with a couple of Ethiopian lads looking after him. Shading the front door stands a large and gloomy tree, sacred to the villagers, who often bring their small offerings and place them under the tree. It is told that once an Italian major, who used to occupy the house, had dared to cut off a branch which was darkening his windows. He died the next day.

Directly above his house, stands the town of Fiché, on the edge of a vast and wonderful gorge, south of the mass of mountains which hide the sources of the Blue Nile. Quite the best view of this amazing scene, is to be had from the lavatory window at the back of the house! I wish I could adequately describe it for you. You look down on a sheer two thousand feet to a tributary of the Blue Nile, with vast crags rising stark and forbidding beyond. Little streams rush down from the hillsides, where they have carved out great gorges and there below they all tumble together into one vast canyon. You might almost imagine yourself to be on the edge of the world as you look out into the immeasurable purple distances and depths. Last night as the light died and the details of rocks and cliffs slowly faded away, a great mass of cumulus cloud stood up in the sky, as rumbles of thunder echoed around the hills and forked lightning flickered in the oncoming dark. It really was perfection.

Between the house and the clinic at the far end of the village, is the Coptic Church, with crowds of beggars, diseased and halt and blind, clustered around the door, holding out their hands for alms. The clinic consists of a small hut for one or two in-patients and a larger hut for out-patients and minor operations. Patients number anything from thirty-five to forty-five a day.

I had been warned that Ken was not beyond playing a practical joke on a newcomer, and the day Jack and I arrived, there he was full of suspiciously good humour. I guessed something was afoot, when he asked us if we would very kindly come and talk to an important relative of the owners, who was staying. "I've already given my diagnosis," Ken added "but this patient needs very special attention," he whispered conspiratorially. Uncertain quite what Ken was cooking up, we followed obediently to see the said patient. Immediately, Ken, assuming affected humility, introduced us and said in his best Uriah Heep voice - 'I would be deeply honoured if the two very eminent 'medical men' who have just joined us, would agree to corroborate my own very provisional diagnosis!'

Somewhat flummoxed, but determined to play along, Jack and I, who have to be the two most medically ignorant men in the entire Unit, were solemnly expected to re-examine the poor chap. With all the gravitas at our command, and trying our best not to laugh, we proceeded to ask him, through an interpreter, any remotely medical sounding questions we could think of. It should be added that our minds were wonderfully concentrated by the fact that the patient had a whole arsenal of pistols, guns and cartridges lying at the foot of his bed. No sooner out of earshot, than we all fell about and Ken decided to re-christen me Doctor Barlow from then on.

We stayed that evening in his really very pleasant house, which had two big rooms. By now the weather had turned around and loud thunder was rattling around outside, as heavy rain pounded on the roof. But Ken had made up a splendid roaring open fire, and we were soon warm, as we eagerly tucked in to a very excellent supper he'd prepared. We talked quite late into the night before retiring exhausted to bed. The next day we drove back and this time, managed to complete the journey with only one puncture!

Till later, love Ralph.

———

As a country, my father falls for Ethiopia – its splendid mountain scenery and outdoor opportunities – as a place in which he thinks he could happily settle and bring up a family – if it weren't for a family and job to return to………

Sunday, April 4th 1943 - continued

I am writing now from what is probably my last Clinic at Ambo, some eighty miles due west of Addis, built around hot sulphur springs which well up between the rocks. It lies in what is known as the Shoa district, the ancient historic area in the centre of the country. The first part of my ride here was splendid, all mountains and fine slopes sweeping down to the valleys, with all sorts of trees and shrubs standing singly in open parkland, and thick growths of bushes along the streams.

Later it became a succession of dull stretches of ploughed land falling back to grass and thistle, with large numbers of rusty old Italian agricultural vehicles strewn along the wayside. Some of the country to the west of here is really grand, all steep tree-covered mountains, and stretches of parkland dotted with trees, rivers and waterfalls.

Once here, it was apparent that the main problem was finding suitable accommodation for the Unit. For the time being they had ended up split between some very unsatisfactory old out buildings and a number of large tents, which was most unsatisfactory because of the danger of infection. Something better would have to be found or else we might reluctantly have to close it down.

We also went to visit a farm school out in the country yesterday, situated high up on a well-watered slope with grand views and fertile land. The school was shockingly run, but nonetheless what opportunities! I can think of many worse places to settle than Ethiopia. A most beautiful country, high up, with a good climate and fertile soil, horses to ride, wonderful birds and plenty of cheap help. In many ways one of God's own countries. How would you like it?! If I hadn't a job to return to – I hope – and if I didn't love England so passionately, and one had money and a job here, it wouldn't be at all bad. It would probably be lonely, and the children's education would be difficult, but they would have freedom, marvellous experiences, horses to ride and a wonderful country to explore. What do you say? It is of course impossible, and quite out of the question, so it hardly matters. We should get terribly homesick, as I am now. "Oh to be in England now that April's there…" Blue skies and clouds, breaking buds, flushes of green, blossoms and migrants coming. How I long for it again! But Ethiopia is a fine country and I have enjoyed my time here, encouraged by all that is being done here.

It has been good seeing so much of Jack and I shall miss him. I think he is by way of being one of my best friends in the Unit and I am so glad that you met him too. I have also come to appreciate Richey much more too. I dismissed him earlier too flippantly. I actually think he is doing a really good job up here.

Back in Addis, I am now in my normal state of awful suspense as to whether or not there will be a plane for me to get on back to Cairo tomorrow. It will be most frightfully inconvenient if there isn't, as I have a hectic few weeks ahead of me before I leave for India and China, and I am not greatly looking forward to it all. I'll close now and write again on my arrival in Cairo.

This brings all my love to you and the children.

God bless, Ralph

The FAU in Ethiopia

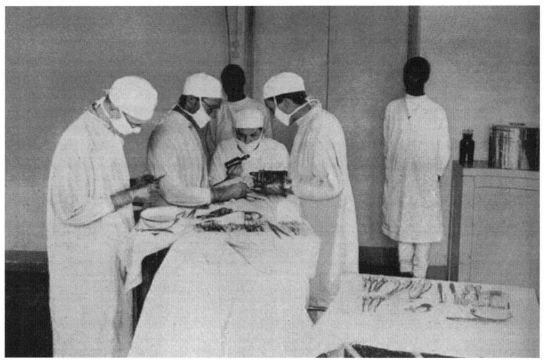

An operation in progress at one of the clinics in Ethiopia.
Photo Friends House Library

On the way to Addis
Harold Waller, Peter Gibson, Barty Knight and Eric Green
Photo Friends House Library

[Textual: My mother refers to 'writing to India', yet all the Air Mail letter cards were addressed to 'FAU, Middle East Force', not India. The answer must be that the Air letter cards arrived quickly, and the long Airmail letters still took up to 2 months. So the latter were addressed to India, and would be awaiting his arrival in Calcutta, while the AMLC's reached him in Cairo before he left.]

And now, to end this chapter, here are two letters from my mother, longing as always to hear news of my father's whereabouts, but which continue to inform my father of news of the family and all their activities – visits to Granny, family photographs, getting cross and a general longing for my father's presence.........

Tuesday, March 9th 1943 – Wolverhampton (34)
Dearest beloved Ralph

 I imagine by now that you are in Ethiopia and I long to hear so much about it. I feel rather out of it all at the moment and find it difficult to follow all your movements. I haven't yet received any news of your visit to Tehran. It seems to me that one can reckon on at least 3 months now for long AM letters to get through. It is disappointing. That is why I now try and squeeze more on the AMLCs. If I write carefully I can get quite a lot of news on the sheets.

I am hoping that you will have a large number of letters awaiting you when you reach India and I really wonder how much longer it will be before Barry and Brandon join you. I only hope the news will not seem too stale and uninteresting when you eventually come to read the letters. I sent off an AMLC yesterday, telling you of our visit to your mother over the weekend, so won't repeat it all. I think it was fairly successful, but rather a strain on everybody in some ways. I felt rather like a chewed rag when I eventually reached Lea Road yesterday lunchtime. I'm afraid your mother will need a long rest as she was quite tired, and also had rheumatism. But she was most kind and looked after us very well. It must have meant a lot of work for her and Lydia, and I can't say it was much of a holiday for me either.

How I long so much for a holiday – just the two of us - away in the country far away from here! I must say though, that the children were very good, but A won't leave me for long just at the moment, which can be tiring. David says he is going to stay with your mother for 20 weeks in the summer! I think she is fond of the children, especially David, but she doesn't say much about our visit. I hope she thought it was worth all the work. She is most thoughtful for our comfort and food etc.

David is very entertaining these days and says some very amusing things. He looked at a picture in your mother's dining room and said "I like that picture of trees Granny", and then after a moment he added – "but it looks pretty lonely!" Then he picked up the cruet and said "this is nice. Is it second hand, Granny?!" We were acting in the nursery last night, and I pretended to cry. "Don't cry mummy, not at your age. You're a grown woman!"

Hilda Ransome quite fell for D and thought him such a darling. "He's so matey", says Hilda!! Antony is a precious dear too, though of course he isn't as sociable as David at the moment. Everyone seems to think they are both very good looking. They are certainly jolly children. Your mother fetched out many of the family photographs. I did enjoy looking at them. Your mother was very lovely to look at in her youth. Her brothers were fine looking men too. Millior always looks rather pious in photos, but you always looked a little darling, so jolly and charming. In one of the family photographs, when you were about 18 months, it might almost be a photo of Antony, although I have never thought he was as much like you as David.

I'm not sure whether it's a good idea to go away with Hilda and the children in the summer. I think it will be difficult to find a place which would suit us all, and everywhere is booked and so expensive. Also, it is such an effort to get there, with so much luggage and Antony liable to be sick when travelling. I do hope he'll grow out of it.

I do wonder whether you were able to sort out the crisis in the desert section? I do think of you often and sympathise so much in all these difficult jobs you are doing. Always remember, my dear one, my faith in you and my belief that you will always succeed. I hope my prayers and thoughts strengthen you, my dearest husband. I know that you will win through and come out successfully on top, as you always do. If only I could share the burden with you and somehow lighten it for you. I would gladly do anything in the world to help you.

I hope you will feel it some compensation seeing Dick, Horace and Duncan when you eventually arrive in India and then China. Please remember me to anyone I know, especially Duncan. I heard from the Woods that they were very pleased to get 3 letters from Duncan last week after a long silence, and I very much enjoyed reading his letters.

I must stop now and take the boys for a walk. They want me to see if we can get our sweet ration! Antony has an appetite like a horse. David is a little better on the whole. More tonight dear one.

Like every parent with two energetic, growing children, missing their father, my mother sometimes feels inadequate and not up to the task. Also a feeling, for all the kindness and help of her sister and brother-in-law, that two years in someone else's house can sometimes be difficult…….

Later….10.30pm

Forgive me, but I am very tired and depressed tonight and cannot write very well. I just feel I want to fall into your arms, and need reassuring that everything will one day turn out alright. Perhaps I am over-reacting from the weekend, but my nerves are 'on edge' as the saying goes. (Though I know you dislike such expressions!) I'm probably over tired, and the children have been very much on top of me today and I so much need your support, encouragement and love.

There are times when I realise how far I fall short of being a good mother. I know I get irritable when I'm tired and don't always have the patience I should have. Forgive me dearest, I am trying to bring them up as you would like, but so often I fail, and I feel so wretched. No, don't smile and tell me I am talking 'through my hat (!), but it is so. I suppose what I need is to live a more Christian life, though God knows I'm not leading a gay or dissipated one! I need more religion in my every day life and I just feel I don't bother enough.

I agree so much with you when you say you are coming to realise more and more that you need religion. It is wonderful to hear you say your faith has increased, and it makes me so happy. Oh dearest, when you return, may we help to build a better world and help each other and our children to live a full life in the true sense.

Tonight I don't know what I really want, except to be with you. I feel I have been here long enough and that we all need a change. Two years is quite long enough to be in someone's else's home, and except that I don't want to remove David from the good PNEU school, where he is so happy, I am more and more anxious to be in a house of our own. I want to live a normal life. How many thousands more must long for the same, as I do?

If you come home this autumn, there will be so much to discuss. I really don't wish to sound ungrateful to W&L, and we all live quite happily here together. But I'm sure W&L must sometimes wish we weren't here all the time as well, and there are times when I just long to be somewhere else.

I know I have much to be thankful for, and W&L have been wonderfully good to us. I'm a very fortunate woman compared with many, and of course, it's been so much cheaper living with my sister and family, than running our own home. But I am now just tired of it all, and so much want our own home again.

To brighter things! I bought some pussy willows today. They look so pretty, and on the dressing table is a most charming little bowl of early spring flowers bought from Swarthmore Road. David really loves flowers, which is nice. I heard a lark at Swarthmore Road singing to herald the spring, bless him. How I know you too long for England, as Browning says "Now that April's there" – well almost! I wish I could tell you more about the countryside, my darling, but here in Wolverhampton, I am far away from such pleasant sites. But one day soon, let's hope.

Goodnight, dearest husband. I just want to put my arms around you and never let you go. I thank God for everything you mean to me.

Continued...Wednesday, March 10th......After a good night's sleep, I'm feeling somewhat better today. It's amazing how one suddenly feels brighter with a more balanced outlook on life. Fortunately, nothing lasts. I feel more able to cope with the children's difficulties, which all seem easier today. Last night I was in the depths. Today, I can see the light! I suppose most of us are like that these days, when the world seems in such a mess.

Everyone seems charmed with David. He often wants to be his own person now, which is understandable as he grows up, though in a household it can be difficult sometimes. But he is very loving and full of fun. All the staff at the PNEU School think he is amazingly clever. One of the teachers said to me - "He's so bright and quick and full of the joys of life". I was impressed in the bus this morning to hear him read out a notice to me, only stumbling once - on the word 'considered'. Usually the average age at which a child reads is 6 or 7, so at 5+ he is progressing well. I do wish you were here to enjoy his companionship. I'm taking the boys into town this afternoon, to buy David a grey summer suit and a mackintosh; and Antony needs a summer coat. I've been snipping off bits of A's hair and now he looks more grown up.

I had another note from your mother this morning and she has sent me J M Barrie's biography to read, which I think I shall enjoy. She says she enjoyed our stay and said – "Since Ralph went away, we have got to know each other so much better and understand each other more now." I think this is true, and I'm no longer afraid of her and can talk to her with ease at last. But I'm never quite sure if she fully accepts me or not. Sometimes, however she seems genuinely fond of me and is very affectionate.

Enid says that although your mother approves of Alfred, in that he is a good Quaker and husband, he irritates her very much. Poor soul, how disappointed she has been in her children's marriages! I told Enid that nothing worries me now. Ralph and I are wonderfully happy and in love and that is all that matters. But I do miss you and your great support and always sensible advice. How lucky I am to have such a husband. I am more than proud of you.

I hope you are feeling strengthened and encouraged by these visits to the other sections, and meeting friends. I just worry that you may get too tired with so much travelling.

I do wonder whether this will reach you sometime around your birthday. If so, it brings my very dear love and many happy returns of the day sweetheart. I shall be thinking of you and long to celebrate the day with you. Forgive me dearest, this is not a very good letter and is written in a rather rambling way, drifting from one thing to another. But it comes with all my love as well as from my mother and W&L. Ever yours Joan

And another letter from my mother full of rejoicing and great delight, as the brocade my father posted from South Africa back in July of 1942, has finally arrived....

Friday, March 19th 1943 – Wolverhampton (Air letter)

Dearest beloved husband
Life seems to get busier and busier, and I haven't yet posted my weekly long letter to you, but I will try and get it off tomorrow. First of all, however, I am terribly excited and thrilled to be able to tell you that I have just received your lovely parcel of brocade!! I was over at 26 collecting some things, and when I got back in the afternoon, there was your parcel, addressed by you and with your dear note inside. There was no other letter with it, so I am afraid I cannot write and thank whoever posted it on. The postmark was Chelsea. But no matter, it is perfectly lovely – charming, and beautiful –all that I could wish for. Truly darling, I am delighted with it. It is just exactly the kind of thing I should have chosen myself. I think you have perfect taste!! I shall have it made up for evening wear one day: it really is exquisite. I wonder where it could have been and how it has managed to turn up after all this time. It could probably tell a tale!

Also your AG about the house arrived yesterday and your mother had her's too. I rang her up last night and we discussed it a little more. I only wish I could move in when she goes to Millior. It would be so much easier for your mother and for me too. If you did come back in the next six to nine months, I would consider moving in. We shall have to wait and see. I haven't mentioned it to anyone, save my mother as yet. But I shall miss 26, which is where I was yesterday, collecting some odds and ends. It was a sunny day and the house looked its dear self. Mr Tritsch keeps the grass cut reasonably well, but that is about all. The ivy and other wall creepers are very overgrown. I must go over again next month and clean out the drawing room, it is so dirty. I took some sandwiches and ate them with the Keens. They gave me a great welcome and made me coffee. They seem well, but I hadn't seen them since last September, and I thought Mr Keen looked very frail and thin. Their garden looks perfect – of course! They both sent dear love to you and were so pleased with your Christmas AG.

[.....] On Wednesday I had a very long letter from Angela, telling me lots of things about your plans and all the trouble you'd had with John Rich going directly to China and with Brandon still here. She also sent me copies of most of your reports to the Square. Just exactly what I've been wanting for months. I am so happy to have them as it has helped me to understand your work so much more clearly. She is going to send me a copy of all future reports.

My darling what difficulties you come up against. I do sympathise. Angela says she wishes she could send a copy of your reports to those in China, to show them just how a report should be written. Since the reports arrived I've spent every moment reading them!

At the concert the other night, I met a Dr Rita Wilson, who is the sister of a man called Mr Applebaum, who went out to Palestine to farm. I seem to remember you and Duncan talking about him. Do you recall? She's an extraordinary person, with any amount of bounce and self-confidence.
Excuse haste. V.d.l. Joan
PS. Your pension at the Office is now £200

Chapter 34
Back in Cairo
April – May 1943

Much to my father's relief, there is a plane which takes him to Asmara, then Port Sudan and across the Red Sea to Jiddah and thence back to Cairo. Once there, he collects some long-delayed mail which cheers him up no end, especially when he learns that the missing brocade has turned up to delight on both sides.....as well as some books.........

Monday, 12th April 1943 – FAU Middle East Cairo

My dearest Joan

To my great relief, not only was there a plane, but at break of dawn next day, I was able to get on it. The first stretch of the journey was down to Asmara where I spent about half a day which was without much note, before having to move on. We then took off for Port Sudan, flying just above a floor of wonderful fleecy clouds, which was rather exciting, before a short hop across the Red Sea to Jiddah. As we took off from Port Sudan, we were all considerably reassured for our safety when they handed out life belts, not least as it was some comfort to think that we should come down gently enough to be in a fit state to make use of them! Jiddah, is known as the Pilgrim's port which is only about 40 miles from Mecca, and I feel sure will be the nearest I shall ever get to the Holy city.

So at last I am back in Cairo, which is getting quite hot right now, but it is looking well with the deciduous trees already covered in fresh green, and many shrubs beginning to flower. I arrived back to find a whole bevy of airmail letters and air cards from you, not to mention a parcel of books. Thank you, thank you. It is really splendid to receive so much news of you and the children. How I wish I could see them. Please thank David for his airmail letter too and tell him I will reply very soon. I am so glad that you agree about moving to Swarthmore Road. I know it will be a wrench to leave 26 and be a heck of an upheaval for you, but I feel sure it is the right thing to do.

I am delighted to have the books – the one on the Crusades and *The Leisure of an Egyptian Official,* though I rather think the book on the Crusades came from your mother, in which case please thank her profusely and I will write separately very shortly. Thank you so much. I can't tell you how thrilled I am that the brocade I sent you from South Africa has finally turned up and that you liked it. I wonder if there was there by any chance a table cloth with it as well, or has that gone to the bottom of the sea?

I find that things have gone quite well in my absence, but there is a hell of a lot to do both in catching up, writing up my report on Ethiopia for the Square and in preparation before I leave for India. So, though London still hasn't yet sent any final instructions through, life continues to be extremely busy. One encouraging piece of news is that I gather Brandon is now on his way, which means that I must start to make some practical arrangements. I gather also that Johnnie Gough is ill in hospital up in Jerusalem. So somehow I shall have to find time to go and visit him, preferably by air.

My forthcoming trips to India and China are in order for me to complete Tom's planned schedule, and I will undoubtedly be away for some time. So yesterday I went to see GHQ to discuss who should take over as No 1 here when I leave. I had been rather dreading the meeting, but in fact it went off better than usual, as these things often do. My position as OCME – Officer for the Middle East section - will now be John Rose. Meanwhile, with Unit work rapidly developing in Italy, it's been decided to appoint Peter Gibson as Officer in charge of an expanded section, to include the Mediterranean, or OC Med in the jargon! So sometime soon Peter will be leaving for Naples, where he'll be based with Jack Frazer as his assistant. All love for now, Ralph

I have put these next letters together, for though my mother's are March and my father's April, they make sense reflecting, as they do, on much the same events, even though some bits of news cross in the post. Here my mother notices that Hatchards bookshop in Wolverhampton is making a big display of 'When We Build Again', a vison of postwar planning, to which my father had contributed, and was being hailed as an enlightened vision of postwar Britain, making my mother a proud wife..........

Friday, March 12th 1943 – Wolverhampton (Air letter)

Darling of my heart

Your AM letter of February 4th (No 31) – (p465) – arrived this morning and I am so grateful for it. I must say they do come in a queer order, in no way sequential, and it is hard sometimes to piece together what is happening and when! David says he would love to come to the Zoo with you, which sounds a good one. [....] You say you envy me the children, and I know how you must long to see them, but these last few days they have rather got on top of me and I would willingly swap jobs for a week or so!!

I went into Hatchards this morning and bought two books for your birthday, which they are posting off today. One was 'Coming down the Wye' by Robert Gibbings, which I thought you might enjoy, being as you are so far away from the English scenery, which you love. I remembered that you enjoyed his other book 'Sweet Thames Run Softly', so hopefully you'll like this too. Also I got a collection of poems by Emily Dickinson, which I hope you'll like as well. God knows when you will get them, as you may be in China when they arrive!

I was interested to see that Hatchards had 'When we Build Again' in the shop and were making a big display of it. It gave me quite a thrill to see your name on the front page! I hadn't realised it was such a big book. In fact it's very well produced, with beautiful paper and some fine photographs.

David is drawing a good deal at the moment. He drew a most elaborate picture yesterday of houses, bombers, guns and parachutes. He is becoming very war minded since he started school!! I have promised to do some gardening with him this afternoon, as your mother gave him some grape hyacinths bulbs and he also bought some seeds of his own. I posted my letter 34 to India yesterday. I'm afraid you will have a great number awaiting you when you eventually reach there!! I do wonder if you are yet back from Ethiopia. The Rhoads (the family Michael Rutter is with in America) wrote saying they had seen a report of yours in the World Friend Review. They think you are doing a fine job, and so say all of us!

On Thursday next I am hoping to go to the Civic Hall to hear the London Philharmonic Orchestra. Win may come with me as well. Mother says she wants to go and see the Noël Coward film 'In Which We Serve'. It's a naval film and considered to be very good. I haven't been to a film for ages.

David is now growing so fast that he needs new clothes, and they really are a price now. The grey suit I bought him cost 46/-; a navy mackintosh coat 46/-; a grey shirt 9/-, and trousers 12/-. Antony only needs a new summer coat.

I had a very nice short note from Dora Tanner thanking me for my letter, but she didn't really say much more.

Must stop now. My darling this comes with all my love. I so long to see you home again. All my love Joan.

The Bournville Village Trust's postwar vision of Birmingham

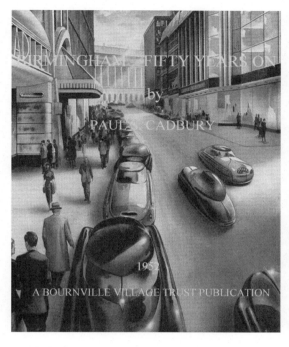

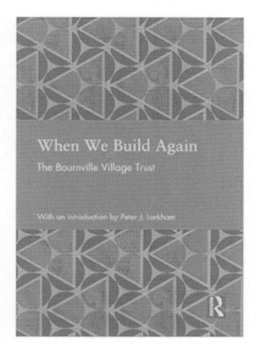

The book to which my father had contributed, and my mother had seen in Hatchards was 'When We Build Again' published in 1943, which was a vision of how planners envisaged the bomb-wrecked city might be rebuilt. It was an important publication instigated by Paul Cadbury and The Bournville Village Trust, and was immediately influential, and the origin of much post-war clearance, adopted in many cities.

In 1952, Paul Cadbury offered his own vision of how the city might look in the year 2000 and after, entitled 'Birmingham – Fifty Years On' and was in the tradition of what George Cadbury had in mind when he first created the BVT in 1900.

Both books were widely seen as an opportunity to deal with slums and overcrowding, providing better developments for hospitals, schools and employment.

More letters arrive from my father, after his return from Tobruk by train, including one for David too, full of my father's little drawings, which gave great joy to all............

Monday, March 15th 1943 – Wolverhampton

Dearest heart

Your AMLC of Feb 24th (p467) was received this morning and both David and I were delighted. It is good of you to take so much trouble to do drawings for him. He was so excited to hear from you and came running upstairs with the letter saying - "Letter from Daddy, letter from Daddy". We laughed a good deal over the drawings, especially the one of you snoring in the train, which does look a bit like you're sitting on the lavatory!

How dearly I would love to be with you seeing all the wild flowers you mention. What a glorious sight it must be. I am glad that at least some of the letters are getting through rather better now. AMLCs take about a fortnight but AM letters are still bad, at nearer two/three months. I still haven't had your Teheran one yet for instance. It is so good of you to write at such length, as everybody appreciates them so much, and for me they are a real tonic. It is the only thing I live for these days as they bring you so close to me.

A letter to David following his return from Tobruk

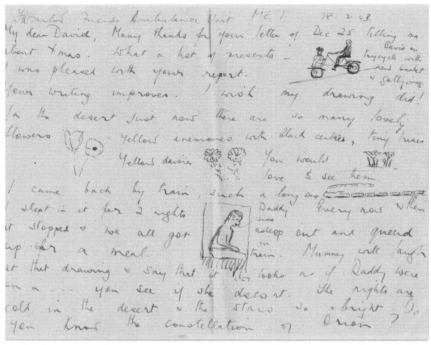

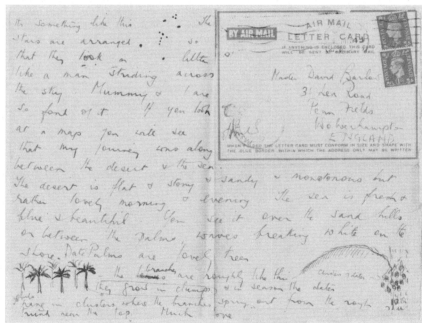

A letter to David from FRB complete with drawings which delighted David, including the one alluded to of him asleep, snoring:

"I came back by train, such a long one. Every now and then, it stopped and we all got out and queued up for a meal......Mummy will laugh at my drawing of me asleep on the train and snoring, and say that it looks as if Daddy were sitting on the......You see if she doesn't!"

I am now thinking of you in Ethiopia, and I do hope all is well with you my sweetheart. Did you see Jack Frazer? How are things going there? Did you fly I wonder, and did you have a good trip? As always so many questions I want to ask! Whenever will you get to India and China? I don't think B & B have yet left!

We are having most glorious weather right now – very cold and frosty first thing but at least bright sunshine in the day, and the almond blossom and forsythia are both fully out now. I have promised Win I'll do some gardening one day soon. When I was over at Selly Oak last weekend, everyone was busy mowing their lawns, and it smelled so heavenly. The chiff chaffs must be here by now. Oh, how I long to get out into the country. You as well, I know, will be longing for the English countryside, at this your favourite time of year. And let's pray that we may all be together this time next year.

Did I tell you Reg is now stationed near Swanage doing special training? I am afraid he will be going abroad sometime soon. He says he is enjoying it, and that they are a fine lot of men, though it's pretty strenuous training I believe.

I have been reading 'A Narrow Street'. Do read it if you can get a copy. It's by Elliot Paul, an American, who lived in Paris near Notre Dame during the 1920s and 30s. He tells the story of the gradual collapse and ruin of France, and visits Spain a good deal also. It is brilliantly told and although quite lewd in parts, tells the story so vividly. He makes the people he describes very real. I found it fascinating. Now I'm reading J M Barrie's biography which your mother gave me. What a weakness he had for beautiful women. But it is interesting, and I always enjoy reading about people. He must have had considerable charm with his Scottish accent and manner, but in other ways he was a very insignificant man to look at! I wonder if you are able to get hold of books.

My darling I do wonder if things are getting easier for you now and hopefully running more smoothly. I do admire the way you are so uncomplaining. Bless you for what you are.

Both the children have colds – not very bad ones thankfully – but they are not quite as bright and happy as usual. Antony is talking well now and is a very amusing child. He loves dressing up, and has a delicious laugh and sense of fun. David gets more and more interesting and attractive. But I do miss your support and help at this time, as bringing them up is not easy. I only hope you will feel proud of them one day.

I wonder if you ever knew a woman called Eileen Pim in the FAU. She is now in War Vics. Would you believe, I was at school with her, and have invited her and her fiancé to coffee next Saturday. I haven't seen her for years, but heard she was in Wolverhampton.

I am glad your desert trip to HSU was successful and pleasant. I am always thinking of you and all send our love, and special love and kisses from me. When, when, when shall we see each other again?

Ever your loving Joan.

———

My father, unsure exactly when he will be departing for India, is anxious to fit everything in while he can, and is now trying to arrange a flight to Jerusalem so that he can visit John Gough, who is ill in hospital there. Meanwhile, it's not all work, as Eric Green and he pay a visit to the Archeological Museum...........

Monday April 19th 1943 – Cairo

My dearest Joan

I'm still trying, without much success to arrange a flight to Jerusalem, so I may have to go by sea. Meanwhile, I went to see Chaplin's *The Great Dictator* the other night. I saw it once before in 1940, but I must say it is a marvellous film and I enjoyed it all over again. What a genius he is. Next week I see they are showing *Desert Victory,* about Monty's victory over Rommel. A bit too close for comfort I think. I'm not sure I really need to see that!

Yesterday, Sunday, Eric Green and I went to the Archaeological Museum. There is no Archaeology being done there now, and is at the moment looked after by just two women. One is a Miss Perkins, who is very talkative and outspoken, but kind-hearted. She is a rather plump lady, and used to be secretary to Dr Reisner, the legendary American archaeologist, who spent much of his life excavating out here, practically up until his death last year. Miss P is in charge pro tem, and is busy supervising his papers and clearing up. The other lady, Miss Ginger, is a bit younger, quite good-looking, rather flat-chested, but very pleasant. We both share a bond because, as I think I told you, our 'perfect' group of servants, originally hail from the Museum and many of their relations still work out here. Incidentally, whenever any one of our servants goes to visit Miss Perkins, apparently they speak of 'the Unit men' in the highest possible terms! Well, of course!

As well as the Museum, there is also an Archaeological Mission house out here. It is up near the desert, and it owns masses of unpublished archaeological material, which is kept in their library and includes two volumes of beautifully painted reproductions of tomb wall paintings. They are really most lovely. The Mission is out beyond the Pyramids past Mena House Hotel, where we are, and has the most wonderful view between the second and third Pyramids, right out over the valley to the cliffs beyond. Altogether we had a fascinating visit.

An old postcard of the Archeological Museum in Cairo, built in 1902

Photo Cairo Museum archives

The View from Mena House Hotel

"The Archeological Mission is out beyond the Pyramids past Mena House Hotel, where we are, and has the most wonderful view between the second and third Pyramids."

Photo Egyyptian Tourist Board

My father, not always noted for sartorial elegance, decides that prior to leaving for India, he needs some new clothes! But surprised by the cost he decides to try and barter! But most of the time is taken up with correspondence and attempts to visit all the colleagues he's going to miss, and a pleasant lunch with the English author, Robin Fedden..........

Continuation of April 19th......Friday, April 23rd 1943 – Cairo

Really there is not much news this week. I have been doing a whole lot of this and that! Coping and catching up with correspondence, which is never ending, and sometimes brings bad news. Yesterday, for instance I had a letter from Maurice Webb in Durban saying it seems that two FAU women, Evelyn Rogers and Eleanor Sawdon*10, were on the boat that was torpedoed off the cost of South Africa recently. I have no more details yet, but it would be tragic if true. So awful for their families. I must try and write to them. I worry so much about you and hope you are all safe.

---

*10 They were on the Laconia, but happily managed to survive and after a time in SA, went on to India

I'm also trying to get ready for my eventual departure, and decided that it was about time I had some new clothes. Don't laugh! So I went down into Cairo today to try and buy some, and was somewhat taken aback by the cost. I reckoned there must be a vast profit on them, so I innocently asked the salesman, if he could offer me a discount on the marked price. Without a second thought or even a protestation, he deducted ten shillings, so the margin must be huge. Somehow I don't think it would work in down town Birmingham!

Lastly, I've been spending time with those I shall miss when I leave, and John Bailey and I went and had lunch today with the well-known English writer Robin Fedden[1], who teaches English here at the University, and his charming wife Renée, who is a most attractive Greek lady. He was a friend of Tom's and I had met up with him earlier and liked him very much. There was another exceedingly pretty Jewish girl there as well, of unknown nationality. The Feddens have a delightful little house near the Pyramids, and gave us all a splendid meal. It was a most pleasant occasion.

I also had an excellent meal with Doug Mackenzie last night. He has found himself a new woman. The relationship seems to be blossoming and has apparently been going strong for some three weeks or so now. Doug says she is 'plain, but awfully nice'! Unfortunately for him, she is a nurse on a hospital ship and has had to go away for a while. How hard abstinence is for everybody, and how much I wish you were here my dearest. You are for ever in my thoughts. Still waiting for a flight!

All love for now, Ralph

"Robin Fedden, who teaches English here at the University, and his charming wife Renée."
Photograph kindly loaned by the Fedden family

In this next long letter, my mother struggles to write to my father, despite the distractions of young children (that'll be David and me!), and her mother listening to the wireless. She pays a bitter-sweet visit to Linden Road, and though realising how much shared happiness is tied up in this their first home together, that maybe with so much that has changed in the intervening years, it is right that they should make a new start in a new home, a reunited family at last.

Also Angela writes a long letter including many of my father's reports to HQ, and in reading these, my mother is full of gratitude that on top of his Unit work, he can still find time to write such wonderful letters back home. In many respects, it this keeping in touch, with the constant reassurances of love and information about the children growing up, and of their daily activities, that helps the relationship to be grounded. It is a love affair that never fades, despite the distance, and which my father constantly revitalises with gifts sent from different parts of the world, as with the long-lost brocade from South Africa, the arrival of which here encourages my mother into still further expressions of delight.............

Friday, March 19th March 1943 – Wolverhapton (35)

 My most beloved Ralph

I am afraid your letter has been held up this week, as I seem to have been terrribly busy. [....] However, I must write tonight as I have lots to tell you. The time is now 9.30pm and I am sitting at the bureau in the drawing room. There are two lovely bowls of almond blossom and forsythia near me. I wish you could see it dear one. Win and Llew are out to coffee and mother is listening to a talk on the wireless, and here am I trying to concentrate on a letter to you, while this man's voice drones on and on!

It's been a grey, dreary day, more like November almost, though we've nothing to grumble at, as the weather has been wonderful for most of the winter. Yesterday was a beautiful, mild spring day, warm and sunny, with that gentle air when the world seems stirring, with everything fresh and new, and one gets renewed hope and courage to travel on.

I was at Linden Road most of yesterday and looking through the drawing room window, I suddenly felt you so near and I was overwhelmed by all the love of the past seven years. I was very sad and yet supremely happy. Can you understand? I thought of all the hours and days we've enjoyed the garden and I wondered if we could ever leave it? Dear house of so many joys and such happiness. Precious days. It was uncanny and yet very wonderful. I felt everything was alright and I knew there would be a future for us. As I was travelling back home, I began thinking more about our moving to Swarthmore Road and felt that it would be the right thing to accept your mother's kind offer to live there when you return. Perhaps it will be a good thing to start in a new place – a united family making a fresh strart together. I feel sure it is right for us to go. Oh, dearest love, how I long to have you here to discuss it all, and to be able to talk it over with you.

Your AGs about the house, both to me and your mother arrived yesterday, and we talked about it a little more last night, although we haven't got any further than you already know. But I do definitely think we should take Swarthmore Road, which I said to your mother, and I hope you will think I said the right thing, my dear one. There is of course, one big drawback, which is that I think your mother may want us to take some of her furniture, and perhaps even expect me to keep some of the house as she has it at the moment. But I must make it my own, after all that is the joy of having a house – to make it essentially a creation of one's own - shared with a husband of course!!! However, this is a minor detail and as I am getting to know and understand your mother so much better, I'm sure we can sort that out!

I already wrote of my joy and great happiness when I returned from Bournville yesterday to find the brocade had arrived. I could really hardly believe it and looked at the parcel and examined it a long time before opening it. There was your dear handwriting and an English post mark, which made my heart miss many beats, I can tell you! Dearest, I am quite in love with it; such exquisite and delicate colouring. It will look lovely made into a dress, and I hope one day in the not too distant future, you will see me wearing it. [....] It is so lovely. Many, many thanks for choosing it and buying me such a lovely gift. It is especially exciting to receive it now, when we had both thought it might be lost at sea.

I told you that Angela had written a very long letter, giving me recent news of the Unit's plans for you as well as sending copies of your reports to the Square. I laugh at A when she says - "We don't usually send them out, but I do think it is different in your case!" I feel <u>most</u> honoured! Joking aside, I must say she has gone to a lot of trouble to give me particulars, and I am more than grateful. It is, of course, exactly what I've wanted ever since you departed. Reading through the many reports, has helped me to understand so much more clearly the work you are doing, and the difficulties you are facing.

I have read them all with the greatest of interest, and immediately feel more closely in touch with you. I have found the ones on the Poles in Persia intensely interesting, especially as I haven't yet received your long letter about that trip. They must have meant hours of work and your precious time and I honestly don't know how you manage to do anything else, besides travelling and writing to me. Your letters are doubly precious to me now. Darling of my heart, I do thank you for all the trouble you put into writing me such long and delightful letters. And I do love to get them and appreciate them more than I can tell you. They are meat and drink to me as I so long for news of you. Bless you for loving me so dearly, and for being what you are, my dear darling Ralph.

Sometimes I feel so very lucky, and in thinking back to the times when I have written to you saying I was depressed, I now feel ashamed that I have ever grumbled. I count my many blessings – so many I have – especially our two dear children. God knows they can be rascals and diffcult at times, but they are darlings and I love them very dearly. How I long for you to share them with me. I do pray you may come back soon, soon, soon.

It is now 10.45pm and W&L have returned and Llew has a call out, and I must get the children's drinks ready for the morning.

More tomorrow. Good night my sweet one.

Continued....Saturday 2.0pm

Ever since you went away, I have disliked weekends. I suppose one reason is that I never get any letters at weekends! Your letters always seem to arrive at the beginning of the week. When we were at home, I always loved the weekends, because you were with me and I had your companionship.

I think I mentioned in my AMLC that your mother wants me and the children to go to Fairbourne with her for 2 weeks in June. She telephoned me yesterday to see whether I would consent to D missing school for a fortnight. I gather she is writing to Wilfred Southall to see whether it is possible for us to go there. I had rather given up the whole idea of going away, as it didn't seem easy to find a hotel or farm, and it is rather a strain taking a child away at Antony's age, especially as he gets so sick when travelling. Win says that Priscilla who was also car sick, was never sick in a train, so perhaps A would be alright too. But I don't mind as long as the children really benefit from the sea air. [....] I wonder how your mother and I would get on together for 2 weeks. We do understand each other better now but...?!

I find it rather difficult writing when I don't know if and when you will ever get my letters. I'm still sending to India and hope someday you will receive them and that all I say won't seem too stale and dull and uninteresting. Of course, by the time you receive this, we may have had our holiday at Fairbourne and be back here again!

David adores writing letters to you, which he does while he is resting after lunch. He writes them entirely alone, without any help, and even though the spelling is sometimes wrong, I know you will understand them. He loves you so dearly and is continually talking of you and asking questions about your travels and what you are doing etc.

He does long for your companionship. I can give him so much up to a point, but you could give him so much more, and as he grows older, the more he needs you. Everybody falls for his charm, and he is so friendly and spontaneous in his talk. Antony is a great talker too now! He is a jolly child with a great sense of fun. He and D are becoming great friends and play together well, except for the fact that D bosses him about rather, but I suppose the elder is always inclined to dominate the others. David is thrilled to think he may be going to the seaside. I don't think he remembers our holiday in Swalecliffe[2], as he wasn't quite two when we went there. [....]

I really must finish now my sweetheart. Antony says he has a tummy ache and is rather miserable. He will liven up again soon and by bedtime will be so rowdy again, bouncing up and down. I'm always telling David that they get far too bouncy before bedtime!!

As always dearest husband, I am just longing for that day when we meet and can all be together and be one united family. I ask God to bless you and guide you and watch over you in your difficult work. Oh how I love you my dear. Ever your devoted and adoring wife Joan.

My father, unable to get a flight to Jerusalem, decides to drive there instead, taking Gilbert Legg along as companion and to assist, which turns out to be a wise move, in view of a very bad journey, in the course of which everything went wrong mechanically that possibly could! He managed to get a room staying in the Eden Hotel, but it turns out to be a mixed blessing, as he has to share with two other officers, who keep him awake as they noisily made heavy weather of late night sex with a less than eager young WRVS lady.

Thursday, April 29th 1943 – Jerusalem (37)

My dearest Joan

In the end I wasn't able to arrange a flight up to Jerusalem, so I decided to drive up with another one of our chaps, Gilbert Legg. And I am glad I did, as he has not only helped with the driving, but been a great support during a really shockingly bad journey. We made Ismailia alright and spent the night there. But yesterday we crossed the canal and had scarcely gone 30 miles when a back wheel started to come off. We put that right as best we could, and then blow me, our back axle broke. I left Gilbert to cope with the car and managed to cadge a lift with a Major who happened to be going to Jerusalem too.

As if our troubles weren't enough, his car then developed carburettor trouble, before breaking its universal joint and finally passing out altogether! A breakdown van took us in to a repair station, but they said they could do nothing. So we proceeded in the breakdown van with the car in tow at about 10mph, with 200 miles still to go. We stopped anything that passed, and after a while got a lift in a staff car for a few miles. Fortunately, the Major was a forceful man used to getting his way, and when the staff car reached its destination, he ordered the regiment to take us on in one of their trucks for another 50 miles.

Meanwhile he had phoned ahead to Jerusalem and arranged for a truck to come out and meet us. Useful sort of chap! When the truck arrived, we insisted on finding somewhere to eat as we were starving, and at 6.30 we sat down to our first meal since breakfast. We eventually made Jerusalem by 9.15, having used five different vehicles and taken thirteen hours. It should have taken seven! Thank God, I have managed to secure an air passage back, as I certainly didn't fancy another journey like that.

Fortunately - as I thought - I got a room here at the Eden Hotel. But it turned out, as I soon discovered, that this meant sharing with two fellow officers. I had a bath and was just going to sleep when the other two chaps came in with much noise and larking about. As I listened, I heard a woman's voice, which I thought was odd. So I decided at once that discretion was the better part of valour, and pretended to be asleep, which seemed an improvement on saying "Have a good time" or "Don't mind me!"

Ignoring my presence, they switched out the light and got straight into bed and proceeded to make very heavy weather of what sounded like rather unsuccessful love making, with much ineffectual bouncing up and down. After a while, she'd had enough, complaining, "it's no good with that other man in the room" and upped and left. I knew it'd end up being my fault! From my grandstand view, it had a certain amusement, but what annoyed me most was being unable to get to sleep! Really, some people have no sense of decency! Tonight I have made sure I have a single room!

Despite last night, The Eden is in fact one of, if not the, nicest hotels I have ever stayed in. It's new without being oppressively modern; it's well-planned and very tastefully furnished, with well-designed furniture, good carpets and curtains. It's also very comfortable and has excellent service, even if the en suite entertainment was not up to much!

I went to see John who is in the General Hospital on the Mount of Olives. It is a really fine hospital and John appears to be very comfortable there I am glad to say, and is now convalescing. When he's fully recovered, the Bishop designate has kindly invited John to stay with him, which will be more restful for him. I was able to sit and talk with him for quite a while and he seemed genuinely pleased that I had made the effort to see him. From where we sat and talked, we looked out over a flowered slope, across the hills to the Dead Sea and the mountains of Moab beyond.

Jerusalem looked really lovely in the fresh morning sunshine, with the green land and the meadows bright with flowers, and we walked for a little round the hospital grounds. From the other side of the hospital one could see the whole of Jerusalem, both the old and the new city, and the surrounding mountains. What a lovely place it is. I am so fond of it. John said he felt a little better and managed to walk back down to my hotel and have some tea, before we ambled over to call on the Lochs. But sadly they were out and so I saw John back to his hospital.

Today I am waiting in the David Hotel, for a lift down to the airport. But as usual there are delays, and with some time to spare, I called on the new Bishop, Weston Stewart, though actually he's only Bishop designate, as he has not yet been ordained, or whatever it is that you do to a Bishop. His predecessor Francis Brown had been tragically killed in a car accident, the previous year. I discussed a proposed joint scheme between the church and the Unit, for one of the Clinics. He was very pleasant and helpful and hopefully something will come of it.

——

I went back to the David Hotel and luckily my lift soon arrived and I had a most lovely run down from Jerusalem to Lydda, the country's main airport.Everywhere was so green, that even the olives, usually such a noticeable feature here, seemed quite drab in comparison. All the fields were awash with colour from white and yellow daisies, to red anemones and wild blue Anchusa. It is undoubtedly quite a country.

Having got here in good time, of course, we waited ages for the plane. But eventually it came and once aloft we flew through some wonderful cumulus clouds, which were most spectacular, and almost made me forget the pain in my ears! Dear love, now I am back in Cairo and I think I must get this letter away to the post. I am also enclosing another piece about birds I have seen, which the Birmingham Post may like as they were kind enough to print my earlier one. I'm afraid this is not a very good letter, but brings all my love. I think of you and the children so much and long only to be back with you all.

I am trying hard to find some little thing I can bring back for David that he'll like, as well as collecting things I can bring for you, my dearest. Knowing the vagaries of the postal system, I send you premature many happy returns for your birthday in June, and you know I shall be thinking of you on that special day. I shan't be able to pick you roses and dianthus as usual, but I shall wish them to you.

All my love Ralph

"We looked across to the Dead Sea and the mountains of Moab beyond."

Photo National Geographic

A rest from the hot sun en route to Jerusalem

"Unable to get a flight to Jerusalem, my father decided to drive with Gilbert Legg (left)
......a great support during a really shockingly bad journey."
Photograph Friends House Library

A long letter from my mother fills in a picture of life at Lea Road – a busy surgery, friends popping in, us children growing up, and a rather chaotic moving of rooms........

Monday, March 22nd 1943 – Wolverhampton (36)

Dearest One

It is 10.30pm and I am in bed. I fully intended to get this off this afternoon, but a Canadian soldier, a cousin of Llew's, called in this afternoon and brought three others with him, so I had no free time. They went into town later, taking David, who was wildly excited to go – how that child adores company! He came back with two more packets of seeds!! As W&L were busy in the surgery, I made some cakes, as we had nothing to offer them. I'm glad to say they were a great success. He has been over here since last autumn and is rather nice. He's aged about 31 and married. He took a great liking to D, who is a charming child I must admit, though I says it as shouldn't! Antony is very friendly too, but from a distance. He gets so wild, he doesn't know how to work off his energy.

I had another long letter from Angela this morning, giving me a little more news concerning the No 1 Mobile Military Hospital Units, which must have driven you quite grey with anxiety. It would be so sad if you had to withdraw because of the problems and people's inability to compromise. I do hope that you will be able to settle it satisfactorily, so that you can leave with an easy mind. It seems that you have more worries than you bargained for, and with so much distance between you and the front, it can't be easy to discuss things and reach a positive decision quickly. It must be even more complicated discussing things with the Square.

I do hope you can keep it all together and not have to withdraw, or that if you must, you have been able to do it with your usual grace and tact. It can't be easy for you to be spokesman for 60 men and to give the Executive a true picture of everything. I must say I think you are marvellous, in the way you deal with everything. You have gone from crisis to crisis, ever since you arrived out there and yet you always succeed and win through. I really think you deserve a halo. I know London has such faith and confidence in your judgment, and in you as Leader.

You know too that I have complete confidence in you darling, and I know you will make it work. I only hope that by the time you read this, that the crisis will have subsided and seem very remote and insignificant. Only I suspect that you will probably have other trying problems to cope with. What it is to be such a responsible person, but I am so proud of you, and Angela tells me that the whole Unit acknowledges the fact that you are the ablest man in the Unit.

And as if that wasn't enough, everything seems terribly complicated regarding India and China. I do wonder if you will go, or whether you will feel it is too difficult to leave the ME. It must also be sickening that you, Brandon and John Rich should all be in 3 different places, so many 1000's of miles apart. Angela did say, that she thought the position of Brandon and Barry was at last looking slightly more hopeful.

On other matters, we have been in quite a whirl today. I told Win that I would move from our bedroom in to the front bedroom, so that W&L could invite friends to stay if they wished. It seemed only fair. But we are in the middle of moving right now, and oh the mess of it all! There is one bed in the front room and Win has put up a small bed for David. We shall be quite comfortable I think. Just at the moment, however, it's a hell of a mess! We're all tired and peevish. We have so many belongings and books galore. D has so many of his own as well, and we all have boxes, and cases.

Poor Win must wish that we were somewhere else, what with our things, and mother's too. How profoundly thankful I shall be to get into our own home again and all our belongings collected in one spot. But that's for another day! At the moment half the things are moved and half not, and I don't' know which job to do first! And what with Vera coming for the weekend, we are all rushing about bumping into each other!

David, of course, is delighted at all of the moving, and so is Antony; they have been very good and collected all their boxes and sorted their things out, which is very sweet. And bless them, they think they are helping, but very often they seem part of the work!! D is developing very rapidly and making quick headway with his lessons. He often picks up a newspaper and reads bits from it. I was quite astonished yesterday when he started reading a piece about the RAF in the Middle East. When we are out walking or on the bus, he's always on the look-out for new words and asking their meaning.

David's teacher told me that she was amused and amazed to hear him say something was 'quite bloody' the other day. He said "Oh, I know it's not a nice word and I won't use it again miss, but you know I heard 1B using it!" It seems he gets wilder and typically schoolboy-ish every day. When I go to fetch him at 12 midday, he is always playing some wild and hilarious game with the others in the garden. They are interested in guns and planes, which is hardly surprising with all that they hear and see going on in the world. Even Antony came rushing at us with sticks the other day, shouting wild noises. He is so full of energy!

It does seem rather strange trying to write news that I know you probably won't read for at least another two months, or maybe more. You will probably receive about six or seven letters all at once, by when they will be so dull and stale. But I feel I must continue to write each week. Writing is a way of confiding in you, and encouraging you in all you do and sending you and the children's love. So, forgive me if I ramble on!

I wonder if you have yet reached Ethiopia. I think the work there must be some of the most interesting the Unit has undertaken. I hope it has been an enjoyable visit too, and not too tiring. I expect you must get very worn out sometimes.

Now for news of our proposed holiday to Fairbourne. Your mother phoned yesterday to say she had written booking rooms at the house where John and Enid stayed once. I am very apprehensive about the whole thing and wonder if it will be a success. Your mother even suggested that perhaps my mother might like to come too, but I don't think she will. I wish she would, as I'm sure the rest would do her good. But she feels that the children, especially Antony, will get to know their Granny Barlow much better without her there too, which may be true up to a point.

If we get a spell of fine sunny weather, it should be quite enjoyable, as we shall be able to be on the sands most of the day and the children will love it. David, of course, is madly excited at the thought of the seaside, paddling and making sand castles! I so wish you could come with us. [.....] Life is so dull without you to share it with.

No more has been said about Swarthmore Road so far. I expect your mother is waiting for Millior and Alfred's plans. I will let you know as soon as I hear anything fresh – that is if I can get in touch with you. I am so afraid I shall hear nothing for months when you reach China.

Tomorrow I am taking David to tea with Margaret Brockbank. Her son Tommy is going to the PNEU School next term. I hope it is a fine day, as it is rather a long way. My mother said she would kindly have Antony, as it's her half day from the book shop. David breaks up for a fortnight today. Next term he goes up into 1B, where he'll feel very grown up.

I feel quite concerned that there is no-one to help with your mending and that you are going about with buttons off and clothes falling to pieces, 'half naked' as you jokingly say! What a good thing the warm weather is coming! Seriously though, can't you find someone to help? You mustn't lose your prestige by going about minus buttons in vital places or large holes in various places!

I think I must finish this letter. I'm wandering badly, and it's not a very good letter. The fact is, dear heart, that there is not a lot of news. Somehow, I seem to make a letter out of nothing! But the main thing is to tell you that I love you and the children miss you so much. I do hope your rheumatism is better now.

God bless you my dearest and take care. Always in my prayers, I send lots of kisses and hugs. All blessings to you from us all.
Devotedly, Joan.
PS.Did I tell you that I had given up smoking for Lent? I don't miss it as much as I had anticpated. I really wanted to prove that I could give it up.

My mother had long-awaited my father's letter from Teheran, and at last it arrives, which she straight way sets about copying for the family. Also the promise of a sheepskin coat piques her anticipation, and heartening news that Barry and Brandon are at last on their way to join my father en route to India, albeit by a somewhat circuitous route (p531)...........

Friday, March 26th 1943 – Wolverhampton (AMLC)

Dearest darling husband
I'm afraid that I have been cursing Llew's cousin, Alan Bendall today, who is calling in most days now for a cup of tea and then stays and stays. W&L go off into the surgery, leaving me to cope with entertaining him, which is annoying when I have so much to do and just want to write my letter to you.

I am so pleased that at last your letter from Teheran - number 24 - (p.402) has just arrived this morning. It is so <u>very</u>, <u>very</u> interesting and I am thrilled to get it. I must say your descriptions of the journey to Teheran and meetings with so many fascinating people, make me very envious. How I wish I could have been there to share it with you. My dear, you really must write these memories into a book. How thankful you must have been to get a passage on the plane both ways, though it sounds as if it were touch and go. I will type extracts from it to send to your family and perhaps also to Gordon Square, as it is such a good letter, I am sure they will like to see it too.

My dearest, how wonderful of you to have bought a sheepskin coat for me. You're a sly one. You told me they were too expensive! A thousand thanks for buying it. I can't wait to see it. It sounds quite beautiful.

I expect you have heard by now that Brendan and Barry have finally left to join you. I do so hope it won't be too long before you all meet up, especialy as John Rich is already in India and flying on to China almost directly.

David said he saw a swallow in the school garden today, but I am not sure he could have done, as March is surely too early for them. But I mustn't discourage him, as he is so keen to emulate your interest, and he loves watching the Great Tits in the garden.

We are awaiting Reg and Vera, who are supposed to be staying this weekend, though I am not sure if they will come, as Vera's mother is sadly worse.

An old chap came to the door asking if we needed any work done, and Llew set him to weed the garden. He isn't very energetic, but goes to it with a will.

I haven't heard any more from your mother about the proposed holiday in Fairbourne. I must finish now and take the boys out for a walk. As always it brings all my love and thoughts.
Devotedly Joan.

And as March comes to an end, my mother - perhaps in anticipation of my father's imminent departure - has written more letters than usual, so that however delayed, there are bound to be at least some that get through to greet his arrival in India, and give my father as she says 'an idea of our home life'. However, as my father didn't yet have a date of departure, my mother continued, as before, to send AMLC's to Cairo and long letters to India........

Monday, March 29th 1943 – Wolverhampton AMLC

Dearest dear
I do so hope you will someday receive all these letters, which I am sending off to you, more in hope than in expectation! I should feel so disappointed if they were all lost. Not that they are especially good letters, but I have written them with care and at some length too, to try to give you an idea of our home life and what we have been doing.

I haven't really any news to tell you, but it's spring and everything is bursting forth all at once. Suddenly, everything is green and fresh looking. How I wish I could describe in detail exactly how the English countryside looks on this early spring day, but I long, as you do, for the country – to walk and walk and feel the warm fresh air and gentle rain upon my face. Today it is raining, but everything is alive and I'm overwhelmed with a longing for you. I have the same awful sinking feeling of depression that I had when you first went away almost a year ago now. I thought I had fought against it so well, and that I could now keep it under, but today it is worse than ever. Oh, my dear how I long for you.

Why is it that we can be separated by thousands of miles, and yet be so bound to each other, that at times, separation is still unbearable? We live from day to day like robots, doing the job in hand, but our real selves are submerged and I know, for me at any rate, I shall not live in the true sense until you return. I am thinking of you so much and hope with all my heart that life is bearable for you and not too complicated. I know how difficult it must be to keep everything running smoothly inside the Unit as well as in your relations with outside. You have all my understanding and support. Do not get down-hearted, as I know with your ability, all will be well.

I am busy copying extracts from your Teheran letter, so I can send it round the family. Don't worry, I'm being very careful. I have read it many times now, as you bring everything to life in your letter in a marvellous way. Your descriptions of scenery and of people are so vivid and real that they almost walk off the page! Thank you so much for all the trouble you take in writing so well and at such length. I and everybody really appreciate it. I think I've had all your letters up to January 28th now.

I think you got somewhat out with your numbering, and until I received your Teheran letter, I thought four were missing as you jumped from number 20 to 24. The last Airgraph I received was March 11th. They certainly seem to be coming through better now. I so hope that when you do eventually reach India, you will find a good number of my long letters awaiting you. I started sending these letters there at the beginning of February with my letter No 30, (p465) and have now sent 7 letters there to date.

The children are very well and full of boundless energy. Especially Antony, who is at a most destructive stage! Your mother was delighted to get your letter, written when you were in Teheran. She has been in bed with a cold, but seems better now. I believe Millior and the baby come to stay with her very soon. Anna will be six months old in a few days' time.

I went to see the film 'Desert Victory'[3] the other day. What a grim business desert fighting is. It seems to me that all the men deserve the VC in such conditions. It certainly made me realise more clearly how the attacks are planned and carried out. It also made me understand so well, what you say in your letter quoting from Mr Colat (p.414) – "It's only when you are in comfort and civilisation, can you truly value life." It is absolutely true. Somethings are looking up, however, as we are now at last seeing eggs in the shops again!

I still haven't heard any further about Fairbourne, though apparently the person in Fairbourne doesn't want children, which rather rules us out. God bless you and watch over you. Dear love my darling, devotedly Joan.

My mother's AMLC's are now less and less behind, as the one above has already arrived in Cairo, but this is the beginning of May for my father, and he has only just had notification that he will be sailing to India, not flying. So he is now doubly busy trying to clear everything up, with an even clearer realisation that the journey will inevitably involve a considerable delay in my mother hearing from him any time soon. Typical of him, having initially dreaded the posting, he is now sorry to be leaving...........

Monday, May 3rd 1943 – MEF Cairo (No 38)

My dear Joan

I wrote you an Air letter last week and posted it, but I am afraid that I have not written since then, as I have been so busy rushing around trying to clear everything up here and see people before I finally leave. By the way, I saw a lovely watch, here, which I've bought for you and will post off today. (p547) This may indeed be the last letter you will receive from me for some time, as I really do not know my movements or even how I am going yet. But I will cable before I go and write as and when I can, you can be sure of that. Until then I suggest that you continue to send mail to me here in Cairo. By the way I've just received your airmail dated March 29, which has come through very quickly. Thank you as ever for writing such newsy letters.

I was really hoping Peter Gibson would be able to come down here before I go, so that we could talk over matters before he goes off to Naples. Unfortunately, it didn't prove possible, but I saw the Red Cross Commander, who has just returned from England and we had quite a satisfactory interview. I'm happy to say that our relations are pretty good at the moment.

In many ways I will be sorry to go, as I feel that I have just begun to know the Middle East, and if our reshuffle of people and jobs goes through as we hope, then we may be on the eve of quite a good period. I am also sorry not to see Barry and be able to settle him in, and I don't like leaving John Rose with so many problems to deal with, though I suppose I am going to have enough problems of my own very soon. Too much to do!

I wish I could properly assess how much I have achieved in the eight months I have been here. God knows I have tried and have worked damned hard. I'm not sure I shall miss people very much, except Eric Green, who I like enormously and has been extraordinarily good to me. John Rose I like and respect too, but he's not become a close friend, like Jack Frazer and Mike Rowntree have, and though I have not seen enough of them, I shall miss both greatly.

Well, I have at last received some travel arrangements and it seems I am to go by ship. So, yesterday, all packed up I came down here to Port Said, to a small hotel, where I shall have to wait, which is always sickening. It is not a very good hotel either, in fact rather crowded and dirty, and I only have a bed in a passage. I suppose Port Said itself is not as bad as it might be. The residential quarter is well enough laid out, and there are numerous old houses with pleasant gardens and grand balconies on all floors, giving the city a distinctive look. Even the poorer houses, laid out I suppose, by the Suez Canal Company for its employees, are in long one-storied rows with balconies and nicely pantiled roofs.

Happily, there is a stiff northerly breeze blowing today, which makes it very tolerable. There is a garden behind the hotel and some rough apology for lawns, suffering badly from lack of water, and mostly comprising patches of clover and trefoil. Everywhere are Palms, Orange trees and Bougainvillea with hedges of a shrub I do not know, and growing in among it a climbing plant with leaves and flowers much like white jasmine, but deep yellow instead of white. As I was waiting around, I saw a pair of Redstarts, two Bee-Eaters and some Doves, and right out on the sands, I think I saw some Whimbrel.

I spent yesterday morning full of foreboding and wondering how long I should have to wait before I could leave. So to while away the time, I went in to Suez in the afternoon and visited the local - very local - picture house and saw *The Corsican Brothers* starring Douglas Fairbanks Jr. It was just like those old cloak and sword novels, with Fairbanks playing a dual role as Siamese twins, separated at birth and raised in different families. He is very good in those swashbuckling parts, and it passed the time – just.

I returned to my hotel and was having some tea, when to my delight, someone came in with my embarkation orders. All my forebodings had proved false, and instead of an overcrowded liner with every inch occupied, instead of a tiny tramp steamer, lo and behold we are in a fair-sized vessel with only about 12 – 15 first class passengers. There are nice double cabins and a good lounge, with deck space. It's early days yet, but it bids fair to be quite a pleasant voyage.

Nor, thank God, is it yet too hot. Indeed I have been quite cold and have been glad of the bush jacket and the extra pullover I bought the other day in Cairo. They are comfortable and practicable and can be worn wither with or without a shirt. I think they actually look quite well. The only fly so far in this particular ointment, is that I have a mild attack of gyppy tummy, the first I've had for ages. This afternoon I sat out in my new clothes, in a deck chair and looked across the dazzling blue sea and the barren hills of the desert that lie between us and the Nile, and as light relief I re-read Sayer's *Busman's Honeymoon*, which is really very funny, and is a good antidote to *War and Peace!* All for now my darling. More tomorrow. Love Ralph

My mother - having not heard for a while, and unaware as yet either that he is about to sail for India, or that he is about to be seriously ill, and so prevented from communicating at all for some while - continues to send him day to day news.......

Wednesday, March 31st 1943 – Wolverhampton (37)

Dearest love

I have written so many AMLCs to you of late, that there doesn't seem much news left for a long letter this week. But I'll see what I can manage, though I haven't had anything from you for some weeks now. The last was your fascinating Teheran letter, which I have just copied and sent to Gordon Square. I did rather tremble to send anything to them, after your remarks about being careful, but I did read it through several times before posting and it seemed all right to me.

These last few days we have had a simply terrific wind, which nearly sweeps you off your feet and by the time you've lost your hat several times and been much blown about, you rather lose your dignity – if I ever had any that is, which I very much doubt!! Also one arrives at one's destination a complete wreck. You know what these March gales can be like in town. They just blow up all the dust and rubbish which isn't altogether pleasant. I can't imagine what a sandstorm in the desert would be like. It must be frightful.

Yesterday, after morning school, David spent the day with the Walker family and I took Antony down for tea. David really loves going there and has a perfectly grand time. They played in the garden and both he and Antony love the climbing frame. Perhaps we should get one as well, one day. After tea they all dressed up and had a very hilarious time. Antony liked the dolls and the pram and was perfectly at home.

You would have been amused at tea time. He had a cup and a saucer – very grown up, as he usually has a mug. Seeing me pass my cup for some more tea, he thought he'd do the same for some more too! I do like the Walker family. They are a delightful family and I hope you'll meet them when you come home. Mr Walker is rather quiet, but most charming and Mrs Walker is an open-air sort of person, charming as well but so natural. The girls are a very good looking lot and David is very fond of Susan and Selma, the two youngest. Mr and Mrs Walker have all the right ideas on bringing up a family and I admire them so much. Mrs W and I have become very good friends, although she is about 10 years my senior.

D is getting invited out a great deal at the moment He was actually invited to another party yesterday, but had to refuse as he was at the Walkers. Tomorrow we go to the Brockbanks for tea, where we should have gone last week, but Mr B was in bed with the 'flu. Then on Saturday he is going to another birthday party and yet another one on April 13. He just loves going out. Term finished a week today on the 7th.

Tomorrow night mother and I are going to the theatre. It is the first week of the new Rep season here and they are doing a comedy called 'Other People's Houses'. I don't know anything about it. On Friday I am invited to the Inglis's house to meet Eva's sister who is married to Dick Webster, who knows you. I expect we shall have some music too. I only wish it wasn't such a long way to walk back in the black-out. I wish you were here to come and meet me! That makes quite a full week for me. Mustn't complain!!

I had a letter from your mother yesterday, saying she has written to another place in Fairbourne, but also enclosing a letter from the person who wrote refusing to have children. It seems this first person has now relented, and may perhaps have us after all! I have written to her, asking her whether she definitely will or not. We'd have to buy our own food, but they will cook it for us. One place wanted to charge 8 guineas a week - without food!!

Your mother has had rather a bad cold and swollen eye. She rather thinks she picked up a germ – someone was sick in the tram and the germ flew straight to her! Poor dear, she seems to pick up other people's germs so easily. Millior comes to stay with her next Tuesday, I believe, for a fortnight's visit with Anna. I shall try and take David over one day during his Easter holidays.

I am a little worried about David being rather flat footed and that perhaps he may need to do some special exercises. [....] I will take him to see a specialist and will let you know what happens. I am so anxious that he shall be good at games and fond of them, and it may be a great handicap to him in later life, if he isn't up to the physical standard of other boys.

On the other hand, he is very forward in his lessons and leaps ahead in most subjects. I wonder how he'll like being in a higher form next term? Antony makes great progress and is quite adorable, and is putting very long sentences together now, and talks most of the day. But he does need quite a lot of watching, as he is so full of mischief. He is also very tidy minded and always puts his things away and shuts the doors on the cupboards. D on the other hand is getting rather untidy, but I'm doing my best to train him – (that makes him sound rather like a horse!) But he now folds his pyjamas before going to school and he washes himself and puts himself to bed now with only the minimum of supervision! He really is a very sensible child. He is always saying how much he wishes you were here, and if I don't know the answer to a question, he says "Daddy would know wouldn't he mummy?" So you see what you are in for when you return. I'm afraid Antony calls anyone in uniform 'Daddy'!! But how are you my dearest?

I wonder if you will be in India or perhaps in China when this letter reaches you. I've no idea how long you are expecting to stay in India, and it is a little difficult to know when to start sending to the ME again. I don't think it's any use sending long letters to China, but I will start sending Aigraphs to India soon.

I spend so much time worrying about you. [....] The trouble is I seem to miss you more and more and sometimes it is quite unbearable. As I mentioned in my last letter, I've had the same horrible sinking feeling that lasted for weeks and weeks, when you first went away. Most of the time I can fight it and get on top of it, but just occasionally I am completely miserable with longing for you, and so lonely without you. Pray God this hell will soon end and you can return to us all. [....] You are just so precious to us and all my loving thoughts are forever with you.

I so long to awaken from this long winter of loneliness and to emerge from my chrysalis! I think I may be myself again as soon as I have you home in our own house. What fun it will be to cook and garden with you and go for walks together. It isn't normal the life we are leading. It will be so much better for the children to be in their own garden again and for you and I to do things with them.

Forgive this rather dull letter but I will try and do better next week.

Goodbye dear heart, devotedly Joan.

Chapter 35
My father sails to India
May/June 1943

On December 8th 1941, Great Britain and the United States were at war with Japan. Christmas day that year saw the fall of Hong Kong, February and March 1942 of Singapore and Rangoon respectively. With Burma and Malaya now in enemy hands, Calcutta and the whole of the eastern seaboard of India came into the front line.

By the end of 1941 the FAU had already amassed valuable experience and technical knowledge, which it was considered could be placed at the disposal of the cities of Bengal and Madras. The moving spirit was Richard Symonds, who had previously been in charge of Unit work in London. Despite some lack of enthusiasm from Friends in India, on account of the volatile political situation in the country, Sir Stafford Cripps took it up with the Viceroy on his visit to India in March 1942. As a man of deep sympathy with Quakerism – two of his grandchildren were at the Quaker inspired Prep school, The Downs in the Malvern Hills with me - he was able to explain that The FAU had no political involvement, and as a cable to the Governor said' "the sole object of Unit members is the relief of suffering and distress, in accordance with Quaker principles." Eventually the Viceroy conveyed the message that "it gratefully accepted the offer on the conditions proposed." But as Tegla Davies writes:

"It was indeed a bold move on the part of any relief organisation to enter the cockpit of India in 1942. No organisation, however ingenuous in its intention to give disinterested service, could proceed to work in a vacuum, regardless of the political struggle for Independence. The very act of going under Government auspices, even though as an independent body, might mean estrangement from a large section of Nationalist opinion."

However, India had been a concern of the Society of Friends for many years, and no-one knew the country better than Horace Alexander, who was at that time on the staff of Woodbrooke Quaker College in Birmingham. He was a personal friend of Mahatma Gandhi as well as other Indian leaders, and was just the person to be able to guide the Unit section in establishing itself in the country.

It was not long since Horace's wife Olive had died and such a project, was exactly what he needed to distract from his personal sorrows. With the intervention of my father and his close friend Duncan Wood, long time friends of Horace, they were able to effect a leave of absence for him from his work at Woodbrooke. And so in June 1942, Horace and Richard Symonds arrived in India, soon followed by five others, all selected individually for their experience in aspects of air raid precautions. They soon made contact with both British and Indian Friends at the Friends Service Council headquarters in Itarsi in central India, who were most helpful. But it was felt essential that they should also establish good relations with the nationalist side as soon as possible. So with Horace's friendship with Gandhi, they were soon able to spend several days as the Mahatma's personal guests and gained his blessing for their undertaking.

Although everywhere they encountered cries of 'Quit India', as they came in a spirit of service, everywhere there was a welcome for them. Their reception and the co-operation from Indian voluntary societies was quite remarkable, and when it was known that they were not connected to the government and that they were respected by prominent Indian figures, they were received with confidence, and before long cables were being sent to London for reinforcements.

Richard Symonds became advisor to the Commander of fighting house fires, while Horace had the wider responsibility of making contacts and new friendships and steering the boat through troubled waters.

Soon files wrapped in red tape began to be moved into the office in 1 Upper Wood Street, Calcutta, into which the Unit had now moved. The office also became a base for many of the China Convoy section en route to China, who were often temporarily delayed there, and provided welcome extra help for the increasing work in India. By December 1942 the ARP services were also called in to deal with a series of devastating night raids with some hundreds of casualties.

Meanwhile, the political situation had worsened with the national party threatening disobedience, and before long Gandhi and those following him were arrested. Gandhi began one of his many fasts and eventually it was agreed that Horace should pay him a visit. He stayed in Poona until the end of the fast, which was the last contact they had with leading figures until well into September 1943. At this stage the Unit might well have withdrawn, but with conditions worsening from night raids and the resulting casualties, with food shortages and the terrible general poverty they encountered, its real job in India was just beginning. They organised canteens, provided food and clothing as well as distributed milk through the Indian Red Cross. My father arrived in India in May, prior to moving on to China. He had known Horace since his childhood, being an early member along with his great friend Duncan Wood of his ornithological group. By this time my father was already beginning to show signs of the debilitating illness that he had contracted in Ethiopia and which beset him for the next few months.

Horace Alexander (1889 - 1989)   Richard Symonds (1918 - 2006)
"Together, they were the moving spirits behind the work of the FAU in India."

Horace knew India well, and was a personal friend of Gandhi and other Indian leaders; Richard, a Rugby scholar, not long down from Oxford, was brilliant with heaps of drive."

Photographs of Horace from family archive and RS from FHL

Here my father writes in his memoirs about the journey out from Egypt and arriving in India at the beginning of May, with the early stages of his illness, describing it as 'a bad dream', which is the nearest he came to describing the truly debilitating effects that he suffered for some five weeks...........

The voyage to India on a small but comfortable troopship – at least as far as first-class accommodation was concerned - was uneventful, except for playing a great deal of very bad chess. I got to know a Greek colonel on board, who was being sent to Bombay, though he had no idea why. I did subsequently discover that he belonged to the wrong political party and the government in Cairo thought that Bombay was a convenient place to send him. During the journey we saw something of each other, as I was the only man on board who made any pretentions to speak French - not that mine is very good – and he had only French and Greek.

At our first port of call we took on coal, and it was remarkable to see the barges coming alongside covered with gesticulating locals. But the speed with which this apparently unorganised crowd got the coal on board was amazing. One or two of them fell into the water, but they seemed unconcerned, and certainly came out apparently no cleaner than they went in.

In India, after an initial period in hospital – which is something of a bad dream – I spent some weeks on the balcony of the Unit's HQ at No 1 Upper Wood Street, which is in the European part of Calcutta. It is quite a big house with a nice garden and plenty of trees. They have furnished it very tastefully and they live well. From my vantage point, I was able to get quite an intimate view of the Section and of the kind of life in one of the better parts of Calcutta.

In this letter written in transit he describes some of his fellow passengers, several of whom have not heard from their wives for months, in comparison with my father's weeks. And he tells how, in the absence of the busy schedule he is accustomed to, how he fills in his time, with reading and re-reading his favourite books........

Monday, May 3rd 1943 - In transit (39)

Dear Joan

In my hotel in Port Said, I got talking to a merchant skipper who had spent the last twenty seven months on a tramp steamer going between various African ports. His was a tale of heat, illness, malaria and danger, alternating with boredom. The last letter he had from his wife, he told me, was written mid-December. What a hard life it is! And I dare to grumble when it's only a week or two.

There is also a Greek on board who has heard nothing of his wife for a year and a half. Neither of them knows whether the other is alive. Poor man. He only talks French and Greek, and I seem to be the only man on board with any knowledge of French, and you know how limited my knowledge of that is. I talked to him, or rather he talked to me, for nearly an hour last night! I can understand all right, but my replies are so bad. But you can tell my dear sister that I have been speaking French!

This is really a very nice little boat, and is not too hot. In fact it is quite tolerable and my fellow passengers seem pleasant enough, if not outstanding. The general food is pretty good - not very good or inspired - but alright. Our breakfast menu, on the other hand, is first class, though it will probably make you envious, as you are suffering such terrible rationing. But here on board this ship, they serve us porridge, fish, eggs, bacon and toast and marmalade. If only my poor upset stomach would settle down, I could enjoy it all.

It is extraordinary how difficult it is after months of being incredibly busy, suddenly to have nothing to do. Of course, that's not entirely true, as I have all the China files to read and get sorted in my mind. But there's no compulsion, and the heat makes one lazy, and such moral stamina as I possess, seems to desert me completely. However, if I devote three hours per day to China and India, as well as time writing to you, then I'll feel justified in relaxing and reading for the rest of the time.

I'm back to reading *War and Peace* now, and it really is a truly remarkable book. I suppose I am about half way through, and am enjoying it so much. Tolstoy makes one think of Shakespeare, and today I read as a sort of comparison with Tolstoy's war scenes, Shakespeare's *Henry V.* The latter, as I think I have remarked to you before, is so much more than a mere glorification of war or patriotic ranting. The whole of war is there, as indeed it is in Tolstoy - its colour and pageantry, its righteousness and glory, its attraction and its thrill, its amazing bravery, courage and endurance - he calls out so many of the best qualities. Yet there is also its folly and waste: the cruelty and suffering, the mistakes and inefficiency and the effect above all, on the soldier.

More later.

———

With no means of posting his letters, my father adds a bit each day, describing how at the first port of call, the local Arab lads manage to swing sacks of coal to each other to refuel the ship; of giving English lessons to a Greek gentleman, communicating only in French; of once again becoming Doctor Barlow advising on cures for varicose veins; and reading a book that has echoes of his own strict upbringing..........

Monday, May 10th 1943 - FAU - In transit (No 39 Contd.)

My dearest Joan

It's a few days since I wrote, but in truth not a lot has happened, although so far the journey has not been too bad, except that we progress rather slowly. At the moment it is very hot, but there is quite a breeze, which makes it bearable. Yesterday was particularly lovely, with bright sun and a strong breeze and white horses on the waves. I had hoped to post a letter when we stopped, but unfortunately it proved not to be possible.

This was our first port of call and we had to take on more coal, which would have amused David. Two big coal barges tied up alongside us with some thirty young Arabs on each. No-one seemed to be in charge and everybody was doing their own thing. Everyone shouted vehemently at each other and at least one man fell in the water. But somehow, in a surprisingly short space of time, they had organised themselves and were working well. They erected platforms up from the barges, with some on board and some down below in the ship's bunkers. They worked in pairs, swinging sack after sack, from one pair to another. And by the end, these Arabs were as black as the coal itself and glistening with sweat and coal dust.

I would not have you think that I am being totally idle. I have been giving the Greek gentleman an apology for an English lesson each morning, for which he is most grateful. I have also made some notes on my time in the Middle East in case I have to give a talk about it, and I've read all the dope on China and India, and made some notes on that, so that I am well prepared. I have written endless letters, and two little essays, but in this heat, any energy is difficult. I have also been playing quite a bit of very bad Chess, which is, I think, a very good game. I'm not a great games person as you know, but I make an exception for Chess.

For the duration of this journey, I have been sharing my cabin with a naval Officer. He is a cocksure, bouncing little Lieutenant from Solihull, but quite nice. I should say that the 'but' in that sentence refers to the first two adjectives, not to 'Solihull'! The 'bounciness' is not his fault! The poor man has varicose veins, and thinking, I suppose, as so many mistakenly seem to, that even if I am not a doctor, I look as though I might know something about the subject, he proceeded to ask my opinion. I felt that here at least I was playing on my home ground. You may remember that the First Aid book we have at home, tells you what causes varicose veins, though I can't actually remember what that cause was right now!

But having told him what I thought the First Aid book might have said, I explained to him that I was fortunate enough to have a brother-in-law, who was a wonderfully clever doctor, and that he had cured my own varicose veins. So I said to him that I was quite certain that if he were to go to his doctor, he would be able to prescribe the same cure for him too. But as he exclaimed in his best Brummie accent - "I am not going to see any old naval doctor. I want to see your brother-in-law, Doctor Llewellyn Rutter," who was apparently the only medicine man for him. So if sometime next autumn, a funny little know-all Lieutenant from Solihull, turns up at Llewellyn's surgery in Wolverhampton, it'll be all my fault! Please warn him in advance!

Of course, apart from teaching English to Greek gentlemen, boning up on India and China, and giving out free medical advice, I have been catching up on a great deal of reading too. This has included Willa Cather's[1] latest book, *Sapphira and the Slave Girl*, which I thought quite good, if rather slight. Once again I tried to read A J Cronin's[2] *The Citadel,* which everyone rates as 'a deeply moving story,' but which I continue to be alone in thinking an awful book.

Ah well, can't like them all. But I never tire of reading Shakespeare, and have just re-read *Coriolanus*, though even I have to admit this is not my favourite of his plays. But then *Henry IV* part 1 definitely is, and I believe to be one of the best plays ever written. I absolutely adore it.

I'm also very fond of *Antony and Cleopatra* as a play, though I don't know quite why. I think it's because the two principal characters are so wonderfully drawn and of course there are some terrific lines. Cleopatra –"I'll set a bourne how far to be beloved." Antony – "Then must thou needs find out new heaven, new earth." And of course Enobarbus' descriptions of Cleopatra - "Age cannot wither her..." and "the barge she sat in....." or "I saw her once hop 40 paces through the public street....." are all terrific. All the high pageantry is there as well as the tragic folly, of a world lost because he loved without moderation – "She once being loof'd/The noble ruin of her magic, Antony claps on his sea wings, and like a doting mallard/Leaving the fight in height flies after her."

But Antony is such a man - such a soldier, poet, lover, yet also such a braggart and libertine. Yet despite all, how loveable he is and how his servants adored him. Then finally the death scene is magnificent – "Give me my robe, put on my crown. I have immortal longings in me." I'm sorry, but it is a grand play. I know it's only a story of a brigand and a courtesan and I am just a sentimental fool, but my, it's a grand play!

Romeo and Juliet, on the other hand, despite some exquisite lines, tends to leave me unmoved. I know everybody loves it, and of course there are beautiful lines – *"She doth teach the torches to burn bright/It seems she hangs upon the cheek of night/Like a rich jewel in an Ethiop's ear",* but on the whole I still don't much like it as a play. I think it's because I find the lovers altogether too adolescent.

Afterwards, as a complete change from Tolstoy and Shakespeare, I read Daphne du Maurier's *Frenchman's Creek*, which I hugely enjoyed. It's really only a cloak and sword novel, but is well written and is sufficiently credible, at least until the end, when it is rather too heavily piled on.

I found a book yesterday called *John Arnison*, by Edward Thompson[3], which I believe is a follow-up to an earlier volume called *Introducing the Arnisons.* They are supposed to be a study in novel form of the nonconformist Churches, especially Methodism. His thesis is, that for two hundred years nonconformists totally excluded themselves from national life, and contributed little to it. They lived a narrow existence concerned almost exclusively with saving their own souls, with the Bible as their sole authority.

He thinks, however, that at one time they represented a tremendous force for good, which in the early years of this century, gradually began to make itself felt through the Liberal party and later through socialism. He now feels, however, that the nonconformist churches are a spent force. I don't think it's a particularly good book, but his theme is a most interesting one.

One catches in it an echo of one's own upbringing; rather narrow, rather shielded from the breadth of adventure, too bounded by a church and a way of thought. It took me a long time to escape, but I have escaped – I think. But it has also a side for which one must be grateful. High standards, integrity and all the good that is in Quakerism. I hope that we can we give that to David and Antony and yet give them freedom? Freedom to read widely and as they will, freedom to leave us early and travel, freedom to choose their own friends, to love at their own liking and when they see fit. And yet with this freedom give them a ballast of good sense and integrity, which will show them instinctively how to use it. I want them to have a full life: friends, country, holidays, reading, university, and yet that they should deserve it and realise their responsibilities. I hope you agree.

Monday, May 17th 1943 - In transit (No 39 contd)

With so much time to sit and contemplate, I think of you more and more my dear, and realise how very much I love you. How wonderful it will be to be with you and the children once again. Do you realise it is almost a year since we had that lovely holiday in Stottesdon and in that time I have travelled thousands of miles round the world, from England to South Africa; from SA to Egypt, Syria, Palestine and the Lebanon; from there to Ethiopia and now on to India and China. And in that time I have never ceased to miss you and long only to be back safe with you in our home once again.

I shall be so glad when all this is over and to be home again, and just to get away from other people, especially people I don't particularly like, and all those objectionable things one dislikes about other people, such as their underclothes and toothbrushes and so many such little things! No doubt they all dislike the same things about me! I do hope you won't find me too solitary and independent after all these months of fending for myself. But I will try to be a good husband to you. All my love Ralph

—

Before my father departed at the beginning of May, he must have collected several of my mother's letters dated April, as in his next letter he refers to my mother being depressed, which she writes about, particularly at the prospect of many more months of separation ahead, as he sails off to India and then China, from where communication is likely to be even more protracted than it is from the Middle East. It seems appropriate, therefore, to include a few of mother's letters here, whilst my father is at sea.......

Wednesday, April 7th 1943 Wolverhampton

My dearest one

I trust you won't have left the Middle East by the time this reaches there, but I am as yet rather at sea as to your movements. I cannot quite see how you can go to Ethiopia and still reach India by the middle of April. Perhaps I shall hear more details from you before too long.

I hate to think of you going further and further away, though I know it is inevitable. I'm afraid I am feeling more than depressed at the moment – everything seems so difficult and the future seems to hold nothing for me but months of separation.

But I shall pick myself up again, and by the time you get this I expect I shall be cheerful again and all will be well. Just think of me and pray for me, as I do for you. I do so hope you manage to sort all the problems out before you leave for India, and perhaps Barry will arrive in time to help you, so that you can go without being weighed down by extra worries to do with the ME.

Thank you so much for your letter written about your holiday in Aswan and Luxor, which arrived the other day. It is so descriptive and I felt as if I had been out there with you. I'm so glad you were able to get a break for your long trip to India and then China.

Yesterday, mother and I took the children over to Sutton to see Bobbie and family. David enjoyed himself immensely and loved seeing everything on the farm – ducks and hens and a goat with a kid just a few weeks old, and of course, Barbara's pony. David had a long ride on it and loved every minute of it.

I heard from London that the Unit have left the Whitechapel Hostel now and have settled in Millfields near Hampstead, which is heaven in comparison apparently!

All for now my dear, lovingly Joan

———

My mother expatiates a little more on my father's letter from Aswan, which helps to lift her out of the rut of everyday life on to another plain; the on-again, off-again holiday to Fairbourne, seems finally to be back on – again! My father has expressed some concern to my mother, over showing too much of his letters to too many people, including his very proud mother, who would rather read them herself than be read to; and so off to a concert………

Friday, April 9th 1943 Wolverhampton (38)

My own darling Ralph

Today there is a terrific gale blowing and tiles are crashing down in every direction, several trees are down and altogether it seems quite dangerous to be out. I hardly recognized myself when I arrived home for lunch with David. My hair was untidy, my face filthy and my mouth and nose full of grit and dust. There was a runaway horse in the centre of the town this morning. I do hate this rough weather – I very nearly got blown off my feet in town, people's hats were tossed across the street and everyone seemed to be dashing in all directions. The garden gate has been wrenched off its hinges and branches from flowering trees are lying all over the garden. I'm going out to a concert at the Civic Hall tonight, but I'm not very keen to venture out, except that I do want to hear the music they're playing tonight. Coming home in the dark with a high wind blowing isn't very pleasant - anything may hit one.

Your long letters 28 and 28a, containing your bird articles on Syria and Egypt, have just this minute arrived by the afternoon's post. I am so pleased to have them and more than happy to know that you enjoyed your holiday so much. I will type them out as soon as I get a moment and send them to the B'ham Post. I'm sure they will be keen to print them.

It is indeed good to hear you talking about the things you love – the birds and flowers, the scenery, wind and sun and the beauty of the world. It is so refreshing to read after having nothing but war news. It has lifted my mind right out of the everyday rut of hurried life into beauty and loveliness, and has brought you so near to me my darling. How I long to be with you and share it all with you. It makes me so happy to know that you were able to be quiet and at peace, even if only for a few days.

I'm sure that it will do you good in the long run and help you over the difficult days ahead. I have only read your letter through rather hurriedly, as I am anxious to get this off for posting. I'm afraid I shan't finish today, as I need to give the children their tea early, and have them in bed before 6.0pm, as my concert starts at 6.30. Everything starts early these days, as the last bus goes at 9.0 O'clock. Putting the clocks on last Sunday makes the evenings so light and pleasant now.

David's school finished today and doesn't commence again till May 6th. He had a very good report, though it says he's not so good with his hands, but is otherwise excellent. We have now finally fixed our holiday at Fairbourne for a fortnight from June 17th. I do so pray it will be worth the effort and be a success. I am a bit doubtful about the whole thing as the trains are anything but convenient, with at least two changes. But if the weather's nice we can be on the sands and it should do the children a lot of good. The only problem is having to keep David away from school, but I don't think he will suffer much, as he is so forward in everything.

Thank you, also for the Newsletter containing the article about Tom and Peter Hume. Tom must be missed terribly by so many people. It seems so tragic that such a gifted person should die so young. I do wonder how Barry and Brandon are progressing. You will be glad to see them and I hope it will ease things for you a little darling. I hope Barry remembers to bring the photos of the boys. I think they are good. I wonder if Brandon is staying in China for the duration?

I am rather coming to the conclusion that it is better to keep your letters entirely to myself, as you seemed rather cross with my sharing them, in case outsiders saw them. But I promise I am very careful, and cut out anything that is at all personal or private. I sometimes find when reading your letters to your mother that I have to censor them as I go along. When I was staying with her and read several bits to her, she asked if she could read them through herself. So I had to cross out several things! I don't really think she ought to ask to read them. Not that I mind sharing them with her, but after all they are private letters and personal to you and me. Actually, she has only read a couple herself, and the rest I have copied out for her and the family to see.

I do know how she feels of course, and how she must long for news of you. My! She is proud of you, but then so am I!! I will take this recent letter and the one from Teheran for her to hear when I go over next Thursday, and then I can read to Millior as well. You really are to be congratulated on your letters. They are so fine, descriptive, expressive, and all that a good letter should be. They will make very good reading all together, when you return. One day, I mean to fetch out all the letters you have ever written to me and read them through in the correct order. One of these days, when I've plenty of time! They tell me all I want to know and I can picture everything so vividly.

Bless you for writing so fully and telling me so much. It is worth all your effort darling, because they mean so much to me and I do appreciate them. Thank you for going to so much trouble.

How I long for you my dearest. Some days I feel life is quite unbearable and useless without you. I miss your help with the children more than I can ever tell you. The burden seems so great at times and I long to discuss so much with you. I particularly miss your good sane advice and wise outlook on life. I know I fail so terribly in bringing them up at times, and I long for your help and encouragement. Speed the day when you return.

I must get some tea, as D& A are all over the table and I can't concentrate any more!

Late Friday night 10.45pm

I'm now in bed having got back from the concert, which was most enjoyable. Malcolm Sargent was conducting again, and Cyril Smith played Rachmaninov's piano concerto brilliantly. I so wish I knew more about music. I'm only really just beginning to undesrtand it, but I find I now want more and more, as it does take one out of the grim present and into another world. I suppose poetry does the same, and we do need these uplifting outlets more and more in these hard and troubling times.

Walking back this evening, the wind had mercifully dropped a little and it was quite pleasant, with a beautiful, starry sky and the new moon looking rather lovely and delicate against a pale blue sky streaked with primrose yellow in the west. But everywhere the roads were strewn with tiles, glass, leaves and branches and many trees down altogether. It really has been a terrific gale.

Antony's cold has been rather troublsome today and I've had to run round with a handkerchief all day. Both D&A have had coughs, but they seem fairly cheerful and lively. We've quite settled in the front bedroom now, and David says he prefers it, as he can see the buses better, also he likes his little bed, which he says is so cosy. It's not really such a pleasant room, but we manage very well and it's easier to keep clean.

I've not read much lately but try and read The New Statesman and the Birmingham Post and Chronicle besides other weeklys and any books W&L may have. I read that things are looking a little better in Tunisia, but I do so long for the end of this war. And I live only for your return.

Always remember I have complete faith in you. Forgive me but my pen has run out and this pencil I'm using instead is now very blunt!!

God bless you my sweet, ever your adoring Joan.

———

One of the mysteries of Barry's and Brandon's arrival or non arrival in Cairo, is partially solved in Barry's (Michael Barratt Brown) autobiography 'Seekers', where he explains – "The journey to the Middle East from London was surprising – to Edinburgh, round Scotland, through the Sound of Mull…..to join a convoy across the Atlantic to New York harbour. There we joined another convoy via Pernambuco, Brazil to pick up fresh fruit, and back across the Atlantic to Freetown on the African coast. Brandon tried to use his influence to fly on direct to Cairo, but this proved impossible, so we made our way to Cape Town. Eventually we managed to reach Durban, and thence by flying boat to Cairo!" Quite why they took such a circuitous route is never explained, nor indeed have I discovered from books, letters or descendants, why Brandon went to China by way of Cairo, instead of via Rangoon as others had done. It has echoes of G K Chesterton's "the night we went to Birmingham by way of Beachy Head."!

Actually, my father left Cairo before they arrived, and only met up with Brandon when he got to China. MBB stayed in Cairo as Relief Officer, working with the Middle East Relief and Refugee Administration (MERRA), to organize opportunities for Greek and Polish refugees.

But in this letter from April 1943, my mother is still assuming that my father is patiently awaiting their arrival in Cairo. Otherwise life rolls on – birthday parties, visits to Granny, fingers cut….and when will you get to China!!.....

Wednesday, 14th April 1943 – Wolverhampton (39)

Darling beloved one

I expect by now you are back from Ethiopia and awaiting the arrival of Barry and Brandon. I hope before too long to get an AG or AMLC telling me of your visit. I long to know so much. I think AMLCs get through much quicker than the AGs. I wonder if there is an AMLC service to India and I wonder what the mail too and from China is like. I fear that I shan't hear back at all once you get there. Do you yet know how long you expect to be away in China?

I wonder so much where you will be when this letter eventually reaches you. India or China? My goodness, by the end of it all, you will have travelled so much and met so many people. I hope that it will cheer you up a bit to meet your old friends. And I hope you haven't been weighed down by too many difficulties and problems. I am afraid that China has been one huge problem for the Unit, but everyone at the Square has great faith that you are the one man who can sort it out.

We are enjoying a lovely spell of warm weather here at the moment. Yesterday was just like summer: glorious sunshine and so warm. Today, though it has been raining a little, it has freshened everything, and it is still mild and pleasant. The garden is really quite gay with the flowering trees – the Japanese Cherry is perfect and covered with blossom. Also the prunus, lilac, white and mauve and the forsythia are still lovely and lots of primroses and primulas are now out as well. In Kipling's words such 'glory in the garden' - which you would love.

Today, Antony has been a real scamp, and if I don't watch him carefully he would pick all the flowersl! He's such a darling, but a real handful. Last Sunday he had an unfortunate accident. He and David were playing in the garden and A picked up a brick and suddenly fell cutting his finger very badly. He's been very brave about it, having it dressed, but Llew says it will take some time to heal.

Yesterday, David went to a birthday party and had a perfectly lovely time. He came home filthy from playing in the garden, bringing a parcel of chocolate and a little book and a packet of seeds. He said the birthday cake had a white and mauve icing with chocolate inside! It was quite a long way to get there, on two buses, and then later fetching him back again at 6.15. I had put A to bed, but he doesn't like being left at home when D goes out and says "Antony too". He enjoys going out as well!

Tomorrow D and I go to Swarthmore Road for the day. We shall go early in the morning after breakfast, because we have to leave fairly early as the buses are so crowded. I have promised D he can wear his new suit. He looks an angel in it and so grown up! He has a school badge on the pocket and a school tie. I wish you could see him. He is adorable.

I was interested to hear him read some of 'Alice in Wonderland' to me while I was changing yesterday. He is making great headway with reading and puts lots of expression into it. I never cared that much for Alice as a child, and David doesn't like the illustrations much. Perhaps he's still a little young for it.

I wonder if you have heard from Dick, and whether he is enjoying his job? Does he expect to stay in India after the war? Or is he looking forward to returning home? There will be so much to talk about when you meet up with him and Horace. I do wish I could be with you and share in all your adventures. You will be a man of the world, so rich in experience when you return and I fear I shall have stood still and stagnated the while. I do hope I won't seem dull with nothing to talk about except the children and the house!

Reading is really the only way I have of enriching my mind, and I have been reading Charles Graves 'A Londoner's Life', which is a diary of the war so far. It's mixed with his personal and poilitical views and is quite interesting. He was a war correspodent in France before Dunkirk.

I do wonder very much what Jeph and Margaret are doing now that they have left Barnt Green. I haven't heard a word and I've no idea where they are. I don't think I told you that the Holdings have a fourth son!!

Do you know it's' just 10 years since I sailed for Egypt and Syria. What a lot of water has flowed under the bridge since then. I was 18 - what a babe, but I did enjoy it! My first trip and experience of travel.

I'm afraid this isn't a very interesting letter, but there's no very interesting news at the moment. I'll try and do better next time. I do miss you so much my dearest. How sweet life will be when you are here home with us all again. God bless you always. All three of us send you love and kisses.
Always your loving Joan.

———

My mother may think her letters are dull and by comparison uninteresting, but my father makes it quite clear that they are just what he needs and wants to hear – news of life at home and of his children. And this due to his developing illness, is the last letter from him for some time ....

Monday May 24th 1943 – In transit (No 39 final)

My dearest Joan,
I'm sorry that you have been feeling so down of late. I appreciate only too well how difficult and often dull and tiring life must be for you, and that my life must seem much more exciting. But I have such confidence in you my dear heart. I do sympathise, and I know that of the two of us, it is you that has much the most difficult of our jobs. I fear life must often get you down, but know that you are constantly in my thoughts and prayers. I do admire you so much, for the way you carry on and look after the boys.

Please thank David for his lovely letters and tell him I am delighted and proud of his excellent school report. I am concerned that he has been having so much trouble with his feet and legs and now with measles too. It must have been such an extra trial for you.

Thank you so much for your marvellous letters. All the trouble you take in writing them is amply repaid by the pleasure they have given me, especially now. Thank you so much; they tell me all that I want to know and it is sweet of you to write at such length when you have so little time in which to do so.

How I miss being in England at this time of year. The bluebells, beech trees, lilac and laburnum, and the garden coming into glory. Do you remember when we were in Dunster in May time, and the wallflowers in the garden there, and all the green of the young leaves and just you and I. Do you remember Ewyas Harold and the roses and the Curlews calling out... "My heart remembers how..." Yes, we have lived, but how I long to do it all again.

There seems some chance of posting this on board which will go from our next port of call, though God knows when or if you'll get it. So I'll close the letter and seal it up for now to make sure it catches the post. As ever it carries all my love to you and the children and to wish you all happiness on your birthday. I shall be thinking so much of you on that day and wishing I could share it with you….may we be together this time next year.
Always your loving Ralph.

With my father in transit and post taking an even more indeterminate time to reach its destination, my mother is increasingly frustrated for lack of knowledge – not knowing how he is, or where he is. All she can do is write and hope that one day her letters will reach my father, and sooner or later she will receive news from him of his plans……….

Tuesday, 23rd April 1943 – Wolverhampton (40)

Dearest heart
I am so longing for a letter or Airmail letter card from you. I long to hear news of your visit to Ethiopia and how you are feeling – tired or depressed or fairly happy? I just wonder what you are doing and thinking since your return, and what your future plans are, both in the short run and in the more distant future. So much I long to know. The last letter I received was March 29th, [p485] which now seems an eternity ago.

It is now 10.0pm and I am in bed! It is just dusk and though it seems early to come to bed, I was very tired and thought I would like to be in bed where I can be alone with you in my thoughts. I write more easily when I am quiet and can collect my thoughts together. So often with the rush of the day's activities, I find it difficult tio concentrate and write a half sensible letter.

Like you I have been thinking about and reliving our last holiday together before you left England, when the whole countryside was so beautiful, and we rejoiced in the wonder of an English spring. I can still see those lovely Shropshire lanes and the views for miles around; the chestnut trees and beeches in all their beauty, and the cowslips and primroses everywhere; and then in the evening being together, reading or talking. How I ache for that to happen again - just you and me alone. I often feel so lonely without you.

Millior and Anna return to London tomorrow, and I know your mother will miss them very much. She is overjoyed with Anna – a little grand daughter at last. David is very fond of his granny too, and never wants to leave her. I think he partly hates to think of her being alone (except for Lydia). He is often asking me if she is lonely.

This afternoon David has had Susan and Selma Walker over to tea. It was a most rowdy party and Antony contributed his full share of the noise and fun! I played lots of games with them – rounders, french cricket, and hide and seek. Antony is so funny, as he is quite determined he's not going to be left out of anything, and trots around with the rest, doing his best to join in their games. He is full of devilment and mischief. When we were playing hide and seek, everyone was found except Antony. I called and called, but couldn't find him. Finally I called "Where are you Antony", and a voice answered "Don't know!" He had somehow got into the surgery, and was sitting on a chair in the Examination Room! He thought it was a huge joke!

David is going out to tea again tomorrow with a boy who is staying up the road. He went there last Saturday and came back looking rather red and guilty. He had a huge tear in his trousers! I think he thought I would scold him, but I wasn't cross, as it was obviously an accident, and he is usually very careful with his clothes.

You will see a big change in him. He's getting much more wild and noisy, which is healthy, but he's sensible and independent and adores company and going out. He doesn't mind about me, which I am pleased about. It shows he is developing along the right lines. He's a dear child.

I took him to the Dentist on Friday and he had a filling done, which he took quite in his stride. He carefully asked about each instrument, to make sure exactly what the Dentist was going to do. But I think what pleased him most was the Dentist admiring his new grey suit. He was really proud of that!!

Last Thursday mother and I went to the theatre to see 'Pride and Prejudice'. It wasn't particularly well done, but it was quite charming in its way. It's actually rather intriguing in these troubled days to realise how people lived in Jane Austen's time. To think people could be so occupied with such trivial and yet to them important things – the gossip, and finding a husband, the social round and dressing up. This wasn't the best production ever, but it reminded me of that heavenly weekend when I came up to London and you and I and Frank Westlake went to see the same play.....and that production really was beautifully done. I wonder if you have managed to see anything at all recently.

I've been reading Siegfried Sassoon's autobiography, "The Weald of Youth", which I'm quite enjoying, but find some of it heavy going. I don't think his style of writing and expressing himself, always make for easy reading.

But it's late now and I am falling asleep, so I shall say goodnight my darling till tomorrow.

Tuesday......

It is a lovely day again today and I have been sorting out the childrens' winter clothes and washing them and putting them away till next year. I must also spring clean the Nursery, as the walls are all covered in the children's pencil marks and chalk scribbles!

Thank goodness for the warmer weather, as the children can play out of doors. Antony's bad finger which he hurt is now healing well and he is being very good about having it dressed.

Darling, I wonder if you remember at the end of 'For Whom the Bell Tolls'[4] when Robert Jordan and Maria part? She doesn't want to leave him and he tells her "We will not be going to Madrid" and she started to cry. "Listen," he said "We will not go to Madrid now, but I always go with thee, wherever thou goest. Do you understand?" She pushed her head against his cheek with her arms around him. "Listen to this well, rabbit" he said. "Thou wilt go now rabbit. But in spirit I go with thee too. As long as there is one of us, there is both of us. Do you understand? For I am thee now, as you are me. Surely thou must feel it rabbit."

The words have given me comfort, though of course I always knew it was so. And yet, so much of me is with thee that I often feel weak and nothing but an empty shell of the real me. You have so much of me with you. It must be so, and I am of course richer because of that. This is a wonderful thought, when two people are as united as we are, they are bound forever, even if separated by thousands of miles - always one.

I wish so much I could look ahead into the future a little. I do wonder what this time next year will bring along, and what we shall be doing. Will the war be over, or still dragging endlessly on and on? Will you be at home or still far away? If only I could make some plans. Everything seems just a dead end at the moment.

Your mother has suggested that if she moves in the autumn – that is if Millior and Alfred find a house suitable – that I move to Swarthmnore Road, as it will be so difficult to store her furniture, and also if she lets the house unfurnished, she can't easily turn people out. But she doesn't feel she wants to let the house furnished just to anyone. It is difficult to know quite what to do for the best.

Of course, if you should return in the autumn, it would be heavenly to make a home for you. And of course, the question of your mother's furniture won't really be a problem. If she takes what she'll need for her rooms with M&A in London, then after the war, the rest can be divided between the family, and we can start to get our own furniture then. Your mother doesn't want to discuss it with everyone at the moment, in case it gets back to Cousin Edward.

Personally, I feel it would be better to tell them our plans now in a tactful way. Of course everything is unsettled, as M&A may not be able to find a suitable house. Are you any wiser as to your plans for the autumn? I wish I knew more.

I have just this minute received a note from the B'ham Post. They have kept both your birds articles - Birds in Egypt, and Birds in Syria - though the Editor says the Syrian one is quite long, and may have to be cut down because of shortage of space. But they hope to use both soon. I'll keep an eye out for them.

Every day Llew's surgeries seem to get longer, booking in more and more maternity cases. People talk about the decline in the birth rate, but it seems to me to be on the increase in most places, especially where there are troops stationed!

W& L go to Criccieth for a week from the last Wednesday in May to the 1st of June. My mother said she may have her holiday that week too, but she has definietly decided that it is better both Grannies do not come to Fairbourne. I think she's is probably right, but I do wish mother would get a holiday, as she badly needs one. However, she keeps well and is a wonderful help to me in so many ways, though of course, she gets tired.

Reg is still in Essex, but thinks he may be posted abroad any time soon. Vera's mother lingers on I'm afraid.

Well, darling of my heart I must stop now. David has just gone out to tea and Antony is pulling everthing off the table, so I must stop and take him for a walk.

I cannot believe it is Easter this weekend. I really hate weekends and holiday times since you went away. It is so very lonely without you. I wish I could see an end to it all.

God bless you my dearest. D & A send their love amd kisses too.
Very devotedly, Joan.

———

In a further group of three AMLCs dated 22,23 and 28th of April, she reiterates her concern of not having heard for some time, and hence not knowing how long my father will be away in India and China or indeed of Gordon Square's plans for his future. Her concern is that she "won't hear at all, once [he is] in China." Meanwhile my father's journey reaches its end as he arrives in Bombay feeling decidedly peculiar……

Chapter 36
Arriving unwell in India
May to July 1943

[Textual: It is rather difficult to be precise about the dates of this period, as records are imprecise and often vary. As a result of his illness, my father's memory is not entirely reliable, talking of one or two weeks in hospital, when it is clear that it was nearer five. The wonderful Polish doctor's report, written in August, some while after my father had recovered, says my father arrived in Bombay at the beginning of May. But my father's letters written on board ship, before he became ill, are dated late May. Horace's letter is also dated May 18th, when clearly he means June – which I have corrected. Then some of my father's letters from Darjeeling are headed Calcutta. My best guess, therefore, is that he arrived in Calcutta in late May, and was in hospital for several weeks, writing his first letters in early June, before moving to Darjeeling.]

My father arrives in Bombay (Mumbai) India sometime towards the end of May, after a long three week sea journey, feeling distinctly odd. At first he booked into a hotel there, but soon decided that it would be better to be ill in Calcutta, where the FAU were based. He cancels the hotel booking and manages to get a train direct to Calcutta (Kolkota) which is a journey of some 30 hours. In the words of the Polish doctor who eventually examined him – "he complained of severe rheumatic pains in his limbs and a fever. Despite which he took the train to Calcutta by when he was scarcely able to stand and had difficulty eating due to a clumsiness in his left hand."

A Major who had been travelling with my father on the boat, seeing that he was very drowsy and in a bad condition, kindly took him round to the Unit HQ in Wood Street, in the European Quarter of Calcutta, whereupon they immediately put him to bed, pending the arrival of a doctor. The following morning the doctor ordered him to hospital, where he remained for some weeks in a very poor condition as he vividly describes later.

The European Quarter of Calcutta, Upper Wood Street
"The FAU HQ.....From my bed on the verandah, I have a good view of life here, with people passing along the streets and occasional carts pulled by buffaloes."
Photo Calcutta Historical Society

My mother meanwhile, is receiving hardly any post, and has little knowledge of his illness, until she receives a couple of belated airgraphs from my father, which are very inexplicit. It is not until she hears from Horace Alexander in mid June that she learns that he has been in hospital, with an as yet undiagnosed illness. Whilst in hospital, he is too weak to write and he does not go into much more detail until he moves up to stay with Harold and Mary Loukes in Darjeeling, by which time he is beginning to recuperate........

Sunday, June 5th 1943 – 1 Upper Wood Street (No 40)

My darling wife

I am afraid that is nearly a month since I wrote to you at all, and as you have probably heard I have been quite ill, but I am getting better now, and getting stronger. I hope you will not worry about me too much, as in a short time I hope to be able to go up into the hills to stay with some friends for a bit of convalescence. I do not yet know fully what has been the matter with me, but I think Horace was wrong to say that I had 'sleeping' sickness, but it may have been 'sleepy' sickness, though I do not know the difference. However, the doctor says that I shall get quite better and that it won't recur. I expect to be away for about 3 or 4 weeks and that when I come back, the opinion is that I should be fully recovered. What the future will be then, I have as yet no clear idea, though there are certain possibilities.

I am still hoping that after my convalescence, I shall be well enough to go on to China, if only for a short time, as to be so near and not go is a really cruel blow, especially after so much planning and with Brandon on his way. Horace has been so good in looking after me and if I had to be ill, I suppose this was as good a place as any. I will know more after my time in the hills and the doctors have seen me again, and I will keep you informed.

I have had a fine lot of letters from you which have been very cheering and I will try and answer some of them shortly, although I suspect that with the oldest ones, it will be mostly too late to comment on them, but I am sorry D has had measles and that you have had so much trouble with his legs and feet. Tell David I will write as soon as I can as well as, of course, to you, just as soon as I get settled.

All my love Ralph

A brief letter to make up for not having written while he was ill, and to remember my mother's birthday (June 17th) and to introduce the Loukes family..............

Monday, June 7th 1943 – 1 Upper Wood Street

My dearest

Not having written for so long, I shall make up to you and try and write more frequently while I can. There is not too much news except that I love you and think of you so much. By the time you get this, you will have had both your birthday and your holiday. I shall be thinking of you so much on your birthday and wishing I could be with you, and hope that the holiday will have been a success.

I am getting a little stronger each day and will be moving up to Darjeeling in the mountains very soon to stay with a Quaker family called the Loukes, whom Horace knows. He is coming up with me. He really has been an angel of mercy and I can't thank him enough. I will write again from there.

All my love Ralph

——

My father never spoke much about his illness, or told my mother quite how ill he had been. This letter to my mother from Horace Alexander is the first intimation she has of his condition, and at this stage he too is making guesses which are not especially accurate, but at least it apprises my mother of the situation...........

18th June 1943

"Dear Joan

I have been looking forward for some time to the day when I could write and tell you of Ralph from first hand observation. But then when I did first see him a few days ago in the hospital, I was so upset, that I had no heart to write to you at all. Now he is a lot better, and although the Doctors don't seem to have diagnosed his case fully, that really didn't matter much, provided he gets strong again.

The nurses think it was largely heat stroke, and I daresay they may be right. We certainly were worried for a couple of days, but I think the treatment he has had in the Presidency General Hospital, where he has been in a single, airy ward under a good fan, has been very good. Anyhow, it seems to be having the desired effect. He admitted to me today, that he had rarely or never felt so bad. His voice is still weak, but he is taking food alright now, and has jolly playful things to say with that nice smile of his.

I can tell you it does me lots of good to go and see him each day, and know we can talk about all manner of things, including the birds he saw in Ethiopia. I have just a faint hope that we might travel to England together in the late summer, but perhaps I ought not to mention that, for fear it doesn't come off. Once he is really well enough to go to China, he ought to pick up. Kutsing is 7,000ft above sea level and has a splendid climate.

I do hope you and the children are well. My love to you all and Ralph's mother and any others of his family you may see.
As ever Horace"

———

After some time of being in hospital and staying at Upper Wood Street, my father feels strong enough to start to recuperate up in the mountains where the Loukes have a house. It is from there that he writes his first letter to my mother, telling her of his illness.......

Thursday, June 17th 1943 - The Yews, Darjeeling (No 41)

Dearest Joan
I can't be sure, but I think I posted my last letter sometime in May, from the boat, and I do hope you may have received it by now. I think it must be nearly five weeks since then, so I will try and make amends. You must be wondering why you have not heard from me, but since arriving here in India, I'm afraid I have been quite ill, though I am at last now gradually improving. I don't think I can properly cover all of that time, but I'll try and give an outline. Though whether you will ever receive this, I have no idea.

The boat journey seemed never ending, and by the time I arrived in Bombay, I was not feeling at all well. I booked a room in a hotel, but I knew something was not right as I was feeling distinctly odd, and thought if I was going to be ill, it would be better to be ill in Calcutta than Bombay. So I cancelled the hotel and luckily managed to get a train directly to Calcutta. But I had a very bad and largely sleepless night, and awoke in a very curious condition.

I couldn't talk properly, I was seeing double and I walked as if I was drunk. Somehow I managed to dress and made my way totteringly to the dining car, where I put more food on the table than in my mouth. I just about got back to my coach and then spent the rest of a very hot day in a drowsy condition, in and out of sleep. All night long I had peculiar dreams, and was extremely glad to get in to Calcutta at 3.0pm the next day.

I remained fully conscious, but just very weak and very erratic in my movements. By the time I arrived in Calcutta, I was in a pathetic state, but luckily a Major who had been travelling with me, very kindly took me round to the Unit HQ at No 1, Wood Street. They put me straight to bed, and immediately called a doctor. He came round first thing the next morning and told me that I must immediately go into hospital. For once I did as I was told, and remained there for the next few weeks. I had a private ward and it was actually a very pleasant place, standing in its own grounds and I was well cared for.

For the first week or two I did little but sleep. I had violent hiccups, I was constipated, and I had all sorts of enemas and injections, and a tube pushed down my throat to enable me to have sustenance. The hiccups went on and on and on, which made me very weak. Apparently, it is all part of the disease, but I had no temperature and didn't feel ill in the ordinary way. I was just generally very low, and I suppose really quite ill. After about two weeks, I started to sit up a bit and even to read a little, and gradually started to feel brighter. Thinking I was getting better, they let me out, and I went back to Wood Street, where I stayed for some time sleeping in a bed on the verandah. I tried to get up from time to time, but everything was such an effort that I remained in bed. It is a pleasant house and very comfortable and I was looked after well.

Luckily the doctor who examined me, knew his tropical diseases. This was Dr Budzislawski, a marvellous Jewish refugee from Poland, who really was extremely good. He took endless tests, which as far as I could gather, yielded few results, but obviously confirmed what he was looking for and he insisted on my staying in bed, and very gradually I began to improve. But for at least another week, life remained a great effort. Eventually, two other doctors also examined me, and the general opinion is that I have had a mild attack of epidemic encephalitis. Happily, I am advised, it seems to have been reasonably slight, which has enabled me to get better quite quickly. During the last week I even managed to get up and dressed, and have had rather a good view of life here, with people passing along the streets, occasional carts pulled by buffaloes, screeching koels**[11]** and the eternal kites. I will write more later when I get a bit stronger. Thank you for all your letters which have cheered me up no end and helped me recover.

All my dearest love. Ralph

———

---

[11] A type of long tailed Cuckoo found in Indian subcontinent

The Presidency General Hospital, Calcutta
and
The Loukes Family

The main Hospital in Calcutta, where FRB spent several weeks recovering from his illness.
Photo Calcutta Hospital archives

Harold and Mary Loukes in 1942 (left)
Right, after the war: Harold with children Christopher and Mary
Photos courtesy the Loukes family

My father was actually ill for about two months, in and out of hospital there, before he started to get well again, "which was something of a bad dream" he writes. This is about as near as he comes to admitting how ill he was. My father hardly ever talked about this period, and skips quickly over it in his memoirs. I do remember, however, him telling me many years later about the terrible hiccups that went on for about two days and had he not stopped, he might well have died.

He had been told all sorts of mixed accounts of what his illness was, some saying it was either 'sleeping sickness' or 'sleepy sickness', though I'm not sure there is much difference. But for a true account of his illness, I have found the record made by the remarkable Polish doctor, Dr Budzislawski, who was the only person to correctly diagnose what was wrong with him. This is the medical report he wrote for the FAU……

"Mr Barlow arrived in Bombay from Egypt [at the end of May] having come from Africa. When leaving the ship he complained of severe rheumatic pains in his limbs and his body and a fever. He noticed that he had double vision which lasted for a day or two. In spite of his illness he took the train on to Calcutta. He felt so ill that he could barely stand on his feet, which he first attributed to the movement of the train. He noticed further, that he had great difficulties with his food, due to uneasiness and clumsiness of his left hand. He spilt the contents of his cup on the table. He has not exactly clear ideas of his journey.

After his arrival in Calcutta he went to bed, and when I saw him he had a temperature of 101.71 and a severe hiccough which prevented him from eating or drinking. He complained of great weakness and inability to sit up and I noticed that he had difficulty in speaking. He told me that he had never been seriously ill before.

[……..] From the signs I observed, I made the probable diagnosis of Epidemic-Encephalitis and sent the patient to hospital. He was sent home after a week or so, when he was greatly improved but still very weak. All the signs observed were still present, except the hiccough which had subsided.

[Some time later] I found his speech improved and his tongue nearly equal on both sides. The right corner of the mouth was also normal again. He could get up from his bed and walk, but his walk was staggering and uneasy. All reflexes were normal and there were no abnormalities in the deep and superficial sensibility. The patient behaved completely normally, but he realised that he had great difficulties in mental concentration. In conversation he felt easily tired. He also noticed that he was unusually irritable, which he had not been previously.

Dr Gil Budzislawski

At times during the editing of my parent's correspondence, I found it extremely difficult to know quite how and where to place their letters in relation to each other, without interrupting the flow of one or the other. As is already apparent from their letters, the time gap between posting and arrival, between receipt and replying, means inevitably that one does not always answer the other. The best I can do is to place them in some sort of proximity, so that they make sense. Later in this chapter when my father falls ill, for instance, there is quite a gap when he is unable to write, which causes my mother much anxiety, so I have placed a whole group of my mother's letters together, as she wonders if he is alright. It is sometime before she gets a cable telling her that he is in hospital, and then more time until my father is well enough to write himself.

So the placing is designed to give an idea of the experience they both would have had in making the most of each letter as it came, often weeks late, often out of sequence and often with gaps of nothing at all. But above all it is crucial to realise that my mother's letters, replete as they are with the mundane minutiae of family life, are exactly what my father wanted and needed to hear, to keep him in touch with the home life he so clearly missed and longed for. In addition, my father, who was often prone to self-doubt and depression, fed off the constant love and encouragement with which my mother filled the pages of her letters. Across the distance, not knowing when or if they would arrive, they remain paeans of love that sustain them both through the traumas of separation.

These were written in May '43 while my father was on the high seas to India, when ports of call where he might be able to post a letter, were few and far between. So all my mother was receiving were the delayed letters from before he left, and no news beyond that, which meant she still had no knowledge of whether he had left Cairo or not, and inevitably she becomes more and more worried.........

Monday 3rd May 1943 – Wolverhampton

Darling mine

I am thinking of you so much – but where are you at the moment? On the high seas, in a train, on a plane, in Calcutta? I wish I knew. I so long to get further news of you. Perhaps one day soon I may get a cable to hear of your safe arrival somewhere. I do pray so. The last airmail letter I received was written from Luxor and Aswan.

By the way, your delightful article on 'Birds in Egypt' (see appendix) was published in last Friday's Birmingham Post, as well as in the Birmingham Evening Mail on the same day, which was the 30th April. Everybody seems to have seen it. Marjorie Watts (B'ham Quaker) phoned last night to say she had read it, and that she had been thinking of you so much. Their youngest son, Ronald, had cut it out, as he is a very keen birder too. And Cousin Dorothy had phoned your mother about it and sent me a copy, together with the letter you had sent her, so that I could read it too, which was kind of her. I felt so proud of you.

Last Thursday I left David with your mother for the day, where he had a lovely time, while I went to clean up Linden Road, which looked rather sad and forlorn, and in a terrible mess. The drawing room was in an awful state, and there were mice droppings everywhere. I gave it as good a clean as I could in the time. Today I took David over to the masseuse, who gave him some exercises to strengthen his legs. She wants us to go once a week for a month or so. But she was confident it would soon improve and be alright. This afternoon we went to get his shoes built up a bit, to help his flat feet. He enjoyed the whole outing and talked a lot about it.

I do hope you are well wherever you are, and that you are managing to achieve all the things you want to do. I know that you will. This brings all my love as ever. Joan

A few days later, an even more frustrated tone enters my mother's writings, reiterating the 'Where are you?' queries of letters of this time. But bravely she continues to recount the ups and downs of daily life and 'remembrance of things past'........

Wednesday 5th May 1943 – Wolverhampton (41)

Darling husband

Are you in India at last? I wish I knew. I do hope I get a cable before long to ease my mind. [....] You have been in my thoughts and prayers all day and I am worried sick about you, and whether you are well. I wish I could be of some help. I have been longing for an Airmail letter, as it is ages since I heard anything. I live so much for your letters, as they mean everything to me. Life is so ghastly at times, that your letters are all I have to brighten my life.

The children have been able to be outside, as we have been having some lovely weather of late. They both play so well together and Antony is going to miss David very much when he returns to school tomorrow. They build all sorts of constructions to hide in, where they are quite alone in a kind of house that is all theirs! Antony follows David in everything, and thinks he is exceedingly clever! While they were playing in the garden I was able to clean the Nursery and wash all their scribble off the walls. It took me all day. It looked so much better afterwards, but was I tired and dirty at the end! Antony has moved in with me just for the moment, as he is rather afraid of the dark, and last night he slept much better I'm glad to say.

David is very keen on his exercises at the moment, and determined to get his flat-footedness better! He is a good child, and I try to give him time each night and morning to help him. I hope to collect his shoes with the built-up wedge in tomorrow, which will hopefully make all the difference. Otherwise the children have kept very fit, for which I am so grateful, and so far they haven't caught measles. David's school fees have gone up though, now he has moved into a higher form and from the summer term it will be £.8.2.4, (c.£350 today) which seems rather a lot, but he is so happy there and gets on so well, that it is worth it.

I haven't heard any more from your mother about the Swarthmore Road house, or what M & A's plans are. I believe they saw a house recently, though more than that I haven't heard. I seem to hear very little about anything at the moment. No doubt I shall when it is all settled. Later this week a ballet company is coming to the Wulfrun Hall, and my mother and I are hoping to go, which will cheer us both up. We are greatly looking forward to it.

These gorgeous spring days remind me so much of our wonderful visit to Kew in Jubilee year, when we went up to London and visited the gardens. Wasn't that a heavenly time? The cherry trees, the rockery, the bluebells, tulips, wallflowers and magnolias were all at their best. I never remember seeing such a wonderful show of flowers or enjoying more marvellous weather. What splendidly good and happy days those were, when we were young and carefree. Can anything so good and lovely ever happen again?

How I wish you were here to hold me and reassure me. I know you are very busy and have such responsibilities, and our being together again, sometimes seems a million years away. But if only I could plan just a little for the future.

Well, my darling, I hope this letter doesn't seem too downbeat or full of trivial things about us all, but that is all the news I have at the moment. Nevertheless, it comes with all our love.

May God keep you safe, my dearest. Ever your devoted and loving Joan.

At last a letter arrives, but it is one from the time just before my father went to Jerusalem to see John Gough, so she is still no further forward in knowing whether he has left for India since writing it. However, Angela sends my mother a copy of FRB's report from Ethiopia, which is widely admired throughout the Unit.

But a suggestion that my father should come home for a short leave in the autumn, doesn't go down well, as it would inevitably involve my father rushing up and down between Wolverhampton and London to attend committee meetings, give talks and then another sad parting before taking yet another dangerous journey back to the Middle East, without being able to spend much time with the family....the idea does not much appeal........

Saturday 8th May 1943 – Wolverhampton (AMLC)

Dearest husband

Here am I waiting for your cable to say you have arrived in India, and now this morning I get your AMLC of 23rd April (p502), to say you haven't yet left! I hope this will reach you before you do leave, but I doubt it. However, here's hoping you will receive it sometime ere long!

Angela has sent me your marvellous Ethiopian report, which I have only dipped into so far, but I am greatly looking forward to reading right though. It really is a masterpiece and the London office is very proud of it and of you. Angela writes – "We do admire it all so much; not only the clear judgments and picture he gives of everything, but the methodical and comprehensive way he sets it all out. It is almost a miracle to have covered so much ground – literally and metaphorically – and in a fortnight!" Needless to say I am inordinately proud too. You must be tired of so much praise, but I am so happy to be able to tell you and pass it on.

As to your coming home for a visit of a few weeks or so in the autumn, I feel dead against it. So much expense, so much travelling, for so short a time. It would be nothing but a round of committee meetings for you, and giving talks, and to and fro from London, that we should probably see little of each other. It's not that I don't want you home. You know the reverse is true. But on the whole I think it unwise. I would find the strain of yet more partings and separations almost impossible to bear again. If London wants you here permanently as Chairman, then that would be different, and of course, you should come. But to come and then go again, would be so difficult for both of us. Is this being unreasonable?

Everything here is in a mess. Winifred is expecting a baby at the beginning of December, (George was born November 30th 1943!) though as yet it isn't absolutely certain, so don't say anything for the moment. I shall obviously have to move to Swarthmore Road – that is when and if your mother goes to Millior and Alfred's - though as far as I know they still haven't found anywhere. Your mother says very little. I shall hate it in so many ways – packing up and moving, changing David's school and so on, and so on. It will also be quite lonely to begin with, having been away for so long. I expect I shall survive, but just now I am feeling rather weighed down with it all. It seems somewehat strange for W & L to start having more children just now, but that is their business of course.

I had an AG from Florence Bayman about 2 days ago – she is so fond of you. My letter to her took 5 months!! So I suppose I shouldn't complain at five weeks! All for now dearest. All my love, Joan

—

Feeling that perhaps her emotions had been expressed too forthrightly, she follows the previous letter with a quick additional one to try and express it better.......

Saturday 8th May 1943 – Wolverhampton (AG)

Dearest darling mine

This is an extra letter to the one I sent off this morning. Just thinking over what I said, I hope you don't think my words over hasty and stupid. It's not that I don't want you home or to see you. You know that is the only thing I want – more than anything else in the world. But I honestly can't feel it would be to anyone's advantage for you to return for so short a time. But of course, none of us knows what the next few months will bring.

Things may yet unfold differently, and we'll see everything more clearly as time goes on. But this is as I see it at the moment. I feel it isn't a good idea for anyone, let alone for you. It would be so exhausting and tiring for you and I don't think you would achieve much by it. But I won't say any more, as I think it will all soon become clearer. This is just as I see it at present, but my darling, you know very well, I wouldn't stand in the way of whatever you think is right. I did speak to your mother on the phone today, and I think she agrees with me. She also said she had an inflamed eye again. I really think she needs a rest.

[....]Bobbie's adopted child Susan is ill, and they suspect 'Pink Disease' too. I do hope it isn't. I would hate to think of them having to suffer the misery that we did over David. Reg is having trouble with his foot and ankle, and he hasn't passed his further medical on account of it. He has to have an X ray taken sometime soon. Otherwise all is well with him, though he is going through some pretty strenuous training.

I am wondering if you will see Barry and Brandon before you leave – surely they must soon reach their destination. Angela says Dick is very depressed. Ever you loving Joan

In mid June my father was also examined by two military doctors - Dr Love and Lt Col Seaward - who both confirmed Dr Budzislawski's original diagnosis. They added "our examination has not revealed any new symptoms, though we noticed that the right side of his tongue is still a little bit flatter than the left side. However, the muscular force in his left arm and foot has greatly improved. The patient is now going for a short holiday in the hills."......

....and indeed, as the report says, my father, accompanied by Horace, moves up into the mountains to stay with the Loukes family. In this letter he describes the joy of being high up in the hills, near Kanchenjunga; the love and care Horace has shown towards him; as well as the mixed opinions about what his future movements should be..........

Friday, June 18th 1943 – Darjeeling (No 42)

My darling Joan

I am now writing from Darjeeling, where I am staying with a family called the Loukes, who have very kindly agreed for me to stay with them and recuperate up here in the mountains. It is a most lovely place and when the clouds clear we are right opposite Kanchenjunga. Harold Loukes is a headmaster of a school, which moved up from Calcutta to get away from the raids. I feel so lucky to be here.

Horace kindly came up with me on Monday evening last. We travelled by the night train, leaving Calcutta about 8.0 o'clock. It was such a lovely change and would have been even more pleasant if I hadn't got a piece of grit in my eye during the night which made it most uncomfortable.

To get to their house, you have to leave the train at the foot of the hills and drive the rest of the steep rise by car. Over a drive of some 2½ hours, you rise thousands of feet, up an amazing, winding road, running through enormous hills, tremendous valleys with rivers in the bottom, and waterfalls on the slopes, all green with the continual rain. When we came up it was teeming torrents of rain.

I'm feeling a little stronger each day and can now write a bit better. As regards the future, at first they said that I was certainly not to go to China with Brandon, and probably not to China at all. Eventually, however, they agreed that a short visit to China would not hurt after a long rest, and that after that, if essential, I could go back to China, but that it might be wiser to return home for a period of leave first. At present it seems therefore, as though if it can be arranged I might go to China in July and then after that, I don't know. We'll have to see. As you can imagine, after so much preparation and planning, I was very disappointed about it and still am, but I suppose it's no good worrying. I had a bed on the verandah and was able to see quite a lot of birds. It really was too hot to be ill though!

Horace has been very good indeed and could not have looked after me better. It's such a pleasure seeing so much of him again. As you can imagine, with my dislike of staying in bed, I got very bored just lying there, especially as I did not feel at all like reading. But gradually I picked up, and recently have read quite a lot again, including a few thrillers and all Bernard Shaw's plays. He is undoubtedly a very clever man and his plays read very well, but I don't know whether they will all last. Maybe some are too topical. But I think *St Joan, Back to Methuselah* and *Pygmalion* will survive. I have also read *A History of India* and *A Spanish Farm* by R H Mottram which is a portrait of the First World War as seen through civilian eyes. It gives a stark portrayal of the reality of love during wartime and is, I think, very good.

I already feel I am starting to get better. Initially I had been badly affected all down my left side with a minor paralysis, but that seems to have improved, and I am able to talk alright again now. I am also walking better, my left hand seems to be OK, and my writing is improving too. I tell you all this because by the time you get this letter, I should be altogether better and there will be no cause for you to worry. I must say I am profoundly thankful to everybody who has looked after me, and feel almost as though I had risen from the dead. Doctors say encouragingly that it will not recur. Praise the Lord for that good news. I promise I am being careful.

I must acknowledge all the letters you wrote to me. I have appreciated them so much. You say there is not much in them, but they tell me just what I long to know and make me very homesick. Thank you for writing so often, especially when you are so busy. All your trouble in writing is amply repaid by all the joy they give me, especially at this time. I am so glad that the jam arrived, though I'm afraid of late I haven't managed to send any parcels. It is good that David is so fond of mother, and I do hope the holiday won't be too much of a strain for you. I was sorry to hear about D's feet; it must be worrying for you. But thank you for looking after the boys so wonderfully, and thank you too so much for sending my bird article to The Post. I am delighted they published it.

Regarding coming home, I do appreciate your anxiety, but the idea would be to report on my visits to India and hopefully China. It would carry much more import if I gave it in person and would be of more value for the Unit. I must do the best thing I can, but ultimately London must decide. I know life is rather grim, and please do understand how much I admire the way you carry on and look after the boys. I know it must often be difficult and tiring, but I have such confidence in you.

I was interested and surprised to hear about Win's expected baby, I understand how that might worry you and all that it will mean for the future. I will write more about that in my next letter. I am so lucky and fortunate in having the best wife in the world. You must know how much you mean to me and how I love you too, and long to be together with you again. I must finish now and will write more about Darjeeling in my next letter.

Dearest love Ralph.

In this letter, my father describes his surroundings with all his former flair and style, conjuring perfectly the beauty of the scenery, and the kindness of the Loukes family.........

Thursday, June 24th 1943 – Darjeeling (43)

Dearest Joan

Darjeeling is an exciting place, for though much of the time the rain is very heavy and everything is blotted out by thick cloud, all of a sudden, there is likely to be a flash of lightening or a gleam of sunshine. In a moment the clouds will thin and a distant shoulder of mountain will come into view, before the cloud returns to shroud it all again. But often the light persists, and as the clouds lift out of the valleys, it catches the green of the trees glistening and wet, with the lower slopes an amazing purple, now visible too. Eventually, the clouds will open to reveal the bluest of blue skies, and great stretches of rugged mountains ahead of us, their tops brilliant in the sun. Everywhere great masses of cumulus cloud tower up into the sky, white and purple and fresh. Then finally, as though a conjuror has magically lifted a veil, the snowy peaks appear, grand and majestic.

Darjeeling is indeed very fine. I think I can best compare it to a place like Wengen, in the Bernese Oberland, where we had such a lovely holiday once. But it's larger, with a steep main street, many hotels, cafés and good shops. There's also a fairly large native quarter, with knickknacks for sale, ponies to ride and even cinemas. Not bad. The army often sends soldiers up here for a leave camp, and there are vast numbers of birds, though very often I find myself quite out of my depth as to what they all are.

We are on a spur about 7,000 feet up, looking right out towards the enormous Kangchenjunga range, with about five snow peaks in the middle, and steep valleys on either side. The other night the sky cleared after dark, and the snows stood clear in the moonlight. The next morning a bar of cloud covered the lower snows, and at first all was quiet and lovely, but without colour, until the most glorious sunrise lit the eastern snow. Then very gradually clouds started to fill the valleys, until the whole vista was completely blotted out. It was ravishingly lovely and quite unforgettable. I only wish I could describe it adequately.

One inevitably compares this with Switzerland, though perhaps I haven't been here long enough yet to form a full impression. It is grand certainly, no doubt of that. But somehow it is too big, too vast and too untamed. Whereas, odd as it may seem, Switzerland, has more character, being more intimate with its villages more in scale and tamed. Of course, this is wonderful too and in some ways more inspiring. Last night for instance, as the sun went down in a sea of angry cloud, the valley clouds turned golden and faded slowly as the sun sank. It was indescribably lovely; probably some of the most stupendous scenery I have ever seen.

I am indeed a lucky man to be here. And the Loukes family are so nice and are being amazingly kind to me. They have made me very comfortable and are looking after me with such care. Harold Loukes is a convinced Friend, clever and very capable, about 31 and his wife, Mary a little older and very pretty. They have two very fine boys, Antony and Christopher, who are a little younger than David and Antony.

They are very well behaved and the younger one, Christopher came up to Darjeeling with me and I bought him a little car for his second birthday which is in a few days. It makes me so want to be back with D and A. And though it doesn't make me any the less homesick, all things considered, I could not be in a better place.

Harold is full of new ideas and I think it speaks well for him that Indian officials and businessmen entrust their children to him. The school is co-ed and caters for children, who but for the war would have been in England, but whose parents want them here. It is I think very successful, though up here quite cramped – there are about 160 children up to the age of 18.

I am heaps better, and on Tuesday I even managed a little gentle gardening in the morning, and then later went down by car with Harold to see about a train to Calcutta for the children. And in the evening I even went to the end of term school concert without suffering any ill effects. Staying here has really done me a lot of good, both mentally and physically.

I have managed to read quite a lot too, while I have been away, including a Sapper[1] story, Flaubert's *Madame Bovary*, too famous to be affected by any criticism of mine. Yes, I enjoyed it in a sort of way, but I was glad to finish it! I also read a good Penguin life of Raleigh.

Yesterday, Harold and Mary went down to Calcutta with the school party, and have left me with the children together with their Indian Ayah. It is a bit of a responsibility and I shall be quite glad when H & M return. I think I will finish now and try and catch the post. Remember, I love you all so much and only look forward to when we are all together again.   As ever, Ralph

Harold and Mary Loukes 1943
Courtesy of the Loukes family

Views of Darjeeling and Kanchenjunga

Views of the mountains that so ravished my father.

"But often the light persists, and as the clouds lift out of the valleys, it catches the green of the trees glistening and wet, with the lower slopes an amazing purple, now visible too. Eventually, the clouds will open to reveal the bluest of blue skies, and great stretches of rugged mountains ahead of us, their tops brilliant in the sun. Everywhere great masses of cumulus cloud tower up into the sky, white and purple and fresh. Then finally, as though a conjuror has magically lifted a veil, the snowy peaks appear, grand and majestic."

Photos National Geographical

For my mother, it's a time when everything is amiss, with no news from any quarter, making her downhearted. No news from my father, no news about Millior and Alfred finding a house, and consequently no news as to when Granny Barlow might move to London......and finally David develops measles.......!

Tuesday 11th May 1943 – Wolverhampton (42)

Darling, dearest one

I haven't heard from you for so long. Maybe your letters will all arrive together; that will be so good, though if I could choose, I'd rather they were spread out more! I do wonder if mine are taking as long to get to you. I know you are so very busy at the moment, but how I long to hear from you, just to know that you are alright. At the moment it all seems so endless with no end in sight. I think I will send this one to the Middle East, as I expect you will be back there again by August, which is about when I expect this will reach you. It is so difficult to write a letter for you to read a few months hence!

I wish I knew what is going to happen for us in the coming months - with Win expecting another baby, it does rather complicate matters. Mother is a bit annoyed about it, as she thinks it the wrong time for her to start having another baby, with the other two still in America. It may mean mother having to give up her job, which she so enjoys and doesn't want to at all. If I move, which I think I must, it may mean moving David in the middle of a term, as W & L will want to prepare the house ready for the event.

I don't know when your mother will move - if and when Millior and Alfred get a house – but when? I don't know if I want to move to live all alone with the children, but I've found one can get used to most things in this life. I only hope bad air raids won't return again, as there is no air raid shelter at Swarthmore Road.

Then too, where shall I send David to school? The High School I suppose, though I don't know how I shall get him there if I have no help. It's all very complicated and worrying, but I suppose it's no good getting upset about it. Things will probably sort themselves out and get easier as time goes by. I do wish I knew more about your plans. Are you going to be away for long?

I'm rather worried about Antony. He's suddenly started to stammer quite badly, and it's made me most depressed. It's such a terrible thing to go through life, with that sort of handicap. David went through a similar stage, but not quite so badly. I think it's that A has so much to say, and can't get it all out quick enough - (which are in long sentences now). Many people say that small children often go through such a stage when they are learning to talk, and soon get over it. But I'm worried in case he doesn't. I do hope he will? He's such a darling and looks the picture of health. I couldn't bear it if he had it for life. I can't think what suddenly brought it on – just a week ago.

As I have had no cable from you, I wonder if you are still in Cairo, or have you left and not been able to send anything? I do hope so, or I'm afraid you'll be so behind with all your plans, and you'll miss Horace. I think of you all day and hope all goes well with you. I'm afraid you must be so tired and rather annoyed about the delay. Bless you. Have courage sweetheart. All will be well.

I had a letter from Michael Cadbury yesterday, giving me a little news of you. He said they were all so pleased at your exceedingly good Ethiopian report, and that you had been able to cover so much ground. He also said that at the staff meeting a week ago, names for the Executive Committee came up again, and your name came up first. There was no doubt about it. Everyone shouted their eagerness for you, while they took some time deciding the other names!!

He also mentioned that the Unit is hoping to have a lunch at Friends House on Friday, May 28th, for parents and relatives of Unit men and asked me if I could possiby go up for it. I suddenly felt I really must try and go. I need to see more people and it would cheer me a good deal to have a change, so I wrote off to Mickey, saying that if I could manage it, I would go. I should have to leave very early in the morning, and return late afternoon, as W & L will be on holiday then, and I mustn't leave mother alone for a night. But I think it would be worth it. How I wish I was going up to meet you. How wonderful that would be my precious husband.

One bright spot in an otherwise gloomy world – mother and I went to the ballet on Saturday and I was able to forget everything for two heavenly hours. I did long for you to see it too. It was performed by Mona Inglesby's International Ballet[2] which tours ballet around the country. It was all charming and delightful. I could have gone every night during their week's stay, but we only managed the last night.

Darling, how kind and generous of you to buy me a watch. You really are naughty, spending more money on me than you ought. But how excited I shall be to see it when it arrives. I do love being spoilt by you. I hope very much you will soon receive the books I sent you for your birthday, though it's always possible you may be in China by then!

David has just gone down to the Post Office to spend some of his pocket money on a writing pad. You'd never believe the amount he writes – letters to you and Granny and drawings. He likes to have lined paper for writing, which isn't always easy to get. He adores going to the shops and is very sensible when he does errands for us. As I've said before, he really is a most sensible child.

Antony is full of fun and rushes here, there and everywhere. He likes to come into my bed just after 6.0 am. I do wish he'd sleep a little longer though! He wriggles about and tries to tease me by hiding things. He' such a darling! I was going to take D to the masseuse again yesterday for more exercises, but it poured with rain all day, and as there was no-one to look after A, which meant I would have had to take him too, I decided to put it off till a finer day.

I've just got Vita Sackville West's[3] new book 'Grand Canyon' out of the Library. It was very well reviewed and should be good. I wonder if you have had much chance to read anything lately. I hope your sea journey to India will give you plenty of time for reading a bit, and a real rest too, which I know you must need so much.

David and I are going to Marjorie Watts[4] for the day on May 26th. I've been promising her that I would go over for sometime, and it seems possible to fit it in between other happenings, before W & L go to Criccieth. Soon after they return I shall be preparing for our fortnight away with your mother. How I wish I was looking forward to it more than I am. At present, I cannot work up much enthusiasm. Perhaps it will be more enjoyable than I anticipate.

I'm afraid this seems a most gloomy letter, but don't make more of it than you need. It is inevitable that we all get these times of wretchedness. It will pass. Nothing lasts. It will all be months away when you eventually get this letter, which makes it all silly and insignificant. So don't worry. Just remember my deep love for you darling. I am so proud of you and all you are doing. I truly thank God for you and all you have meant in my life. I just long to pick up the threads and live a united life again with you and our children one day soon. All I ask and pray is for you to be back here with us. God bless you and keep you and watch over you, my own dearest Ralph.
I send you all our love, Joan
PS. 12th May David has measles!

And quickly followed by a brief note to confirm David's measles.....though my mother is still waiting for news from my father..........

Wednesday 12th May 1943 – Wolverhampton (AG)

Darling Ralph

Just a brief follow up to my last letter to confirm that David has indeed got measles and is covered in spots. It had to come sometime, and I suppose it is a good thing to get it over. Now I expect Antony will get it in a day or two.

I am so anxious for news of you and to know where you are. I don't really know where to send these letters. Are you on your way? I haven't had a long letter or even a cable or anything for weeks and weeks. I just long for something, to know that you are alright and safe. I think I am going to send letters to the Middle East again, as by the time they arrive - probably in August - you should surely be back in Cairo by then.

I am writing this in the Nursery, sitting by David's bed. He's very interested to learn that you had measles too when you were young. I read to him most of the time. But how I wish you were here to read to him – I am slowly going hoarse from reading!

I just wish I could get some more up-to-date news of you. Dearest love from me and from the children. Devotedly Joan.

At last my mother gets news that my father is ill, though she knows very few more details as yet.......

Tuesday 18th May 1943 – Wolverhampton (AG)

Dearest Ralph

I am pleased to have heard at last that you have arrived in Calcutta safely, as I have been so anxious for news. But I am very concerned to hear that you are ill again and in hospital. I do hope that you will recover soon and that you are not too wretched and miserable. How I wish I could come and look after you and bring you some lovely flowers to brighten the day.

I hope you found some of my letters awaiting you on your arrival. How happy you must have been to meet up with Dick and Horace, though I fear perhaps you were not well enough to enjoy it to the full. David is much better now, and Antony still not yet ill. Everyone sends all their love. Love Joan.

Mona Inglesby and Henry Danton in *Les Sylphides,* which my mother saw at the Civic Hall, Wolverhampton. "I went to see Mona Inglesby's International Ballet, which tours ballet around the country. It was all charming and delightful. [....] I could have gone every night"

Photo Henry Danton collection

In this letter we get a sense of how hard it is to write anything other than generalties. When letters take so long to arrive, it is nearly impossible for instance, to give advice – such as here, imploring my father to get better before rushing off again – realising that he will already have 'rushed off' by the time the letter arrives! She now knows my father is ill, but not how ill; David and I are at home ill with the measles; and my mother is not able to make any plans for the future; and not able to take up invitations from friends, all of which conspire to make life in Wolverhampton very trying and testing.......

Thursday 20th May 1943 – Wolverhampton (44)

Dearest heart

I am thinking of you so much since learning of your illness, and praying that you will soon be well again. Do take care of yourself and make sure you fully recover before you go rushing around everywhere again! A lot of good my saying this, when you won't receive this for some months yet! I had been hoping for a cable, but it seems I hope in vain. Do send me a cable when you get back to Cairo.

I just wish I knew how long you are expecting to be on these journeys. I seem so very out of touch with you. Life is just hellish at the moment. I thought that I had accustomed myself to your absence and a dull life, but these last weeks I have missed you more and more and the ache gets worse. Oh, God! How much longer must we endure this separation?

Some days I feel absolutely at the end of everything. There is no chance to plan or look forward. It is all so far away. I'd love to know what we are to do about your mother's house. I haven't heard anything of her plans, or Millior's and Alfred's plans for their house. Oh, how I long to have our own home, to have my husband back home, and for a normal family life again. I am really sick of travelling round, living in other people's homes. I want you and everything which that means. When, oh when, will you return to me?

This week I am finding it so difficult to snatch a moment in which I can write, as David is recovering from measles, and Antony is poorly, waiting for the spots to develop. D got over his remarkably quickly and Llew says it will be alright for him to go in the garden this afternoon, as it so sunny. He is longing to go back to school again, now that he feels better.

Life has been quite tough of late, knowing you were ill, and with the boys ill too. Ah well, one plus – at least the weather has been good this week! It is such a shame that the children have been indoors during it all. It is a nuisance that D is missing so much school this term – especially as the fees are now so heavy. I do wonder where I shall send him when we return to Birmingham.

I know I mustn't complain. People can be very kind, the Inglis's especially, who invited me to go with them to a concert at the Civic Hall, to hear the Liverpool Philharmonic with Malcolm Sargent[5] conducting, which was most enjoyable and relaxing. It was a very hot evening and not as crowded as usual, but I did love it. And tonight, if Antony isn't too poorly, mother and I are going to the theatre to see a play by St John Ervine, which W & L enjoyed very much. So I have much to be thankful for.

May 21st..........I have just received four letters from you today, which have cheered me up no end, especially the one describing your visit to the Hadfield Spears Section. How beautiful the flowers must have been, and how heavenly to see such glory in the desert. I do think Pat Barr and his wife are so lucky to be out there together. How many more romances I wonder. What a funny time you had in The Eden Hotel in Jerusalem. You don't seem to have been embarrassed by all the goings on! The others should have been!

I really long to hear of your meeting with Dick and Horace, and what the Unit Section in Calcutta is like? Is Dick happy there? Angela says he is rather depressed. She also told me that she is changing her job, and taking a course in post war Relief. I am glad that Barry and Brandon have now reached South Africa, though it will still be some time before he reaches Duncan and company out in China. It sounds as though you will miss seeing him too.

Michael Cadbury rang to say that they have another son – Duncan James. Apparently, the baby arrived three weeks early, and the nurse didn't turn up until it was all over. Luckily Michael was home for the weekend, and had to turn to and help the doctor himself! Heather hasn't been very well since the birth and Mickey asked if I would like to go away in June with Heather, just the two of us, without the children while the family and the nurse looks after Andrew and the baby. It would be nice, but there would be no-one to look after our children.

At the moment I'm sitting on Antony's bed while he has a rest, though I'm afraid he is rather poorly and isn't eating anything, but the spots still haven't appeared. David has been playing in the garden happily, though what with still getting over the measles and missing school, he is being a bit trying at the moment. How I wish you were here to help.

Mother and I did enjoy the play last night. It was very amusing and quite well done. There was a lovely programme on the wireless the other night, called 'Bird Song from a Surrey Wood' with Nightingales, Thrushes, Blackcaps, Blackbirds and Robins. The countryside must be quite perfect these late spring evenings, with the full moon rising and all peaceful, except the sound of the birds. I must finish now and look after Antony. God bless you always. Joan.

A three page Airgraph from my father offering sympathy, love and support as well as reassurance that he is recovering; together with some more definite answers to her questions about plans for the future, including a prospective homeward journey………

Saturday, June 19th 1943 – Darjeeling (AG)

 My darling I have sent you quite a few AGs which I hope you have had. I am now feeling a lot better – the magnificent scenery up here helps my spiritual well-being greatly! And the Loukes are so kind. I am afraid that my news will have given you such a worrying time lately, and your recent AMLCs have sounded rather grim. Believe me I do understand and sympathise. I wish I could help more. I have tried my best to keep you informed, and you know you have all my love. I do love to get your letters.

Two important points. My return is rather in the balance, though it seems likely. But I don't think either you or I can decide. I think we must put the facts before Gordon Square and let them decide. If I do go to China, it means that I will have seen all the Unit's foreign sections, which will be of great value to London if I do return. First hand reports are so much better than the written ones.

Please understand though that the only thing I want to do is to come home. I am so homesick and want to be with you as much as you with me. I know you realise that I must do what seems best. Please don't misuderstand me my dearest, but the best plan would be for me to go to China, return through the Middle East and then home, perhaps going out again later if needs be. However, it's all in the melting pot.

Concerning Swarthmore Road. You must do as you think best, provided that you can get someone to come and live with you for a short while, and that we have enough money. With these provisos, I think it is a good idea and of course I shall agree with you. I miss you so much and love you more and more. God bless. As ever Ralph

"How you would love the markets here."
Photo Calcutta archives

By now my father is beginning to relax and to recover - enough to begin to settle into the family life of the Loukes, and even to looking after their children and taking part in the youngest son Christopher's 2nd birthday, reminding him, as it does, of his own family back home.

He has also been able to take stock of the work the Unit has been doing in India, meeting most of the personnel, who have been kindly visiting him in Darjeeling. He is now looking forward to going to China, which the doctors have finally given their permission for.....if only for a short visit.........

Saturday, June 26th and into July1943 – Darjeeling (No 44)

My dearest Joan

There is not much more news since I last wrote. The last few days, we have been having some really glorious weather, and I have been able to fully appreciate what must be one of the finest views in the world. Yesterday about 5.0pm, the sun was in the west, and from where I sat, I could see the Darjeeling spur in the foreground. The sky was a clear deep blue, with the whole horizon from south-east to south-west filled by mountains. The foreground was full of the heavy green of the tea plantations; the middle distance a haze of purple and blue with the sun lighting up here a valley and there a cliff; and in the distance to the west, mountains in a sea of fleecy clouds, and to the east, nothing but pile on pile of beautifully shaped and shaded cumulus.

But topping all, the whole of the central area was filled with range after range of snow-capped mountains, now clear of cloud save for two layers just below the snow. A totality of white, not dazzling, but pervaded by a soft evening shade, of white intermixed with blue and purple. Wherever you looked was so supremely lovely, that nothing one felt, could ever better it. Before breakfast the next day, it was dazzlingly clear, the sky pale blue and the eastern hills a blue mass with jagged lines against the sky.

Far below us in the east was a mass of cumulus clouds gathering in the valley. Almost more beautiful than my beloved Switzerland, this enormous view of high snow-capped mountains, continually changing in cloud and sun, is unforgettable. How lucky am I to have seen what I have seen. How could I fail to feel better in such a place? The earth is indeed lovely and how I wish and wish you could be here to share it with me.

Now with Harold and Mary back from Calcutta, everyone is celebrating the youngest boy Christopher's 2nd birthday, and with some assistance from me, Harold made him a fine doll's house. I must say they've given me a real tonic and made me feel part of a family. It could never be the same as being with you and our two boys, but it was so sweet of them to include me. It cheered me up no end.

They were also very sweet about my birthday too, and the children gave me little presents as well. It was so kind of them all. Last year on the boat, I forgot all about it. Mary has also given me a knitting needle holder decorated with Kashmiri paintings for you. I do hope I will be able to bring it back with all the other little things I've collected. I shall be sorry to leave here as they have not only looked after me, but made me feel so much at home and part of their family.

I ventured into Darjeeling myself this morning, to see if I could find a few toys for the children and perhaps something for the party. How you would love the fruit market here, with its long sheds, full of stalls covered with all sorts of fruit from oranges and grapefruit to bananas and pineapples, as well as a whole assortment of fresh vegetables.

So many visitors have taken the trouble to come up here to see me, which has been heartening and made me feel slightly less useless, including Horace and Dick Symonds of course, Jean Cottle, Brian Groves and Eleanor Sawdon. Horace has done really well as Section leader, though Richard Symonds has been tremendously supportive as well and the section support for both of them has been most encouraging.

On the political side, though Horace is well-known and respected by the Indian people, the political deadlock has made it impossible for him to do very much. He is very glad he came and it has given him new insights, but I think he is anxious to get back home now, though his departure will be a serious loss, which will throw an extra burden on Richard. It has been great to see Richard again, who remains much the same as ever, though perhaps rather more mature now. I think he has done an excellent job and is well thought of. I do like him very much and I think Horace has grown fond of him as well.

Jean, the only trained nurse out here, has also done some excellent relief work, especially after the terrible floods following the cyclone in Bengal province, near Midnapore. She is very much as I remember her, a hard worker, rather too easily put down and apt to be prejudiced, but I think her recent engagement to Alex Horsfield, with whom she has been working, may have softened her. Like me she has unfortunately now been laid up by bad ill health as well. Brian Groves is quietly and efficiently doing a responsible job in the Information Office, handling food and clothing. He is such a nice fellow, but I do wonder how he will ever settle back to running the tramways system back home!

Eleanor Sawdon has not been out here very long, but I do find her quite difficult to get along with. Probably my fault too. The rest of the people, I don't think you'll know, but I must say my first impressions are that they have all done very well, often in very trying circumstances. But more of all this later, as I hope to have the chance to take a longer look at all the good work going on, when I get back from my long-planned trip to China, which the doctors have at last allowed me to do, if only for a short stay.

I know you have been worried about me, and probably think I'm mad to go to China, but I'm only going with doctor's permission, and I promise to be careful and go steady. But if all goes well, I might be home in September or October. Wouldn't that be wonderful? Horace is being rather firm with me, and insists that if I do go to China, I should return home to England with him though Cairo. So doctors willing, I am hoping to go about the middle of the month. Then spend a week somewhere with Duncan, before joining the men to assess the situation out there. All being well I will then fly out mid-August back to Cairo, join up with Horace and together take the boat back to England. I know there may be slips date-wise, but it would be so splendid. I can think of nothing else. Seeing you and the family and meeting you at Wolverhampton station. That would be really the best.

I have now received several marvellous letters from you, for which my continued thanks. You have no idea how much joy they have given me, especially in the last few weeks, when I have been so low. Regarding my coming home after China, I will write more later, but I do have several reports I need to give to the Square, and it would obviously be much better and of more value, if I could deliver them in person. Of course it would be wonderful, but as you say, I must also do the best by the Unit, so ultimately I'll have to see what London says.

I'll send an air letter as soon as I know more. So now I am rapidly trying to get ready to fly off to China, though I am rather dreading it, as it will involve a lot of meetings. I will have to pace myself carefully, as I still get tired easily. But it will be so good to see Duncan again and I'm looking forward to that. All for now, all my love, Ralph

No further news from India, but David and I having measles prevents my mother going to Friends House in London, which she'd been so looking forward to. However, the good news is that I stop stuttering and David's garden provides welcome bunches of flowers.......

Monday, 31st May 1943 – Wolverhampton (45)

My dearest darling
News is still so slow coming through, and I haven't heard any more for a long time. I rush to the hall every time the post comes and grab the letters, hoping against hope that there will be one for me. I really do hope to hear soon, as I understand that Air letter cards are coming through in only two weeks now. I still seem to be so completely cut off from you, when all I want to know is if you are well again. Are you still in Calcutta? God bless you darling, wherever you are. I pray for you in all your difficult jobs and hope that things are going well for you. I do wonder where we shall all be this time next year.

The children are progressing well – Antony's spots eventually developed of course, but have not quite disappeared yet. He and David have been in the garden this morning, as we have been having the most perfect spring weather imaginable. Albeit, yesterday morning there was a terrific thunderstorm, which dashed things about a bit, but today is almost unbelieveably fresh with garden scents everywhere, which are a real tonic.

Of course with Antony still not yet completely free of the illness, I haven't been able to get up to London. I told you I had been really looking forward to going up for a special lunch at Friends House for Unit relatives and spouses. But I just couldn't leave mother to look after the two boys. I have been rather depressed about it, as I had been longing to get out for the day and to meet other people - people you know and who know you. I haven't been out of Wolverhampton for more than a year now, which makes life pretty dull at times. Nothing seems to be going quite right or according to plan at the moment. Not to worry, I'll recover and be my bright self by the time this reaches you. I'm never down for long.

A few moments ago I heard footseps and went to see who it was, as I imagined the boys asleep or resting. But when I looked, there was A on the landing having dressed himself, with both legs in one trouser hole, shoes on the wrong feet and soap in his hair and all over his face and on his jersey! He is a scamp, but at least it's a sign that he is getting better!

It was 'Wings for Victory'[6] all last week, raising money for more bombers, and Wolverhampton was so crowded. There were displays everywhere, with brass bands playing, and planes on display, and an exhibition in the Civic Hall. It would be the week that I had to collect our new Ration Books from the Art Gallery!

They have been doing one letter each day, and Thursday was the letter B. But of course, there are thousands of B's, making it probably one of the worst days of all! I had to wait for over 2 hours! However, I am thankful to have done it, even though the wait did seem an eternity. Afterwards I collected a new gas mask for Antony, which is enormous and difficult to carry, especially on a crowded bus.

One really good thing has happened though, which I am so thankful for, is that Antony has stopped stuttering, thank God. He was really dreadful for about three weeks, and then stopped as suddenly as he had begun. It's curious that both he and David should do it when they were both around 2 years old. I am so relieved that it has now gone away.

David has been cultivating a small area of W & L's garden as his own small garden, and it has been so colourful these last few days. He came indoors yesterday with a bunch of stocks, pansies and saxifrage for mother and a pink rose for me, which he presented as a special treat.

Oh, flowers, flowers. How I love them! How many bouquets you and I have picked in so many different places – Switzerland, the Lakes, Dunster, and our own garden. I picture in my own mind, so many lovely flowers, and now the pinks and catmint are coming into flower, as we are almost in June.

Darling of my heart, I love you so much, and _so_ much. I hold you close to me and kiss you and love you and tease you. I long for you more and more. If I close my eyes I can imagine you are sitting in the chair opposite me, with your pipe and a book and perhaps a cup of coffee and a ginger biscuit. After a while we shall wander into the garden together, arm in arm, and you'll ask me if I think you are a good gardener, and I shall say – "You are wonderful, but don't you think that plant ought to be put a little further from the pansies!" Oh, for those joyous carefree days when we were young and gay.

I've been reading the actor Esmond Knight's[7] autobiography, 'Seeking the Bubble'. He was in the navy and blinded while serving on the 'Prince of Wales'. It's a fascinating account of his life up until last year, and ends with him wondering what the future might hold for him. I thought it very good. I've also got Virginia Woolf's, 'The Death of the Moth' to read. I really ought to get on with other tasks such as mending and knitting, but when I get an interesting book, I just read on until it is finished, and I can't tear myself away!

Well, God bless you sweetheart. I thank the Lord for the best husband in the world. Take care my darling. Ever your own devoted Joan.

———

An illustrated letter to David from Darjeeling

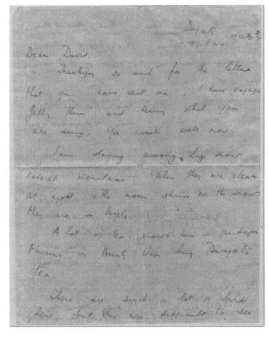 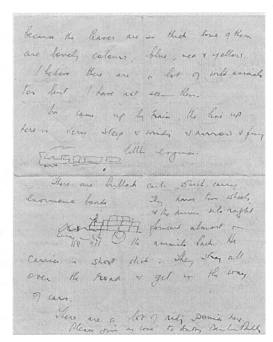

Darjeeling   27.6.1943

Dear David

Thank you so much for the letters that you have sent me. I have enjoyed getting them and hearing what you are doing. You write well now.

I am staying among huge snow covered mountains. When they are clear at night, and the moon shines on the snows, they are so lovely.

A lot of tea grows here – perhaps Mummy or Aunty Win buy Darjeeling tea.

There are such a lot of birds here, but they are difficult to see, because the leaves are so thick. Some of them are lovely colours.

I believe there are a lot of wild animals too but I have not seen them.

We came up by train - the line up here is very steep and winding and [it has] funny little engines.

There are bullock carts which carry enormous loads. They have two wheels and the driver sits right forward almost on the animal's back. He carries a short stick. They stray all over the road and get in the way of cars.

There are a lot of riding ponies [too].

Please give my love to Antony.

Dear love Daddy

David adored his father and would spend hours writing to him; letters, which Dad equally loved to receive. In return he sent David many letters, often illustrated, as here, with pictures of animals or birds, trains or carts, much to my brother's delight. Though no great illustrator, the pictures had a naïve quality that conveyed great joy to the recipient!

My father, always trying to prevent my mother from worrying, is constantly reassuring her that he is getting better. In truth, he is slowly getting better, but is actually desperately keen to complete his survey of all the Unit bases and in particular his promise in his own mind, to complete Tom's mission to China...........

Monday, June 28th 1943 – Darjeeling

My very dear wife

I am getting better quickly now and I am extremely comfortable and well looked after here by Harold and Mary, who are very good to me. I do like them both very much, and hope they don't tire of having me about.

Most of the staff and children are from Calcutta or district and went down to Calcutta yesterday at the end of term. They had great difficulty fixing up the train, and then at the last minute, part of the line was washed away by a landslide. So I do hope they got down alright. They were both run down by the end of term and two days in Calcutta will do them good. I know how glad they were to get away for a rest. I am helping the Ayah to look after the children for three days. I hope all goes well! The children are very good though Anthony can be rather a handful. All this makes me so homesick.

It is beginning to look as though I should be able to go to China in July, though it is not 100% certain yet. I would probably return through Cairo.

I do hope you are getting my letters and Airgraphs....I haven't heard from you for a while, and I do so love to get your letters. They help me very much. I love you so much. Your love, your sane and sensible attitude which you always adopt, is such a help and strength to me. I could not have gone on if you had cracked or grumbled. You will never know how much you have helped me.

My dear love to all, Ralph

My mother has received some cables from both my father and Horace and learns a little more, though obviously not yet very much more of my father's condition.........

Friday, 4th June 1943 – Wolverhampton (AMLC)

Darling mine

I have just received the two cables from you and from Horace, for which so many thanks. I was *so* pleased to get them, as I have been so very anxious for news, knowing you were ill in hospital. I only hope it is really true that you are much better. It must have been wretched arriving in India so ill. I do sympathise and think of you. Are you out of hospital yet? I do hope you can get away soon to the hills for a good rest, where it is cool and pleasant.

My darling, do please go carefully when you are well again, and don't do too much rushing around, I beg of you, please. You are so especially in my thoughts now, when you are not well. I only wish I could be with you and look after you. Oh that you were safely home with me, so that I could make sure you were being properly looked after. You need me to be with you – I know you do. Just as I need you with me.

Will you still go on to China, I wonder? I'm so afraid you will be completely worn out with so much worry and travel. I think you ought to come home for good in the autumn dearest. Seriously I do.

I only hope now that you are so much better, that you will be able to enjoy Dick's and Horace's company. Make sure you thank Horace so much for his cable. It must be good to have familiar faces round you and those of friends you like so much.

The boys are well again, but need a holiday. Well June 17th is not far away now and David is so excited. Your mother has kindly managed to get spades for the boys and I think I can make buckets out of old syrup tins! I'm busy now getting all our things together.

W & L returned yesterday from their holiday in Criccieth, where they had a good time, and now look well, and very brown.

I've really enjoyed reading Virginia Woolf's 'Death of the Moth'. It's a collection of essays and short stories and makes a pleasant change from a novel.

David and Antony and all at Lea Road send you their love. Ever your loving Joan.

In this AG my mother is beginning to get insistent that my father should come home after he has recovered sufficiently, and complete his recuperation at home.........

Friday, 11th June 1943 – Wolverhampton (AG)

My darling Ralph

I am still so anxious for more news of you. It is quite exasperating to be so cut off with no definte news. I keep wondering what you are doing, whether you are still in hospital, if you are really feeling better, and well....what has really been the matter with you. It is all very well to say 'don't worry', but of course I <u>am</u> terribly worried.

You simply must come home for good when you are fit again. This is the third illness in just a year, and you can't go on indefinitely like this. I am afraid that you have been too ill to write, but I hoped that Horace or Dick might have sent me more Airgraphs. I have been so worried I can't settle to anything.

There is so much to do before next Thursday when we go away. How I wish we had already been and were now back home again! I still don't know any more about Swarthmore Road. I simply must get into a house of our own again. Please come back to me soon, my darling I do need you so terribly. God bless you and watch over you. David and Antony send you kisses. All love Joan.

———

It is perhaps worth pausing here for a moment, to consider the question of how far my father had recovered, and whether he was fit enough to travel on to China in the near future. After the war, his sister Millior and others felt that he should have been sent home after his time with the Loukes, and not allowed to go on to China, while still suffering some after effects of his illness.

However, it is apparent from reading between the lines, that my father, who was never a good patient, was himself at least in part instrumental in persuading the powers that be that he had recovered sufficiently to make the trip to China. He was examined again both by Dr Budzislawski as well as by the two military doctors, and it is instructive to note in their Military medical report below, the phrase – "he pronounced himself fit for work."

So, though it is possible that he might have recovered more speedily had he returned home, there is no real evidence that undue persuasion was exercised.

Lt Col Seeward and Dr Lowe wrote on July 16th 1943........

"We confirmed that Mr Ralph Barlow has made further progress and pronounced himself fit for work. He still walks with a slight stagger, but no pathological reflexes could be detected on him. There is still a slight wasting of the left forearm and the reflexes on the left arm were perhaps slightly brisker than on his right side. His intelligence however, is completely normal. It was generally agreed that he could proceed to China on a mission without harm to his health, provided he could travel comfortably."

In addition there are three other letters that corroborate that due care and diligence regarding my father's well being, was taken at all times. Firstly, there are two letters from Mary Loukes to my mother, one in June and the other in July. The first states firmly that it is 'an impartial view', whilst the second says 'from an unbiased witness', realising perhaps that others possibly had some vested interests:

22nd June 1943 The Yews, Darjeeling

Dear Mrs Barlow

You may have already heard from Ralph that he is staying with us for three or four weeks' convalescence. My husband and I thought you might like to have an impartial eye-witness account of how he seems to be. Of course, not knowing what he is like when completely fit, we can't tell how much further he has to go to be quite better. But we can say that he is very cheerful, and seems to be enjoying himself thoroughly, has a very good appetite –(the source of a good many family jokes), sleeps well, (we firmly drive him off to bed every afternoon), and he goes for quite long walks.

His only obvious disability is that he can't walk very fast yet, and I think he feels that he is not getting on as rapidly as he'd like. But that's a common state of affairs when anyone is recovering from a bad illness, don't you think? And he must certainly be a great deal better than he was in Calcutta.

Quite apart from anything else, we are delighted to have him with us. Our two small sons (aged four and three quarters and two, respectively, treat him as entirely one of the family, which in the case of the elder one particularly, means a great deal of bossing about!

[....] It is my small boy's second birthday today – great excitement in the family, especially on the part of the elder offspring. Christopher, the younger, has enjoyed it all far more than Anthony did at his age. Ralph has also been an integral part of the celebrations to all our delight. Funny isn't it that our two family's children should both have the same names – Christopher's second name is David!

I do hope that we shall meet you and the family when we settle back in the UK.

All good wishes, Mary Loukes.

Harold and Mary Loukes
who cared for my father at their home 'The Yews' in Darjeeling
Photograph courtesy of the Loukes family

Mary and her husband Harold, ran schools in Calcutta and Darjeeling, and together they looked after my father in their home in Darjeeling, including him as a member of the family. They were exceedingly kind and caring for his health and were not people to make exaggerated claims of his well-being. Both they and the family remained friends long after the war. Two of their children, Anthony and Mary have been wonderfully helpful in finding photographs from that period........

5th July 1943 The Yews, Darjeeling

Dear Mrs Barlow

I thought you might like to hear from an unbiased witness, how very much better Ralph is. We were very worried about him for a week or ten days after he first came, as we had no medical data about him. Horace was very vague and alarming, and we had no idea how likely he was to overdo things, or what would be likely to happen if he did. But for more than a week now we have been quite certain that he is very much better, and we are perfectly happy about his going down to Calcutta next week, though we shall not be surprised if the doctor says he still has to go rather slowly. Horace wants him to go to China for a very short time, but we feel that it would be better to go for a longer time and not have to rush while he is there. However, the doctor will decide.

You will realise how much better he is when I tell you what he did yesterday. It looked such a promising morning that I got him out of bed at a quarter to seven, and we went for about half an hour's walk to the top of a view-point, and got back just in time for breakfast. Then in the evening he went off by himself and walked a good eight miles he told us when he got back, to our great astonishment. I think he made himself a bit tired, but all the same he walked another five miles this morning quite happily. So you see his walking has improved enormously, and that was the last symptom of the illness that we could see.

We were grateful beyond words for the two days holiday that Ralph gave us when he offered to look after the family. We've only been away together for one night since Anthony was here, as although we've had several good offers from friends, we've felt that we couldn't leave Anthony with anyone he didn't particularly like. But he was so attracted to Ralph that we were quite happy about it this time, and it was lovely to shake a leg loose, even for so short a time.

We left Ralph with a visiting kitten to look after as well as two small boys, and since we came back, another has been added to the household as a permanent member. The visitor is a very well-bred small Siamese, and very handsome, but although ours is only a stable cat, he's a pretty little thing, black with a white front and white feet. The two of them give us endless fun in their games together.

The weather is being fairly kind to us just now, and we do hope it gives Ralph a really good show before he goes. We are both so very much looking forward to meeting you in the not far distant future. I have a strong impression that we have a great deal in common, and will get on well together. I know how hard it must be for you, with Ralph so far away and the boys needing their father so much. My Anthony is playing up terribly at the moment, so I must end here and give Harold a break and make some tea.

Best wishes from us both, Mary

The last letter is from Richard Symonds, Horace's right hand man in Calcutta. This is of particular interest from a health point of view, as this letter gives the lie to the notion that the Unit put pressure on my father to start work again too soon, before he was fully recovered. It shows, in fact, how very solicitous people were for my father's well-being.....

16th August 1943

Dear Joan Barlow

I have known that Horace has been keeping you fairly well posted with Ralph's progress, but I thought that you might welcome a letter from me as well, since I was in charge in Horace's absence, when the final consultations took place with the three doctors concerned, and I hope that they have related the contents to you.

I should like to make it quite clear that throughout Ralph's sickness, both Horace and I have been certain that any errors of judgment which were made, must be on the side of safety. Thus, although the doctors were prepared to allow Ralph to go back to Cairo as OC Middle East after two months' light duties, I urged Tegla Davies very strongly to recall him to England, and this recommendation has, I understand, been accepted.

As regards China, letters from Duncan Wood and Kenneth Bennett, who are senior officers there, make it clear that they entirely appreciate the advisability of confining Ralph's activities to consultations rather than visits. None of the three doctors had any doubts on the question of Ralph's proceeding to China. He had four or five days after his return from Darjeeling, and was completely his old self, both socially and as regards business. I tried to avoid bothering him with the latter, but he insisted on giving me some embarrassing moments in investigating our finances!

I am very glad from the Unit's point of view that Ralph is going home, because I think that both his experience and temperament are going to help enormously at HQ in their relations with Foreign Sections, and also in the planning of post-war relief, which I gather is becoming increasingly important. And, I know personally how much he is looking forward to getting back to his family life, as I am sure you can imagine. I know that the prospect is making him face his present work, very happily.

I haven't written before, as I felt Horace knew you better than I did, but I have done all I can here to help to see that the best medical advice and treatment available could be obtained, and to ensure that no course of action should be prescribed for Ralph, which did not allow a very wide margin of safety. Please do not hesitate to let me know if there are any other points which I can clear up.

Yours sincerely,
Richard Symonds.

A postscript from my father in a letter to my mother.........

Dearest....The doctor said that a short time at home would be the best possible cure. How grand it will be to get home. I picture it all so vividly – you and the children, and England. It will indeed be wonderful – After so long, the best thing I can imagine....[.....] Ralph

The next few weeks - in July and early August - see my father getting stronger and stronger, and preparing to go to China, pending a final decision on his health. My mother, is still feeling more and more isolated with an absence of letters. She writes "I feel like a widow, with not a letter since April" ....

Monday, 5th July 1943 – Wolverhampton (AMLC)

My darling husband

As I think of you, I picture you and Horace up in Darjeeling, enjoying the cool and peace of the hills. I hope the birds there are good too, but trust, knowing your weakness, you aren't being too energetic. It is so good to know that you have Horace with you, and please tell him how happy I am to know he is taking care of you, and how grateful I am for all he has done for you.

All the same I feel sure you really need a woman's love to take that special care of you, and how I have longed to be with you. It is so wretched to be so far away. I do pray that you are getting stronger each day. Take courage, my dear, I am sure all will be well, and that you will soon be back home with us.

We returned from Fairbourne last week. It was a very hot and tiring journey, and everywhere was so crowded. But I think the holiday was a success, and it was certainly very good of your mother to take us away. In the last week the weather was beautiful and I think it did us all good. Indeed, we are now quite sunburnt!

The night before we left, David said to the landlady "I've got a sudden sad feeling I don't want to leave my dear friend Mrs Lewis." He is a real charmer and always knows the right thing to say! He started back to school this morning and was so delighted to see everyone again. He had so much to say that the teacher had to tell him "No more talking until lunch time, David!"

My dearest Ralph, may God bless you and bring you safely back to me. This comes with all my prayers and love. Devotedly Joan.

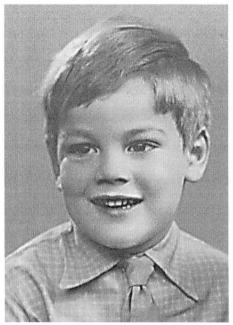

David aged 6   Antony aged 2½

The photographs of my brother and me, that were sent to my father.

My father eventually receives the photos of David and me that our mother had taken and given to Barry (MBB) to deliver to my father when they met up in the Middle East. Because of the difficulties of travel, firstly due to the delays in finding suitable transport, and secondly because of the circuitous route he took out there, they never met up in the ME, as my father had already left for India, by the time he arrived. So, as my father writes, Barry sent them in a letter some six months after my mother had given them to him!

My father looks after the two Loukes' children whilst Harold and Mary have a break...and some further news of future plans.........

Friday, 2nd July 1943 – Darjeeling (AG)

My dear wife

I have just received a letter from Barry enclosing the photos of the children. I am so glad to have them. How splendid they both look. I left David still a baby and now he is a boy, and a very handsome boy too; and Antony looks an angel too. I know how much work it is for you and how tired you must often be, but I have such confidence in you. You have every right to be a proud mother.

As I wrote previously, the Loukes are in Calcutta now, and I am responsible with the Ayah for the boys. She looks after Christopher, the younger one completely, whilst I spend time with Anthony the elder. Yesterday I took him down to the station. Both the children are very good, but I shall be glad when the parents come back. Other people's children are a great responsibility.

I am a great deal better now. It has done me so much good staying here both mentally and physically. I hope you may find me a nicer person when I return. More understanding and patient and tolerant. Looking back I must have been rather a bad husband, particularly latterly. I will try and do better in future. You have always been such a good wife, for which I am eternally grateful.

It looks now as though I should leave here about July 14th to return to Calcutta, and then leave there about the 20th for China. I gather Brandon is having rather a difficult time there and is anxious for company. I shall go very carefully, and only when the doctors say I can. But I think they will give me the clearance to go as I am so much better. Brandon suggests that Duncan and I should go away for a few days, to give him a holiday and for me to see his point of view. I should leave there in August and return through Cairo.

It seems likely that I shall then come home. I have had a long letter from Barry in Cairo, urging me to, so that I can tell London about all the foreign sections. He seems to think that I might have to go out to the ME again after that, but we shall see. If that materialises, and of course, it may not, I should be back home in October or November, which would be marvellous. I really have been lucky to get better so quickly, and to have such a pleasant place to convalesce. Just imagine if I had been ill in Calcutta, or even worse in Bombay! God has been very good to me. Perhaps an answer to a prayer.

There are lots of birds here, but they are not that easy to see, with all the foliage, and the bad weather and all the activity. The Himalayas in spring and autumn, and further up the mountains, must be a paradise. It is of course fine here, but perhaps not quite as lovely as Switzerland! But then I am biased! In 1939 we were both in Sweden at this time. How grand that was. Where shall we all be this time next year?

I do hope your holiday with mother went well. All my love to you and to my mother and yours. Horace is leaving in August, and I will cable before I leave Calcutta and when I reach China. All my love Ralph.

My mother writes of how the family is thinking of my father on his birthday, and hoping especially that he is really better, before departing for China. With only winks and nudges from my father and others that he could be home by the end of the year, my mother has bought wholesale into the idea that he'll be home by the autumn, which gives her great happiness........

Friday, 9th July 1943 – Wolverhampton (AMLC)

My darling Ralph

Today is your birthday and I wish with all my heart that I could be with you, giving you all our love for a happy day. I'd be bringing you a special bouquet of flowers in your honour – scabious, sweet peas, gypsophola and roses. Let's pray that soon I may have that great pleasure. We are all thinking of you on this your special day and talk of you all the time.

I do so wonder if you are truly better yet, and whether you are still up in the hills. I pray that your time in Darjeeling has given you new strength and hope for the future. I just wish I could be with you and spoil you.

Right now I have so much to think about during the next weeks and much to plan and arrange. That you might be back with us in a few months, fills me with great happiness and excitement. But do I dare to look forward too much? I cannot believe I shall see you in so many weeks' time. It is all too wonderful to contemplate. To be able to look up and see you walk into a room, bringing so much joy and happiness with you and gaiety and fun. That will all be so wonderful.

The children are all fit again now and David is growing up so rapidly and developing well. Antony so adorable and bubbling with fun and merriment. They certainly keep me busy!

Vera's poor mother died a week ago, which is a relief, as she suffered so, and Vera was getting very tired and worn out. Reg has now been posted near home, which must seem like a miracle to them.

I don't know what has happened to our summer, but we are all shivering and there is so much rain. Your mother is going to London to stay with Millior on Tuesday, so that she can look at a house that they have in mind. I shall be very sad to take David away from his school, but I daresay he wil settle in happily somewhere else.

I so long for more news, but I expect one day soon I shall shout with joy at the sight of your handwriting. God speed that day.

God bless you and watch over you. We all send so much love.
Ever your devoted Joan.

———

Christopher and Anthony obviously got on well with my father, and he loved feeling part of a family again, but he was also quite relieved when H & M returned.........

Monday, 5th July 1943 – Darjeeling (AG)

My darling wife

Harold and Mary are back, for which I am quite glad, though in fact everything went alright and the children were very good, and Harold and Mary had a very good time in Calcutta. Mary was delighted to see the photographs of the children, and said how charming they looked....David like me and Antony like you. She also said 'How pretty Joan is'. Don't snort, but receive a compliment!

It is curious being in a home again after so long. So much is coming back to me, and I am suddenly very homesick and want you all so much. When I come home, I will try and be nice. I don't think I have always been as good as I could be. I think I was probably right to go abroad, but I know it has been very hard on you and the children. But I wonder if I was as nice as I could have been before I left. If I wasn't, I apologise again, and promise to do better.

I've had a long leter from Duncan, who suggests that when I get to China, I should have a few days holiday with him first, which sounds a good idea, and would be really nice. He sends his love to you.

Harold and Mary said how much better I looked when they got back, and I must say, I do feel better.

I've just finished reading W C Braithwaite's[8] monumental 2 volume history of Quakerism, which I enjoyed very much. It is a great work of scholarship and very readable too. I must remember to tell Alfred.

Dear love to you and the children. Your loving husband, Ralph

My mother continues to be frustrated with not hearing much about my father's state of health, and though excited as the prospect of him returning home, is not quite certain if it is definite, or as she says, 'castles in the air'………

Friday, 19th July 1943 – Wolverhampton (AMLC)

My darling

Thank you so much for your AG of June 28th (p562), which I received this morning. You say you hope I am getting all the AG's you have sent. In fact this is only the third I have had since you were ill. Maybe some are lost. I realise that you haven't been able to write much of late, but I do sometimes feel like a war widow! Oh, God! I just feel out of touch with everything, as though I was not only miles, but years away from you as well! I don't know how you are feeling, or what you are thinking, or what you are really planning to do. I have been so terribly worried about you. All I want is to know that you are well and strong again.

I was so grateful to Mary Loukes for writing to me (P558/9). It's the first sensible letter I've had from anyone, giving me the details and the news I've been wanting to know for weeks. I believe it takes a woman to give the details. She told me that your appetite is now amazingly good! I am so glad to hear that!

I think I'd better send this to Cairo, as I doubt if it will reach Calcutta in time. I think this is probably the last you will receive. That is, if it is true that you really are returning, as I haven't heard anything definite from you as yet. I wish I knew more, so that I could plan ahead just a little. Tegla sent me a copy of an AG you had sent him (dated June 14th), which says you are extremely anxious to return to the ME. Michael Cadbury and Tegla have both been very good in writing to me.

David is going to spend a week with your mother as soon as he breaks up. I wonder if you have thought where we should send him to school, when we are back in Birmingham.

Well, there is not much more news. We are all well here and we all think of you all the time. Shall I really see you in – how many weeks?! I pray it is true and not just castles in the air. All my dear love for now and the children send theirs too. Joan

———

My father is gradually getting ready to leave Darjeeling. Here he talks of his fondness for the wonderful mountain scenery, for the kindness of the Loukes family and how he'll miss both; and of his proposed schedule for getting to China and afterwards back to Cairo and so home, and his impatience to see my mother and us children.......

Thursday, 8th July 1943 – Darjeeling (AG)

My very dear, dear wife,
It seems some time since I heard from you. Probably the mail is getting held up, but I do so love to get your letters. I love you so much dearest one, so, so much.

Horace is being rather firm with me, and is insisting that when I have been to China, I should return home through Cairo and thence back home with him. God willing – and the doctors too - I hope to go to China about the middle of the month - in about a week's time. When I get there, I shall then spend a week somewhere with Duncan, and then following various meetings, fly (?) to Cairo mid August.

If all goes well, I might be home in September or October. I know there can be many a slip, but wouldn't it be marvellous? I can think of nothing else. Seeing you at Wolverhampton station, and then the family. It's all too good to be true. What shall we do?

The Harold Massingham[8] book, *The English Countryman,* that you sent me for Christmas (!) has at last arrived. Thank you so much for it. You are good in sending me things. Reading that and being with Harold and Mary and their two children, makes me so long to be back and in our own home again, and with my own family. You and the children and England. That will indeed be good. The best thing in our lives after so long.

H & M are very devoted to their children and bring them up so well, and I shall be very sorry to leave them, as they have been so good and kind to me. Tell David that they have a lovely little Siamese cat, which is so playful. He would love it. I bought Mary some rather pretty table mats as a token of my gratitude. I also bought some nice dress material, which might make a suitable present for somebody. Harold has gone down to Calcutta again, but will be back shortly, and has kindly agreed to come down with me when I leave.

The scenery here really is very special when the weather clears. Last night, all of a sudden, a valley and distant mountain range came into view for an hour or two. Instead of thick mist and heavy cloud, with visibility scarcely a mile, you suddenly got a view of the valley, and the mountains, streams and forests for miles and miles in the light of the evening sun, under high-piled, beautiful, shadowed cumulus clouds and blue sky. This morning we climbed up to a stunning viewpoint before breakfast. There was sun and blue sky, and the clouds just beginning to come up as well. I can't describe it, but it was just magnificent. When it clears it is quite stupendous......but, dare I say it, it's not quite as beautiful as my beloved Alps!! How I wish you were here to share it with me.

Dear one, this brings all my love for you and the children; all my sympathy for your difficult job at this troubling time; and all my longing to see you very soon.
Always your loving Ralph

FRB on reading William C Braithwaite's *The History of Quakerism:* "It is instructive for a change to read something of the history of one's own society, to see Quakerism set in perspective, in the mystic tradition, a tradition which later generations have tended to overlook. To read this in parallel with Margaret Irwin's novels, proves, if proof were needed, what a rich and varied century was the seventeenth. This book is a history to be proud of, and there is no excuse for not reading it; it is most readable."

"How I shall miss Darjeeling"

"Suddenly we got a view of the valley, and the mountains, streams and forests for miles and miles in the light of the evening sun, under beautiful, clouds and blue sky."

Photo National Geographic

This time it's my father who has been missing letters from my mother, which seem to have been taking their time, but at last two arrive and he attempts to answer some of the questions, and though he talks of being home in the autumn, it's still hedged about with the conditional tense.........

Friday, 9th July 1943 – Darjeeling (AG)

My dear wife

Yesterday I had an AG from you and an Airmail letter. Thank you so much for them. The one you sent to Cairo No 45 (p553) has arrived here tremendously quickly. I haven't written any letters of late, only AGs, as they get through more quickly. I fear you have had a very trying time of late, what with the boys having measles and Antony stuttering, which I hope may have cleared up by now. I do so sympathise. I know what you mean, when you say that you can get used to anything. How I agree! When I think of the things I have got used to in the last 3 years since I joined the Unit!

Regarding houses, I may yet be able to help, if I am back in the autumn, which seems very likely. We will sort things out. I expect you think I'm mad to go to China, but I promise I will only go as long as the doctors allow me to, and I promise I will be careful.

Mary says she will write to you again before I leave here. The family were so sweet about my birthday, with everyone giving me a present, which was so kind of them, especially as I forgot all about it on board ship last year! They could not have been kinder to me.

Richard tells me that he is sending the doctor's note to London and I have asked Tegla to send you a copy of it too. The last few days have been so lovely, with cumulus clouds over the mountains, making them indescribably beautiful. I will miss this wonderful scenery. As I've said before, if only you were here to share it with me.

But enough about me. How are you dearest? I do hope life isn't too complicated and troublesome. You are for ever in my thoughts and prayers.

All my love to D and A, and to your mother, and to you my darling.   Ever yours Ralph

Finally, my father says his farewells and leaves Darjeeling for Calcutta - and as with many previous partings, subsequent to an uncertain beginning - with much regret. Now, however, there is an eager anticipation of returning home.........

Darjeeling railway, the end of the Himalayan line, built in 1881
Photo Darjeeling archives

Thursday, 15th July 1943 – Upper Wood Street, Calcutta (AG)

Darling Joan

I came down to Calcutta here last night by train. An easy journey, and as Harold came with me, I was well looked after. The long run down to the station to catch the train we did by bus, which was rather lovely, especially once we got below the clouds, when we were afforded a splendid wideangle view over the plains.

Nothing much happened in the last few days before I left, but last Tuesday, I took Harold and Mary out to dinner, which was very pleasant. I must say in many ways I was very sorry to leave, as I love this place and have grown very fond of the family. I thank God I was able to stay here, as it has done me so much good. I expect to see the doctors tomorrow, and all being well, leave for China on Monday, and then spend a few days with Duncan when I get there. Horace is away now, but Richard is here and will look after me until I am free to leave and get a flight to China. Always in my thoughts, and I am so thrilled at the prospect of returning home and to being with you again.
All my dearest love Ralph.

And so on to China, for the next and last journey he will make before returning home.

Chapter 37
China and the China Convoy
July/August 1943

The Sino-Japanese War had led to deteriorating conditions in China, on account of which, a section of the Unit had been in China since the spring of 1941, when agreement had been reached for the FAU to deploy 40 volunteers to deliver medical aid to the wounded. At first they were moving supplies up the Burma Road, supplying two surgical teams to work with the British and Chinese armies in Burma.

Both Hong Kong and Singapore had already fallen to the Japanese earlier that year, and then proceeded to invade Burma, thus cutting the backdoor route for military and other supplies. So for all intents and purposes, China was now blockaded, and after the Burma Road was closed, the only option was the huge military airlift by American transport planes based in India, to ferry war supplies, at considerable risk, for the Nationalist government's defence of China, against Mao's communists. The airlift was over 'the hump' - the hazardous mountain range of the southern spur of the Himalayas – down into the now booming little town of Kunming, from where the Unit distributed supplies to civilian hospitals in West China. This entailed long hours of truck driving on difficult roads, with journeys often taking up to ten days, and more if mishaps occurred, and due to the shortage of petrol, the majority of the trucks were converted to charcoal, thereby losing much of their power. Sometimes they found it difficult to even reach the top of a ridge and there were many bandits on the road. It was undoubtedly a hard life.

The Unit had provided two surgical teams to work with the Chinese army in West China, but the Chinese were not well supplied with doctors and the Unit medical teams settled into existing hospitals, looking after the sick and wounded. They also looked after the civilian population during times when they were less busy, and it is estimated that 80% of medical supplies to China were distributed by the FAU. Following the fall of Burma, they regrouped, becoming known as the "China Convoy", led by Peter Tennant and Duncan Wood, arriving in China by a variety of routes in 1942, full of enthusiasm but perhaps more in faith than expectation. They encountered many problems along the way, from ambulances that had been ordered, and proved too wide for the roads, to disputes regarding high level appointments without sufficient consultation, and arguments about distribution of work. There were other difficulties too, caused by long distance communications and financial problems, but the main trouble was the question of the personalities that made up the party. No section of the Unit was more conscious of its democratic unity, but there were those who could see that a more pragmatic approach was sometimes necessary if things were not to decline into anarchy. Gradually London began to lose confidence in the China set-up, both in its decision-making and in its long-term policy-making, which is when it was decided to send my father out there together with Brandon Cadbury to sort the situation out.

My father's visit had been delayed by his illness, but in July 1943 he had recovered sufficiently to make the journey. His old friend Duncan Wood was there to greet him and to brief him on the situation and within a few days, he had convened a major staff meeting of Unit members from all over China. On the last day of July 1943, with my father in the chair, the members were made to face up to the poor administrative history of the group, whereby corporate Quaker decision making had often got in the way of clear direction. This proved to be a turning point in the Convoy's history. Considerably better, though probably not fully recovered, and still easily tired, my father was nonetheless determined to complete his mission in Tom's place, and so set out in mid-July to fly to Kutsing.

As so often with my father during his time in the FAU, he seemed to be waiting for a plane to take him somewhere – whether it be Tehran, Ethiopia or back to Cairo – and now still stuck in Calcutta, he is awaiting a flight to China.........

Thursday, July 15th 1943 - 1 Upper Wood Street, Calcutta (45)

Dearest Joan

I fear I am getting worse as a correspondent. I suppose because I am still not 100%, and also I think that perhaps I may be home before the letters get there. But God knows, I doubt it. My flight to China has again been postponed, and I am in one of my black depressions. You'll have to excuse pencil, but there doesn't seem to be any ink anywhere!

But for once, he doesn't have to wait long and is soon flying over 'The Hump' [1] and landing at Kunming airport, where he meets up with Peter Tennant and Duncan Wood..........

(No 45 Contd)........Friday, July 16th

Mercifully, I didn't have to stay long in Calcutta, which I do think is a loathsome city: so dirty and noisy. The plane left Calcutta for China at some unearthly hour yesterday. We flew for an hour or so over flat flooded plains, with thatched villages on the higher ground and a patchwork of fields and broken hilly ground.

At our first stop, we were delayed for an hour, which was terrible as it was frightfully hot. But the next hop over the 'Hump', (the airlift route to China over The Himalayas) was supposed to be the worst, which I rather dreaded as the plane rises to 18,000 feet and it can often be very rough and would normally play havoc with my ears. However, as it turned out, we had a comparatively calm and easy flight, with splendid views out over the mountains.

In fact I had a very comfortable trip out with quite wonderful cloudscapes. Sometimes we had a clear view of the land with billowing clouds piled on a distant horizon, golden in the sun. Sometimes the world was floored by a whole ceiling of cloud, like a landscape under the snow, stretching as far as one could see; white, plain and fantastic cloud shapes, like trees under snow.

Occasional open patches, through which one could see the earth beneath. Sometimes vast towers and pillars of cloud rose into the sky, with precipices, cliffs and gorges. Whenever the sun caught them, they were a dazzling white. Towards evening it cleared somewhat, and there were piles of golden clouds, blue sky, and the rivers and floods below made a golden path to the setting sun. What a fantastically beautiful, but unreal, insubstantial and un-human world it is.

By the time we arrived at Kunming[2] airport, I was quite tired, but not unduly so. I was met by a welcoming party and taken to a small hotel for the night. Duncan came in that evening, and it was really good to see him again after so long. Of course it was good meeting up with the others too, but D is D - the same as ever, and after I'd settled in, we went out for a stroll together. In fact I am not doing much for the moment, besides talking to Duncan and trying to find out all I can about the situation here.

Later he and Peter Tennant took me out to a Chinese restaurant for supper where the food was very good, with a great variety of dishes, which we all dug into, though I fear I couldn't manage the chopsticks at all, and soon abandoned the pretence and used a spoon instead!

The next day, as had been arranged, my father would spend some little time with Duncan, partly so that he could ease himself into the long rounds of talks, and partly to familiarise himself with the situation and problems in China.........

(No 45 Contd)........Saturday, July 17th Kunming

It was such a pleasure meeting up again with Duncan and we spent a whole day bird watching above the lake outside Kunming. We went out in a very decrepit and crowded native bus to Lake Dian, a big freshwater lake not far outside the city. The lake is vast and stands in a huge plain with ranges of mountains rising out of it, and we climbed a little way up the mountain near the lake, where we ate our picnic lunch and admired the view. The hillside on which we sat, was rocky, covered with bracken and low bushes and wonderful wild flowers. Just below, on the slope across from us, was a flat strip, planted with rice, which is a bright vivid green. The lake itself was calm save for the occasional ripple, and beyond was a level, wide plain and then more hills. It was overcast but the clouds were high and there were occasional rainstorms and bursts of sun. The colouring of lake and mountain was quite superb, and the whole scene very lovely. But best of all we saw a number of birds, including a Chinese Heron and an Oriental Stork. It really is so good to see Duncan and to enjoy such simple shared pleasures again.

In a couple of days, we are going up to Kutsing[3], where I expect to meet Brandon and John Rich. Right now we are in the middle of the rainy season here, though it is not seriously heavy yet and in fact yesterday turned into a lovely day. From what I've seen so far, of the country round about, it is a rather beautiful, plateau land, with mountains rising some 7,000 feet up. More tomorrow, all my love, Ralph

Lake Dian, also known as Lake Kunming
"The lake is vast and stands in a huge plain with ranges of mountains rising out of it.
It is not far from where we were staying in Kunming itself, and proved ideal for Duncan and me
to spend some time birding together."
Photograph Friends House Library

The problems in China went back to the very beginning of the FAU out there, and started with a group of people, who were not entirely temperamentally suited to work togther. An understanding of this is essential to appreciating the problems my father had to sort out. Here, in his report for Gordon Square, my father discusses the background, and the real heart of the problem, which as so frequently in Quaker managerial disputes, resolved itself into the dilemma Quakers faced between democracy and pragmatism, especially in times of war...........

There were few sections of the FAU that clung together so persistently as what became known as the 'China Convoy'. Once in China, they longed to come home, and once back home they longed to be back. In China they felt there was a real need for them, and such was the shortage of trained personnel that any job they could do, there was no-one else there to do it, whereas back home there were many who could and did take their place. But in addition, there was a camaraderie, born of the nature of the country itself.

The 'Convoy' encountered much poverty, squalor and disease, graft and corruption. Everything other than what they were used to back home. The Chinese were initially uncooperative and carried the qualities of long-suffering to aggravating lengths. Gradually, however, the country asserted itself, so that despite the poverty and squalor, there was a growing fascination with China, which the whole 'Convoy' experienced.

At the beginning money was a problem, but Tom Tanner's visit to America in 1942 had encouraged the American Friends Service Council and various other sources such as the United China Relief Fund, to open their purses, and within the Unit there was also growing enthusiasm to serve in China. Eventually, Peter Tennant was appointed as Commandant, and he began to gather together a special group of people around him, including Selby Clewer as Quartermaster and Duncan Wood as Group Leader in charge of Personnel.

The Joint China Committee of the FAU, however, was concerned that no-one among this group, really possessed the desired knowledge of China or indeed Chinese, that the Committee regarded as essential. However, through the unlikely source of two shortly to be famous literary names, Wystan Auden and Christopher Isherwood, a name was recommended to the FAU. This was Dr Robert B McClure, whom the pair had encountered during their visit to China in 1938. They had been commissioned by Random House to write a book on the Sino-Japanese war in China, which was published in 1939 as *Journey to a War, and* contained verses by Auden and prose by Isherwood, and a series of war photographs.

According to them, Bob McClure was "a stalwart, bullet-headed Canadian Scot, with the energy of a whirlwind and the high spirits of a sixteen year old schoolboy," and a whirlwind was exactly what the Unit discovered when he joined them. He had been born in China to missionary parents and educated at Toronto University, and when a cable had been despatched to him, asking if he would take charge of the Convoy, he replied at once that he had 'already bought his ticket'! The trouble was that the Joint China Committee had invited Bob McClure to lead the Convoy without any reference to the Convoy itself. This created much righteous indignation and threatened the very future of the group.

Peter Tennant, the appointed so-called 'Commandant', was a fervent old school supporter for the Unit's democratic Quaker decision-making process, which he had helped to build up back home in London, insisting that important decisions should always be decisions of the group, or at least after the group had been consulted. McClure on the other hand preferred a more pragmatic and realistic approach to decision-making, and inevitably these two approaches clashed.

No sooner had Bob arrived than he encountered problems, and he wrote back to London - "There is a great desire in the Unit – which is easily understood amongst a group of thinking men - for 'democratic control'. I'm all for it. But there is a fine line between that and 'a lack of firm leadership'. It cannot be had both ways. I quickly made the firm decision that the men should settle down and start work. As a consequence there now seems to be a much happier atmosphere."

This is the classic conundrum faced by Quakers in times that require quick and firm decisions, and which I have often complained about. Quaker business methods are well-known and admired for their collective way of decision making, but this is not necessarily the best way in a war situation. As I wrote elsewhere:

"I found myself on the one hand convinced of the importance of the Quaker message and methods and certain that it should be given to the world as a way of life through worship and service, but on the other critical of committee methods, traditional phraseology, bad choices of personnel, woolliness and isolation from the world. I still feel this very strongly."

Christopher Isherwood (left) and W H Auden at Victoria station in 1938 on their way to China, commissioned by Random House to cover the Sino-Japanese war. They had met Bob McClure in China and recommended him as the person to lead the China Convoy.

Photo by John F Stephenson/Getty Images

This then was the situation my father discovered, through his own investigations, through his long talks with Duncan, as well as being fully briefed by all the leading personnel concerned. Following the quiet days he spent with Duncan, walking, birding and generally restoring his energy, my father called all the leading Unit members who were working in different parts of China, to come together in Kutsing, in order to thrash out their various problems as well as the future direction of Unit's policy in China.

Sensing difficulties between the two factions, my father obtained pre staff statements from Bob McClure, Peter Tennant, John Rich and others. These revealed the problems and dissatisfactions inherent in a Unit which relied on an ideal of personal responsibility, to try to combine clear direction with democratic control. My father listed 'inadequate sense of direction', 'excessive individualism', 'lack of discipline and lack of thoughtfulness for others' among things that needed to be sorted out. He was also concerned to establish what the aim of the Unit's work in China was to be. Was it working too much for the Chinese and not sufficiently with the Chinese?

So it was that on the last day of July 1943, the conference commenced with my father in the chair. It reviewed in detail the Convoy's administration and programme of work, and as a result the old Executive Committee was abolished, together with the offices of Commandant and Adjutant. In its place a new structure was established consisting of a Chairman, Personnel Officer and an Executive Secretary. Leonard Tomkinson from the Friends Service Council, with his long experience of China was to be Chairman. Duncan Wood Personnel Officer and Ken Bennett Executive Secretary. Bob McClure became Director of the Unit's Medical work with Peter Tennant as Field Inspector.

The FAU Hostel in Kutsing, Yunnan Province, designed by Selby Clewer
"The Unit has three one-storeyed huts here, one containing cubicles for three beds or berths, one living quarter and one for the servants."
Photograph Friends House Library

The team that sorted out the China Convoy

FRB
Chairman of the Committee

Peter Tennant
'Old school democrat'

Photos FHL

Robert (Bob) McClure – pragmatist
"A stalwart, bullet-headed Canadian Scot,
with the energy of a whirlwind"
Photograph McClure family

Brandon Cadbury
"Who even with an extra burden of
work did extremely well."
Photograph courtesy of Rupert Cadbury

In a letter home, my father describes the journey up to Kutsing and the countryside, the FAU set up there, waiting for Brandon to arrive from Chunking, and setting out the problems as London saw them.......

Tuesday, July 20ᵗʰ 1943 - Kutsing

Dearest Joan

We all came down here to Kutsing yesterday by truck, which is about 200 miles. 'All' are Duncan, Peter Tennant, Brian Jones myself and some others and so we had a truck full. Luckily I managed to find a comfortable seat and so was not too tired. It was a charcoal burner and so went very slowly and took us about eight hours. On our way, part of the cargo suddenly started to smoulder. Luckily Peter was quickly able to extinguish it in the ditch, but inevitably, the finger was pointed at me, for starting it, with ashes from my pipe! I admit that I have been known to start the odd fire on occasion, but I always pleaded not guilty to this one!

The weather just now is lovely, very hot during the day but cool at night. Everywhere the country is a high plateau with ranges of hills rising out of it. All the way we were driving through hills, either steep and bare, or covered with fir trees. Down in the valleys, were banks of bushes along the roads. Where there was any flat land, there was cultivation, all terraced with earth walls to hold in the water, and everywhere there was rice growing - sometimes just planted, sometimes a brilliant fresh green, sometimes darker. When it is very young the bright green spears stick up through the water which reflects the sky. It was a most beautiful run. But I was also struck by the general squalor and poverty everywhere. The villages are filthy and small. Kutsing itself is a small town, surrounded by a great stone wall, and Duncan and I walked round part of it this morning and sat in a pavilion looking out over the town to the view below with its rice fields and the distant hills and wild flowers. It was stunning.

The Unit has three one-storeyed huts here, one containing cubicles for three beds or berths, one living quarter and one for the servants. I have been here four days now, talking to people, reading files and writing reports. Save for the vast quantities of fleas, bugs and mosquitoes, life has some advantages, as it is a pleasant enough place and the weather is really lovely. Very hot during the day, but cool at night.

Brandon is still in Chungking, but we are expecting him with John Rich very soon, and then we shall have a whole lot more meetings. At the last Staff Meeting we established a new set up for the future, with a Council of four, of which Leonard Tomkinson - from the Friends Service Council, who was also a China expert - as Chairman and Duncan and two others in place of McClure and Tennant. In view of the tension between these two, I think this was probably a good move.

I have been trying to explain to them why London had so little confidence in the administration, but even so, I expect when we all meet again next week, the Council will take one view, John Rich another, probably supported by Brandon. Luckily Duncan, is an ideal Personnel Officer and much respected, so with a bit of luck, we might find a medium way. He is just the same, very patient, very thoughtful and very wise. He sees the funny side of everything and it is a real joy to see him again. He is far and away the soundest man out here. So although there are many problems to sort out here, it's not disaster and overall I am quite impressed by the organisation here. I probably shouldn't have come, even with the doctor's permission, but talking with D, I think there are things I can do which can be of considerable help. I hope so anyway. However, I'm alright and taking it slowly. If all goes well, we might even sort things out by next week, when I am hoping to be able to leave.

As ever all love my dearest, to you and the children, Ralph

A letter from my mother, happy that he arrived safely in China, and looking forward to my father's ultimate return, and imploring him to care and not tire himself out...........

Monday, 22ⁿᵈ July 1943 – Wolverhampton (AMLC)

My dearest Ralph

I received your cable this morning, saying that you had reached China. I was so pleased to get it and to know that you are well enough to travel and are safe. I rang Tegla, who was glad to hear from me, as he hadn't yet heard of your arrival in China. I know you have so much responsibility in sorting all the problems out in China, and I do hope all the negotiations will go well for you. I hope you find Duncan well and enjoy some quiet days with him too. It will be so lovely when you are back in Cairo and on your way home, as the main thing is to get you home safely – oh, joy of joys! So do go carefully on the way back, and don't be rash, my dearest.

I received three of your airgraphs this morning, and I am so happy to have them and to know that you are getting on so well. Unbelievably they took six weeks to get here! You certainly sound more cheerful. I am glad you enjoyed looking after the Loukes' children in Darjeeling, while their parents were in Calcutta, but of course you could, as you were always so good with David. It was good for you to be right away from the Unit for a time. Tegla sent me a photograph of Harold and Mary (Loukes), which I was delighted to have. They look a charming couple, and I wish so much I could have been with you in Darjeeling. I hope you will keep in touch with them. I have written to Mary to thank her for all they did looking after you.

I also had an airgarph from Horace, which I was exceedingly happy to get, and I am so indebted to him for all his care of you during those many anxious weeks. I am so thankful that he was able to be with you, and I have written to him too

I went over to Linden Road for a while yesterday to collect a few things that Win might like, and had lunch with your mother, who had just got back from London and seemed well. The 'Sunnybrae' garden is a glorious sight right now – scabious, phlox, yellow daisies, roses, ceanothus, honeysuckle and delphiniums. I am sure we will be able to make the house very nice. She told me that Millior and Alfred have now decided on a house in Golders Green and your mother seemed happy about it.

David finishes school on the 28ᵗʰ and he is then going over to 'Sunnybrae' on August 5ᵗʰ, to stay with your mother, and is very excited at the prospect. I am going to stay with Jeph and Margaret the following Thursday, as she wants me to see their adopted son, Richard, which will be nice, and then I will go on to collect David from No 6 to bring him back to Wolverhampton. Llew kindly gave David an old watch a few days ago, and ever since it has gone without stopping and D is thrilled with it, as he can now tell the time. I think you will see a big change in both him and Antony. They have both grown up so rapidly and A is as lively as can be.

You talk about being home for two months! But I have much much more to say about this, and we shall be firm! After such a serious illness too. You must realise that your health comes first, and that if you are not fit and well, you cannot give of your best to anyone. We must go away together when you return, if you feel up to it. I wonder where we could go? Just you and me. Wouldn't that be heavenly? I shan't let you do too much!! All I long for is to see you again, and have you with me. Oh, my dearest one, it will be so wonderful. David asks so many questions about your journey home, and we are all longing to see you. So please, please, take care of yourself on the journey home and rest sufficiently.

I really ache to see you. I almost daren't look forward to it too much. All my love Joan

Maps of China

Above - Map of Yunnan Province and the towns FRB visited
Kunming and Kutsing to the North East (now called Qujing)

Map showing relationship of Yunnan to the rest of China
Images Google Maps

Members of the 'China Convoy'

FAU HQ in Kutsing with l. - r. Brian Jones, Ken Bennett and Duncan Wood
Photograph Friends House Library

In his memoirs, my father writes of this period......

Things that stick in my mind of my time in China, was first of all the extraordinary feeling of isolation of China from the rest of the world. I recall hearing on the wireless of the fall of Mussolini, but it seemed like a happening almost from another world. But I was impressed by the generally friendly atmosphere, especially in the section at Kutsing and once Brandon arrived from Chungking we had a complete orgy of meetings, which on the whole, did, I think achieve something.

And here in another letter home, he describes something of the meetings.......

Thursday, 5th August 1943 – Kutsing

My dearest Joan

I have now been here for ten days, and as soon as John Rich and Brandon eventually joined us, we fell into an orgy of meetings, which I think have gone well. I took the chair, which was perhaps rather foolish, but I have survived. Hitherto a state of considerable chaos has prevailed here, though I don't quite know why they have made so many stupid mistakes, and I am hoping that the new Council we have set up, should make a change. We have washed quite a lot of dirty linen and I hope laid a basis for collaboration to build on, though there is still some way to go. However, considering the divergence of views, I think I did rather well, though I says it as shouldn't.

Unfortunately, we have been so busy that I have not been able to see much of China, and I was determined not to get too tired (without success), but I did enjoy the visit. Kutsing is pleasant enough, though not very interesting and sleeping in our tents every night, I got bitten to death with the hordes of mosquitos that came in every night, despite the nets we put up. I am filled with unbounded admiration for the people who have worked for months in such conditions.

Having been here for a while, I must say I found the friendly atmosphere of the section most reassuring. Now I am almost ready to return to Calcutta and suddenly I am feeling very homesick. It seems ages since I received any letters from you. In fact not since before I left India, so I have sent you a cable to see if you are alright. I trust that you have received that.

I just keep remembering our life together; our lovely home and children and you and all our holidays in Switzerland and Sweden and Dunster, and of course our wonderful honeymoon in the Lakes. How much I have to be grateful to you for. There must be so much more I could say, but I will only tell you how much I love and miss you, and hope it won't be long before I will back home again.

All my very dearest love as ever, Ralph

FAU trucks in Kunming in Western China.
Photograph Friends House Library

To give an idea of the complexity of the situation, and the sensitivity of the nature of the meetings my father chaired, I have included a substantial section of his report for Gordon Square, as it goes to the heart of much of the FAU's work overseas, where conditions can be so different to those that members were used to back home. The report, the result of what he called 'an orgy of meetings', highlights the many problems and the solutions proposed. Following the previous mismanagement and unhappiness, the changes my father brought about - in administrative machinery, in personnel, and liaison with London - mark the beginning, against the odds, of the next phase of the Convoy's work in China: a period of confidence and maturity............

Although my visit to China was restricted by illness, I feel that I was able to get some idea of the situation and to complete most of the job I went there to do. But I must praise Brandon who has had an extra burden of work to do, which he has done extremely well.

At the outset, it seemed that the various sides were so far apart that we would never reach agreement. But in the end our initial meetings in Kutsing and later in Kunming were successful. There's no doubt that the state of affairs in the China party was most unsatisfactory. Morale was low, discipline was bad, the general efficiency was not of a high standard, and relations with other bodies both Chinese and foreign, were badly handled.

Brandon expressed these views ably. It is also apparent that Bob McClure, though an extraordinarily able and vital personality, is not suitable to command an FAU party. It is also obvious that it is impossible for Peter Tennant and Bob to work together as a team. The result was that there was no clear leadership to the party and that they had allowed democracy to develop into anarchy. The party had to face very great difficulties in adapting themselves to a new country. They were upset by the general standards of Chinese living, the hardships of life on the road, the food, and the attitude of the people. They needed a much longer period to acclimatize themselves as well as time to gain a fuller appreciation of what they were doing.

Although general relations had been much improved, along with some improvement in Chinese speaking, and in living with the Chinese people, I believe the Convoy was still felt to be too much a foreign organization superimposed on China. It was working too much for the Chinese, and not sufficiently with the Chinese, or if necessary under them. This involved a considerable change in both attitude and in procedure.

So the old Executive Committee was abolished, along with the positions of Commandant and Adjutant. Instead we established a Council of four, consisting of Chairman, Personnel Officer, Executive Secretary and one other. Naturally, it is not ideal, but I think that it is the best possible, and it is most important that we should give it our confidence and that we should encourage them to have confidence in us.

Leonard Tomkinson, the FSC worker, who had been its first Liaison Officer, was now to become Chairman. He is not the personality that McClure was, but he had a great knowledge of China, sound judgment, and a good idea of what the Convoy ought to be. Ken Bennett was made Executive Secretary, and I think he will carry on the business side very ably. Duncan Wood is to be Personnel Officer, a position he is admirably suited for and someone in whom the Convoy has great confidence and who is the key-stone of the arch. The fourth member was Wil Jenkins, who impressed me greatly and who would be the Unit's representative in Chunking. Bob McClure is to move sideways to be Director of the Unit's growing medical work.

It was also agreed, albeit reluctantly, to appoint an American administrator. And in the circumstances, having an American, John Rich there, was important, although I am not at all clear how far the Americans generally fully understand the Unit's point of view, or whether they have fully worked out in their own minds the difference between a Unit which provides work for COs, and simply a piece of work undertaken by the AFSC. But I think that John did appreciate this difference and I hope that he will be able to interpret it to the American Friends.

If that comes about, it will demonstrate America's growing interest and acceptance of responsibilty for the Convoy's work in the future, so that it will gradually assume the character of permanent Quaker work and not just that of emergency FAU work, and I think that we should look to handing over our work more and more to the Americans.

Finally, it was fairly apparent that there was no immediate job for Brandon. On the other hand, I do feel that his presence in China over the next four or five months, will be invaluable, both to watch over the developments which we have planned during these meetings, and to see the inauguration of, and to get to know, the new American administrator, when he is appointed. His subsequent return to London, especially if he can return through Ethiopia and the Middle East, would also be most useful.

Sunday, 8th August 1943

[.....] I returned to Kunming in an appallingly slow and overcrowded train, in which the fleas and bugs were most trying! The airtrip back, however, was most comfortable.

FAU Trucks outside a Pagoda in Kunming

FAU trucks outside a Pagoda in Kunming
Photograph Friends House Library

Chapter 38
And so back to India and on to Cairo
August - September 1943

My father writes of his return from China to Calcutta.........

I returned to Calcutta by air, and stayed some 10 days first at No 1 Wood Street, which was almost unbearable because of the heat, and then most happily with the Loukes again up in Darjeeling, which was a blessed relief, while I awaited an onward flight to Cairo.

Back in Calcutta, which my father found as 'foul as ever', he rejoins Horace and meets up with the Governor of Bengal, and sees several high level people, along with something of the work of the India Section, which forms the basis of his report to the Square. Eventually he escapes the heat of Calcutta to go back up to Darjeeling.........

Tuesday, August 10ᵗʰ 1943 – No 1 Upper Wood Street, Calcutta (No 46)

Dearest Joan

I have just returned from China and am now back here in Calcutta. The air trip back turned out to be one of the most comfortable as well as one of the easiest trips I have had. This is the first time I have had a moment to sit down and write a proper letter to you, though I have no idea when you might get it.

I hope you have received at least some of my letters while I was away in China. I was there for nearly three weeks, and with endless meetings, it proved quite a strenuous time. I'm afraid I got very tired, but I have come to no harm. It was so good seeing Duncan again, and he said he would write to you, and I wonder if you have heard from him yet. He is much the same as ever and still looks very young. He is doing an extremely fine job and is universally respected. I was also glad to see Brandon, and I think together we achieved some useful changes.

Back here in Calcutta, I cannot say that my general impression of the city has changed very much over the times I have visited it. The climate is as foul as ever; very hot and damp. I have never felt really well here, or had any energy to do anything, and I find it so depressing. Indeed I feel more tired now than I did when I got back from China a week ago! It is greatly to the credit of the section here, that they have accomplished so much.

During this first week back, while waiting for a flight, I have busied myself meeting a variety of Unit people, and seeing something of the fine work they are doing here, and yesterday I visited Brian Taylor's Office and saw the children's canteens that have been set up to ease the famine. I also met a number of local influential people, including Ian Stephens, who is the highly thought of Editor of the English language Calcutta Statesman. He has made quite a name for his brave campaign in exposing the horrors of the terrible Bengal famine. He is widely thought to be a bit of an eccentric, but I liked him and certainly admire what he is doing. I also met Mrs Brown, who runs the Red Cross out here, and the Indian Editor of the Muslim newspaper. All very interesting people.

No 1 Upper Wood Street, the FAU HQ, is pleasant enough and quite a comfortable house, where the Unit live well, though the servants are not up to the ones that looked after us in Cairo! The European part of the town is quite pleasant, and the shopping streets, Government buildings and the Maidan Park, are all impressive. The native quarters, however, seem very crowded, and though the small shops and busy back streets are quite interesting, the suburbs are terribly squalid. And everywhere you go there are vast numbers of American troops, being typically very rowdy. Calcutta, during the monsoon season, when so much of the country is under water, is a really depressing experience, and the signs of starvation in the streets are frightening.

It has been good to see Horace again, though I don't know quite how long we shall be here. We have been able to do quite a bit of work together, including visiting the Governor of Bengal, Richard Casey[1], who spoke well of the Unit, and we had a really pleasant and helpful interview. He is actually rather a distinguished Australian statesman, having been a much decorated soldier in the First World War. I think he was in the diplomatic service for a while, before he was appointed Ambassador to the United States. Churchill then invited him to join his war cabinet and sent him out here to oversee relief, following the Bengal famine. He has generously agreed that the Australian government will supply some trucks to the FAU, of which Christopher Taylor is shortly to take delivery.

Sadly, Horace told me that he has decided to return home, which will be a terrible loss to the FAU out here. His year's sabbatical from Woodbrooke is already at an end, and I think he feels that he would be more use back home raising awareness of the famine and poverty out here and stirring up the English government. He will be greatly missed, and yesterday there was a very nice farewell party for him in the splendid Bishop's House, a place of great mental peace in Calcutta, and hence a suitable measure of his standing here, with everyone expressing their regret at his departure and thanking him for all the good work he has done. He has been an extraordinarily valuable member of the Section.

I discovered today, that as per usual, our flight has already been postponed. This was a terrible blow, as the thought of staying any longer in Calcutta filled me with despair. But joy of joys, Harold and Mary came to my rescue and kindly offered to put both Horace and me up, in their home in Darjeeling. It is really most good of them and will make the rest of my time here much more pleasant. I think I should have died if I had been forced to stay another day in Calcutta. Up in the mountains, it's so blessedly cool and peaceful, and they are so hospitable. I shall miss them a great deal. But I have really no idea how long I shall stay there, or how I shall get out, but I'll write to you of my plans as soon as they are more definite. I now very much doubt if I shall be home before October. Excuse such a poor letter, but I have so little energy. I'll write again soon.
Dearest love Ralph

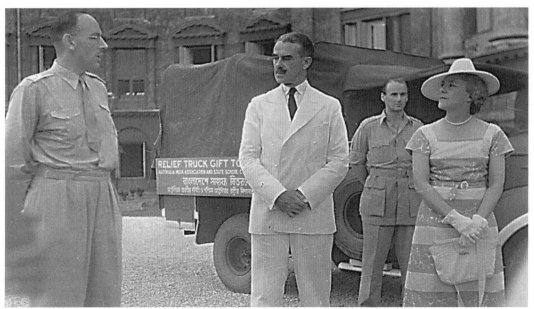

Richard Casey, Governor of Bengal with his wife Ethel,
presenting a new Relief Truck to Christopher Taylor 1943
Photograph Friends House Library

583

A fitting farewell for Horace at the splendid Bishop's Palace

The Bishop's House in Calcutta
"A place of great mental peace, very suitable for a fitting farewell party for Horace."
Photograph courtesy of Indian Tourist Board

During the couple of weeks back in India before my father returned home, he was able to make an appraisal of the Unit's work out there, which he delivered to Gordon Square on his arrival in London in October. This completed his survey of all the major theatres of Unit activity including China and now India, which he was doing in lieu of Tom Tanner. At the heart of the report was a summary of Horace's invaluable work and influence, and the possible future of this Section.........

I must emphasise firstly, that during much of my time in India, I was not well, which inevitably coloured my outlook on events. Secondly, these are my personal impressions; the main report must, of course, come from Horace. I am not competent to decide on the value of his political work, but despite some notoriety, it has undoubtedly been extremely valuable, winning general respect, both from Government officials in Bengal and in the UK. [....] The reaction of this on the work of the Section has been of great importance, bringing it in touch with politicians which has enabled it to maintain its position between the Government and the non-offical bodies, which it held with marked success. [....] The removal of Horace's influence and ability will be a serious loss, which will throw an extra burden on Dick Symonds, whose ability and drive has also contributed very greatly to the success of the work out there.

[....] There is of course, any amount of work still to do, particularly regarding the famine and flood relief work in Midnapore, where they are doing a very vital job, and it would be a pity if so much work and good will were allowed to lapse. [....] As a result, I think that sometime in the next twelve months, subsequent to a further review of the value of the work still to be done, the Society of Friends should consider taking over responsibility for this work, and run it from a Friends' centre there, for which the Society would bear a considerable part of the cost, always bearing in mind, that the FAU is not the Society.

After a week of blessed quiet and rest in Darjeeling, there seems to be a possibility of a flight, and Harold and Mary accompany Horace and my father back down to Calcutta. But as so often in this part of the world, the flight is postponed and they are forced to stay on in Calcutta, much to my father's disgust. But he takes the opportunity to have a final medical report, which advises him to take life quietly, and use his time at home in England to fully recover.........

Wednesday, August 25th 1943 – No1 Upper Wood Street

My very dearest wife

After a week of blissful peace up in the mountains, Harold very kindly accompanied Horace and me down to Calcutta, as there seemed a possibility of a flight. But no sooner here, than it was postponed again, and I am in one of my black depressions, having to stay in Calcutta yet again. I wish in many ways we'd stayed in Darjeeling, instead of coming back to this bloody place. I've also had a bit of a tummy upset, but once again they have been very kind and looked after me. I think they are rather fond of us and Mary was delighted to get your letter, and will reply very soon.

John and Mary Burtt have just arrived, which is very nice. They had a very good journey out here, and were delighted to have heard from you too. They are here to follow up the Unit's work, in lieu of Horace, now he is on his way home. They will take charge of the Upper Wood Street office and supervise Government canteens and voluntary kitchens, so vital now in the midst of the terrible famine. Alex Horsfield is now here as well with Jean, as secretary of the Central Relief Fund. So there is a strong team developing here, which is good news. It has been lovely to see so much of Dick Symonds, who is doing a fine job here.

Before coming home, you will be pleased to know that I saw the doctor again, and he was positive that I would be fully recovered in two months, if I took things quietly, and I promise I will. He has given me a full report of my illness since he first saw me, which I am to give to my doctor at home. I also understand that it is of sufficient interest to Indian doctors for it to appear in a medical journal. Imagine 'the Barlow case' written up in Indian medical history!!

I am so looking forward to seeing you again. Please give my love to the children and to Win and Llew. I hope Win keeps well. Tell them both that the American John Rich, who was with us in China, knows the Rhoads family where the children are in America, and speaks well of them. I wonder how long after I leave here, I will get home. I will go on writing in case I am further delayed, which is perfectly possible.

All my love for now, and I'll write again tomorrow
Ralph

———

These next are the last letters my mother wrote before my father's return, and as they all cover a lot of the same ground, I have taken the liberty of editing them into two letters. My mother was now eagerly anticipating my father's return, and her excitement is palpable, even though she is talking of September, while my father is thinking of October – but as always letters cross, and these from early August would most likely only just reach Cairo before my father left at the end of the month. As ever they bring my father up-to-date with the activities of family and friends, and as she receives more and more recent letters from India, she learns more about his illness, as well as of his time in China....

Friday, August 6th 1943 – Wolverhampton (AMLC)

 My dearest darling Ralph

I am thinking of you now in China, and hope so much you have been able to have some little time alone with Duncan, before embarking on the business meetings. I just pray that you are not having to do too much travelling, or undertaking too many meetings. But knowing you, I expect this is a forlorn hope!

I am so excited over future plans that I can hardly wait for September. It is all too wonderful and I lie awake at night planning and planning, and thinking of you. How I long for your return and to be able to take care of you here. David and Antony talk of you continually and are most excited at your coming home. I hope your return journeys go smoothly.

Here it's been busy, busy. I have just returned from Selly Oak, having left David quite happily parked with your mother. He seemed quite excited at the thought of spending a week there. I shall miss him terribly, but in many ways I think it will be good for him. He is such a sensible boy, so interested in everything, and really loves company. He has recently become mad on caterpillars, and has given me the responsibility of looking after them while he is away! I hope they don't die, or I shall get into serious trouble!

Your mother made us very welcome and I stayed one night, just to settle D in, and also to discuss things about the house. Heather asked if David could go up to play with Andrew, so on my way back in the morning, I left him there happily playing with A. Heather's new baby is a bouncy youngster – Duncan – who is very lively and healthy.

When I got home, Antony gave me a very warm welcome, and has been very good while I was away.

In discussion with LPA (L P Appleton at the BVT), we recently decided to give the Tritsch's notice, because of the necessity of getting our belongings out. They have until the end of September. I rather dreaded the outcome, in case they made a fuss, but apparently they are being very quiet and accepting everything as inevitable, now that you are coming home! So that is a great relief.

Win and Llew had a rather worrying letter from America today, saying that Priscilla is very unhappy and suffering terribly from homesickness. The Doctor advises her immediate return home[2], but it is difficult for W & L, as they don't know how best to get her back. I feel so sorry for them. I do hope some plan opens up for them soon.

I recently received an airgraph of yours dated July 9th and also one from Mary Loukes. It was so sweet of her to write and I am very grateful to her for all her kindness and help. How thoughtful of them to give you presents on your birthday. I must say they both seem very fond of you and I am so happy that you were able to be looked after by such charming people. She has given me real news about you, which is wonderful.

I have been reading the Earl of Lytton's book on India, 'Pundits and Elephants', which is facinating, and I am sure you would enjoy it, especially now you've been there.

I am sorry if some of my recent letters have been rather miserable, but you must realise that by the time you get them, I will have recovered. But just lately, I have missed you so terribly my sweetheart. Do take care of thyself – forever in my thoughts and prayers.

All my dearest love, Joan

———

At last my father hears that there is a flight the next morning, much to his relief. The plane turns out to be a flying boat, and once they've taken off, he describes in some detail, the route they take across Northern India, Pakistan, Baluchistan, Iraq and landing on the Dead Sea, and so to Cairo...........

Friday, August 27th 1943 – No 1 Upper Wood Street, Calcutta

My very dearest wife

Hurrah, hurrah! I have just heard that there is a flight to Cairo with seats for Horace and me tomorrow morning, which is great news as I am so anxious to get back now. All that remains is for me to pack up and say final farewells, especially to the Loukes for their kindness and hospitality on two occasions.

Continued.......Saturday, August 28th

Harold kindly took us both to the airport, which was a great help. Our plane turned out to be a flying boat, which is a novelty for me, and is very comfortable. Soon after we had left Calcutta, we saw the great width of the Hooghly River in the rising sun, which was most impressive. Unfortunately, we flew too high to see much else, either coming down at Allahabad or later in Gwalior in Madhya Pradesh state, in Central India.

In the evening we landed in Karachi, which is a not an unpleasant town, though situated in dull and rather bleak country. We spent the night in quite a good hotel but were off again very early the next morning. Again we hardly saw anything, until we came down on the shores of Baluchistan, in the south-west of Pakistan, which all seemed very barren.

We then flew on up the Persian Gulf, where it was almost unbearably hot, before reaching Basra in Iraq that night, coming to land on the Shatt al-Arab, the great river at the confluence of the Tigris and the Euphrates. On one side of the river is mile after mile of date palms, while on the other the cranes and landing stages of Basra. There is rather a grand new hotel there, where we stayed and which we found most comfortable. At the back is a garden where dinner was served by the light of the flood lamps, and in the front is another garden, which goes right down to the river. Here Horace and I sat out, eating the first dates of the season, watching the Bee Eaters and Terns on the river.

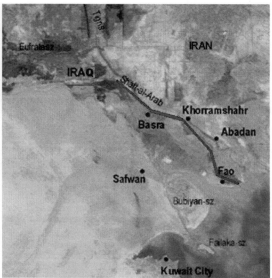

Right - showing Basra on the Shatt al-Arab, the great river at the confluence of the Tigris and the Euphrates.

Above – "Horace and I sat out eating the first dates of the season on the banks of the river!"

Map of India, Pakistan and S W Asia
Flight from Calcutta to Cairo by Flying Boat

Black line Map showing my father's flight from Calcutta to Cairo
Via Gwalior in central India, Karachi, Basra, RAF Habbaniyah landing on the Dead Sea
Image World Atlas

Our next stop was RAF Habbaniyah, just west of Baghdad in western Iraq, which is right on Lake Habbaniyah, on which we landed. We then flew on over the valley of the Tigris and Euphrates, which is not as inspiring as it sounds, passing over the remains of Babylon. From there on it is nothing but a very long and dull four hours of desert, before we eventually came down on the Dead Sea - a barren desolation. We had lunch in a café on the shore and at last made Cairo about 3.0 o'clock.

It was a good but very tiring trip, though in many ways it was rather pleasant to be back in Cairo. Coming back, I find that I rather like it. Compared with some other cities, it is clean – in comparison only - and well run - again comparatively - and the climate is good. All seems to be going well here and John Gough has done a very fine job, as has Michael Barratt Brown in relief work. Henry Headley, bless him, came in from Kassassin, and it was wonderful to see him. He always makes me laugh.

The new FAU seems just what we want – an all FAU unit. We have already had quite a reunion of old friends and colleagues, with Michael Rowntree here from somewhere west of Tripoli, Jack Frazer from Ethiopia and John Gough from Beirut. I am having long talks with them both jointly and separately. I had dinner with Jonnie Gough at the Auberge, with Eric at the St James, and with Jack Frazer at Mena House.

On Saturday I went up to Gezira Sporting Club to watch cricket with Barry Jones, and Horace and I and Michael went out in a taxi to try and see some birds and the only one of any note we succeeded in spotting, was a Wheatear, down by the Pyramids. However the deltas looked very lovely by the evening light. Unfortunately both John Rose and Douglas McKenzie were in hospital. But it is looking as though I may be here for about three weeks before I finally manage to leave, but Horace is going on as soon as he can.

I have found that the state of the Unit has changed considerably since I was here last. John Rose has been ably coping in my former role as OCME, and the Relief and Refugee Association, which had hitherto been dealing with refugees, such as the Poles I saw in Teheran, are now preparing to deal with a further large influx from Yugoslavia, as well as making preparations for those shortly to arrive from the liberated Balkan countries.

Army work, which had previously been the backbone of all the Unit's activities in the Middle East, is beginning to assume a secondary place, and preparations are in hand for a big increase in the numbers of Unit workers which has taken place in the last twelve months. The Hadfield Spears Unit is now operating in North Africa, while back in England a fresh Unit Section is already getting ready to come out to work with the French. I must say everything seems to be in capable hands and I feel I can safely leave in a few days and return to London. I'll write another letter at the end of the week.
All my love, Ralph

———

My mother, so delighted at my father's imminent arrival, keeps writing each letter as though it were the last, but each time there is a delay, as a flight is held up or my father stays longer than anticipated. She is also concerned about getting the Tritsch family out of the Linden Road home, as her sister is expecting the two elder children back from America, as well as the birth of the new child in November or December, and will want to prepare the house. This will mean that my mother and David and I will have to move back to Birmingham in time for my father's return. As my father's sister hasn't yet settled on their new London home, Granny Barlow is unable to move to London. So it is unlikely that my mother will be able to move into Swarthmore Road before November. A Cox and Box situation, if ever there was one, which drives my mother slightly mad! ....

Wednesday, August 11th to Friday, August 27th 1943 – Wolverhampton (AMLC)

My dearest husband
I was so happy to get your cable from Calcutta yesterday, and more than glad to know that you are safely back from China. I do hope you are really well and not too tired from your three weeks away. I phoned Gordon Square immediately. Tegla was at Yearly Meeting, but I spoke to Michael Cadbury, who said he would go straight into Yearly Meeting and announce that you were back! I am so excited and thrilled to think that you will soon be home. It really is too wonderful and I am bursting with plans. D & A are both very excited too. Oh, it is good, good, good. Please do take special care of yourself and make sure you get sufficient rest on the journey home.

Your mother says David is having a marvellous time at Swarthmore Road and is so good and sweet. Isn't it splendid he is so happy and not missing me? It is very good for him to be independent. He really does love going to places. Antony misses David very much, but he has been quite good amusing himself. I took him to the Walker's for tea, which he enjoyed very much. It is so quiet though with only one son here....mere child's play after having two to look after!! I am going to Jeph and Margaret's tomorrow morning and will then fetch David back.

Thank you for your long letter No. 37 (p506) which arrived this morning together with your Bird essay, which was the very devil to read!! I have enjoyed reading both the letter and the essay so much and will try and type them out. You do write such excellent letters. What a marvellous report the doctors gave you before you went to China. You have indeed made a wonderful recovery. But I still think you must take things quietly for some time.

I keep saying that this letter or that letter is going to be the last I shall write, but I still go on writing, as you continually get delayed. How annoying all the hold ups must be. I do hope you won't get too many more and that I really will see you in September. David keeps asking when he is going to get a letter from you. He does so love to hear from you. You would laugh at his chatting to his many bus driver friends. They all wave at him and pass the time of day. He will miss them when we move. He is reading very well now.

I haven't heard any more from the Tritsch's and wrote him another note yesterday, saying we needed the house by the 1st of October at the latest, and would he please let me know the date he intended to leave. LPA thinks he doesn't intend to move! But we really do need them out soon, so that I can get it ready for your return. Also Win is expecting the baby at the beginning of December, and it's quite likely Mike and Prill will be back from America[2] soon, as W & L have gone to London today to see Noël Hunnybun, who has just returned from the USA, hoping that she can advise them about getting the children back. I can't see us moving into 'Sunnybrae' until November, as Millior and Alfred haven't yet got things fixed. My head is in a whirl, and I wish I had everything clear. No doubt it will sort itself out in time. But.....!

I am trying to smarten myself up for your return! Shall we have altered much do you think? I am wondering if it would be possible for me to come up and meet you in London on your return. Perhaps you could phone me or wire when you landed? It would be wonderful if I could, and perhaps we might spend two or three days doing things together, if you weren't too tired. I leave it to you.   All my love for now, Joan

This next letter really is my mother's last! And it is full of happiness at the news of my father's return. As usual my mother's letter also brings my father up-to-date – David's stay with his Granny, visiting friends, more letters from India, and worries about moving. In the event, probably because the Tritsch's weren't able to find somewhere else to live immediately, my father's homecoming was at Wolverhampton. And so, as so often in life, early worries prove wasted energy, and they never did return to Linden Road, but moved straight into No 6 Swarthmore Road in the November........

Wednesday, September 1st 1943 – Wolverhampton (AMLC)

My dearest one
This definitely will be my last letter until I see you! I had been rather anxious without any recent news, but yesterday morning, Michael Cadbury telephoned from London to say they had received a cable of your safe arrival in Cairo. I was terribly excited and so relieved. Now I'm fairly bursting with happiness as there's a good chance we shall meet later this month. I do, do hope so. David is thrilled and even Antony is excited and keeps saying "Daddy coming home". I have a new coat and dress for your return, and I hope you'll like them. I wonder if you'll find me much changed.

I can't tell you what it's like, except it is just a very warm feeling of happiness, like a dream. I have pictured it all so many times, and now it is coming true. Richard Symonds sent me a letter (p560) from Cairo all about you and how you were, which was kind of him and much appreciated. It's wonderful to know that you are so much better.

I've just received four long letters from you, two written on the boat to India, and two written at the Loukes. They were such good letters and I have so enjoyed reading them. They tell me so much more than the Airgraphs, especially of what you are feeling and thinking. I almost wept to read the account of your illness. How awful it must have been to feel so ill and not know anyone when you arrived in Bombay. How I long to have you back home, so I can look after you properly. Oh when shall I see you? I get so terribly excited at the thought of you being home again.

590

David had a very, very happy time staying with your mother, who said he had been very good. Even Lydia remarked how well behaved he was and everybody told me "How well trained he is!" I asked him if he had missed me much, and he said "Well, not <u>very</u> much!" Bless him. I really think your mother did enjoy having him. She said he had been such good company. They did so many things – going to the Lickeys, the Manor, the Yachting Pool[3], to Meeting on Sunday, and to John and Enid's, where Roger showed him his train set.

Your mother told me a funny story about when she and David had been doing some spelling together, and she had written the word ALE. David said "I know, it is like Beer, horrid stuff. Don't you ever take any Granny, or it might become a habit!!" He couldn't have said anything to please her more, and I felt it was rather a feather in my cap! Though God knows I've never talked to him about it.

When he got home, he ran straight into the yard to look at his caterpillars, which mercifully hadn't died under my care!

I enjoyed my time with Jeph and Margaret and looked after the new baby for her, while I was there. They gave me a great welcome and it made a real change for me. Reg and Vera have been staying at Sutton, and came over here for the day yesterday with the children. Reg is still stationed near home and able to live at home with Vera, which is nice for both of them.

I'm hoping and praying that the Tritsch's will move out of 26 very soon, so that I can prepare everything for your homecoming. I don't think we can move to 'Sunnybrae' until November, as Millior and Alfred are having a lot done to their new house.

The children are well and are such dears and send hugs and kisses to you too. Well my dearest, God keep you safe and watch over you till we meet again - very soon now I pray.

Always your loving Joan

Granny Barlow with my father and his first born, David at Linden Road 1937.
David had always been very fond of his Grandmother since he was a baby.

After nearly 3 weeks my father completes his business in Cairo, calls a halt to the many requests on his time to see people, decides that a sea journey will be more restful than a flight, and books a cabin on a boat instead, which is shortly leaving Suez for Liverpool......

Tuesday, September 7th 1943 – Cairo

Dearest Joan,

I'm afraid I have been so busy seeing people while I have been here, I just haven't had the time to write. Forgive me, as so many people have wanted to see me before I leave, that my time here keeps having to be extended. It really does look as if I shall be here for another two or three weeks before I can get on a boat home. If I tell you that just yesterday I saw Captain Archibald, and Mrs Bryant at the British Red Cross, Lord Moyne, the Middle East Minister of State, and Sir William T Mathews of the Middle East Refugee Association, you will have some idea of the pressures.

I was also, would you believe, invited out by the talkative Miss Perkins at the Archeological Museum to have tea at the Pyramids. It's all been rather tiring and I was really quite glad not to be flying on with Horace, who left a few days ago. I hope by the time that you get the airmail I posted the other day, you will have heard from Horace, who will have explained why I have stayed on here a bit longer. It's partly because there is quite a lot to do, and much that needs to be completed before I go, in particular meetings with John Gough, Jack Frazer and Mike Rowntree. I did not want it to seem as though I was rushing away.

Secondly, I thought a sea voyage would be more acceptable and relaxing than undertaking further flying; the long air trip from India was really very tiring. I am also trying to buy some clothes before coming home, so as to save on coupons. However, I think I have now managed to call a halt to all these visits and finally fixed up to get a cabin on a boat leaving Suez in a few days' time. Unfortunately this will mean having to spend most of two days and a night in that frightful transit camp at Suez.

———

Continued.......Friday, September 10th 1943 - Cairo

The transit camp was every bit as ghastly as I remember it and I was glad to leave there, I can tell you. So after I'd had an early breakfast at 6.30am, I hastened to get on board about 7.0, as it would have been too awful to have had to spend one more night in that place. I'm not quite sure which day we are sailing, but I must say the prospect of returning home is thrilling and of seeing you and the children. I send all my love for our anniversary on the 17th, and shall be thinking of you so much. Seven such happy years.

I am guessing that there will be so many things to clear up when I get back, that I think I will come to see you all straight away and stay a few days, which will be wonderful. But then I shall almost certainly have to go on up to London, and probably spend about a week there, before taking some proper home leave. I really am getting better now and this voyage will, I am sure do me good. But being home with you will do me most good of all.

Well, this appears to be quite a fine ship, and I have a decent cabin, a single one which has been adapted to take four, but actually there are only three of us. One of them, is a Cable Company employee who seems to have spent all his life travelling, and had lived for some time on Ascension Island. Poor man he was most upset to have lost his rather nice felt hat, so that his only head covering, in which he would eventually leave the ship and proceed on to Edinburgh, is a sola topee!

The boat is very full of POWs who have just escaped from Italy and are on their way home, plus a number of sick and wounded Officers. There are also nurses, WAAF's and ATS's all being repatriated; Palestinian officials and Police going home on leave; and Merchant Navy and Royal Navy personnel going back to Blighty![4]

Happily, it is a very comfortable ship, which is just as well as it is proving to be a very dull and boring journey. A day through the canal, a day at Port Said, and about four days through to Algiers. We were able to see only very little, bar the island of Pantellaria, the searchlights of Malta and the dim outline of the African coast.

Continued.......Friday, September 20th 1943

We were stuck in Algiers for nearly a week, which was very tedious for all on board, as we were unable to go ashore. After we left there, we are due to call at Oran in north-west Algeria, where I will try and post this, before we finally sail on through the straits of Gibraltar and so on up to Liverpool. The voyage has been totally uneventful, save that one of our large escort boats dropped some depth charges. I hope you will get this before I get back home. I am so longing to see you again.   With all my dearest love Ralph

There were no further letters, but my father writes in his memoirs of the sheer joy of arriving home........

We landed on a beautiful day at the beginning of October. It was an unforgettable experience going up the Channel and getting one's first sight of England again. I don't think I shall ever forget the thrill as we came into Liverpool and docked at the same quay from which we had left. The joy of being really back in the UK again has never left me. How well I remember driving through Liverpool to the station, sending off a number of telegrams to Joan and Gordon Square, and then travelling down to London in an English train. After sixteen months of being abroad and away from the family, it was the most exhilarating experience imaginable. After a night in London, I went to Wolverhampton, the scene that I had so often pictured in my mind, with Joan and the boys meeting me on the platform, and later back at Lea Road, unpacking the presents I had brought.

The Mersey and the Liverpool docks c. 1943
"I shall never forget the thrill as we came into Liverpool and docking at the
same quay from which we had left."
Photo Liverpool archives

Chapter 39
Back in England
October 1943 – December 1944

This chapter is taken from a combination of my father's memoirs written for his children, plus the report he made for Gordon Square. It details his joyful return home, a short holiday alone with my mother in one of their favourite places, moving house to Swarthmore Road, and three months sick leave. He then returned to Gordon Square for most of 1944, in the position of Officer for Overseas Work, while continuing his role as Deputy Chairman, before being invalided out in December 1944.......

When I arrived home, I was, like all the other people back from overseas, full of a desire to tell Gordon Square a lot of things they probably already knew, but were too polite to say, and no doubt wasted a lot of paper on reports! I then went on sick leave for three months, during which Joan and I went for a glorious week together to Dunster, where we had been so happy in 1940. We did little, but it was as lovely that autumn as we remembered from before, and our week was indeed good. When we got back, we moved into my mother's former home at 6 Swarthmore Road, which was a considerable undertaking.

It was of course, wonderful to be in our own home again, and to be with Joan and the boys after so long away and to have a period of calm and readjustment. Inevitably, because the war was still ongoing, there was always a feeling that overshadowed everything, that it might be only temporary.

In January '44 I went to London to Chair the monthly Staff Meeting, once again as Deputy Chairman, as Tegla was away on an extended visit to the Mediterranean and then jointly with Paul Cadbury to North-west Europe. I was asked if I would take on the role of Overseas Officer, with responsibility for all overseas work and correspondence, and I started work almost at once.

Civilian Relief became the central prong of the Unit's work in 1944 and 1945, beginning in Italy and Sicily and slowly gathering momentum. Not all the FAU's other work came to an end. For instance, the China Convoy remained at full strength until 1946, when it was taken over by the AFSC; and in India a small number of Unit members remained, dealing with the results of the natural disasters of floods and famine. But in November '44 both the Ethiopian Section and the Syrian clinics were put on notice of withdrawal, to be handed over to local administrations. For the most part, therefore, during these last years of the war, the Unit was concentrating on the Far East and relief work in Europe. As per usual with a new position, my father is unsure whether he will be any good, and of course, when he leaves the Unit in '45 he is reluctant to leave! ....

The Unit and its later work in 1944

Initially, having had a job in the field for so long, it was difficult to avoid a feeling of general uselessness, receiving and reading endless correspondence. But gradually I started to enjoy it and immensely appreciated working with Ronald Joynes, whose long experience of the Overseas Office was invaluable. He was a cheerful soul, who had a pleasant, clear mind and we spoke the same language.

Our object was to give Overseas Sections as good a service as possible of news, answering their questions, and generally creating a feeling of responsibility and trust. I tried to be au fait with the countries in which the Unit was working and to disseminate news to other bodies. Actually, though I says as shouldn't, I think the Unit Office in London was as well informed as any of the Unit offices.

International co-operation

Clarence Pickett
Photograph AFSC

Sir Herbert Emerson
Photograph IGCR

Roger Wilson
Photo courtesy Wilson family

It was increasingly clear that only by international co-operation, could relief be organised on a large enough scale to tackle the immensity of the problems. Hence we worked very closely with Sir Herbert Emerson, the Director of the Inter-Governmental Committee on Refugees (IGCR), with Roger Wilson at Friends Relief Service, (FRS - The former War Victims Relief) and with the leading American Quaker, Clarence Pickett of the American Friends Service Council.

During the twelve months I was working in London, the Unit saw big relief developments. Initially, this was in Italy thanks to Peter Gibson's drive, where he got the Unit in, despite a Red Cross monopoly. There they were principally dealing with refugees from other countries as well as Italian refugees displaced by fighting. In Sicily also the Unit undertook a very useful survey of hospital services. Italy also offered to house many Jewish refugees, and I met up with Sir Clifford Heathcote-Smith[1], who was also working for IGCR in connection with finding them homes there.

In the autumn Pickett visited London, and he struck all of us as a really big man. He was very anxious to co-operate with the FSC (Friends Service Council) in future work in India and happy for the AFSC to takeover what might be left in China. I had several meetings with him – including a very nice dinner at the Euston Hotel! – and I introduced him to the Executive and arranged for him to meet British Friends at a conference at Edward and Dorothy Cadbury's home, Westholme, Bournville. Under Pickett's leadership, the AFSC had become one of the leading voices on peace and social justice around the world.

Middle East

The Unit was also working on relief in the Middle East, where after a difficult initial period, during which Michael Barratt Brown had decided to leave the Unit to work for the Middle East Relief and Refugee Administration (MERRA), they settled down under Lewis Waddilove's capable leadership, and together with Keith Linney and Arnold Curtis did an excellent job in the refugee camps, where they were employed in welfare, cooking, catering and nursing, as well as all the other things so necessary in large camps of refugees. After the Germans withdrew from the Balkans, they gradually moved to undertake work in Greece, where an advance party had already gone when I left in December 1944.

India

Inevitably, I still had a lot to do with the India Section, through my close contacts with Horace Alexander, and Gandhi's close associate and Secretary of the Indian Conciliation Group, Agatha Harrison. Together we liaised with the High Commissioners and the India Office. During this period there were several changes of personnel in the India Section.

The first was in June when Dick Symonds was over on leave, and he received an offer of a job as Special Officer for Relief and Rehabilitation in Bengal under the Governor, Richard Casey. As the offer came as a direct result of the work he'd undertaken with the Unit Section out in India, I thought it only right that he should accept it. Christopher Taylor, who had been Chairman of the Friends Relief Service in London, subsequently took over from Richard as head of the India Section, where he remained until July '44. The Section had done a good job and had acquired a deal of experience in famine relief, and were now taking over more and more responsibility for rehabilitation.

Horace Alexander (2nd left) and Agatha Harrison (4th left) seen here with the Mahatma

Far left - Rajkumkari Amrit Kaur, who was to become the first Minister of Health and far right Pyarelal Nayar, Gandhi's secretary.
Photograph Dinodia photos

China

Following my visit to China in '43 and the many meetings I had chaired there, I was keen to try and build up confidence between there and London, and I think that on the whole I succeeded. In fact during my twelve months, I think the China Section worked very well. Many of their earlier difficuties had been surmounted under Duncan Wood's and Ken Bennet's able direction and they had consolidated their efforts well.

In the process of creating better relations, I saw a lot of senior diplomats and experts on China, including George Kitson head of the Far Eastern department of the Foreign Office, the Chinese Ambassador, the legendary Vi K Wellington Koo, Leonard Tomkinson, the man who we appointed Chairman of the Council in China, and the Quaker authority and Swarthmore lecturer, Harry T Silcock. The needs of China were simply immense, and the Unit, by providing medical planes and transporting supplies were doing a little to meet at least two of the most pressing.

Allied Armies - Civil Affairs Branch

The Allied Armies, through their Civil Affairs Branch had initial responsibility for relief in liberated areas, and had drawn up a programme of relief for N W Europe, involving a request for a large number of British voluntary personnel. We decided to send Robin Whitworth, the Unit's Overseas Relief Officer, out to Brussels to co-ordinate, and through complicated negotiations, skillfully carried out by him, a contingent of 55 Unit members under the leadership of Gerald Gardiner[*12] went to Europe to deal with refugees uncovered by the advancing allied armies. This was the largest single group the Unit ever sent overseas. One section, for instance under Richard Wainwright, in liaison with Entr'aide Française, did a very useful job distributing vital stocks of medicine and clothing through the FAU office in Bayeux, before the onset of winter.

There were any number of international committees being established at this time, such as the United Nations Relief and Rehabilitation Administration (UNRRA), and their proliferation led to the establishment of a supervisory body to co-ordinate their many disparate efforts. This was the Council of British Societies for Relief Abroad (CBSRA) and Members of the Unit including myself sat on its General Purposes Committee. The problem with large organisations was that their official machinery often ground slowly, and small organisations such as the FAU could frequently move more rapidly and get to work while official machinery was still ponderously gearing up for action.

Talking to Friends House

One of my other chief preoccupations during this period, was with the Society of Friends. Soon after I returned from the Middle East I had spoken at Meeting for Sufferings. Later I spoke at Yearly Meeting and I wrote many articles for The Friend and The Wayfarer.

I believed that the Society had been presented with a great opportunity by the Unit, but I thought that to make the most of it, it needed to be less vague and woolly, more realist, and have a more clearly defined policy.

The Unit was often critical of the Friends Relief Service, and during these months, it had in many ways the best staff that it ever had. Yet much of its policy seemed half-hearted. It had a job to do, but failed to do it. By the autumn, Jack Ryan had returned to America, Charles Carter was Overseas Secretary and Roger Wilson was in Paris.

[*12] Later Lord Gardiner, Harold Wilson's Lord Chancellor.

Overseas Work

There was much talk of co-operation for overseas work, and several of us had a conference at Christopher Taylor's house Througham Hall in Gloucestershire, but nothing came of it. FRS did a real job in this country, and will I think do a real job overseas, but it has had a lot of teething troubles.

I also thought that it was tragic that the Friends Service Council was so cautious and unadventurous. I didn't particularly mind if they took over much of the Unit's work, but I was anxious that they should make use of our experienced personnel. I regarded it as a major personal triumph, that when I left, they were prepared to take on Unit people including the Burtts and later Alexander, who remained in Calcutta, and to sponsor the education team of Selby Clewer and his wife in Ethiopia. I believe that in some way, I helped to make these changes possible.

———

As my father mentions during his year at Gordon Square, he had a lot to do with the Society, and in an article he wrote for The Friend, he confronts some of his concerns and considers from his experience, the implications and significance of the Unit's work overseas......

The Friend - January 1945
The Friends Ambulance Unit Overseas by F Ralph Barlow

"Many Friends must wonder how far the Unit overseas succeeds in making any pacifist witness. On my way back home, a man on the boat, who was most sympathetic to our pioint of view, told me he thought the Unit's position was untenable, and that a real pacifist witness can only be made by completely standing aside. I know that certain Friends feel that our compromise has been too great.

They may be right; but, after visiting all Unit sections overseas, I have come to the conclusion that the Unit does succeed in making a very real witness. This is particularly the case in our co-operation with the Army in the Middle East, where the whole basis of our work depends on the authorities accepting our position as pacifists and appreciating what we can and cannot conscientiously do. To those who do not share our views, it is not the degree of compromise, but the fact of our pacifism that matters.

However infinitesimal, comparatively speaking, the Unit's achievements may be, it is impressive that a band of young and largely inexperienced young men, holding unpopular views, has been able to build up the work it has, in centres so widely separated as Whitechapel, Beirut, Cairo, Addis Ababa, Calcutta and Kutsing. It is also a remarkable tribute to the liberal mindedness of the country in which we live. Irrespective of what has been achieved, and this is by no means negligible, it has value and meaning as an indication of what men of goodwill can do in a world of war.

In what other ways has it achieved its purpose? It has enabled nearly eight hundred CO's to give service where it is needed, which was the hope of Paul Cadbury when he refounded the Unit at the beginning of this war. It has enebled them to share the life of those millions of our fellow countrymen and women who are serving overseas. But we must not be blind to the fact that our sacrifice is smaller than that which is demanded of the fighting forces. Unit sections suffer danger, hardship, separation from home and isolation, but they do not suffer the two worst aspects of a soldier's life, boredom and monotony without hope of relief and the ever present danger and courting of death.

I would not however minimise the strain, often unconscious, of life abroad, which the fighting forces and pacifists share alike. The absence of all home associations is a very real strain and one which does demand some internal resource and power. Some find contact with foreign people and with differing standards very unsettling. In a few days or weeks, Unit members must settle into and start work in a new country; there is little time for acclimatisation. Often a man will find his conscience no more at rest by going abroad; rather the contrary.

How far do Unit members meet these difficulties? Moral standards are inevitably lowered in time of war. My impression is that the Unit has stood the test. Lack of money may have something to do with this. Devotion to a cause is still there, however, even though rarely mentioned, despite the deadening effect of four years of war and two more years' absence from home. In places Unit devotionals are still a very real thing; in places they are very lifeless. In attempting to conduct its religious meetings after the manner of the Society, the Unit is taking a very difficult path, and it is not surprising that it often fails; it is perhaps more surprising that it so often succeeds.

It is interesting to consider the hopes for the future of Unit members overseas. First, I think, they look forward to returning home; some to their previous jobs, (especially the specialists) all of them to their families. For the former, whatever excitement there may have been in doing unfamiliar tasks, has worn off and they want to return to jobs they are trained for and can do. Many will want to become good citizens and to do their service as such. Others will want to go in for relief and social work. These are fewer, however; four years of their lives have passed, and many feel that they must make a place for themselves and their families.

It should be realised however, that there is, in the Unit, a vast mass of material potentially of great value to the Society. Will the Society have the imagination and wisdom to capture it? How it can best do so I do not know, but many who have been abroad are still loyal members or are anxious to be loyal members. They are however more cynical and more realist. They dislike any suspicion of cant and hypocrisy, and the wrapping up of things in words. Their contact with their fellow men in the services, with others of different denominations within the Unit and with people of other religions, make them demand a clear and real faith. Has the Society a message for such people? Are its feet sufficiently on the ground? I know that the approach must be mutual, that the Unit too must show much wisdom, tact and forebearance.

Of our debt to the Society we are all conscious. The word 'Friend' in our name is a tremendous asset. We are grateful for what it means to us and hope that we are conscious of the responsibility it imposes. There is another side to the picture however, which Friends shoud realise. With all its mistakes and impetuosities, the Unit has honourably carried the name and something of the spirit of the Society into areas where it was hitherto unknown, and has taken new life to exisiting centres. Ethiopia is an instance of the former, the East End, Syria and India of the latter. Travelling round the world, one is continually humbled and astonished at the reputation which the Society enjoys. The Unit shares that reputation, and it is, I think, fair to say that in the last four years, it has contributed to it.

Yet the Unit is not the Society of Friends. So much of its valued membership comes from other churches, bringing their own high traditions. These members respect the Society, but are critical of it in a friendly spirit. But we are, I think, agreed that the Society, if it so desires, must and should be the inheritor of the Unit's more permanent work.

The Unit is essentially an emergency organisation, brought together by the war, and only waiting for the emergency to end before it spearates again. Time and again, however, it has become involved in commitments of a more long term nature.

It will be a pity if all this work should come to an end. Does the Society wish to build on any of the foundations which have been laid, or the foundations which we hope to lay in relief work? Probably rightly the Society is loth to go ahead of concern; finances and personnel are scarce, the field is great. But there is an opportunity for the Society which it can grasp if it shows imagination, clear thinking, and some speed of action. It is an opportunity which should be taken soon, if the services of many qualified workers are to be secured. Friends' relief will, as before, depend to a great extent on the few mature and experienced Friends, but there will be so many younger, less experienced people anxious to work under the Quaker star. And there are those who may come under conscription Acts after the war.

It would be interesting to have the judgment of an unbiased observer. Personally, while fully alive to all the shortcomings of the Unit (as only an inside observer can be) I feel that it has justified itself at least on the three following counts. It has not only provided employment for a number of COs, but in many cases it has enabled them to feel that they are giving really useful service. It is undertaking work which would otherwise remain undone. It is making a gesture which is not insignificant, amidst the tragedy of a world at war."

—

Looking back on the Gordon Square he knew when he first joined, together with all his close friends, he looks back and looks forward.....

The Unit Past and Present

In many ways the Unit is very much the same as it ever was, and the Executive Committee still discusses many of the same things as before – the nature of women's work and how best to implement HQ's orders, but there has been a subtle change, although I find it very difficult to define. I think it is more than merely a nostalgia for the good old days. I think the Unit is duller – perhaps more efficient, more concerned with doing a job – and consequently it spends less time looking inwards, talking or thinking about itself.

Also of course, so many people who had made life interesting, have gone overseas. I think as well, many are rather tired and war-weary, and certainly much of the abounding enthusiasm of the early days seems to have gone; it makes life easier, but duller. Unlike the previous period in London, I now had no special friends in the Unit.

It has been the aim of Ronald Joynes and myself so far as possible to keep in touch with overseas sections and to keep them in touch with what is happening here and to see that parties going overseas have some clear knowledge of what they are going to do. Ronnie Joynes has, of course, reduced the business of getting parties overseas to a fine art.

Another noteworthy feature of these months, is the way in which members of the first Camp are again playing a part in Unit affairs at Headquarters. There has been too, I hope, a closer approach to the Society of Friends. We are greatly in its debt, and we on our part have given something to them too.

The past twelve months have seen a great development in the numbers on relief in the Balkans and the formation of an entirely new section in the North-West; and ambulance and hospital work being done quite close to the front line by the two sections with the French.

These developments, together with the continuing work of the other overseas sections, have provided plenty of work, but it was very easy to feel completely useless sitting in an office at Gordon Square and to get the impression that members in the field are doing all the work. This useless feeling should not, I think blind us to the real importance of work at HQ, and all honour is due to those who have uncomplainingly borne the brunt of dull administrative routine for so long.

I was still getting very tired, and I cannot imagine that I was 100% effective. The Unit Doctor said that I should take things slowly, and I did take weekends off at home in Birmingham. But by the year's end I was finding it a struggle, and I and others felt that I ought to see a specialist.

A photo of FRB taken prior to his starting back at the BVT in 1945

Photograph by Morland Braithwaite

Chapter 40
Invalided out
&
Letters of Praise and Appreciation
December 1944

This chapter begins with one of the few letters from this period which my father wrote from Gordon Square, in September '44. It is interesting, that he is already talking about leaving the Unit to live at home, prior to any Doctor's advice that he do so. His reasons, importantly, involve primarily the feeling that he should give more time to my mother and us children. But he is obviously aware that his health is not 100%, and hence his input is limited, as is his finance, in which connection, it is worth remembering that he is still only on half salary from the BVT. He promises to be home for good by Christmas......

Sunday, September 10th 1944 – Gordon Square

My darling wife

I don't much like staying up in London over weekends, as there seems nothing much else to do, and the feeling that I ought to come into the office. It really is a damned nuisance having to go to Welwyn this evening. When asked back in April if I would go and talk there, September seemed so far away, that it was quite alright to agree. Now, of course, the chickens have come home to roost. I think I am also supposed to give a talk at Leighton Park in October.

I didn't tell you I think, that the evening I got back here, I went to Antoine's for supper, and there was Sydney Bailey, a Unit member just back from China and America, having dinner with Kingsley Martin[1], the New Statesman Editor. Sydney kindly invited me to join them. I hadn't met him before, but he was most interesting especially on America and Russia in connection with Mao[2] and Chiang Kai-Shek[3]. Remind me to tell you.

I have been thinking a lot about us, and I just want to promise that I will make a real effort to get out of the Unit by Christmas. I say this is for the following reasons:
   a) Because you quite rightly think that it is time.
   b) Because I think you have every right to expect me to give you more help with the children.
   c) Health – I do feel a lot better since the holiday, but perhaps not 100%.
   d) The BVT Estate Office – I need to get back.
   e) Finance – I have been on half salary long enough

So unless any very unexpected difficulty arises, I should be home for Christmas.

As the eighth anniversary of our wedding approaches, I would like to say now, what I shall be able to say in person next week-end. Thank you for being such a wonderful wife. You are all and more than I could have hoped for. They have been eight very wonderful years. I love you more now than ever. I love your comradeship, your humour and keen interest in everything, and your charm and tenderness.

I am deeply grateful for our sons and the way you have brought them up, and for the way you have run and managed everything over the last difficult years. And I am so grateful to you for letting me go to the Unit. Understand my darling how much I love and admire you.
May God keep you safe. Your ever loving husband.
Always yours, Ralph

———

Later in the month he wrote to Tegla Davies, who was away visiting Sections abroad, along the same lines, beginning the process of leaving the Unit that he had promised my mother........

Saturday, September 30th 1944 – Gordon Square

PERSONAL

My dear Tegla

I think it might be desirable to write you a personal note about my position as I see it. [....]

With regard to my own health: on the whole I feel better than I did before I went on leave – although that is not saying much! I am obviously able to do a fairly full day's work, but I do get frightfully tired, and I still crawl around the place like an old man! So that I think that at some suitable stage after your return, it would be a good idea if I could see a specialist.

It seems to me that there may be three things that he might say. Firstly, that I am all right, and that I am making a fuss about nothing. Secondly, that I ought to have a longish period of leave, and then carry on in the Unit. Or thirdly, that if I am really to get better, I ought to be invalided out.

In the event of his saying the first or second, it will still be necessary to decide what should happen to me. In the event of his saying the third, the position is fairly clear.

We then come to the other reasons. Firstly, my wife is naturally anxious for me to live at home, and I do feel that I ought to do so for her sake and for the sake of the children. Naturally, I should like to do so. Secondly, Bournville would also like me back, and Mr Appleton is leaving in March. Lastly, I feel it about time I started to earn more money [....] and a proper salary would be a great help!

[....]I hope the above notes will be of some help

Yours ever, Ralph

Here my father talks in his memoirs about the prospect of leaving and his mixed feelings of both wanting to stay and his need to get back home......

I was very doubtful about the rightness of leaving the Unit. I was not well and perhaps I did not fully realise how far from well I was. But I suppose I thought that as long as the Unit wanted me at Gordon Square, I should carry on. I did not want my health to be an excuse for getting me back to Bournville, and I did not want all my friends to feel that I was deserting them.

Christopher Taylor – on behalf of the Unit – felt very strongly that I should see a specialist, and that if he thought that I would recover best at home, then I should be invalided out. He thought that it was important in the interests of my family and for the future that I should get fully well, and that although I probably could carry on, it might be permanently detrimental to my health.

Paul Cadbury thought the same, though I felt he was possibly biased towards Bournville. Joan was also strongly of the opinion that I ought to leave. So following advice from all quarters, I went to see a specialist, who did advise me to leave and live at home, and so on December 5th 1944, I left the Unit with many expressions of regret and much kindness.

Once the decision had been taken, my father received, as he says 'many expressions of regret' from all levels of the Unit – both the Executive and ordinary members. It is a measure of my father's standing that not only is he held in enormous respect by those he has worked with, but also by senior management everywhere.

My mother often calls him 'the most capable and respected member of the Senior Management' or the 'only person to take Tom Tanner's place', and it is easy to think this is a wife's hyperbole. But these letters from the entire Unit, give the lie to that, as such sentiments are echoed in these many letters of regret at his leaving, and all talk of the gap he will leave. As our Grandmother wrote to my mother....."Dear Joan [....] Thank you for letting me see these letters. You must keep them to show the boys when they grow older, so that they will learn about their father from all the heartfelt tributes both to his dear self and to his work."

So rather than just reproduce a few of them, it seems important to print several of them to show exactly the stature of the man who, we his children, are privileged to call our father.

So I begin with one from the person who began it all, Paul Cadbury, founder of the FAU......

Friends Ambulance Unit Gordon Square – December 6 1944

 Dear Ralph

I am so sorry that you are leaving the Unit on medical grounds, though I feel sure it is the right decision, despite my certain knowledge that you are one of the few men in the Unit who cannot be replaced. [.....]

I must also thank you for the work you have done for the Unit since you joined – perhaps more helpful to me than you will ever realise.

This is just to let you know that I shall miss you at Gordon Square, and to wish you well.

Next from Tegla Davies, who served in the Unit from 1940 until the end of the war, holding senior positions including acting Chairman. He also chronicled the history of the Unit in WW2 in his book 'The Friends Ambulance Unit', published in 1947.........

Friends Ambulance Unit Gordon Square – December 3rd 1944

My dear Ralph

You know how I feel about your going and I have sensed over the last few days, you have felt about having to go. The Unit gets hold of one [....] Most of all I want to thank you for your loyalty.

You must know that I feel you have so many admirable qualities for Unit administration; but what I have appreciated most of all is your old fashioned loyalty to the Unit as an idea and to me personally. You have been a tremendous and irreplaceable help to me, especially over the last year. Today the place seems emptier now that you've gone.

Take care of yourself Ralph.

Yours Tegla

PS. Final bit of news – Gordon Square was burgled last night. They stole a typewriter and a camera – but greatest of all losses was Ronnie Joynes' Homberg hat! All future meetings will have to wait until a new hat is procured!

Then in no particular order, are letters from colleagues and friends who had worked alongside him in the Unit both in London and abroad, or in association with him in his dealings with allied organisations such as Friends House, The British Red Cross, the Friends Service Council and the American FSC:

Agatha Harrison, close associate of Mahatma Gandhi and fighter for Indian independence........

Cranbourne Court SW11 – December 4th 1944

Dear Ralph

I have just found out from Horace that you are leaving the Unit. I somehow can't imagine 4 Gordon Square without you, and I shall miss you personally very much indeed.

I am sorry that it is a matter of your health and I do hope that you will soon be back to your normal strength.

When you are next in town, do please give me a ring, so that I can look forward to the pleasure of your company again soon.

Ronald Joynes, colleague in the Middle East and at Gordon Square, London........

Friends Ambulance Unit 4 Gordon Square – December 6th 1944

My dear Ralph

When a chap like you leaves the Unit, there are so many things one wants to say, yet most of them are very hard to express. When the possibility of your leaving was first raised, I found it hard to talk to you in the way I really felt.

On the one hand I felt your health must certainly come first, on the other I didn't see how we could manage without you. I still don't see. I didn't want to say – 'yes you should go' – too often, in case you thought we were trying to get you out! On the other hand, if we didn't encourage you, you might not have gone at all! Seems silly now, doesn't it?

I was glad to read in your note that you had enjoyed the time we had working together. Me too – and we did manage to see the brighter side of things as well, didn't we? I feel with old Tegla back, it's likely to be rather a serious office, but perhaps we can educate him!

Take care Ralph, and think of me sometimes in this 'school' here! I must say every day it does seem more and more like one. The other day, I almost threatened to take one of the China party to see the Headmaster!!

The place already seems dead without you, and I can't think how we shall manage. I have only just begun to realise how much we owe to you and how much I depended on our daily discussions and 'grumbling sessions'.

I do hope you can take things easily, and will soon be really fit again.

Very sincerely

Henry Headly, colleague in the Middle East............

FAU Central Mediterranean Forces Italy - December 10th 1944

Dear Ralph

We have just heard that you have left the Unit and I need hardly say, that to me at any rate, it has come as a real blow. I know it has been on your mind for some time, but somehow I could never really imagine it happening. I realise that to a great extent our confidence in Gordon Square administration, was really confidence in yourself.

Ever since you came out to the Middle East, I seem to have been passing bucks on to you, and leaving you to carry cans of one sort or another, and I have always appreciated the helpful and sympathetic way in which the said bucks and cans were accepted.

May I thank you personally for what you have done for the FAU, and so indirectly for me. On the other hand, I must say that I am glad to hear that you have taken the step you have, if it means that it will help you in your recovery. I'm sure you will enjoy a bit of leave and getting back to your old job.

I hope Joan and the family are all well, and I send you all best wishes for Christmas and the New Year.

Yours

Henry

From Brandon Cadbury, close associate both in London and in China........

December 19th 1944 – Chunking

From Brandon Cadbury

Dear Ralph

Thank you for writing to inform me of your departure from the Unit. I am personally very sorry and I know London will certainly miss you very much indeed, as will I. It has always been good working with you and the Unit owes you a great debt of gratitude. [....]

I wish you and your family every happiness now, for the New Year and the future.

Sincerely

Brandon.

From Michael Rowntree of the Hadfield Spears Unit.........

December 10th 1944 – FAU Dover

Dear Ralph

Thank you for writing. It's going to be bloody grim without you at Gordon Square.

Wherever we have been together, whether in the Middle East or London, your friendship has been one of my abiding legacies from the Unit. But more, your wisdom and judgment as well as the spirit you brought to all your work, has been one of the great qualities of your leadership, and your withdrawal is a great blow to the Unit.

But now, we all just want to hear that your health is on the mend and that you will soon be your old self. My love to Joan and all the family.

With true good wishes

Mickey.

Clarence Pickett, American Friend and Chairman of the American Friends Service Council............

Friends Relief Service, Friends House, London – December 5th 1944

Dear Ralph

It has been a great satisfaction to come to know you and to work with you, and I hope you may be able to visit us in the States before too long, both on the concerns of Friends and in the interests of housing, when I will be happy to make arrangements for you to meet people in the National Housing Agency.

Although you are leaving the FAU, I am sure that spiritually you cannot leave it and, in my own mind, I shall think of you, as we have further occasion to deal with the Unit. You have been very helpful in letting me share the information brought back by various members of the Unit who have been travelling abroad.

Very sincerely yours

Clarence

From Michael Barratt Brown, with whom he worked in London and the Middle East......

December 10th 1944 – Gordon Square

My dear Ralph

[..... Thank you for your note...you didn't have to write, as you know how much I have always enjoyed working with you, and how I deplore the fact that what I may almost claim to be our partnership, should now come to an end. [....]

I do hope you have a really good rest now and get completely fit again. God knows you deserve a break. All my good wishes to Joan and you.

Yours ever

Michael.

From Bartie Knight, with whom he worked in London and latterly in Ethiopia....

December 10th 1944 – Gordon Square

Dear Ralph

I am so sorry that I didn't have a chance to say good bye. You are one of the few people in the Unit whom I shall always seek out, as I have such respect for you and all you have done for the Unit. I wish you a speedy recovery.

Yours ever

Bartie.

From Christopher Taylor with whom he worked in the UK and in India.....

December 11th 1944 – Calcutta

My dear Ralph

It is very sad to learn that you are leaving the Unit. It will be a great loss. I want you to know with what affection and respect you are looked upon by all of us here. You have made a truly great contribution. How you managed to carry on the duties of Chairman as well as the Overseas Office, is remarkable. I know you'll be keen to get back home and will soon regain your strength and be able to rejoin the BVT. Yours

Christopher

Robin Whitworth, former BBC Producer and FAU colleague in this country and abroad, who returned to the BBC after the war ....

Broadway, Worcestershire - December 2nd 1944 (Overseas Relief Officer)

My dear Ralph

The significance of your loss to the Unit is obvious [....] but I also want to say on a personal level, how very sorry I am that the time has come for you to leave. There are many good people in the Unit, but so far very few who take such a balanced and comprehensive view of things as you, and so few who one can regard as really kindred spirits. I will miss you a lot.

The Unit is enough to drive me crackers sometimes, and in many ways is bad for me. But yet I believe that it may be accomplishing something really important. As I've said before: it is important that there is an FAU now, and it may be even more important that there has been an FAU after the war. So one goes on trying to do one's best, such as it may be.

You have certainly done yours, and the time has undoubtedly come for you to retire from it - not only because it would be unwarrantably quixotic for your health to be further jeopardised. But also because I think you are now called to even more important work, and I think the work you will soon be taking up is very important in its wider implications.

Do have a real rest. You really deserve one, and a period of relaxation and recreation will enable you to be all the more useful in the future. [....]

I send you my good wishes and I hope we may always keep in touch.

Yours

Paul Sturge, General Secretary of the Friends Service Council............

Friends Service Council - December 2nd 1944

Dear Ralph

We at FSC are very sorry indeed that you should be retiring from the FAU on health grounds, but of course we are most anxious that you have every chance of making a full recovery. We have very greatly valued having you as our main contact with the FAU and only wish it could continue – your deep knowledge of the Society's concerns has been a real advantage.

[....] Later, when you are back to your full health, we should very much like to maintain your contact with the Council's work because of your knowledge of the whole of the FAU set-up and personnel, which would be of enormous value to our work. [....] In particular we hope you will remain on the India Committee with your special connections in that field.

But these matters are all for another day. For now we wish for nothing more than for your full recovery.

Yours ever

From Richard Wainwright, sometime the Unit's Chronicle Editor and later with FAU Central Mediterranean Force, who places my father in the list of the significant leaders of the FAU, along with first Tom Tanner, then FRB and Tegla Davies.......

December 4th 1944 – FAU Antwerp

My dear Ralph

I have just heard from Tegla of the doctor's report on your health, and of the very wise decision which has followed. I would first like to say how much I hope that a good rest will give back to you the energy which you have given out so prodigally in the interests of the Unit.

The last four months must have been an awful strain for you, but I hope it is of some satisfaction to you to know that you leave the Unit pretty firmly established in most of the significant areas of the world, thanks to the leadership of first Tom and then yourself and Tegla. The section here asks to join me in good wishes to you, and in thanks for helping to put us onto the right footing out here. As ever

From John Gough, first in the Lebanon office, then with the Hadley Spears Unit and as Training Officer in this country.........

December 9th 1944 – Hadfield Spears Clinic, Syria

My dear Ralph

I am extremely sorry to hear that you are leaving the Unit, though Tegla had warned me it might happen. [....] You can just imagine how much I shall miss knowing that you are in the adminstration in London.

I have not forgotten the many difficult, as well as amusing times we have been through together, and I do hope that it won't be very long before we can meet again in England. The interest you have always taken in our work in Syria and the many encouraging letters you have sent me, are things I shall not forget.

As you know, we inevitably get depressed in the work we are doing, and your notes of appreciation have made a great difference to me personally. Perhaps it is the best tribute I can pay to you, to say that I do endeavour to encourage our own people as far as possible on the same lines, and I am glad to be able to say that I can write letters of appreciation to them with complete sincerity, as despite their various failings, I do think the Unit can be proud of their achievements, and we owe that to you.

I send you my greetings and wish you a speedy recovery. Yours ever

From Roger Wilson of Friends Relief Service.....

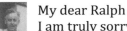
My dear Ralph

I am truly sorry that your health isn't what it ought to be. I fear that we in the FRS must share some responsibility, for we too, placed our burden upon you. All of us at FRS always felt more confidence in any job when we knew that you were in charge. So our good wishes for a thorough recovery and working together again very soon.

This from Peter Gibson, who my father succeeded as Relief Officer in London, and then in the Middle East, where Peter was liaison Officer with the Army under my father as OCME. My transcription below is an amalgamation of three different letters expressing Peter's feelings about my father's leaving. I reproduce the letter below, as PG obviously relishes using the headed paper left over from the days of Il Duce………

December 10th 1944 – FAU CMF Italy

My dear Ralph

[….] You do not need to feel guilty (about leaving) in any way whatsoever. Don't you think you've done more than could be expected of anyone, and that during Tegla's absence you were carrying a huge burden which must have been such a strain for you? You must know without being told, that you have always had the confidence of all us, more than any other person in the Unit. Need I say more?

Yes, I would love to come and stay with you for a night if I may - being the rude so-and-so I am, I was going to invite myself anyway! I hope that steeling myself to a day in Birmingham, will show you how much I love you. Take care of yourself. We all love you, and here is a little offering from Jack and me. If there had been a second bottle in Italy, you should have had it. Likewise if there were any Vodka, it would be thine, and if you don't drink the enclosed in one sitting, then we shall be ashamed of you. And I promise not to say what an old Quaker humbug you are! – (Oh, slipped up there, didn't I?) Happy Christmas.

I hope you like the notepaper, and will hang it on the wall beside your Africa Star, China and Indian medals, OBE and goodness knows what else.

Take care of yourself and Happy Christmas, Love

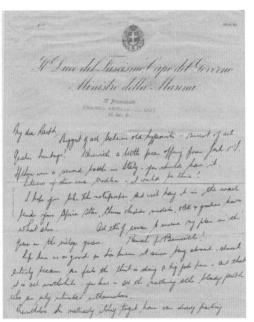

The headed paper reads:

Il Duce del Fascismo. Capo del Governo
Ministro della Marina

Il Presidente
Friends Ambulance Unit
C.M.F.

Translation:

The Leader of Fascism
Head of Government
Minister of the Navy

The next two letters are something of 'a puzzlement'. They are from Jack Frazer and Michael Cadbury and refer to 'Dear foul mouth' and 'foul mouthed epithets'! These have always worried me, but can only be an in-joke to tease my father. Dad was never one to be pompous, or stand on ceremony, but neither did he ever swear more than an occasional 'bloody'. My conclusion, therefore, is that coming back into the Gordon Square Office as Deputy Director, after some time abroad, he felt he should insist on certain standards. I guess that probably he said once too often ..."Now, now. Less of the foul-mouthed language!" Hence a degree of mockery entered the office banter, referring by reversal to the 'foul-mouthed Deputy Director'!

One's inclination is to feel that the very surprise of its being there, rather distracts from the letter. But it would be petty-minded indeed to edit it out. Surely, best to take it for the jolly banter it is, and enjoy the obvious jokiness with which it is written!

So here first is the letter from Jack Frazer, one of my father's closest colleagues both in London in the early days in the Rest Centres and later in Ethiopia. This letter was actually written before my father's illness had seriously deteriorated, though JF is obviously aware of the possibility of him having to leave the Unit.......

October 29th 1944 FAU Central Mediterranean Force, Italy

My dear 'Foul-Mouth'

[....]Believe it not, FRB is the only Unit person who I've ever been really happy in working under as sort of lieutenant – and that's saying a lot, since I yet have a very high and warm opinion of those others – (Tom) Tanner, Richey (Mounsey), John (Gough), Peter (Tennant) and all the rest.

I often feel so totally inadequate to do much of the work and consequently end up hating it as well! But there's no use moaning. It's just necessary to reconcile oneself to the fact that the only solution is that the war should come to an end!

But hell...what right have I to grumble, when you, you old sod, have had to carry so much of a heavier burden for so long, and with the added disadvantage that you've been far from fit. Not only do you do your work far better than any other Unit person could possibly hope to do, but you also take on your shoulders so much of a personal responsibility for anything that goes wrong. [....]

I also know that Ruth (later Jack's wife) very much enjoyed being able to see you occasionally, and I do feel grateful for the friendship you've shown to her. I think you'll realise without my saying it, that the thought uppermost in my mind is that should it be necessary for you to leave the Unit on medical grounds, then that will be one of the biggest losses which the Unit, and in particular foreign sections, could possibly suffer.

Don't misunderstand me, for though I realise what an enormous loss it will be for the Unit if you leave, nevertheless, I aslo feel strongly that above everything else you must most definitely do what is advised by your doctors. There's not the slightest doubt in my mind about that. The Unit has already let you go further in 'giving of yourself' than it ought to have allowed you to do. More than anything I had hoped that you would be well enough to continue, both from the Unit's point of view, but also it is so disturbing to hear that you are not yet your old self. [....]

So take care of yourself old friend and do what you are told by the quacks and make sure you get better. God bless, yours as ever

Jack.

And secondly, here is the letter from Michael Cadbury, a colleague with FRB at Gordon Square, London and at Failand in Bristol, reiterating the 'foul-mouthed' soubriquet. Michael, who in later life assumed the roles of Chairmanship of several Quaker Trusts, was not remotely of that ilk: jolly, hail fellow well met, but never one to my knowledge of him, to indulge in bad language.........

Failand House, Bristol 8, FAU Training Centre - December 6th 1944

My dear Ralph

It was with very mixed feelings that I heard that you had been given your cards, and were now a free man. We shall miss you in the Unit more than can be accounted – despite the 'foul-mouthed epithets and boorish manners' that you introduced to the Square!! Poor old Tegla is going to have a job to cope with everything, and it's good to know that you are in the background.

I do so hope that you will really make good progress under the careful eye of Joan, and will soon quite recover your old self.

The kind way you have kept me in touch with things since you got back and I left London, has been very much appreciated, Ralph. It has meant a tremendous lot to me to be allowed to have some idea of what has been going on in London.

I am very anxious to go abroad, and had always treasured the idea of going abroad with you, but as you know the prospect of being stuck out in Europe for two or three years at this stage of the war, is more than I feel I can ask Heather to face, after four and a half years on her own.

If you are able to face a trip down here, it will be very good to see you, and it might be regarded as part of your cure! This comes with very best wishes for your complete recovery, and may you thoroughly enjoy your well earned retirement.

Yours

Michael

These are just a representative few of the many, many letters that came in from all over the world, including other members of the Unit such as Lewis Waddilove, Gordon Cox and John Fleming from the Middle East, Elliott Burgess-Smith from Italy, Bill Spray and Hamilton Mills with the FAU American Army base in France, Stephen Thorne, Secretary of the Society of Friends, Gordon Thompson, Director of the British Red Cross Society, Colin Bell from China, Harold Watts from the FAU Council, John Saunders, Russell Brayshaw, and Eric Gargett, all echoing the same sentiments.....

"....the Unit will always remember you as a fellow who meant every word that he said, for which reason you must have sensed the huge amount of confidence which we all had in you." (Harold Watts)

"...You are simply irreplaceable, and of the leaders of the Unit, you are the one in whom I have always had completest confidence and with whose eminently balanced viewpoint I have never disagreed." (John Fleming)

"...It was with a sense of a great loss that I concurred with the decision that you should be invalided out. It will be a loss to the Unit indeed at a time when it will be felt most. I always felt that in Egypt you bore the full weight of the Unit's conscience, and our struggle came to a focus in you. And in India too, you probably haven't realised just how deep rooted the confidence in you has been. We all send you our very good wishes. (John Burtt)

"...I expect you'll be fed up with hearing and reading words of praise, but as just an ordinary member of the Unit, I want to say that I owe you a great deal of gratitude for all your wise words in Council, and with so many of us, I say a big thank you and wish you well." (Bill Spray – Later Headmaster of Leighton Park School)

"...We aren't so rich in leaders who command everyone's confidence, that we can feel your departure as anything but a great loss. (Gordon Cox)

".... I personally shall miss you a very great deal and no reconstruction of the Overseas Office can possibly fill the gap. The fact is that we shall continue without you, but I do not intend to let you forget that I am your 'creation' in the job of OCME. If anyone in the Unit should be given a break, it is you, and I sincerely hope you will benefit from it. For heaven's sake start looking after yourself and do not get entangled in Advisory Committees! As ever... (John Rose)

In addition to these letters, there were many that were sent to my mother as well, which in addition to saying how much he will be missed, also thank her for being such an understanding wife, including ones from Tegla Davies and Michael Cadbury and this one from Paul Cadbury back in the summer of '44.......

June 21st 1944 - Birmingham

Dear Joan
It has been on mind to write to you for some little time, but news of Ralph has been scrappy. I'm afraid he has had a very bad time, but he is well on the way to recovery.

Ralph has undertaken an immense responsibility on behalf of the Unit, and I should like you to know how greatly we all trust his judgment and rely on his strength of character.

[....] This is an anxious time for you and I do hope you will get in touch with me at once, if there is anything I can do to ease your worries.
Yours

Paul S. Cadbury

Tegla Davies, who became a good friend of my parents post-war, also had the grace to write to my mother and say what FRB's leaving meant to them all back at Gordon Square. It was a close-knit community, and the loss of one member, in John Donne's famous words 'diminshes me'...........

December 3rd 1944

Dear Joan
Yesterday was a sad day for us at Gordon Square, because it was no easy thing to say good bye to Ralph. But I am sure that the time has come when it is right for him to leave. I am writing a note to you, because I want to thank you for the way in which you have co-operated with us over the last year and let us keep Ralph, although many a time you must have felt very inclined to make a fuss and insist on taking a 'strong line'!

In the case of married members of the Unit, it is only too easy to forget that it is the wives at home who have very much the thin end of the stick. You must have felt constant worry and anxiety over the last year, but (if I may say without appearing patronising) you have been very good about it, and we do appreciate your attitude. We were especially grateful that he was able to go to China so soon after his illness, as he was the one man who could do the job which we had originally asked Tom Tanner to do.

Heaven knows Ralph is the last man we can really spare from the Unit, and that is why we have hung on to him so long. I have always known that the confidence of the Unit, and particularly of overseas sections in the administration, is greater when he is there. And I had hoped for a long time that while he was at Gordon Square, he would be able to make slow but sure progress towards complete recovery. But on coming back from my trip and seeing him, certainly no worse, but apparently not much better either, I came to agree with those who felt it was only fair to him and his family to encourage him to go, particularly since the doctor's report was reassuring and suggested that, given the right conditions, he would recover his strength.

I am more certain that this is the right course than I think he is himself. He, with his very good loyalty to the Unit, has perhaps felt that he ought to carry on and postpone his return to a more natural and normal life. We've discussed it with him, and discussed it at great length among ourselves, and we do agree that we ought now to take the strong line and make him take more care of himself. I have particular cause to be grateful to him for the loyalty and support which he has always shown me, and for shouldering the whole burden while I was away. This needs no reply. With two children and a husband to look after, you will be a very busy woman indeed!
All good wishes

Then this letter from Michael Cadbury from September 1943, who had kept in touch with my mother for much of the last year, keeping her updated about my father's health and when he would be home, and generally being a good friend………

September 7th 1943

My dear Joan
[....] I have had a cable to say that Horace was able to get an unexpected flight home, as Ralph had some winding up business to complete in Calcutta. I know that this will be a disappointment to you, but he is being well cared for by everyone out there including John Rose, John Gough, Barry, Peter Gibson, Jack Frazer and Mike Rowntree - all of whom – will, I know look after him, fête him and act as a general tonic to him, to offset the difficult decisions awaiting him there, which will have been held over for his wisdom to decide while he is there.

The thing I was afraid of was that you might get garbled messages through about Horace and wonder what was happening to Ralph. I hope all your plans for the new home are going ahead. It must be an exciting time for you with the prospect of Ralph coming back and being together in your own home again, almost like getting married again! It will be so good for us all to have him back and we are intending to leave him alone while he recovers!

Much love

And to our mother from 'Granny Barlow', now living with Millior and Alfred in London, giving words of praise for her bravery and for the love she gave to us children……..

December 13th 1944 – 17 The Park NW11

My dear Joan

How good of you to let me see these letters. I have loved reading them. It makes our hearts rejoice doesn't it, to read these affectionate tributes to Ralph's self and his work. They brought cheer to me in these dull winter days. It will help him also to know how they all agree in thinking he should rest and recover, reluctant though they are to part from him. How very nice of Clarence Pickett to write – I foresee an American visit in the future!

John (brother) says that already Ralph's voice sounds a bit less tired on the phone. I do hope callers and visitors will not come in too much, though I know he will very much welcome seeing Mike Rowntree.

I do echo Tegla's letter to you. I have often felt that you have been very brave in bearing up so cheerfully through all the happenings of the past years. The moving away from home, then back again, then the final closing of your own home and dwelling in other's homes and all the anxieties you have borne month after month, as well as caring for the boys and surrounding them with love. Now comes your reward with a husband back and once more in a home of your own. How many thousands of wives must be longing for such happiness!

It is so terribly sad to think of the numbers of children to whom the father is almost a stranger.

*Yrs affectionately
M.E.B,*

I think it's also worth adding this letter from 1942 to my mother from Maurice Webb, which he wrote after meeting my father in Durban. I quoted the opening sentence in the chapter on my father's stay in Durban (p236), as it clearly illustrates the respect in which my father was held. Despite his doubts of his own capabilities, this letter clearly shows the impression he made after only a short time.

Dear Joan

Last Monday evening a voice on the telephone said: "You will not know me but I am with the FAU…" I said; "You are Ralph Barlow", having been prepared by a cable from Gordon Square. Ten minutes later Ralph was in our home and I hope that he felt at home. We were certainly very glad to meet him and have been very glad of the chance that has come to us to get to know him.

Ralph has a big job with his 33 men and the wait over here has thrown much work onto him. Except for a cold he is well. We have met nearly all, if not quite all, the members of his party (two are in the next room now) and it has been fine to note how affectionately Ralph is regarded by them all, the real respect coupled with friendship that obtains between his party and him. He is making a fine job of leadership.

Yesterday we had a good and helpful meeting for worship in our home, which a large part of the party attended. Ralph spoke very helpfully. He spent the afternoon at this desk and I rather think he wrote to you. I hope he felt that he could write happily, in quiet surroundings. Anyway he left his pipe behind, if that is a sign of his being at home!

This afternoon I was able to give him a short run round our town and a glance of our housing and other problems. I think that when he saw the jobs we have to face here, he was glad that his work is in Bournville!

We do not know how long the party will be here. There are times when Ralph thinks that they have been forgotten and will be left here for the rest of the war! But it is likely that one day soon they will move on and we shall have another visit from the FAU to look back upon. We shall always be glad that we have had this time with Ralph and hope that the contact will continue.

I do not know what Ralph has told you about Durban and this part of South Africa, but we think it a good part of the world and have rejoiced in being able to introduce him to it. But much as he may have liked Durban (and I suspect he has liked it not a little, for there are times when its more like a lovely dream than a mere city) he will, I know, be glad to to get back home and to you.

Yours sincerely

Then there was the official minute of the Executive Meeting:

Friends Ambulance Unit
Minutes of the Executive meeting
Held at 4 Gordon Square, London W C 1
Monday, November 27th 1944

Present: Tegla Davies, Ralph Barlow, John Bailey, Robin Whitworth, Oswald Dick, Ian Nicolson, William Moore, Gerald Gardiner, and Michael Rowntree.

Minute 3041
F RALPH BARLOW
The Chairman reported on the result of Ralph Bartlow's recent examination by a specialist, and it was clearly recommended that in the interests of his future health, Ralph Barlow should be released from service with the Unit. It was therefore agreed to accept his resignations on health grounds from December 2nd 1944.

The Committee wished to record on its own behalf and on behalf of all Unit members its appreciation of Ralph Barlow's services as a member and Officer of the Unit and as Deputy Chairman of the Executive Committee. In particular it stressed the great debt which the Unit owes to him on account of the manner in which he has discharged his heavy responsibilities since his return to this country and while not fully recovered from his illness.

The Committee hoped that the irreparable loss which the Unit would suffer by his resignation would be mitigated to some extent by having the benefit of his advice as a member of the Council as in the past. It also expressed its good wishes to him for the future and wished him a speedy amd complete recovery.

———

Perhaps it is appropriate to end this series of tributes with one final letter. This time from a person he scarcely knew - Peter Hume's widow, Frances……

December 16 1944 - York

Dear Ralph Barlow
You may be surprised at having a letter from me, whom you only know by name.

But I feel constrained to write and tell you how sorry I am to learn you have been obliged to leave the Unit because of indifferent health.

I know from the old days, of what Peter told me, of your work and how, when I hear from one or two friends of Peter's, what a great loss your leaving means to them all, I should just like to send my little tribute to one who has worked faithfully and sacrificed health so willingly, in the wonderful work of the Unit.

I send my loving thoughts and best wishes to you and the family and for your better health.

Yours very sincerely

Frances Hume.

And there were many others who made it known how much my father would be missed, including………………

Michael Crosfield

John Saunders

Clarence Dover

Some of the many others who expressed their heart-felt thanks and appreciation.
Photographs Friends House Library

Chapter 41
What did we achieve?
1945

Under pressure from the Unit and from friends and family, my father finally left the Unit on December 2nd 1944 on health grounds. He gradually settled back into family life, and relaxed and recuperated, slowly recovering his health - going on a birding trip to Scotland with Horace and enjoying time with the family and getting to know us all again. He started back at the Bournville Village Trust again in the spring of 1945. Here he writes in his memoirs of being back at home........

Although I had many regrets about leaving, I did not share other people's forebodings that I should find my life at home dull. Indeed, despite such concerns, I did not find any difficulty in settling down – and I hope the family found none in receiving me. To live at home without fear of any further partings hanging over my head, was quite marvellous. At last one could fully enjoy the pleasures of life at home, really be able to become a true part of it - so different from short leaves or the odd weekend. A large part of the ease of settling back and of the joy of being home, was of course, due to Joan, who is undoubtedly, the most wonderful wife imaginable.

I have two charming children of whom I am very proud, and I am very grateful to Joan for bringing them up so well and looking after them so ably while I was away, and coping with all the concomitant problems of living in different houses and keeping the children alert to my presence and my love for them.

Antony is still very young, but altogether very charming, and understandably still shy of me. David and I probably have more in common. In some ways he is old for his age and is very forward, constantly asking questions, and loves doing things with me. He is a very sensible child, quite highly strung, but with flashes of an angelic nature. Altogether they are three people to make any man happy. I hope I can be a good father to them. We are indeed lucky. A reunion and a return after so long wandering and waiting, seemed almost too good to be true. We are very fortunate and very thankful.

This is taken from my father's report for Gordon Square just after he left the Unit in December 1945, and draws together his thoughts both on the Unit as a body, and his time in it ....

In the course of these notes, I have traced the development of the Unit as it appeared to me from fairly early and rather chaotic enthusiasm to its present state. It is very easy to see the faults of the Unit writ large; its inefficiency – although any contact with other bodies shows that it is by no means as inefficient as many with whom it works; its lack of discipline – although one cannot fail to be impressed by the loyalty of its members; its lack of staying power – although here again it is remarkable the way the Unit members have stuck to a dull job, and it is apparent that, although much of the early enthusiasm may have waned, there is still something there.

The Unit is perhaps too conscious of itself and what it has done, and of late has received an embarrassing amount of publicity, which is no doubt bad for us. On the other hand, I think one can point to certain things which the Unit has learned. At one time I used to think that the Unit was something of an anachronism and a nuisance to the authorities, which, because we lived in a liberal country, had to be accommodated and to be tolerated, but now I think that on the whole, it is something more, and I believe there is a place for a voluntary organisation, even in a world totally organised for war. It is at least something of a gesture.

Although the Unit is, in the last resort, not a democracy, it has learned something about self-government; particularly, I think, this is true of the China section; and with much painful effort this has been achieved without the complete sacrifice of efficiency, and I think, that while upholding a certain standard of efficiency, the Unit has not lost its respect for the value of individual personality.

Another remarkable thing is that to which I have already referred – namely, a very strong Unit loyalty and tradition, which springs in the first instance, I think, from the succession of training camps, and the loyalty of individual members and the lack of personal ambition. In the early days we were not quite sure what we could or could not do, and were apt to go beyond our resources, but of late I think that we have come to understand the importance of limited aims; we have realised that we are only an emergency body and that, on the whole, it is a mistake to take on work with long-term implications.

Looking at the work of the Unit in different parts of the world, it is extraordinary how in nearly every case, it has developed on different lines and yet, although in many cases we must have been within an ace of failure, it is noteworthy that any group of Unit members set down at a given place have, on the whole done a good job, and it is no small achievement that a comparatively small group of young men should have established the work they have in centres as widely separated as Whitechapel, Rome, Cairo, Beirut, Addis Ababa, Calcutta and Chungking. I know too that the success of the Unit, such as it is, is very much the success of the whole body of members and not of any few individuals.

In certain detailed matters, too, the Unit has acquired a certain amount of experience, about working overseas for instance, and experience of individual countries; of clinic work in Syria and Ethiopia, famine relief in India, transport in China; and I think we should try to see all this work against the pattern of the present day world rather than as a lot of piecemeal pieces of work.

Every so often in the Unit one pulls up painfully grown roots; I am used to it now and so I find the final parting easier. I expect that we all have our own personal feelings towards the Unit. There has been much depression, much frustration, very much anxiety and worry and much disappointment, but my debt to the Unit is very great. It has been in many ways an exacting mistress, and those of us who are married must have much sympathy for our wives, but, though the war and the Unit have taken much away from us, there are, I think, certain things that we can be grateful for.

It has brought us experiences which we should not have had otherwise, and if we think of the work that many of us would have been doing as CO's but for the Unit, we must be grateful for the experience that it has brought us, of administering a body such as the Unit, or of conditions of work in different parts of the world, and perhaps, above all, we must be grateful for the experience of meeting all sorts of different people in the Unit and for the friendships we have made.

In considering the future, I think we should think not so much what the Unit will do, but what we ourselves are able to make of the experience which the Unit has brought us and how, with what we have learned in the Unit, we can conduct ourselves in the years to come.

―――

What follows is a more personal assessment that he wrote for the benefit for his children, and covers not just the Unit but his personal beliefs and ethics........

I was brought up in strict Quaker surroundings. These must have affected me more than I realised. My debt to my parents is tremendous, especially my father. Also, though very critical, I have a very real respect for and to the Society. My theology is very uncertain. What do I believe? In a God of goodness and truth and beauty, evidenced through Christ; through good lives; in beauty, nature and art.

Concerning the divinity of Christ, I am less certain. I love to read the Gospels, but with so much of beauty, there are nevertheless things difficult to understand. I realise that such a deistic, humanistic religion (for it comprises service) is very suspect to the true believer. How far it helps me I do not know. I shall never be an adventurer or an explosive force, always safe, traditional and conservative. There is always enough native caution to damp down any ardour built up by religion! Also I am rather self indulgent, so perhaps my religion does not provide me with what I need. Be that as it may, the enthusiasm of the mystics and evangelists leaves me cold.

Certain points of ethics I do believe. I think a person should accept responsibility for whatever they undertake, and perform it as best they can. I also think reliability is a surprisingly important virtue – doing what you say you will do. In this mass organised world I think efficiency is important. Above all I think relations to others – sympathy, understanding, and kindness - matter profoundly. I believe it is our duty to do as best we can in whatever station we are in, and that that is the test of a person, not great doings. If a person cannot conscientiously do a humdrum, unexciting job, he has not the qualities required in life generally.

I have been influenced by other creeds quite a lot. I respect the tradition, the certainty and the devotion of Catholics, and I admire the beauty of Anglicanism. In my time in the Unit, my beliefs have changed considerably. Beginning perhaps as a more orthodox Quaker, I shared in and derived much benefit from devotionals and religious services of various sorts which members attended - some good, some not so good, some a complete waste of time. I got quite a lot of interest out of the Divine Service held on board the various troop ships on which I travelled, where members were glad to get a place to themselves, which I think were on the whole successful. They seemed to bring me closer to home and to Joan. In alien surroundings they also had meaning.

I remember one held in the camp at Durban, which was particularly good. We also used to attend Sunday morning meeting in Maurice Webb's house, which was remarkable, if for nothing else, for the view out over Durban to the sea. And the Christmas morning service in Cairo Cathedral, packed with Service men and women, was remarkable. Perhaps the most interesting of all was the service which I attended with Michael Rowntree, Freddie Temple, Stephen Verney and Michael Shewell, in the small Nestorian church in Tel Tamer. Communion was celebrated by a visiting Anglican Canon, in a small building with tiny windows. He conducted the service with dignity, and in those surroundings, the beautiful wording of the English prayer-book, was more than usually impressive. I began to feel however, that our services, while sometimes held in the spirit, were more often a dry formaility. We did not have enough of 'that of God' in us, and were too much equal in age and experience.

From the time of my illness however, my interest has waned. In Darjeeling I acquired new interest and respect in Quakerism from reading Rufus Jones and William Charles Braithwaite, but my religious life, such as it was, atrophied.

I returned home in this mood. My whole self submerged in the delight of getting home again, and I wanted nothing more. I found myself on the one hand convinced of the importance of the Quaker message and methods, and certain it should be given to the world as a way of life through worship and service, but on the other, critical of committee methods, traditional phraseology, bad choice of personnel, woolliness and isolation from the world.

I still feel this very strongly, and I wonder too how far the meeting for worship really 'speaks to my conditon'. Here I know the remedy lies partly in my own hands, but I have not the spiritual depth, to give the sort of ministry that is required, and too many doubts to give anything at all. Yet I think that in the future my service will be with Friends. Of religion I have little certainty, but of the need and demand for service, I am quite certain.

At one time, in order to stay in the Fire Service, I nearly gave up my pacifism. In the early days of the war, I might have fallen on either side of the fence. That I did come down on the pacifist side, I do not regret, although I often tired of feeling a possible pariah. But I have never been a rabid pacifist. I believe it is right for me, but each must decide for himself, and I cannot persuade or criticise another.

I recognise the obligation of England, bound by treaties to fight for Poland; I am grateful for the protection and food which the armed services give me; I understand the call to defend my native land; I realise the evils of a German victory may be greater than the evils of war; I see how Germans behave to Polish people and to Jews; I am stirred both in the present and in my historical mind, by England's stand.

I hope I am not deterred from fighting by cowardice or squeamishness. Yet I believe Christ meant pacifism, and I cannot square war with his teaching. I find it too hard to break away from my traditional Quakerism. The inhumanity and callousness of war grows, and I cannot believe that so great an evil as war can bring lasting good. After five years of war, the world must be a worse place.

Yet I am in doubt. Pacifism seems so illogical, so pitifully inadequate. So safe and privileged and protected. We pacifists can never share the full hardships and dangers of the forces. As an Officer I was especially safe, though I would not underestimate the hardships of travel, the difficulties of my job, nor the sacrifice of separation from home. I remember only too well, the difficulties and the periods of black depression. However, I think the Unit has provided me with the right sort of wartime service. It has I should think been a very different Unit from the last. More integrated, much more self-governing, more pacifist. Yet my pacifiism is nearer the last Unit – I think!

I owe much to the Unit. I got on in it on my own merit, and it has given me experience and self–confidence. I have made my way, stood on my own feet and done a job. I have gained knowledge of all sorts of people and places. Why did I get on? I was not a pioneer, I did not create. I came to the fore to administer, run and in a small way develop a going concern. The answers are partly seniority, partly Quakerism, conscientiousness, and some administrative ability. What more I know not. This experience has made a different man of me. It came almost too late. I should have had it at University or directly after.

Coming when it did into a happy, married life, it nearly broke me. It must nearly have broken Joan too, but she stood up to it, in face of all sorts of difficulties, kept her courage, did not let me, who had a much more interesting and varied life, grow away from her, and brought David and Antony up wonderfully. And now we are reunited again, and our marriage has survived the storms of war, and is as wonderful as ever. But this is not the end, only a breathing space. The world will terribly need our services. What form that will take and how it will come, I do not know.

Tributes on the deaths of Ralph and Joan Barlow

After the war my father devoted his life to the BVT, Scouting, and of course, the family. Sadly, though he relished his retirement, partially due to his wartime illness, and partially maybe to a life time of smoking, he died at the comparatively young age of 70 in 1980; my mother, on the other hand, following his death, assumed and continued to cherish much of my father's work, and died at the ripe age of 93 in 2007. Here are two tributes to two very special people.

THE FRIEND   1034   AUGUST 15, 1980

Ralph Barlow

Those who tend to undervalue the contribution of birthright Friends—and "birthright concerns"—to the witness of our Society should ponder the life and work of F. Ralph Barlow who died on July 11, two days after celebrating his seventieth birthday. Of impeccable Quaker stock—his father, John Henry Barlow, was clerk of London Yearly Meeting—he spent nearly all his life in that most Quakerly of British cities, Birmingham. After graduating from Birmingham University in 1932, he joined the staff of the Bournville Village Trust, which George Cadbury had founded in 1900 as a pilot project arising from his concern to "provide improved dwellings for the working class".

Ralph was secretary and manager of the trust from 1945 until 1973, a period of very rapid growth in its responsibilities, when the number of dwellings on the Bournville estate more than doubled in response to the post-war drive to meet the housing shortage. The trust continued to be a pilot project, gaining and sharing valuable experience in such matters as green belt management, town planning and the conservation of natural amenities—a special interest of Ralph's. Ralph also ensured that what had become a large enterprise remained a Quaker concern. His professional knowledge of housing questions opened many opportunities for personal service: in inner-city development with the Birmingham Copec Housing Trust, in housing for the elderly at Bryony House and in the work of the West Midland Rent Assessment Panel, with all of which he remained actively associated right up to the time of his death.

The war took him out of Bournville and into the Friends Ambulance Unit to which he made an outstanding contribution, as a camp leader, as commandant of the large contingent sent to the Middle East in 1942 and as emissary of headquarters to the outlying FAU sections in Ethiopia, India and China. It was in the course of his visit to India that he contracted a fever which permanently impaired his health and eventually left him, as he used to say, "rather slow on my feet". Thus, he accomplished his life's work under a severe handicap (yet, astonishingly, he found the energy to add Scouting to his other preoccupations).

Ralph and his wife Joan spent the autumn term of 1977 at Woodbrooke. Thereafter, Woodbrooke became the concern closest to his heart. He rejoined the Woodbrooke Council and, just before his death, had completed his work on the past 25 years' history of the college which became almost his second home—certainly, his second garden, the future of the trees being his special care. It was at Woodbrooke that he died.

At Woodbrooke, too, a large company met to give thanks for his life, his work and his loves—poetry and drama; "Match of the Day" (he was a keen Aston Villa fan); gardening, a life-long interest pursued with great skill; and, above all, birdwatching, a passion derived from school days at The Downs and Leighton Park and from the precious guidance of Horace Alexander. All of these he shared generously, not only with his close-knit family, but with a much wider circle to which many besides the writer were privileged to belong.

J. DUNCAN WOOD.

A final tribute to my father
from his life-long friend Duncan Wood in the Quaker journal The Friend

And my own tribute to my mother for The Guardian's 'Other Lives'

The Guardian

Joan Barlow

Tue 17 Apr 2007
Antony Barlow

My mother Joan Barlow, who has died aged 92, was a Quaker who lived a truly Christian life and did everything to the best of her ability. The last of four children of a printer who died young, she was born, educated, married and lived within a very small area of Bournville, on the south-west edge of Birmingham.

Her mother struggled to bring up her children, working, and taking in lodgers. Joan was bright, and, after Bournville junior school, won a scholarship to Sibford Quaker School. She then became a secretary for two Birmingham Quaker headmasters, at King Edward's and Camp Hill schools.

It was at the local Quaker dramatic society that she met Ralph Barlow, son of the first manager of the Bournville Village Trust, the organisation representing the model village set up by chocolate maker George Cadbury. Ralph and Joan married in 1936 and Ralph, taking over his father's job, remained in it for the rest of his life.

When she married, Joan gave up her secretarial work, she believed a mother's first task was as a home maker, and their home was always a loving and happy environment. The couple were members of organisations such as the old Midland Institute, the Quaker Book Club and the Essay Society where members would read their topical essays to the rest of the group. Keen gardeners and theatre lovers, they took their children to the old Birmingham Rep as well as to Stratford. Overseas students at the Birmingham Quaker College, Woodbrooke, always found a warm welcome at the Barlows'.

When Ralph retired both he and Joan studied Quakerism and the Bible at Woodbrooke. After Ralph's death in 1980, Joan took over many of his duties, ensured that her beloved husband's work should not be forgotten and supported the foundation of the Ralph Barlow Rooms in Bournville and the Ralph Barlow house in north Birmingham, providing housing for the less well off.

Joan was on many committees, including the Middlemore Homes for orphans and was chief commissioner for the Birmingham Girl Guides. Since the early days of her marriage, she catalogued everything that she did, books she had read, plays she had seen, world events - even the weather - in her daily diary. It is a lasting memory of her life and a valuable social document.

Joan's wider family was equally important and her own children were always part of the diaspora of first and second cousins and aunts and uncles. Everyone who knew her loved her. She is survived by five children and 13 grandchildren.

Chapter 42
What happened to them after the war?

The people who served in the FAU were a remarkable group of people who came from a variety of backgrounds. Some, like my father came from old Quaker families, with pacifism in their DNA, others from Methodist families such as Tegla Davies, Jack Frazer and Ronald Joynes, still others from old church families including Freddy Temple and Stephen Verney, or from no religious background whatsoever. But all wanted to make a difference, and do something other than fighting. My father here looks to the future in an article he wrote for The Friend at the end of the war.........

What are the hopes for the future of Unit members? First, I am sure they look forward to returning home; some to their previous jobs, all of them to their families. For the former, whatever excitement there may have been in doing unfamiliar tasks has worn off, and they want to return to work they were trained for. Some will want to go in for relief and social work; others will feel they must make a place for their families.

There is in the Unit a vast amount of material potentially of great value to the Society. Will the Society have the imagination to capture it? Many who have worked abroad are still loyal members or are anxious to be loyal members. They are, however, more cynical and more realist. They dislike any suspicion of cant and hypocrisy, and the wrapping up of things in words. Their contact with their fellow men in the Services, with others of different denominations within the Unit, and with people of other religions, makes them demand a clear and real faith. Has the Society a message for such people? I know that the approach must be mutual, that the Unit too must show much vision, tact and forbearance.

Of our debt to the Society we are all conscious. The word 'Friend' in our name is a tremendous asset. We are grateful for what it means to us and hope that we are conscious of the responsibility it imposes. There is another side to the picture, however. With all its mistakes and impetuosity, the Unit has honourably carried the name and something of the spirit of the Society into areas where it was hitherto unknown and has taken new life to existing centres. Ethiopia is an instance of the former, the East End, Syria and India of the latter. Travelling around the world, one is continually humbled and astonished at the reputation which the Society enjoys. The Unit shares that reputation, and it is, I think, fair to say that in the last four years, it has contributed to it.

The Unit is not the Society of Friends; much of its valued membership comes from outside Churches. But we are, I think, agreed that the Society, if it so desires, must and should be the inheritor of the Unit's more permanent work. The Unit is essentially an emergency organization, brought together by the war, and only waiting for the emergency to end before it separates again. Time and again, however, it has become involved in commitments of a more long-term nature. It will be a pity if all this work should come to an end. Does the Society wish to build on any of the foundations which have been laid, or the foundations which we hope to lay in relief work? It is an opportunity which should be taken soon, if the services of many qualified workers are to be secured.

Personally, while fully alive to all the shortcomings of the Unit (as only an inside observer can be), I feel that it has justified itself at least on the three following counts. It has not only provided employment for a number of COs, but in many cases it has enabled them to feel that they are giving really useful service. It is undertaking work which would otherwise remain undone. It is making a gesture which is not insignificant, amidst the tragedy of a world at war.

In the light of my father's questions in this article, I wanted to include short biographies of the later lives of those who worked alongside him, which show so clearly how the Unit influenced their lives and answer his queries in such an affirmative way. In so many cases their time spent in the Unit was such a crucial experience that many took the decision, as my father hopes in his article, to remain in relief work rather than return to their former careers. Even for those that did resume their careers or continued with their peace-time training, the period in the FAU remained an important part of their later life.

I have endeavoured to trace as many FAU members as I could, but despite my best efforts, some remained determinedly illusive. My heartfelt thanks to the families and descendants of all FAU members who have so kindly and generously helped with these biographies and in tracing old photographs, whose names are recorded beneath their photos; and my equally heartfelt apologies to the families of all those not mentioned, especially Arnold Curtis, Glan Davies, Eric Green, Frank Gregory, Peter Gibson, Michael Hacking and Douglas Mackenzie.

The FAU memorial at the National Memorial Arboretum, Staffordshire erected in 2013
Designed by Rosemary Barnett, it is dedicated to the work of the FAU in two world wars.

The 17 Unit members who lost their lives in WW2, are represented by 17 stars set in the memorial floor, which, of course, include those mentioned in this book such as Norman Booth, Leslie Barnes, Denis J Frazer and Raymond 'Nik' Alderson. Photo courtesy NMA/Barry Turner

My father wrote this in an article on the FAU in 1945, summing up its achievements......

In spite of its shortcomings and failures, the Friends Ambulance Unit believes that it has not been unsuccessful in its efforts to relieve some of the sufferings caused by war. It believes that its members have a place in the evolving pattern of the world today. It is not unremarkable that eight hundred young men and women have been able to work so extensively in so many widespread fields. It is a tribute to the sincerity of this nation, in claiming to fight for freedom of conscience that they have been allowed to serve in so many ways, in accordance with the principles which they sincerely and firmly believe to be right.

The Postwar careers of Unit Members and other affiliate Friends

Horace Alexander (1889-1989)

From as far back as 1918, Horace had been on the teaching staff of Woodbrooke College, teaching international relations, and remained so until he was asked to head up the India section of the FAU in 1942.

On returning from India, he returned to Woodbrooke, where he continued to teach, as well as working behind the scenes in conflict resolution and playing a significant part between the Indian leaders and the British Government in the years leading up to independence in 1947. His first wife, Olive Graham died from MS in 1942, and in 1958 he married an American Quaker, Rebecca Bradbeer (1901-1991), moving in 1968 to live in Pennsylvania to be near her family.

He was also one of the most influential ornithologists of his age, with his work with the early RSPB and the West Midlands Bird Club. He died six months after his 100th birthday.

(Details courtesy of 'Gandhi's Interpreter' by Geoffrey Carnall. Photograph of Horace and Rebecca courtesy of ARB and HGA family)

John Bailey (1910-1997)

After the war, as with a number of CO's, John had difficulties finding a job. He had been trained as a metallurgist and with the help of a University friend, he was able to join the Aluminium Development Association, where he remained for many years. Folowing his work with ADA, he joined the Aluminium Wire and Cable Company, often travelling to America for them. Before the war he had married Edna G Bailey (1914-1990), and she also joined the FAU London office.

In 1946 they both moved to north London, where they were amongst the founders of Finchley Meeting, raising money for the building fund and overseeing its construction. Indeed both worked on behalf of Friends and Quaker issues all their lives. John became an Elder, and Clerk of Hampstead Monthly Meeting and served on the revision committee for Christian Faith & Practice, while Edna was an Overseer, as well as being especially involved with the children in the meeting's 'Quaker Grey Club'. There were four children, Beth, Cherry, Ruth and Charles, enlarged to four when they fostered Martin, and all have memories of the family's political involvement from Aldermaston Marches to Greenham Common. On John's retirement, they moved to Wiltshire, joining Bradford-on-Avon meeting, again working tirelessly for the meeting. John died in York.

(Details thanks to Beth Allen, eldest daughter of John and Edna Bailey. Photograph Friends House Library)

F Ralph Barlow (1910-1980) and Joan M Barlow (1914-2007)

Post-war, my father returned to the Bournville Village Trust as its Secretary and Manager in the job description of the time, or CEO in today's terminology. It was a post, which he held until his retirement in 1973, but up until his early death, he continued to be involved with Birmingham housing through the COPEC housing Trust, and the Rent Assessment Panel. For several years he was also a Commissioner for Birmingham Scouts. He remained a devoted ornithologist all his life, passing on his love to his children, especially Nick.

My mother continued working for Friends, being Secretary of the Old Scholars at Woodbrooke for many years, and ensured her husband's memory was kept alive, opening the Ralph Barlow room in the Dame Elizabeth Hall, and alongside Sir George Young MP, then Secretary of State for the Environment, the Ralph Barlow Gardens in the West Midlands.

She lived a long and busy life, relishing being the matriarch of a large family of children, grandchildren and great grandchilderen. She died aged 93 in 2007. There were three other children born postwar, Stephen (1945), Rosemary ('47) and Nicholas ('58).

(Photograph of my parents taken by ARB in 1965)

Patrick Barr (1908- 1985)

When he came down from Oxford, he worked first as an engineer, before moving to acting in 1936 to work at The Old Vic. As a CO he'd joined the FAU in 1939, where he distinguished himself with his work aiding the free French in North Africa, for which he received the Croix de Guerre.

After the war he resumed his career in a production of Noël Coward's *Private Lives,* and his tall good looks, ensured he was hardly ever out of work. He was soon taken up by television and was twice named 'Television Actor of the Year'. Throughout the 60s and 70's he appeared in over 70 films, but seldom deserted the stage for long, and in 1970 he joined The Royal Shakespeare Company, and continued to act into old age. He and Anne 'Jean' Williams who he'd met while in North Africa with the FAU, remained married & their daughter, Belinda, married the theatre photographer, John Timbers.

(Photograph courtesy of family)

Michael Barratt Brown (1918-2015)

After the war Michael became a leading figure in the development of the New Left, a pioneer in industrial worker education and the drive for workplace democracy; later he was very active in the movement for Fair Trade.

He was one of the founders of the New Left Review in 1960, of the Peace Foundation established by Bertrand Russell in 1963, and of the Conference of Socialist Economics in 1970. In 2005, towards the end of his long life he met up again with Annette Caulkin, whom he'd known from FAU days and they remained together until she died in 2012, aged 97.

(Details courtesy of Michael's autobiography *Seekers* and DBB)

(Details and photograph courtesy of Michael's son Daniel Barratt Brown)

John Burtt (1910- 2003)

John was descended from a very old Quaker family dating back to the beginnings of the Society, and had been to the Quaker Schools Saffron Walden and Bootham. From Bootham John went up to Merton College, Oxford where he read Greats. On coming down he went first as a student teacher back to Saffron Walden, where one of his contemporaries was Mary Close, who in 1936 became his wife. After Saffron Walden he got a post at Calday Grange Grammar School in the Wirral.

Being the only CO in the school, his position soon became untenable and in 1940 he joined the FAU, working in the East End at Poplar Hospital, then as Warden of the Unit Hostel in the East End and later in charge of one of the training camps at Manor Farm, in Northfield. Mary meanwhile set up a residential refuge in Lymm, in Cheshire for disabled women from Liverpool, who were at particular risk from the regular bombings. When Horace Alexander decided to return home from India, John and Mary were jointly sent out by the FAU and the FSC to follow up the Unit's work there in the Society's name. They both threw themselves into emergency relief work and stayed there until 1945.

At the end of the war, John returned to teaching first at his old school Bootham as Head of Classics, remaining there until 1953. Their daughter Mary was born in 1946 and they adopted a boy, James a year later. Then on leaving Bootham, John was appointed as Head of Whitley Bay High School on the Northumberland coast, at that time rather a run-down school. In a very short time he had completely turned it around and raised the standard, such that pupils were soon gaining places at leading Universities. He eventually retired in 1970, shortly before the school became a Comprehensive. Sadly, Mary died in 1973 not long after his retirement. John remained in the area and continued as a regular member of Monks Eaton Quaker meeting, where they had both worshipped for many years.

(Details and photograph courtesy of Barbara Phillips, daughter of John Burtt)

Brandon Cadbury (1915-2011)

Brandon arrived home from China in 1946 and decided after a seven year absence he would not resume his pre-war career as a solicitor. Instead he joined the family business, first as a trainee and then in 1951 joining the board, taking responsibility for the Bournville Works Council and the five Overseas subsidiary companies.

He left Bournville in 1969 after the merger with Schweppes and retrained as a probation officer, retiring in 1981. In 1990 he and his wife Flavia moved to mid Wales, where he died in 2011 and Flavia in 2013. There were four children including Rupert, who kindly wrote the Foreword to this book.

(Details and photograph of Brandon and Flavia courtesy of their son Rupert Cadbury)

Jack (1912-1989) and Tessa Cadbury (1909-1999)

Jack initially worked at the Academy of Natural Sciences in Philadelphia, his specialty being butterflies and moths, but at the outset of the war he joined the American Friends Service Committee, which brought him to the UK to undertake relief work, particularly amongst the many families bombed out of their homes. He was based at Gordon Square, which is where he met the then Tessa Rowntree whom he married in 1942.

After the war they moved back to America, and Jack continued to work for AFSC until 1954. He then returned to the natural sciences, and both he and Tessa travelled round the states of America studying moths and birds, notching up some 600 species and meticulously recording them. On several such occasions they teamed up with Horace Alexander. Both my parents, and later my brother Nicholas, also a keen ornithologist, stayed with them at their home 'Spung Hollow' in Rancocas Creek, New Jersey.

(Photograph of Jack and Tessa Cadbury with daughter Alison, courtesy of the JC Estate)

Michael Cadbury (1915-1999)

After the war in 1946 he joined the family firm, initially as senior representative in Birmingham and then in 1948 in London. In 1950 he was made a Director with specific responsibilities for Exports, Young people and Education, which took him all over the world.

In 1966 he became Chairman of the British Cocoa, Chocolate and Confectionary Alliance and spokesman for the industry to the Minister of Food. In 1969 he was the Sales Director for the Company, finally retiring in 1975. He was for many years a Governor of Leighton Park School and was appointed High Sheriff of the West Midlands (left). Heather died in 2005. There were three children, Andrew, Duncan and Janine.

(Details and photograph courtesy of Michael and Heather's son Duncan Cadbury)

Annette Caulkin (1918-2012)

Annette Coooper as she was, joined the FAU in 1940 working in the East End during the blitz, where she met David Caulkin, whom she was to marry. David subsequently decided to leave the FAU and joined up, and was tragically killed right at the end of the war, leaving Annette with two children, Simon and Anne.

After the war she worked for a time at the Canadian Red Cross Hospital in Taplow. Later she joined the National Film Finance Corporation, editing and assessing scripts for possible production, for which she received an MBE.

Much later, in 2005, now in her eighties, she met up again by chance with Michael Barratt Brown and renewed a friendship dating back to their FAU days, although for the intervening 65 years, they hadn't seen each other! They proceeded to share their lives, sometimes in London, sometimes in Derbyshire for the next seven years, until she sadly succumbed to Alzheimers.

(Details and photograph courtesy of Daniel Barratt Brown)

Selby J Clewer (1917-2001)

Before the war Selby studied architecture at the Birmingham School of Architecture, where he won the Pugin Prize. He joined the FAU in 1940 and volunteered for the China Convoy, arriving in Rangoon in July 1940, later moving to China, where he was responsible for the design of what became the Convoy's HQ in Kutsing (now Chuxiong City). In 1943 he returned to the UK and that year married H Dorothy Street, before going out to Ethiopia, where he designed the Princess Tsehai Memorial Hospital.

In 1944 his wife joined him, and they remained there until 1953, when he returned to the UK. He joined the Society of Friends, and became the Chief Architect of the BVT, where his many designs included a number of places for worship, including the chapel of St Francis of Assisi's Church, Bournville, the Methodist Church in Quinton, and the Quaker Meeting House in Redditch. When he retired in 1973 he was appointed Administrator of Hanbury Hall and he and his wife raised the profile of this historic house. In later life he and Dorie moved to Ice Cottage in the grounds of the Hall, before finally moving to Studley, where he died in 2001.

They had a wonderful, 'crazy' family, as daughter Jo describes them, comprising their own, adopted and foster children, a splendid and happy mix.

(Details and photograph courtesy of Jo Carter, Selby and Dorie's daughter.)

Michael 'Mick' Crosfield (1920 -2014)

Michael Crosfield, known to most as 'Mick' was the son of two well-known Quaker families – his mother was Eleanor Cadbury and his father Bertram Crosfield, Managing Director of the Daily News. He interrupted his studies at Cambridge University and joined the FAU, becoming a member of 'The China Convoy', air-lifting medical supplies 'over the Hump' and then transporting them throughout the country, often on the famous charcoal-fuelled lorries.

After the war he trained as a film-maker and initially worked in research before graduating to script writing and directing. In 1951 he married Noni Jabavu, a writer from South Africa, adopting her daughter Tembi and moving with the family to Uganda shortly after, where he made documentary films on behalf of the government. Later they moved to Jamaica, where he directed an excellent film on the island's independence. When he returned to the UK he set up Viewpoint Productions Film Company, and two of their films were subsequently nominated for Baftas.

He bought a house in Covent Garden which he restored, and was a leading opponent of the GLC's redevelopment plans, which along with others, they succeeded in overturning. He and Noni divorced and he married Sally, with whom he had two children, Sophie and Sam. He was widely known as a man of independent and courageous thought.

(Photograph courtesy of PA)

Tegla Davies (1912-1970)

Tegla grew up in North Wales, and went on to study Classics at Oxford, before working as a schoolmaster in the late 30's. He joined the FAU at the beginning of the war, and after Tom Tanner's sudden death, became Chairman of the Executive, a position he held with distinction for three years. After the war he wrote the official history of the Unit entitled simply *Friends Ambulance Unit,* published in 1947.

Through members of the Cadbury family, whom he had known in the Unit, he was offered a position at the Bournville factory, heading their management training department, which he continued to lead and develop until his sudden death from a heart attack in 1970. He was also a dedicated member of the Methodist church and for many years a lay preacher. He married Sheila, and they had three children, Quentin, Mark and Clare. Mark's son is the children's author Stephen Davies. Shela died in1999.

(Details and photograph courtesy of Tegla and Sheila's son Mark Davies)

Jack B Frazer (1916-1970) and Denis J Frazer (1922-1944)

Jack was one of three children of Joseph and Florence Frazer, along with his elder sister Eileen and his younger brother Denis, part of an old Methodist family from Bath. Jack joined the Unit in 1939, while Denis joined in 1941 at the age of only 19. Denis, who had become a much loved and respected member of the FAU, was tragically killed in France by German machine gun fire in 1944, heroically trying to rescue a French soldier. He is buried in Strasbourg and was awarded the Croix de Guerre posthumously. His death deeply affected his brother Jack.

Before the war Jack had been active in the Methodist church, involved with the Sunday School movement, and like Denis, his pacifism was firmly grounded in his faith. By this time, he was already articled to Meade-King and Co, a firm of Solicitors in Bristol, to whom he returned after the war, and in which he eventually rose to become a senior partner.

When he joined the Unit he was initially in charge of one of the early training camps up at the Manor Farm, Birmingham, which was when my father joined in 1940. From then on, they worked together in the East End and again in Ethiopia, cementing a lifelong friendship. After the war in 1946, he married Ruth Heyneman, moving together to live in the Bristol suburb of Westbury-on-Trym, which is where their daughters Janet, Hilary and Susan were born in 1948, 1952 and 1955. Janet sadly died of cancer in 2010. After the war Jack resumed his active participation in the life of the local Methodist church, and was appointed a board member of the respected Wesley College in Bristol. He was also a keen tennis player, but sadly an underlying heart condition precluded playing in later years, and ultimately brought about his early death at 54. Ruth eventually remarried, dying in 2002 at the age of 81.

(Details and photograph courtesy of Jack and Ruth's daughter Hilary Skelton, with initial help from researcher Margaret McGregor.)

Gerald Gardiner (1900-1990)

In 1939 Gardiner first joined the Peace Pledge Union, before volunteering to join the FAU in 1943. He soon became involved in assisting refugees in the turmoil of north-west Europe in the last years of the war. He had been called to the Bar in 1925, a profession to which he returned postwar, when he was made King's Counsel. He was involved in a number of high profile cases, including acting as Defence Counsel in the trial of the publishers of *Lady Chatterley's Lover.*

He became a Labour politician in Harold Wilson's government and was appointed Lord Chancellor, becoming one of the most reforming people to hold the post, being responsible for the creation of the role of Ombudsman and helping to advance women's rights. He was made Baron Gardiner in 1964 and in later years he became Chancellor of the Open University. He married Lesley Tronson and they had a daughter. When his wife died in 1966, he married the film producer and director Muriel Box, who eventually published his biography. *(Details and photograph courtesy of National Archives)*

Henry T Headley (1918-1996) *

Henry was a member of a large and well-known family from Ashford in Kent, the name being familiar to Friends as that of the printing company, started by Henry's Uncles, which until a few years ago, printed the Quaker journal The Friend. Henry had three brothers: Lewis, who ran a grocery business in Ashford in succession to their grandfather and their father Percy; Patrick who farmed in nearby Sturry, on land still farmed by Patrick's son Peter; and Philip who was a doctor.

When Henry returned to Ashford after the war, he was able to draw on his wartime experience in the FAU, which as well as driving mobile medical units in the Middle East, had included considerable maintenance work, which no doubt inspired him to set up a very successful building business T Henry Headley, which for many years served Ashford and the surrounding area. The firm eventually closed in 1983 following Henry's retirement. He and his wife Mary remained loyal members of Ashford Meeting and two of his six children still live in the town. The other four live in Australia, where Mary came from. Mary died in 2016. They remained close friends of my parents all their lives. (* Being the third son, his middle name was Tertius!)

(Details courtesy of Henry and Mary's son Harry and Ashford Meeting's Testimonial.)

Ronald Joynes (1917- c.1999)

Coming from a CofE background, Ronald Joynes was one of a number of non-Quakers to join the FAU. He had left school at 16 to train as an Accountant, and during much of his time in the Unit his many postings involved his accountancy and administrative skills.

Post-war he completed his training, setting up his own very successful Accountancy business, based in the City of London. Until the FAU was closed down, he maintained close links with them, auditing the remaining funds on behalf of the Society.

He also acted on a voluntary basis for a Social Centre in Dagenham with pacifist connections, forging exchange links with German students post-war, and also with the former Shaftesbury Society, providing holidays for the disabled. Peggy, whom Ronald had known since they were children, married him immediately after the war. They were a devoted and much-loved couple, and were close family friends all their lives.

(Photograph of Henry and Mary Headley – left - together with Ronald and Peggy Joynes with Joan Barlow – centre - taken in 1981 – Barlow archives)

Barty Knight (1917-2012)

After spending much of his FAU time in Ethiopia running clinics as well as teaching, he ended his Unit life in India finally leaving there in 1947. After the war he spent the rest of his career in the field of education, teaching first back in Addis Ababa in Ethiopia. Then for the next twelve years he held the post of Education Officer in Tanzania. After that he joined the British Council as Language Officer for the British Council, which took him to Alexandria for two years, before working for the Education Department at Leicester University.

In 1968 he was appointed Principal of Broumana High School in the Lebanon, which he and his wife Audrey ran with distinction until 1975. On his leaving there, he was made an OBE for his services to Education. His later years were spent lecturing in Jeddah and lastly as visiting Professor in the University of Alexandria. He finally returned to this country in the early 80's, retiring to Hereford, to be near some of their four children, where he enjoyed tending an allotment and where for a time, Audrey continued to teach music. He died shortly before he was 95.

(Details courtesy of Barty and Audrey's eldest daughter Celia Almond. Photograph courtesy of Broumana High School)

Gwendoline 'Gwendy' Knight (1909-2009)

Barty's sister, Gwendy, as she was always known, was involved with running a training course for the women's section of the FAU. She had trained as a doctor at the London School of Medicine, and after the war Dr Knight returned to work as resident Medical Officer at the retreat in York.

When her father died in 1945, she left to move down to Cowes to care for her mother. For many years she had two jobs – working as a psychiatrist for half the week in Portsmouth mental hospital, and for the rest of the week working in Newport, IoW for what was known as the Child Guidance clinic. She also worked for the island's mental hospital for adults. When she retired, she and her younger sister Beth moved to Brigflatts in Sedbergh, Cumbria, where they lived at 'Rosebank', the house next to the Quaker Meeting House. They later moved to Hereford when Barty and Audrey did. Gwendy died a few months short of her 100th birthday.

(Details and photograph courtesy of Barty and Audrey's daughter Celia Almond. Barty with Gwendy (left) and Beth Knight.)

C Keith Linney (1912-1992)

Keith came from an old Quaker family, the son of the Tasmanian cricketer, George Linney. He arrived in England at a young age, and went to the Quaker schools of Sidcot and Stramongate, where he first showed his cricketing talent. His parents moved to Somerset and he was snapped up by the county and offered a professional contract in 1931. As a good left-hander he was a potentially useful asset, but the county never really developed his talents, often putting him in as a tail-ender. Eventually he transferred to Wells City, though still making the occasional professional appearance for the county. For a time he was a teacher and coach at Dunstable School, before joining the Quaker shoe company of Clarks as Chief Cashier until the outbreak of war. In 1937 he married a work colleague, Dorothy M Gibbs-Barrett; there were no children.

Following his Quaker principles he joined the FAU in 1940, working in the shelters for those who had lost their homes, first in London and then in Birmingham. He was then sent out to the Middle East, where he helped in looking after the many refugees in camps set up by the Unit. After the war, he joined the United Nations Refugee Agency, where he was the Director of Shipping for the international refugee operation. He later acted as a consultant on shipping and ship valuation for a number of governments, before becoming a Director of Cunard Lines. For a while he was also a Trustee of Martins Bank. On his retirement, he settled in Tunbridge Wells, and died at the age of 80.

(Details thanks to Stephen Hill and his book 'Somerset Cricketers 1919-1939', published by Halsgrove. Photograph Friends House Library)

Harold Loukes (1912-1980)

Harold was a British Quaker academic who, when he came down from Oxford, spent ten years teaching at the University of Delhi and at the New School in Darjeeling, where he was headmaster. It was during this period when, with his wife Mary, they provided a loving and caring home for my father to recuperate.

In 1945 he returned to the UK, and taught at Oundle, Leighton Park and Thorne Grammar School, where he was Head of English until 1947, before being appointed a lecturer in the department of Education at Oxford. In 1951 he was made a Reader in Education, a position he held for the next 30 years, writing many books on religious education, several of which dwelt on Quaker faith. He was also editor of 'Learning for Living' from 1961- 1964, to which he brought his liberal Quaker model of Christian upbringing to the reform of county school religious education during the sixties. His approach based on his own experience exerted great influence, which can still be detected in today's secondary schools.

There were four children, Anthony, Christopher, Nicholas and Mary, of which sadly Nicholas and, most recently Mary died.

(Prior to her death in 2020 Mary, and subsequently Anthony, both helped greatly in my research, with post-war details and family photographs.)

Mary Loukes, née Linsell (1911-2012)

Mary met Harold at Oxford where she was studying botany. They both did their teacher training, got married and went out to India. She performed all the duties of a headmaster's wife while also teaching biology in the school and bringing up three children. When they returned to England and had another child she had her work cut out to look after the family without the three servants they had in India. However she was able to teach part-time when they moved to Oxford. She also sang in the Bach Choir and was a keen gardener.

When the children had left home she and Harold moved to Wytham, a small village outside Oxford. She continued with the gardening, played the organ in the church and was chair of the village hall committee. Mary was able to return to botany and took part in field research for the publication of *The Flora of Oxfordshire.* After Harold died she continued to go to Scotland every summer where she loved mountain walking. When she could no longer manage her house and garden she moved to a nursing home in North Oxford where she celebrated her 100th birthday.

(Details and photographs of Harold and Mary courtesy of their son Anthony Loukes)

E Richey Mounsey (1912-1986)

During his time in the FAU he worked out in Ethiopia where he was on the staff of the Medical Directorate, and where he also set up a fund to help educate the local boys.

After the war he worked in North East England in the Coal business for some years, before moving to Dalbeattie in South West Scotland, where he was the Manager of Craignair granite quarry. He never married.

(Details courtesy of John and Edna Bailey's daughter Beth Allen and Selby and Dorie Clewer's daughter Jo Carter. Photograph Friends House Library)

Alexander 'Sandy' Edward Libor Parnis CBE (1911-1994)

'Sandy' Parnis, as he was always known, joined the Unit direct from the Civil Service, where he went straight after coming down from Clare College, Cambridge. In 1937 he became acting Vice Consul in Paris, before joining HM Treasury. Hardly surprising then that following the 11th Camp, he became Unit Treasurer.

After the war he returned to the Treasury in 1945, spending the rest of his career there, holding several important Secretarial posts, including that of the Gower Committee on Houses of historic or architectural interest; and of the Waverley Committee on the export of works of art. Away from HM Treasury he was Secretary of the Churches Main Committee, Treasurer of Cambridge University for nearly 10 years, and assistant Secretary of the Grants Committee. He was made a Fellow of King's College, Cambridge.

(Details courtesy of Clare College, Cambridge and Richard Seebohm. Photograph Friends House Library)

John Frederick Rich (1902-1973)

John was a prominent American Quaker, who became an influential figure through his work for Quaker relief efforts during the Spanish Civil War, as well as in his capacity as Public Relations Director of the American Service Committee (AFSC). He led efforts to assess the devastations resulting fromt the Civil War, and formulated a plan to help Spanish refugees.

John had been born in London in 1902, one of the five children of Max and Esther Reich, who had emigrated to the USA in 1915, changing their name to Rich. He became a naturalised citizen in 1928, the same year that he married Virginia Percy, with whom he had two children, Edward and Elizabeth. He graduated from Haverford College in 1924, and after leaving, held a variety of posts, firstly as a teacher, then a journalist, before joining the Bell Telephone Company as partof their Public Relations staff.

It was in 1936 that he was appointed PR Director of the AFSC, which in many ways defined his life. During his time in Spain, he kept a diary, and on his 37th birthday in 1939, he wrote – "I am glad to have been involved in the Spanish Civil war, and to have contributed something to the peace process. If I died today, at least I could say that I had contributed something worthwhile." This was a clear expression of his deeply held belief in the Quaker Peace testimony. He continued to travel widely, carrying out work overseas for the AFSC in China, where he worked with FRB, and in India, up until 1946. After the war he set up his own company, the John F Rich Company in Philadelphia, which offered consultancy services in fund raising and public relations. For many years, he was the honorary secretary of the British Schools and Universities Foundation in New York, served as a trustee of the Britsih Cathedrals and Historic Churches Foundation, and was a member of the Rotrary Club of Philadelphia.

(Details and photo courtesy of Sarah Horowitz, Curator of Quaker Collections, Haverford Col PA.)

Michael H Rowntree (1919-2007)

Michael - who was Arnold's son and Tessa's brother - together with Michael Barratt Brown, had worked closely with Paul Cadbury in re-establishing the FAU in 1939, and held a number of leadership roles in the Unit, including co-ordinating the FAU work in Germany.

After the war he first went into journalism, joining the Oxford Mail and Times, eventually becoming its General Manager. In 1967 he stepped down, though remaining a Director, to devote time to other work including Oxfam, which he served in various capacities for 60 years, ending up as its Chairman. He was also involved with the Rowntree family Trusts and was a Trustee of the Friend. As mentioned in my book, he was a much-valued birding companion to my father throughout their time in the Unit, to whom my father often deferred, and he remained so all his life. He married Anna Crosfield and they had three children, Jenni, Scilla and Hugh.

(Details courtesy of Michael and Anna Rowntree's daughter Jenni. Photograph courtesy of Oxfam)

Angel Sinclair-Loutit (1921-2016)

While in the FAU, Angela de Renzi Martin, as she was then, worked in the Gordon Square office London, and later in refugee camps in Egypt, where she met Kenneth Sinclair-Loutit, a doctor, whom she married in 1946. They first moved to Toronto, where Kenneth trained in Public Health. As he took on work of increasing importance with WHO, or as an adviser to Unicef, she moved around the world with him, from Canada to Thailand, France and Morocco, often undertaking voluntary work herself, such as running nursing services in Morocco.

In 1972, she returned to London with the three children, but sadly without Kenneth, and she set about training as a psychiatric social worker. She lived in South Kensington with Jessica, her youngest, while the boys, David and Stephan were at University. She later settled in Islington, where she became active in campaigning for local issues, such as saving the Whittington Hospital from closure or similarly Gillespie Park in Highbury, regularly writing to the Islington Gazette on their behalf. She remained a member of CND and of the Labour party, and was till her death at 95, a colourful figure of the left, smoking heavily and writing campaigning letters.

(Details and photograph courtesy of Jessica Sinclair-Loutit)

J Richard C Symonds (1918-2006)

Richard's wartime service in the FAU and the Deputy Directorship for Relief and Rehabilitation of the Government of Bengal (1944-1945) were the experiences which led him to a life of service for the United Nations. He worked in a variety of departments all over the world, including in relief for UN Relief and Rehabilitation Administration (UNRRA), in technical work for the UN Technical Assistance Board (UNTAB), and in development for the UN Development Programme (UNDP).

His field service, which took him to both East and South Africa, was punctuated with a stay at Oxford University's Commonwealth Studies, before returning to the UN with work in population control.

Reaching UN retirement age, he was made a Senior Associate Member of St Antony's College, Oxford, writing a number of books on his time in India and Pakistan. His first marriage to Anne Harrison ended in divorce in 1948, after which he married Juanita Ellington with whom he had two sons, one of whom died. When Juanita died in 1979 he married Ann Spokes.

(Details and photograph courtesy of the United Nations)

Christopher Taylor (1904-1984)

After the war Christopher returned to Bournville, where he was a manager in the Sales Department with special responsibility for the Outside Sales Staff. Travelling widely to meet with Representatives in different areas of the country, he discussed sales strategies and supported them if moving to a different location. He ran memorable Annual Conferences for the Representatives, and when they retired he wrote them a personal letter.

When he retired himself, he was delighted to receive from the Representatives a full set of Ordinance Survey maps, bearing their signature where they worked. He was Treasurer of the Friends Service Council for 30 years and travelled in the service of Quaker Work Overseas. He also travelled in the UK speaking to Quaker Meetings and encouraging the raising of funds for FSC. Ably supported by his wife Hannah, and with a different committee meeting almost every night of the week, he continued to work alongside my father at COPEC Housing Trust, and as the appointed Quaker Trustee at the Bournville Village Trust, where he forged close links with staff and teams.

(Details and photograph courtesy of Christopher and Joy Taylor's daughter Clare Norton)

Freddy Temple (1916-2000)

Frederick Temple, always known as Freddy, came from a remarkable church family with two Archbishops of Canterbury as forebears – his Grandfather, Frederick, and his famous Uncle William. After his time in the FAU, he too had a distinguished ecclesiastical career.

Immediately postwar he studied at Trinity Hall, Cambridge to prepare for Holy Orders. From 1947 to 1951 he was a curate in the Nottinghamshire parishes of Arnold and Newark, before becoming Rector of St Agnes Church in Manchester. In 1953, he went out to Hong Kong as Dean of the Cathedral, and Temple was deeply involved in community affairs, as well as those of the Church.

In 1959 Archbishop Fisher invited him back to the UK, to become his senior Chaplain at Lambeth, and Freddy accompanied him on his historic trip to Jerusalem, Istanbul and Rome, where Fisher was the first Archbishop since the Reformation to visit the Pope. He left Lambeth in '61 to become Bishop of Portsea, where he stayed until 1970, on being made Archdeacon of Swindon and eventually Bishop of Malmesbury. Following his retirement in 1963, he remained an honorary assistant Bishop in the dicocese of Salisbury. He and his wife Joan had two children, a son and a daughter.

(Details and photograph courtesy of Rooftop Publishing)

Peter Tennant (1913-2001)

After the war he first joined the Civil Service, working on housing and New Towns, but he and his wife Valerie (née Nettlefold) soon found this unsatisfactory, and moved with his three daughters, Alison, Fiona and Sheila to Callander in Perthshire, where he remained as a hill farmer for the next 27 years. He was considerably ahead of popular opinion, already experimenting with natural cultivation, and extensive tree planting.

For many years he was a member of Perth meeting, which involved a 90 mile round trip, but in the 1960's a meeting started in Dunblane only 19 miles away, of which he became a staunch member. In later years he and his wife moved to near Ballycastle in County Antrim, where he involved himself with the Corrymeela Community, helping those who had suffered through the NI conflict and working in the wider aspects of peace making. In 1994 he and his wife moved back to Scotland, where he died.

(Details and photograph of Peter on his farm shearing sheep, courtesy of Alison Burnley, Peter Tennant's daughter)

Stephen Verney (1919-2009)

Stephen was the 4th of eight children of Sir Harry Verney, 4th Baronet. Unlike his brothers, however, who joined the armed forces, Stephen was a CO and interrupted his university studies to join the FAU in 1940. He served in North Africa and the Middle East, mostly in Syria and the Lebanon, where he worked in mobile clinics and building hospitals. In the Christmas of 1941 he memorably led a choir, singing carols to the hospital patients. He became disillusioned, however, when a local Arab swindled him when buying wood for a new hospital, and joined MI6, ending up in Crete, where his knowledge of Greek became useful, working among the partisans in German occupied territory. He succeeded in rescuing many captives, including Kostas Mitzotaki, who remained a life-long friend and was to become Prime Minister of Greece.

After the war he resumed his classical studies at Oxford, before training for ordination. He subsequently worked in various tough inner-city housing estates in Nottinghamshire, before becoming Canon in residence at the new Coventry cathedral, where he helped to make it a centre of creativity and theological thinking. In 1970 he became Canon of St George's Chapel, Windsor. He had married his first wife Scilla in 1947, and they had three daughters and a son. Her death in 1974 affected him deeply. In 1977 he was appointed Bishop Suffragan of Repton, where his pastoral skills had full rein, and his scholarship resulted in books such as *Into the New Age* and *Water into Wine* on St John's Gospel. It was said of him that he was 'classless', respecting all people, no matter what race, creed, gender, orientation or age.

(Details and photograph courtesy of The Times)

Roger Wilson (1906-1991)

As well as remaining closely involved with Friends War Victims Relief post-war, he went on to a distinguished career in education, holding the chair of Professor of Education at Bristol University for over twenty years. Along the way he also advised third world governments on educational and social services programmes; fulfilled a twelve month UN mission to the Congo following independence, led opposition to apartheid and helped to establish a multi-racial university in what was still then Rhodesia. He and Margery celebrated their diamond wedding in 1991, not long before he died. There were two children Anthony and Elizabeth, both closely involved with Friends.

(Photograph courtesy of the Wilson family)

Duncan Wood (1910-2006)

Having taught at his former school Leighton Park before the war, Duncan resumed his career there in 1946, staying until 1952, and as well as teaching History and Latin, he was an inspirational leader of the Bird Group.

In 1952 he and his wife Katharine and their daughter Rachel moved to Geneva, joining the staff of the Quaker United Nations Office, representing the Society at the UN for the next 25 years, as well as running an international summer school for young Quakers, one of which I attended. On his retirement in 1977 he and Katherine settled in Arnside, Cumbria, close to the family.

(Details and photograph courtesy of Rachel Malloch)

Richard Wainwright (1918-2003)

Richard had joined the liberal party whilst up at Cambridge, and his beliefs had been greatly influenced by the social condition of the 1930's. He joined the FAU at the beginning of the war, remaining till late in 1945, and so just missed the general election of that year. But he was to become a popular Liberal MP, pivotal in the post-war revival of the party.

He was able to make the aspirations of the party, first under Jo Grimond and later Jeremy Thorpe, accessible to the public. He was popular with party members, encouraging young talent, and taking on heavy speaking and campaigning engagements.

He worked for many years on the Joseph Rowntree Social Service Trust. He and his wife Joyce were devastated when their son Andrew committed suicide, and set up a Trust in his memory. There are three other children: Martin, who edited the northern edition of The Guardian, Tessa, and Hilary, who edited and now co-edits the radical journal Red Pepper. Dr Matt Cole, Professor of History at B'ham University wrote a biography of him 'Richard Wainwright, the Liberals and Liberal Democrats: Unfinished Business' in 2011.

(Details and photograph courtesy of the Wainwright family)

Humphrey Waterfield (1908-1971)

Just before Humphrey joined the FAU, his parents tragically took their own lives, a devastating blow for him. He joined the FAU in 1940 and was deployed to the Middle East, Algeria and lastly to France, where he was taken prisoner, and spent six months as a prisoner in Strasbourg. His war diaries are now in the Paul Mellon Centre. Whilst up at Oxford in the twenties, he had studied History, getting a first class degree, but had already decided to become a painter and studied at Ruskin College, before going on to the Slade.

Prior to this, with money inherited from his parents he bought three acres of land in Essex, building a studio there, where he moved in 1938. He transformed the site, which he called Hill Pasture, into one of the great gardens, which his close companion, Nancy Tennant, tended whilst he was in the Unit. After the war he continued to paint and to design gardens, keeping a meticulous garden notebook. He became friends with the war artist Edward Bawden, but never achieved his success. He was, however, highly respected as a garden designer, being described in *The Garden* magazine, as "the most sensitive and original designer of his generation."

(Details and photograph courtesy of the Paul Mellon Centre)

Robin Whitworth (1911-1996)

Educated at Eton and Oxford, Robin joined the BBC working with such well-known producers as Val Gielgud and Archie Harding. By the time he joined the FAU in 1939, he was already a well-established Radio producer, having made a number of acclaimed programmes such as the Christmas day broadcast of 1935 'Unto Us' and a special tribute on the death of King George V in 1936.

He made no secret of his pacifism, agreeing not to publicise his views, but on joining the Unit, he was initially made Director of Publicity, before being put in charge of shelter work in Liverpool, establishing homes and relief centres in some of the poorest parts of the city. Towards the end of the war, he was appointed Executive Officer for Overseas Relief, in which capacity he was sent out to Brussels in 1944 to co-ordinate a programme of relief. He returned through Paris where he continued regotiations with Entr'Aide Française for Unit members to undertake transport work for emergency transport of food supplies.

Before the war he had married Cecily Blunt, with whom he had a daughter, Mary who became a fund-raiser for Oxford University. At the end of the war he rejoined the BBC as Features Producer, and one of his major post-war projects was to make a series of 10 half hour programmes with Solly Zuckerman entitled 'Look Ahead', exploring scientific inventions that would change our lives over the next 10 years. He then joined BBC TV as Head of Documentary and made a much-praised programme following the building of the new Coventry Cathedral. Other posts included Organiser of Women's programmes, and Manager of Programme Contracts, finally retiring in 1971.

(Details courtesy of The Times. Photograph of RW in his garden with author Barbara Strachey courtesy NPG)

Henry J Cadbury
Accepting the Nobel Peace Prize in 1947 on behalf of the FAU

HC delivered the Nobel lecture having accepted the Peace prize in 1947 on behalf of
The Society of Friends for their relief work in two world wars.

Henry J Cadbury, American Quaker and Biblical scholar.
He and his wife Lydia became firm family friends

Appendix 1
Birds

After writing about his time overseas and his travels and his later thoughts on the Unit and his beliefs, my father chronicled the birds he had seen, three of which the Birmingham Post published. Here he introduces the subject........

One of the things which added greatly to the interest of all my visits was, of course, the birds, especially in Syria, Ethiopia and India. I did have some extraordinarily interesting times seeing many varied species. I think that I saw some 250 varieties while I was away, which is, of course, less than the total seen by Duncan Wood while he was in China, or Michael Rowntree in his journeying round the Mediterranean; and Horace Alexander in India saw an astonishing total. I sent home to Joan three articles on birds I had seen in Egypt, Syria and the Middle East, which The Birmingham Post were good enough to publish, and which I reproduce below.

BIRDS IN EGYPT

———

KITES, HOODED CROWS – AND SPARROWS

——

From a correspondent

Most of the morning I have sat on a rock rising steeply from the Nile. Here, in February, in Upper Egypt, the sky is cloudless, the sun warm but tempered by a cool breeze, the air wonderfully clear. On either side is a long reach of the river. To the south, black rocks, smooth and glistening, stand in the stream; opposite is an island covered with palms; to the north, where the river curves out of sight, is a small town with feluccas moored along the front; on the far bank rise the bare sandy cliffs, which mark the beginning of the desert. The river is muddy, but even so takes on some colour from the sky. White-sailed yachts pass up and down.

Always there are Kites flapping to and fro, or wheeling high up in the sky; their shrill mewing cry, so common a sound in Egypt, goes on from dawn till dusk. These are African Kites: once I supppse, the red Kite was as common in London. Hooded Crows caw and squabble among the palms trees.

A large party of Sand-Martins passes, flying high and apparently with purpose. Are they in the middle of their long journey, and in a month's time will they be hawking for flies over English streams and pools in clear March sunshine, or blown by a north-east wind? It is a pleasant thought, but perhaps they are after all only local birds, like those which seem to be resting among the stones of a ruined temple on the opposite island, and are flying around now in company with red-breasted Swallows.

A common Sandpiper settles on the mud below me. I can hear a Chiff-Chaff and a Willow Warbler calling in the hotel garden behind. Perhaps if and when this arrives, the sandpiper maybe flitting along some Scottish stream, and the warbler may be singing in an English wood.

Occasionally a Kestrel or a large Falcon, probably a Peregrine, flies past. Coming up in the train, I saw several black and white Egyptian Vultures, but I have seen none here. Nor surprisingly, have I seen any of the Kingfishers which are so common in the delta. There are two common species, one like the English bird; the other, the pied, much larger. He is a fine sight as he hovers in the air, black and white wings beating quickly and long beak pointed down; then suddenly he dives, there is a splash and away he flies with a fish.

A white bird, about the size of a large gull, appears flying steadily down stream low over the water, strong pointed beak, head drawn back to the shoulders, long legs out behind. An Egret, one of the commonest birds of this country. They can be seen standing in groups in the fields, clustered like strange white flowers in the top of some tree, or flying home in flocks of six or a dozen to a roosting-place.

Back in the garden, sheltered from the breeze, the sun is hot and the air full of scents: the bees are busy in the bougainvillea; there is a sound of running water from the irrigation taps. Doves call incessantly with a curious double note. The shadow of a kite moves swiftly across the ground. Here in all places, more ubiquitous than the balloons and the black-out, there are sparrows. Wherever one goes – South Africa, Egypt, Syria – there are Sparrows, chirping, fighting, bathing in the dust; the same here as in Whitechapel or Aston. As common in its way, a Little Owl calls from the island.

Now there is a bird on the wires about the size of a Shrike, but less stoutly built, with a short neck, long pointed stout beak, apparently some yellow on its underparts and the middle tail feathers longer than the others. Certainly a Bee-eater, a lovely graceful bird rare in England, but not unknown.

England is thousands of miles away. But some of these birds (Warblers, Sandpipers, and Martins) may make the journey in the coming weeks. Those of us who are here will not see them in England this year, save in memory. But perhaps in the future we shall again hear the first chiff-chaff in the usual corner of the Lickey Woods, near Kendal End or Barnt Green. Or see the first party of sand-martins flitting over a sheltered corner of Bittell Reservoir, so early that the winter duck will not yet have left and goosanders and wigeon will still be preening themselves out in the middle. Or we shall hear turtle doves in the woods near Chaddesley Corbett. Then we shall remember that we saw them on their journey under the hot winter sun of Egypt. Perhaps we shall remember too the Kites and Egrets and Vultures; but I, at any rate, shall not miss them much, though it would be good to see a Bee-eater in Worcestshire.

F.R.B.

Sand Martins
Photo Alamy

Appendix 2
Birds in Syria

The Birmingham Post May 20th 1943

COURSERS, RED-BACKED SHRIKE, BULBULS AND SQUACCO HERONS
From a correspondent

Early last autumn my work took me on a long trip through Syria. Good fortune gave me a fellow ornithologist (Mike Rowntree) as a companion. Our vehicle was an open truck, admirably suited for birding in a hurry.

As we drove over desert tracks, Cream Coloured Coursers ran away from us, or if we approached too near, took wing and flew for a short distance. About the size of a Mistle Thrush and coloured as their name implies, they are handsome birds with a bold black eye stripe. Often they are hard to pick out against a light background.

Great flocks of Plovers went on feeding, apparently little frightened of the car, but taking flight as soon as we stopped and got out. They were sociable Plovers, in size, flight and habit like Lapwings, but with different markings. With them were Dotterell, smaller, duller, but distinguishable by a white eye stripe. Often in the distance flocks of Sandgrouse would appear, flying with the rapid unmistakeable flight of the grouse family, Otherwise birds were few save for Larks and friendly Wheatears bobbing on stones, gay and brave on those enormous wastes, which seemed to stretch endlessly on either side and whose loneliness seemed made more lonely by a Bedouin either driving a donkey and a few camels, or sitting beside his miserable-looking black tent.

At our destination we were able to walk for a couple of hours beside a fine river, which flowed through a great stretch of flat land. Wooden water wheels, creaking as they turned, irrigated the land, and Arabs stood on wooden platforms slinging stones into the crops to frighten the Sparrows. The crack of the sling and the sound of the falling stone moved them for a time, but they quickly returned. One was reminded of David and Goliath, but the persistence of the Sparrows was surely more difficult to cope with. There were great masses of cloud and broad stretches of blue sky, and the wide plain had a mellow autumnal air. Over the water a pair of Pied Kingfishers hovered and dived for fish, while a European Kingfisher sat motionless on a branch. Warblers called in the Willows and hawked for flies, and from some Poplar trees we put up a Nightjar and a Red Backed Shrike. Then as we moved away, two Lapwings flew over the plough and were joined incongruously by two Magpies.

As we returned to the village the countryside lay in the full glory of the evening sun. Herds of black sheep and goats, cattle, brown, black and white, and donkeys were all being driven down to the river to drink. The village was mud built, the houses having domed mud roofs, as timber is so scarce there. Fierce dogs rushed out of the houses to bark as we passed.

This stretch of country is a big migration route. Most of the birds seen were similar to English species, but probably those we saw would be working their way south from Eastern Europe. In all this country there are many members of the hawk tribe. The biggest are the Eagles and Vultures; sitting on some rock, they look enormous, then they flap lazily off and later can be seen ascending in great spirals till they look small against the sky. Kites are everywhere, mostly Black but there are a few Red, a much handsomer bird, with a long forked tail. Then there are Pallid Harriers, the cock a lovely bird with grey and white plumage. On the telegraph wires are countless Kestrels and sometimes those graceful little falcons, the Hobby and the Red Footed Falcon.

Our route back took us near the upper waters of the Euphrates, where it flows through a wide valley, mostly barren save for a rough growth of bushes near the water, and occasional groups of trees. On one side are the cliffs of the desert. We reckoned that we could spare an hour by a muddy pool if we made it up by driving late by moonlight, before sleeping out beside the truck.

I have spent many days birding in many parts of England and Europe, but few produced such a wealth of birds as did that hour. To detail the species would be merely boring. But in one corner, a pair of Black Winged Stilts with black and white bodies on fantastically long legs, waded in the water. On the far side were two Great White Herons and as we watched, several Squacco Herons came down too. There was an Avocet; there were flocks of small waders such as Stints, Dunlin, Ringed Plover and Marsh Sandpipers; there were Greenshanks and Black Redshanks. And out in the open water, ducks were splashing and preening themselves – Wigeon, Teal, Shoveler, Common and Ruddy Shelduck – all enjoying the evening sun as ducks do.

Reluctantly as the light faded, we tore ourselves away and returned to the truck where the long suffering third member of our party had prepared a meal. As we ate it in the darkness, the redshanks were still calling and occasionally a Wigeon would whistle or a Mallard start quacking. Then a Little Owl hooted and we wondered if we might see an Eagle Owl, a species said to occur in the desert. We did not however; perhaps the Gods considered they had already been kind enough.

In the great mountains where the air is fresh and where the purple shadows of the clouds move across the grey stone, and from whose summits one can look down to the great stretch of blue sea, we saw few birds. Along the coast too we saw little, just a few Gulls, and Chats and some Bulbuls calling in the gardens. But any lack of birds is simply compensated for by the beauty of the sun-soaked grey rocks, the olive trees grey and green as the wind moves their leaves and the clear blue sea with white-sailed barques moving steadily along the coast.

F.R.B.

A Squacco Heron
Photo Birds of Syria

Appendix 3
Birds in the Middle East
Birmingham Post April 1943
From a Correspondent

To anyone who watches birds, it is interesting to see in the records of earlier civilisations of the Middle Eastern countries, mention or drawings of the very birds that can be seen today. The following notes, refer to some of these. They are in no sense a detailed study of the subject, nor is the writer anything more than an amateur, who has noticed birds on his travels.

Take the first of those amazing paintings on the walls of the tombs of kings, queens and nobles in the Valley of the Kings, and elsewhere in the neighbourhood of Luxor. There, together with scenes depicting the progress of the dead monarch or official through the underworld, often in company with animal and hawk-headed Gods, are drawings of ploughing, harvesting and threshing. The visitor can see too pictures of servants carrying to their Lords, piles of fruit from orchard and vineyard, or bringing in deer, duck or fish from the chase. Other drawings show flocks of duck rising from the reeds, prominent among these are Pintail, drawn and painted with amazing accuracy. In other paintings are birds obviously meant to represent Shrikes and Hoopoes. In the quantities of small figures carved in relief or bas-relief on the rock walls, delightfully cut figures of Owls and Ibises appear frequently.

Travelling through the Nile Valley today, one can still see Pintail, Shoveler and Teal on the river or on lakes or pools. Once from a lake in a desert oasis, the writer saw twenty Pintail get up and fly round in single file, behind them was a black cloud rising in the sky, and as they passed in front of it, the sun shone full on them, showing up the details of their lovely colourings and graceful form. So must the ancient Egyptian artist have sometimes seen them too. And there are still gaily coloured Hoopoes walking among the palm trees and Little Owls sitting quietly on some wall or bank. As you come out from the dark tombs into the full sunshine, there are Swallows round the village houses and Swifts wheeling high in the air as they must have done for thousands of years.

One can stand on top of a ruined temple and look out over the flat river valley green with crops, the groups of palms and mud villages, to the lines of trees that mark, the river and to the hills of the desert beyond, while Pigeons coo from the Dove-cotes and Kestrels play and scream among the ruins. Is it a Kestrel's head that the Hawk-headed God wears? Or perhaps more probably it is a Peregrine or a Lanner.

The ancient Egyptians were wonderful craftsmen, but their art was fettered by tradition and accepted method, having reached a certain stage early in their history, it seems not to have progressed further. As in drawing the human form, they would draw the body facing and the head in distorted silhouette, so in bird drawing, although in some respects amazingly accurate, they seemed to have been unable to fit the wings of a bird in flight correctly on to its body.

Guides show you on the walls of a temple, the record of the great expedition which Queen Hatsheput sent to the land of Punt, which is said to have brought back to Egypt animals and trees then unknown. One wonders how in that voyage, presumably through the Red Sea, sufficient water was carried to keep the precious cargo alive; and whether, if then as now, Swallows and Blue-Headed Wagtails settled on the rigging and hawked for flies. On the walls of tombs and temples, are drawings of men said to represent the Jews. In the Bible, records of the Jews' Exodus, their wanderings in the desert and their subsequent occupation of and life in Palestine, there are various references to birds.

One remembers how after their sojourn in the land of Egypt, the children of Israel wandered in the wilderness of Sinai and how the Lord sent manna and flocks of Quail to assuage their hunger. In the streets of Cairo, when the Quail migration is in progress today, men with open baskets containing six or eight of these birds, can be seen offering them for sale,

The Psalmist wrote "For the Stork, the fir trees are her house". In spring, Storks pass up the Nile Valley and can be seen standing in the desert in hundreds, rising in clouds when disturbed and after wheeling round, continuing their journey. Later they can be seen still on migration on the edge of the Sinai desert, walking solemnly among the Bedouin Corn. Corn sown after the ground has received a shallow scratching from the primitive ploughs and left to grow or not at the mercy of the rains. In good years the desert seems quite green in places before the corn is cut.

When the Lord was questioning Job, he says "Doth the Hawk fly by thy wisdom and stretch her wings towards the south? Doth the Eagle mount up at thy command and make her nest on high? She dwelleth and abideth on the rock and the strong place. From thence she seeketh the prey, and her eyes behold afar off. Her young ones also suck up blood and where the slain are, there is she" Which Hawk, I wonder, is referred to. Is it the Kestrel again? Or is the reference to spreading her wings to the south, an early migration observation, and is the writer thinking of the Hobby or Red-footed Falcon? If the Eagles mentioned seek out the slain, were they not more probably the Vultures that can still be seen? Though one likes to think that when David, lamenting over Saul and Jonathan, says "they are swifter than Eagles", it really is Eagles that are meant and not the unattractive, greedy, carrion-eating Bald-headed Vulture.

There is too, that lovely passage from the Song of Solomon, which anyone who has been to Palestine in spring must appreciate – "For lo, the winter is past, the rain is over and gone; the flowers appear on the earth; the time of the singing of birds is come and the voice of the turtle is heard in our land'; the fig tree putteth forth her green figs, and the vines with the tender grape, give a good smell. Arise my love, my fair one and come away."

Although I have never heard a Turtle Dove in my brief experience of Palestine, I have always presumed that that is what was meant. Am I wrong? The writer of that passage knew and felt that Palestine is especially lovely in spring, when the meadows are bright with flowers and the fruit trees are coming into leaf, against the dark green of the Cypresses and grey green of the Olives.

F.R.B.

Turtle Doves
Photo Alamy

Appendix 4
Finance

In compiling this account of my father's time in the FAU, I have often wondered about the financing of the Unit's many undertakings, and I can't do better than quote Tegla Davies' book 'The Friends Ambulance Unit', which has an illuminating end-section on the matter. However, the nitty gritty of day-to-day transactions remains something of a black hole. My father often refers to 'filling up with petrol', or 'staying at the best Hotel in town' and taking so-and-so out to lunch. Quite how an officers' impress worked I am less than clear. But I suspect the obvious answer is most probably the correct one. Namely, that some came via the military, and for the rest Gordon Square would either transfer money to a local Bank, or make an arrangement, so that the person in charge would, on a signed authority, be able to withdraw money in the local currency sufficient to buy food, petrol and pay for necessary expenses. This would be topped up from time to time.

As to the origin of the financing, Tegla has this to say, and I quote verbatim:
"The underlying principle of financial policy was while the Unit never refused work which it believed to be necessary and desirable, simply because it was unpaid, contributions were sought wherever possible from the bodies for which the work was done. Thus activities were extended as far as possible without the loss of independence and the freedom to undertake work, such as that of the India section, which would have been prejudiced had it been financed too heavily from official sources. Often work was begun at Unit expense because it was felt to be necessary, and later, contributions sufficient to make the work self-supporting, were received from the body concerned, when it recognized the value of the work."

The Finland expedition, which cost some £20,000 was met wholly from private subscriptions.
Relief work in England was financed entirely by the Friends War Victims Relief Committee, with funds derived from the American Friends Service Committee, until the amalgamation of the FWVRC and the Home Relief Section of the FAU, with the work becoming the responsibility of the new Friends War Relief Service. Those working in hospitals received board and lodgings from the hospitals.
The China Convoy, which was much the most costly section.....was financed entirely by special grants from the British Government, from America and later from Canada.
The Ethiopia Section, apart from an initial outlay on equipment, was covered by grants from the Ethiopian Government.
The Middle East Sections – those sections working with the forces in the ME were financed in two ways. Those working with the British Army received their full maintenance and replacement of equipment from them; initial equipment, expenses and allowances were drawn from Unit funds. Those working with the Free French likewise.
The India Section was financed partly from the British government via the Viceroy's Office, partly from the Bengal government, and partly public donations, through such avenues as BBC appeals.

By 1943 the policy of securing contributions towards their work was bearing fruit. For instance the Council of British Societies for Relief Abroad, negotiated a deal whereby 50% of expenditure on overseas relief work would rank for a grant from the Foreign Office. So by 1945 the Unit's financial position was such that it was possible for the £10,000 recouped under this agreement, to be used to finance further relief projects in Europe.

The support from donations from all classes of the community was remarkable, ranging from a few stamps and a tin of threepenny bits, to a single gift of £10,000; from OAPs as well as large businesses; the peak of the donations being reached in the winter of 1943/44 with the Bengal Famine appeal and the BBC 'Week's Good Cause' raising £15,931 and £7,200 repectively. It was a striking tribute to the generosity of the British people, that a body like the Unit could draw funds from so many sources during the most destructive war in history.

Notes

If a chapter is not listed, it means there are no notes!

Introduction

1. The Downs School – a Quaker inspired school in the Malvern Hills.
2. Horace G Alexander (1889-1989), an influential Quaker, close friend of Gandhi and Nehru, connected with the struggle for independence. One of the best ornithologists of his generation.
3. Rachel Wood - Daughter of Duncan and Katherine Wood. Now Rachel Malloch.
4. Serins – small finches with short stubby bills and forked tails.
5. Christopher Cadbury (1908-1995) the grandson of George Cadbury, married to Honor Milward (1909-1957). Four children – James, Roger, Virginia and Peter.

Chapter 1- Family Background

1. Phyllis Deborah Barlow – FRB's elder sister, died at the age of two in 1909 a year before his birth.
2. 'The Black and Tans' - A force of temporary constables recruited to assist the Royal Irish Constabulary during the Irish War of Independence, but became notorious for reprisal attacks on civilians as well as arson and looting. Their actions swayed public opinion against British rule.
3. Dame Elizabeth Cadbury - (1858-1951) George Cadbury's second wife, born Elizabeth Taylor and a first cousin of FRB's mother, Mabel Barlow (née Cash)
4. From the 'Life and Times of Llewellyn and Winifred Rutter 1997, interviewed by Sir Michael Rutter.
5. Soldanellas – light purple Alpine flower.
6. Suresnes - A housing commune in the western suburbs of Paris.
7. Frankley Beeches - A prominent landmark near Northfield, Birmingham (Near the jnct of M42 and M5) with a stand of Beech trees given to the City by George Cadbury. It now belongs to the National Trust.
8. Munich – An agreement signed by Neville Chamberlain in 1938, conceding the Sudentenland region of Czechoslovakia to Germany. After Hitler invaded Poland, Britain declared war on Germany on September 3 1939.
9. Mr & Mrs Tritsch – Polish refugees who rented 26 Linden Road from parents during the war.
10. Enid Barlow - (née Priestman) married to FRB's brother, John.

Chapter 2 – The Auxiliary Fire Sservice

1. Wards – Electrical shop on Bournville Green
2. Raddlebarn Road – in Bournville, Birmingham
3. Dunkirk – the evacuation of Allied soldiers during WW2 from the beaches and harbour of Dunkirk in N France, between May 26 and June 4 1940.
4. Great Charles Street - With Suffolk St leads into Victoria Square in the centre of Birmingham.
5. Branch – A Fireman's word for the nozzle attached to the end of the fire hose that directs and regulates the water flow.
6. Home Guard – A defence organisation operational from 1940 – 1944, comprising local volunteers, otherwise ineligible for military service, usually owing to age, hence their nickname of 'Dad's Army'.
7. Beaconwood – a house in the Lickey Hills, south west Birmingham, the home of Christopher and Honor Cadbury, where Antony was born in January 1941.

Chapter 3 – The Friends Ambulance Unit WW2

1. The Friend – A weekly Quaker magazine, published continuously since 1843.
2. Manor Farm – Bristol Road, Northfield Birmingham, the former home of George and Elizabeth Cadbury. They moved there from Woodbrooke in Selly Oak, Birmingham in 1894, when it became a Quaker college. George and Elizabeth lived together at the Manor Farm until George's death in 1922. During WW2, Elizabeth Cadbury let the FAU use the grounds for a training centre. She continued to live there until her death in 1951, aged 93. It was then sold to Birmingham University as a hall of residence. It was badly burnt down by arson in 2014 and again in 2017.

Notes

Chapter 4 – Getting started

1. ARP – Air Raid Precautions, an organisation set up in 1937 dedicated to the protection of civilians from the dangers of air-raids.
2. Dr Hubert Rutter was the father of FRB's brother-in-law, Dr Llewellyn Rutter, who had married Winifred Barber. He gave most of the early medical lectures at FAU training camps at Manor Farm.
3. Living in America – When Tom Tanner joined the FAU, his American in-laws, William and Gertrude Adelbert Jones arranged for Tom's wife, Dora and their 2 children Stephen and his sister Virginia to be moved from Glasgow to New Jersey for the duration of the war, away from the bombing.

Chapter 5 – FRB joins the FAU and his first camp at Manor Farm

1. Keith Linney – born in Tasmania to an old Quaker family. He went to Stramongate and Sidcot Quaker schools. A good all-round left-hander for Somerset. After the war he worked for the UN.

Chapter 6 – Poplar Hospital

1. Fircroft College – Residential College, founded by George Cadbury Jr, grandson of Cadbury's co-founder John Cadbury.
2. H A L Fisher – English historian, educator and Liberal politician.
3. Roger Fry – English painter and art critic (1866-1934), member of the Bloomsbury group. An advocate of new developments in French painting which he called Post-Impressionism.
4. Alfred Braithwaite – like FRB's brother, John (see note in Ch 14), Alfred (b.1901) wasn't required to register as a CO until 1941. In 1939 he was Chairman of the Conscription Committee, and after appeal he was given unconditional exemption on the grounds that he was acting as lawyer for many of the CO's at their Tribunals.

Chapter 7 – A New Year Dawns and the arrival of a new child

1. Sidcot School – Quaker co-educational school for boarding and day pupils in Somerset.
2. Mr Dobinson – Charles Dobinson, Headmaster of King Edwards Five Ways, B'ham. The author's mother was his secretary, before getting married. His son Humphrey was at LP with David & Antony.
3. HMS Illustrious – Leading Aircraft carrier in the Mediterranean fleet in WW2.

Chapter 8 – A Country Posting

1. CEMA – Committee for the Encouragement of Music and the Arts set up in 1940. J M Keynes was the first Chairman. It became the precursor of the Arts Council.
2. Tai Yang – Chinese for Sun.
3. Lord and Lady Dillon – Brigadier Eric Fitzgerald Dillon, 19th Vicount Dillon CMG, DSO (1881-1946). Irish Peer and British Officer, served in WW1. He and his wife Nora Juanita (née Beckett) known as 'Nita', had two children. The eldest, Michael Eric Dillon married Irène Marie du Plessis, and had 8 children. He succeeded his father as 20th Viscount Dillon. Their daughter, Pamela m. William Onslow, 6th Earl of Onslow and their daughter, Lady Teresa m. Auberon Waugh, who had a daughter Daisy.
4. Lord Gort - Field Marshal John, Standish, Surtees, Prendergast, Vereker 6th Viscount Gort VC, GCB, CBE, DSO and 2 bars. MVO, MC – senior British Army Officer.
5. Duff Cooper – Alfred Duff Cooper, 1st Viscount Norwich, GCMG DSO, PC, known as Duff Cooper. Conservative MP, diplomat and author. Later worked with de Gaulle as leader of the Free French.
6. General Charles Noguès – C–in-C North Africa, and after the Allied invasion of N Africa, High Commissioner.
7. Allied invasion – During WW2 Algeria, along with most of N Africa, were under the control of Nazi Germany and Vichy France. On Nov 8 1942, the Allies launched the first major offensive of the war, led by General Dwight D Eisenhower. The Allies retook Morocco along with Algeria, establishing the liberation of N Africa.
8. Lord Belisha – Lord Hore-Belisha, controversially appointed to replace Duff Cooper as Sec of State for War. Remembered for his introduction of Belisha beacons at Zebra crossings.

Notes

Chapter 9 – Finding a home for JMB and the end of Cheveley

1. Noël K Hunnybun (1889-1984)a well-known Social worker, who had worked at The London Hospital when FRB was there, and she joined up with Quakers and other COs, such as Tessa Rowntree, in advising on re-housing families from the East End into Cambridgeshire homes away from danger. She had also advised on placing British children in American homes, and so had knowledge of Win and Llew Rutter's two children who were in America, and was able to help in getting them home.
2. Archie Wavell - Archibald Percival Wavell, Ist Earl Wavell (1883-1950), GCB, GCSI ++. Senior Officer of the British Army. Served in both World Wars with distinction. Famously published his anthology of poems *Other Men's Flowers* during the war, which has never been out of print.
3. Oswald Garrison Villard (1872-1949) an American liberal journalist and Editor of the New York Evening Post. A civil rights activist and founding member of the Civil Rights movement.
4. 'Who stole my heart away?' – From the 1925 musical 'Sunny' by Jerome Kern and Oscar Hammersetein II: 'Who stole my heart away/Who makes me dream all day/ Dreams I know can never come true'....etc
5. Lady Bracknell – A character in Oscar Wilde's comedy '*The Importance of Being Earnest*'.
6. J B Priestley – Well known playwright of such plays as *An Inspector Calls,* as well as of popular books such as *The Good Companions.* Left wing commentator, his famous Postscripts broadcast during the war, boosted morale.
7. Robert Ransome – sadly died from cancer 2018.
8. Unity Mitford (1914-1948), the 5th of 7 children of Lord Redesdale, including Nancy, Diana and Jessica. A British socialite, and supporter of Nazism, known for her relationship with Hitler. When war broke out, she attempted suicide in Munich. She never fully recovered.

Chapter 11 – A holiday in Ewyas Harold and Relief Officer

1. L P Appleton – The 2nd Secretary and Manager of the BVT, preceding FRB.
2. Hugh Walpole (1884-1941)a popular novelist – most famousl for *Mr Perrin and Mr Trail* (1911)
3. W E Henley (1849 – 1903) a jingoistic and patriotic writer, most famous for *Invictus* (1875)
4. John Masefield (1878-1967) a prolific writer: became Poet Laureate, famous for his sea poems.
5. Baedeker Raids – Named after the popular travel guides, from a comment by a German Foreign Office spokesman, who is reported to have said "We shall bomb every bulding in Britain marked with three stars in the Baedeker Guides."
6. FWRS - Friends War Relief Service, later abbreviated to FRS.
7. Neave Brayshaw – Quaker thinker, and historian, taught at Bootham School and in the early days at Woodbrooke. Wrote biography of George Fox and a short history of the Society of Friends.

Chapter 12 – Relief Work Part 2

1. Kingsmead College – one of four colleges which were part of the federation of Selly Oak Colleges in Birmingham, devoted to theology, social work and teacher training, including Fircroft, Westhill and Woodbrooke. Kingsmead was founded in 1905 for the training of missionaries. Woodbrooke and Fircroft are the only two still surviving.
2. Pipe – There is a letter from Duncan to FRB from Glasgow on his way to China dated 28th Nov 1941 – "Dear Ralph, Just a line to say that I am smoking your pipe with very great satisfaction. There is only one other thing to say, and that is that you have given me fresh courage and hope for this journey, and I know I shall have the support of your thoughts in all the days to come...."
3. Homosexual – the use of the word 'gay' for homosexual didn't come in till the mid 1960's.
4. FRSC – Friends Relief Service Council
5. BRCS – British Red Cross Society
6. Lady Limerick – Angela Pery, Countess of Limerick (1897-1981) leader of the International British Red Cross.
7. Lady Mountbatten – Edwina Mountbatten (1900-1960), the last Vicereine of India, wife of Lord Mountbatten.

Notes

Chapter 14 – Deputy Chairman and Missions hither and yon

1. Stafford Cripps (1889-1952), had Quaker sympathies - later Sir Stafford, Labour party politician and member of Churchill's wartime cabinet. Influential diplomat in Russia and later in India.
2. Violet Markham (1872-1959) a writer and social reformer. First woman JP, she became Deputy Chairman of the Assistance Board in 1937.
3. Robert Bridges (1844-1930) the Poet laureate from 1913. His poems reflected a deep Christian faith and he wrote many well-known hymns including 'Oh sacred head, sore wounded'.
4. Marcel Pagnol (1895-1974), a widely regarded as one of France's greatest film makers.
5. John Barlow (FRB's brother) – because of his age (b.1901) he was not required to register until 1941, after which he was seconded into The National Service Hostels Corporation from Cadbury's, where he was then working, with a remit to supervise the running of the hostels for 'war workers'. He later joined the Home Guard (aka Dad's Army), rising to the rank of second Lieutenant.

Chapter 15 – Long months of waiting

1. Vera Brittain (1893-1970) a Voluntary Aid Detachment (VAD) nurse, writer and pacifist. Her best-selling book, *Testament of Youth* recounted her experiences in WW1.
2. Hasel Mundy – Susi Hasel Mundy was the younger sister of Gerhard Hasel, who was a 7th Day Adventist. Hasel's childhood experiences in Nazi Germany are told in *A Thousand Shall Fall*.
3. Rubáiyát – *The Rubáiyát of Omar Khayyám*, the title given by Edward Fitzgerald to his translation of the 11th Century Persian poet.
4. Julian Bell (1908-1937) an English poet, son of Clive and Vanessa Bell. A pacifist, he was killed in the Spanish Civil War. Both Julian and his brother Quentin were at LP with FRB.
5. Quentin Bell (1910-1996) an English art historian and writer, younger brother of Julian. He held Professorships of Fine Art at a number of Universities.
6. Aldous Huxley (1894-1963) an English writer and Philosopher. Wrote some 50 books including *Chrome Yellow, Brave New World, The Doors of Perception* and *Grey Eminence,* about a French monk.
7. *The Gay Galliard* – An historical novel by Margaret Irwin (1889-1967), *The Gay Galliard* is the story of Mary Queen of Scots.
8. Cousin Anna – Lady Anna Barlow (née Denman) (c.1874-1965), the widow of Sir John Emmott Barlow, the 1st Baronet and second cousin to FRB. A welfare reformer, & liberal party supporter.

Chapter 16 – Still waiting to leave

1. Lin Yutang (1895-1976) a Chinese novelist, philosopher, and translator. He wrote in English and Chinese, and published best-selling translations of classic Chinese texts. His first novel, *A Moment in Peking,* written in English, covers the turbulent events in China from 1900 to 1938.
2. Ronald Lockley (1903-2000), a Welsh ornithologist and naturalist. He wrote over 50 books including this major study of Shearwaters.
3. David Astor (1912-2001) - The Hon David Langhorne Astor, English newspaper publisher, the third child of the very wealthy American/English parents Waldorf Astor and Nancy Langhorne.
4. Frances Lloyd – MBB's 1st wife, d. of Ted and Margaret Lloyd. They separated in 1940. He then m. Eleanor Singer. When she died in 1998, he & Annette Caulkin from FAU days, got together.

Chapter 17 – Overseas and Round the Cape to Durban

1. Evelyn Waugh (1906-1966) an English novelist, travel writer and journalist. Particularly famous for early satires *Black Mischief, Scoop* and *A Handful of Dust,* as well as *Brideshead Revisited* and the second world war trilogy *Sword of Honour.*
2. Henry Nevinson (1856-1941), a war correspondent and suffragist, he was a co-founder of the FAU in WW1, he helped to expose slavery in W Africa.
3. Sir Barry Jackson (1879-1961), a Theatre Director and founder of the Birmingham Repertory Theatre, and with Bernard Shaw, The Malvern Festival. Many famous names such Laurence Olivier, Ralph Richardson, Edith Evans, Albert Finney and Derek Jacobi started at the 'Rep'.
4. Essay Meeting – In the days when Quakers frowned on the theatre and music, they devised their own entertainment, including a monthly Essay Society, when members wrote and read out an Essay. Another such was a Book Club, which for Birmingham Friends was called the QQ, standing for Quindecim Quakeri, being limited to 15 members.

Notes

Chapter 17 contd

5. H G Wells (1866-1946) a novelist, historian and science fiction writer. Best known works include novels such as *The History of Mr Polly*, and *Kipps*, as well as science fiction books *The War of the Worlds* and *The Time Machine*.
6. L P Jacks – (1860-1955) English educator, philiosopher and Unitarian minister.
7. Winifred Fortescue (1888-1951) a British writer and actress.
8. Bernard Shaw (1856-1950) an Irish playwright and polemicist. The most influential writer of his generation with plays such *Pygmalion*, *Saint Joan* and *Man and Superman* and *The Doctor's Dilemma*, which debates the medical ethics of saving one person rather than another.

Chapter 18 – Durban at last – 'The Kindness of Strangers'

1. Gordon Square – The FAU London HQ, aka 'The Square', Bloomsbury, London WC1.
2. The Mount – Quaker girls school in York, sister school of Bootham.
3. Oundle – a co-ed boarding school in Northamptonshire, founded in 1556.
4. Howard K Smith (1914-2002), an American journalist, and well-known Radio and Television reporter. His book *Last Train from Berlin*, was an eye witness account of Germany immediately pre-war. It became a best seller.
5. Maurice Webb – A Quaker CO who left England to join a publishing firm in Durban and founded the Durban Literary Group. He became a leading figure in South African Quaker circles.
6. Florence Bayman (c.1900 -1984/5) a South African Friend, who worked for the Rand Daily Mail under their legendary campaigning Editor, Laurence Gandar. After the war she came to live in Bournville and became a close family friend. She had a daughter Cynthia Loft in Denmark.
7. Dr Herbert Standing (1857-1943) a Quaker medical missionary and palaeontologist in Madagascar, where he was Headmaster of the Friends High School there.
8. Francis Braithwaite – the youngest son of Fred Braithwaite, cousin of Alfred. FRB was at LP with Francis' elder brother Arthur.
9. John Steinbeck (1902-1968), an American writer noted for *Tortilla Flat, Canary Row* and *East of Eden*. He won the Nobel Prize for Literature in 1962.
10. Quote – From Wordsworth's famous "Sonnet Composed on Westminster Bridge" 1802.
11. Douglas Reed (1895-1976) a British journalist and novelist with largely anti-Semitic themes.
12. The Woodlands – A home for older people in Wolverhampton run by Quakers. Victorian house leased by the Society of Friends in 1941, initially for older people who had been bombed out of their homes. From 1945 it was bought by the Society and became a permanent home for the elderly. Granny Barber (d. 1966) and Llew's mother (d. 1978) both spent their last years there.
13. Sidney Howard (1891-1939) An American playwright and screenwriter, who won a posthumous award for the screenplay of *Gone with the Wind. The Silver Chord* was a major stage hit

Chapter 19 – And so to Cairo

1. Philip Holding – The Holdings were a Quaker building company, who built many of the houses on the Bournville Estate. Dick Holding and his wife Mary, were close friends of my parents.
2. Alan Cadbury – son of William and Emmeline Cadbury, elder brother of Brandon, grandson of Richard Cadbury.
3. Moorestown – A township of New Jersey and suburb of Philadelphia, with strong Quaker links.

Chapter 20 – Cairo and Alexandria

1. Lydia – Lydia Brookes, a personal maid to MCB, who stayed on with us when MCB moved to London. Her husband had been killed in WW1.
2. Norman Birkett (1883-1962) - Later Lord Birkett. British barrister, Judge and politician. One of the Judges at the Nuremburg trials after the war.
3. Ernest Sawdon – Ernest and Eleanor Sawdon had been missionaries in China and Head of the Chunking Friends School.
4. Max Beerbohm (1872-1956) - Sir Henry Maximilian Beerbohm, English essayist and Caricaturist, writing under the name of Max Beernbohm. His only novel is *Zuleika Dobson*.
5. Octavia Hill (1838-1912), a pioneering social reformer and co-founder of The National Trust in 1895.

Notes

Chapter 20 contd

6. Hadfield Spears Unit – Anglo French volunteer medical unit, sponsored by Sir Robert Hadfield and Lady Spears.
7. *Pygmalion* – By George Bernard Shaw. Later made into the musical *My Fair Lady* in 1964.
8. Frederic Prokosch – (1906-1989) American writer, known for poetry, novels and memoirs.
9. Wilfred Littleboy – Wilfred and Winifred Littleboy. Highly respected Quakers, who both made a great contribution to Woodbrooke. He was Chairman of the Council for many years. He was imprisoned in WW1 for being a CO.

Chapter 21 – Travelling to visit the Hadfield Spears clinics

1. Khabur river – The largest tributary of the Euphrates in Syria, originating in Turkey.
2. Latakia – The principle port of Syria
3. Patrick Barr (1908-1985), a British actor whose career spanned over 50 years. He appeared in over 100 films and numerous television series, and frequently on the stage.
4. Humphrey Waterfield (1908-1971) a passionate gardener and painter, who created gardens in this country and France.
5. NAAFI – Navy, Army and Air Force Institutes: an organisation that ran the catering facilities for British military bases.
6. Beersheba – (Hebrew/ Be'er-Sheva) The largest city in the Negev desert of southern Israel.
7. AMLC – Air Mail Letter Cards; a thin lightweight piece of foldable and gummed paper for writing a letter via airmail, in which the letter and the envelope are one and the same.
8. Airgraph – a means of reducing the weight of mail carried by air. The letter was written on special Airgraph forms. It was then photographed and sent out as a negative on rolls of microfilm.
9. Vichy France – the French state headed by Marshal Pétain, which moved from Paris to Vichy in the unoccupied 'free zone'. But from 1940, when Pétain signed a treaty with Germany ending the war between them, the Vichy government collaborated with Hitler.
10. Henri Dentz – I have no enlightenment on what this night have been, but Dentz was eventually convicted of being a collaborationist, which carried the death penalty, but de Gaulle commuted it to life imprisonment, and he died in prison in 1945.
11. Emile Cortas – One of four children of Tannous and Mariam Cortas, a Lebanese family of Quakers, who taught at the Quaker school in Broumana. My mother got to know them all when she was in the Lebanon with her sister and brother-in-law, Dr Rutter in 1932. Emile and his brother and sister Michel and Najla often came over to the UK post war, and stayed with my parents. They had a canning business.
12. Marshall and Annie Fox – The Fox's had been out in the Lebanon since 1908, and closely involved with Broumana High School.
13. Broumana High School – A Quaker co-educational day and boarding school, established in 1873.
14. David Stafford Allen – Edwin and Hilda Ransome (née Stafford Allen) were great family friends
15. Trachoma – An infectious disease, which causes damage to the eyelids and can lead to blindness.

Chapter 22 – The Desert and Bedouin Tribes

1. Joice and Sydney Loch – Joice was an Australian journalist and humanitarian worker, who worked with refugees in Poland, Greece and Romania before and during WW2. She married Sydney Loch, a Gallipoli veteran and humanitarian worker. Together, they set up a refugee camp for Poles in Haifa.

Chapter 23 – Further Journeys into Syria

1. Druse – A religious group that emerged in Egypt around 1017. Their faith is often described as a mix of Islam, Buddhism and Hinduism. They recognise all major Prophets such as Moses, Jesus and Mohammed.
2. Justinian (482-565 CE) the Eastern Roman Emperor from 527 to 565.
3. Homs – A city in western Syria.
4. Circassians – An ethnic group native to Circassia, along the NE shore of the Black Sea, many of whom were displaced in the course of the Russian conquest of the Caucasus in the 19th century.
5. Nestorians – A Christian based group that emphasises a distinction between the human and the divine. Founded by Nestorius (386-450 CE) Patriarch of Constantinople from 428-431 CE

Notes

Chapter 23 contd

6. Benno Moiseiwitsch – (1890-1963) Russian/Ukrainian born British pianist, known especially for his interpretations of the late Romantic repertoire, especially Rachmaninov. Famous for his lyrical phrasing, elegance and easy virtuosity.
7. Stephenson – Robert Louis Stephenson – From his 'Songs of Travel'. 'Whaups' is an old English word for Curlews.
8. Barrows Stores – A Quaker run up-market store in Bull Street, B'ham from 1849 – 1973.
9. The Desert Song – 1926 Popular Operetta by Sigmund Romberg & Oscar Hammerstein II.
10. A Little Book of Healing – Mary Webb (1881-1927) An English romantic novelist and poet of the early 20th century. Her work is set in the Shropshire countryside. Diagnosed with Graves' disease at the age of 20, she found that her love of nature helped her healing.
11. *The Flax of Dream* – a novel by Henry Williamson in 4 volumes telling the story of William Maddison from schooldays to WW1 and post war. It is largely autobiographical.

Chapter 24 – The Military and Blood transfusions

1. Ibn Saud (1875-1953), known in the Arab world as Abdulaziz, he was the founder and first monarch of Saudi Arabia
2. Alamein – October/November 1942, the 8th Army, now led by Lt Gen Montgomery, won a decisive victory and boosted the morale of the Allies and marked the end of Western Desert campaign.
3. Leavitts – Leslie and Margaret Leavitt, Principals of the International College, Beirut 1946-1970.

Chapter 25 –Thoughts of a Quaker CO at war – An Exacting Mistress

1. Ashley Dukes (1847-1930) was a popular playwright both in the West End and on Broadway, *A Man with a load of Mischief* being the most popular. In 1933 he started the Mercury Theatre in Notting Hill, London and produced T S Eliot's *Murder in the Cathedral* there. In 1918 he married Marie Rambert, who founded Ballet Rambert.
2. *The Just So Stories* – By Rudyard Kipling, published in 1902, they are considered a classic of children's literature, and amongst his best known works.
3. Charles Morgan (1894-1958) was a novelist, playwright and journalist. His books, he said 'dealt with Art, Love and Death' and include *The River Line* and *The Voyage*. He was also a Poet and for nearly 20 years the Drama critic of The Times.
4. Marjorie Rawlings (1896-1953) was an American author who wrote on rural themes, including her best known novel *The Yearling,* which won the Pulitzer Prize and was also filmed. *Cross Creek* was an autobiographical study of her neighbourhood and got her into a libel case which she lost.
5. *Mrs Miniver* – Originally a book by Jan Struther (1901-1953) who also wrote hymns such *Lord of all hopefulness*. But *Mrs Miniver* was famously filmed starring Greer Garson and Walter Pidgeon. It depicts how the life of an unassuming housewife in rural England is touched by the war.

Chapter 26 –The Worst Job in the World

1. Annette Caulkin – Annette Cooper married David Caulkin during the war. He was killed a week before the end. They had two children. She later met up again with Michael Barratt Brown.
2. Harold Massingham (1888-1952) was a British writer on the countryside. Also a poet.
3. Freya Stark (1893-1993) was an explorer and travel writer especially about the Middle East and Afghanistan. Her wartine experiences were described in *Letters from Syria*. She was made a Dame in 1972.
4. Pearl S Buck (1892-1973) was an Amerian writer and novelist, she was the daughter of missionaries, and spent most of her early life in China, and her most famous book *The Good Earth* depicting peasant life in China won the Pulitzer prize and in 1938 she won the Nobel prize for literature for her writings on Chinese life. She was also a prominent advocate of women's rights.
5. Philip Gibbs (1877-1962) was a prolific English journalist, novelist and war correspondent. His novel *Sons of the Others (1940)* starts at the outbreak of war and takes it until Dunkirk.
6. Joan Grant (1907-1989) was an English author of historical novels, the most well known being *Winged Pharaoh* dealing with Egyptian history.
7. *The Root and the Flower* – A trilogy set in Moghul India (1556-1605) by distinguished British novelist L H Myers (1881-1944).
8. Robert Herrick (1591-1674) was a lyric poet, best known for his book of poems *Hesperides*, which includes the ever popular *Gather ye rosebuds while ye may.*

Notes

Chapter 26 contd

9. Siegfried Sassoon (1886-1967) was one of the leading poets of WW1, decorated for bravery on the Western front. His poems depicted the horrors of war. Also famed for his fictionalised autobiographies *Memoirs of a Foxhuntuing Man* and *Memoirs of an Infantry Man*. His trilogy of real autobiography including *The Weald of Youth* were also widely acclaimed.
10. Marguerite Steen (1894-1975) was a British writer of biographies, especially of creative people such as Ellen Terry and Hugh Walpole. She also wrote about bullfighting in *Matador* and a long saga on the slave trade *The Sun is my Undoing*
11. Alice Meynell (1847-1922), a British writer, editor and critic, now mostly remembered as a poet.

Chapter 27 - To Teheran and Back

1. ATS – The Auxilliary Territorial Service, the women's branch of the British Army in WW2
2. Ferdowsi (940-1020) was the great Persian poet and author of the epic poem *Shahnameh*.
3. Mennonites – A Christian group named after Dutch teacher Menno Simons (1496-1561). Persecuted by the RC church, they are early Protestants and believe in pacifism.
4. Sir Arnold Wilson (1884-1940)a British Commissioner in Baghdad (1918-20), administrator in Mesopotamia after WW1, and Iraqi revolt against the British in 1920. Died in action in WW2.
5. Tommies – Tommy Atkins (often just 'Tommy') is slang for an ordinary soldier in the Br. Army
6. Droshkies – A light, low, four-wheeled, open vehicle used mainly in Russia.
7. Seton Merriman (1862-1903), the pseudonym of Hugh Stowell Scott, a prominent English novelist, best known for *The Sowers*, set in Russia.

Chapter 28 – The deaths of Tom Tanner and Peter Hume and the aftermath

1. Neil Gunn (1891-1973), a prolific novelist, critic and dramatist, who was one of the leading lights of the Scottish Renaissance of the 20's and 30's. Arguably the most influential Scottish writer of the first half of the 20th century. *Silver Darlings* was an historical novel dealing with the Highland Clearances.
2. Corder Catchpool (1883-19552), an English Quaker and pacifist, actively engaged in relief work on the Western front in the First FAU. He was later imprisoned as an absolutist. After the war he worked with the War Vics in reconciliation with Germany, then as a welfare co-ordinator.

Chapter 29 – Life in Cairo carries on and FRB goes down with Jaundice

1. ENSA – The Entertainments National Service Association, set up in 1939 by Basil Dean and Leslie Henson, to provide entertainment for British armed forces in WW2 both at home and abroad.
2. Virginia Woolf (1882-1941) an English writer considered to be one of the most important writers of the 20th century. Her works included *To the Lighthouse, A Room of One's Own, Orlando* and *Jacob's Room*. The essay *Death of a Moth* was influenced by the death of her brother. She was troubled by mental illness and drowned herself.
3. Antoine de St Exupéry (1900-1944) French writer, journalist and pioneering aviator, best known for *The Little Prince,* and *Night Flight*. During his time in America he wrote *Flight from Arras*, widely acclaimed in the States. He died in a plane crash while on reconnaissance duties for the free French.
4. Anton Chekhov (1860-1904) a Russian playwright and Doctor, whose plays including *The Cherry Orchard, Uncle Vanya* and *The Seagull* are considered classics. Also one of the best short story writers of all time. He died of TB.
5. T S Eliot (1888-1965), considered by many to be one of the most influential poets of the 20th century. His most famous poems being *The Waste Land* and *The Four Quartets*. He was also a renowned writer of verse drama such as *Murder in the Cathedral* and *The Family Reunion*. Born in Boston, he moved to the UK in 1914 and became a British subject in 1927. He was also a renowned writer of critical essays.
6. Allen Maw – My mother's first boyfriend prior to meeting FRB. His parents were missionaries.
7. J M Synge (1871-1909) an Irish playwright, a key figure in the Irish literary revival and a co-founder of The Abbey Theatre. *The Playboy of the Western World* is his best known play.
8. Louis Pasteur (1822-1895) a French biologist and chemist renowned for his discoveries of the principles of vaccination and pasteurisation.
9. Samuel Butler (1835-1902), a satirical English writer. *Erewhon*, one of his best known books (1872), is a satire of Victorian society. Erewhon itself is almost 'Nowhere' backwards!

Notes

Chapter 29 contd

10. Constance Holme (1880-1955) an English novelist and playwright. Her books are set in the old English county of Westmoreland. *The Lonely Plough* was one of the earliest books published by Penguin Books.
11. Nora Wain (1895-1964) was from a Quaker family in PA, she was a best-selling writer and journalist writing books on her time spent in China in the 20's and Germany immediately prewar. Whilst in China, she met and married the Englishman George Osland-Hill. He had a daughter from a previous marriage Mary Osland-Hill.

Chapter 30 – Leave in Aswan and Luxor

1. Queen Alexandra Sisters – Full title - Queen Alexandra's Imperial Nursing Service which looked after wounded servicemen.
2. Apologia pro Vita Sua (1801-1890), the autobiography of John Henry Newman, an English theologian, Catholic priest and Cardinal. Controversial figure, canonised in 2019.
3. Elroy Flecker (1884-1915) James Elroy Flecker, an English poet, novelist and playwright.
4. Colossus of Memnon –Two massive stone statues of the Pharaoh Amenhotep III, who reigned in Egypt during Dynasty XVIII c. 1350 BCE
5. Baksheesh – In the ME money given to beggars, sometimes as a form of bribery.

Chapter 31 – Back in Cairo and another impasse with the Army

1. Lord Woolton – A prominent businessman appointed Minister of Food by Neville Chamberlain in 1940. He stayed there until 1943.
2. Wadi – Arabic word for a valley or dry riverbed, or that only has water in the rainy season.
3. Thomas Grey (1716-1771) an English poet. From his *Elegy written in a Country Churchyard.*
4. Louis Bromfield (1896-1956) an American author and conservationist; an early environmentalist.
5. H G Wood – The father of Duncan Wood and his brothers and sister.
6. Veronica Lake (1922-1973) a very striking American film actor best known for her femme fatale roles with Alan Ladd.

Chapter 33 – Ethiopia

1. Jehu-driven – Kings II Chapter 9 verse 20: "For the driving is like the driving of Jehu, the son of Nimshi, for he driveth furiously."
2. Shepheard's Hotel – The leading hotel in Cairo, and one of the most celebrated in the world from the middle of the 19th century, until it was burned down in 1952 in the Cairo fire.

Chapter 34 – Back in Cairo

1. Robin Fedden CBE (1908-1977) an English writer, diplomat and mountaineer. He served as a diplomat in Athens and then in Cairo, where he taught English Literature at Cairo University. He was known as one of the Cairo poets and co-edited the literary journal *Personal Landscape* with Lawrence Durrell. After the war he worked for the National Trust becoming Deputy DG.
2. Swalecliffe – A popular seaside resort in Kent, where Reg and family had their first home.
3. 'Desert Victory' – 1943 Wartime documentary film of the allied campaign to drive Italy and Germany from North Africa including the battle of Alamein.

Chapter 35 – My father sails to India

1. Willa Catha (1873-1947) an American writer, well-known for her novels of frontier life on the great plains, including *O Pioneers!, The Song of the Lark, Death Comes to the Archbishop* and *The Slave Girl.* She was awarded the Pulitzer Prize in 1923 for *One of Ours* a novel set in WW1.
2. A J Cronin – *The Citadel* published in 1937, ground-breaking for its treatment of medical ethics, it won the National Book Award in America.
3. Edward Thompson (1886-1946) a novelist, poet, journalist and historian of India. He was a liberal advocate for Indian culture and political self-determination. He wrote novels about a Wesleyan family the Arnisons, the first, *Introducing the Arnisons* in 1935 about growing up Wesleyan in late Victorian and Edwardian England.
4. *For Whom the Bell Tolls* – Novel by Ernest Hemingway, published in 1940, tells the story of Robert Jordan, a young American in the International Brigade, attached to the anti-fascist guerrilla in the mountains of Spain.

Notes

Chapter 36 – Arriving Unwell in India

1. Sapper (1888-1937), the pseudonym of Herman McNeile, British soldier and novelist who won fame with his thriller *Bull-Dog Drummond* (1920). Several sequels, but none as popular.
2. Mona Inglesby (1918-2006) a British dancer, choreographer and director of the touring company International Ballet, which kept ballet alive in the regions during the war.
3. Vita Sackville West (1892-1962) an English author and garden designer, especially remembered for the famous garden at Sissinghurst.
4. Marjorie Watts – Harold and Marjorie Watts, Birmingham Quaker friends
5. Malcolm Sargent (1895-1967) an English conductor, regarded as the leading conductor of choral works, and famous as chief conductor of the Proms for nearly 20 years. Knighted in 1947.
6. Wings for Victory – People were encouraged to do their bit during WW2, and 'Wings for Victory' week was a fundraising scheme established in 1943 to raise funds to purchase bombers for the British war effort.
7. Esmond Knight (1906-1987) a very successful stage and film actor pre-war. Badly blinded in the war, but regained some sight later. Due to people like Laurence Olivier, who cast him as Fluellen in his film of *Henry V*, he went on to act in many subsequent films as well as on stage.

Chapter 37 – China and the China Convoy

1. The Hump – The name given by Allied pilots in WW2 to the eastern end of the Himalayan Mountains, over which they flew military transport aircraft from India to China, to supply the Chinese war effort of Chiang Kai-shek and the units of the US Air Forces based in China.
2. Kunming – The capital and largest city of Yunnan Province.
3. Kutsing – now Qujing

Chapter 38 – And so back to India and onto Cairo

1. Richard Casey (1890-1976)-Sir Richard, KG,CH, DSO Australian statesman, who was a distinguished army officer, long-serving cabinet minister, Ambassador to the US, member of Churchill's war Cabinet and Governor of Bengal. Post war he was Governor General of Australia.
2. Return from America (1944) – Michael and his sister Priscilla Rutter went to America during the war, living with different families, the Rhoads (Michael); the Allens and then the Andrews (Priscilla). Priscilla was not happy with the latter. According to their father (Interview with Win & Llew by Michael Rutter1995/6) "Negotiations to get the children back in 1944 – first an agreement for Prill to join Mike at the Rhoads - took an eternity [....] Then the journey itself lasted an incredible time. The boat sailed first to Lisbon, where it stayed for several weeks, while waiting for a flight to Limerick. Then eventually to Croydon Airport, where I met you."
3. The Yachting Pool – A pool in Bournville, that forms the centre of a pleasant public area, popular for sailing model boats on, walking round and relaxation. It was created on the initiative of George Cadbury Jnr, to develop an area of marshland by unemployed men in the 1930's, who were ineligible for unemployment benefit. It was opened in 1932.
4. Blighty – Popular term for servicemen to describe their home, especially Britain or England. Supposedly derived from an Urdu word meaning foreign, during the time of the Raj and by extension 'going home to Britain'.

Chapter 39 – Back in England

1. Sir Clifford Edward Heathcote-Smith (1883-1963) – he held many senior positions including Consul General to Alexandria from 1923-1943. Later leading representative of Inter-Governmental Committee on Refugees (IGCR).

Chapter 40 – Invalided Out

1. Kingsley Martin (1897-1969) a British journalist, who edited the left-leaning political magazine the New Statesman from 1930- 1960.
2. Mao (1893-1976) - Mao Zedong (often westernised then as Mao Tse-tung) also known as Chairman Mao. A soldier, theorist and statesman, who became the founding father of the People's Republic of China, which he ruled from its inception in 1949 till his death. A Marxist-Leninist, whose theories, strategies and policies are now known as Maoism.
3. Chiang Kai-Shek (1887-1975) a Chinese nationalist politician, revolutionary and military leader of the Republic of China, first in mainland China, and then after Mao became Chairman, in Taiwan.

Index

The letter p next to a number, indicates a photograph

Antony Barlow

One of the five children of Ralph and Joan Barlow, Antony is a descendant of one of the oldest Quaker families, whose ancestor James Lancaster, was one of the Society of Friends founder, George Fox's closest advisors.

His first book, *He is our cousin, Cousin*, published in 2015 traced the long history of his Quaker family, which has been handed down by countless generations of his Quaker ancestors. Through their memories and that of relatives and family archives, he told a remarkable story of fighting persecution and prejudice, defending Quaker principles, opposing slavery, standing up for Conscientious Objection and helping the wounded in the Friends Ambulance Unit in both World Wars. This book has now been made into a fascinating documentary film *A Family and Friends.*

His second book in 2018, *Three Remarkable Quakers*, chronicled the lives of three of his ancestors – Samuel Bowly, Professor John Barlow and John Henry Barlow - all of whom have merited a Blue Plaque for their achievements. This present book takes up the subject of The Friends Ambulance Unit using the correspondence of his parents during the Second World War.

Antony's career has been in the field of Arts administration with The Royal Academy of Dancing, London Festival Ballet, The Young Vic and with his own Arts Consultancy company which managed the Publicity and Press for international tours with Rudolf Nureyev, Mikhail Baryshnikov, Natasha Makarova, as well as the Kirov and Bolshoi Ballets. He now manages a number of international musicians.

Photograph courtesy of Rob Reichelt

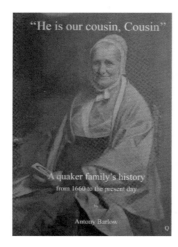

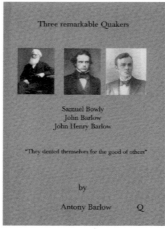

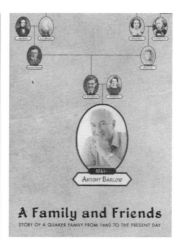